SOCIOLOGY

AQA A-level
Year 1 and AS
Student Book

Steve Chapman
Martin Holborn
Stephen Moore
Dave Aiken

CONTENTS

TO THE STUDENT

The aim of this book is to help make your study of AQA advanced Sociology interesting and successful.

Sociology is an attempt to understand how society works. Fortunately, there are some basic concepts that simplify this ambitious task but some of the sociological theories involved are often abstract and will be unfamiliar at first. Getting to grips with these ideas and applying them to problems can be daunting. There is no need to worry if you do not 'get it' straightaway. Discuss ideas with other students, and of course check with your teacher or tutor. Most important of all, keep asking questions.

There are a number of features in the book to help you learn:

- Each topic starts with an outline of the AQA specification points covered within the topic. This will tell you in which chapter you will find coverage of each point.

- Each chapter starts with a Learning Objectives box to show you what you will learn and the skills you will use throughout the chapter.

- Important words and phrases are given in bold when used for the first time, with their meaning explained in an *Understand the Concept* box. If you are still uncertain, ask your teacher or tutor because it is important that you understand these words.

- Throughout each chapter, you will find evaluation questions. They are written in bold and separated from the main text. You should use them as an opportunity to stop and evaluate what you have learned. These questions often make interesting discussion points.

- Throughout the book, you will find *Focus on Research* features that provide real-life sociological studies and questions to answer about each.

- You will also find *Focus on Skills* features which give you the opportunity to test your ability to pinpoint important information and use key words to inform your response.

- At the end of each chapter, you will find the *Check your Understanding* feature. This is a list of questions which enables you to consolidate your learning and check your knowledge of relevant sociological theories and issues.

- After each *Check your Understanding* feature, there is a *Take It Further* challenge. Here, you will have the chance to put your new-found skills and knowledge into practice.

- Each topic ends with a section called *Apply your Learning*. This is a chance for you to put your knowledge to the test with a mix of short information recall questions as well as longer, more involved ones.

Good luck and enjoy your studies. We hope this book will encourage you to study sociology further after you have completed your course.

1 EDUCATION

AQA Specification

Candidates should examine:

AQA Specification	Chapters
The role and functions of the education system, including its relationship to the economy and to class structure.	Chapter 1 (pages 3–14) covers the key theoretical approaches. Chapter 2 (pages 15–30) deals specifically with class. Chapter 6 (pages 68–85) looks at how these issues play out in relation to contemporary policies.
Differential educational achievement of social groups by social class, ethnicity and gender in contemporary society.	Chapters 2 (pages 15–30), 3 (pages 31–40) and 4 (pages 41–55) deal in detail with these issues.
Relationships and processes within schools, with particular reference to teacher/pupil relationships, pupil identities and subcultures, the hidden curriculum, and the organisation of teaching and learning.	Chapter 5 (pages 56–67) covers these aspects in detail.
The significance of educational policies, including policies of selection, marketisation and privatisation, and policies to achieve greater equality of opportunity or outcome, for an understanding of the structure, role, impact and experience of and access to education; the impact of globalisation on educational policy.	Chapters 2 (pages 15–30), 3 (pages 31–40) and 4 (pages 41–55) consider the effects of policies on access to education. Chapter 6 (pages 68–85) deals specifically with policy issues, but there are important links with the theories discussed in Chapter 1 (pages 3–14).

1.1 THE ROLE OF EDUCATION IN SOCIETY

LEARNING OBJECTIVES

> Understand Marxist, functionalist, social democratic and neoliberal perspectives on the roles and functions of education (AO1).

> Apply these perspectives to contemporary British education (AO2).

> Analyse the relationship between the education system, the economy and the class structure in Britain (AO3).

> Evaluate the strengths and weaknesses of Marxist, functionalist, social democratic and neoliberal perspectives on education (AO3).

INTRODUCING THE DEBATE

In England, for anyone born after 1 September 1997 it is now compulsory to stay on at school until the age of 18. But why is such a long (and expensive) education thought necessary? It is widely believed that all the time and effort devoted to education is good for individual pupils and equally good for the wellbeing of society as a whole. For example, for the individual it might open up opportunities and lead to higher pay, while for society it can help the economy to grow. Functionalist sociologists have a very positive view of education, in line with these widely shared beliefs. Marxists, however, have a very different view, seeing education as serving the interests of a small, higher-class minority and not those of society as a whole. This chapter will examine the ideas and the evidence to see which view is more credible.

The education system is one of the most influential institutions in society. It takes individuals from the age of 4 or 5, or even younger, for six or so hours per day, over a period of at least 13 years in England. It bombards them with a vast amount of knowledge, attitudes and skills.

These are acquired either formally through set lessons, or informally through the hidden curriculum – the processes involved in being 'schooled' and the various interactions that take place while in school (for more on the hidden curriculum, see the section in this topic on the Marxist approach). By the time they finish compulsory education, most pupils will have spent well over 15,000 hours in lessons.

1. Is there anything that occurs in schools that you feel has no purpose? If so, what?

2. What have you really learned at school or college this week? Who will gain from your acquiring this knowledge, set of attitudes or skills?

COMPULSORY EDUCATION FOR ALL

It may seem normal today that all children are entitled to lengthy and free state education, but this has not always been the case. Private schooling was always available for the upper and middle classes who could afford it, but it was not until 1880 that education was available to everyone up to the age of 10.

Forster's 1870 Education Act declared that school boards could be set up in districts where school places were inadequate. Between 1870 and 1880, about 4000 schools were started or taken over by boards. The school boards were replaced with around 300 Local Education Authorities in 1902, by which time about 20,000 board and voluntary schools served 5.6 million pupils. The Fisher Education Act of 1918 made the state responsible for secondary education, and attendance was made compulsory up to the age of 14. The school-leaving age was raised to 15 in 1947, then to 16 in 1972, and for everyone born after 1997 it is now 18.

One of the main reasons for the rapid expansion of state education in Britain has been a belief that improved education was necessary for economic success. There was concern in the late 19th century that Britain was falling behind competitors such as Germany in manufacturing industries. Improving education would ensure that Britain had the skilled workers necessary to compete effectively.

Education was also thought by some to have a key civilising role. This was seen as important, as voting rights were extended to the majority of men in 1884, and to all men over the age of 21 in 1918 (as well as women over 30). People hoped that if the mass of the population was better educated, they would make better informed decisions about who to vote for. The state education system would also teach values and beliefs, which would help to ensure that they were shared by the population as a whole.

The expansion of education was supported by reformers who campaigned for the poor. They saw education as an escape route from poverty, so they believed that state education could help to produce a fairer society in which everybody had opportunities to succeed.

Different groups put the emphasis on different reasons for spending more on state education. These long-standing differences over the purpose of education still exist today.

Since the 1960s, post-16 education to age 18 in school sixth forms and further education colleges has expanded dramatically, as has higher education (see Chapter 6). By 2011/12, UK government expenditure by the Department for Education (DfE) amounted to over £56 billion or about 8% of government spending (Rogers, 2012).

Do you agree that making education compulsory up to the age of 18 will benefit the individual and society (for example, by boosting the economy)? Give reasons to support your answer.

So why do modern societies invest so much in schooling the next generation? Sociologists are divided in their views about this. Most agree that education is important, both in teaching skills and in encouraging certain attitudes and values, but they disagree about why this occurs and who benefits from it.

Functionalist approach

Functionalism was the first sociological perspective to be developed, starting in the 19th century. The initial work of French sociologists such as August Comte (1798–1857) and Emile Durkheim (1858–1917) was then developed in the 20th century in the USA by Talcott Parsons (1902–79) and others. Using different approaches, they examined:

> how societies managed to stick together and work successfully without falling apart

> how shared values and beliefs (for example, about right and wrong) helped members of society to work together

> how institutions such as the family and the education system worked to create predictable and orderly societies.

Some functionalists, such as Durkheim, recognised that things could go wrong with social order, but they stressed that institutions were generally positive and usually 'functioned' to meet the 'needs' of society. They paid less attention to inequality, conflict and social divisions than most other sociologists.

Functionalists argue that education has three broad functions:

1. **Socialisation** – Education helps to maintain society by socialising young people into key cultural values such as achievement, competition, equality of opportunity, social solidarity, democracy, religion and morality. Writing in the late 19th and early 20th century in France, Durkheim was particularly concerned that education should emphasise the moral responsibilities that members of society have towards each other and the wider society. For example, he believed that the teaching of history is crucial in developing a sense of loyalty to your own society. It encourages pride in the achievements of your nation and a sense of shared identity with those who are citizens of the same nation-state. In Durkheim's view, the increasing tendency towards individualism in modern society could lead to too little social solidarity and possibly anomie (a state of normlessness or lack of shared norms). This emphasis can be seen today through the introduction of Citizenship and the maintenance of Religious Education as compulsory subjects.

UNDERSTAND THE CONCEPT

Socialisation is the process through which individuals learn the norms, values and culture of their society; that is, they learn how to behave in order to fit in with their society. Primary socialisation – the earliest stage – usually takes place in families. Education is one of the most important agencies of secondary socialisation.

Parsons, discussing the US education system in the mid-20th century, also recognised the social significance of education. He suggested that it forms a bridge between the family and the wider society by socialising children to adapt to a **meritocratic** view of achievement. In the family, particularistic standards apply – a child's social status is accorded by its parents and other family members. However, in wider society, universalistic standards apply – the individual is judged by criteria that apply to all of society's members. Education helps ease this transition and instil the major

value of achievement through merit. According to Parsons, education therefore helps to produce a value consensus – a general agreement about basic values in society. The value consensus helps to produce order and predictability in social life, ensuring that members of society share the same basic goals.

UNDERSTAND THE CONCEPT

A **meritocracy** is a society or system in which success or failure is based on merit. Merit is seen as resulting from a combination of ability and effort or hard work. In principle, this could be seen as a fair system but it is difficult to define and measure merit, and the prior existence of inequality makes it very difficult to have a system which genuinely rewards merit.

2. *Skills provision* – Education teaches the skills required by a modern industrial society. These may be general skills that everyone needs, such as literacy and numeracy, or the specific skills needed for particular occupations. As the division of labour increases in complexity and occupational roles become more specialised, increasingly longer periods in education become necessary.

Functionalist theory ties in closely with human capital theory, an economic theory which claims that investment in humans through education and training acts very much like investment in new machinery. Just as new machines may be able to produce a higher quantity of better quality products, so better educated and more highly skilled people can create more wealth through their work.

3. **Role allocation** – The functionalists Davis and Moore (1945) argue that education allocates people to the most appropriate job for their talents, using examinations and qualifications. Their argument is based on the principle of meritocracy. Davis and Moore argue that some jobs are more important to society than others. For example, those taking key decisions such as chief executives of large corporations play a crucial role in society. Education helps to identify the people capable of doing such jobs. The examination system encourages competition, individual achievement and hard work. It is closely linked to a rewards system that ensures those doing the most important jobs are awarded the highest pay. The high rewards for some jobs are justified because the system is based on merit and it benefits society as a whole to have the most capable people in the most important jobs. This is seen

to be fair because there is equality of opportunity – everyone has the chance to achieve success in society on the basis of their ability.

Role allocation is the process of deciding who does what within a society or a smaller social setting. The examination system plays a part in this, and the whole process of interviewing or direct recruiting of individuals for jobs is there to vet and select people for particular roles.

Criticisms of the functionalist approach

In general terms, the functionalist perspective on education has been criticised for emphasising the positive effects of the education system and ignoring the negative aspects. Functionalists tend to ignore aspects of education that may be dysfunctional (harmful to society) and that may benefit some social groups more than others, and to ignore conflict in the education system and wider society.

In terms of socialisation, the functionalist view seems most applicable in societies where there is a single dominant and shared culture. In multicultural societies where, for example, different ethnic groups have different cultures and values, it may be hard to reconcile differences through education.

Furthermore, functionalists tend to assume that education succeeds in socialising individuals in the system. A number of studies suggest that not all pupils conform to the values promoted at school (see, for example, the discussion of Paul Willis in Chapter 2).

In terms of skills provision, there has been a long-running debate in Britain about whether British education teaches pupils the right skills, and how successful it is in getting pupils to learn skills at all. It has often been argued that vocational education has low status in Britain, with the result that the education system does not produce the skills needed for the economy.

Many sociologists argue that **globalisation** is increasingly significant. In a globalised economy, British companies and workers have to compete with companies and workers around the globe, yet critics argue that Britain lags far behind some other countries in training its workers. For example, 2012 research (Pisa) placed the

UK 26th out of 65 countries in terms of maths ability among 15-year-olds, 23rd for reading and 20th for science. Even if societies need the education system to provide the workforce with skills, that does not always mean that it will succeed in doing this.

Globalisation involves all parts of the world becoming increasingly interconnected, so that national boundaries become less and less important. Information, ideas, goods and people flow more easily around the world. If the economy is becoming more global, then British companies have to compete not just with other British companies but with companies from around the world. The same applies to educational institutions. For example, British private schools and universities compete with countries around the world (including the USA, Europe and China) to attract pupils or students.

The functionalist claim that education successfully allocates individuals to roles in a fair and meritocratic way has been very strongly disputed. This view ignores various ways in which social divisions, such as those based on gender and ethnicity, might affect educational achievement (see Chapters 3 and 4). It assumes that all individuals have the same opportunity to receive high-quality education and ignores the existence of private education, which gives the wealthy more opportunity to select schools for their children. As we will see in Chapter 2 social class has a strong effect on educational opportunity – a point strongly supported by Marxists. They dismiss the view that education or indeed role allocation in general is meritocratic.

Marxist approach

Marxist ideas originated in the 19th century with the German revolutionary communist Karl Marx (1818–83), but his ideas have influenced generations of social scientists since then. Those who have largely followed his ideas are known as Marxists, while those who have been influenced by his work but have then developed somewhat different ideas are known as neo-Marxists.

Marxists see capitalist societies, such as Britain today, as dominated by a ruling class. The ruling class consists of the wealthy, who own what Marx called the means of production (the things needed to produce other things such as land, capital, machinery and labour power). The wealth of the ruling class enables them to dominate and control the non-economic parts of society – what Marxists call the superstructure.

For Marxists, education is seen as an important part of the superstructure of society. Along with other institutions (such as the mass media, family, religion and the legal system), it serves the needs of the ruling class who control the economic base. This base shapes the superstructure, while the superstructure maintains and justifies the base (see Figure 1.1.1).

For Marxists then, education performs two main functions in capitalist society:

1. It reproduces the inequalities and social relations of production in capitalist society. For example, it generally trains pupils from working-class backgrounds to do working-class jobs while providing elite education for the children of the wealthy, preparing them to take up positions of power in society.

2. It serves to **legitimate** (justify) these inequalities through the myth of meritocracy. It persuades members of society that their positions (particularly their jobs) reflect their ability, while in reality they largely reflect class background. (See Chapter 2 for a discussion of class inequalities in achievement).

UNDERSTAND THE CONCEPT

Legitimation is the process of justifying or gaining support for an idea, policy, and institution or social group. It often involves justifying an inequality or a form of exploitation, perhaps by portraying it as natural (for example, saying men are naturally stronger than women) or as fair (for example, claiming that it is always the most able who get the best-paid jobs).

The Marxist Louis Althusser (1971) disagrees with functionalists that the main function of education is the transmission of common values.

He argues that education is an ideological state apparatus (ISA). Its main function is to maintain, legitimate and reproduce, generation by generation, class inequalities in wealth and power. It does this by transmitting ruling-class or capitalist values disguised as common values. For example, in Britain and other capitalist countries, pupils are encouraged to accept the benefits of private enterprise and individual competition without question. To Marxists, these parts of the capitalist system provide much greater benefit to the ruling class than to other members of society. Along with other ISAs, such as the

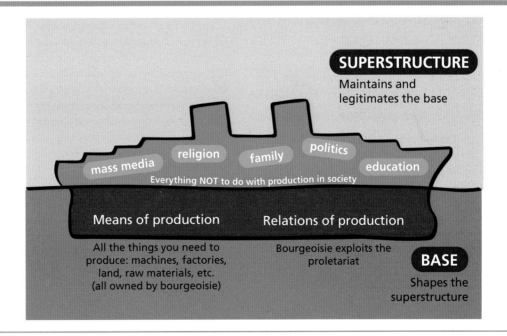

Figure 1.1.1 *Marxist view of the superstructure of society*

media and the legal system, education reproduces the conditions needed for capitalism to flourish without having to use force, which would expose it as oppressive. Instead, **ideology** achieves the same results by exerting its influence subconsciously.

UNDERSTAND THE CONCEPT

An **ideology** is a set of beliefs that promotes the interests of one group (for example, one class) at the expense of others. For example, if the working class are persuaded by ideology that they only deserve very low wages, then this serves the interests of the ruling class.

Pierre Bourdieu (1977) argues that the working classes are effectively duped into accepting that their failure and limited social mobility are justified. The education system tends to value the culture of middle and upper classes much more than that of the working class (for example, classical music and 'serious' literature rather than popular culture). The cultural attributes of the working class are rejected because the system is defined by, and for, the middle classes who, in turn, succeed by default rather than greater ability. Their cultural assets are seen as worthy of investment and reward and hence have greater value as cultural capital. A process of cultural reproduction takes place in which the culture of the middle class is reproduced and given higher status than working class culture through the education system (this is discussed in more detail in Chapter 2). Bourdieu sees this as a form of 'symbolic violence' against the working class.

Do you agree that the curriculum content in the British education system devalues the culture of the working class in particular and less powerful groups in general? Use examples in your answer.

Correspondence theory

Bowles and Gintis (1976) argue that education is controlled by capitalists and serves their interests. From a study of high school children in the USA they argue that there is a close relationship between schooling and work, because schooling is used to prepare children to work in capitalist businesses. The correspondence theory states that education corresponds to employment.

Capitalism requires a hardworking, docile and obedient workforce which will not challenge the decisions of management. Bowles and Gintis believe that education prepares such a workforce through the hidden curriculum, or the hidden, informal messages and lessons that come from the way schooling is organised. It works in the following ways:

> Conformist pupils are awarded higher grades than those who challenge authority or think creatively.

> Schools teach acceptance of hierarchy since teachers give the orders and pupils obey, just as workers obey managers in the workplace.

> Pupils are motivated by the external rewards of exam success just as workers are motivated by wages, since neither pupils nor workers experience satisfaction in learning or work because it is directed by others and they have little control over it.

> Both work and education are fragmented, or broken into small pieces, so that workers and pupils have little overall understanding of production or society. This keeps them divided and, in the case of workers, prevents them from setting up their own businesses in competition with their employers.

Like Bourdieu, Bowles and Gintis see the idea of meritocracy as a myth – people are conned into believing that success or failure is based on merit, whereas in reality their class background determines how well they do in education.

Criticisms of the Marxist approach

Marxism in general, and Bowles and Gintis in particular, have been criticised in a number of ways. They tend to emphasise class inequality in education and pay little or no attention to inequality based on gender or ethnicity. The idea that education corresponds to work has been criticised by Brown (1997), who believes that much work now requires teamwork rather than obedience of authority. Reynolds (1984) believes some education encourages critical thinking, for example, Sociology. Some neo-Marxists such as Willis believe that the hidden curriculum is not always accepted (see 'Neo-Marxist perspectives' in this chapter). They claim that it is debatable whether education is really controlled by the ruling class. Elected local education authorities and teachers have some independence and do not have to follow the wishes of capitalists all the time. Some of the evidence used to support Marxism is dated and may not be representative. For example, Bowles and Gintis conducted their research in 1976 in the USA, and it may not be applicable in Britain in the 21st century.

BUILD CONNECTIONS

The question of whether education provides a route to greater social mobility and therefore leads to a more open class system is crucial in a number of debates around class stratification. The easier it is to move up the class system through success in education, the more open and meritocratic the system is.

Partly as a result of such criticisms, a variety of neo-Marxist (or new Marxist) approaches to education have been developed.

Neo-Marxist perspectives on education

An example of neo-Marxism applied to education is the work of Henry Giroux (1984). He disagrees with the conventional Marxist approach of Bowles and Gintis because he does not believe that working-class pupils passively accept everything they are taught, but actively shape their own education and sometimes resist the discipline imposed on them by the school. Schools are sites of ideological struggle by different classes and by different ethnic, religious and cultural groups striving to ensure that education provides the things they wish for.

Capitalists have more power than any other single group but they don't have all the power. The most influential neo-Marxist study of education is a study of a group of boys (or 'lads') in a Midlands comprehensive school in the 1970s. Paul Willis (1977) conducted the study using interviews and participant observation in the school. The boys studied formed a group that took up an anti-school stance, opposing the norms and values supported by the school. The 'lads' saw themselves as superior to teachers and conformist pupils who they called 'ear 'oles'. They were not interested in getting academic qualifications. At school, their main aim was to do as little work as possible while entertaining themselves by 'having a laff' through bad behaviour. Their anti-school culture was sexist (looking down on women) and racist (looking down on ethnic minorities). They valued traditional working-class masculinity, which emphasised toughness and saw manual work as more valuable than non-manual work such as office work. Willis followed the lads into their first jobs, which were overwhelmingly unskilled manual jobs, often in factories. He found that in these jobs there was a shop-floor culture which was very similar to the counter-school culture. They both involved lack of respect for authority and 'having a laff' to cope with boring and tedious work over which they had little control. However,

it was clear that although the 'lads' rejected aspects of ruling class ideology, their rebellion against school meant that they still ended up reproducing class inequality since they moved on to working-class jobs.

Neo-Marxist perspectives suggest that the hidden curriculum is not always accepted and that education does not always succeed in socialising pupils into dominant values. It suggests that both functionalism and Marxism exaggerate conformity in education. Furthermore it is clearly the case that not all pupils conform at school. However, Willis's study is small-scale and dated. Working-class pupils may not reject school as often today.

Comparing Marxism and neo-Marxism with functionalism

Despite the criticisms of both Marxism and neo-Marxism, it can be argued that these perspectives are just as relevant today as they were in the past. The influence of business on education may be stronger than ever. For example, local authorities have lost some of their power over education because they no longer run colleges, free schools or academies. The Marxist Glenn Rikowski (2002, 2005) argues that there has been a 'business takeover' of schools. In the UK, this has involved businesses sponsoring academies, the subcontracting of many school services (for example, educational psychology services) to private businesses and an ever-growing emphasis on competition between schools. In terms of the curriculum, there is more emphasis on NVQs and BTEC in schools. (This is more fully discussed in Chapter 6).

However, Marxists and neo-Marxists may exaggerate the harmful effects of education as much as functionalists exaggerate the beneficial effects. Like functionalists, they also take an extreme view on the hidden curriculum, seeing it as entirely benefiting capitalism (while functionalists see it as entirely benefiting society as a whole). Neither Marxists and neo-Marxists nor functionalists base their ideas on detailed research into the content of schooling today, nor do they acknowledge that education may have different effects for different groups at different times (see Chapter 5 for more on processes in schools). Marxists and neo-Marxists emphasise class above gender and ethnicity, while functionalists ignore social divisions altogether. Like functionalists, Marxists and neo-Marxists tend not to put forward suggestions for improving the education system. Functionalists tend to assume that education already functions well, while Marxists assume that education could only become fair and just if capitalist society were overthrown and replaced by a communist society. Neither therefore

FOCUS ON RESEARCH: THE BRITISH COHORT STUDY AND THE MILLENNIUM COHORT STUDY

The British Cohort Study is a longitudinal piece of research that takes as its subjects all those living in England, Scotland and Wales who were born in one particular week in April 1970. Data were collected about the births and families of just under 17,200 babies; since then, there have been five more attempts to gather information from this group. With each successive 'sweep', the scope of enquiry has broadened and it now covers physical, educational, social and economic development. In 2000, a new cohort study (The Millennium Cohort Study) began, which initially collected data on 19,000 children born in 2000/1. This study has conducted interviews with the parents, cognitive tests on the children and interviews with their class teachers. By 2012, there had already been five sweeps of data collection when the children were different ages.

Data have been collected in a variety of ways. In the British Cohort Study's 1986 research, 16 separate methods were used, including parental questionnaires, class teacher and head teacher questionnaires, and medical examinations. The participants completed questionnaires, kept two diaries and undertook some educational assessments. The Millennium Cohort Study used interviews with parents, cognitive tests on children and interviews with class teachers.

Over the period of the research, the sample for the British Cohort Study reduced to 15,500, while the 2012 research for the Millennium Cohort Study involved a sample of just over 12,000.

Jo Blanden, Paul Gregg and Steve Machin have used data from The British Cohort Study to compare the life chances of British children with those in other advanced countries, and the results are disturbing. In a comparison of eight European and North American countries, Britain and the United States have the lowest social mobility (movement between classes).

Social mobility in Britain has declined, whereas in the USA it is stable. Part of the reason for Britain's decline has been that people who are better off financially have benefited disproportionately from increased educational opportunity.

Comparing surveys of children born in the 1950s and the 1970s, the researchers went on to examine the reason for Britain's low, and declining, mobility. They found that it is partly due to the strong and increasing relationship between family income and educational attainment. For these children, additional opportunities to stay in education at ages 16 and 18 disproportionately benefited those from better-off backgrounds.

For a more recent group born in the early 1980s, the gap between those staying on in education at age 16 narrowed, but inequality of access to higher education has widened further: while the proportion of people from the poorest fifth of families who obtained a degree has increased from 6 per cent to 9 per cent, the graduation rates for the richest fifth have risen from 20 to 47 per cent.

Analysis of children in the Millennium Cohort Study at age 7 suggested that class inequality was continuing to have a major effect on educational achievement (Sullivan *et al.* 2013). Even at such an early age there were marked class differences in children's cognitive scores and analysis of the statistics suggested that these were very largely determined by the income, social class and previous education of the parents. On the other hand, parenting style made little difference to test scores.

Based on Blanden *et al.* (2005); Sullivan *et al.* (2013)

Questions

1. Explain how the British Cohort Study and the Millennium Cohort Study are longitudinal pieces of research.

2. These studies both used large samples. Identify one advantage and one disadvantage of having a large sample.

3. It is sometimes claimed that longitudinal research is very useful for understanding changes over time. Identify two reasons why this may be the case.

4. Could taking part in a study such as this affect the way participants behave, and therefore affect the results? Give reasons for your answer.

5. What do these studies suggest about the functionalist view that education is meritocratic and allocates roles efficiently in modern societies?

suggests how education could be improved in existing societies. Other perspectives on education do make more concrete suggestions for how education could be improved, and these alternative perspectives will be discussed next.

Social democratic perspectives on education

Functionalism and Marxism are quite extreme views of education, but many sociologists and educationalists take a more moderate view. They argue that education does need to be changed to improve, but that this does not require a revolutionary change in society. However, they disagree over the direction of change.

Social democratic perspectives are associated with educationalists and politicians who would like to see greater equality resulting from the education system. An example of this is the British Labour governments of the 1960s and 1970s, who introduced and expanded comprehensive schools (see Chapter 6). Social democratic perspectives continue to influence those educationalists, sociologists and politicians who stress that schools must give extra help to those from disadvantaged backgrounds.

Supporters of social democratic perspectives believe that in addition to promoting economic growth, education is essential to promoting equality of opportunity in a meritocracy. However, they believe that education is not automatically meritocratic and that governments need to intervene to ensure that people from all social classes have the same chance to fulfil their potential in the education system. To achieve this, the government may need to make some changes in society as well as in the education system. From this viewpoint, a society that has too much inequality can never provide equal opportunities – the richest will always use their wealth to gain advantage (for example, by buying private education). To some extent however, this can be counteracted. By taxing the wealthy more and spending the revenue on state education, it is possible to give those from working-class backgrounds a good chance to succeed.

They believe this can be achieved, for example, by expanding higher education to make more places available for working-class pupils, by introducing comprehensive schools (so middle-class pupils can't gain an advantage by going to selective state schools), and by providing extra educational help for those from disadvantaged backgrounds. Social democrats such as Halsey and Floud were very influential in the 1960s and 1970s when Labour governments followed some of these policies, but they have also continued to have some influence on Labour governments and the Coalition government since then.

Critics have argued that social democratic policies have not been particularly successful in helping the working class to do better in education. Despite the introduction of many new policies to achieve this, the gap in attainment between classes remains large (see Chapter 2).

Wolf (2002) questions whether more and more government spending on education will automatically lead to economic growth. For example, Switzerland has relatively low education spending but high economic growth.

The strongest critics of social democratic viewpoints have probably been neoliberals. According to many neoliberals, greater equality in education can lead to standards being undermined; education becomes levelled down, and the most able students (for example, in mixed-ability classes that progress at the pace of the slowest learners) are not given the chance to reach their full potential.

Social democratic views are also criticised by some feminists, who believe they concentrate too much on class inequalities and not enough on gender inequalities.

Neoliberal/New Right perspectives on education

Neoliberal (sometimes called New Right) perspectives have probably had the most influence on British education in recent years. Neoliberal views are very much in favour of private business and the **free market** because they believe that competition between companies drives innovation and encourages success. Like functionalists and social democrats, they see education as important for a successful economy, but they think that state education can be inefficient and a drain on a country's resources. High government spending on education and other services is seen as undesirable because it requires high taxes. These taxes ultimately come from company profits, and high taxation therefore makes companies less competitive.

UNDERSTAND THE CONCEPT

The **free market** refers to a system in which people are free to buy and sell what they wish. In the free market, producers have to provide what consumers want or they will not be able to sell their products. Firms compete with one another to attract customers so that, at least in theory, consumers get the products or services (including education) they want, and the quality continually improves.

Chubb and Moe (1988) believe that state education is unresponsive to the needs of pupils and parents and tends to have low standards. In contrast, private education has to please its customers in order to survive and therefore standards are high and there is constant pressure to improve further.

Market liberals believe that rising standards are essential as a result of globalisation. If countries are going to compete in an increasingly global economy, workers lacking high levels of skills will lose their jobs to more skilled workers in other countries.

These views have influenced all British governments to a greater or lesser extent since 1979.

Neoliberals take a less positive view of education than functionalists, believing that education needs to be run more as a business. However, their views are strongly opposed by both Marxists and social democrats, who see state education as the only way to provide opportunities for pupils from all classes. From their point of view, private education puts profit before the wellbeing of pupils and will always favour the rich above the poor. Furthermore, this will tend to waste working-class talent and therefore harm the economy.

Postmodernism and education

Despite their differences, the perspectives examined in this section so far (functionalism, Marxism, neo-Marxism, social democratic perspectives and neoliberalism) all agree that there is a single, best direction for the education system. All can therefore be seen as 'modern' approaches to education. Modern perspectives see human problems as being able to be solved by rational planning and thought. They believe that scientific methods and the development of clear theories can analyse problems and come up with solutions. They therefore tend to argue that there is one single true or best way to develop education. Postmodern perspectives, on the other hand, deny that there is any single, best way of tackling problems. They see societies as developing greater variety and pluralism, and they question whether any single, planned approach to education and other issues is

desirable. (For more discussion of postmodernism, see Topics 3, 4 and 5).

This perspective has been applied to education by Usher, Bryant and Johnston (1997) in the context of adult education.

Education for adults has been particularly responsive to the need for greater choice and diversity – for example, by the use of flexible and distance learning. No single curriculum is assumed to be useful for all learners. As a result, a vast range of courses is provided by educational institutions such as FE colleges, The Open University and Adult Education colleges. This allows learners to pick and mix different combinations of courses to suit their own objectives and lifestyles. Furthermore, education is no longer separate from other areas of life. It has become integrated into leisure and work. It can therefore have many different meanings to those who take up adult education. In these respects, adult education is typical of postmodern society, which is characterised by a blurring of the boundaries between different areas of life, greater choice and variety, and the rejection of any kind of plan imposed from the centre on individuals.

Postmodern views can be criticised for exaggerating the changes in education. For example, Haralambos and Holborn (2013) point out that there is actually a greater centralisation in some aspects of education, particularly the national curriculum, rather than greater diversity and choice. The budget for adult education in the UK has been cut and, for example, the range of evening classes available for adult students has declined. They also criticise postmodernists for ignoring the way in which education may be shaped more by big business than by the needs and wishes of individual learners.

Keeping in mind neoliberal, Marxist, functionalist, social democratic and postmodern arguments, identify advantages and disadvantages of business leaders having direct involvement in state education. Do you think the advantages outweigh the disadvantages or vice versa? Give reasons for your conclusion.

FOCUS ON SKILLS: COMPETITION, EXAMS AND THE PURPOSE OF EDUCATION

Eton College in Berkshire

Barrowford Primary School in Lancashire

In August 2014 Tony Little, headmaster of Eton, Britain's most prestigious private school, attacked England's exam system saying that it was 'unimaginative' and claiming that it was not succeeding in preparing pupils for working in the modern world. He argued that it was too much like the exam system in Victorian times and focused too much upon test scores and too little on the content of education itself. Little said that education needed to be about more than 'jostling for position in a league table' which could lead to schools putting too much emphasis upon test scores, which were in any case not always a reliable guide to the quality of the education that pupils had received. He argued that the exam system 'obliges students to sit alone at their desks in preparation for a world in which, for much of the time, they will need to work collaboratively'. Little supported the head of a primary school at Barrowford in Lancashire who had sent out a letter to all Year 6 pupils telling them not to worry about their SATs results because the tests couldn't assess what made them 'special and unique' as individuals.

Michael Gove (a former education secretary) supported more traditional exams with less use of coursework. He justified this in terms of Britain falling behind the highest achieving places in the Programme for International Student Assessment (Pisa) tests, which placed England some way down the international rankings for essential skills such as literacy and numeracy. Shanghai, in China, topped the tables. However, Tony Little argued that the Chinese themselves were concerned that their education was too narrow and that, ironically, they were trying to learn from Britain and develop a more 'all-round education' rather than focusing too much on literacy, numeracy and science.

Questions

1. **Identify** the central differences between the views of Michael Gove and Tony Little.

2. **Explain** the similarities and differences between Tony Little's views and the neoliberal perspective on education.

3. **Apply** Marxist perspectives to explain the differences between working-class and elite education suggested by this article.

4. **Evaluate.** Do you agree with the claim that the exam system in England does not prepare pupils for work in the modern world? Justify your answer.

CHECK YOUR UNDERSTANDING

1. Which act made state education compulsory up to the age of 14?

2. Give three of the main reasons why education was first made compulsory in Britain.

3. According to functionalists, what are the three main functions of schools?

4. What does Althusser consider to be the main purpose of education, and how is it achieved?

5. Why, according to Bowles and Gintis, do white, middle-class pupils do better?

6. How does Willis's work appear to support the views of Bowles and Gintis?

7. Give three reasons why what goes on in schools would appear to contradict the view of Bowles and Gintis that there is a correspondence between school and work.

8. Suggest two similarities and two differences between neoliberal and functionalist perspectives on education.

9. Analyse how functionalists and Marxists differ in their views on the relationship between education and the economy.

10. Evaluate Marxist and functionalist theories by identifying two strengths and two weaknesses of each theory.

TAKE IT FURTHER

Interview a range of your teachers. Ask them to explain the values which they consider are encouraged by the following aspects of school organisation and routine: assemblies, speech days, sports days, school uniform, registration, house competitions, school rules, prefects, detention.

Evaluate the extent to which their responses subscribe to functionalist, Marxist, social democratic or neoliberal views of education.

When conducting the interviews, try to make sure that you do not lead the teachers in any way. Keep your questions neutral and don't express support or criticism of their responses.

1.2 CLASS AND EDUCATIONAL ACHIEVEMENT

LEARNING OBJECTIVES

> Understand the patterns of achievement in relation to social class in Britain (AO1).

> Apply theories of differential achievement to class differences in Britain (AO2).

> Analyse and evaluate competing theories of social class differences in achievement (AO3).

INTRODUCING THE DEBATE

Although some sociologists have argued that ability and effort determine how well people do in the education system, there is much evidence to show that social class exerts a strong influence too. Those from higher-class backgrounds tend to do better than those from lower-class backgrounds, even when you factor in such things as measured intelligence or previous qualifications.

Despite efforts by governments to reduce the inequalities over many years, they remain stubbornly large. Sociologists have therefore analysed the factors which link social class and educational achievement. Some emphasise factors outside school such as the income and lifestyle of the families to which children belong. Others emphasise factors in schools such as the content of the curriculum and the ways in which teachers treat pupils from different class backgrounds. In this topic, you need to evaluate the strength of these different arguments based upon the available evidence.

CLASS: PATTERNS OF ACHIEVEMENT

Differential educational attainment refers to the tendency for some groups to do better or worse than others in terms of educational success. Social class differences were the first to be investigated by sociologists, perhaps because these differences have been very noticeable for many decades. Differences between ethnic groups and between females and males are a more recent focus, and these are explored in Chapters 3 and 4.

Government educational policy over recent decades has largely focused on raising the standards of teaching and learning in schools, and there is research that suggests that the quality of a school does have an impact on achievement across all social classes. Such research, however, needs to be put into context.

Large-scale statistical research by Webber and Butler (2007), involving more than a million pupils, found that the best predictor of achievement was the type of neighbourhood that pupils lived in. The more middle class and affluent the area, the more successful the school tended to be. More than half of the school's performance could be explained by the type of pupils who attended.

John Jerrim (2013) analysed government statistical data on class and test results. He found in his research that even the most talented were being left behind in education if they came from a lower-class background. He concluded that in terms of reading ability, "High achieving boys from the most advantaged family backgrounds in England are roughly two and a half years ahead of their counterparts in the least advantaged households by the age of 15" (Jerrim 2013, p.3). This suggests that, without class advantages, talent is often not enough to succeed.

Material deprivation

Although state education is technically free in Britain, **material deprivation** can still have a significant impact on educational achievement.

UNDERSTAND THE CONCEPT

Material deprivation refers to a lack of resources and a lack of the ability to purchase goods and services, compared with other members of society. In an educational context, this includes:

> resources that can directly help students to succeed in the education system (for example, materials for school, private education and private tuition)

> resources that make it easier to achieve success indirectly (for example, high-quality and spacious housing and a good diet).

Material deprivation can also affect the ability of parents to provide a cultural environment that is helpful to their children's educational success. For example, if parents have to work long hours due to low wages, they may be less able to spend time reading to young children.

Many sociologists have identified ways in which material deprivation can have a negative impact on educational success. For example, in a study of the effects of poverty on schooling, Smith and Noble (1995) list the 'barriers to learning' that can result from low income. These include the following:

> If families are unable to afford school uniforms, school trips, transport to and from school, classroom materials and, in some cases, school textbooks, this can lead to students being isolated, bullied and stigmatised. As a result, they may fall behind in their school work.

State education itself may be free, but supplementary costs can be considerable.

> Low income reduces the likelihood of pupils having access to a computer with internet access, a desk, educational toys, books, space to do homework and a comfortable well-heated home.

> The marketisation (see Social policy and social class) of schools means that there will be better resourced, oversubscribed schools in more affluent areas, while socially disadvantaged students are concentrated in a limited number of increasingly unpopular schools.

> Older working-class students are more likely to have to work part-time to support their studies, or to have to care for younger siblings if informal childcare networks break down, affecting their attendance at school. Middle-class parents, on the other hand, can more easily afford to pay for childcare.

Research by Washbrook and Waldfogel (2010) for The Sutton Trust looked at the impact of material deprivation on the scores of five-year-olds in vocabulary tests. They found that 31 per cent of the difference in scores between children from middle-income and low-income families was explained by material deprivation.

Donald Hirsch (2007), in a review of research, found that students from better-off backgrounds had a variety of advantages:

> They were more likely to have structured out-of-school activities such as playing organised sports, having music lessons and going to theatre groups.

> These activities (which are often costly) helped students from better-off backgrounds to learn particular skills. They also gave them greater confidence in school, helping them to achieve higher grades.

> They had more space (such as their own bedroom), making it easier for them to do homework successfully.

> They were more likely to benefit from private education.

Hirsch discusses research by Sutton *et al.* (2007) in which pupils between the ages of 8 and 13 were interviewed about their experiences of education. One group of pupils lived on a disadvantaged housing estate, while the other group went to private school. Hirsch summarises the findings: "The more advantaged children described a much richer set of experiences in school, inside and outside the curriculum, while for the disadvantaged children issues such as discipline and detention were more apparent" (Hirsch, 2007, p.4). The quality of the school, according to Hirsch, only explained about

The quality of housing stock and the class make-up of an area have a significant effect on achievement in local schools.

14 per cent of class differences in achievement. Material inequality outside school, however, also impacted on the pupils' experiences and confidence inside the school. Based on material inequality, the pupils in the study had already developed stereotypes of 'chavs' and 'posh kids'. Those who thought they were seen as 'chavs' did not expect to do well.

Whatever the general significance of schools for class differences in education, there is no doubt that being able to afford a private education greatly increases the chances of an elite university education. One of the most direct ways in which material advantage can affect educational opportunity is through private education. Only about 7 per cent of pupils in Britain attend private schools (Kynaston, 2014) and for most parents the fees are unaffordable. Kynaston points out that around a third of private-school pupils do get reduced fees, and some schools provide free places based upon academic ability rather than ability to pay. However, only about one in twelve receives a means-tested bursary and most of those still have to pay more than half the fees. Fewer than 1 per cent pay no fees at all and get a free place provided by scholarships. According to Kynaston, with most boarding schools charging some £20,000 or more per annum, private schools remain accessible only to the very well off.

Between 1980 and 1997, Conservative governments in the UK offered an Assisted Places Scheme to help some high-performing students whose parents could not afford the fees to attend private schools. In total, 75,000 pupils benefited from this scheme (Whitty, Power and Sims, 2013). A study by the Sutton Trust (Whitty, Power and Sims, 2013) compared students who took places on the scheme with similar students who went to state schools. They found that students attending a private school did gain better results at GCSE and A-level, and were likely to be accepted into Oxford or Cambridge with lower grades than students from state schools.

Being able to afford private education does therefore seem to offer significant advantages, and this is reflected in research by the Sutton Trust (2010), which found that private-school students were 55 times more likely to get into Oxford or Cambridge and 22 times more likely to get into a high-ranked university than state-school students entitled to free school meals (Sutton Trust, 2010). However, referring to this research, Kynaston (2014) notes the Sutton Trust finding that once they get to university former state-school pupils tend to do better than former private-school pupils. He argues that private-school pupils are often over-promoted within education because of the advantages their better resources afford them. In effect then, Britain has two school systems, one very largely reserved for the wealthy, educating 7 per cent of pupils, and one for the remaining 93 per cent. Many sociologists argue that, as a result, class inequalities are entrenched within a dual system of schooling.

According to a questionnaire by Reay *et al.* (2005) many working-class students intended to apply to their nearest university because they felt they could not afford the costs of travel and accommodation away from home.

For middle-class parents who cannot afford private-school fees, an alternative is to pay private tutors. According to Mike Britland (2013) the use of private tutors is booming in Britain. They are increasingly used not just for exam preparation, but also during the summer holidays to ensure that children do not slip backwards educationally during the long break. Parents may also be able to buy a house in the catchment area for a very successful state school (see Social policy and social class).

Material deprivation has an impact at every level in the education system and in part explains the class differences in achievement. However, it interacts with other factors outside and inside the education system in shaping the educational chances of different classes. These factors will be examined in the sections that follow.

_____

'Money alone can't guarantee educational success, but it is very hard for poor families to get a high-quality education.' How far would you agree with this statement? Justify your answer.

Cultural deprivation theories

As an alternative to explaining variation in educational achievement in terms of material differences, one can explain them in terms of cultural differences. Some theories see working-class culture as failing to provide the necessary attributes for educational success and therefore argue that the working class are culturally deprived.

The idea of **cultural deprivation** is based on the view that different classes have different cultures. These alleged cultural differences suggest that the working class place too much emphasis on enjoying themselves and living in the moment rather than on putting in the hard work and making the sacrifices necessary for educational success. According to Barry Sugarman (1970):

> People in the working class are oriented towards the present time, and are unable to defer gratification. As a result, they are unlikely to sacrifice immediate income by staying on in education in order to gain higher wages and a better job in the long term.

> The fatalism of the working class means they do not believe that they can improve their prospects through their own hard work.

> Their collectivist approach makes it less likely that they will pursue individual success through the education system; instead they will seek it through collective action, for example, through trade unions.

Early research by sociologists such as David Lockwood (1966) claim to identify distinctive subcultures associated with the middle class and the working class. Some of the main features of the subcultures are outlined in Table 1.2.1.

UNDERSTAND THE CONCEPT

Cultural deprivation means being deprived of cultural attributes necessary for educational success. For example, the working class may lack attitudes and values necessary for success in education. They may also lack the knowledge to succeed because they have not benefited from the same informal education from their parents.

They may even lack the ability to speak, read, write and think in ways which will help them in education because of the way they have been brought up. Unlike theories of material deprivation, the crucial factor here is not lack of money and material resources, but lack of the necessary cultural knowledge, aptitudes, attitudes and values.

A number of research projects have supported cultural deprivation theory.

	Working class	Middle class
Time orientation	Present-time orientation: live life in the moment rather than worrying about the future.	Future-time orientation: think ahead rather than living in the moment.
Attitude to gratification	Seek immediate gratification: enjoy yourself now, for example, spend your wage packet as soon as you get it.	Accept deferred gratification: content to put off pleasure now in order to achieve greater pleasure in the future, for example, saving for a deposit on a house.
Collectivism versus individualism	Success achieved through collective action, for example, a union going on strike.	Success achieved through individual action, for example, studying or working hard.
Attitudes to luck	Your chances in life are based upon luck or fate (fatalism).	Your chances in life are based upon your ability and hard work; you make your own luck.

Table 1.2.1 Social class subcultures

Leon Feinstein (2003) used data from the National Child Development Study to examine the effects of cultural and other factors in shaping educational achievement. Feinstein found that financial deprivation (having poorer parents) had some effect on achievement, but that cultural deprivation was much more important. The crucial factor was the extent to which parents encouraged and supported their children. This largely determined how well they did.

Feinstein found that supportive parents have a much greater effect than financial deprivation on children's educational achievement.

Research by Goodman and Gregg (2010) for the Joseph Rowntree Foundation used data from four longitudinal studies (The Millennium Cohort Study, the Avon Longitudinal Study of Parents and Children, the Longitudinal Study of Young People in England, and the Children of the British Cohort Study) to investigate the link between poverty and low attainment in children from birth through secondary school years. They identified a number of cultural factors that helped to explain low educational achievement among poor children. They included:

> the quality of mother-child interactions and the amount of time parents spent with children

> how often parents read books to young children

> attitudes to education (for example, whether parents encouraged their children to aspire to higher education)

> the overall value placed on education by the parents

> the extent of negative behaviour by the children (for example, truancy, antisocial behaviour, smoking) as opposed to positive behaviour (such as participation in sport and in clubs or reading for pleasure)

> parental involvement in schooling (for example, by attending schools, helping with homework and discussing school reports).

The report did not attribute low achievement entirely to cultural factors, but identified material deprivation (for example, lack of educational resources, lack of private tuition) and child–teacher relationships as important too. However, it did see cultural factors as the most important of all.

Basil Bernstein (1972) believes that a particular aspect of culture – speech – shapes educational achievement. He distinguishes two types of speech pattern: **restricted codes**, which involve simpler use of language, and **elaborated codes**, which involve more complex use of language.

UNDERSTAND THE CONCEPT

Restricted codes are used in a type of shorthand speech where meanings are not made fully explicit. They use short, simple and often unfinished sentences. The listener has to fill in some meanings and these codes are not well suited to expressing complex ideas. This type of speech code is more typical of the working class who are more likely than the middle class to communicate verbally in their jobs and less likely to need to write reports.

In **elaborated codes** the meanings are filled in and made explicit; sentences tend to be longer and more complex. They are more likely to be used in middle-class jobs where there is more need to write reports and produce documents. According to Bernstein, this type of speech code encourages more developed and sophisticated reasoning.

In education, elaborated codes are necessary for exam success in many subjects. As many teachers are themselves middle class, they are more likely to use elaborated codes. Being socialised in households that largely use restricted codes holds back working-class children in the education system, making it more difficult for them to achieve academic success. The lack of these skills, which are vital for educational success, may make working-class children feel less confident than middle-class children in a school environment.

Criticisms of cultural deprivation theory

Cultural deprivation theory has been heavily criticised. Critics have questioned whether there really are such big cultural differences between social classes in the contemporary world. Furthermore, the validity of some of the research has been questioned. Blackstone and

Mortimore (1994) argue that research has not measured parental interest in education adequately. Instead, teacher assessments have often been used and these may not reflect the real level of interest of parents. Furthermore, working-class parents may feel less able to visit schools because they feel uncomfortable interacting with middle-class teachers, and schools with more middle-class pupils tend to have more organised systems for parent–school contact.

Qualitative research by Gillian Evans (2007) who carried out observations and interviews on a working-class council estate in London found that most working-class parents placed a very high value on education and did encourage their children to do well. As a middle-class parent herself, she found no difference in positive attitudes to education among mothers in different social classes.

Bernstein has been criticised by Gaine and George (1999) who argue that he oversimplifies the difference between middle-class and working-class speech patterns. They claim that class differences in speech patterns have declined since Bernstein did his research. Also, they found that many other factors apart from speech affect educational attainment.

Cultural conflicts and cultural capital

Cultural deprivation theory has also been heavily criticised by those who believe that it blames the working class for their own failure in a society and educational system that is stacked against them. From this point of view, the working class and the middle class may have different cultures, but that does not mean that working-class culture is inferior, it is simply different. The problem for the working class is that the education system largely operates in terms of the culture of the middle and upper classes. Working-class skills, knowledge, ways of speaking and behaving are devalued by the education system, which gives them

less chance of success. So, they lack the necessary **cultural capital** to succeed.

UNDERSTAND THE CONCEPT

Cultural capital involves the possession of cultural characteristics that can give you advantages in life. Educational qualifications are an obvious example, but cultural capital can also take less obvious forms. Your accent, the way you walk, your vocabulary, and your knowledge of arts, fashions and cultural trends can all help you to fit in with those in elite positions, in order to gain access to elite schools and universities. It might help you succeed at a job interview or in running a business and this in turn can help you gain access to another type of capital – economic capital.

Pierre Bourdieu (1984) believes that the possession or lack of possession of different types of capital shapes opportunity in society. Capital can be defined as any assets that can improve your chances in life, and all types of capital can affect your achievement in the education system. As such, Bourdieu adopts a Marxist approach but extends it to include several different types of capital, not just economic capital, which Marx himself saw as the key to understanding society.

Bourdieu identifies four types of capital, which are summarised in Table 1.2.2.

All these types of capital can help in education and all reflect class inequalities in society. However, cultural capital is particularly useful. The education system is biased towards the culture of higher social classes. Students from these classes have an advantage because they have been socialised into the dominant culture. They therefore possess more of the cultural capital useful for

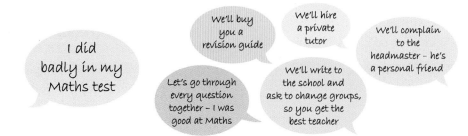

Figure 1.2.1 A parent's response to a problem at school may depend on the type of capital they possess.

Type of capital	Definition	Example	Role in education
Economic capital	Ownership of wealth.	Owning valuable houses, shares, having an income.	Paying for private education or additional tuition.
Cultural capital	Having the educational qualifications, lifestyles and knowledge of arts and literature that are valued in society.	Having a degree-level qualification or higher, enjoying educational holidays, having a knowledge of classical art and literature.	Parents have knowledge and experience to help their children in education. They can provide an educationally stimulating home environment, so children become familiar with knowledge that is valued at school.
Social capital	Possession of valuable social contacts.	Knowing teachers, head teachers, professors.	Parents may know how to help gain admission to the best educational institutions or to find expert help.
Symbolic capital	Possession of status.	Being seen as respectable by the community.	Could help with admission to private or selective schools.

Table 1.2.2 *Bourdieu's types of capital and their role in education*

success in the education system. This view is supported by a variety of research.

Research by Gillian Evans (2007) found that middle-class mothers were able to use their cultural capital to give their children a head start. The mothers tended to have high-level educational qualifications themselves and a good understanding of how children could be stimulated to learn in pre-school years. They used their own educational knowledge to incorporate more learning activities into their children's play.

Ball *et al.* (1994) showed how middle-class parents are able to use their cultural capital to play the system so as to ensure that their children are accepted into the schools of their choice. The strategies used included attempting to make an impression with the headteacher on open day, and knowing how to mount an appeal if their child was unsuccessful in their application to a particular school. However, these researchers accept that material advantages are also important and both cultural and material factors interact with factors inside schools (for more discussion of this research, see Focus on skills: Educational choice and markets).

Bourdieu's concept of cultural capital was tested in research by Alice Sullivan (2001). She carried out a survey on pupils approaching school-leaving age in four schools in England and received questionnaire data from a total of 465 pupils. The occupation of the parent in the highest-status job was used to determine the class of the children, and parents' educational qualifications were used to measure their cultural capital. A number of measures of pupils' cultural capital were used. Pupils were asked about books they read, television

programmes they watched, music they listened to, whether they played a musical instrument, and attendance at art galleries, theatres and concerts; they were also tested on their knowledge of cultural figures and on their vocabulary.

Sullivan then examined which of these factors affected educational performance in GCSEs and identified that pupils were more likely to be successful if they:

> read more complex fiction.

> watched TV programmes such as arts, science and current affairs documentaries and more sophisticated drama.

Both of these activities helped pupils develop wider vocabularies and greater knowledge of cultural figures, and this was reflected in exam performance.

Some cultural activities were not helpful in exam performance:

> Watching programmes such as soap operas and game shows did not improve GCSE results.

> Attending cultural events and involvement in music had no significant effect, suggesting that these activities should not be considered important aspects of cultural capital.

Sullivan found that pupils' cultural capital was strongly correlated with parental cultural capital (that is, their educational qualifications), which in turn was closely linked to their social class. Graduate parents in higher professions had children with the most cultural capital and these children were most successful in exams.

Evaluation of cultural capital theories

Unlike cultural deprivation theories, cultural capital theories do not assume that working-class culture is inferior. They also identify ways in which the education system may be biased against working-class culture and therefore link factors inside and outside educational institutions. They also make some valuable links between factors inside and outside the education system itself, for example, by looking at how schools value or devalue different cultures.

However, they still have their limitations.

They fail to fully acknowledge the importance of factors inside school and the way that different groups are treated once they enter the schooling system. They also generally ignore or underestimate the direct influence of material factors in education.

With the exception of Bourdieu, they fail to acknowledge the way that material factors shape different cultures. Material inequalities are perhaps the main reason that different class-based cultures develop. For example, an inability to defer gratification might reflect the lack of well-paid secure employment. If working-class parents don't have the same skills as middle-class parents to help their children, they don't have the money to compensate for this by paying for private tuition, a comfortable spacious home, educational trips and so on. Furthermore, the extra power that comes with greater resources helps to explain why education might have a middle-class bias. Therefore cultural differences and cultural capital reflect the underlying material differences between classes.

Do you think material or cultural deprivation is the main factor affecting educational achievement, or are they equally important? Explain and justify your answer.

Factors inside the education system

The importance of schools

Both cultural and material explanations of the way different classes achieve in education see factors outside the education system as responsible for class differences. However, a number of researchers have argued that processes within school may be just as important. These factors include the quality of education provided in predominantly working-class areas, the organisation of education and the way that working-class pupils are treated by teachers in the education system.

There is some evidence that schools can make a difference to working-class achievement, and governments have tried to address underachievement in working-class areas. Perry and Francis (2010) reviewed the literature that looks at explanations for the achievement gap between the working and middle classes. They note that a lot of emphasis has been placed by the government and organisations such as Ofsted on improving 'failing schools', particularly those in working-class areas. From the viewpoint of Ofsted, well organised schools with high-quality teachers who successfully motivate students can make all the difference and provide real opportunities for working-class students. Schools deemed to be ailing can be placed under 'special measures' and given 'notice to improve'.

However, in 2013, Sir Michael Wilshaw (Chief Schools Inspector in England and head of Ofsted) made a speech accepting that schools were still failing poor students in many areas (Adams, 2013). According to Wilshaw, there had been improvements in some large cities, but poor students in schools in affluent areas and in smaller towns were being left behind. He said: "These poor, unseen children can be found in mediocre schools the length and breadth of our country. They are labelled, buried in lower sets, consigned as often as not to indifferent teaching." Wilshaw also thought that there was a problem in attracting the best teachers to schools in disadvantaged areas; if this issue were tackled, this could help to increase achievement for the poor. Another solution was to partner weaker schools with more successful establishments.

Ofsted believe that high-quality teachers are vital to the success of poorer students.

While there have been a number of government initiatives to address underachievement in schools, some sociologists have seen general government education policies in recent years as likely to increase educational inequality, not reduce it (see Chapter 6).

Interactionist perspectives on education

The interactionist perspective focuses on processes within schools and other educational institutions to explain differential achievement. It examines how pupils and teachers react to one another in the education system and argues that these interactions hold the key to understanding educational achievement.

From this perspective, small-scale interaction between individuals shapes people's behaviour. While interacting with others, people interpret behaviour and attach meanings to the behaviour of those around them. This in turn affects people's image of themselves (their **self-concept)**, and self-concept in turn shapes behaviour. For example, if pupils are labelled as deviants (people who contravene social norms or break rules) their behaviour will tend to be seen as a deliberate attempt to cause trouble. The reaction of teachers will lead to the pupils seeing themselves as deviants and because of this they will tend to act in more deviant ways.

UNDERSTAND THE CONCEPT

Your **self-concept** is the sort of person you think you are, whether lazy or hard-working, successful or a failure, and so on. To interactionists, your self-concept is strongly influenced by what others think of you (or at least what you believe they think of you). You might not always accept other peoples' view, but it is difficult, for example, to think of yourself as clever or hard-working if people keep telling you otherwise.

According to the interactionist perspective, teachers may **label** pupils (that is, they classify pupils into different types and then act towards them on the basis of this classification).

A variety of studies have found that labelling can have a negative impact on the educational progress of pupils. For example, Hargreaves, Hester and Mellor (1975) found that factors such as pupils' appearance, how they respond to discipline, how likeable they are, their personality and whether they are deviant leads to teachers labelling pupils as 'good' or 'bad'. These labels are associated with class, and working-class pupils are more likely to fit the stereotype of the 'bad' pupil. Once a pupil has a label, teachers tend to interpret that pupil's behaviour in terms of the label, and the pupil tends to live up to the label they have been given.

UNDERSTAND THE CONCEPT

Labelling occurs when particular characteristics are ascribed to individuals on the basis of descriptions, names or labels. These labels are simplified descriptions and often draw upon common stereotypes about certain types of people. These are usually negative ones (for example, scrounger, delinquent, chav and so on). Labels may be expressed publicly or become public knowledge, which leads to other people making assumptions about individuals. For a variety of reasons, the labelled individuals tend to then live up to their label. Their behaviour is often interpreted negatively and their low status makes it more difficult to conform.

This results in a **self-fulfilling-prophecy**, in which the label results in the behaviour predicted by the teacher. This is illustrated in Figure 1.2.2.

UNDERSTAND THE CONCEPT

A **self-fulfilling prophecy** occurs when something happens because people expect it to happen. Sometimes prophecies (or predictions) can change the course of events. For example, predicting that a pupil will succeed in education may give them self-confidence and enhanced motivation, making their success all the more likely.

Class and labelling

Many interactionists claim that social class background affects the ways in which teachers label pupils. Middle-class pupils tend to fit the teacher's stereotype of the ideal pupil better than working-class pupils, and therefore working-class pupils are more likely to be labelled as deviant or lazy. Labelling is often based on factors such as appearance and attitude as much as actual behaviour.

Labelling can lead to pupils being placed in different ability groupings within school. Working-class pupils may be more likely to be placed in lower sets, bands or streams. Lower groupings are likely to be seen as less able and more likely to be disruptive. This can lead to the formation of pupil subcultures, with lower streams or sets more likely to form anti-school subcultures.

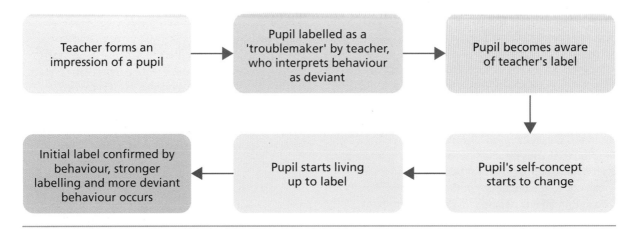

Figure 1.2.1 *The self-fulfilling prophecy*

Amongst these pupils, academic work is not valued and peer groups encourage deviant behaviour and discourage hard work. This is illustrated in a number of studies.

BUILD CONNECTIONS

Labelling is perhaps an even more important issue in the study of crime and deviance (covered in the second year of this course). A number of sociologists argue that many people commit crimes but only the few who are caught and labelled are likely to become long-term and serious criminals. This is because they lose opportunities to succeed in society and end up seeing themselves as criminals and deviants. They therefore live up to the identity and expectations society has given them.

Teacher expectations

In a famous study, Rosenthal and Jacobson (1968) gave false information to primary school teachers in the USA about the intelligence quotient (IQ) of pupils. Teachers were told that some pupils who recorded low IQ scores had a high IQ and vice versa. The progress of the pupils was then measured. This study therefore took the form of a field experiment in which researchers deliberately manipulated a real-life situation to see what the results would be. The researchers found that pupils who teachers believed to have a high IQ made greater progress than those who were believed to have a low IQ, regardless of what their actual IQ was. This suggested that a self-fulfilling prophecy can occur. Those predicted

to do well make good progress because teachers give them more encouragement or have higher expectations of them than those expected to do poorly.

In another experimental study, Harvey and Slatin (1976) used photographs of children from different social classes and asked teachers to rate their likely performance in education. Pupils from higher social classes were seen as more likely to be successful than pupils from lower social classes, indicating that labelling on the basis of appearance may take place. This suggests that teachers can make judgements on the basis of the most flimsy (and possibly irrelevant) information about pupils.

Most labelling is more subtle than this today, but it may still have significant effects on pupils' achievement.

Streaming and setting

Dividing pupils and students by ability level can create or reinforce labels and have significant effects on their achievement. In an early study, Stephen Ball (1981) studied the banding system in a comprehensive school. Pupils were placed in one of three bands based upon reports from their primary school. However, working-class pupils were more likely to be placed in lower bands than middle-class pupils even when their measured ability at primary school was the same. The behaviour of pupils in lower bands deteriorated quickly once they started secondary school. Teachers had low expectations of the lower bands and directed them towards practical subjects and lower-level exams. Expectations of those in higher bands were much greater and they were encouraged more towards academic success.

More recent research by Ireson and Hallam (2009) measured how likely it was for pupils in different sets to have a positive self-concept (or opinion of themselves). They used questionnaires to study pupils aged 14 and 15 in 23 secondary schools. They found that those in higher sets were more likely to have a positive academic self-concept (for example, believing that they could learn things quickly). This also made them more likely to look positively at staying on in education.

A mixture of case studies and survey evidence found that sometimes extra resources (such as better staff to student ratios) were given to lower sets to compensate for problems they might face. Furthermore, most staff insisted that academic criteria were used to allocate pupils to sets. However, the survey research found that it was often not the students with the lowest prior attainment who were in the lowest sets and they argued that: "The mismatch between prior attainment and attainment group suggests that in practice there is strong social interference in teacher judgement and the school processes of set allocation" (Dunne *et al.*, 2011, p. 505). Indeed those eligible for free school meals (and therefore from low-income, usually working-class households) were significantly more likely to be placed in lower sets than those who were not eligible. According to this research, class still plays a major role in allocation to sets.

Knowledge and streaming

Streaming and setting can also affect the type of knowledge that students can gain access to, and can result in working-class pupils being denied the chance to gain the knowledge that makes educational success possible. Nell Keddie (1971) observed classes from different streams studying the same humanities subjects in a London secondary school. In the lower streams, teachers simplified the content to the extent that

learning was largely based on common-sense ideas. Higher streams were taught more in terms of abstract concepts, giving them a greater opportunity to develop their understanding. Questions from pupils in higher sets were taken seriously and answered in detail, but in lower streams those asking questions were often misinterpreted and their questions seen as an attempt to disrupt the class. As a result, they were often ignored or dismissed as irrelevant.

Similarly, research by Gillborn and Youdell (1999) in two London secondary schools found that working-class and black students were more likely to be placed in lower sets than middle-class and white students even when they had been gaining similar results. The pupils in lower sets were often denied the chance to sit higher-tier GCSE exams, meaning they could not get GCSE grades above a C grade, so it would be more difficult for them to progress on to some higher-level courses.

For more on streaming and setting, see Chapter 5, 'The organisation of teaching and learning'.

Pupil subcultures and social class

In early research, David Hargreaves (1967) studied streams in a secondary school and found that students in lower streams who had been labelled as more likely to be troublemakers rebelled against the values of the school. They developed a non-conformist delinquent subculture in which getting into trouble was valued by their peer group and doing homework and conforming in class was looked down on. According to his research, there was a clear polarisation of pupils, with pupils tending to divide themselves into two camps with opposite views.

Similarly Paul Willis (1977) found in the Midlands secondary school he studied that an anti-school peer group developed which rejected the values of the school. Arguing from a neo-Marxist viewpoint, Willis found that there were pronounced class divisions in the school and these were closely linked to wider inequalities of opportunity for those from different backgrounds. The 'lads', who were largely from unskilled backgrounds, were hostile to the 'ear 'oles', who were more likely to be from middle-class backgrounds. The 'lads' saw little point in school work when they expected to take manual labouring jobs. They saw manual jobs as proper work, and middle-class jobs as 'pen pushing' so they had little time for academic work or the values of their school. Willis argued that labelling and streaming made little difference. It was the position of the boys from different class backgrounds in the class structure that shaped their attitudes to schooling and the formation of subcultures, not the way teachers treated them or the way schools were organised.

FOCUS ON RESEARCH: CHAVS, CHARVERS AND TOWNIES

Research by Hollingworth and Williams (2009) examined the way in which some working-class pupils were labelled and devalued as 'chavs' by their middle-class peers. The study involved interviews with white, urban, middle-class families whose students went to one of three inner-city comprehensive schools: 'Norton' (in north east England), 'Riverton' (in south-west England) and a London school.

They interviewed 124 families with parents and children together, 180 mothers or fathers individually and 68 students individually. The students were aged between 12 and 25, and those who had left school talked about their previous school experience. In all the schools the students could identify distinct subcultures: 'hippies' or 'poshies' (Norton), 'goths' and 'emos' (Norton and Riverton), 'skaters' or 'jitters' (Norton and Riverton), 'rockers' and 'gangsters' (London), and 'townies' or 'chavs' or 'charvers' (predominantly Norton and Riverton) (Hollingworth and Williams, 2009, p. 470). Most of these groups were predominantly middle-class, but those seen as chavs, charvers or townies were invariably working class. None of the working-class pupils gave themselves these labels – they were imposed on them by others from non-working-class backgrounds, and the middle-class students were keen to emphasise that they did not belong to these three groups. Indeed they looked down on what they saw as their immoral, anti-social behaviour and their poor taste. They saw them as arrogant, flashy, loud, uninterested in learning and lacking in self-control. While the middle-class students saw themselves as investing in their educational future, they saw the working-class pupils who were chavs, charvers or townies as lacking in the desire to succeed and therefore likely to fail.

Questions

1. Examine the subcultures (if there are any) in your own school or college. What are the similarities and differences compared to the subcultures found in this research?

2. Evaluate whether the type of school used in the research (inner-city comprehensives) could explain the similarities and differences you discussed in answering question 1.

3. Identify the possible advantages and disadvantages of using interviews to study subcultures?

4. Suggest an alternative research method for this type of research and explain why it might be useful.

5. On the basis of this research, explain the view that it is not just teachers who can give pupils negative labels.

6. Applying this research, analyse how the labels attached to some working-class pupils might affect their educational progress.

Research by Mairtan Mac an Ghaill (1994) examined working-class students in a Midlands comprehensive. Because the school divided pupils into three sets, three distinct male, working-class peer groups developed rather than two:

› In the lowest set the main subculture was that of the 'macho lads'. They were academic failures who became hostile to the school, showed little interest in school work, and were usually from less skilled working-class backgrounds.

› In the highest set, the predominant subculture was of the 'academic achievers'. They were academic 'successes' usually from more skilled working-class backgrounds. They tried hard at school and were aiming to progress to higher levels of study.

› The middle set was dominated by the 'new enterprisers'. They had a positive attitude to school and school work, but they saw the vocational curriculum as a route to career success rather than academic subjects.

Evaluation of interactionist perspectives

Although interactionist perspectives have been very influential, and they show that factors operating within school can have a significant impact upon educational achievement, they have been criticised in a number of ways:

> By concentrating on processes within the education system, they fail to explain where wider class inequalities come from. They tend not to look at the wider context that gives rise to stereotypes of the working class, inequality in access to successful schools, and so on. They therefore ignore or downplay factors outside the schools. (Paul Willis, who combines the study of interaction in schools with Marxist analysis, is an exception here.)

> Labelling theory sometimes sounds **deterministic**: success and failure seems to be entirely determined by the attitudes of pupils, which gives pupils little apparent control over their own achievement. It is clear that not all pupils live up to labelling by teachers. For example, a study by Margaret Fuller (1984) found that a group of black working-class girls who were labelled as likely failures responded by working harder to achieve success. Rather than a self-fulfilling prophecy taking place, they rebelled against the low expectations of their teachers.

UNDERSTAND THE CONCEPT

Most people feel that most of the time they can choose how they behave. However, sociologists tend to claim that, to some extent, social factors can explain behaviour. This suggests that people don't have a free choice and that their behaviour is shaped by outside forces. **Deterministic** theories take this view to the extreme. They don't acknowledge that individuals have any choice about how they behave instead arguing that circumstances shape what they do. For some, labelling is a deterministic theory which claims that people will always live up to a label imposed on them by other people. However, most labelling theorists recognise that sometimes individuals will refuse to live up to their labels. These labelling theorists do not therefore support a deterministic version of labelling theory.

> Some interactionists may have simplified models of pupil subcultures and do not identify the full range of responses to schools. By identifying just two or three subcultures, they ignore groups and individuals

who don't fall neatly into one category. However, not all interactionists fall into this trap. For example, Peter Woods (1983) identified eight different groups in schools. 'Opportunists', for example, fluctuated between trying to gain the approval of their teachers and of their peer group.

> Many of the studies have been based on male peer groups and are less useful for understanding female groups (see Chapter 4 for more discussion on gender differences in education).

> Interactionist approaches tend not to look at the effect of social policies in any detail, yet these too can have a major impact on whether factors in the education system promote greater equality of opportunity or make class differences in achievement more pronounced. These are discussed in the following section, Social policy and social class.

Think about relationships and peer groups in the school or college where you study. Are there distinct peer groups? Do they tend to be based on streams or sets and are they linked to social class? Are there more than two or three subcultures? What do your observations suggest about interactionist theories of class and achievement?

Social policy and social class

Educational policies relating to class can be divided into two main types:

> those specifically aimed at reducing class inequalities

> more general policies that have had an impact on class inequalities in education even though this is not their main aim.

Many policies aimed directly at reducing class inequality have been based upon cultural deprivation theory (which sees working-class culture as lacking the necessary attributes to promote success in education). These policies have led to the idea of positive discrimination in the form of **compensatory education** – where the working class are given extra help in the education system to compensate for the supposed inadequacy of their socialisation. A variety of schemes have aimed at providing extra help for the working class such as Sure Start, launched In 1998. Sure Start has provided additional pre-school education to try to compensate for any lack of educational stimulation from parents.

However, critics such as Whitty (2002) believe that all these schemes tend to place blame for failure on the child and their background and ignore the effects of inequality in society as a whole. Many schemes have lacked resources and have failed to tackle the poverty which is the underlying cause of educational inequality. (See Chapter 6 for more discussion of these and related policies).

UNDERSTAND THE CONCEPT

Compensatory education is additional educational provision that is intended to fill gaps or counter weaknesses in the knowledge and skills that the working class are seen as having.

From the time the Conservative government came into office in 1979, the education policies of successive British governments have been influenced more by neoliberal perspectives than by any other set of ideas (see Chapter 1). These policies have involved increased **marketisation** and greater competition between schools, colleges and universities. Since educational institutions are funded according to how many pupils or students they can attract, they have to act like businesses and offer the most attractive 'product' to 'consumers' (pupils, students and their parents/guardians). The consumers of education do not directly pay for most state school and college education, but they have been encouraged to exercise choice, making them more like the customers of businesses. The consumers are assisted in choosing schools by information such as inspection reports and league table standings.

UNDERSTAND THE CONCEPT

Marketisation involves trying to get state-run services to be organised more like private companies, in which goods or services are bought and sold in a market. Individuals don't pay for state education but if learners can choose which institutions (schools, colleges, universities) they attend, and the government rules that money follows the learners, then the institutions will be forced to act like businesses. They will have to compete with each other to attract 'customers' (learners) just as private businesses do. In theory, they will have to constantly improve to keep ahead of or catch up with the opposition, therefore driving up standards.

These policies encourage educational institutions to try to attract the 'best' students who will do the most to boost their league table results. The process of attracting the most able students has been called 'cream-skimming' (Bartlett and Le Grand, 1993). Middle-class and upper-class students are generally seen as more desirable than working-class students. At the same time, marketisation encourages pupils, students and their parents to try to get places in the most successful institutions. Middle-class parents have more resources to manipulate the system to give their children the best possible chance of getting into the 'best schools'. This tends to create a polarised school system with successful schools often over-subscribed and therefore well-funded with largely middle-class students, and less successful schools undersubscribed and largely working class. A number of studies suggest that these policies can lead to greater inequality in the education system, particularly between social classes. Recent research by Lloyds (discussed in Meyer, 2013) found clear evidence that well-off parents were paying extra to live in the catchment areas for the most successful state schools. Houses near the best-performing state secondary schools cost an average of £31,000 more than houses in neighbouring areas outside the school catchment area.

Research by Gillborn and Youdell (2000) found that one result of increased competition was a tendency to neglect the education of the largely working-class pupils who were seen as having little chance of getting a C grade or higher in five GCSEs (a crucial measure of school performance used in league tables). Instead schools concentrated on those who were just below this level of achievement in order to bring them up to C grade level and maximise their league-table performance. (This process is known as educational triage – pupils are divided into groups and some are prioritised. Resources are concentrated on the pupils where the institution has the best chance of improving its league-table standing, while others are neglected, for example, because they are unlikely to achieve five C grades even with extra help.) As a consequence, there was little attempt to boost the performance of lower sets. Working-class and ethnic minority pupils were more likely to be allocated to lower sets than white, middle-class children, further increasing their educational disadvantages.

Based on the evidence provided in this section, suggest two ways in which the educational achievement of working-class pupils could be increased. What problems might there be in getting the policies to succeed?

FOCUS ON SKILLS: EDUCATIONAL CHOICE AND MARKETS

Stephen Ball *et al.* (1994) conducted studies on the effects of educational reform introduced by Margaret Thatcher's Conservative government. They found that some groups took more advantage of the introduction of markets than others. Some parents were more likely to get their children into the school of their choice.

Middle-class parents were usually privileged/skilled choosers. They had the time and social contacts to make informed choices about which were the best schools. Many had the money to pay for private education if necessary or to move home to be in the catchment area for the most successful state schools. (Catchment areas are the geographical areas from which individual schools allow applications from pupils to attend the school.)

Working-class parents were usually disconnected choosers. They had much less opportunity to get children into the school of their choice. For example, they often had limited access to private cars, so it was harder for them to get their children to a non-local school. Some also lacked the knowledge of admission policies necessary to manipulate the situation to and get their children into the 'best schools'. Usually, they couldn't afford to buy a house in the catchment area for a good school, where housing was more expensive. As a result, they often chose the local school for their children and based their decisions on the happiness of their children rather than on the academic reputation of the school. They assumed that children would feel more comfortable studying with friends, living close to schoolmates and attending a school mainly populated by children from a similar background.

Ball *et al.* found the new policies had a number of negative effects upon the education system. All schools tried hard to attract the most academically able students to boost league-table results. Less attention was paid to students with special educational needs. Time and resources were devoted to improving school image to attract pupils rather than to helping the most educationally disadvantaged. Cooperation between neighbouring schools became less common. Most schools tried to portray a traditional academic image, for example, by enforcing rules about school uniform, so there was in fact little real choice for parents. In addition, because the capacity of individual schools is limited, many parents, particularly from the working class, did not get their first choice of school.

Questions

1. **Examine.** Which factors made it more difficult for working-class parents to get their children into the highest performing schools?

2. **Examine** why working-class parents usually ended up sending their children to a local school.

3. **Analyse** ways in which marketisation might lead to a more divided education system. (Are there winners and losers in competitive systems? How could this affect schools?)

4. **Analyse** the reasons why educational policies might lead to working-class pupils falling further behind middle-class pupils in education. (Think about whether the middle class have more opportunity to manipulate the system.)

5. **Evaluate** the view that marketisation disadvantages working-class pupils. Are there any ways in which it could help to improve the standard of the education they receive? (Supporters of the system suggest it drives up standards for everyone. Is this a credible argument and why?)

CONCLUSIONS

Despite all the attempts to reduce differential achievement based on social class it remains stubbornly high. In part this may be because it is impossible to eliminate inequality of opportunity in a society which is very unequal. Factors outside the education system (material and cultural factors) interact with factors inside (such as labelling, setting, the curriculum and the development of subcultures) to mean that the odds are stacked against working-class success. While some individuals can certainly break through the barriers and succeed, the overall pattern of class differences has not changed significantly in recent decades. Some policies aimed at reducing class inequalities may have made some difference, but the general trend towards competition and marketisation has, if anything, made the situation worse.

Social class alone does not shape educational attainment; it interacts with other social divisions, particularly ethnicity (see Chapter 3) and gender (see Chapter 4). However, it is probably the most important single factor. Gillborn and Mirza (2000) have estimated that class has twice the effect on educational achievement of ethnicity and five times the effect of gender.

CHECK YOUR UNDERSTANDING

1. Briefly explain what is meant by material deprivation.

2. Suggest two ways in which material deprivation might hold back educational progress for children even before they start school.

3. Identify and briefly explain three ways in which some sociologists see the working class as culturally deprived.

4. Which two types of speech code are distinguished by Basil Bernstein? Briefly explain each speech code.

5. Suggest three possible criticisms of cultural deprivation theory.

6. Explain how Bourdieu's idea of cultural capital differs from the idea of cultural deprivation.

7. Explain three ways in which interaction within schools may lead to differences in educational achievement.

8. Identify and explain two policies designed to reduce inequality in educational achievement.

9. Analyse the differences and similarities between cultural and material explanations of differential achievement.

10. Evaluate the claim that factors inside education largely determine achievement by identifying two arguments in favour of this view and two arguments against.

TAKE IT FURTHER

Identify a popular and oversubscribed school and a relatively unpopular secondary school close to where you live. Use a website such as Zoopla or Right Move to compare property prices in the two areas. Does your research suggest it is more expensive to live in areas close to popular secondary schools? How could this be linked to theories of material deprivation?

1.3 ETHNICITY AND EDUCATIONAL ACHIEVEMENT

INTRODUCING THE DEBATE

Class is not the only social division that has an impact on educational achievement; **ethnicity** is also important. Britain has an ethnically diverse population with some large minority ethnic groups, such as those of Indian and Pakistani origin and Black Caribbean groups, and smaller minority ethnic groups such as the Chinese. Some minority ethnic groups outperform White British ethnic groups in education, others do less well. Some long-established minority ethnic groups have become more and more successful in education while others have made less progress.

The patterns and trends are complicated but sociologists have sought to understand and explain them in terms of the differences between ethnic groups. As in the case of social class, cultural differences or material inequality could be important, but so could racism both inside and outside the education system. Many of the explanations put forward to explain differences in achievement therefore parallel those used in explaining class differences, but the particular factors that affect ethnicity and educational achievement are not necessarily the same as those shaping class inequalities.

TRENDS IN ETHNICITY AND ACHIEVEMENT

Some minority ethnic groups continue to have lower levels of achievement than the average, while others have above average levels of achievement. This is not always consistent at all levels of education. For example, many minority ethnic groups have high levels of participation in higher education. However, inequalities can be measured in different ways and the evidence suggests that those from minority ethnic groups have lower than average chances of studying at the more prestigious universities. The patterns are further complicated by the intersection (or overlap) of different types of inequality with ethnicity, particularly gender and social class. For example, there is

31

evidence that boys from African Caribbean backgrounds have lower levels of achievement than girls from African Caribbean backgrounds.

UNDERSTAND THE CONCEPT

Ethnicity refers to groups within a population regarded by themselves or by others as culturally distinctive; they usually see themselves as having a common origin. This could be linked to nationality or supposed 'racial' differences between groups of people, but ethnicity is a distinct concept in its own right. Ethnic groups may share some practices or beliefs (for example, religious beliefs). Minority ethnic groups are the smaller ethnic groups in a society while a majority ethnic group is the largest grouping (for example, White British in the UK). The ethnicity of majority groups may be taken for granted, but ethnicity is just as important for these groups as for minorities.

MATERIAL FACTORS AFFECTING UNDERACHIEVEMENT

Although ethnic groups are characterised by cultural differences, there are also differences in the material position of different ethnic groups. Those from different ethnic groups may have an above average chance of living in poverty or having working-class rather than middle-class jobs. So rather than differences in achievement being directly caused by cultural differences between ethnic groups, they could be caused by some ethnic groups being, on average, better off than others. In other words, material inequality or class differences could be the main factor underlying differences in achievement by ethnic group.

According to Lina Platt (2011, p.85) the highest hourly rates of pay for male full-time employees in the UK were for Chinese ethnic groups, followed by Indian, White British, Black Caribbean, Bangladeshi and Pakistani groups. This is quite similar to patterns of educational achievement, and suggests that some groups do better simply as a result of living in higher-income families. However the patterns do not fit exactly. For example, you might expect African Caribbean males to do better in education given their relative income.

These inequalities in income reflect differences in entitlement to free school meals (FSM) as shown in Table 1.3.1.

Ethnic group	Per cent entitled to FSM
White British	12.5
Mixed heritage	21.1
Indian	9.7
Pakistani	28.0
Bangladeshi	38.5
Black Caribbean	25.2
Black African	33.6
Any other group	30.8

Table 1.3.1 Ethnicity and entitlement to Free School Meals (FSM) 2012–2013
Source: Department for Education (2014)

To analyse the relationship further, one can examine how eligibility for FSM interacts with ethnicity and achievement – how do low-income families from each ethnic group perform in the education system? Figure 1.3.1 shows that in all ethnic groups, the poorer pupils who are eligible for FSM do less well than the better-off pupils who are not eligible for them. This helps to explain differences in ethnicity and educational achievement. Whatever their ethnicity, children from poorer backgrounds do less well, and some ethnic groups (particularly Bangladeshis and Pakistanis) tend to have lower than average wages. However, it is also clear that low income affects some groups more than others. In particular, it affects White British pupils more than other groups because the gap between FSM and non-FSM children is much bigger than in other groups. This can't be explained simply in terms of material factors. Other factors, perhaps cultural ones, seem to counteract low income at least to some extent among ethnic minorities. Some cultures might compensate for the negative effects of low income more than others.

A similar pattern was demonstrated in research by Gillborn and Mirza (2000) that looked directly at the effects of social class on ethnic groups in the education system. The data from Youth Cohort Studies between 1997 and 1998 showed that there was a strong relationship between social class and achievement in all ethnic groups. In all groups, children from middle-class backgrounds did better than those from working-class backgrounds. However, African Caribbean pupils (particularly boys) did less well than their peers in other ethnic groups even when class was taken into account, while pupils from Indian, Pakistani and Bangladeshi groups did better.

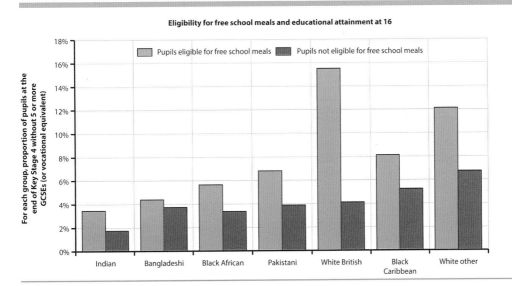

Figure 1.3.1 *Achievement at GCSE of students eligible for free school meals, analysed by ethnic group*
Source: National Pupil Database, DfE (2011)

The relative success of pupils from some minority ethnic groups could be explained in terms of cultural capital. Tariq Modood (2004) argues that many ethnic-minority parents have more cultural capital than is typical for their income or class position. If they are recent migrants to the UK, they may have been downwardly mobile or they may not be able to get jobs in line with their skills, experience and qualifications due to discrimination, or because they lack familiarity with British culture. As a result, they may be better educated than most White British parents from the same class background and can therefore provide more help for their children in their education. Other factors might explain the relative underachievement of African Caribbean pupils, including processes in the education system itself, and these will be examined in later sections.

Would you agree that coming from a low-income family disadvantages children from all ethnic groups, but some more than others? What evidence is there to support or contradict this claim?

CULTURAL FACTORS, ETHNICITY AND ACHIEVEMENT

A number of cultural factors, it has been suggested, are important in explaining the relationship between ethnicity and educational achievement. Some people believe that minority ethnic groups may be either deprived or advantaged educationally as a result of distinctive features of the culture of their ethnic group. However, these views should be treated with some caution. It shouldn't be assumed that all members of an ethnic group share exactly the same culture and there may be differences between males and females in each group. Nevertheless, there may be some broad cultural differences that have an impact.

Parental attitudes towards education could be one important factor. British Chinese pupils and students are more successful than any other ethnic group in the British education system, and there is some evidence that this could be due, at least in part, to support that they receive from their families. Research by Archer and Francis (2007) found that the parents of Chinese pupils placed an exceptionally high value on education.

Research conducted by Tehmina Basit (2013) found that cultural factors had an impact on educational achievement in British Asian communities (of both Pakistani and Indian origin and Muslim and Hindu faiths). Basit studied three generations: grandparents, parents and children. She collected data on attitudes to education among British Asians in the West Midlands. She used **focus groups** for her research with the children (who were aged 15–16) and in-depth interviews with the older generations. All the participants placed a high value on education and saw free state education as a 'blessing' because it generally offered more opportunities than were available in their countries of origin. They therefore tended to put considerable effort and resources into helping their children. Even the relatively poor parents had managed to provide space to study, desks, computer and internet access for their children, and most of the children had their own rooms. Parents expected their children to work hard and, many being well qualified themselves, actively helped their children with their studies.

Basit comments that: "It was strikingly clear that education was viewed as capital that would transform the lives of the younger generation. This educational capital was believed to be the most significant asset a young person could acquire and the families provided a range of support mechanisms to enable the young people to realise this aspiration" (p. 719). While all the grandparents were from working-class backgrounds, some of the parents had gained middle-class jobs (albeit usually modestly paid ones) via educational success, and they wanted, and expected, their children to be at least as successful. Although the parents could not afford to move to expensive areas to gain access to the best schools, they did try to help their children

get into selective schools, sometimes by arranging private tuition.

The research on British Chinese and British Asian families suggests that stable, supportive families who are very keen on educational achievement may be the key to understanding the relative success of some minority ethnic groups in education. However, some research suggests that all minority ethnic groups are enthusiastic about education compared to the White British ethnic majority. Research by Connor et al. (2004) found that among Year 13 students positive attitudes to education were strongest among Black African students planning to go on to higher education.

UNDERSTAND THE CONCEPT

Focus groups are a type of group interview in which a carefully selected group of people are asked to discuss particular issues. They allow a more in-depth exploration of group attitudes than individual interviews and they reflect the ways in which interaction with others affects opinions in social life.

BUILD CONNECTIONS

Changes in family life will clearly have an impact on the relationship between family and education. The increased diversity of families (see Topic 4, Chapter 5) has been most discussed in relation to White British families, but there is also some evidence that diversity is increasing within minority ethnic groups as well. For example, there may have been some increase in divorce and lone parenthood among British Asian families and this could affect the relationship between family life, culture, ethnicity and educational achievement. There is family diversity within, as well as between, ethnic groups, and this illustrates the danger of making generalisations about culture and education.

Despite apparently strong encouragement from families, African Caribbean pupils and students have tended to do less well in education than those of Indian origin. According to a DfE report (Wanless Report, 1997) Black pupils, (particularly boys):

> are significantly more likely to be permanently excluded from school than other ethnic groups

> are 1.5 times as likely as White British pupils to be identified with behaviour-related special needs

> are disproportionately put in bottom sets even though this does not reflect ability

> are much less likely than average to be identified as gifted and talented.

Some sociologists have attributed these problems partly to cultural factors outside schools. Tony Sewell (1997) argues that they are related to the relatively high proportion of Black African pupils raised in lone-parent families (see Chapter 5 for details). Basing his ideas on research with 11–16-year-old pupils in a London school, he claims that being brought up by a lone mother can lead to some boys lacking male role models and the discipline provided by a father figure. As a result, they may be attracted to gangs that encourage an aggressive and macho form of masculinity which does not value respect for authority. These attitudes tend to result in a lack of concern for academic achievement and a rejection of the values of school. Although this only affects a minority of Black African pupils, it depresses the overall performance of Black minority ethnic groups.

Sewell's research neatly links factors external to the education system, such as family life and gang culture, with the education system itself (see 'Labelling, stereotyping and subcultures, in this chapter for more detail on the subcultures he studied within schools). However, Sewell has been strongly criticised for blaming Black Caribbeans for their underachievement rather than concentrating on the inadequacies of the education system itself, and for allowing his work to divert attention away from racism. These views will be explored in the next section (Labelling, racism and pupil responses).

Evaluate the view that 'blaming lone parenthood for the underperformance of some African Caribbean boys in education is blaming the victims of an unequal and racist society'. You could consider whether coming from a lone-parent family necessarily disadvantages children in education.

Certainly the apparent underperformance of Black Caribbean children in education should not be exaggerated. Compared to White British people, minority ethnic groups have a larger proportion of members with working-class backgrounds in higher education. This is particularly true for Pakistanis and Bangladeshis – nearly two-thirds of the entrants to higher education from these groups came from households headed by manual workers or the unemployed (Modood, 2004). Furthermore, some African Caribbean pupils have very high attainment and make excellent progress.

On the other hand, some White British pupils have extremely low attainment, particularly those from economically disadvantaged groups, and make poor progress. For example, national statistics highlight the fact that only 24 per cent of White British boys entitled to FSM achieved five or more GCSE grades at A* to C, even lower than the 27 per cent of African Caribbean boys entitled to FSM who achieve this (DfE, 2007). Also, White British working-class pupils in inner-city areas have recently emerged as the group making the least progress over the secondary phase of education.

FACTORS INTERNAL TO THE EDUCATION SYSTEM

Labelling, racism and pupil responses

While some differences in the educational achievement of ethnic groups can be attributed to factors outside the education system, factors within the system clearly play a part as well. This section examines these factors.

Unequal outcomes and institutional racism

Some researchers have suggested that pupils from different ethnic minorities are treated differently by both teachers and other pupils. A range of research suggests that this may have a particularly negative impact on boys of African Caribbean origin. Research by Steve Strand (2012) using data from the Longitudinal Study of Young People in England found that in Britain, African Caribbean pupils did significantly less well in education at the age of 14 than their White British peers. This held true even when allowances were made for differences in social class background, family, school and neighbourhood factors. The study also found that African Caribbean pupils were less likely to be entered for higher level GCSEs than their White British counterparts.

A number of factors may have accounted for this. African Caribbean pupils were more likely to have been excluded from school and to have had a statement of special educational needs. But even taking these factors into account, for every three White British pupils entered for higher-tier exams in Maths and Science, only two African Caribbean pupils were entered. This seems to provide evidence of teacher bias in decisions about exam entries.

Some sociologists attribute such findings to **institutional racism**. David Gillborn (2002) argues that schools are institutionally racist, as teachers interpret policy in a way that disadvantages Black pupils. For example, setting, schemes for gifted and talented pupils, and vocational schemes for the less academic all underrate the abilities of Black children, relegating them to low-ability groups, a restricted curriculum and entry for lower-level exams. The increased marketisation of schools (see Chapter 6) has led to what some writers have called an 'A to C economy'. According to Gillborn and Youdell (1999) this creates a rationing of education: teachers are forced to focus on those in danger of not realising their potential and fostering them to enable them to achieve a C grade or above. They therefore neglect both the 'no-hopers' and the 'high achievers', leaving them to their own devices. Many Black pupils are judged, often unfairly, to be 'no hopers'.

David Gillborn (2008) argues that racism affects some ethnic minorities much more than others. Thus 'model minorities' – such as Chinese and Indian pupils – who are seen as having positive attitudes to education – are treated differently from minorities who are seen as a potential problem. Institutional racism may, furthermore, be entrenched in the organisation of schools and the way that power is distributed within them. For example, Ranson (2005) highlights the unrepresentativeness of school governing bodies, which are 'disproportionately White, middle-aged, middle-class, middle-income, public/ community service workers'. For these reasons, ethnic inequalities in education are often given a low priority.

UNDERSTAND THE CONCEPT

Institutional racism is a form of discrimination within organisations that unfairly disadvantages those from relatively powerless and disadvantaged ethnic groups. Institutional racism occurs not because of the attitudes of individuals, but because of the systems, cultures, policies and/or structures of the organisations themselves. This results in organisations (such as schools, universities, corporations or hospitals) failing to provide the same quality of service and opportunity to ethnic groups. For example, a school that failed to deal effectively with complaints of racist bullying, or failed to provide a curriculum equally suitable for all ethnic groups, could be seen as institutionally racist.

Labelling, stereotyping and subcultures

Possible reasons for apparent underperformance by some African Caribbean pupils can be found in studies which suggest that these pupils (especially boys) are often given negative labels such as 'unruly', 'disrespectful' and 'difficult to control'. Gillborn (1990) found that African Caribbean pupils were more likely to be given detentions than other pupils. This was because the teachers interpreted (or misinterpreted) the dress and manner of speech of African Caribbean pupils as representing a challenge to their authority. In perceiving their treatment to be unfair, the pupils responded, understandably, in accordance with their labels.

Jasper (2002) goes further, and suggests that the expectations that White female teachers have of Black boys' behaviour dictate the form and style of the teaching that they offer; a style less conducive to learning than

they offer to other groups. O'Donnell (1991) showed how the various ethnic subcultures have distinctive reactions to racism, prejudice and discrimination, which may have different effects on educational performance. African Caribbean males often react angrily to and reject the White-dominated education system, gaining status and recognition through other means. Indians show their anger, but do not tend to reject the education system. Instead, they succeed because they use the education system to their advantage.

According to O'Donnell and Sharpe (2000) in responding to teacher's labels, racism and poor economic prospects, Black males construct a form of masculinity that earns respect from peers and females. This macho response may have little relevance for males in general, with the decline in manual work and increasing opportunities within the service sector. However, for young Black men, with more limited employment prospects, opposition to schooling still has some relevance in highlighting their masculinity and alternative attributes of success. Despite their relatively high academic self-concept (Strand, 2007), educational success is seen as a feminine thing. The way for them to get respect is through the credibility of the street. In Sewell's words, the young man wants to be a 'street hood'. Success in the school room marks the Black boy out from his peers or classmates and is likely to make him the target of ridicule or bullying. According to Sewell, educational failure becomes a badge to wear with pride. Aspects of this view have been reflected in concerns about the development of 'gangsta' culture and the absence of positive Black male role models at home as well as in schools.

A similar response has been identified among some Asian youths – in particular, Bangladeshi boys, whose economic prospects once they leave school are generally bleaker than those of other Asian groups. O'Donnell and Sharpe (2000) recognised that this macho 'warrior' perception by peers existed alongside perceptions of other Asian youths as 'weaklings' who conformed to the demands of the school or 'patriarchs' whose loyalty lay with the prescriptions of the male-dominated Asian family.

Connolly (1998) also examined the treatment in school of boys of South Asian origin. He found that teachers tended to see some South Asian boys as immature rather than as seriously deviant. Much of their bad behaviour went unnoticed by teachers and was not punished to the same extent as that of Black boys. The South Asian boys, therefore, had difficulty in gaining status as males, which made it more difficult for them to enjoy school and feel confident. However, teachers did have high expectations

FOCUS ON SKILLS: INSTITUTIONAL RACISM AND HISTORY TEACHING

Only three black people who want to be history teachers were accepted for postgraduate teacher-training courses last year, according to damning statistics that critics claim expose 'institutional racism' in the British education system.

The figures are part of a wider picture in which just 17.2% of black African applicants and 28.7% of black Caribbean applicants were taken on by teacher training institutions across all subjects, against 46.7% of white applicants.

The revelation provoked claims of racism in the system, with one of Britain's first black professors calling for the government to do some 'soul searching' over the state of the profession.

According to the annual statistical report by the Graduate Teacher Training Registry (GTTR) published last week, 30 black Caribbean, African or mixed-race people applied to read for a postgraduate certificate in education in history in 2013. One mixed-race applicant was accepted as were up to two black Caribbean or black African applicants – at best a 10% success rate. This stands in stark contrast to the 506 white people accepted for history teacher-training courses from the 1,937 who applied – a 26% success rate. A further 19 applicants from other ethnic minority groups, including Indian, Pakistani and Bangladeshi, were awarded places. The ethnicity of 17 successful applicants was unknown.

Professor Heidi Mirza, who is of Caribbean origin, said that the government should be concerned by both the low number of black applicants and the lack of success of those that apply. Nationally, while 17% of pupils in the UK are from black, Asian and ethnic minority backgrounds, only about 7% of teachers are.

Mirza, author of *Respecting Difference: Race, Faith and Culture for Teacher Educators*, said: 'Diversity in

our teacher workforce is crucial if British children are to be well prepared to be global citizens and successfully compete on the world stage.

'We need to do some soul searching in our teacher education provision and look at the insidious ways institutional racism keeps potential black, minority ethnic and refugee teachers from getting on and through their courses. I do think there is a hidden crisis in teacher education, which has slipped under the wire of Gove's reforms in education.'

Professor John Howson, blogger and a former government adviser on teacher recruitment, said that he was particularly concerned by the lack of black history teachers because it limited the variety of perspectives being heard in classrooms on Britain's colonial heritage. A poem from John Agard, "Checking out me history", about the dominance of the history of white males in classrooms resonates deeply with many in the black community.

Mirza said there was significant evidence that discrimination was a major factor. She cited a survey on 'Leadership aspirations and careers of black and minority teachers' in which more than half of the sample reported some sort of discrimination. Another survey found that black and Asian teachers were half as likely to be head teachers and deputy head teachers as white teachers.

Source: Boffey, D. 'Institutional racism and history teaching' *The Observer*, 22 March 2014

Questions

1. **Identify** and summarise evidence in this article that suggests there may be institutional racism in teacher recruitment, training and career progression.

2. **Analyse** the effects that this might have on different ethnic groups in the education system. (Do you think, for example, that other ethnic minorities are likely to become history teachers?)

3. **Analyse** what effect this might have on the curriculum. (For example, is the history of other minority groups prominent in the history curriculum?)

4. **Evaluate** the strength of the evidence of racism in schools, based on this article. (How convincing and how broad is the evidence?)

of their academic potential and they were often praised and encouraged.

Although much of the research focus has been on ethnic-minority boys in the education system, the position of girls has also been studied. Connolly (1998) found in his investigation of three classes of 5 to 6-year-olds in a multi-ethnic, inner-city primary school that some negative stereotypes are not just confined to boys. Like Black boys, Black girls were perceived by teachers as potentially disruptive but likely to be good at sports. The teachers in one school tended to 'underplay the Black girls' educational achievements and focus on their social behaviour'. Like their male counterparts, they were quite likely to be disciplined and punished, even though their behaviour did not always seem to justify it.

While few would argue that teachers display overt racism, Wright (1992) found considerable discrimination in the classroom. She observed Asian and African Caribbean children in primary schools and found that teachers paid Asian pupils, especially girls, less attention. They involved them less in discussion and used simplistic language, assuming that they had a poor command of English. Teachers also lacked sensitivity towards aspects of their culture and displayed open disapproval of their customs and traditions. This had the effect of making the girls feel less positive towards the school. It also attracted hostility from other pupils, who picked up on the teachers' comments and attitude towards the Asian pupils.

Wright (1992) observed that primary school teachers often paid less attention to Asian girls.

Despite this, teachers did have high expectations of Asian pupils with regard to academic success. According to Connolly (1998), South Asian girls, though generally successful in the education system, may be overlooked because of their perceived passivity, or they may feel marginalised and left out of discourses relating to intimacy, love and marriage because of stereotypical assumptions about Asian family life. Connolly also challenged the stereotypical assumptions many teachers made, noting

that the behaviour of South Asian girls pointed towards a similar mix of work and avoidance of work, and obedience and disruption, making their behaviour largely indistinguishable from that of their female peers. It would appear, therefore, that high expectations may to some extent be responsible for creating a self-fulfilling prophecy in terms of Asian girls' relative success.

Some evidence indicates that many Black girls are anti-school, but pro-education. They resent low teacher expectations and labelling, but are more determined to succeed than many other groups, especially Black boys.

Mirza (1992) notes how some Black girls respond to the failure of the school to address their needs by rejecting the help of teachers, which they regard as patronising and, though sometimes well-meaning, misguided. For example, the girls were entered for fewer subjects 'to take the pressure off' or given ill-informed, often stereotypical careers advice. The girls respond outwardly by appearing to reject the values of the school through their dress, attitudes and behaviour. In terms of academic achievement, however, in Mirza's study, the rejection of teachers' help and limited involvement in lessons were seen to place the girls at a disadvantage academically, even though they preserved high self-esteem. They were not victims of overt racism or labelling. They were simply held back by the well-meaning but misguided behaviour of most of their teachers.

However, research by Margaret Fuller (1984) found that there could sometimes be a positive reaction to negative labelling. The group of Black girls in her study managed to use their rejection by the school to motivate them to be successful, and they were able to overcome the barriers put in their path to achieve high grades.

While teachers may have certain expectations of minority ethnic groups, some of which may have been detrimental to their success, pupils of both Asian and African Caribbean origin are, according to Connolly (1998), often victims of racism from White pupils. The impact of this on educational commitment and performance is inevitably negative.

Other sociologists argue that racism, at least in the overt sense, cannot be a complete explanation for ethnic group differences in attainment. Modood (2003) argues: "If racism leads to the victim being turned off school and dropping out, why do Asian men and women have such high staying-on rates and make academic progress?" This does not discount the possibility of social stereotyping or institutional racism against some ethnic groups, but does highlight the importance of being sceptical with regard to generalised explanations.

FOCUS ON RESEARCH: AIMING HIGH (TIKLY *ET AL.*, 2006)

In 2003, the government set up a programme called 'Aiming High' to help raise the achievement of African Caribbean pupils. It provided extra resources to 30 schools where African and Caribbean pupils were performing below the average for all pupils between the ages of 11 and 16. In 2006, a team of sociologists led by Leon Tikly evaluated the success of the project.

Tikly's team used postal questionnaires to generate quantitative information about setting, examination tiers and rates of exclusion. The questionnaires were returned by only 18 schools at the start of the project and 11 at the end. One third of the sample (10 schools) were subsequently involved in semi-structured interviews with, for example,

governors, headteachers, pupils, parents and teachers. These generated qualitative data about the extent to which schools recognised and valued ethnic diversity and the ways in which they treated ethnic-minority pupils in relation to behaviour and discipline. Those that were most focused on these issues appeared to have fewer behavioural problems and lower exclusion rates.

Source: Tikly, L. *et al.* (2006)

Questions

1. Identify the quantitative and qualitative methods used in this research.

2. Analyse the advantages and disadvantages of using postal questionnaires for this type of research.

3. Evaluate the extent to which you think the results of this research can be generalised to other schools. (Is a sample of 10 schools sufficient to make generalisations?)

4. Evaluate the benefits of participating in the programme for those schools that valued ethnic diversity.

5. Analyse the reasons why their policies made a difference? How could extra resources help?

The curriculum

Some sociologists have argued that the curriculum – what is taught in schools – actually disadvantages ethnic minorities. The knowledge that they encounter at school may not connect with their own cultural experience, while ethnocentrism, resulting from the use of out-of-date material, could be potentially offensive by reflecting old colonial values and racial stereotypes. In pioneering research, Bernard Coard (1971) showed how the content of education also ignored Black people. The people who are acclaimed tend to be White, while Black culture, music and art are largely ignored. Coard argued that this led to low self-esteem among Black pupils. However, this assertion was refuted by both the Swann Report (1985) and Stone (1981), who noted that, despite feeling discriminated against by some teachers, African Caribbean children had been able to maintain an extremely positive self-image.

More recently, efforts have been made to address the neglect of other cultures in the curriculum. **Multicultural** education, which acknowledges the contribution of all of

the world's cultures, has become more common, although it has been criticised for focusing only on external factors ('saris and samosas') and failing to address the real problem of racism. Ethnic-minority languages still do not have the same status as European languages.

UNDERSTAND THE CONCEPT

Multiculturalism sees ethnic diversity as a positive aspect of society. It encourages the celebration of cultural diversity and believes that a society should adapt to accommodate the cultures and lifestyles of different groups. For example, schools should embrace the variety of diets, religions and festivals of major ethnic groups. Multiculturalism has been criticised for paying too little attention to inequality and racism. David Cameron criticised multiculturalism in 2011 for discouraging the integration of different ethnic groups into British society and culture, causing social divisions (Pilkington, 2011).

The National Curriculum itself has also been criticised for being ethnocentric – especially in its focus on British History and Literature. Geography also emphasises Britain's positive contribution to the rest of the world, rather than the negative consequences of unfair trade and employment practices. Changes introduced by the Coalition government in 2014 marked a renewed emphasis on a traditional curriculum (for example, studying Shakespeare and British Literature in English) leaving even less room for a multicultural curriculum.

Tikly *et al.* (2006), in their study of 30 comprehensive schools, found that a significant number of African Caribbean pupils noted their invisibility in the curriculum and were exasperated by the White European focus. Moreover, when Black History was acknowledged within the curriculum, many pupils reported their frustration with the tendency to focus on slavery.

However, while the curriculum may be ethnocentric, it is unlikely that this is the only factor in the underachievement of ethnic minorities, as it is not the case that all pupils from ethnic-minority backgrounds underachieve to similar degrees. Indian and Chinese pupils' achievement, for example, is above the national average.

To what extent should the content of the curriculum in British schools reflect the ethnic diversity of Britain? For example, how far should pupils concentrate on British History and 'classic' English literature (largely written by 'dead white men')?

CONCLUSIONS

Although ethnicity may be less important than social class in influencing patterns of educational achievement, it remains a significant factor. The evidence suggests that material differences between ethnic groups partly, but not wholly, explain differences in achievement. Other factors outside the education system, such as cultural factors, may partly explain differential achievement by ethnic group, but they interact with factors inside the education system, including institutional racism. Ethnicity also interacts with both gender and social class in affecting achievement. To complicate matters further, there can be diversity within ethnic groups, and the dividing lines between ethnic groups are not always clear-cut. For example, an increasing number of households are headed by parents from different ethnic backgrounds.

CHECK YOUR UNDERSTANDING

1. Identify one ethnic group that does better than average at GCSE and one group that does less well than average at this level.

2. Identify the ethnic group least likely to be entitled to free school meals and the ethnic group most likely to be entitled to them.

3. Briefly define 'ethnicity'.

4. Explain what is meant by 'institutional racism'.

5. Outline the attitudes of Chinese parents towards the education of their children based upon the research of Archer and Francis.

6. Explain the link between family life and low achievement among male Black African pupils suggested by Tony Sewell.

7. Identify and briefly explain four factors internal to the education system that might shape patterns of educational achievement within different minority ethnic groups.

8. Explain three ways in which African Caribbean pupils may be disadvantaged by the operation of the educational system in Britain.

9. Explain two reasons why the relationship between ethnicity and educational achievement is far from straightforward and needs to take account of other social differences.

10. "Factors internal to education largely determine the educational success of ethnic groups." Evaluate this claim.

TAKE IT FURTHER

Analyse the content of a sample of text books at your school or college. Focus on visual images, examples and case studies. To what extent do they recognise the variety and contribution of ethnic groups in contemporary Britain? Is there any evidence of an ethnocentric (pro-White British) bias in the curriculum?

1.4 GENDER, EDUCATIONAL ACHIEVEMENT AND SUBJECT CHOICE

LEARNING OBJECTIVES:

> Understand gender and educational achievement (AO1).

> Understand gender and subject choice (AO1).

> Apply this understanding to contemporary Britain (AO2).

> Analyse the reasons for gender differences in achievement and in subject choice (AO3).

> Evaluate competing views on these differences (AO3).

INTRODUCING THE DEBATE

In the 1980s, **feminists** argued that education systematically discriminated against females, leading to their doing less well in higher levels of education (A-level and above) than males. Since then, the position has changed, and females outperform males in most (but not all) aspects of education in Britain. However, that raises two questions – why the change and why are females, in general, more successful?

Plenty of explanations have been put forward, and you can probably think of some common-sense ideas yourself, but that doesn't mean that the research will support these explanations, or that the reasons are straightforward. Furthermore, while gendered inequalities in achievement are relatively small, differences in subject choice remain very significant.

UNDERSTAND THE CONCEPT

The **feminist** theory of society claims that women are disadvantaged and exploited by men, while men are dominant and run society in their own interests. Gender inequality is seen as the central feature of society rather than, for example, class differences. There are different types of feminism. For example, Liberal feminism is a version of feminism which is relatively moderate and believes that the position of women in society can be improved through reform rather than radical or revolutionary change. (For example, this might involve schemes to encourage girls to study scientific, mathematical or engineering subjects in higher education). On the other hand, Radical feminism believes that the dominance of men in society is so well established that revolutionary change is needed to make a real difference.

TRENDS IN GENDER AND ACHIEVEMENT

According to Michele Cohen (1998), girls have educationally outperformed boys in the early years of schooling since mass education was introduced in the UK. However, girls have not always had the same opportunities to progress to higher levels of education. Before 1877, no British university accepted female students. Women were only allowed to attend university lectures at the discretion of lecturers. Women were first awarded degrees in 1920 at Oxford and 1921 at Cambridge.

Even in secondary education, opportunities for women were still somewhat limited after the Second World War. For example, under the **tripartite system** that dominated British education between 1947 and 1964 girls tended to do better in the entry exam for Grammar Schools (the 11+) than boys. However, there were no more places for girls than boys, so girls often had to achieve higher marks than boys in order to be accepted. One justification for this deliberate discrimination was that boys 'mature later'. Another was the view that women's careers were seen as secondary to their role as housewives and mothers once they married and had children.

Margaret Thatcher, later Prime Minister, graduated in Chemistry from Oxford University in 1943 – just 23 years after women were first granted degrees from Oxford.

UNDERSTAND THE CONCEPT

The **tripartite system** is a form of secondary education introduced by the 1944 Education Act. It involved taking an IQ test at the age of 11 (the 11+). Those who did well in this test were admitted to a grammar school, where they received an academic education and had the opportunity of gaining formal qualifications. Those who did reasonably well and who were technically minded or creative were admitted to technical schools (although not many of these were actually built). Those who did less well were admitted to a secondary modern school from which they received a vocational certificate. Most of the pupils in secondary moderns left school at the age of 15 with few qualifications. The tripartite system began to be replaced in the 1960s by the comprehensive system.

Despite the limited opportunities for women in the past, since the early 1990s, official statistics have shown that girls outperform boys at most levels of the education system and as more opportunities for progression by girls have opened up, the gender balance in educational achievement has shifted. Nevertheless, the situation is complicated and it isn't as straightforward as one sex outperforming the other.

For example, as Table 1.4.1 shows, in 2011 at Key Stage 2 girls did better than boys in reading and writing, although there was no difference in the percentage achieving Level 4 in Maths.

	English	Reading	Writing	Maths
Girls	86%	87%	81%	80%
Boys	77%	80%	68%	80%

Table 1.4.1 *SATS: Level 4 achievement by gender at KS2 in 2011*
Source: DfE (2011)

In 2013, girls did better than boys at GCSE level (in terms of achieving A* to C grades) in every subject – often by a significant margin – other than Maths. For the same year, at A-level, girls were more likely to get A* to C grades in every subject other than French (boys had a slight advantage here). Girls were also more likely to pass every subject apart from Economics and Media and film. However, it should be noted that many of the differences in rates of achievement are quite small at A-level.

In terms of A-level, if we examine performance across A* to E grades, there are only three subjects in which there is more than a 1 per cent gap between boys' and girls' overall achievement. Moreover, both 2012 and 2013 saw boys gaining slightly more A* grades at A-level than girls. It is therefore dangerous to exaggerate the problem of underperformance by boys at this level.

In 2010/11, there were more female (55 per cent) than male (45 per cent) full-time undergraduates enrolled at university. In 2012, women were a third more likely to start a degree than their male counterparts. Moreover, female undergraduates consistently perform better than males at this level, as shown in Table 1.4.2.

	First-class	Upper 2nd	Lower 2nd	Third	% First & Upper 2nd
Male	27385	72490	45985	12130	63%
Female	34220	105935	54330	11800	68%

Table 1.4.2 *Class of degree achieved by gender in 2012*
Source: Higher Education Statistics Agency (2013)

With regard to the number of students achieving first-class and second-class degrees, the gender gap has remained consistent, with women outperforming men by about 5 percentage points.

Again though, the significance of these differences can be overestimated. As Haralambos and Holborn (2013) point out, the performance of boys and young men in education has been steadily improving and at some levels, specifically GCSE and A-level, the gender gap narrowed in the first decade of the 21st century, with boys making up ground on girls. McDonald *et al.* (1999) argue that the generalisation that girls outperform boys applies most strongly to working-class children; among the middle classes the gender gap in achievement is either very small or non-existent. Moreover, the gender gap is wider in comprehensive schools than in selective schools.

Similar gender gaps can also be seen between ethnic groups. The difference in achievement between boys and girls is far wider among African Caribbean children than among other ethnic groups, such as Indians.

Recent results at KS2, GCSE and A-level suggest that boys' underachievement is not the problem it once was. The gap between male and female achievement is narrowing. Furthermore, gender is only one of three key social influences on achievement – the evidence with regard to boys suggests that their social class and ethnicity are just as important. International evidence suggests the UK's record with regard to gender equality in education is better than many other countries. The Organisation for Economic Co-operation and Development (OECD) found that in the Programme for International Student Assessment (Pisa) tests in 2013, the gender gap in achievement (with girls outperforming boys) was lower than in most other countries. But there are still some significant differences and the reasons for these will now be explored.

GENDER AND ACHIEVEMENT

This section examines the reasons for differences in educational achievement between males and females. As in the case of class and ethnicity, factors influencing achievement may be external or internal to the education system itself, or a combination of the two. However, both inside and outside education children's behaviour is **gendered** as a result of differences in the socialisation of girls and boys. The next section examines the way in which gender socialisation underlies gender differences in education.

If an area of social life is **gendered**, then it is experienced differently by males and females – it differentiates between males and females and gives them different advantages/disadvantages. For example, work is gendered if the expectations of male and female workers are different, or if different jobs are thought suitable for males and females. To say something is gendered does not necessarily imply that one gender is always advantaged at the expense of the other; but it does imply that there is systematic inequality and difference.

Patriarchy literally means, 'rule by the father', but it is usually used by feminists to refer to a system in which men have more power than women and therefore shape how societies are run. Patriarchy does not just operate through political or economic control, but also through culture, so that both men and women may come to see male dominance as natural. Patriarchal power has been analysed and challenged by feminists who seek to undermine patriarchy both in education and in society as a whole.

Gender role socialisation

Early socialisation (primary socialisation in the family) takes place before a child enters education, but socialisation continues inside and outside school for older age groups and it impacts on and interacts with factors internal to schools.

Factors linked to socialisation that influence gender differences in educational achievement are present from birth. Edwards and David (2000) suggest that gender-differentiated primary socialisation gives girls an initial advantage in both primary and secondary schools, but still tends to create a male-dominated or **patriarchal** society. (For example, the willingness of boys to break rules can lead to their dominating classrooms.) Girls may have better language skills than boys because mothers talk to baby girls more frequently than baby boys. Edwards and David suggest that there is some evidence that girls are taught by their parents to conform to more formal standards of behaviour than boys, which familiarises them with what is expected in the classroom. For example, at home, they are taught to sit still, to be quiet, to read and to listen.

Consequently, by the age of 7, girls within the education system are more likely than boys to pay attention in class and to be self-disciplined in supervised play. By the time they enter secondary school, girls have often developed a compliant motivational style, which means they are prepared to conform to classroom rules and to get on with their work independently. Moreover, they are experienced in listening and speaking, which puts them at an advantage because the classroom is essentially a linguistic environment.

Early socialisation appears to be reflected in attitudes and behaviour as girls progress through school:

> Research by Burns and Bracey (2001) found that girls at secondary schools generally work harder and are more motivated than boys.

> Research suggests that, on average, girls put more effort into their work and spend more time on homework. They take more care with the presentation of their work. They are better organised, and they consequently meet deadlines more successfully than boys.

> Research shows that, from the age of 6, girls read more books than boys, and this trend continues throughout their lives.

It is not just primary socialisation in families that influences gender roles in education; **peer groups** can also have a significant influence. These influences occur both inside and outside the education system. Hannan (2000) shows that girls spend their leisure time differently from boys. Whereas boys relate to their peers by doing (that is, by being active in a range of ways), girls relate to one another by talking. This puts girls at an advantage, because most subjects require good levels of comprehension and writing skills. Girls are also happy to help each other. It is an acceptable part of being female.

A **peer group** is a group of friends and fellow pupils. The concept of 'social control' refers to the penalties that the peer group can impose on boys or girls who do not conform to group expectations about how males and females should behave at school and in the classroom. For example, they may be negatively labelled, shunned or bullied.

The socialisation of boys is significantly different from that of girls:

> Edwards and David (2000) found that, at home, parents allowed boys to be noisier and more attention-seeking than girls. They found that this mode of socialisation often translated into primary school boys more likely to break rules and less bothered than girls when told off by teachers.

> Edwards and David also found that by the time they started secondary school boys often had trouble sitting still and concentrating. They were only able to deal with short-term tasks and were far less prepared to get on with their schoolwork than girls.

> Many boys believed school work should be done at school and, unlike girls, were not prepared to draft and redraft assignments.

> There was also some evidence that boys' behaviour was often shaped and policed by their peer group. The culture of such groups tends to be organised around masculine or 'macho' values. These set out rules of behaviour for boys that mean they are subject to social controls from other boys. For example, this may mean not showing emotion or talking about personal feelings.

Evidence from Frosh et al. (2001) suggests that boys who are members of these cultures regard schoolwork as 'feminine' and 'unmanly' and have a tendency to engage in hyper-masculine behaviour, such as back-chatting teachers, being disruptive in class and bullying the more academic boys. Showing an interest in school work was deemed silly, soft and weak. Bright, diligent boys were often subjected to homophobic abuse. On the other hand, masculine status was associated with being sporty, funny and 'up for a laugh'. Kirby (2000) argues that it is noticeable from research that boys who do well at school are often helped at home, away from the view of the peer group. Boys often consider it weak to request help from a

teacher and it is also especially difficult for a boy to accept help from another boy.

Some research indicates boys' overconfidence may blind them to what is actually required for educational success. Research by Kindon and Thompson (1999) indicates that boys interrupt more frequently and answer more often, even when they do not know the answer. Moreover, boys are surprised when they fail exams and tend to put their failure down to bad luck rather than lack of effort. On the other hand, girls are more realistic, even self-doubting, and try that much harder in order to ensure success. However, according to Francis (2000), boys are no longer likely to consider themselves more able than girls, as was the case in the 1970s and 1980s. Francis also notes that boys are more likely to have career aspirations that are not only unrealistic but less likely to require academic success (such as professional footballer) whereas girls' career ambitions more often require academic success (such as doctor) which drives their commitment to schoolwork.

Studies of working-class boys in school by Hargreaves (1967) and Willis (1977) showed how such boys were fatalistic in accepting school failure as inevitable. Some of them developed anti-educational coping strategies, such as setting up anti-school subcultures or having a laugh at the expense of teachers and more academic boys.

There is evidence that some of the anti-school cultures inside school may develop into street gangs involved in territorial street violence, drug-dealing and mugging. Evidence from a variety of studies of juvenile gangs in London by Kintrea and from the profiles of those convicted for their part in the 2011 London riots and looting (Lewis et al., 2011) overwhelmingly show participation by males who had left school with few or no qualifications.

Kirby (2000) has suggested that communicative play through organised social games has been replaced with TV, DVD and computer games. In addition, there has been a decline in family discussion time, through occasions such as mealtimes. Both changes have reduced opportunities for boys to catch up with girls in terms of language development. He points out that while modern computer games (more popular with boys than girls) may exercise already advanced spatial and visual abilities, they do little to address language deficiency.

Is talking at family mealtimes in decline in most families?

SOCIAL CHANGE AND PATTERNS OF ACHIEVEMENT

A number of factors have been suggested as possible causes of changes in the relationship between gender and achievement. Many of these are linked to broad social, economic or cultural changes in the UK.

Social change and the effects on girls

Some feminist sociologists, such as Helen Wilkinson, relate girls' relative success in the past 30 years to post-industrialisation, which has transformed the attitudes of young women and depressed the expectations of males.

The last 30 years have seen a feminisation of the economy and the workforce. Jobs for women in the service sector of the economy (financial services, retail, mass media, health, welfare and education) have expanded. As a result, girls may believe that the future offers them more choices. They are provided with the incentive to seek economic independence, and careers are now a real possibility.

Wilkinson's argument is that female aspirations underwent a radical transformation in the last two decades of the 20th century. She suggests that young women experienced a '**genderquake**' in terms of profound changes in their attitudes and expectations about their futures, compared with those of their mothers and grandmothers. Their aspirations are no longer restricted to family life. Instead, most teenage girls are committed to education and qualifications, and aspire to careers and economic independence.

UNDERSTAND THE CONCEPT

Wilkinson uses the word 'genderquake' to refer to the dramatic change in attitudes towards work and careers experienced by females over the course of three generations. She argued that young women at the start of the 21st century have radically different attitudes towards education, work and family to those of their mothers and grandmothers.

Sue Sharpe's surveys of young working-class females in London support Wilkinson. Her study of working-class girls in London (*Just Like a Girl*, 1976) found that most girls held very traditional ideas about womanhood and prioritised 'love, marriage, husbands, children, jobs and careers, more or less in that order'. When the research was repeated in 1994, she found that the priorities had changed to 'job, career and being able to support themselves' above all other priorities. Studies of girls in primary and secondary schools also illustrate this change in emphasis.

According to Francis and Skelton (2005): "The majority (of primary and secondary school female pupils) appear to see their chosen career as reflecting their identity and as a vehicle for future fulfilment, rather than as simply a stopgap before marriage". The growth in employment opportunities and the rise in young women's occupational ambitions have increased their incentives to gain educational qualifications. Studies of both primary and secondary school pupils show that many girls are now looking towards jobs that require degree-level qualifications (Francis and Skelton, 2005).

Both Wilkinson and Sharpe noted that feminist ideas were filtering down through the media and education system and ultimately into family life, so that these movements (although not always recognised and supported by young women in the early 21st century) were partly responsible for increased opportunities for females in education and work. The work of feminist sociologists in the 1970s and 1980s led to a significantly greater emphasis on equal opportunities in schools than there had been before.

Changes in employment and the attitudes of girls and women have been accompanied by changes in the family, such as:

> long-term increases in divorce

> increased age at first marriage

> increased age of women at birth of their first child

> the growth of lone parenthood

> more individuals living alone.

Ulrich Beck (1992) sees these changes as part of the growth of risk and uncertainty, which leads to greater insecurity for males and females alike. Both relationships and jobs are insecure and cannot be relied on to last in the long-term. According to Beck, this creates a more **individualised** society in which both men and women have to be self-reliant and, to a greater extent, financially independent. This further increases the incentives for girls to achieve educational qualifications so that they don't risk reliance upon a husband and are sufficiently well qualified to cope with the uncertainties of the labour market.

UNDERSTAND THE CONCEPT

Individualisation – This involves a process in which group membership and collective identities (based, for example, on class, gender, sexuality, ethnicity, religion or region) become less important. Individuals have more freedom to choose different lifestyles and tend to have less loyalty to the social groups to which they belong. This does not necessarily mean that collective identities are no longer of any importance, but it does suggest that people will feel the need to be more self-reliant and will think more about the choices they have in deciding how to live. This process is associated with the ideas of sociologists such as Ulrich Beck and Anthony Giddens.

FOCUS ON RESEARCH: GIRLS AND THEIR AMBITIONS

Carol Fuller (2009) conducted an in-depth study of a single-sex girls' school in the south-east of England with a high proportion of pupils from minority ethnic groups and a largely working-class intake. The school was in an area with high levels of deprivation and had been deemed to be unsatisfactory by Ofsted. Fuller's study focused on Year 10 and Year 12 pupils and she used participant observation, focus groups and both structured and semi-structured interviews. She said that: "This multi-method approach was adopted with the view that it would produce much richer data than using one method alone" (Fuller, 2009, p.3). The participant observation was conducted in student common rooms, the staff room assemblies, lunch areas and in tutor groups. The focus groups helped Fuller to devise questions for the 'in-depth, semi-structured interviews with students' (p.3). The

interviews themselves focused on 'the value placed on education, students' expectations for themselves in terms of achievement and their life course, and how these views impact on students' perceptions of themselves' (p.4).

The school organised pupils into five sets. Fuller found that it was possible to identify three groups of girls. The low aspirers wanted to leave school at 16, they were generally in the bottom two sets, and they thought that much of what they learned in school was not directly relevant to them. Although they thought it was risky not to have qualifications, they found school work, especially coursework, stressful and they lacked confidence in their ability to succeed. They expected to work in jobs such as shop work, or as a nursery nurse assistant, and these sorts of jobs were typical of their work placements (which Fuller describes as being both gendered and classed). Some of the girls hoped to achieve fame, for example, by becoming singers. However, relationships were more important to them than careers, and their boyfriends and the prospect of eventually becoming a mother gave many their sense of future direction.

The middle aspirers intended to continue in education after the age of 16 but not to continue to higher education. Most opted to do vocational rather than academic courses, but some chose A-levels. All felt that they needed further qualifications to give themselves a strong enough position in the labour market. This group mainly came from the second and third sets and were lacking in confidence that they could do well enough to continue on to do degrees. They aspired to steady jobs with a measure of job security, for example, hairdressers, qualified nursery nurses or chefs. Some who had chosen A-levels were thinking more in terms of administrative roles, for example, as bank workers or receptionists. Friendship networks were important to these students, and whether they stayed on at the same school, or moved elsewhere to study, was influenced by their peers.

The high aspirers were defined as those who wanted to progress to higher education. They were mainly but not exclusively in the top set and were generally confident in their own ability. While those with less ambitious aspirations largely accepted teachers' judgements about their ability, the high aspirers believed they could succeed even when teachers were less positive about their progress. These students were the most individualised group, willing to move to a different institution for A-Level study if they thought it would improve their chances of success. Many of them had quite vague career plans but they were certainly aiming for professional jobs of one sort or another. While friendships and relationships were important to them, self-reliance and financial independence were higher priorities. Fuller therefore supports Beck's view that society has become more individualised (see Social change and the effects on girls).

Because the sample were all female, and from broadly working-class backgrounds, Fuller argues that the differences cannot be explained simply in terms of class and gender. Many of the aspirations, especially for low and middle aspirers were gendered, but different groups were making different choices about how they wanted and expected their lives to progress. They were reacting to their position as girls from working-class backgrounds in an economy dominated by the service sector, but in in different ways. Fuller's research suggested that two key factors explained differences in aspirations. The first was the amount of emotional support (or emotional capital) provided by their families. The second was the girls' perceptions of themselves and particularly the amount of self-esteem and self-confidence they had in school settings. This in turn was connected to their relationships with teachers. Thus factors both inside and outside school, along with structural changes in the labour market, helped to explain why some girls, but not all, had high aspirations and were focused on educational success.

Questions

1. Identify the particular contribution made by each research method (participant observation, focus groups and interviews) to the research.

2. Explain the claim that: "This multi-method approach was adopted with the view that it would produce much richer data than using one method alone". (What might have been overlooked by using only one method?)

3. Analyse ways in which this research could explain improvements in the educational performance of girls.

4. Evaluate, on the basis of this research, the view that the aspirations of girls remain highly gendered.

5. Evaluate Fuller's view that factors inside and outside school help to explain the achievements and aspirations of girls.

Social change and the effects on boys

There is some evidence that social changes associated with a more individualised and post-industrial society have lowered the expectations of boys, and that boys in the early 21st century consequently lack confidence in themselves and experience low levels of self-esteem. Some commentators, notably Mac an Ghaill (1994), suggest that working-class boys are experiencing a 'crisis of masculinity'. They are socialised into seeing their future male identity and role in terms of having a job and being a 'breadwinner', but the landscape has changed:

> The decline of the manufacturing industry and the rise in long-term unemployment make it increasingly unlikely that males will be the main earners.

> New jobs in the service sector are often part time, desk-based, and suited to the skills and lifestyles of women.

> In some families, females may be the primary breadwinners.

Consequently, traditional masculine roles are under threat.

Wragg (1997) believed that pessimism about the world of work, induced by declining job prospects for males, has filtered down to primary school boys and undermines their desire to work hard. Jackson (2006) believes that working-class male adolescents may conclude that education and qualifications are irrelevant because they can see that the jobs they will end up doing are unskilled or semi-skilled at best and not very well paid. Such boys are likely to look for alternative sources of status. This may be achieved by exaggerating their masculinity through involvement in delinquent anti-school subcultures. Street credibility is gained by not subscribing to an academic ethos, and even for getting excluded from school.

Jackson's research found evidence that these changes had a particularly strong effect on working-class boys. She used interviews and questionnaires to study masculinity and femininity in eight schools. She found that the schools were dominated by a culture of **hegemonic** (or dominant) **masculinity** that valued toughness, power and competitiveness. Academic work was seen by boys as being essentially feminine and therefore 'uncool'. Boys tended to mess around to impress their peer group rather than concentrate on the work – acting out a culture of laddish masculinity. Some boys did want to succeed but to avoid being seen as 'uncool' they worked mainly at home. This disadvantaged working-class boys who had poorer facilities at home, for example, less space or poorer computing facilities and internet access. Working-class boys were particularly affected by changes in the labour market. Lacking the prospect of employment to give them a sense of identity, they used laddish behaviour to restore a sense of masculine pride.

UNDERSTAND THE CONCEPT

Hegemonic masculinity is the dominant version of what it means to be masculine in a particular culture. In contemporary Britain it might be seen as involving rationality, heterosexuality, competitiveness and a desire for control over others. It emphasises strength over weakness. It is not the only version of masculinity, and many men do not conform to these ideas – for example, the cultures of gay men might offer an alternative, as might those of peace-loving vegetarian men – but the alternative forms of masculinity tend to have lower status than hegemonic masculinity in education and society as a whole.

Francis and Skelton (2005) argue that these underachieving boys are often vulnerable, confused and insecure. They suggest that while the underachieving boy

may appear tough on the outside, seeking to impress and boost his self-image, on the inside he is insecure and has low self-esteem. This can be reinforced by a lack of educational success.

FACTORS WITHIN THE EDUCATION SYSTEM

The 1980s saw a greater emphasis on equal opportunities in schools, which resulted in the monitoring of teaching practices and resources for sex-bias in order to ensure more girl-friendly schooling. This was the direct result of the work of feminist sociologists such as Stanworth (1990) and Spender (1983), who carried out observation-based research of teacher–pupil interaction in the late 1970s and 1980s. They concluded that schools reinforced gender inequalities in wider society because teacher expectations and the resulting labelling led teachers to discriminate against females. This discrimination took many forms:

> Spender found that when boys questioned or challenged a teacher they were often met with respect whereas girls were criticised as being too assertive and 'unladylike'.

> Spender also claimed that boys' and girls' work was often judged by different standards. The same work got better marks when teachers were told a boy had written it.

> Stanworth found teachers gave more time and attention to boys and expected more of them.

These feminist studies were influential in terms of social policy and led to schools and colleges introducing equal opportunities policies aimed at being more sensitive to the educational needs of females. Weiner (1995) has argued that teachers have more forcefully challenged stereotypes since the 1980s and many sexist images have been removed from learning materials. Consequently boys, especially in mixed schools, are also more aware of equal opportunities and the unacceptability of sexist behaviour.

Pedagogy

The school environment
Research by Rothermel (1999) has found that, among home-educated children, boys are as successful as girls. This suggests that what goes on inside schools plays a crucial role in boys' underachievement.

Epstein (1998) identifies a 'poor boys' discourse that blames schools for failing to cater for boys. Teachers, the exam system, and female concerns and interests ignore boys' learning needs and fail to appreciate and understand their masculinity, especially during primary school. To resolve this, proponents argue that schools should be made more 'masculine', and attention and resources should be directed from girls to boys.

Some sociologists have suggested that the school environment has become feminised. Some research suggests that primary-school environments, which are female-dominated and may have an emphasis on neatness and tidiness, exert a less positive influence on boys, and may even be alienating to them. However, recent research by Carrington et al. (2007) suggests that the gender of the teacher has little or no impact on boys' or girls' learning.

Sukhnanda et al. (2000) report that boys generally feel they receive less support, encouragement and guidance from teachers. They feel that teachers have higher expectations of girls and are more critical of boys for non-academic reasons, such as bad behaviour and scruffy presentation. Consequently they view schools as alien places.

Abraham (1995) argues that schools fail to confront traditional notions of masculinity and that teachers may even collude with pupils in traditional gender stereotyping. In Abraham's study deviant boys were more popular with some of the teachers than academic boys and girls. According to Mitsos and Browne (1998), teachers are not as critical with boys as with girls. They may have lower expectations of boys, expecting work to be late, rushed and untidy, and expecting boys to be disruptive. These expectations may have a self-fulfilling effect, depressing the achievement of boys.

However, not all sociologists see the school environment as favouring girls. Coffey and Delamont (2000) argue that schools have always been patriarchal. In 2014, most senior staff in schools and colleges were male, the discourse of education remained fundamentally male – hierarchical and competitive – and the ethos of most schools, especially secondary schools, was still resolutely masculine – authoritarian, regulatory and sexist. For example, there are still schools that will not allow girls to wear trousers.

Some sociologists suggest that although girls are doing better in exams, they may not be getting the best education. Myhill (2000) argues that girls' success may be down to their being passive and compliant learners, but that boys may be getting the better education because teachers interact more frequently with them. Moreover, girls' greater conformity in the classroom may be a positive attribute in the school but a barrier in the workplace because, as Myhill points out, 'few company executives, politicians and lawyers would be described as compliant and conformist'.

The evidence also suggests that the experience of school may be more negative for girls. Girls may be doing better in most tests but they are more at risk of sexual abuse, depression, self-harm and eating disorders.

The curriculum and assessment

Some sociologists have highlighted the role of the curriculum in shaping the learning outcomes of boys and girls. Some significant changes that may have had an impact include the move from O-levels to GCSEs in 1988, and subsequent changes in the balance between exams and coursework. Initially GCSEs increased the proportion of marks that could be gained through coursework in many subjects, but more recently the coursework component has been reduced in both GCSEs and A-levels. In 2013 the Coalition government announced changes to A-levels: limits were imposed on opportunities for resits, and the exam system was shifted towards end-of-course exams in both GCSEs and A-Levels. There were parallel changes in the curriculum, with some moves towards a less traditionally academic curriculum. However, the same government subsequently reasserted the importance of traditional academic subjects and subject content. These changes may have had different impacts on boys and girls.

Pirie (2001) has argued that the pre-1988 O-level was an exam geared towards boys, with its 'high-risk, swot it all up for the final throw' approach to assessment. By contrast, the coursework involved in GCSEs and some A-levels requires organisational skills and sustained motivation – skills that girls seem to be better at than boys. This could help to explain why the performance of girls improved more rapidly than that of boys in the years following the change in the exam system. Reviewing the research, Machin and McNally (2006) comment that the change to GCSEs did coincide with improvements in the performance of girls relative to boys. Furthermore, they cite research which suggests that girls do tend to do better in coursework while boys are better at doing end-of-course exams. They suggest therefore that this shift may have been key to changing patterns of gender and achievement in GCSEs. The return to a greater emphasis on exams may partially explain the narrowing of the gender gap under the 2010–15 Coalition government. Greg Hurst (2014) notes research that suggests boys overtook girls in GCSE Maths performance following a change in emphasis towards end-of-course exams from 2009.

It is suggested that curriculum changes in terms of subject content may have been more to the taste of girls than boys. Discussing English, Bleach (1998), for example, observes that girls tend to favour fiction over non-fiction and creative writing over factual writing, whereas boys are more likely to prefer reading non-fiction and writing factual responses. Boys dislike lengthy fiction, especially the pre-20th century texts that are an essential part of the national curriculum at GCSE and A-level. Bleach concludes that that the English curriculum in schools, on balance, favours girls' strengths over boys'. Since reforms introduced by Education Secretary Michael Gove in 2014 required more study of classic English literature such as Shakespeare, it seems likely that this imbalance may increase.

Arnot (1998) argues that most girls prefer tasks which are sustained, open-ended, process-based and realistic rather than abstract. Project and source-based work, which have become more prominent in Humanities, are therefore ideally suited to girls' preferences. In contrast boys prefer to give brief, commentary-style answers to clear questions. Moreover, girls like tasks which require extended responses, such as investigations. Tasks such as these have become more commonplace in Mathematics and the Sciences in the early 21st century. Boys generally prefer memorising unambiguous facts and giving 'correct' answers at speed. Boys perform significantly better on multiple-choice tests than girls.

Boys generally achieve higher marks on multiple-choice tests than girls.

The literacy hour (which was introduced nationally in 1998) and the numeracy hour (introduced in 1999) may have had some impact on the achievement of boys and girls in primary schools. According to Machin and McNally (2006), the evidence suggests that these initiatives had a bigger positive impact on the gender

which had been less successful in the relevant subjects. Thus the literacy of boys improved faster than that of girls, while girls made more progress than boys in maths, contributing to a narrowing of the gender gap.

Based on the evidence in this chapter and your own experience, do the current curriculum and the associated assessment methods unfairly favour boys, girls or neither? What changes, if any, would you introduce to make them fairer in terms of gender differences?

Subject choices

Patterns of subject choice

Despite relatively narrow gaps between boys and girls in terms of achievement, very considerable differences in subject choice remain. Skelton, Francis and Valkanova (2007) comment that: "at the moment that subject choice is introduced (be it as particular subject options in addition to the National Curriculum at Key Stage 4, or at post-16) the statistics continue to show highly stereotypical trends for young men to pursue certain subjects (typically technical and science-oriented subjects) and young women others (typically caring, or arts/humanities/social science subjects)" (p.20). Feminists such as Anne Colley (1998) see this as a significant problem. For example, when girls select their A-level subjects, this affects their choice of university degree and may lead to different career paths compared to boys. Anne Colley argues that such choices mean that females more often end up in low-status and relatively low-paid professions compared with males. Certainly an examination of A-level exam entries, as shown in Table 1.4.3, confirms the first part of Colley's hypothesis: there are significant differences in subject choice. Males are particularly likely to choose Physics, Economics and Maths, while females predominate in Biology, English and Sociology. In other subjects the gender differences are less marked but still significant, with more males than females doing Chemistry, Business Studies, and Design and Technology.

	Biology	Physics	Chemistry	Business Studies	Economics	Design & Technology	Maths	English	Sociology
Males	26,988	28,190	26,988	16,270	17,464	9,031	63,305	25,196	7,561
Females	33,195	7,379	24,830	11,403	8,675	6,610	38,576	64,246	23,127

Table 1.4.3 *- 2013 A-level – Number of Exam Entries by Gender*

Source: Joint Council for Qualifications (2013)

Similar patterns are found at university: more young men study Engineering, Architecture and Computer Science at undergraduate level, while young women are a big majority among students of subjects allied to Medicine (e.g. nursing and physiotherapy), Education, Creative Arts and Design, and Languages. The differences don't always lead men towards the more prestigious and highly-paid jobs (there are now more women than men studying Medicine, Dentistry and Law, for example), but they are likely to contribute to significant differences in the careers of men and women.

Colley (1998) argues that factors influencing subject choice are partly outside the education system. She stresses the influence of the family, and of influential peers who also subscribe to gender stereotypes, over subject choices at GCSE and A-level. For example, research indicates that parents still believe that certain toys and games are suitable only for one gender or the other. This may result in females in mixed comprehensive schools being 'steered away' from courses traditionally dominated by males and vice versa.

The education system itself, however, may well reinforce gender differences in subject choice. Colley also argues that although the national curriculum reduced gender differences in subject choice, traditional cultural beliefs about femininity and masculinity may still be held by teachers, lecturers and career advisors, especially in mixed schools. These cultural beliefs may be passed on to pupils via teaching styles. For example, the subjects to which girls tend to be drawn are taught mostly by women in secondary school. These female teachers may use the discursive teaching styles that girls prefer. In contrast, the teachers of subjects more popular with boys are more likely to be men, who may be more reliant on formal teaching styles because of the nature of the subjects they teach. Colley notes that girls in single-sex schools are twice as likely to study Maths at university because these cultural pressures are likely to be compensated for by the positive female role models offered by teachers and peers.

The combined influence of factors inside and outside school leads to subjects becoming gendered – they develop an identity as essentially male or female that is hard to change and makes it problematic either for boys to choose 'feminine' subjects or for girls to choose 'masculine' ones. However, Colley believes that subjects may shift gender identity if the curriculum changes. For example, the increased use of technology in music has meant it has come to be seen as more 'masculine' than it was previously.

Is music becoming a more 'masculine' subject with greater use of technology?

Skelton, Francis and Valkanova (2007), reviewing research in the area, argued that 'gender stereotyping' and 'differential constructions of gender among pupils and teachers' (p.20) are probably the most significant factors. They cite research by Lucey (2001, cited in Skelton, Francis and Valkanova, 2007) that English is often socially constructed as being more 'naturally' female than male. They say, the: "gender discourse is so subtle that behavioural characteristics become taken for granted and naturalised" (p.20). Rolfe (1999, cited in Skelton, Francis and Valkanova, 2007) found this was reinforced by unconscious stereotyping in careers advice, and some evidence of this was also found in Fuller's research (Fuller, 2009) into a single-sex girl's school in the south-east of England (see Focus on research: Girls and their ambitions).

FOCUS ON SKILLS: GIRLS AND PHYSICS

Some feminists claim boys dominate science classrooms.

Half of mixed-sex state schools have no girls choosing physics as an A-level subject, research shows.

The report by the Institute of Physics reveals that no 16-year-old female GCSE pupils, from 49 per cent of co-educational state schools, went on to take the subject at A-level.

Girls at single-sex schools were nearly two-and-a-half times more likely to take physics A-level.

The lowest figures were for schools without a sixth-form, whose pupils were the least likely to take the subject when beginning their A-level studies elsewhere.

The institute used records of A-level exams sat last year, and tracked back to find out what type of school candidates attended at GCSE level.

In the Institute's report, *It's Different for Girls*, Prof Sir Peter Knight, president of the institute, said: 'Physics is a subject that opens doors to exciting higher education and career opportunities. This research shows that half of England's co-ed comprehensives are keeping these doors firmly shut to girls.

'Perceptions of physics are formed well beyond the physics classroom: the English teacher who looks askance at the girl who takes an interest in physics or the lack of female physicists on television, for example, can play a part in forming girls' perceptions of the subject.'

The proportion of girls choosing A-level physics has been consistent, at about 20 per cent for more than 20 years, but the report said that evidence from the database helped to confirm the source of the problem.

Clare Thomson, curriculum and diversity Manager at the institute, said: 'The importance of having a sixth form in your school for uptake of physics is related to the availability of specialist physics teachers – a factor we know contributes to enjoyment of and engagement with the subject across both sexes.

"Schools that have a sixth form are more likely to have specialist physics teachers on their staff and these teachers' confident and enthusiastic teaching of the subject inspires a greater number of students to progress on to A-level physics and beyond."

The institute makes a series of recommendations, including that gender equity in subjects should be part of Ofsted inspection criteria.

Caroline Jordan, the head of Headington School in Oxford and chair of the Girls' Schools Association education committee, said: 'In single-sex schools you simply do not see girls making choices that are gender biased and this is particularly so in physics, where girls get to tackle everything.

'In co-ed schools boys can grab all the equipment and give the impression of being in charge, while girls find themselves consigned to writing down results.'

Helen Fraser, chief executive of the Girls' Day School Trust, said: 'For a girl to choose physics in a co-ed school is often viewed as a brave choice or a risky move. Teenage girls (and boys for that matter) are often desperate to fit in with their peer group, and can be concerned at the prospect of doing anything that might make them stand out from the crowd, which makes a girl studying a subject which some might view as "unfeminine" much more of a social risk.

'The key ages for this sort of self-consciousness are the years from age 13 to 16, just when pupils are choosing which subjects they want to take for their GCSEs and A-levels.'

Source: Woolcock, N. 'Half of co-ed schools have no girls studying A-level physics', *The Times*, 4 October 2012

Questions

1. **Assess** what evidence there is here that the choice of Physics as an A-level subject is strongly gendered.

2. **Evaluate** the extent to which the type of school or college where Physics is studied affects gender differences in the take-up of the subject.

3. **Analyse** two possible factors inside the education system that may affect the chances of girls studying physics. (The answers are contained in the extract).

4. **Analyse** two possible factors outside the education system that may affect the chances of girls studying Physics. (There are answers given in the description of the research).

5. **Apply** the evidence and arguments in this chapter to evaluate how successful the proposals put forward by the Institute of Physics would be likely to be if implemented. (You can think about whether they have taken account of all the possible factors)

6. **Evaluate** the view that gender differences in subject choice are unlikely to be significantly reduced until gender differences in employment have ended; changes in the education system will never be enough on their own. (You can think about how far subject choice is affected by factors other than career opportunities for males and females.)

CONCLUSIONS

Many feminists believe that the current concern about boys and achievement is simply a **'moral panic'** that distracts from female achievement. Weiner *et al.* (1997) suggest that newspaper reports about 'failing boys' reflect a middle-class concern that working-class black and white boys are leaving education with few or no qualifications and consequently may develop into a potentially socially disruptive underclass. These concerns were aired again after the 2011 London riots and looting.

UNDERSTAND THE CONCEPT

Moral panic refers to public anxiety that is usually generated by mass media reports. It involves an exaggerated and often somewhat irrational fear about a phenomenon that is portrayed as new or growing (even if it is neither). It usually links in with widespread anxieties about social changes, for example, the changing roles of men and women in society or NEETS (young people not in education, employment or training).

Some critics have argued that the whole question of equality of educational opportunity has now been largely reduced to gender and the focus on boys. However, as noted earlier, social class has over five times more effect on educational attainment than gender, and ethnicity has twice the effect (Gillborn and Mirza, 2000). According to some researchers, the focus on boys has diverted attention not only from underachieving girls but also from pupils disadvantaged by their class and/or ethnic background. For example, Osler (2006) argues that a more important issue is reducing the number of school exclusions among working-class boys and certain ethnic minorities.

Moreover, Osler also argues that the current focus on boys' underachievement is hiding a serious problem of exclusion and underachievement among girls, which is increasing at a faster rate than that of boys. For example, African Caribbean girls are often hailed as one of education's success stories. Yet girls classified as African Caribbean are more vulnerable to disciplinary exclusion than their White female peers.

Do you think concern about 'underachievement' by boys in general can be seen as a moral panic which takes attention away from problems for girls and other types of educational inequality? Justify your answer with reference to appropriate evidence.

CHECK YOUR UNDERSTANDING

1. When were women first admitted to a British university?

2. Are males or females more likely to achieve first- or upper-second-class degrees?

3. What do the most recent statistics suggest about changing patterns of gender and achievement?

4. Identify and briefly explain three ways in which socialisation might prepare girls better for primary education than boys.

5. Identify and explain two ways in which peer pressure might hinder the educational progress of boys.

6. Explain what is meant by individualisation and suggest one way in which it might explain the increasing success of girls in education.

7. Using material from Carol Fuller's study, explain how factors inside and outside education can interact in shaping the aspirations of different groups of girls.

8. Explain how changes in the use of coursework in British school education might help to explain changing patterns of achievement.

9. Identify one subject that is predominantly studied by girls and explain two sociological reasons why it might be more attractive to girls than boys.

10. Give three arguments against and three arguments in favour of the view that education is no longer significantly gendered.

TAKE IT FURTHER

Find a boy in your school or college who takes a subject usually regarded as 'feminine' and a girl who takes what is usually seen as a 'masculine' subject. Ask them why they take the subject, how difficult they find it and whether the gender balance or image of the subject put them off at all. Compare your findings with other class members and discuss whether subject choice has become less gendered over time. You may wish to use semi-structured interviews for this research.

1.5 RELATIONSHIPS AND PROCESSES IN SCHOOLS

LEARNING OBJECTIVES

› Understand relationships and processes in schools (AO1).

› Apply this understanding to contemporary Britain (AO2).

› Analyse the impact of these processes on schooling and pupils (AO3).

› Evaluate competing views on these processes (AO3).

INTRODUCING THE DEBATE

The preceding three chapters on class, ethnicity and gender have shown that some sociologists see relationships and processes within school as playing a significant role in explaining differential achievement. Chapter 1 showed that the hidden curriculum can play a role in the values that pupils learn in school. This chapter returns to these issues and develops your understanding of them in greater depth. It examines how the experience of schooling for pupils, involving both pupil–pupil and pupil–teacher interaction, can have a significant impact not just on achievement but also on the development of different subcultures and identities. Pupils spend many years attending schools, making them an essential part of growing up, helping to shape the adults that pupils become. However, this is not just a passive process of socialisation: pupils play an active role in the processes too.

THE HIDDEN CURRICULUM

Chapter 1 showed us that a 'hidden curriculum' exists in which children are socialised into various norms and values. This chapter explores in more detail how the hidden curriculum is transmitted, the messages it conveys and how different groups of pupils respond to it. Some pupils accept it unquestioningly, while others, like the girls of St Trinian's, (or the 'lads' in the Paul Willis study discussed in Chapter 2) may reject it and gain pleasure from disrupting the school's attempts to socialise them.

The hidden curriculum involves messages and ideas that schools do not directly teach, but which children learn, and which are part and parcel of the normal routines and procedures of the organisation. It concerns unpublicised features of school life, and involves norms, values, beliefs and practices that are taken for granted.

These may appear to be common sense, and they can be part of the overall ethos of a school, which could be reinforced by the school's managers, its teachers and its processes.

We saw in Chapter 1 that functionalists value not only the *formal* curriculum that develops the skills and knowledge needed by modern industrial society, but also the *hidden* curriculum, because, at least in theory, it helps foster cooperation, healthy competition (but not at the expense of solidarity) and the spirit of meritocracy. Marxists and feminists, and **anti-racists**, are critical of many aspects of the school curriculum for the way it legitimates (or justifies) ruling-class, male or White dominance, and helps to maintain and reproduce dominance by these groups.

UNDERSTAND THE CONCEPT

Anti-racists believe that racism remains very significant in societies such as Britain, and emphasise the importance of revealing and challenging racist practices. These racist practices may be hidden, denied by those in authority and unintentional. They may be the result of institutional racism (see Chapter 3, Labelling, racism and pupil responses) as well as individual racism. Anti-racism plays a similar role in challenging ethnic inequality as feminism does in challenging gender inequality.

Cotton, Winter and Bailey (2013) argue that the hidden curriculum in contemporary education places the highest value on *efficiency* and *value for money* rather than the promotion of greater *equality* and *opportunity*. Educational institutions may make only token attempts to promote equality, while the endlessly repeated messages and continual emphasis on the importance of hard work, discipline and being successful reveal the real underlying message of education. Many of these messages emphasise inequality and hierarchy.

How is the hidden curriculum transmitted?

This occurs through the standard, everyday aspects of school life, such as:

> the hierarchy of management that places mostly White, generally male head teachers at the top, female classroom practitioners in the middle and

Black, working-class service workers, such as kitchen staff and cleaners, near the bottom (and pupils at the very bottom!)

> an insistence on punctuality at key points within the rigid pattern of the day

> wearing a uniform, which imposes the identity of the school over that of the individual

> the various sets and levels defined by age and ability

> elements of the curriculum and the school's pastoral system

> the organisation of the classroom, for example, with the teacher at the front for pupils to look up to, with the teacher in turn looking down on them

> the expectations teachers bring with them about particular categories of pupils.

The hidden curriculum can even be detected in the organisation of services within the school and the physical layout of the school. Cotton, Winter and Bailey (2013) have discussed these types of process in relation to university Geography courses (although it can just as easily be applied to schools). They found that while undergraduate courses in Geography placed a strong emphasis on sustainability, the way waste and energy was managed in many universities gave it a relatively low priority, in comparison with their concern about cost and convenience.

Taken together, the various elements of the hidden curriculum shape pupils' experiences, producing particular outcomes which are positive for some, while being negative for, and often challenged by, others. They encourage certain values and beliefs and discourage others.

However, it should not be assumed that the hidden curriculum always gives a single, unambiguous message. From a neo-Marxist perspective (see Chapter 1, Neo-Marxist perspectives on education), Henry Giroux (1984) argues that schools are sites of ideological struggle. That is, they are places where different political and moral views may co-exist and be in competition. Thus, whatever the overall ethos of the school, individual teachers may have different views and give different informal messages about what is important in education. For example, some teachers may value punctuality and conformity less than others, some may place more emphasis on equal opportunities than competition and some may even criticise or flout school rules.

From your own experience of schooling, evaluate the view that there is a single, consistent, hidden curriculum in schools. Can you think of examples to contradict this? What are some of the different messages you get from schooling?

PUPIL SUBCULTURES

Some groups in schools accept the rules and the authority of teachers without question, while others may devote much of their energy to rule-breaking and avoiding work. You have probably encountered examples of both during your compulsory education. Sociologists are interested in these **subcultures**. Why do they form, and what effect do they have on their members, other pupils, teachers and schools?

Some researchers, such as Peter Woods, believe that there can be a wide variety of ways of adapting to school, leading to the formation of varied subcultures.

UNDERSTAND THE CONCEPT

Subcultures are groups within wider social groups (for example, within British society) whose attitudes, lifestyles and values are shared by the subculture members, and are significantly different from those in wider society. This might include, for example, different tastes in music, leisure activities and clothing or different attitudes towards groups in authority. Of course, these groups will also share much in common with others in the wider society/culture but they are sufficiently different to be seen by themselves and/or others to be a separate subculture.

On a general level, all subcultures have things in common: their members gain status, mutual support and a sense of belonging from the subculture. According to Hargreaves (1967), anti-school working-class subcultures are predominantly found in the bottom streams of secondary schools. In fact, he argued, they are caused

Ingratiation	Pupils who try hard to win the favour of teachers and have very favourable attitudes to the school.
Compliance	Pupils who accept school rules and discipline and see the school as a useful way to achieve qualifications but who do not have wholly positive attitudes to the school. Typical of first year pupils.
Opportunism	Pupils who fluctuate between seeking approval from teachers and from their peer group. This may be a temporary adaptation before a more settled attitude develops.
Ritualism	Pupils who go through the motions of attending school but without great enthusiasm and without much concern for academic success or gaining the approval of teachers.
Retreatism	This is a deviant adaptation in which pupils reject the values of school and 'mess around' at school but without wanting to directly challenge the authority of teachers.
Colonisation	Common in later years of schooling, this adaptation involves trying to get away with as much as possible without getting into too much trouble.
Intransigence	This involves the rejection of academic success as being important and a rejection of accepted standards of behaviour at the school.
Rebellion	The goals of the school are rejected and pupils devote their efforts to achieving different goals (for example escaping school, or attracting boyfriends/girlfriends).

Table 1.5.1 *Peter Woods: Eight ways of adapting to school*
Source: P. Woods (1983) *Sociology and the School: An Interactionist Viewpoint*, London, RKP.

by the labelling of some pupils as 'low-stream failures'. Unable to achieve status in terms of the mainstream values of the school, these pupils substitute their own set of delinquent values, by which they can achieve success in the eyes of their peers. They do this by, for example, not respecting teachers, messing about, arriving late, having fights, building up a reputation with the opposite sex, and so on.

Writers such as Hargreaves and Willis refer to the pro- and anti-school cultures as homogeneous, coherent groups that share their own uniform sets of values. Peter Woods (1983), however, suggests that this is too simplistic. He argues that pupils use a variety of adaptations, depending upon the ways in which the values of the school are accepted or rejected. Some pupils may partially accept aspects of the school's values but reject others. It is now recognised that responses will also differ within and between the different categories of pupils, and in different school situations. The study of school subcultures is therefore a lot more complex than it used to be.

BUILD CONNECTIONS

The idea of adaptations was first developed by the American functionalist sociologist Robert Merton in the study of crime and deviance in the USA. He believed that there were various ways of adapting to a situation in which everybody started out wanting success but only a few achieved it, and where those from working-class backgrounds had less chance to do well than others. The situation is similar in schools. Not everyone is going to be near the top academically, the most popular or the best at sports, so there are likely to be different ways to adapt to school life depending on how successful you are in different spheres.

Male subcultures

The anti-school male subcultures of the early 1970s (see Chapter 2, Pupil subcultures and social class) made a degree of sense in that their members nearly all got jobs, despite their lack of qualifications. Their coping strategies – what the 'lads' in Willis's study called 'having a laff' – also equipped them for the monotony of the work they were destined for.

The economy has changed, however, and relatively few working-class jobs remain in manufacturing. Has this changed the anti-school subculture of the 'lads'? There is certainly evidence of some changes, but also some continuities and anti-school subcultures continue to exist.

Research by Hollingworth and Williams (2009) (see Chapter 2, Focus on research: Chavs, Charvers and Townies) suggests that working-class peer groups with anti-school attitudes still exist, though they are now seen as 'chavs' rather than 'lads'. The research also suggests that there is a greater variety of middle-class subcultures within schools, based upon different types of consumption and leisure (for example, listening to different types of music). Thus middle-class groups included 'skaters', 'poshies', 'hippies', 'emos' and 'goths'. There was also some regional variation in the subcultures, although all the middle-class groups had at least reasonably positive attitudes to the value of education.

Studies of subcultures have increasingly emphasised their complexity rather than simply seeing them as working-class or middle-class, pro or anti-school. For example, they have added in issues of sexuality and have paid more attention to issues of identity (see Identity in this chapter).

School subcultures may be becoming more diverse than they were in the past.

Mac an Ghaill (1994) illustrated the complexity of subcultural responses by examining the relationship between schooling, work, masculinity and sexuality. He identified the following range of school subcultures.

The 'macho lads'

This group was hostile to school authority and learning, not unlike the 'lads' in Willis's study. Willis had argued that work – especially physical work – was essential to the development of a sense of identity. By the mid-1980s, much of this kind of work was gone. Instead, a spell in youth training, followed very often by unemployment, became the norm for many working-class boys.

The academic achievers

This group, who were from mostly skilled manual working-class backgrounds, adopted a more traditional upwardly mobile route via academic success. However, they had to develop ways of coping with the stereotyping and accusations of effeminacy from the 'macho lads'.

The 'new enterprisers'

This group was identified as a new successful pro-school subculture, who embraced the 'new vocationalism' of the 1980s and 1990s (see Chapter 6). They rejected the traditional academic curriculum, which they saw as a waste of time, but accepted the new vocational ethos, with the help and support of the new breed of teachers and their industrial contacts. In studying subjects such as Business Studies and Computing, they were able to achieve upward mobility and employment by exploiting school–industry links to their advantage.

'Real Englishmen'

These were a small group of middle-class pupils, usually from a liberal professional background. They rejected what teachers had to offer, seeing their own culture and knowledge as superior. They also saw the motivations of the 'achievers' and 'enterprisers' as shallow. While their own values did not fit with doing well at school, they did aspire to university and a professional career. They resolved this dilemma by achieving academic success in a way that appeared effortless (whether it was or not).

Gay students

Finally, Mac an Ghaill looked at the experience of a group neglected entirely by most writers – gay students. These students commented on the heterosexist and homophobic nature of schools, which took for granted the naturalness of heterosexual relationships and the two-parent nuclear family.

School pupils being educated by Sir Ian McKellen on tackling homophobic bullying

Female subcultures

Mac an Ghaill refers to the remasculinisation of the vocational curriculum. By this he means the higher-status vocational subjects such as Business Studies, Technology and Computing, which have come to be dominated by males. Girls are more often on lower-level courses – doing stereotypical work experience in retail or community placements, for example. In Mac an Ghaill's study, although girls disliked the masculinity of the 'macho males', most sought boyfriends. Lower-class girls, in particular, even saw work as a potential marriage market. More upwardly mobile girls saw careers more in terms of independence and achievement.

Griffin (1985) studied young White working-class women during their first two years in employment. Rather than forming a large anti-authority grouping, they created small friendship groups. Their deviance was defined by their sexual behaviour rather than 'trouble-making'. Most importantly, there was not the same continuity between the school's culture and that of their future workplace as there had been for the lads in Willis's study. Instead, there were three possible routes for the girls, which they could follow all at the same time:

> the labour market – securing a job

> the marriage market – acquiring a permanent male partner

> the sexual market – having sexual relationships, while at the same time maintaining their reputation so as to not damage their prospects of finding a suitable husband.

However, it is also clear that many female pupils have positive attitudes towards schools and their subcultural affiliations reflect this. For example, Heidi Mirza (1992) in a study of 62 Black women aged 15–19 in two secondary schools found that they had very positive attitudes towards achieving success although many thought that some teachers were racist. They sometimes therefore formed subcultures based on their ethnicity which valued education but had less respect for schools as an institution.

Ethnic subcultures

As the study by Mirza demonstrates, ethnicity interacts with other social divisions, such as gender and social class, in shaping the formation of subcultures. Ethnic-minority subcultures were also discussed in Chapter 3. However, it is worth reiterating here some of the key issues. For both males and females, their subcultural responses to school reflect a rejection of differential treatment on the basis of their ethnicity and gender. Such responses enable them to cope with and counter the negative experiences they suffer, and to redeem themselves, sometimes to their educational cost.

Some black boys reject school and education in favour of a culture of conspicuous consumption and street credibility, while black girls may strive to achieve in alternative ways, as they reject their teachers' low expectations of them.

In some cases, members of other ethnic groups, such as Bangladeshi males, have adopted aspects of black subcultural responses. For example, Louise Archer (2003) found that Muslim boys in four schools in North West England sometimes drew upon African American 'gangsta' culture, which valued talking tough and having a macho identity. However, they were also affected by ideas on masculinity which emphasised the importance of the breadwinner role within families. Therefore, even though they sometimes felt that they were victimised and even subject to racism by some teachers, they were generally still keen to achieve academic success.

All groups have substantial numbers of conformists who attract little attention. However, it is clearly the case that the actual or perceived membership of subcultures in school has an impact on pupils' experience of schooling and their achievement, in a variety of ways. The situation can be highly complex and it is difficult to generalise. However, there is considerable evidence that teachers do respond to groups of students differently, whether they project a particular identity or not. Teachers bring with them certain expectations about particular groups and they may ascribe characteristics erroneously (incorrectly), which in turn can have particular consequences.

LABELLING AND THE SELF-FULFILLING PROPHECY

As we saw in Chapter 2, teachers' expectations can have the effect of creating a self-fulfilling prophecy, whereby whatever they anticipate (or predict) comes true because it is what they expect. This happens in one of two ways:

> Pupils accept the label teachers give them as being true and internalise it as part of their self-concept, seeing themselves as, for example, having low ability.

> They react against the labelling process and thus conform to negative assumptions, by exhibiting poor behaviour and/or underachievement.

The self-fulfilling prophecy was a very influential concept throughout the 1970s and 1980s, and led to considerable educational reform. Educationalists began to acknowledge that placing pupils in different classes or schools on the basis of ability could considerably damage the prospects of less able pupils. Since the 1990s, these concerns have been given a much lower priority as the quest for higher grades and league table positions has become more important (see Chapter 6).

TEACHER–PUPIL RELATIONSHIPS

As the section on pupil subcultures in this chapter showed, teachers' perceptions and subsequent interactions with students have a significant impact on pupils' educational experiences.

Teachers prefer to teach pupils whom they perceive to be well behaved, well motivated, well mannered, reserved and compliant. They tend to reward such pupils with praise, good marks and subsequent placement in higher sets. Such pupils tend to be middle-class and White, not because of overt prejudice but because teachers tend to judge them by their own cultural standards, being generally members of the White middle classes themselves.

We saw in Chapter 2 how interactionist sociologists identified teachers' perceptions of the 'ideal pupil' as one who conforms to middle-class standards of behaviour. However, this earlier research (Becker, 1971) noted that teachers did not consciously ascribe low ability to working-class pupils. Rather, as is also confirmed by more recent research, teachers have a 'common-sense understanding of ability' which they think to be fair and without particular bias. Gillborn and Youdell (1999) suggest that teachers systematically discriminate against working-class pupils by failing to recognise their intelligence because they do not exhibit it in the right way. Instead, they use their blinkered judgement to allocate working-class pupils to lower sets and foundation-tier examinations. Such pupils may respond with resentment, perceiving their treatment to be unfair. This may cause hostility, discipline problems and reduced motivation, impacting negatively on achievement and their relationship with their teachers.

We also saw in Chapter 3 how differential treatment by teachers of particular ethnic-minority pupils can have negative consequences for the teacher–pupil relationship and for learning. Many ethnic-minority pupils, in particular, feel angry at the way they tend to be singled out for punishment when White pupils are often just as guilty. This too may lead to anti-school sentiments and negative subcultural responses that make interaction with teachers even more confrontational. Many Black pupils, particularly boys, get drawn into this downward spiral of disengagement from schooling (Connolly, 1998).

There has been extensive research on whether teachers' expectations affect school performance, particularly in the USA. This research has been reviewed by Nicole Sorhagen (2013).

The review found that inaccurate teacher expectations (where they thought the pupils were more, or less, able than they were) did lead to long-term effects and a self-fulfilling prophecy for many children. The effects were greater for children from low-income families than those from high-income families, and greater with respect to maths than reading.

However, such labelling does not always have an impact. Various studies suggest that some children become all the more determined to do well in order to disprove the teachers who have labelled them negatively.

THE ORGANISATION OF TEACHING AND LEARNING

The way pupils are allocated to teaching groups – on the basis of sometimes unfair judgements made by teachers – shapes what pupils are taught and their ultimate success, both in terms of the qualifications that they achieve and their subsequent progression opportunities. These groupings can in themselves involve labelling and self-fulfilling prophecies. The main methods of grouping are as follows:

> Mixed ability – where pupils of all abilities are taught together. Teaching tends to be differentiated to allow weaker pupils to engage, while stretching and challenging the more able. Proponents feel that there are both social and educational benefits. This approach allows for a broader social mix, reducing conflict in society and ensuring that labelling on the basis of behaviour does not affect attainment. It also recognises the fact that ability is not fixed, as children develop in spurts rather than all at the same rate.

> Streaming – where pupils are grouped by ability for most or all of their lessons. The top stream is the most academic group; the bottom streams contain the lowest achievers. Supporters believe that this ensures that the most able are not held back and the least able can be given the extra support they need.

> Setting – where pupils are placed in ability groups for particular subjects and so may be in the top set for one subject and a lower set in another. This is the most common form of ability grouping in secondary schools in England and Wales, especially as pupils approach GCSE, as it helps teachers to prepare pupils for a particular examination tier.

> Within-class grouping – where the teacher makes ability groups within the class – is more common in primary than in secondary schools. However, research into primary schools has shown that pupils are aware of which ability group or table they have been put into, and this does impact on motivation and self-esteem.

Although within-class grouping is common in primary schools, it has been shown to have an effect on pupils' motivation levels.

Numerous writers have suggested that the influence of league tables has increased the tendency for schools to separate pupils on the basis of ability. Ireson *et al.* (2002) note that such grouping is not always based on attainment within specific subjects – it has also been based on behaviour and used as a means of socially controlling particular groups of pupils. Ireson's research survey indicates that setting tends to be beneficial for the more able pupils in the top groups, while those in bottom sets generally receive little challenge or stimulation, and so can easily become demoralised, disruptive and disaffected.

Evidence from the Evaluation of the DfE African Caribbean Achievement Project (Aiming High) (Tikly *et al.*, 2006, p.217) does appear to indicate that African Caribbean pupils are underrepresented in higher-ability sets, higher test and examination tiers, and in gifted and talented cohorts.

Although there has been a lot of research on the academic, social and personal outcomes of grouping pupils by ability, there has been little from the pupils' perspective. Research by Hallam *et al.* (2004) illustrates the impact of ability grouping as pupils perceive it. Six pupils, of high, moderate or low ability, mixed in gender, in each Key Stage 2 class were interviewed in each of six primary schools adopting different combinations of grouping practices, including streaming, setting, within-class ability and mixed-ability grouping.

At primary level, the authors found the following:

> In reading, most pupils wished to be in the top group because it gave them status and a feeling of superiority. However, most pupils (excluding the top groups) preferred whole-class or individual work because they didn't like to feel left out.

> Social adjustment, social attitudes and attitudes toward peers of different ability were 'healthier' among children in non-streamed classes.

> The more streams there were, the more negative the attitudes of those in the lower streams.

> Pupils of below-average ability who were taught by teachers who believed in streaming could become friendless or neglected by others.

According to the authors, what research there is on ability grouping in secondary schools suggests the following:

> Streaming may play a major role in polarising pro- and anti-school attitudes among pupils (with higher-level students being pro and lower ones anti).

> Setting may produce more negative than positive consequences among Maths students, with a high proportion of students wanting to move sets or change to mixed-ability teaching.

> Ability grouping – when it involves setting – is the preferred form of grouping among secondary pupils, but the greater the level of mixed-ability teaching in the school, the more it is the preferred option among students.

The research on ability grouping does suggest that, overall, it has relatively little impact on school achievement levels, but that those in the top sets do a little better than they otherwise might, while those in the bottom sets do a little worse. The winners tend to be the White middle classes; the losers, working-class and ethnic-minority pupils. Streaming and setting had been in decline throughout the 1970s and 1980s. As Chapter 6 shows, however, since results were first published in league tables for secondary schools in 1992 and for primary schools in 1997, many schools have felt obliged to return to various systems of ability grouping. This is because schools now operate in a marketplace where they compete for pupils and resources.

IDENTITY

Identity is concerned with how individuals see themselves and how they are seen by others. This is closely related to membership of social groups. For example, we have identities in terms of our gender (masculine or feminine), ethnicity, sexuality, nationality, social class, religion, and so on. Identities partly flow from how others see us, but our own sense of identity may not always coincide with the views of others. Identities can be quite complex and changeable as our view of ourselves interacts with the views of others.

UNDERSTAND THE CONCEPT

Kath Woodward (2000) sees **identity** as based upon the similarities individuals feel they have with other individuals, but also the differences. Your identity is often defined in opposition to groups with which you do not identify, as well as in terms of a sense of similarity with groups that you do identify, with. Because of this, identity is not just a psychological phenomenon, it is also social. Many aspects of identity only have meaning because they involve belonging to particular social groups (for example, ethnic groups or supporters of a particular football team). Furthermore, as Richard Jenkins (1996) claims, identity is not purely personal but also depends upon how other people think of us. This inevitably has some influence on how we see ourselves. Therefore the social identity given by others is linked to our personal identity, or the way in which we see ourselves.

FOCUS ON RESEARCH: BLACK MASCULINITIES AND SCHOOLING

Tony Sewell (1996) conducted research in comprehensive schools in London. The bulk of the study took place in what Sewell refers to as 'Township School'. This school was a boys' comprehensive for children aged 11–16. There were 61 students of Asian origin, 63 of African origin, 140 of African Caribbean origin, 31 mixed-race students, 127 White boys and 23 'others'.

Sewell gathered his material through an ethnographic approach using semi-structured interviews and observation. At the time, he was in his early 30s and describes himself as Black. He is careful to point out that he was able to build very good relationships with the boys and was able to mix with them socially. He describes this process as being able to 'chill'.

Sewell found that some Black pupils were disciplined excessively by teachers who were socialised into racist attitudes and who felt threatened by these students' masculinity, sexuality and physical skills. Furthermore, the boys felt that their culture received little or no positive recognition (see Chapter 3, Cultural factors, ethnicity and achievement, for more detail on this study and its findings).

Questions

1. **Explain** why sociologists such as Sewell often change the names of the schools in which they conduct research.

2. **Outline** and **explain** two reasons why it was important for Sewell to build good relationships and 'chill' with the boys.

3. **Assess** to what extent Sewell's own social identity may have helped his relationships with the boys.

4. **To what extent** do you think the boys would have been completely honest with Sewell? Explain your answer.

5. **Analyse** the potential dangers for a researcher in identifying too strongly with the group being studied.

Identity can be linked to differential achievement, for example, in terms of whether individual pupils identify themselves as being academic or non-academic. However, it extends much further than this and is linked to many other issues in education, such as the friendship groupings that children form and how education influences ideas of masculinity and femininity. Some researchers on education have moved away from looking at narrower issues of, for example, pupil–teacher interaction and labelling, and have instead studied how different identities are formed in a school setting.

An example is a study conducted by Robert Young (2012) of 'Neds'. The word 'Ned' is short for Non-Educated Delinquent and is used in Glasgow and other parts of Scotland to refer to a young 'thug' or 'layabout' and has similar connotations to the word 'Chav' in Britain.

Young says that explanations for the existence of 'Chavs' and 'Neds' tend to fall into two categories.

Structural accounts emphasise the importance of social structures, such as class structures, for explaining the existence of these groups. From this point of view, social changes, such as the decline in unskilled and semi-skilled work, are largely responsible for the contemporary male working-class subcultures that reject the values of school and wider society.

Agency-based theories emphasise the active choices made by individuals as they form social groups and develop their own subcultures and identities. From this point of view, identities are more creative and individual.

UNDERSTAND THE CONCEPT

There is a long debate in sociology about whether social life can be explained in terms of **structure** or **agency**, or a combination of the two. Structures involve relatively large-scale features of society, which are hard for individuals to change and which constrain peoples' choices and options. For example, feminists believe that patriarchal structures shape the lives of women, and Marxists believe that class structures limit opportunities for the working class. Agency refers to the (apparent) ability of individuals to act how they choose, change their behaviour and sometimes change society. Interactionist sociologists tend to emphasise agency. Many sociologists now accept that structure and agency are both important. People make choices, but those choices are limited by their circumstances (for example, how much money they have), and these circumstances are shaped by structures.

Young found that some pupils seemed to choose the 'Ned' identity as a way to gain respect from their peer group.

Young conducted a survey of 22 Scottish schools to examine which of these approaches was more plausible. Pupils were asked about a range of youth styles, such as whether they read books, thought schools were a waste of time, liked hip hop music, skipped school, hung around on streets or drank Buckfast (a fortified wine). They were also asked about family life, the social class of their parents or guardians and where they lived. Young found that those with 'Ned' characteristics were more likely to be boys and to come from deprived areas. However, this was not always the case: a significant number were girls and were from more affluent backgrounds. Some pupils seemed to be choosing the 'Ned' identity even though they did not come from the typical background because being a 'Ned' was thought by some respondents to earn you 'respect' from your peer group and was considered, at least to some extent, to be 'cool'. Therefore Young concluded that while structural factors were important, some pupils actively chose a 'Ned' identity. This affected the peer groups they associated with and their relationships inside and outside education.

An emphasis upon identity is also found in the work of Mac an Ghaill (See Male subcultures and Female subcultures in this chapter) and in the work of Connolly, which is discussed in Focus on skills as well as in Chapter 3.

A focus on identity can be helpful as an alternative to the narrower processes of labelling and the self-fulfilling prophecy, and the formation of subcultures. It can help to:

> link factors inside and outside schooling

> move beyond the assumption that children are neatly divided into specific subcultures

> show how different social divisions (for example, class, gender, sexuality and ethnicity) interact within schools

> link pupil interaction with family, peer groups and teachers in helping to understand how different individuals and groups negotiate life in school.

However, the greater complexity of this approach might make it more difficult to identify and acknowledge some of the direct ways that discrimination and labelling limit the achievement of some groups in the education system.

Do you agree that gender and ethnicity are two of the most significant factors shaping the identity of school pupils? How far do these identities in turn shape attitudes to school work?

FOCUS ON SKILLS: RACISM, GENDER IDENTITIES AND YOUNG CHILDREN

Connolly's 1998 study of primary-school children emphasises the diverse influences on the way that gender and ethnic identities are formed by factors inside and outside school. The research was based on the study of three classes of 5–6 year olds in a multi-ethnic inner-city primary school. It used observation, interviews with parents, staff and governors, and group interviews with the children. Connolly looked at how factors both inside and outside schools helped to shape the identities of girls and boys from different ethnic groups.

Black boys

Teachers were more willing to criticise the behaviour of Black boys than that of other groups. They felt that some of the Black males in the school were in danger of growing up to be violent criminals, and saw them as a threat to school discipline. However, they also took positive steps to encourage them to participate in school activities such as football.

The boys also brought their own values and attitudes to school, for example, those relating to masculinity. These contributed to their sense of identity and helped build a sense of loyalty to their peer groups.

Black girls

Black girls were also perceived by teachers as potentially disruptive but likely to be good at sports, music and dancing. Boys in the school tended to regard girls as being quite passive, including Black girls. However, the girls themselves were not always passive in accepting these characterisations. For example, on one occasion a group of Black girls 'captured' a White boy they found annoying and paraded their captive around the school.

South Asian boys

In the local community and in the school, non-Asians tended to see the Asian community as having a more distinctive lifestyle than the Black community, as well as being more law abiding and conformist than other ethnic minorities. Some teachers contrasted what they saw as the close and supportive Asian families with the high rates of single parenthood amongst other groups in the area. Partly for these reasons, South Asian boys tended to be seen by teachers as immature rather than seriously deviant.

There was a tendency for other boys who wanted to assert their masculinity to pick on South Asian boys. The South Asian boys had difficulty in gaining status as males. This made it difficult for them to feel confident at school.

South Asian girls

South Asian girls were seen by other pupils to be even more obedient and hard-working than South Asian boys, although Connolly's observations showed that their attitude to work was not significantly different from that of other female groups. Some were diligent and hard-working while others were less conscientious, and some were quite disruptive and uncooperative.

South Asian girls had a relatively low status among their peers. They were seen as feminine in terms of their passivity and obedience, but they were not seen as potential girlfriends by Black and White boys because their culture was considered too alien. However, they enjoyed high status for their academic ability.

Questions

1. **Explain,** using an example, how factors inside and outside school influenced identity formation in this study.

2. **Explain.** Using one example from the study, explain how gender and ethnicity interact in forming identities.

3. **Analyse** how the identities of these groups may have affected their academic progress. (Consider the ways in which you see yourself and are seen by others and how this influences educational achievement).

4. **Evaluate** the usefulness of focusing on identities rather than relying on a more straightforward labelling theory of schooling.

CONCLUSIONS

The research discussed in this chapter demonstrates that factors inside schools can have a significant impact upon the way that pupils perceive their own schooling, ability, and ultimately achievement. Pupils form their identities in interactions with other pupils, with teachers and in the context of school organisation. This inevitably shapes their experience of schooling and the levels of achievement that they attain. As Chapters 2, 3 and 4 have demonstrated, this can have an effect upon the relationship between social class and attainment, gender and attainment, and ethnicity and attainment.

However, there is a danger in some of this research that the influence of factors within schools can be exaggerated. Factors external to the education system, particularly material inequality and cultural differences, also have a significant impact upon achievement. Interactionist approaches that concentrate upon interaction within schools may pay too little attention to wider power structures (linked to social class, patriarchy and ethnic inequality) that help to explain the patterns of achievement found within the education system. While schools may be able to go some way towards reducing the effects of these wider social inequalities, they cannot eradicate them entirely. Social class in particular continues to have a strong influence upon achievement regardless of how schools themselves may be organised or how they may help teachers interact with their pupils.

Some versions of labelling theory may also be too deterministic (that is, they assume that achievement will be determined by the labels given to pupils). As we have seen, not all pupils accept and live up to the labels attached to them. Some challenge these labels and some of those who have been negatively stereotyped may try particularly hard to succeed.

The most credible attempts to explain patterns of behaviour and patterns of achievement within the education system acknowledge that factors inside and outside the system interact with one another to shape the outcomes. Research founded on the concept of identity can help to illustrate and make sense of the complex processes involved in explaining the ways in which pupils experience and react to education.

CHECK YOUR UNDERSTANDING

1. What two things do Cotton, Winter and Bailey claim are the main values taught by the hidden curriculum in British schools?

2. How does Henry Giroux characterise schools? Briefly explain the implications of this for the hidden curriculum.

3. Briefly explain the meaning of the word 'subculture'.

4. Outline and briefly explain three adaptations to schooling suggested by Peter Woods.

5. Explain how class might be linked to any two school subcultures.

6. Explain two ways in which subculture formation might be shaped by factors outside school as well as inside schools.

7. Give a short summary of any one piece of research which suggests that streaming or setting might affect achievement.

8. Explain what is meant by identity.

9. Using the research of Connolly, explain how identity formation was linked to gender and ethnicity in any two groups of pupils.

10. Evaluate why processes within school should not be examined in isolation from factors outside school when studying education.

TAKE IT FURTHER

Visit the Ofsted website at www.ofsted.gov.uk and find the latest full inspection report for your school or college. Identify and summarise its findings on relationships within the school/college, particularly pupil–pupil and pupil–teacher relationships. Evaluate its findings and write your own response to the Ofsted report explaining how far your own experience of the school fits with their assessment. Briefly suggest reasons why your 'insider' view might be different to their 'outsider' view. Compare your findings with those of your classmates.

1.6 SOCIAL POLICY AND EDUCATION

LEARNING OBJECTIVES

> Understand educational policies, including policies of selection, marketisation and privatisation, and policies to achieve greater equality of opportunity or outcome (AO1).

> Understand the impact of globalisation on education policy (AO1).

> Apply this understanding to contemporary Britain (AO2).

> Analyse the impact of the above policies on the structure and role of education, and students' access to and experience of it. (AO3).

> Evaluate competing views on the advantages and disadvantages of these policies (AO3).

INTRODUCING THE DEBATE

An enormous amount of public money (and a lot of private money too) is spent on education and children now have to spend at least thirteen years in education or training. Since state education began in the 19th century educational policies have been frequently revised, but has all this money and all these changes actually improved British education? This chapter examines changes in policies introduced by education ministers such as Michael Gove (pictured above) and evaluates how effective they have been. In particular, it looks at the increasing influence of neoliberal ideas that support greater competition in and privatisation of education and considers whether this shift has led to more or less equal opportunities and whether it has improved the quality of the education provided in Britain. Is Britain's education system up to the job of educating its citizens for life in a globalised 21st century world?

1944 TO 1965

The 1944 Education Act (sometimes called the Butler Act after the Education Minister at the time, Richard Butler) marked the beginning of the modern state education system in the UK, with the introduction of compulsory state education up to the age of 14. This opened up secondary education to all social classes, rather than restricting it to those who could afford to pay for it privately. Up until the end of the Second World War, those with the most access to education and the opportunities it provided were the sons and daughters of the middle and upper classes. The policy was part of the establishment of the Welfare State, following a report by William Beveridge in 1942. Beveridge argued that the state needed to tackle five Giant Evils and one of these was 'ignorance'. Ignorance resulted from the lack of secondary education for many, leading to a lack of opportunity for these children. As part of the new educational policies, the tripartite system was established, which provided the cornerstone of state secondary education for several decades.

The tripartite system

As part of the aim to create a 'land fit for heroes' after the Second World War, Butler's Education Act of 1944 introduced secondary education for all pupils. The act may have had no effect on the public schools, but it did aim to abolish class-based inequalities within state education. A tripartite system was to be introduced, providing three types of secondary school, each suited to one of three supposed levels of ability:

› grammar schools for academically able pupils

› technical schools

› secondary modern schools for everyone else.

Underpinning this system, at least in theory, was the idea of equality of opportunity. All children would take an IQ test at the age of 11 in order to discover which kind of school most suited their abilities. The government accepted the view that intelligence was innate (in-born) and could be scientifically measured. While only those who passed the 11+ test went to grammar or technical schools, each of the three types of school was supposed to have similar standards of provision and to be considered as equal ('parity of esteem'), as each school would provide the most suitable education for the development of each type of learner, irrespective of their background.

Problems of the tripartite system

1. For most pupils only two types of school were available – grammar and secondary moderns. Few technical schools were built because of the cost of equipping them.

2. Grammar schools, attended by around 20 per cent of pupils, were seen as the most prestigious type of state secondary school. They specialised in academic subjects that led to university and a well-paid job. The 75 per cent of pupils who attended secondary moderns were seen as 'failures'. Some were not allowed to take exams, so were denied opportunities to progress. There was no 'parity of esteem', but instead a huge wastage of talent.

3. Some pupils ended up in secondary modern schools irrespective of their ability. Girls generally achieved better marks than boys in the 11+, yet the pass mark for girls was set higher as there were fewer girls' grammar school places available (many grammar schools being single-sex). In some parts of the country, as little as 12 per cent of pupils could get grammar school places, while in South Wales there were places for 40 per cent (Ball, 2008).

4. The social class divide remained intact. Most grammar school places were taken by middle-class pupils. The mainly working-class pupils in secondary moderns were effectively labelled 'failures' and so lacked the means and motivation to succeed. Consequently a number of reports (for example, the 1959 Crowther Report) suggested that a lot of working-class talent was being wasted and the system was producing too few skilled workers.

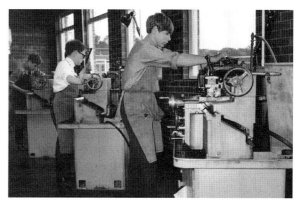

Grammar schools followed a traditional academic curriculum including Latin.

Secondary modern schools offered a more vocational curriculum for those who had failed the 11+.

The system still had its supporters. It served many middle-class families very well, so that even today it survives in some areas of the country. In 2011, there were still 161 grammar schools educating 158,000 pupils or 5 per cent of secondary-school children (Chitty, 2014). The Conservative Party has considered the idea of opening new grammar schools at various times, but the number has not expanded. Grammar schools did provide some opportunities for social mobility for those working-class pupils who passed the 11+ test. Some recent research has gone so far as to suggest the system gave working-class pupils more chances than they have today, although this claim is controversial.

Discuss whether there is any justification for keeping grammar schools today.

1965 TO 1979

Comprehensive schools

The tripartite system had not succeeded in creating equality of opportunity. Social democratic perspectives (see Chapter 1) were very critical of what they saw as the highly divisive tripartite system. Sociologists such as A.H. Halsey (Halsey, Heath and Ridge, 1980, and Halsey, Floud, Arnold and Anderson, 1961), conducted research suggesting that social mobility had stalled. From this perspective, it was thought that what might bring meritocratic ideals closer was to abolish selection at the age of 11 and to educate all children in the same school, regardless of their class, ethnicity, gender or ability. These views influenced the Labour governments of the 1960s and 1970s, and in 1965 a Labour government instructed all local authorities to submit plans for comprehensive reorganisation. Facilities were upgraded so that the new comprehensive schools could provide a broad curriculum and more sporting and recreational activities. Comprehensive schools were introduced gradually depending on the individual local authority, and, as we have seen, in some authorities selective grammar schools were retained.

Problems of comprehensive schools

1. In practice, comprehensive schools did not live up to all of their ideals. Admissions were largely based on geographical catchment areas, often inhabited mainly by one social class, so social mixing at school was limited. Also, the tripartite system continued in some areas and independent education remained an option for the most wealthy.

2. Most comprehensive schools organised their classes by ability, for example, by streaming. Because of the links between social class and achievement, this meant that higher streams were dominated by middle-class pupils and lower streams by working-class. Sociological studies by writers such as Hargreaves (1967) and Ball (1981) showed that the class divide that existed between grammar and secondary modern schools was reappearing within comprehensives (see Chapter 2, Factors inside the education system, for more detail on the effects of streaming and setting).

During the 1970s, comprehensive schools came under increasing attack. From the social democratic perspective, class differences were not budging, so equality of opportunity still remained some distance away.

The loudest criticisms came from what has become known as the Neoliberal/New Right (see Chapter 1, Neoliberal/New Right perspectives on education). They criticised comprehensive schools for their alleged lack of discipline, poor results, large classes and failure to prepare pupils for the world of work. It was claimed that mixed-ability schools dragged down the performance of the most able and that lack of parental choice was a problem. If all children went to the same type of school, then there was no opportunity to choose a type of school that would be particularly suited to the individual child. In line with New Right/neoliberal thinking, state schools had a **monopoly** and therefore had no incentive to compete with one another and improve. Teachers effectively had a job for life, with a guaranteed stream of pupils fed to them by the local authority, and therefore they had no incentive to improve either. It did not matter that there seemed little evidence to support some of these criticisms (for example, exam results were improving during this period); momentum for change grew. In 1979, the Conservative Party won the general election, and Margaret Thatcher became prime minister.

1979 TO 1997

Education and the New Right

New Right policies became increasingly influential during the Conservative governments of 1979 to 1997. New Right policies favour the use of market forces as a method of distributing resources. In a free market, consumers can choose from a range of products. Producers compete to produce the best product at the best price. In this way, schools compete to attract pupils and educational standards improve.

The government's first actions, however, involved trying to tackle the growing problem of youth unemployment.

Vocational education and training

The Conservatives felt that youth unemployment was the result of schools' failure to teach appropriate work

skills. This 'skills crisis' was to blame for Britain's economic decline. A number of schemes were developed that aimed to reduce youth unemployment, increase young people's skill levels and make them more aware of the world of work. For example, Apprenticeships and Training Schemes combine 'on the job' training alongside part-time study with the aim of achieving National Vocational Qualifications (NVQs) and possibly other accreditations and skills. These became known as the '**new vocationalism**'.

Criticisms of the new vocationalism

Vocational education and training have had many criticisms, particularly from neo-Marxist writers. Finn (1987) argued that there was a hidden political agenda to vocational training in this period:

> It provided cheap labour for employers and kept the pay rates of young workers low.

> It undermined the bargaining power of the unions (because only permanent workers could be members).

> It reduced politically embarrassing unemployment statistics.

> It may also have been intended to reduce crime by removing young people from the streets.

Critics such as Phil Cohen (1984) argued that the real purpose of vocational training is to create 'good' attitudes and work discipline rather than actual job skills. In this way, young people come to accept a likely future of low-paid and unskilled work. Those young unemployed who view training schemes as cheap labour, and refuse to join them, are defined as irresponsible and idle, and are 'punished' by the withdrawal of benefits.

It was argued that vocational training led to a low-paid workforce.

According to Cohen, it was not proven that young people lack job skills. Many had already gained a lot of work experience from part-time jobs. Youth unemployment was the result not of a shortage of skills, but of a shortage of jobs. Critics also pointed out that the sorts of skills taught to Youth Training Scheme (YTS) trainees were only appropriate for jobs in the secondary labour market, that is, jobs that are unskilled, insecure, and pay low wages. Such jobs offer little chance of promotion, employer investment is very low, and labour turnover is consequently very high.

In practice, it is lower-ability students who tend to be channelled into vocational courses. The new vocationalism thus introduced another form of selection, with working-class and ethnic-minority students being disproportionately represented on these courses.

Training schemes were also criticised for failing to break down traditional patterns of sex stereotyping found in employment and education; nor were they encouraging girls to move into non-traditional areas. In fact, according to Buswell (1987), they were structured so as to reproduce gender inequality. She pointed out that the types of schemes into which girls were channelled, such as retail work, led to occupations where they were low paid when young, and would work part time when older, reflecting women's position in the labour market. This problem has persisted up to the present day. For example, according to figures from the DfE, 6 per cent of Apprenticeships in hairdressing in 2006 were taken up by males compared with 94 per cent by females. Retail fares slightly better with a 38/62 percentage split, whereas in construction crafts, the male-to-female ratio is 99 to 1.

The 1988 Education Reform Act and other reforms

The influence of the New Right is clearly seen in this Act, the most influential in education since 1944. It introduced a new emphasis on competition and choice in education. It had six key elements.

Marketisation

Competition between schools was to be encouraged. The greater the competition, the greater the incentive for schools to improve. Successful schools could expand; unsuccessful schools would have to improve or face the possibility of funding cuts and, ultimately, closure. Parents would, in theory, be given a real choice between schools. These aims would be achieved through open enrolment (which allowed successful schools to expand to the limit of their physical capacity) and formula funding so that the money given to schools was based on the number of pupils they attracted.

Testing

Parents would need a way of judging the quality of schools. It was decided that all pupils would sit national tests at the ages of 7, 11 and 14. These, along with GCSE and A-level results, would be used to draw up league tables so that parents could make an informed choice of school.

The National Curriculum

In order to develop meaningful standards for comparison and to ensure that all pupils received teaching in appropriate knowledge and skills, a National Curriculum was introduced. This prescribed knowledge in a range of subjects that every school would have to teach. In addition, the influence of local authorities on education was reduced. Schools could decide how to manage their own budgets and even opt out of local authority control altogether, enabling them to make their own decisions about which pupils to admit, and even introducing selection if they wished.

League tables

A significant reform introduced after the Act was the introduction of league tables. These were designed to provide better information to parents (along with regular school inspection reports) so that they could choose the best schools for their children. It also put pressure on schools to improve their performance to attract pupils. A crucial measure of success was the achievement of 5 or more GCSEs at C grade or above for secondary school pupils.

Diversifying school choice

In order to give parents more choice of school (and to reduce local authority control of schooling) a greater variety of schools began to be introduced. Existing schools could opt out of local authority control and become grant maintained (these schools were funded directly by central government). City technology colleges were introduced in some inner-city areas to try to improve educational standards and offer choice. These institutions concentrated on Maths, Science and Technology and were partly funded by the private sector (which helped start the process of **privatising** educational services).

Private education

The government was supportive of private education and thought that it would be useful if some talented children who would otherwise go to state school were given the opportunity to attend private school. To this end they introduced an Assisted Places scheme in 1980 (it ran until

1997) which helped pay the fees for these children out of state funds. This gave a boost to the private school sector (for more discussion see Chapter 2, Material deprivation).

The New Right government was supportive of the private-school sector.

UNDERSTAND THE CONCEPT

Privatisation involves moving functions previously provided by government into the private sector to be run by businesses for profit. The most obvious privatisations in the UK have involved the selling of utilities (such as gas, electricity, the post office and water) to shareholders, and the privatisation of companies such as British Airways (BA). Many of these privatisations took place under Margaret Thatcher's government in the 1980s. However, schools increasingly buy services (for example, counselling, catering and Educational Psychology services) from private providers. Private companies are increasingly involved in running schools (see Multinational companies and education in this chapter).

Criticisms of New Right policies on schooling

1. Concerns were expressed over the damaging, stressful effects of testing children so often and the idea that testing could distort what was taught so that schools would 'teach to the test'.

2. The whole system could not operate like a true market because parents were not paying for education and could not select schools based on price. Instead it was an artificial market (or **quasi market**). League tables in particular gave incentives

to manipulate the rules to get the best possible results. For example, schools could try not to take on weak pupils, not to enter some pupils for exams, to concentrate on the 5 GCSEs at C grade measure to the exclusion of other aims, and to expel difficult pupils to improve the image of the school. Competition might also force schools to spend large amounts of money on marketing rather than on the education of pupils.

UNDERSTAND THE CONCEPT

Quasi-markets are artificial or pretend markets used to try to make state-run services run like businesses, even when their 'products' are not bought and sold. For example, schools are funded as if parents were consumers, so that each school gets a sum of money when parents agree to send a child there. One problem is that the price paid for the service is fixed – however much children and parents like or dislike the school, the school gets the same amount of money. Schools, can't compete on price and it is difficult to change schools because the alternatives might be full or too far away.

3. Some critics felt that the 1988 Education Reform Act was motivated by the Conservative government's desire to reduce the power of Labour-controlled local authorities rather than to improve education.

4. Very few extra places were available in popular schools, so in practice many parents had very little or no choice of school.

5. It has been argued that class differences were reinforced by the 1988 Education Reform Act. Middle-class parents were able to use their cultural capital (see Chapter 2) to make sure that their children got into the best schools. Research by Stephen Ball et al. (1994) showed that middle-class parents were better able to impress at interview, write convincing letters and manipulate the system, for example, by making multiple applications to schools. They could also use their economic capital (money) to pay transport costs if better schools were further away, and even move nearer their favoured school if necessary. With their emphasis on standards rather than equality of opportunity, there were few attempts to address such class or other social divisions which contributed to inequality of opportunity.

6. Competition and increased emphasis on school diversity reintroduced a divisive education system which the comprehensive system had tried to eradicate. A certain amount of selection was introduced in some schools and oversubscribed schools were sometimes able to engage in **cream skimming** (selecting the best pupils), leaving other schools with fewer motivated and academically able pupils. As a result some schools went into a spiral of decline while others became ever more successful.

UNDERSTAND THE CONCEPT

Cream skimming refers to selecting the best while leaving the rest behind. Just as you might want the cream from a pint of milk, leaving the skimmed milk behind, you might try to choose the most able pupils for your school, leaving other schools with pupils less likely to do well. This loads the dice in league tables in favour of the schools that can do this, and against those that can't.

1997 TO 2015

In the period between 1997 and 2015 there were two different governments, both of which were influenced by New Right/neoliberal thinking and policies but without embracing them fully.

1. Between 1997 and 2010 there was a Labour government. However, the leaders (Tony Blair and, from 2007, Gordon Brown) described the government as 'New Labour' suggesting that they were no longer going to follow completely social democratic policies alone but would combine them with elements of New Right or neoliberal policies.

2. From 2010 to 2015 a Coalition government was in power. It was led by the Conservatives (David Cameron was prime minister) but had the support of the Liberal Democrats (Nick Clegg was the deputy prime minister). It largely followed Conservative neoliberal policies but with some concessions to the Liberal Democrats, so some policies were influenced by more social democratic thinking.

David Cameron and Nick Clegg announcing their Coalition agreement in Downing Street in 2010

NEW LABOUR: NEW RIGHT/NEOLIBERAL INFLUENCES

New Right/neoliberal thinking continued to influence the New Labour government elected in 1997. Many of the policies begun by the Conservatives were continued and developed. One example was the expansion of specialist schools.

Specialist schools

Schools have been encouraged to specialise in particular subjects. The aim has been to increase choice, encourage competition, raise standards and allow schools to excel at their specialisms. No longer do school pupils have to attend what Tony Blair's Press Secretary, Alastair Campbell, referred to as the 'bog standard' local comprehensive school.

State secondary schools could apply to become a specialist school in one of ten specialisms – Art, Business and Enterprise, Engineering, Humanities, Languages, Mathematics and Computing, Music, Science, Sports and Technology. Schools had to raise £50,000 from sponsors, which was matched by government funding. Once a specialist school, they could select up to 10 per cent of their pupils from those who showed an aptitude for their specialism.

In 1997, New Labour inherited 196 specialist schools from the Conservatives. Ten years later, there were 2,500 – about 80 per cent of all secondary schools in England.

Increased choice

Along with specialist schools, academies were introduced in 2001 and community schools and foundation schools were allowed greater control over their own affairs than other types. Chitty (2014) comments that by the time New Labour left power in 2010, there was a very complex secondary education system with nearly twenty different types of school.

Work-related learning and vocational education

Another strand of policy inherited from the Conservatives was a focus on work-related learning and training. A number of initiatives illustrate New Labour's continued commitment to the aim of improving the skills of the workforce in order for Britain to remain competitive in the global marketplace. One way of trying to ensure that Britain had a suitably skilled workforce was to enact legislation that raised the age at which children were

allowed to leave education or training to 17 in 2013 and 18 in 2015. This brought with it various initiatives to allow schools and colleges more options in providing vocational education and training (see Table 1.6.1).

Labour's former education secretary David Blunkett

New Deal for Young People (NDYP)	In 1998, Labour introduced the NDYP, with the aim of reducing youth unemployment. The programme was designed for 18–24-year-olds who had been unemployed and claiming Jobseeker's Allowance for six months. They were provided with Personal Advisors to guide them through the various options involving education, training, voluntary work or a subsidised job. They lost benefits if they refused all options.
Apprenticeships	Labour also expanded the Apprenticeship scheme and young apprenticeships at Level 1 for 14–16-year-olds in schools and colleges were also introduced.
Vocational GCSEs/AVCEs	These replaced GNVQs in an attempt to create parity of esteem with academic courses.
Increased flexibility programme	Pupils at Key Stage 4 (14–16-year-olds) were allowed to attend college for one or two days per week to follow vocational qualifications not available at school.
Diplomas (formerly Specialist diplomas)	These involved a combination of vocational and academic learning studied alongside other complementary qualifications and embedded skills. The Diplomas were discontinued in 2010.

Table 1.6.1 *Labour's work-based education and training initiatives*

PRIVATISATION OF EDUCATION

Perhaps the most obvious New Right influence on New Labour education policies was a move towards privatising aspects of education. Conservative governments between 1979 and 1997 introduced greater private sector involvement into some aspects of education. For example, city technology colleges allowed businesses to set up and run some state schools, and academies also allowed state involvement. Ofsted school inspections were also contracted out to private companies (Ball, 2013). But marketisation gathered pace under New Labour.

A programme of new buildings for schools and colleges was partly financed by the Private Finance Initiative (PFI). Private companies did the building, but in return were given contracts to repay the investment and provide maintenance for 25–35 years. The colleges, schools or local education authorities (LEAs) had to pay the ongoing costs. The academies programme, which began in March 2000, allowed greater business involvement in the running of schools than ever before. Furthermore, some companies were given contracts to run aspects of the education system. The private company Capita was given a contact in 2004 to manage the strategy to improve literacy and numeracy and an American firm, Educational Testing Service (ETS), was given a contract to manage Standard Achievement Tests (SATs) testing for pupils aged 11 and 14. From the perspective of New Labour, these marketisation measures offered the promise of greater efficiency because companies could compete to be given contracts. The PFI promised extra investment in education beyond what the government felt it could afford to invest at the time.

NEW LABOUR: SOCIAL DEMOCRATIC INFLUENCES

By no means all of New Labour's educational policies have reflected New Right thinking. The influence of social democratic viewpoints has also been apparent. Here are some examples of policies that aimed to reduce social exclusion and promote equality of opportunity.

Academies
In 2001, it was proposed that academies should be established in partnership with employers and other sponsors to replace failing schools and provide high-quality education for all in deprived areas. The best teachers would be encouraged to work in these schools and there would be a high level of resourcing. Sponsors would be able to have a say in how the school was run and what curriculum was on offer. In the sense that academies represent private companies becoming involved in state education, and therefore a degree of privatisation, there is also a neoliberal influence visible in this policy.

Sure Start
This term describes a wide range of programmes targeted at giving young children a better start in life. Free nursery education was made available, and Sure Start children's centres would bring together a range of educational and other support services in disadvantaged communities. The intention was to tackle cultural deprivation and counteract the material deprivation which placed working-class children at a disadvantage before they even started school.

Education Action Zones
These were established in some of the lowest-performing inner-city areas and involved cooperation between a variety of groups (including schools, the LEA, businesses and parents) to try to raise standards.

Private schools
The government was hostile to private education and ended the Assisted Places scheme shortly after coming to power. Although there was some discussion about removing charitable status from private schools, this never happened, but private schools were encouraged to provide expertise to help state schools to improve.

Nursery education
In another attempt to ensure a good start in education for all social groups, government support for pre-school nursery education was increased.

Educational Maintenance Allowances
Students between the ages of 16 and 19 in full-time education and training could apply for an Educational Maintenance Allowance of up to £30 a week. These were available to families on lower incomes and aimed to encourage young people to stay in education.

Vocational education
Under New Labour, there was a greater emphasis upon breaking down the divide between the academic and vocational so that vocational qualifications (traditionally more likely to be undertaken by working-class pupils) gained in status and became a route to university. This was particularly evident in the introduction of Diploma qualifications towards the end of New Labour's time in power.

Higher education
A stated aim of the government was to increase the number of students in higher education. The target was that 50 per cent of young people would be entering higher education by 2010. To meet this target, university facilities were expanded, funded by the replacement of student grants with loans, to be repaid once the graduate's salary had reached a certain level. Also, students had to meet some of the cost of their tuition fees. Financial support for less affluent applicants was available.

New Labour aimed to increase the number of young people in higher education.

So, was the government's plan to encourage a wider range of young people to apply to university working? In one sense it was: the percentage of young people from manual working-class backgrounds going to university increased from 11 per cent in 1991/2 to 19 per cent in 2001/2 (*Social Trends 34*). However, over the same period, the percentage from middle-class backgrounds increased from 35 to 50 per cent. Statistics from the Higher Education Statistics Agency show that by 2004/5 only 28.7 per cent of young entrants to university came from lower socio-economic groups. If anything, overall, class inequalities in higher education were increasing (McNight, Glennerster and Lupton, 2005).

What is more, a range of research evidence shows that university students from a working-class background are more likely to:

› study at local institutions with limited course options

› live at home while studying

› study part time

› have family or work commitments

› incur high levels of student debt

› drop out of their initial choice of course.

EVALUATION OF NEW LABOUR POLICIES

The influence of New Right/neoliberal ideas on government thinking has meant that competition and choice was seen as the key way to improve educational standards. However, as Sally Tomlinson has pointed out, in practice, the middle class has gained most from these policies (Tomlinson, 2005). They were best placed to ensure that their children attended the best performing schools and continued to do well. In addition, the focus on exams and league tables meant that much education had become, as Tomlinson put it, 'examination techniques, rote learning and revision'.

New Labour has also been criticised for introducing greater privatisation of education. Critics have argued that this removes democratic accountability. Unlike LEAs, private companies are accountable to their shareholders rather than the local electorate. Companies, unlike LEAs and central government, have to make a profit, so private provision can in fact work out more expensive. Chitty (2014) suggests that the long-term costs of PFI have created financial difficulties for parts of the education system. He also questions the efficiency of some private providers. For example, ETS failed to deliver accurate marking or to deliver marks on time. The ETS contract was cancelled as a result.

In terms of vocational education, there were positive policies to expand apprenticeships, and the NDYP had some success in getting the unemployed into work (although still fewer than 50 per cent and in many cases the jobs did not last). Attempts to overcome the divide between vocational and academic qualifications were not successful: small numbers took up the new Diplomas, which were in any case scrapped by the Coalition government after 2010. It continues to be difficult to get places in more prestigious universities with vocational qualifications.

Social democratic influences on educational policy have resulted in the directing of resources towards deprived groups and areas. This may have resulted in some improvements although some areas have benefited more than others (McNight *et al.*, 2005). Data discussed by Ball (2013) suggests that under New Labour there were overall increases in the proportion of students getting five or more GCSEs at C grade, and improvements in achievement for some ethnic minorities. However, the gender gap remained large, with boys still lagging well behind girls, and class differences were not significantly reduced. Ball suggests that whatever the direct effects of educational policy, continuing high levels of child poverty (though New Labour did reduce this somewhat) and of inequality meant that education could not compensate for the effects of low income on the educational performance of those from lower classes. So while New Labour had some success in raising achievement and tackling some forms of inequality of opportunity, their record was inconsistent.

The changes in higher education under New Labour reflect the overall pattern of their policies on education: opportunities increased for everybody, but class inequalities remain stubbornly present. Back in 1971, Basil Bernstein wrote that 'education cannot compensate for society' – in other words, education will tend to reflect social inequalities rather than eliminate them. That seems to be the story of education under New Labour.

Why do you think New Labour policies had only limited success in reducing inequality in education?

COALITION POLICIES

After the 2010 election, no single party had an overall majority and a coalition government was formed between the Conservatives (the dominant partners) and the Liberal Democrats. The education minister was a Conservative

(Michael Gove) and many of the policies reflected New Right/neoliberal thinking.

New Right/neoliberal inclined Coalition policies

Academies and free schools

Michael Gove rapidly extended the academy programme, while changing the form it took. Under the New Labour government it had been aimed at failing inner-city schools, in order to help tackle deprivation and inequality of opportunity, but from 2010 academy status was opened up to all schools that had achieved an 'Outstanding' grade in Ofsted inspections. In addition, religious groups, parents' groups and teachers (among others) could set up new schools with approval. These were known as free schools. Academies were independent of local authority control, while free schools had a good deal of control over their ethos and curriculum. By August 2014, there were 331 free schools open or approved (Woolcock, 2014). Free schools were given scope to have distinctive content for some of their curriculum. The early schools included a school in West London opened by the journalist Toby Young with a grammar-school style of education; Jewish, Hindu, Muslim, Sikh and Christian faith schools; and in Lancashire, the Maharishi School (based upon the teachings of the Maharishi Mahesh Yogi, where pupils learnt meditation and yoga alongside a more conventional curriculum) (Chitty, 2014). Both academies and free schools could have their own admissions policies (if approved by the Minister) and manage appeals procedures.

The growth of academies created opportunities for more privatisation of schooling, with some academies operating in chains run by businesses.

FOCUS ON SKILLS: FREE SCHOOLS ARE FAILING TO SERVE NEEDIEST

David Cameron opens a free school in Birmingham in 2013

Free schools are opening in disadvantaged areas but taking in fewer poor children than other local schools, according to a report by education experts.

It found that, while the state schools set up by parent, teacher or community groups were likely to open in places of deprivation, their intake was better off than the average local child.

Francis Green, professor of labour economics and skills development, said: "It appears that, so far, the places in reception at free primary schools are being filled by children who are somewhat less disadvantaged and more advanced in their development than the average.

"This outcome may be disappointing for the government, which had hopes that its free schools policy would be a vehicle for delivering social justice."

Today's report by the Institute of Education, based in London, also highlighted that children started at primary free schools ahead of their peers academically. This meant it would be important to judge the 'value added' by the schools as the children progress, academics said, rather than just looking at overall results.

It added: "The government's anticipation that free schools would emerge in disadvantaged neighbourhoods is, on average, vindicated.

"Looking at the neighbourhoods of free schools, one can see that there is a slightly higher proportion of children entitled to free school meals when compared to the rest of England – 22 per cent compared with 17 per cent at secondary level, and 18 per cent compared with 16 per cent at primary.

"However critics' concerns that the schools might become socially selective are also supported. Within the neighbourhood, fewer pupils actually attending the free schools were eligible for free school meals – only 17.5 per cent for secondary schools and 13.5 per cent in primary schools.

"The net effect is that the free secondary school pupils themselves are close to average for all secondary schools, and the free primary school pupils very slightly better off."

The authors of the study, funded by the Economic Social Research Council, claim it is the first academic analysis of the social composition of all free schools over the first three years of the programme.

It used the national pupil database to examine data for 88 primary and 63 secondary free schools that had opened by September 2013.

The New Schools Network (NSN), the organisation that advises free school groups on their applications, criticised local authorities for failing to use their powers to set up new schools, despite the current shortage of primary school places.

Analysis by NSN has shown that a minority of local authorities has set up free schools or academies, compared with other groups.

Tristram Hunt, Labour's shadow education secretary, said: "David Cameron's ideological free school programme is damaging our education system. By spending taxpayers' money setting up free schools in areas with surplus places – when we have huge pressures on primary school places – and presiding over a widening of the attainment gap between the poorest children and the rest, we are seeing school standards suffer under this Tory-led government."

Martin Freedman, director of economic strategy at the Association of Teachers and Lecturers (ATL), said: "Free schools have brought in selection by the back door and become the elite institutions we feared

they would be, dominated by children with the pushiest parents."

Source: Woolcock, N. 'Free schools are failing to serve the neediest' *The Times*, 7 August 2014

Questions

1. **Interpret** the meaning of the statistical evidence included here and summarise it.

2. **Interpret** what Martin Freedman might mean by 'selection by the back door'.

3. **Analyse** the differences between the arguments put forward by supporters and critics of free schools. (Look out for the key areas in which they do not agree, in terms of the effects of free schools, and particularly in terms of which pupils they are serving.)

4. **Evaluate** the view that, on balance, free schools might make little difference to opportunity, inequality and standards in education. (Consider, for example, whether they have become 'elite' institutions, whether they are really helping more disadvantaged children and whether they are improving results or just selecting relatively more 'able' pupils.)

Reforms to the curriculum

Gove also favoured a more traditional and rigorous curriculum. To this end he 'toughened up' A-levels by removing opportunities to retake exams, making students sit all exams at the end of A-level courses, revising the curriculum, and separating AS from full A-levels so that students had to take a more difficult exam for their first year work if they wanted to gain a full A-level.

In 2013 a new National Curriculum was introduced with a strong emphasis on traditional learning styles and content. For example, 5-year-olds had to study fractions, and in English there was more emphasis on grammar and spelling.

League tables were reformed for secondary schools. The English Baccalaureate (or EBac) was introduced. It stipulated that certain subjects, regarded as academic, had to be passed to gain the qualification. League tables were based on the percentage of pupils who attained GCE A* to C grades in English, Maths, two sciences, a

modern language (French or German, for example) and History or Geography.

Reforms to vocational education

Educational Maintenance Allowances (which gave money to students from poorer backgrounds to stay on in education) were scrapped. This was part of the austerity measures designed to shrink the size of the state and cut government spending.

Rather than trying to increase the status of vocational qualifications, the Coalition downgraded the value of many of them. For example, they decided that just 125 vocational qualifications could be counted as GCSE equivalent compared to the 3,175 that had previously been accepted. The emphasis in vocational education was on stopping schools and colleges using them as easy, less academically rigorous options to boost league table performance. The Diploma system, introduced towards the end of New Labour's time in government, was abruptly dropped.

Student protests against EMA cuts

Tuition fees in higher education

In higher education the most striking policy was the large rise in tuition fees from a maximum of £3,225 in England to a maximum of £9,000. (Scottish students studying in Scotland, however, paid no fees). Students were able to take out loans to meet these fees (and could also borrow some money to meet living costs) but the loans had to be repaid (with interest) once they started earning over £21,000 per year. Higher education became much more like any other market-based service, with individual students using their fees to fund the service rather than much of the cost being met out of government funding. In addition, rules on recruitment were relaxed so that by 2014, universities were able to expand and take on more students if there was sufficient demand from well-qualified applicants.

Michael Gove: a controversial minister

Many of these Coalition policies were described by Michael Gove as an attack on an 'educational establishment' he characterised as 'the blob'. From the point of view, the establishment had failed to enforce rigorous standards and a rigorous curriculum making it too easy to get qualifications, many of which he saw as being of dubious value. To Gove, an apparent increase in the qualifications of the workforce hid declining standards and he was determined to reverse this. However, he was a controversial minister and many of his policies were strongly opposed by teachers unions and others. In 2014 he was moved from his education post and replaced by a less controversial minister, Nicky Morgan, although she largely continued his policies.

Social democratic inclined policies

Not all the policies adopted by the Coalition government reflected the New Right/neoliberal agenda of privatisation, a return to valuing a traditional curriculum above vocational education, cuts in spending, and greater choice and competition schooling. The Liberal Democratic partners in the government did get significant concessions in two main areas.

Compensating for disadvantage in schools

One important new policy was the pupil premium. This policy involved providing extra resources for schools related to the number of pupils and students who were on low income and therefore eligible for free school meals (FSM). The intention of this policy was to compensate children from low-income families for their educational disadvantage by providing extra educational resources. By 2013/14 the pupil premium amounted to a not insubstantial £900 per pupil (*Education Journal*, 2013). It was also designed to fit into a wider social mobility strategy in which it was hoped that there would be better opportunities for disadvantaged children to end up in middle-class jobs. Head teachers were given considerable choice as to how this money was spent so long as it was designed to boost the performance of children from relatively poor families.

Compensating for disadvantage in higher education

Arguably, the Liberal Democrats also had some influence in higher education despite the introduction of much higher fees. Children from families on low and medium incomes could get maintenance grants (which would not be repayable) to help cover the costs of living while at university and larger loans were also available for those from low-income families. Students were not required to repay anything until after they started earning £21,000 and all debts were wiped out after 30 years. Students who did not end up in well-paid jobs would therefore be

FOCUS ON RESEARCH: THE EFFECTS OF UNDERGRADUATE FEE RISES

Student protests against university fee rises

The following summary is taken from the 2014 report of the Independent Commission on Fees, which was set up in the aftermath of fee rises. The results are based upon statistics produced by the university admissions system, UCAS, and upon a survey using online questionnaires. The methodology of the survey is described as follows:

"Ipsos MORI surveyed a total of 1,728 adults aged 16–75 in England from 13th – 17th June 2014 via its Online Omnibus Survey. The survey data were weighted by age, gender, region, social grade, working status and main shopper to the known profile of the English population aged 16–75. Of the respondents, 889 were male and 839 were female, 1,009 were working and 719 were not working."

Executive summary of the report

Application rates for 18-year-olds in England have continued to recover from their depressed level in 2012, with rates in 2014 1.9 percentage points above their 2010 levels.

The proportion of the 18-year-olds population taking up places at university has also recovered in all countries of the UK.

Mature student numbers remain substantially depressed in terms of the take-up of university places. Eighteen per cent fewer people aged 25+ took up places in 2013 than in 2010.

Over 100,000 fewer students over the age of 25 started part-time higher education courses in 2012/13 than in 2009/10 – a reduction of 43 per cent.

This was part of a more general decline in part-time higher education, with 41 per cent fewer part-time enrolments overall in 2012/13 than in 2009/10.

The gender gap in applications and acceptances has continued to increase. In 2013, 21 per cent more female than male 18-year-olds entered university. This gap is largest among disadvantaged applicants, meaning disadvantaged boys are particularly under-represented.

The gap in application and entry rates between advantaged and disadvantaged students has narrowed slightly, but remains unacceptably large – particularly for the most selective universities:

In 2010, English school-leavers from the least disadvantaged backgrounds were 3.2 times more likely to enter higher education than those from the most disadvantaged. In 2013 this ratio was 2.8. In 2010, the number of English school-leavers from the least disadvantaged backgrounds entering the 30 most selective universities in the UK (the Sutton Trust 30) was 7.3 times higher than the number entering from the most disadvantaged areas. In 2013 this ratio had narrowed to 6.8. However, for the 13 most prestigious UK universities (the Sutton Trust 13) the ratio was 9.8 and remained at 9.5 in 2013.

Source: The Independent Commission of Fees (2014)

Questions

1. Outline and briefly explain the type of sampling method that was used in this research.

2. Analyse the value of using the statistical data on background, university admissions and applications to examine the effects of fee rises on student applications. (Do you think, for example, these are the key variables likely to be linked to changes in applications? Can you think of others that might be relevant?)

3. Evaluate the sampling methods used in the opinion poll. (Consider how representative or 'typical' the sample was likely to be of all relevant students.)

4. Evaluate the view that fee rises have had little effect on class differences in higher education, but have increased age differences in opportunity. (You will need to look carefully at the statistics here.)

unlikely to repay the full amount of the loan for tuition and maintenance loans. Some commentators, including the Liberal Democrat Minister who introduced the scheme, Vincent Cable, argued that it was like a graduate tax in many respects, ensuring that those who benefited from higher education with high wages paid for the privilege. Furthermore, the government also continued the policy started under the previous Labour government to widen access to higher education, requiring all universities charging fees above £6000 to implement schemes to encourage those from under-represented groups to go to university.

Evaluation of Coalition policies

The limited lifespan of the 2010 to 2015 Coalition government gave relatively little time for its policies to take effect and for those effects to become clear. However, there was no shortage of critics of many of their policies.

> The National Union of Teachers (cited in Haralambos and Holborn, 2013) argued that free schools and academies tended to reduce the budget available for other schools, undermined democratic accountability (since they were not run by LEAs) and widened inequalities. They pointed to the Finnish educational system, which is widely seen as having some of the best schools in the world even though there is no competition in their system.

> Parental choice under the Coalition was limited in many areas and it remained difficult for children from disadvantaged backgrounds to get into some of the most popular and oversubscribed schools.

> The removal of Education Maintenance Allowances was criticised by Alan Milburn (Coalition adviser on social mobility) for lowering staying-on rates in further education for children from disadvantaged backgrounds (Wintour, 2012, cited in Haralambos and Holborn, 2013). This outcome was unsurprising: eligible students lost financial support to help them pay the costs of education and compensate for their lack of earnings.

> The effects of the pupil premium were also questioned. One report (Ratcliffe, 2014) found that although 53 per cent of teachers in a survey said their school was using the money to raise the achievement of disadvantaged children, the remainder said it was being used for other purposes, such as helping to plug the funding gap left by reductions in government funding or to help all pupils regardless of their family income.

One way of measuring the effects of government policies on class inequalities is to look at the **attainment gap** between children who get free school meals (FSM) and those who do not (non-FSM).

UNDERSTAND THE CONCEPT

The **attainment gap** is a relatively simple measure of class inequalities in educational attainment at school. It is measured by looking at the difference in the percentage of non-FSM and FSM children achieving five or more GCSEs at C grade or above. The bigger the gap, the greater the inequality. It does not measure class or income directly, but relies on the imperfect measure of entitlement to FSM. As not all those eligible claim FSM, and some poor families earn just too much to be eligible, it is a far from perfect measure.

The attainment gap stood at 26.7 per cent in 2012/13, down slightly from 27.5 per cent in 2010/11, suggesting the policy may have had some impact, though it may have been counteracted by other policies introducing more competition (Watt, 2014).

Why do you think the attainment gap changed little under the Coalition government? Can you suggest policies which might have reduced the gap more?

GLOBALISATION AND EDUCATION POLICY

The idea of globalisation has become increasingly influential in sociology and in many other fields. Globalisation refers to the idea that the world is becoming more interdependent and countries (or nation-states) less self-contained.

One of the most influential sociological definitions of globalisation was put forward by Roland Robertson in 1992 "Globalisation as a concept refers to both the compression of the world and the intensification of consciousness of the world as a whole" (Robertson, 1992, p.8). What Robertson is drawing attention to here is the idea that the world, at least from the viewpoint of humans, is becoming a smaller place. Individuals have become much more aware of areas beyond the local area in which they live, the borders between countries have become less significant as boundaries, and movements of people, ideas, products and cultures around the globe have become more common.

The Headquarters of the United Nations in New York City

Impact on British society

There are many different theories of globalisation, but all agree that it is no longer adequate to analyse social life from the viewpoint of individual societies. For example, British society is not isolated and self-contained; it is heavily influenced by outside factors:

› politically, the European Union (EU) shapes government policies and laws

› many residents are immigrants

› there are many foreign tourists in Britain

› produce, fashions, films, books, ideas, and so on from other parts of the world influence people in Britain

› many companies operating in Britain are foreign-owned.

Therefore to understand what happens in Britain, you also have to look beyond its shores and examine global influences. Similarly, what happens in Britain increasingly influences other parts of the world too.

Globalisation and schools

The impact of globalisation is not as immediately obvious in education as in some other areas of social life. On the surface, education remains largely under the control of national governments in the UK and elsewhere, but there are a number of significant ways in which globalisation may have affected British education.

Some of these are identified by Anthony Kelly (2009), reviewing competing theories on the effects of globalisation on education policy:

› National governments, including the British government, feel increasingly obliged to tailor education policy to meet the needs of the economy. In particular, they increasingly feel that education has to produce workers who are able to compete in a global economy by having skills that will be valuable in a global market.

› This in turn tends to put less emphasis upon social (rather than economic) objectives. Social objectives would include, for example, a concern to produce a more integrated and cohesive society, to increase equality of opportunity, or to make individuals into good citizens. Similarly, concerns such as passing on important knowledge or appreciating culture may be marginalised in an education system geared to global economic competitiveness.

› There is the possibility that education systems throughout the world will become increasingly alike as all governments try to achieve the same objectives. Anthony Kelly argues that education systems have to vary to meet individual circumstances and cultures, but there is something of a worldwide trend towards privatisation, marketisation and competition in education systems (see The 1988 Education Reform Act and other reforms in this chapter for a discussion of marketisation).

› Kelly also refers to the adoption of similar school improvement programmes in different parts of the world, often driven by large multinational corporations.

› These trends can lead to the professionalism of teachers being undermined, as managers and consultants are seen as having more expertise in these programmes than individual teachers. Similarly, local democratic accountability (for example through LEAs in the UK) will be seen as less important and less desirable since meeting local needs is secondary to competing globally.

Globalisation in higher education

In addition to the points identified by Kelly, it can also be argued that educational institutions increasingly have to run as businesses if they market their products (education) internationally or globally and aim to thrive and prosper. This may be difficult for local state secondary or primary schools, but Stephen Ball (2012) points out that universities have increasingly marketed themselves to a global audience, often setting up overseas branches. Universities are particularly keen to attract overseas students because they pay high fees, while having branches overseas allows universities to expand. For example, Liverpool University has set up a joint venture in China near Shanghai, and Nottingham, Newcastle and Southampton have developed universities in Malaysia. Private schools may also have become increasingly reliant upon overseas pupils, particularly from China and

Hong Kong. In this process, students can be viewed as commodities to be bought and sold to different educational institutions for profit.

Multinational companies and education

Most of the changes produced by globalisation in education policy are, according to Stephen Ball and others, closely linked to the dominance of neoliberal perspectives that increasingly treat education as a business. Indeed, Stephen Ball points out that there is increasing involvement by private companies in education, and that these companies are often multinational and operate across many different countries.

To Ball, national governments have less control over education than in the past. Instead education is run through networks which involve private companies as much as local and national governments.

All these arguments suggest that one of the main effects of globalisation is to shift policies even further towards neoliberal perspectives, but this might not always be the case. For example, increased migration, which can be seen as part of globalisation, can lead to a more multicultural curriculum and understanding of different cultures in educational institutions. It can also lead to an increased emphasis upon equality of opportunity, fostering the talents of every individual in order to make the country more competitive.

National governments can still decide how to respond to globalisation and choose a range of educational policies with different objectives. National politics and competing perspectives on education still matter and can make a difference to the sort of education system that is provided by the state in the UK and elsewhere.

BUILD CONNECTIONS

Globalisation has affected social life in many different ways, which will become evident whatever topics you cover. For example, some British families have extended families living around the globe, some crimes (such as computer fraud) are often carried out by criminals abroad against British people, and conflicts between members of different religions can have an impact on Britain (for example, conflicts in Syria, Israel/Palestine and Iraq).

CONCLUSIONS

British education has tended to suffer from frequent changes of direction and contradictory policies. While some policies have aimed to increase equality of opportunity, and may have had some success in helping those from less advantaged backgrounds, other policies have had the opposite effect and have tended to cancel out the more favourable ones. Similarly, the general direction of educational policy has often changed when there has been a change of political party (or in the case of the Coalition, parties) in power.

As Chapters 2, 3 and 4 have shown, there has been some progress in reducing inequalities based on gender and ethnicity, but rather less in reducing those based on social class, even though these have been a central focus for many policy changes. This was reflected in a Sutton Trust Report in 2011 (cited in Chitty, 2014) which showed that just five schools – the four private schools Eton, Westminster, St Paul's Boys and St Paul's Girls, and a state sixth-form college in Cambridge – sent more pupils to Oxbridge than did 2,000 other state schools and colleges in the UK combined.

Over recent decades, there has been a general increase in the number of pupils and students achieving various levels of qualification, suggesting that standards have been improving. However, whether this represents a real increase in the educational level of British pupils and students has been challenged by some, who think it merely reflects the 'dumbing down' of standards. Despite more than 50 years of educational change and innovation since the 1944 Education Act, the British education system remains very hierarchical. The experience of those who attend private schools and gain places at Oxford or Cambridge is still rather different from that of pupils in even the most successful state schools in low-income areas.

Discuss the view that despite very many changes in the British education system, the outcomes have changed relatively little.

CHECK YOUR UNDERSTANDING

1. What were the three types of school under the tripartite system? Explain their differences.

2. Give three common criticisms of the tripartite system.

3. Briefly explain why supporters of social democratic perspectives saw comprehensives as an improvement on the tripartite system.

4. Identify three policies of the 1979–97 Conservative governments and briefly explain how they fitted New Right/neoliberal thinking.

5. Explain what is meant by privatisation and give an example of the privatisation of education.

6. Explain two changes to vocational education introduced by the New Labour government.

7. Suggest two criticisms and two strengths of the marketisation of British education.

8. Identify and briefly explain two effects of globalisation on the British education system.

9. Explain what free schools are, and give one argument against them and one argument for them.

10. Identify and briefly explain one way in which Coalition policies may have promoted equality of opportunity and one way in which they may have undermined it.

TAKE IT FURTHER

Carry out an interview with an experienced member of your school or college staff. Ask them to describe the impact that the following changes had upon their educational career and experiences: school/college inspections, league tables, competition between schools/colleges, the introduction of academies and free schools, parental choice, and the rise in tuition fees.

APPLY YOUR LEARNING

AS LEVEL

1 Define the term 'cultural capital'.   [2marks]

2 Using **one** example, briefly explain how 'setting' differs from 'streaming' in schools.   [2marks]

3 Outline **three** functions performed by education, according to functionalist sociologists.   [6 marks]

4 Outline and explain **two** ways in which material deprivation can impact on educational achievement.   [10 marks]

5 Read **Item A** below and answer the question that follows.

ITEM A

School subcultures and educational achievement

Research suggests that pro- and anti-school subcultures are a common feature of many schools. Such student subcultures can have a significant impact on the educational achievements of their members.

Some research in the north-east of England, for example, found that members of a subculture known as 'charvers' rejected their secondary school and deliberately aimed to fail their GCSEs. Charvers were mainly from a deprived background, but didn't lack confidence or self-esteem. Rather, status within the subculture was dependent on a rejection of schooling and their social standing within the subculture was more important to them than gaining qualifications.

Other pupils who didn't belong to the subculture were nevertheless affected by it because they were afraid of being bullied if they were seen to have done their homework or to be answering questions in class.

Applying material from **Item A** and your knowledge, evaluate the view that working class underachievement is a product of membership of anti-school subcultures.   [20 marks]

A-LEVEL

1   Outline **two** ways in which the education system reproduces social class inequalities from one generation to the next.   [4 marks]

2   Outline **three** reasons why the labelling of pupils may lead to their underachieving.   [6 marks]

3   Read **Item B** below and answer the question that follows.

ITEM B

Gender and achievement

In the past, boys did well at school and girls underachieved. It is widely believed that today that pattern is reversed.

However, while it is true that girls as a group tend to outperform boys in terms of educational achievement, many boys achieve highly and conversely many girls underperform.

Analysis of attainment data shows that the picture is not straightforward and that there are other factors that have a greater bearing on educational achievement than gender considered on its own.

Applying material from **Item B** and your knowledge, analyse why it is a myth that 'all boys underachieve and all girls now achieve well at school'.   [10 marks]

4   Read **Item C** below and answer the question that follows.

ITEM C

Educational attainment by ethnicity

It is a fact that educational attainment varies with ethnicity, though it is not the case that White pupils consistently perform better in school than Black, Asian and minority ethnic groups (BAME).

Instead, the picture is more complicated, with children of Chinese and Indian origin as a group generally performing better than average and children of Pakistani and Black Caribbean origin often doing less well.

Applying material from **Item C** and your knowledge, evaluate the view that ethnic differences in educational achievement are a product of factors inside schools.   [30 marks]

You can find example answers and accompanying teachers' comments for this topic at www.collins.co.uk/AQAAlevelSociology.

2 SOCIOLOGICAL RESEARCH METHODS

AQA Specification	Chapters
Candidates should examine:	
Quantitative and qualitative methods of research; research design.	Chapter 3 (pages 109–116) covers qualitative research. Chapter 4 (pages 117–127) covers qualitative research. Chapters 1 (pages 89–96) and 2 cover research design.
Sources of data, including questionnaires, interviews, participant and non-participant observation, experiments, documents, and official statistics.	Chapter 5 (pages 128–140) covers questionnaires and interviews. Chapter 4 (pages 117–127) covers participant and non-participant observation, and experiments. Chapter 6 (pages 141–151) covers documents and official statistics. Sources of secondary data are also covered in Chapter 6 (pages 141–151). The strengths and limitations of these sources are discussed in the relevant chapters.
The distinction between primary and secondary data, and between quantitative and qualitative data.	This is introduced in Chapter 1 (pages 89–96). More detailed discussions are found in Chapters 3 to 6 (pages 109–151).
The relationship between positivism, interpretivism and sociological methods; the nature of 'social facts'.	This is covered in Chapter 2 (pages 97–108), but related discussions can also be found in Chapter 1 (pages 89–96).
The theoretical, practical and ethical considerations influencing choice of data, choice of method(s) and the conduct of research.	Chapter 2 (pages 97–108) covers this.
Students must be able to apply sociological research methods to the study of education.	This is covered in Chapter 1 (pages 89–96) but followed up in relation to specific methods in Chapters 3 to 6 (pages 109–151).

2.1 RESEARCHING SOCIAL LIFE

LEARNING OBJECTIVES

> Understand the purposes of sociological research. Analyse the different types of data (AO1).

> Apply this understanding to researching in the context of education (AO2).

> Analyse ways of evaluating research (AO3).

INTRODUCING THE DEBATE

We generally experience our everyday lives as being relatively easy to understand and quite predictable. We have quite a good idea of what we think will happen if we don't hand in a piece of work if we are studying, how others will respond to us in the street or in a shop, and we may assume that we have a deeper understanding of how the world around us works. For example, we may believe that if we study hard, we will get good qualifications and that will probably lead on to a well-paid job. However, sociologists don't assume any of those things, they study them. In order to study them in a way that convinces others that they have produced worthwhile knowledge about them, sociologists use systematic research methods to try to uncover how the world really works. This section introduces these processes and begins to examine the principles on which the research methodology is based in order to explore some of the different types of methodology.

GETTING YOU THINKING

Big Brother is a television series in which a group of people are required to live together in a house for a period of several months. During that time all their activities and conversations are monitored. Edited versions are shown to a television audience, which then votes contestants out of the house each week, until the last remaining 'survivor' is declared the winner.

1. Do you think that people who live in the *Big Brother* household are representative of the country as a whole?

2. Do you think the people in the household act naturally? If not, why do they behave the way they do?

The television series Big Brother monitors housemates' actions at all times. It can be argued that this will have an effect on their behaviour.

3. Does *Big Brother* therefore give a 'true' picture of what life would be like if a group of young people lived together? Explain your answer.

4. Do you think that a lot of what goes on is 'edited out' by the producers? What kinds of things are left out? Why?

5. *Big Brother* could be seen as a type of experiment. How might a sociologist change an experiment such as this to produce more useful data?

INTRODUCTION

Sociologists try to provide insights into the social world that the ordinary person would not normally have. All members of society try to understand the social worlds around them and become skilled at living in those worlds, but they tend to rely heavily on their *common sense* or *personal experience* in understanding society.

Sociologists may see the way individuals make sense of social worlds as important, but most don't see this as sufficient on its own to understand the ways in which social worlds work. Common sense and personal experience, they argue, are based on our own limited experiences and don't allow us to see social worlds in wider contexts and from broader perspectives (see Table 2.1.1). Individual members of society generally make do with an understanding that lets them get on with their lives and make day-to-day decisions, but they usually don't delve deeper or question their own assumptions about how social worlds work.

Sociologists use research methods to help them produce what they hope will be more in-depth and credible knowledge about social worlds. Many believe that carefully selecting particular research methods can help to produce knowledge that goes beyond personal opinions, can challenge individual biases and uncovers patterns that would normally remain hidden. However, the activities of sociologists do not stop at undertaking research – once they have uncovered these patterns, they then seek explanations for the relationships between them. This process of constructing explanations for social patterns is known as 'theorising'. Theories are produced and are then evaluated using further research. They may be supported and gain in credibility, or contradicted and criticised, which undermines their credibility. Sometimes theories emerge from research, and sometimes they are produced simply through the imagination of the sociologist, but however they are initially produced, they will be more likely to stand the test of time if research is used to back them up.

A useful distinction between sociological research and common sense can be made in terms of **subjectivity and objectivity**.

UNDERSTAND THE CONCEPT

Subjective knowledge is based purely on the opinion of the individual (the subject). It is knowledge based on how they see things from their point of view. **Objective** knowledge is based on the characteristics of the object, or thing, being described and should be independent of the personal opinions, wishes, biases and experiences of any individual. Sociologists are bound to take account of the subjective opinions of individuals, because these opinions help to shape how people behave. However, when describing the actual social world, sociologists try to be objective, in order to put their personal views to one side and collect evidence about how things really are. It may be impossible to be completely objective but if the information can be checked by other people (who might have quite different views or biases) and they agree that it is an accurate representation, then something close to objectivity might be achieved.

WHAT DOES SOCIOLOGICAL RESEARCH SET OUT TO DO?

Sociological research does three main things: gathers data; establishes makes correlations; and suggests, confirms or contradicts theories.

Gathering data

The first task of research is to gather information about the social world. This very basic function is the starting point for any kind of sociological understanding. Knowledge can take the form of statistical information, such as the numbers of marriages and divorces. This type of data is known as quantitative data. (This sort of research is conducted in the UK by the Office for National Statistics (ONS), a government organisation that collects data.) Research can also include observations of people in social situations – such as Alice Goffman's study of life in one of the USA's most disadvantaged neighbourhoods in Philadelphia (2014) – or people talking about their own lives – such as Ken Plummer's biographical research into the lives of gay men (1995). Data of these types of information are known as qualitative data.

However, we need to be wary about accepting these data at face value. As we shall see later, what is a 'fact' for one person may not be for others, as they may use different theories and methods to interpret the facts. A well-known example of this issue is research on suicide by Émile Durkheim (1897, reprinted in 1952). He collected a large number of statistics and then based his theory of the causes of suicide on these statistics. However, much later, other sociologists looked at exactly the same statistics and produced very different interpretations of these same 'facts'. They argued that the statistics on which Durkheim had based his research were fundamentally flawed. These sociologists said that in only a few cases can we know for certain whether the death was suicide or not. In many cases, it is unclear: did the person truly intend to take their own life, or was it an accident, or, even, murder? The real research, they argued, was in studying how coroners go about making their decision as to whether or not to classify a death as suicide (J. M. Atkinson, 1978).

Common sense	Sociological research
What is common sense for one person is not common sense for another.	Research is based on evidence.
Common sense derives from personal experience and people have limited experience.	Research can be conducted in areas where most people have little experience.
Common sense is not concerned with being objective.	Research is concerned with being objective.
Common sense can be based on false beliefs and information.	Research can be tested.
Common sense is often based upon memories, which may be faulty.	Research can compare memories with other evidence to check their accuracy.

Table 2.1.1 *Research and common sense: why common sense is faulty*

Much effort is made in sociological research to make sure that the data gathered is as clear and accurate as possible, but sociologists always approach any

data – whether in the form of statistics, observation or narrative – in a very cautious way. Some reasons for this are given below.

Do you agree that sociological research is likely to produce better data than common sense? If so, what are the crucial factors that make it more credible and how can you ensure it doesn't just reflect the views of the individual sociologist?

Establishing correlations

Research can go further than just gathering information. It can help us to explore relationships between different elements of society. At its most basic, it can be in the form of simple correlations. Sociologists describe a correlation as the situation where, when one social event occurs, another one tends to do so as well. This is clearer if we use an illustration. Bennett and Holloway (2005) conducted a national research project over a number of years, which involved testing the urine of people immediately after they were arrested by the police while they were being held in police cells. The results of the urine tests demonstrated that the offenders had a very high chance of showing evidence of illegal drug use (as well as alcohol use). The statistical results therefore show that there is a correlation between drug use and crime, as when one social event (committing crime) occurs, then another (taking drugs) tends to do so as well.

Cause and effect

The immediate conclusion that most people would draw from this correlation is that drug use causes crime. But this may not be true. It could be argued that people who commit crime are more likely to take drugs – and indeed there is considerable evidence to support this argument (Pudney, 2002). We could also argue that people who like to do drugs also like to commit crime. Therefore a completely different social event causes people both to commit crime and do drugs. There is considerable evidence for this explanation too (Hough and Roberts, 2004).

Just because statistics demonstrate that two social events tend to occur together – a correlation – it does not mean there is a causal relationship (that one thing causes another). Identifying and agreeing a causal relationship between social events is often complicated and linked with developing a sociological theory.

BUILD CONNECTIONS

Some of the difficulties in establishing causal relationships are illustrated in the section on education. Many factors seem to be statistically connected to poor educational attainment, but the actual causes are disputed. For example, coming from a low-income family seems to make it less likely that pupils will succeed in getting five or more GCSEs at C grade and above, but is this a direct result of lack of money, or because those with a low income have a culture which makes it difficult for them to do well in education, or is it that those on low incomes tend to be labelled and discriminated against at school? It is only by doing detailed research to explore the independent effects of these different factors that the possible causes can be untangled and sociologists can be confident that they have found convincing explanations.

Developing theories

The final role of research is to support, contradict or help to develop sociological theories. (A theory is simply a general explanation of social events.) Researchers gather information and statistics which help sociologists explain why certain social events occur. This often involves providing an explanation for correlations. So, if a correlation exists between drug use and crime, various theories can be developed. One theoretical explanation for heroin users having high rates of burglary is that they need money to pay for their drug habit. An alternative is that burglars have a high income and so are more likely to have a pleasurable lifestyle that involves using drugs. A third theoretical explanation could be that people with unhappy home backgrounds turn to crime and drugs. Pudney (2002) tackled this problem in a research project on whether young offenders started taking drugs before they committed crimes or after.

SOURCES AND TYPES OF DATA

Data can come from either primary or secondary sources. **Primary data** are produced by sociologists whereas **secondary data** are not.

UNDERSTAND THE CONCEPT

Primary data are collected directly by the researchers themselves. The most common methods of producing primary data are surveys, observational studies, questionnaires, interviews and experiments. Because these methods are actively chosen by researchers, they usually help researchers to obtain exactly the sort of information that they require to test and develop theories (if it is possible to collect the required information at all). However, collecting primary data can be expensive and time-consuming, and there can be many ethical or practical problems that make it difficult or impossible.

Secondary data are sources which are used by sociologists but have been collected by other people. These include official and commercial statistics; radio, internet and TV; historical and official documents; and personal letters and diaries. Because this sort of data already exists, using it often does not involve the same time and expense as producing the primary data. However, since it was not produced by sociologists to examine particular theories, the type of data which is available is often limited and may not suit the purposes that sociologists wish to use it for.

There are two types of data (see Table 2.1.2):

> **Quantitative data** is the term used for statistical charts and tables.

> **Qualitative data** is the term used to describe data in the form of observation or other published or broadcast sources.

Types of data	Sources of data			
	Primary research		Secondary research	
Qualitative data	interviews	observations	historical documents	TV programmes
Quantitative data	statistical surveys		official statistics	

Table 2.1.2 *Types of data*

UNDERSTAND THE CONCEPT

Quantitative data are any data based on numbers, whatever those numbers represent. In an educational context, for example, quantitative data could include league table results, absence and truancy figures, figures on the types of groups applying to university, and so on.

Qualitative data are non-numerical data and can be based on words (for example, transcripts of interviews or descriptions of social scenes), take the form of images (for example, photographs) or could be a combination of the two (for example, a video diary). Quantitative data often appears to be more objective but this isn't necessarily the case because they are only as good as the procedures used to collect the statistics in the first place (see above on suicide statistics). In most studies a combination of qualitative and quantitative data are collected, although the main emphasis can be on one type or the other.

Many people feel more comfortable with qualitative data than with statistics but most sociologists think that both methods have their place. In educational research, when might a quantitative study omit valuable information and when might a qualitative study do the same?

EVALUATING DATA

When conducting research or reading sociological research reports written by others, sociologists are always very critical of the methods employed and the data used. They know that if the methodology is weak, then the research may well be inaccurate. All sociologists are committed to making sure that their research is of the highest quality and achieves what it sets out to do. When sociologists evaluate research, they need to look at its reliability, validity, representativeness, generalisability and objectivity. We will look at each of these in more detail.

Reliability

The nature of sociology means that it has to use a variety of very different methods, in a range of circumstances, to study people. In these circumstances, it can often be quite difficult to compare one piece of research with another and sociologists accept this. However, what is

always expected is that if the same piece of research were repeated by different sociologists, then it should produce the same results. If this is not the case, then we could not rely upon the evidence produced.

Sociologists, therefore, always ask questions about whether or not the research, if repeated, would be likely to produce the same results – the issue of reliability. If it is easy to repeat the research and reproduce something like the original conditions (replication) then it is possible to achieve greater reliability. If the research is gathered in unique conditions requiring lots of interpretation by the individual researcher, then replication becomes impossible, although it is possible to compare it with similar but not identical research.

Some research methods are much more likely to produce results that can be repeated. Well-designed questionnaires are probably the method most likely to produce similar research results each time and are therefore regarded as highly reliable. At the other extreme, when a lone sociologist engages in participant observation (that is, joins a group of people and observes their behaviour), the research is likely to be far less reliable, as it is affected by the specific circumstances surrounding the group and the relationship of the observer to the group. Overall, quantitative methods tend to be more reliable, qualitative methods tend to be less reliable.

Validity

The second crucial factor in evaluating research is the extent to which it is **valid**, that is, how far it gives a true picture of the subject being studied. In evaluating a piece of research, sociologists will ask whether the methods used were those most likely to get to the truth of the matter. Interestingly, validity and reliability do not always go hand in hand. We saw before that questionnaires are likely to be highly reliable, but this does not necessarily mean that they are valid. For example, when asked about embarrassing subjects, such as sex or criminal activity, people often lie. Therefore, if the study were repeated, the results might be the same, yet they would never be true! Observational studies are usually difficult to repeat and so are fairly unreliable, but if the observation has been done well, then it may actually be very valid.

UNDERSTAND THE CONCEPT

Giving a true picture of what is studied is not a straightforward concept. A range of factors, as discussed in this chapter, can affect whether something is **valid** or not.

Another issue is whether statistics really measure what they claim to measure. For example, crime statistics claim to measure the actual amount of crime, but in reality they only measure crimes that have been recorded by the police. This type of validity is known as construct validity, and depends upon defining things properly. Another type of validity, ecological validity, concerns whether people in a study are behaving naturally. If they are outside of their normal setting (for example, in a laboratory) they are likely to behave unnaturally and the results would therefore lack ecological validity. Similarly, questionnaires may lack ecological validity: people might be lying in questionnaires or they might not act as they say they would when faced with a real social situation. It may be impossible for any research to be totally valid because all research, in one way or another, represents a shorthand description of a social world or part of it.

The issue of whether research gives a true picture of social life is always controversial and sociologists who adopt different approaches to methodology have different views on what gives validity. To some, validity comes from immersing yourself in the social life of those you are studying and seeing it from their point of view (for example, through participant observation). To others, this is likely to give a distorted, untrue and invalid picture of the social world because the researcher might become too involved and see things from a subjective point of view. To those who prefer quantitative methods, you can achieve greater validity by being more objective and avoiding becoming too involved with the groups being studied. This means the observer can be more detached (for example, by simply handing out a questionnaire to a respondent). Differences of opinion over what is considered valid go to the heart of disputes over the best way to collect data.

Would you agree that aiming for reliability often leads to a loss of validity because things we can define and measure precisely can't do justice to explaining something as complicated and unpredictable as social life? Give examples to support your answer.

FOCUS ON RESEARCH: CHOICE IN HIGHER EDUCATION

Diane Reay and her colleagues (Reay *et al.*, 2001) wished to study the choices and views of people entering higher education, focusing on people who were not school leavers and were from traditional middle-class backgrounds.

The researchers studied people from six different educational institutions. They gave out 502 questionnaires and followed this up with 53 interviews with students and 'a small number of interviews with parents' and others. The study drew upon the 'qualitative' interviews with the 53 students, who Reay says were 'not representative of the sample as a whole'. The students were asked to define their ethnicity themselves and the result was that only 23 of the 53 people in the sample defined themselves as being 'White'. One of the interviewees defined himself as 'Irish', rather than any other category such as 'White'.

The students were also classified by the researchers into social-class groupings. The researchers used the registrar-general's five-point scale, but in order to simplify things, did not use one of the categories (III Non-manual).

Questions

1. The researchers quantify various elements of the research, but not the 'small number' of interviews. Why not?

2. If the students are not 'representative', how easy is it to generalise?

3. What problems can you identify regarding 'self-definition' of ethnicity?

4. The researchers adopted the reliable registrar-general categorisation, but chose to leave one grouping out. What implications could this have for their research?

5. Suggests ways in which you could improve the research design.

Representativeness

The third crucial element in any evaluation is that of representativeness. Does the sample of people chosen for the research reflect a typical cross-section of the group or society the researcher is interested in gaining information about? If the respondents in the study are not representative, then it is simply not possible to generalise to the whole group or society (see below). For example, if sociologists wish to talk about the population as a whole, then the chosen group must be representative of society as a whole. Similarly, if they wish to comment on people who are students, then the study must be of a representative group from this section of society.

Overall, the larger the numbers of people in the study and the more sophisticated the methods used to select these people, the greater the chance of the study being representative.

Generalisability

The aim of much (though not all) sociological research is to produce knowledge which can aid us in understanding the behaviour of people in general – not just the specific individuals being studied. If the knowledge gained from studying the group cannot be generalised to all society, then it has limited use. This is why many sociologists are concerned that the people they study are typical or representative of a cross-section of the society or social group they wish to generalise about.

Objectivity and the researcher

The final key element in ensuring that research is of a high standard is the extent to which the researchers have ensured that their own values and beliefs have not had any influence on the design or the carrying out of the research. This is known as objectivity. If sociologists allow their own values to intrude into the research process, then this will seriously weaken the research and will certainly impact upon the validity of the research. We cannot say that all values should be kept out of research – that would be impossible – but there should never be intentional bias. No research, however careful, can provide a complete and totally unbiased account of the social world, but it certainly aims to be a great deal more credible and valuable than the very limited perspective produced by common sense.

FOCUS ON SKILLS: ANALYSING RESEARCH

The following three studies are examples of educational research using different methods of researching social life. Read the short description of the studies and answer the questions that follow.

Study 1

Paul Willis (1977) used a combination of observation and group interviews to examine the lifestyle and beliefs of a group of boys with anti-school values in one secondary school in the Midlands, England. Willis' research aimed to understand why the boys had negative attitudes to school and he related his findings to differences in the opportunities for different social classes. He spent several years conducting the research (for more details see Topic 1, Chapter 1)

Study 2

David Gillborn and Deborah Youdell (2000) studied racism in education, using a combination of interviews and observations in several London schools. They compared their findings with the picture of racism revealed in sources such as school policy statements, local authority guidelines, antiracism, and the minutes of staff meetings and working parties.

Study 3

Michael Rutter (1979) used questionnaires to collect large quantities of data from 12 inner-London secondary schools. He was looking for correlations between achievement, attendance, behaviour, and factors such as class size and number of staff. He found that schools could have an impact upon educational achievement independent of the social class of the pupil intake.

Questions

1. **Explain** how each of these studies used primary data, secondary data, or both.

2. **Analyse** whether each of these studies produced quantitative or qualitative data, or both.

3. **Analyse** how representative each of these studies is of the school population of England and Wales.

4. **Evaluate** whether each of these studies could be repeated and can be seen as reliable.

5. **Evaluate** whether each of these studies could be seen as giving a true picture of what was studied and could therefore be seen as valid.

CHECK YOUR UNDERSTANDING

1. Explain the three main aims of sociological research in your own words.

2. Give two reasons why sociological research is more trustworthy than 'common sense'.

3. Explain the difference between a 'correlation' and a 'causal relationship'.

4. What term is used by sociologists for statistical data?

5. Explain the difference between primary and secondary data.

6. What does it mean to say the results of research are generalisable?

7. Give two examples of:

   (a) primary data

   (b) secondary data

8. Explain why is it important for a sociological study to be 'valid'.

9. Explain two types of validity.

10. Briefly explain why research can never be regarded as completely valid.

TAKE IT FURTHER

Divide into small groups. Explain what sort of data you would collect for each of the following types of study. Justify your choices.

1. A study of pupil subcultures in an inner-city state school.

2. A study of the effects of changing the Educational Maintenance Allowance on staying-on rates in further education colleges.

3. A study of the attitudes of pupils from different ethnic groups towards the study of English Literature at GCSE level.

4. A study trying to uncover factors leading to truancy.

2.2 CHOICES IN RESEARCH: METHODS, PRACTICALITIES, ETHICS AND THEORIES

LEARNING OBJECTIVES

> Understand practical, ethical and theoretical factors in research design and implementation (AO2).

> Apply this understanding to research in the context of education (AO2).

> Analyse and evaluate the relative importance of the impact of practical, ethical and theoretical factors in research design and implementation (AO3).

INTRODUCING THE DEBATE

Imagine a sociology teacher told you that you had £10,000 and three months to conduct some sociological research of your choice. How would you go about choosing what you would study and how you would study it? These are the sorts of issues covered in this chapter. Of the infinite number of things that could be researched, only a few actually are, including some unexpected ones (for example, social class and Christmas lights, the informal rules of public swimming pools, or people's emotional reactions to watching *Big Brother*). Why these topics and not others? And why certain methods and not others? Some of the reasons discussed in this chapter include the practical (for example, whether you could finish on time and within your budget), the ethical (for example, whether you would be able to carry out experiments on humans), and the theoretical (for example, whether you see sociology as a scientific subject or more like a humanities subject). Research creates knowledge and knowledge shapes our beliefs about the world around us. This chapter will help you to understand the way that humans make sense of the world around them and come to believe some things but not others.

ISSUES WHEN UNDERTAKING RESEARCH

In Chapter 1, we found that attempts to carry out objective research and the creation of theories comprise the key elements that distinguish sociology as a distinct academic subject. However, the reality of actually undertaking research and creating theories is complex and full of pitfalls. Several important issues arise:

1. Why do some topics of research occur again and again (for example, young people and offending), while other issues are rarely explored (for example, the breaking of ecological rules by multinational companies)? Could it be that the more commonly researched issues are easier, or perhaps cheaper or more interesting for sociologists to look at? More worryingly, is funding less likely to be obtained for research into subject areas that threaten the interests of more powerful groups?

2. Why do sociologists choose to use some research methods rather than others? Sociologists have a wide range of methodological approaches to use. These range from questionnaires handed out to thousands of people, which are then subjected to statistical analysis, to a sociologist spending time with young, homeless people and being part of their lives. Which method is more useful in which circumstances? Are there any implications for the research project in using one method rather than another?

In this chapter, we seek answers to these questions and provide a few signposts to help guide us through the complex issues of ethical and theoretical debates and their relationship to research methods. We then examine the particular issues surrounding the choice of research methods in researching education, looking at the practical, ethical, and theoretical factors which apply in the educational context.

THE CHOICE OF RESEARCH AREA

Before starting their research, sociologists have to choose which topic to study. There are an almost infinite number of topics which could be studied, and each could be looked at from a variety of different angles. So what leads researchers to choose one study rather than another? A number of factors are likely to be important.

1. The choice will be affected by the values of the researcher. A person's own position in society might influence what they consider to be a worthwhile

topic, for example, their sexuality, social class background, gender, ethnicity or whether they have a disability or not. Researchers are unlikely to study issues which they think are unimportant so, for example, researchers such as A.H. Halsey in the 1960s and 70s would have investigated the tripartite system because they valued equality of opportunity for social classes in the education system.

2. Sociologists have their own interests as professionals. They generally want to further their careers, produce work that will be respected and admired by their peers, and keep their jobs. For all these reasons, they will tend to research topics that attract research funding. Much of this comes from research councils – such as the Economic and Social Research Council (ESRC), which funds a lot of sociological research in Britain – channelling money that originally comes from the government. The councils' decisions are also influenced by government priorities, which is why some subjects are frequently researched (for example, ways of improving standards in education) and other topics get less attention (for example, student protests).

3. Sociologists will be influenced by developments in sociology and in society. Some topics become more fashionable within sociology, or are seen as being particularly important in certain eras. For example, the influence of feminism led to the disadvantages suffered by girls in education to be widely researched in the 1980s but in recent times the supposed underachievement of boys has been researched more. New government policies also tend to lead to new research so, for example, new types of schools such as academies and free schools have become the subject of research in recent times.

4. Sociologists are inevitably influenced by the practicalities of carrying out research. Research that is totally impractical, very difficult, expensive or time-consuming is less likely to be carried out than research which is relatively practical, easy and cheap to do.

5. Similarly, research that presents serious ethical difficulties is less likely to be conducted than research that does not. So there is less likely to be research on issues such as sexuality in schools than issues such as exam performance (where there is also a lot of existing and easily accessible data). Furthermore, merely by choosing an area, the researcher might be confirming some people's

prejudices about a particular issue. For example, many sociologists are concerned about the extent of research into the 'negative' side of African Caribbean life, with studies on school failure, lower levels of job success and even the claimed higher rate of criminality. Critics argue that merely by studying this, a continued association is made between race and criminality or race and failure.

6. Sociologists who hold strong theoretical beliefs about society are highly likely to study the topics that they consider the most important, and far less likely to be interested in other areas. The following are relatively simple examples of how particular theories of society can be linked:

> Feminist sociologists see it as their role to examine the position of women in society, and to uncover the ways in which patriarchy, or the power of men,

has been used to control and oppress women. Consequently, their choice of research projects will be influenced by this. For example, they are more likely to study gender divisions in education than other social divisions.

> Marxist and other **critical sociologists** argue that the most important area of study is the question of how a relatively small group of people exploits the vast majority of the population. They will study issues such as the concentration of power and wealth, and the importance of social class divisions.

> Functionalist-oriented sociologists think that society is based on a general consensus of values. They are interested in looking at the ways in which society maintains agreement on values and solves social problems. Therefore, they will look at the role of religion or schools in passing on values.

FOCUS ON SKILLS: OBSERVING PRIMARY CHILDREN PLAYING

Between 2009 and 2010, Chris Richards (2012) carried out organised research observing children playing in London primary schools. It was decided to observe different age groups and to look at gender differences in play in a playground setting. This was chosen as a place where children had some freedom but were also subject to adult supervision, and were aware that adults might intervene if the play was seen as dangerous or problematic in some way. The researchers were interested in how adult supervision affected the children's play and how gender differences in play might be affected by the media. Two researchers visited the school on a regular basis and videoed what happened

in the playground. They also allowed the children to use camcorders themselves to video their own play. One of the findings was that when enacting roles in the playground 'girls mostly figured as mothers, teenagers, teachers, princesses, witches, dancers and pop singers, and boys tended to be professional footballers, soldiers, zombies and superheroes' (Richards, 2012, p. 287).

Questions

1. **Explain** in your own words what you understand to be the purposes of this research.

2. **Analyse** why the sociologists might have thought it was important to carry out this study. What sort of theoretical perspectives might have influenced their choice of research project?

3. **Analyse** the ethical and practical problems they would have have had to overcome before carrying out this research.

4. **Evaluate** whether in your view the methods used were ethically acceptable. Why might some people object to the methods used in this research?

5. **Evaluate** whether the methods chosen would produce valid data about this topic.

Is there any way to decide whether one topic is more important than another for sociological research or is it just a matter of opinion? Is there anything too trivial for sociologists to study?

UNDERSTAND THE CONCEPT

Critical sociologists believe that the role of sociology should be to study society in order to uncover injustice, exploitation or oppression. They don't think that sociologists should stay neutral, but need to take a stance favouring those who are disadvantaged in society, exposing the actions of their oppressors and arguing for change. Marxism is a version of critical sociology that emphasises class inequality and oppression, while feminism emphasises gender-based oppression of women. Other critical sociologists might concentrate on the oppression of ethnic or sexual minorities or those with a disability, or look at how multiple forms of oppression interact.

PRACTICAL, ETHICAL AND THEORETICAL FACTORS AND CHOICE OF RESEARCH METHOD

Once a sociologist has chosen a topic to study, they then have to choose the appropriate research methods and design the actual research. These aspects of research can be influenced by practical, ethical and theoretical factors and are summarised in Figure 2.2.1, along with the factors driving choice of topic and the interpretation of results.

The relationship between practical issues and research

Perhaps the most obvious factors affecting the choice of research methods are practical ones. There are a number of practical issues that recur in many research settings. Here we will look at some of the main types of practical issue.

1. Money is always an issue. As well as looking at whether it is possible to find funding for research, there is also the question of how much the research will cost. Generally, the larger the number of people who are going to take part in the research, the more the research will cost. However, this also depends upon how much it costs to conduct

research with each person. Handing out a simple questionnaire, collecting it and analysing the results using a computer may be less costly than travelling to diverse locations and interviewing a small number of people in depth. Researchers have to meet expenses and if they employ others to help conduct the research, this can be very costly. Sometimes secondary sources provide a useful and cheap or even cost-free alternative to conducting primary research.

2. Time is also an important issue. As a minimum, while conducting research, researchers have to meet their own living costs. The longer the research takes, the greater the financial commitment they make, especially if they are not employed by a university or research organisation. Even if they are, then someone is paying their wages, and the more time the research takes the longer their employer will be paying them to do it. So time often equates to money. However, there may be other reasons why time is an issue. Researchers may be keen to complete research and publish findings to further their career, or they may have only a short time to carry out research because of other commitments. Whatever the reason, it is quite likely that research that will use up a lot of time will not get done.

3. A third crucial issue is whether it is actually possible to do the research: can the researcher gain access to particular social situations or individuals who will be willing to take part? There are many situations where a researcher might be barred from observing (for example, meetings of senior management in educational institutions or cabinet meetings of the British government). If the researcher wants to use questionnaires or interviews, then they have to locate the appropriate participants and get them to agree to participate. Some participants might refuse and some might be unable to understand the research or to answer complex questions (for example, very young children). Issues of access and gaining the cooperation of participants quite often prevent researchers from carrying out the kind of research they want to do, so they have to find indirect ways of getting the information they want, or even choose a different topic.

The relationship between research methods and ethics

Research can have a powerful impact on people's lives. It can do so in both harmful and beneficial ways. Therefore, researchers must always think very carefully

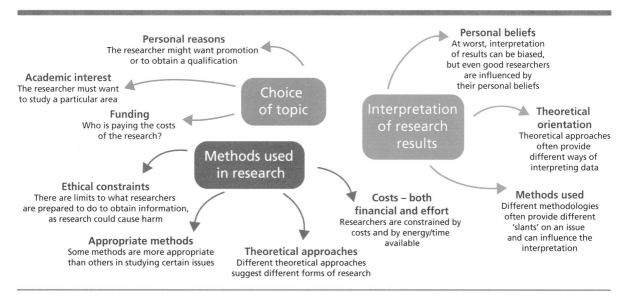

Figure 2.2.1 *Influences on the research process*

about the impact of their research and how they ought to behave, so that no harm comes to the subjects of the research or to society in general. These sorts of concerns are generally discussed under the umbrella term ethical issues.

The following are some of the key ethical issues.

Gaining consent

The subjects of research must normally be able and willing to give informed consent to being part of the research project. To do this they must be aware that the research is happening, understand it and be in a position to agree to take part. This can be a problem if these subjects are very young, lack the mental capacity to agree, or if informing them of the research would invalidate it. For example, very often if those being researched know the purpose of an experiment it will affect their behaviour and the results will not be valid.

Effects on the people being studied

Research can often have an effect on the people being studied. Before setting out to do research, sociologists must think carefully about what these effects might be (although it is not always possible to anticipate such effects).

One of the reasons why sociologists rarely use experiments, for example, is that they may lead to the subjects being harmed. For example, subjects may find themselves behaving in immoral ways, which could give them a negative impression of themselves.

Confidentiality

It is often important for some aspects of the research to remain confidential, especially when it could harm the respondents or an institution if others became aware of their responses. For example, a teacher might have their career affected if a head teacher were aware that they had made negative comments about a school in interviews, or a school might be unhappy if accounts of disruptive behaviour by pupils were publicly associated with the school. For these reasons, researchers may need to guarantee that some details of who took part will be withheld.

Effects on the wider society

It is not only the people being studied who could be affected by the research. For example, the families of those being researched may have information given about them that they wish to keep secret. Victims of crime may be upset by the information that researchers obtain about the perpetrators, as they may prefer to forget the incident. Research may even be used to justify policies that ultimately cause harm, so researchers need to consider who might make use of the research findings and what they will use them for.

Issues of legality and immorality

Finally, sociologists may be drawn into situations where they commit crimes, or help with or witness deviant acts. For example, while undertaking research on a prisoner in the USA, Kenneth Tunnell (1998) discovered that the

101

prisoner had actually taken on the identity of someone else (who was dead) in order to avoid a much longer prison sentence. The prison authorities became suspicious and investigated the prisoner's background. Though Tunnell knew the truth, he felt that he owed the prisoner confidentiality and deliberately lied, stating that he knew nothing about the identity 'theft'. As a result, the prisoner was released many years early.

Most researchers consider it immoral to lie to those they are studying about whether they are conducting research and/or what their research is about. Many researchers therefore refuse to do secret research or to mislead those being studied (partly because they can't give informed consent in these circumstances).

Most research that takes place today has to be considered by an ethics committee, for example, in the university where the researcher works or in the institution where the research will be carried out (for example, the health service). Many such committees are very cautious about granting approval if they fear they could be sued for granting permission, and this limits the range of research that is allowed.

Many studies which have produced interesting results in the past might not get approval today. Do you think it is right to be cautious in approving research which could have ethical issues? Is it worth taking more risks because the research might help to make the world a better place?

BUILD CONNECTIONS

Issues of criminality and deviance that will be addressed in the second year Crime and deviance topic are becoming increasingly important in school contexts. Not only might pupils or students be involved in deviant and criminal behaviour (for example, violence in playgrounds or the supply and use of drugs), there is increasing concern over serious abuse by teachers in boarding schools (both physical and sexual abuse). While much of this offending by teachers may be historic, researchers need to be aware of safeguarding issues when conducting research with children.

The relationship between theories and methods

Various theories may point to different areas of interest, but theories also nudge sociologists into different ways of studying society. Theories in sociology usually fall into two camps – structural and social action theories.

Structural approaches and positivism

Structural approaches, such as functionalism and Marxism, say that the best way to understand society is to view it as a real 'thing', which exists above and beyond us all as individuals. It shapes our lives and provides us with the social world in which we live: our role is generally to conform. This kind of theoretical approach emphasises that any research ought to bear this in mind and that the researcher should be looking for general patterns of behaviour – which individuals may not even be aware of. It adopts a type of top-down approach which looks at how the organisation of society tends to affect individuals.

UNDERSTAND THE CONCEPT

Structural approach looks at how society as a whole is put together and operates. It examines the major institutions and how they relate to one another. Functionalists and Marxists tend not to examine the behaviour of individuals, but some structural approaches (for example, some versions of neo-Marxism) accept that the actions of individuals are important, as well as social structures.

The research methods used by sociologists with such an approach tend to be those that generate sets of statistics (such as questionnaires), known as quantitative methods (see Chapter 3). Sociologists sympathetic to the use of these more 'scientific' methods are sometimes known as **positivists**.

UNDERSTAND THE CONCEPT

Positivism is an early influential approach in sociology, advocated by Auguste Comte as early as the 1840s and by Émile Durkheim (1897), which suggests that sociology can be scientific. The same methods used in studying the natural world can be used in studying the social world. This approach supports the use of quantitative methods.

Positivists believe the following things.

> There are objective social facts about the social world. These facts can be expressed in statistics. Facts about who passes exams, for example, are seen as no different from facts about the temperature of the oceans.

> You can look for correlations (patterns in which two or more things tend to occur together, for example, high social class and high achievement in education).

> Correlations may represent causal relationships (one thing causing another, for example, low income causing poor educational performance).

> It is possible to discover laws of human behaviour – causes of behaviour which are true for all humans everywhere and throughout history. (An example might be that higher social classes always, on average, get higher qualifications than lower social classes.)

> Human behaviour is shaped by external stimuli (things that happen to us) rather than internal stimuli (what goes on in the human mind) – the theories that educational achievement is shaped by family income, or how you were disciplined as a child, for example.

> To be scientific, you should only study what you can observe. It is therefore unscientific to study people's emotions, meanings or motives, which are internal to the unobservable mind.

> This approach supports the use of methods such as questionnaires and official statistics that provide factual, statistical data.

Interpretive approaches

Bottom-up approaches, such as interactionism (see Topic 1, Chapter 5), stress that the only way to understand society is to look at the world through the eyes of individuals as part of social groups, as it is the activities and beliefs of individuals that make up the social world. Research must start at 'the bottom' and work upwards. The sorts of research methods favoured by those who advocate this approach (known as **interpretive** sociologists) tend to be those that allow the researcher to see the world from the same perspective as those being studied (known as qualitative methods – see Chapter 4). An example is participant observation (see Chapter 4).

UNDERSTAND THE CONCEPT

Interpretivism is concerned with how individuals interpret the world around them before they act. It asks why people behave in certain ways as well as looking at how they behave. It generally accepts that people have some choice about how they behave and that their actions are not totally determined by social structures. Interpretivism often sees interaction in small groups as important for understanding society.

Interpretivists usually advocate the use of qualitative data to interpret social action, with an emphasis on the meanings and motives of participants. (For example, they would be interested in how people feel about education and what their motives are for choosing particular subjects.)

Interpretivists often see sociology as different from the natural sciences, in that it requires an understanding of meaningful human behaviour. (Children choose how to behave in classrooms but chemicals can't choose how to react if they are heated by a Bunsen burner, for example).

From this viewpoint, people do not simply react to external stimuli but interpret the meaning of stimuli before reacting. An understanding is therefore required of people's unobservable subjective states, such as motives, emotions and beliefs. (For example, do people see a low exam mark as the fault of the teacher or as their own fault? Are they motivated to try harder or to give up?)

This sort of information cannot be reduced to statistical data. Methods therefore have to be used to reveal these meanings, motives, emotions and beliefs, such as in-depth interviews or participant observation.

Triangulation and mixed methods research

Although some sociologists are largely in favour of using quantitative methods and others prefer qualitative methods, in practice many sociologists now use a variety of methods if they think this will be useful. This mixing of methods has become known as methodological pluralism (using several methods together) or in some specific contexts, **triangulation**.

Using a variety of methods can improve the validity and reliability of a single piece of research. The results gathered using one method can be checked against those derived from another and the advantages and disadvantages of quantitative and qualitative approaches can be 'balanced out'.

So, quantitative researchers may well back up their work by including some observation or some in-depth, unstructured interviewing, whilst qualitative researchers may well engage in some structured interviewing or draw upon quantitative secondary sources.

UNDERSTAND THE CONCEPT

Triangulation involves looking at the same thing from a variety of different angles to build up a three-dimensional picture of it and to cross-check that the impression produced from one angle is the same as that produced from another angle. The term comes from surveying, where examining land from different viewpoints enables you to map it in three dimensions.

FOCUS ON RESEARCH: ETHNOGRAPHIC STUDIES IN EDUCATIONAL RESEARCH

In *Young, Gifted and Black* (1998), Mairtin Mac an Ghaill carried out two ethnographic studies in inner-city educational institutions in which he worked. The first study looked at the relations between white teachers and two groups of male students with anti-school values – the Asian Warriors and the African Caribbean Rasta Heads – and the second study looked at a group of black female students, of African Caribbean and Asian parentage, called the Black Sisters.

Why study this subject?
Originally, Mac an Ghaill wanted to study Irish school students for his PhD, but no university supervisor was available to help him do so. He was advised to study students of African Caribbean origin instead and agreed to this. He then began his study of (male) Asian Warriors and the African Caribbean Rasta Heads.

His later study of ethnic-minority females was also not planned. As Mac an Ghaill puts it: "I had not intended to carry out a study of black female students. In fact it

would be more accurate to say that they chose me." Mac an Ghaill was teaching sociology at the time in a sixth-form college and, because he was seen to be on the side of the students, the Black Sisters were happy to talk to him about their views of racism.

The relationship between theory and method
Mac an Ghaill started his research by accepting the then current sociological explanation for the underachievement in school of young people of African Caribbean origin; namely that there were cultural differences with the dominant white culture. Initially, therefore, he wanted to research the problem of young African Caribbean students as trapped between two cultures.

Because Mac an Ghaill wanted to understand the nature of the cultural differences, he decided to use participant observational methods, which would give him a close insight into the values and beliefs of the students. As Mac an Ghaill says: "Intensive participant observation of the anti-school Rasta Heads led me to shift my theoretical perspective, identifying racism rather than the students themselves as the main problem in their schooling.

"Adopting a Black perspective – that is, the view that the Black community experiences the social world in a systematically different way from Whites – was vital here. It enabled me to reinterpret the students' subcultural responses, not as primarily causal of their academic underachievement but as symptoms of their coping with a racially structured institution."

Although he used participant observational methods, he also collected a range of quantitative information, including data on school absences, lateness, suspensions, the ethnic composition of students in academic/non-academic teaching groups and examination results. As the study developed, he used this material, linking it with what the students told him, to provide a deeper understanding of the students' perspectives.

Objectivity

During the research, Mac an Ghaill became friendly with the students. As he explains it himself: "Over the research periods the Rasta Heads, the Warriors and the Black Sisters visited my home regularly. The experience of talking, eating, dancing and listening to music together helped to break down the potential social barriers of the teacher–researcher role that may have been assigned to me and my seeing them as students with the accompanying status perception."

Mac an Ghaill does not claim to be value-free in his research, and states that he was committed to helping the students to overcome the racially-based barriers they faced in life.

Practical issues and research

Mac an Ghaill was able to gain entry into the research because he was a teacher in both educational

institutions over the period of research. Beyond that, his sympathy and support for the students convinced them that he was a trustworthy person who was 'on their side'. Mac an Ghaill also lived in the area and was recognised as a local. However, there was always tension between his role as a teacher and that of a friend and researcher of the young people. He found that in the staffroom he became the defender of the ethnic-minority students and a critic of the institutional racism he believed existed in the school and wider society. This position sometimes caused conflict with other members of staff.

Questions

1. Which factors influenced the choice of subject Mac an Ghaill studied?

2. What was the relationship between theoretical perspective and methods?

3. What methodology did Mac an Ghaill use?

4. Do you think that Mac an Ghaill found it difficult to remain objective in his research? Give reasons for your answer.

5. How did 'practical issues' impact upon his research activities and his relationship with staff and students?

RESEARCH IN THE EDUCATIONAL CONTEXT

The general issues relating to the selection of research methods apply in all contexts; however, there are some specific issues that tend to come to the fore in an educational context.

Research in education can involve the study of a variety of groups. However, the groups most frequently studied are:

> educational staff, such as teachers and head teachers

> the consumers of education, pupils and students

> the parents of school pupils.

Research may be carried out inside educational establishments, such as schools, colleges and universities, or outside those establishments, particularly when the research involves parents.

The particular group being studied, and the context within which the study takes place, has an impact on the practical, ethical, and theoretical advantages and disadvantages of conducting educational research and

these in turn influence both the choice of topic and the choice of method.

Research into educational staff

Practical issues

A common problem in conducting research into educational staff is gaining access. Access to educational staff may be limited by lack of time. Teachers are often hard-pressed during working hours and may feel they have little time to devote to being interviewed. Furthermore, schools are hierarchical institutions and teachers are only likely to be willing to take part in research with the permission of their line managers. This may restrict the availability of respondents in interview or questionnaire research. Senior educational staff are themselves subject to scrutiny; for example, head teachers are responsible to school governors. This may restrict their ability or willingness to take part in research. They may also be unwilling to take part in case the research portrays the institution in a bad light, putting their jobs and careers at risk.

Research has to be designed in such a way that it fits in with the working life of teachers or other educational professionals, does not use up too much of their time and doesn't seem to threaten the reputation of the institution. If it is not possible to gain access to respondents, then the research will have to be abandoned.

Ethical issues

In conducting research, researchers should ensure that they do no harm. It is possible that unguarded comments by educational staff may affect their career progression. It is therefore very important to maintain confidentiality for staff who take part in research.

Observation of teachers in staff rooms has ethical problems if all members of the teaching staff have not consented to take part in the research. For these reasons, an educational researcher might also avoid using observational methods to research situations such as school assemblies, where it is hard to control who is present and to get everyone to agree to participate.

Theoretical issues

When teachers or lecturers are observed, they may act unnaturally. Teachers are likely to associate the presence of an outsider in their classroom with Ofsted inspections. In these circumstances, teachers may act in ways that are not typical in order to impress the observer. This raises questions about the validity of classroom observations. However, carrying out interviews will not necessarily overcome problems of validity. In interview research, there may be a degree of interviewer bias and teachers may give cautious answers rather than express their true opinions, particularly if are concerned about the confidentiality of the data.

Another problem may be the representativeness of staff who are permitted to take part in research. For example, the teachers or lecturers permitted to take part in the research may be hand-picked by more senior staff in order to give a positive impression of the institution, making the findings unrepresentative. Researchers might reject particular methods because of such factors, for example, they might avoid classroom observation. Researchers may also design their research so they can obtain a sample without approaching the school or other educational institution.

Research into pupils and students

These are perhaps the groups who are most commonly studied in educational settings.

Practical issues

Access to studying children may be limited if schools or parents are not willing to give consent for them to take part in research. In most circumstances, researchers will also need to undergo a Disclosure and Barring Service (DBS) check to ensure that they are suitable people to have close contact with children. Researchers also have to conform to the demands of educational organisations, so the timing of their research is dependent upon when schools, colleges or universities are operating and when they are permitted access to them. Researchers may also need to get approval for the research from parents and the school rather than just being able to get consent from the participants, as is the case with research into adults.

There are particular problems researching young pupils, since they may lack the skills or confidence to fill in questionnaires or to answer complex questions. Research has to be designed to take account of the abilities of particular respondents, which may limit the range of information the researcher can collect or the length of interviews. Researching young children can be particularly time-consuming and therefore potentially expensive, as they may have a tendency to stray from the central points of the research.

Ethical issues

There are specific ethical issues with studying young children because, as children are considered particularly vulnerable, it is especially important that research does not harm the children. For example, the researcher must ensure that children do not suffer any psychological distress during the research. Researching pupils and students could be interpreted as doing them harm if it distracts them from their education and therefore potentially impedes their performance.

There can be particular problems with gaining informed consent from young participants in research, since they may not fully understand the purpose of the research. Keith Punch (2009) points out that adults are generally in positions of power over children, so it can be difficult for children to refuse requests from adults to take part in research. Furthermore, the British Sociological Association guidelines state that the consent of children should be obtained as well as that of their parents. The guidelines also state that 'researchers should have regard for issues of child protection and make provision for the potential disclosure of abuse'. Researchers will therefore need to think carefully when choosing whether to research children and will be obliged to take ethical factors into consideration if they are going to get ethical approval for the methods they would like to use.

Theoretical issues

Researchers are always concerned with trying to ensure that the data they produce is as reliable and valid as possible. But this can be a problem when children are being studied and may lead to their rejecting methods they would otherwise choose to use, or rejecting topics they would like to study. The researcher has several issues to consider.

> There may be problems with young children expressing abstract ideas or understanding questions based upon those ideas. It could be difficult to tell whether responses are based upon a genuine understanding of the question, and this could affect the validity of the data.

> Theoretical issues with research into the consumers of education partly depend upon their age, but educational consumers of all age groups in schools, colleges and universities occupy relatively low-status positions. They have little power, which may make it difficult for them openly to express their views. This could affect the validity of their responses.

> In classroom observation, the presence of the observer may well affect the behaviour of pupils or students, as well as the behaviour of teachers and lecturers. Therefore, even research that takes place in a natural setting may produce unnatural behaviour.

> The representativeness of samples may be problematic. Because access to children is dependent upon the willingness of parents and teachers to allow researchers to question them, it may be impossible to get a representative sample, and this will make it difficult to generalise from the findings of the research.

Research into parents

Although less common than research into pupils/students and educational professionals, research into the parents of school pupils is sometimes conducted, particularly when researchers are interested in the influence of home background on educational performance or the choices made by pupils/students about what to study and where.

Practical issues

Gaining access to a sample of parents is not likely to be straightforward. Unlike pupils and educational professionals, parents are not usually present in schools and other educational institutions. This makes it difficult to gain access for research purposes. There are practical difficulties in getting details of parental addresses and finding ways to approach them to secure their cooperation. This might limit sample size and encourage researchers to use more qualitative methods. Researching parents using interviews is likely to be time-consuming because in all probability each home will have to be visited separately at a time convenient to the parents, who may well be working during the day. However, alternative methods may be completely impracticable. Researchers are unlikely to be able to observe the behaviour of parents when discussing education with their children or assisting them with homework, because this takes place in private family settings that are not accessible to them. Interviews of one sort or another are therefore perhaps the most common method used to study this group.

Ethical issues

Ethical issues are less of a barrier to research with this group than practical considerations. Researching parents is much less ethically problematic than researching pupils because parents are more likely to be able to give properly informed consent than children. However, the general ethical issues concerning research still apply, such as the problem of maintaining confidentiality.

Theoretical issues

There are particular problems in obtaining a representative sample of parents. Some groups of parents, particularly those who are more involved with their children's education, may be more willing to take part in research than other groups. Thus, for example, research data might exaggerate the degree to which parents assist children with homework or take an interest in their schooling.

If questionnaires are used, then there may be an uneven response rate from different groups of parents, and this will affect the representativeness of the data.

Parents may also feel that they need to appear actively interested in their children's homework if they are going to create a good impression for the researcher, and this may affect the validity of any responses. Researchers sensitive to such issues will design the research carefully and may, for example, use triangulation to test the validity of the findings.

CHECK YOUR UNDERSTANDING

1. Briefly explain any two factors that influence the choice of research topic.

2. Explain, in your own words, what is meant by the term 'ethical issues'.

3. Briefly explain any two practical issues that can affect the choice of method, apart from money.

4. Explain how any one theoretical approach might influence the choice of research topic.

5. Explain how any one theoretical approach might influence the choice of methodology.

6. Identify and describe three differences between positivism and interpretivism.

7. Identify and explain one ethical issue relating to interviewing young children.

8. Identify and explain one practical issue relating to interviewing teachers.

9. Identify and explain one theoretical issue relating to observing classrooms.

10. Explain what is meant by 'triangulation', and explain two advantages of using triangulation in researching the reasons for class differences in educational attainment at GCSE level.

TAKE IT FURTHER

Choose a topic for an educational research project and briefly explain the methods you would use to collect the data. Explain what ethical, practical and theoretical problems might arise with the topic and methods. Swap proposals with another student and evaluate the strengths and weaknesses of the other student's plan.

2.3 QUANTITATIVE RESEARCH METHODS

INTRODUCING THE DEBATE

We are surrounded by statistics from governments, politicians and organisations, and they are often used to encourage us to think in a particular way. Marketers and political parties make much use of them and often spin them to give a particular slant. Sociologists use statistics too, but how are they produced, can we believe them and, if so, why? Can sociology be an objective subject like the natural sciences and even use experiments to test its theories? This chapter discusses these questions both in the context of education and more generally.

Sociologists choose different methods of research depending upon which method seems most appropriate given the circumstances, their theoretical preferences, the practical and ethical issues, and the resources available to them. The approach covered in this topic is quantitative research. This stresses the importance of gathering statistical information that can be checked and tested. It therefore emphasises reliability.

Quantitative research usually involves one or more of the following:

> surveys

> case studies

> experiments

> comparative research.

Although these methods tend to collect quantitative data this is not always the case, depending on the exact techniques used to put them into operation.

Quantitative research methods are most often chosen by sociologists who believe that sociology should attempt to be similar to the natural sciences in the way that it carries out research. Sociologists who prefer the natural sciences model of research argue that the closest they can get to scientific research is if they use highly advanced statistical methods, which can, they argue, factually prove the relationship between different social events. Therefore, statistical analyses have demonstrated beyond doubt that social class, ethnicity and gender are all directly related to educational success. As discussed in Chapter 2, one such approach to sociological research is known as positivism.

Positivists reject qualitative research, which is based on the principle that people construct the social world through their perceptions of what is real or true. Positivists argue that knowledge can only be generated through obtaining verifiable and objective information about the social world.

SURVEYS

Social surveys

A social survey involves obtaining information in a standardised manner from a large group of people. Surveys usually obtain this information through questionnaires or, less often, through interviews. The information is then analysed using statistical techniques. There are three possible aims of social surveys. They can be used to:

> find out 'facts' about the population – for example, how many people have access to the internet. This is known as a factual survey. A good example of a factual survey is the British Crime Survey, which takes place every two years and asks people about their experience of crime. This survey has helped sociologists gain a fuller understanding of patterns of crime. We now know a lot more about issues such as people's fear of crime, the factors affecting the reporting of crime and the likelihood of different social groups becoming victims of crime.

> uncover differences in beliefs, values and attitudes – for example, whether young people have a more positive view of the internet than older people or whether they think a university education is important for their life chances. Often this is called an attitudes survey and an example is the annual British Social Attitudes Survey, which asks a variety of questions, for example, about attitudes to family life.

> explain aspects of social life – for example, explaining why some people choose to apply to university and others do not. This is known as an explanatory survey.

Before a full social survey is carried out, it is usual for a researcher to carry out a pilot survey. This is a small-scale version of the full survey, which is intended to:

> help evaluate the usefulness of the larger survey

> test the quality and the accuracy of the questions

> test the accuracy of the sample

> find out whether there are any unforeseen problems.

Longitudinal surveys

Social surveys are sometimes criticised for only providing a 'snapshot' of social life at any one time. Sociologists often

want to understand how people change over time and in these circumstances the typical cross-sectional survey (as these 'snapshot surveys' or 'social surveys' are sometimes called) is not appropriate. Longitudinal surveys get around this problem by studying the same people over a long period of time – sometimes as long as 20 years. Such surveys provide us with a clear, moving image of changes in attitudes and actions over time. The Longitudinal Study of Young People in England is a longitudinal survey that began in 2004 and will continue to track the sample throughout their education and onwards. In 2004, students in Year 9 (born 1989/1990) were interviewed and completed a questionnaire regarding their views on education. In all, over 15,000 young people were interviewed. Since then, the interviews have been carried out annually. The information obtained is used to plan educational provision, among other things.

Longitudinal surveys suffer from a number of problems.

> From a practical point of view, they are very expensive and time-consuming.

> Once they have started, you cannot collect retrospective information, so you have to be sure you have the right questions and have identified any potential issues from the start.

> Theoretically, a major problem is that respondents may drop out of the survey because they get bored with answering the questions, or move causing the researchers to lose track of them. If too many people drop out, this may make the survey increasingly unrepresentative, as the views of those who remain may well be significantly different from the views of those who drop out.

> People may change their behaviour as a result of taking part in a survey. They might reflect more on their own behaviour than those who are not taking part, and therefore choose to alter behaviour as a direct result of participation.

Surveys, whether longitudinal or not, rely upon asking questions, whether in written questionnaires or in interviews. The different types of question and the advantages and disadvantages of this type of research will be discussed in Chapter 5.

Sampling

It is usually impossible for sociologists to study the entire population they are interested in. The word population in the context of sampling refers to everybody (or everything) relevant to the study. For example, the relevant population in a study of A-level sociology students in England would be all the A-level sociology students in England. The sampling unit is the individual example of the thing to be studied (for example, an individual or a school). Because it would often be too expensive, time-consuming or difficult to get cooperation to study the entire population, sociologists need to find a way of studying a smaller proportion of the population whose views will be likely to mirror the views of the whole population. There are ways of ensuring that the smaller group studied (the sample) is typical – or representative – of the entire population, but sometimes the researcher deliberately sets out to get a non-representative sample.

Types of sampling: techniques for obtaining a representative sample

> Random sampling – this is based on the idea that, by choosing randomly, each person has an equal chance of being selected and so those chosen are likely to be a representative cross-section of the population. A simple random sample involves selecting names randomly from a **sampling frame**.

UNDERSTAND THE CONCEPT

A **sampling frame** is a list from which a sample is chosen. If the sampling frame is inaccurate, this can lead to errors in the final findings. Therefore, it needs to be a true and comprehensive list of the relevant population. Examples of commonly used sampling frames are electoral registers (lists of people entitled to vote, which are publicly available) or the Postcode Address File.

A simple random sample does not guarantee a representative sample – you may, for instance, select too many young people, too many males or too many from some other group. You rely upon chance for your sample to be representative, so you need a sizeable sample to make this most likely. For this reason, many sociologists break down their list of names into separate categories (for example, males and females) and then select from those lists. This can help them to ensure that, at least in terms of chosen characteristics, the sample is proportionate to the population as a whole.

> Systematic sampling – this is a variation on random sampling where every *n*th name (for example, every 10th name) on a list is chosen.

> Stratified random sampling – this is where the population under study is divided according to known criteria (for example, it could be divided into 52 per cent women and 48 per cent men, to reflect the sex composition of the UK). Within these broad strata, people are then chosen at random. The strata can become quite detailed – for example, with further divisions into age, social class or geographical location.

> Quota sampling – this is where the researcher establishes how many people they want in a sample with particular characteristics and then finds a selection of relevant people to fill these quotas. Often this is used when sampling people in the street or in opinion polls, however administered. It is useful for studies of large groups (for example, the British population as a whole) because it can allow a reasonably representative study using a small number of people. For example, the typical surveys of voting preferences in journals and newspapers use a quota sample of approximately 1,200 to represent the entire British electorate.

Would you agree that the results of any research involving sampling cannot really be relied upon, because not everyone has taken part and you can't know for sure how typical or atypical the participants are? Bear in mind that opinion polls immediately before elections usually get very close to predicting the actual result.

> Non-representative sampling – sometimes researchers either do not want a cross-section of the population, or they are unable to obtain one. In such cases they may use one of the following methods.

– Snowball sampling – this method is used when it is difficult to gain access to a particular group of people who are the subjects of study, or where there is no sampling frame available. It involves making contact with one member of the population to be studied and then asking them to name one or more possible contacts. An example of this is Robert McNamara's study of male prostitutes in New York (1994) where he asked prostitutes to identify others, gradually building up enough contacts for the research.

= Theoretical sampling – Glaser and Strauss (1967) argue that it is sometimes more useful to study non-typical people, because they may help to generate theoretical insights. Feminist sociologists have deliberately studied very atypical societies, where women occupy non-traditional roles, in order to show that gender roles are socially constructed – if they were based on biology, you would expect to see the same roles in every society. The different types of sampling and their main advantages and disadvantages are summarised in Table 2.3.1.

Type of sampling	How it is conducted	Advantages	Disadvantages
Random	Every sampling unit has an equal chance of being chosen – for example, names are drawn out of a hat.	Technically, it is the most representative type of sampling, relying upon statistical odds to ensure representativeness.	You need a large sample to ensure that it is statistically likely to be representative.
Systematic	A method is devised to enable systematic selection from a list, for example, every 10th person is sampled.	It avoids having to pick the sample from a hat or using a computer list of random numbers.	It is not truly random.
Stratified random	The population is divided into groups according to important variables such as class, gender and ethnicity, and the sample is then chosen in the same proportions as their prevalence in the population.	It allows you to be confident that your sample is representative while using a relatively small sample.	It is only possible if you have a sampling frame which contains details of the significant characteristics of the population you are studying.
Quota	Quotas are established which determine how many people with particular characteristics are studied. Once a quota is filled no more people in that category are included.	It has the advantages of stratified random sampling but can be conducted without the use of the sampling frame.	It may be less representative than random and stratified random sampling because the accessibility of potential respondents affects their chances of being included in the sample.
Snowballing	A member of a sample puts the researcher in touch with other potential members of the sample.	It is used mainly with groups who are hard to identify or access, for example, criminals.	It is very unlikely to be truly representative because it is based upon people who have contact with one another.
Theoretical	People are chosen for the sample who have particular unusual characteristics.	It is useful for testing some general theories.	It makes no attempt to be representative and therefore you cannot generalise from the findings.

Table 2.3.1 *The advantages and disadvantages of different types of sampling*

FOCUS ON RESEARCH: SURVEY RESEARCH ON PARENTS AND EDUCATIONAL ADVANTAGE

In *Parent Power?*, a study of how parents use money and skills to help children succeed in education, Becky Francis and Merryn Hutchings (2013) used survey data. The study was based on an online survey of 1,173 parents of children aged 5–16 years who attended school. It was carried out for the Sutton Trust by the polling organisation, YouGov. The sample was taken from members of the public who are on YouGov's panel of people willing to take part in polling on various subjects for a small fee. YouGov selected parents who lived with their children to take part; they took account of the proportions who were male and female and invited people from different social classes (or as they call them, social grades), taking account of how many people in the general population are in those classes. However, those in the highest group (social grade A, consisting of higher managers, administrators and professionals) were over-sampled because the study was particularly interested in parents from this class. (Over-sampling involves asking a higher proportion than you would in a representative sample from one group of particular interest, and then adjusting the results to take account of this at the end. It allows you to make more reliable statements about groups who would otherwise make up only a small proportion of the sample).

Respondents were sent an email asking them to participate and those who responded positively were included. YouGov ensured that 50 per cent of the sample was male and 50 per cent was female. Although this sampling method got a spread of people from different classes, the sample did not closely match the proportions in the population as a whole (because it depended on who agreed to participate), with some classes over-represented in the sample and some under-represented. Furthermore, they found that Black and minority ethnic groups made up only about 12 per cent of their sample, while about 24 per cent of school pupils come from these backgrounds.

For more information on this study visit the Sutton Trust website.

Questions

1. What was the sampling frame used in this research?

2. Suggest ways in which the sampling frame may not have been representative of the population as a whole. (Think about the sort of people likely to be on the YouGov panel.)

3. What type (or types) of sampling were used in this study? (You may find more than one type was used.)

4. Evaluate the overall strengths and weaknesses of the sampling procedures. (Think about how representative the sample was, and whether it could have been more or less representative.)

5. Suggest ways in which the sampling could have been improved.

CASE STUDIES

A case study is a detailed study of one particular group or organisation. Instead of searching out a wide range of people via sampling, the researcher focuses on one group. The resulting studies are usually extremely detailed and provide a depth of information not normally available. They can provide an in-depth picture of how a small (or micro) social world works. A good example is Paul Willis's study of a group of anti-school boys (see Topic 1, Chapter 1). However, there is always the problem that this intense scrutiny may miss wider issues. The group might not be representative and they may change their behaviour because they are being studied intensively. Case studies can be useful for coming up with new ideas and theories, which you can then test in further research.

EXPERIMENTS

Experiments are very commonly used in the natural sciences (for example, in physics and chemistry). An experiment is basically research in which all the variables are closely controlled, so that the effect of changing one or more of the variables can be understood.

UNDERSTAND THE CONCEPT

Experiments can test theories in precise conditions controlled by the researcher, ideally in a laboratory. The researcher develops a hypothesis – a prediction of what will be found – which is then tested.

Experiments involve trying to isolate the effects of independent variables (possible causes) on a dependent variable (the thing to be explained). A control (in which everything is held constant) and an experiment (in which one independent variable is changed) are compared, allowing scientists to find precise causes. Experiments can be replicated (reproduced exactly) to test the reliability of findings.

For example, if you were testing the effect of sunlight (the independent variable) on the growth of plants (the dependent variable) you would experiment on two identical (as far as possible) groups of plants exposing one group (the experimental group) to more sunlight that the other group of plants (the control group). In terms of independent variables, such as the type of soil, temperature, and how much they were watered, the experiment and control groups would be kept in identical conditions. That way you would be sure that any difference in growth really was the result of light and you could exactly repeat the same experiment (replicating it) to check that you got the same results time after time.

Here, the researcher would observe the effects of sunlight (the independent variable) on the growth of a plant (the dependent variable).

Experiments are widely used in psychology, but much less so in sociology. There are several reasons for this.

› It is impossible to recreate normal life in the artificial environment of an experiment.

› There are many ethical problems in performing experiments on people, for example, they may cause the people harm or you may need to lie to them to ensure the validity of the experiment.

› There is the possibility of the experimenter effect, where the awareness of being in an experiment affects the behaviour of the participants. This means that experiments may not be valid.

› Experiments cannot be used to study long-term or major social change – you can't get a whole society into a laboratory.

Occasionally, sociologists use field experiments, where a form of experiment is undertaken in the community. Rosenhan (1973, reprinted in 1982) sent 'normal' people to psychiatric institutions in the USA in the late 1960s to see how they were treated by the staff. (Rather worryingly, the staff treated ordinary behaviour in institutions as evidence of insanity!)

Because of the practical, ethical and theoretical problems with experiments, sociologists often carry out comparative research instead.

COMPARATIVE RESEARCH

The sociological version of an experiment is the comparative method. When a sociologist is interested in explaining a particular issue, one way of doing so is by comparing differences across groups or societies, or across one society over time. By comparing the different social variables in the different societies and their effects upon the issue being studied, it is sometimes possible to identify a particular social practice or value that is the key factor in determining that issue.

Émile Durkheim (1897/1952) used the comparative method in his classic study of the different levels of suicide in societies, concluding that specific cultural differences motivated people to commit suicide. In order to arrive at this conclusion, Durkheim collected official statistics from a number of different countries and then compared the different levels of suicide, linking them to cultural differences, including religion and family relationships, which varied across the different countries.

Comparative research uses the same logic as experiments but focuses on what has actually happened rather than artificial situations set up by a sociologist. There are problems with this, however. You cannot control or manipulate variables and you can't always control what data is available. As a result, you have to make the best of what information is available and because that is often imperfect, you can't be absolutely sure you have found the true causes of something. However, comparative research can still yield very valuable and quite convincing evidence to support or contradict particular theories.

Discuss the view that because comparative research is commonly used in sociology, sociology can be considered to be a scientific subject.

BUILD CONNECTIONS

Experimental and comparative methods are both found in scientific research. Scientists cannot always use laboratory experiments to study large-scale or long-term phenomena (for example, evolution or the birth of the universe). This means that scientists need to adopt more varied methods so that science is perhaps closer to social science than it might immediately appear to be. These issues will be revisited in the later parts of the A-level course (Book 2) when we look at whether sociology can be considered a science.

FOCUS ON SKILLS: COMPARATIVE RESEARCH ON ACADEMY CHAINS

Manchester Academy

Becky Francis, Merryn Hutching and Robert De Vries (2014) conducted research comparing different academy chains (where a single body ran three or more academy schools) and comparing academy chains with schools in general. Their findings were published in a report entitled *Chain Effects*. To make the comparisons they examined existing data on:

› GCSE exam results in terms of the grades obtained by disadvantaged pupils (those getting free school meals) in their five best GCSEs

› the proportion obtaining five or more GCSEs including English and Maths

› the amount of progress made in English and Maths

› the proportion obtaining the English Baccalaureate.

They also compared the different types of chain to see whether any particular type tended to have more success than other types in raising the achievement of pupils from poor households. They found that academy chains did less well than the average for all schools in raising achievement for poor pupils, but some were very successful and these were likely to be chains that had not expanded too quickly, and that had staff with lots of experience of managing school improvement.

For more on this study visit the Sutton Trust website.

Questions

1. **Explain**. Demonstrate your understanding of the comparative method by explaining why this study is an example of comparative research.

2. **Analyse** some of the different independent variables that were used in this study.

3. **Analyse** the main dependent variables used in this study.

4. **Analyse** reasons why this research could not have been carried out as a field experiment.

5. **Evaluate** the possible weaknesses and limitations of this research.

6. **Evaluate** the strengths of this research.

EXPERIMENTAL RESEARCH IN THE CONTEXT OF EDUCATION

Experimental research has been used to investigate a range of topics in the education system. However, the most common type of research is to do with labelling theories

of education and the effects of teacher expectations upon pupil performance. Some examples are discussed below (see Topic 1, Chapter 2 for further details of the studies).

Rosenthal and Jacobson (1968) gave false information to primary school teachers in the USA about the IQ of pupils. They found that pupils who were believed to have a high IQ by teachers made greater progress than those who were believed to have a low IQ, regardless of what their actual IQ was. This suggested that the self-fulfilling prophecy can occur.

Harvey and Slatin (1976) used photographs of children from different social classes and asked teachers to rate their likely performance in education. Pupils from higher classes were seen as more likely to be successful than pupils from lower social classes, suggesting that labelling on the basis of appearance does take place.

Practical problems

Laboratory experiments are very difficult to conduct because of the problems in gaining permission to conduct experiments and take children out of school. You might need permission from teachers, head teachers, parents and children themselves. The research by Harvey and Slatin (1976) was a type of laboratory experiment but it was conducted on teachers rather than pupils. Laboratory experiments are usually confined to studying older students rather than young children. Field experiments, such as those by Rosenthal and Jacobson (1968), are more practical but it may be difficult to get permission from schools and teachers to conduct them.

Ethical problems

There are major ethical problems in conducting the types of experiments described above, particularly if they involve school pupils. The research by Rosenthal and Jacobson may have damaged the educational progress of some pupils labelled as having low ability, and informed consent wasn't possible.

Theoretical problems

The experiments involve the creation of artificial situations which may lead to their lacking in validity. Attempts to reproduce the Rosenthal and Jacobson study have produced inconsistent results, suggesting that such research may not be very reliable. A lot may depend on the particular ways in which the labelling is put into practice by the teachers, showing that it is very difficult to control variables in field experiments.

Is it ever ethical to conduct sociological research on young children? Is it really any different to social policy, which continually tinkers with the education system without being too sure what the effects will be?

CHECK YOUR UNDERSTANDING

1. What is meant by 'quantitative research'?

2. Explain the importance of sampling.

3. Why are random samples not always representative?

4. Explain what is meant by 'quota' sampling? Give one drawback of this method.

5. Identify and explain, in your own words, two types of sampling other than quota and random sampling.

6. Give an example of a situation in which a sociologist might use each of the following types of sampling:

   (a) snowball sampling

   (b) theoretical sampling.

7. Give three reasons why sociologists rarely use experiments.

8. Describe one example of a study that used an experiment in studying education, and explain two problems with the study.

9. Describe one example of a research project that has used the comparative method.

10. Explain two reasons why findings based upon comparative research may be less convincing than findings based upon experiments.

TAKE IT FURTHER

Devise a plan to conduct an experimental study on encouraging males and females to choose non-typical A-level subjects. You will need a control group and an experimental group. What practical, ethical and theoretical problems might you face? Would it be ethically sound, in your view, to treat the groups differently?

2.4 QUALITATIVE RESEARCH METHODS

2.4

LEARNING OBJECTIVES

> Understand the principles of qualitative methods of research involving observation and questioning (AO1).

> Apply this understanding to researching in the context of education (AO2).

> Analyse and evaluate the strengths and weaknesses of qualitative methods of research both in general and in an educational context (AO3).

INTRODUCING THE DEBATE

'Proper' research is often thought of as being quite scientific, perhaps involving experiments in laboratories or the analysis of statistical data. From this point of view, simply hanging around and watching what people do, joining in with them or talking to them in a fairly informal way all seem like they are far too casual to be seen as a form of research. Yet many sociologists prefer doing research like this and, more than that, they see it as invaluable for producing worthwhile knowledge that can help us to understand social worlds. To give you an example of how valuable it might be, think about how much you could help an outsider to understand the peer groups you belong to by giving an insider's view of the friendship groups in your school or college. Would your understanding not be far more valuable than the results of some questionnaires handed out to your friends? Some sociologists certainly think so and that is why they choose qualitative methods of research.

Sociologists may choose to keep their distance from those they are researching, sometimes in an attempt to remain objective. They may use questionnaires, interviews and surveys to obtain a clear view of their research topic. On the other hand, there are sociologists who are more interested in experiencing the emotions and a sense of actually being there. These sociologists set out to immerse themselves in the lifestyle of the group they wish to study. Other researchers seek a more in-depth engagement with their subjects, even if they don't actually study them in their natural social environment. They may do this through in-depth interviewing.

Because these types of research are generally less focused on in statistics as support for the arguments being investigated (that is, through quantitative research), and more focused on the qualities of actual social life, they are known as qualitative research. Qualitative approaches are based on the belief that it is not appropriate or possible to measure and categorise the social world accurately – all that is possible is to observe and describe what is happening and to offer possible explanations. This approach is therefore generally used more by interpretive sociologists rather than positivists and others who see sociology as scientific.

TYPES OF QUALITATIVE RESEARCH

Common forms of qualitative research include:

> certain types of observational study

> informal or unstructured interviews

> focus groups.

In this chapter we will concentrate mainly on observational studies, as some of the issues surrounding asking questions and discussion are covered in Chapter 5. However, we should remember that, strictly speaking, qualitative research can include a wide variety of other approaches, such as video and audio recording of activities.

Although there is still some debate, the general consensus is that qualitative research is a naturalistic, interpretative approach concerned with understanding the meanings that people attach to actions, decisions, beliefs, values and so on, within their social world. It is also about understanding the mental mapping process that respondents use to make sense of and interpret the world around them (Ritchie and Lewis, 2003).

One of the most common forms of qualitative research consists of observational studies in which particular groups of people are closely observed and their activities noted. The belief is that exploring the lives of people in detail can lead to insights that can be applied to the understanding of society in general. Observational studies derive from **ethnography**, which is the term used to describe the study of the lifestyles of social groups.

UNDERSTAND THE CONCEPT

Ethnography was originally associated with the work of anthropologists who studied simple, small-scale societies by living with the (usually tribal) people and observing their daily lives. However, ethnography can also be used to study the cultures or subcultures of groups of people within more complex societies, such as the USA or the UK. It aims to provide rich descriptions of those lifestyles, of their cultures, values and social divisions, and often to explain why they have developed these ways of living given the context in which they live their lives.

OBSERVATIONAL RESEARCH

Observational research is a general term that covers a range of different research techniques. Observational studies vary in two main ways (see also Figure. 2.4.1).

1. The extent to which the researcher joins in the activities of the group – i.e. the researcher may decide to be a participant or not. The choice is between participant observation (taking part in the activities) and non-participant observation (merely observing the activities).

2. Whether the researcher is honest and tells the group about the research, or prefers to pretend to be one of the group – i.e. will the researcher engage in overt or covert research? The choice of approach has a significant influence on the practicalities of carrying out observation in ethnographic research.

An observer in a classroom

COVERT

Laud Humphries (1975) studied homosexual activity in public toilets. He pretended to be a gay voyeur.

Amy Flowers (1998) got a job as a telephone sex line worker and studied the ways in which the women learned to mask their feelings and emotions when talking to clients. Neither employees nor managers knew about her research.

NON-PARTICIPANT

PARTICIPANT

Heidi Safia Mirza and Diane Reay (2000) studied two African-Caribbean 'supplementary' schools, run by the African-Caribbean-origin community for their children. The researchers attended and observed the classes (as well as using in-depth interviews).

Stephen Lyng (1990) studied 'high risk' groups (sky divers and motorcyclists) to find out why they took part in these activities. Lyng never hid the fact he was an academic but joined in with all the dangerous activities.

OVERT

Figure 2.4.1 *Types of observational research*

Covert and overt methods

Before researchers begin their work, they must decide whether they wish to conduct the research in a covert or an overt way.

Does the researcher inform everybody that they are doing research and fully disclose its purpose (overt research)? Or, at the other extreme, do they pose as a member of the group and keep the research entirely secret for its duration (covert research)? Many researchers adopt a position in the middle, telling some but not all members of a social group, or saying that they are doing research but being vague about its exact purpose. Even if you want to be open, it might be hard to explain yourself to everyone you come into contact with. However, you might tell some key informants (such as gang leaders) who can pass on the information to others, or vouch for your presence in the group.

The advantages of covert research

> Forbidden fruit – Researchers can enter forbidden areas, be fully accepted and trusted, and immerse themselves totally in the group being studied. This can generate a real sense of understanding of the views of the group.

> Normal behaviour – The group will continue to act naturally, unaware that they are being studied (although the fact that the researcher is among them will inevitably have some effect).

The disadvantages of covert research

> Danger of discovery – If the researcher's true role is uncovered, it may place the researcher in danger. At the very least it is likely to mean that the research will not be able to proceed further.

> Ethical dilemmas – Firstly, there is the issue that it is wrong to study a group without telling them. Secondly, if the group engages in illegal or immoral activities, the researchers may have to engage in these activities as well. They could then find themselves in possession of knowledge that it may be immoral to withhold from the authorities (for example, knowledge of serious crime).

The advantages of overt observation

> The confidante – As someone who has no role within the group, the researcher may be in the position of the trusted outsider and receive confidences from group members.

> Honesty – The researcher is also able to play an open, clear and honest role, which will help minimise ethical dilemmas.

> Other methods – Researchers can supplement their observation with other methods, such as interviews and questionnaires.

The disadvantages of overt observation

> Outsider – There will be many situations where only a trusted insider will be let into the secrets of a group. Anyone else, even a sympathetic observer, will be excluded.

> Changing behaviour – It is particularly likely that the subjects will change their behaviour if they know they are being studied.

Is it ever ethical to carry out covert research? How could it be justified? Can people ever act naturally if they are being observed? If not, how can this problem be minimised?

CARRYING OUT ETHNOGRAPHIC RESEARCH

The process of carrying out ethnographic research involves solving some key problems, largely of a practical nature, but there are also ethical and theoretical implications.

Joining the group

An observational study of homeless people, such as Blackman's, might involve visiting an advice centre in order to find participants.

Observational studies may involve groups of people on the margins of society, and the first problem is actually to contact and join the group. The sociologist has to find a place where the group goes and a situation in which they would accept the researcher. Shane Blackman (1997) studied a group of young homeless people, whom he met at an advice centre for young people. Sometimes sociologists make use of gatekeepers – members of the group who can help the sociologist become accepted and introduce them to new people and situations. Andy Bennett (2004) describes how his route 'into' the hip-hop scene in Newcastle was facilitated by a local breakdancer who also worked as an instructor at a community dance project. Through this contact, he gained access to, or learned of, key figures in the scene. He would accompany the gatekeeper and a number of his dance students and other friends to around a dozen weekly hip-hop nights held in a bar.

Acceptance by the group

There are often barriers of age, ethnicity and gender to overcome if the group are to accept the researcher. Moore (2004) researched young people 'hanging around'. He was initially unable to gain full acceptance because of his age. He overcame this by using young, female researchers.

Recording information

When researchers are actually hanging around with a group, it is difficult to make notes – particularly if engaged in covert research. Even if the group members are aware of the research, someone constantly making notes would disrupt normal activity and, of course, the researcher would also be unable to pay full attention to what was going on. In participant observational studies, therefore, researchers generally use a field diary. This is a detailed record of what happened, which the researcher writes up as often as possible. However, the research diary can also be a real weakness of the research.

Research diaries

In participant observational studies, researchers generally use a field diary. This is a detailed record of what happened, which the researcher writes up as often as possible. However, the research diary can also be a real weakness of the research.

Ethnographic researchers do not keep regular hours. Their observation may well go on into the night and it can be difficult to write up a diary each evening. Therefore, there is plenty of time to forget things and to distort them. Most observational studies include quotes, however, as it is impossible to remember the exact words, the quotes often reflect what the researcher thinks the people said. This may be inaccurate.

Maintaining objectivity

In observational research, it is hard to remain objective. Close contact with the group under study means that emotions almost always emerge. In the introduction to his study of crack cocaine dealers, Bourgois (2003) comments on how these dealers are his friends and how much he owes to the 'comments, corrections and discussions' provided by one particular dealer. Such input from those being studied might help to produce a more rounded and valid account, but it can also compromise the researcher's objectivity.

Influencing the situation

The more involved the researcher is with the people being studied, the greater the chance of influencing what happens. Stephen Lyng (1990) joined a group of males who engaged in 'edgework' – that is, putting their lives at risk through skydiving and (illegal) road motorcycle racing. Lyng became so entangled in this style of life that he actually helped encourage others into life-risking behaviour.

Participant observation

The most common form of observational study is **participant observation**, where the researcher joins the group being studied in one role or another.

UNDERSTAND THE CONCEPT

The idea of **participant observation** is particularly associated with the Chicago School – researchers at the Chicago University sociology department from the 1930s onwards. The idea was that members of the sociology department should go out into the city and join in while observing social life in a rapidly expanding city. The sociological perspective of symbolic interactionism (see Book 2, Topic 2) emerged out of this approach. It is an approach that gives particular significance to the meanings people attach to social life as they experience it.

BUILD CONNECTIONS

There is a close connection between observation / participant observation as research methods and labelling theories, such as those discussed in the chapter on processes in schools (see Topic 1, Chapter 2). Labelling theories place emphasis on how people's images of themselves (self-concepts) develop during interaction with others. It is difficult to study this without being present as this interaction between people unfolds. Labelling theory is itself closely connected to symbolic interactionism (Book 2, Topic 1).

The advantages of participant observation

Practical issues

It may not take much preparation to conduct participant observation, especially if it involves social groups the researcher is already familiar with. It may also make it possible to study some groups who would not take part in other types of research, for example, cults and sects, or criminal gangs.

Ethical issues

Through day-to-day engagement with those being studied, the researcher is in a better position to understand the needs of the subjects than researchers using other methods, and to ensure that they do them no harm. They may even be able to help the subjects out in various ways, for example, by offering advice or helping with practical tasks.

Theoretical issues

> Experience – Participant observation allows the researcher to fully join the group and to see things through the eyes (and actions) of the people in the group. The researcher is placed in the same situation as the group under study, fully experiencing what is happening. This can result in the researcher being better able to understand the perspectives of the group than other researchers.

> Generating new ideas – Often this type of observation can lead to completely new insights and generate new theoretical ideas, unlike traditional research, which undertakes the study in order to explore an existing theory or hypothesis. The researcher can be much more open-minded than they can be when devising experiments or questionnaires.

> Getting the truth – One of the problems with questionnaires, and to a lesser extent with interviews, is that the respondent can lie. Participant observation prevents this because the researcher can see the person in action. It may also help them to understand why the person would lie in a questionnaire or interview.

> Digging deep – Participant observation can create a close bond between the researcher and the group under study, and individuals in the group may be prepared to confide in the researcher on issues and views that would normally remain hidden.

> Dynamic – Questionnaires and interviews are 'static': they are only able to gain an understanding of a person's behaviour or attitudes at one precise moment. Participant observation takes place over a period of time and allows an understanding of how changes in attitudes and behaviour take place.

> Being naturalistic – It is easier for the researcher who participates to use the concepts and language of those being studied, and to reflect their priorities, than it is for the researcher who uses questionnaires, where they have to impose their own structure and priorities in writing the questions. The research is therefore 'natural' – it reflects real social life.

Interpretivists therefore see participant observation as one of the best, if not the best, method for understanding social life and producing a valid account of what it is really like for particular groups. It helps the researcher to understand the unobservable meanings and motives of others by going through some of the same experiences as them, and allows them to better explain why people live and act as they do.

The disadvantages of participant observation

Practical issues

Participant observation studies tend to be very time-consuming and therefore expensive. For example, Alice Goffman (2014) spent six years in a low-income Black neighbourhood in Philadelphia studying the effects of drug enforcement laws on the community. If the researcher has an interest in a particular aspect of social life (say racism in classrooms or criminal behaviour by gangs) then they may waste a lot of time waiting to observe the type of behaviour they are researching. There can also be significant problems of access to some groups. The researcher may be the wrong age, sex or ethnicity to join a group, or the group may be closed to outsiders. As a consequence, many participant observation studies are concerned with the least powerful groups in society – typically groups of young males or females who engage in deviant activities. Some critics (for example, Marxists) argue that the information obtained does not therefore usually help us to understand important issues in society concerning the powerful.

There can also be practical problems with recording the data, for example, finding time and space to write up field notes.

Ethical issues

One problem with participant observation is that the researcher may need to take part in illegal or immoral behaviour in order to fully participate within the group. It may also be impossible to seek informed consent from all those who will be observed in the research. If the research is covert, then researchers will have to mislead all the participants about their motives for being there. It can also be difficult to maintain the anonymity of those being studied; the descriptions are often so detailed it could well be possible for a reader of the research report to work out who they are.

Theoretical issues

> Bias – The main problem with participant observation lies with bias, as the observer can be drawn into the group and start to see things through their eyes. This may blind the observer to the insights that would otherwise be available.

> Influence of the researcher – The presence of the researcher may make the group act less naturally because they are aware of being studied. Of course, this is less likely to happen if the researcher is operating covertly, but just by being there they will have some effect on the interaction that takes place.

> Reliability and validity – Critics have pointed out that there is no way of knowing objectively whether the findings of participant observation are reliable and valid or not, as it is not possible to replicate the research, and the interpretations rely very much on the individual researcher. The findings rely upon the selective memory of the researcher (they cannot possibly remember everything) and the way they choose what they consider to be significant. Ultimately, it is just one person's interpretation and somebody else might see things very differently.

> Representativeness – Participant observation is usually used to study small groups of people who are not typical of the wider population (you have to study people who are gathered in one place). It is therefore difficult to claim that the findings can be generalised across the population as a whole.

Positivists therefore argue that the data from participant observation is subjective, unrepresentative, and unreliable because it is impossible to replicate. The data itself is contaminated by the presence of the researcher, so from their point of view, it is not a valid research method for a subject which they see as scientific.

Non-participant observation

Some researchers prefer to withdraw from participation and merely to observe.

Advantages of non-participant observation

> Bias – As the researcher is less likely to be drawn into the group, their views are less likely to be biased by becoming too involved in the group or **going native**.

> Influencing the group – As the researcher is not making any decisions or joining in with any activities, the group may be less influenced than in participant observation.

Disadvantages of non-participant observation

> Superficiality – The whole point of participant observation is to be a member of the group and experience life as the group experiences it. Merely observing leaves the researcher on the outside and may limit their understanding.

> Altering behaviour – People may well act differently if they know they are being watched and in many situations it is not possible to observe without explaining why you are there.

Evaluate the view that what participant observation lacks in reliability it makes up for in validity.

Going native involves the researcher becoming primarily a member of the group they are studying rather than an observer. There is a risk that a researcher who goes native becomes so immersed in the social group that they can no longer stand back and analyse the group impartially; instead, their research uncritically accepts the attitudes, values and understandings of those being studied. Of course, individual group members might understand their social groups well, but most researchers believe that their understanding can also be distorted, for example, by self-interest and justifications they give for their own poor behaviour. If the researcher becomes 'one of them', they may be unable to see beyond these sorts of biased viewpoints.

QUALITATIVE INTERVIEWING

Informal, unstructured interviews

Interviewing techniques are discussed in some detail in Chapter 5, but it is worth stressing here that informal or unstructured interviewing is a very important part of qualitative research. The aim of informal interviews is to allow the interviewee to provide descriptions and explanations of their behaviour and social worlds in their own words and in their own way. They often try to focus on a particular issue with one person and to guide them into explaining how they perceive that issue. It is useful to view such an interview as a sort of 'controlled conversation'. Qualitative interviews tend to use open questions, which allow the respondent to talk in some depth, and to choose their own words.

Sometimes, the conversations are recorded (with the respondent's permission) and the sociologist listens again to the interview and makes notes at a later stage. If a large number of interviews are conducted, sociologists tend to use special software that analyses conversations and collects words or themes that recur.

Interviews can also be used to supplement data produced through participant observation, allowing the researcher to explore areas of social life that they have not been able to witness. For example, they can discuss past events or events that occur in private, which could not be accessed through participant observation. However, interviews can only be used in conjunction with participant observation if the research is at least partly overt (otherwise they would be unable to explain why they wanted to carry out an interview).

One of the main advantages of unstructured, qualitative interviews is that they allow a person to talk in depth about their views and it is often possible to get a real sense of a person's understanding of a situation. Often new ideas are generated, which the researcher had not previously thought of. Interpretivists generally favour this type of interviewing over questionnaires or highly structured interviews, because they allow the interviewee to report on their motives for behaving in particular ways and the ways in which they interpret and give meaning to the world around them.

These sort of internal and unobservable parts of human consciousness are seen by positivists as beyond the scope of sociology – they don't believe that scientific research can study things where you can't observe and check independently what a person says. Furthermore, data from unstructured interviews doesn't easily lend itself to statistical analysis (unless the responses are coded (see Chapter 5), so it is difficult to generalise from them.

FOCUS ON RESEARCH: GANG LEADER FOR THE DAY

The 'projects' in Chicago where the research was conducted

Sudhir Venkatesh (2009) was a young researcher who started trying to do questionnaire research into Black drug gangs in the housing blocks (or 'projects' of Chicago). He ventured into the projects armed with a questionnaire, but was soon surrounded and himself questioned by members of a gang, the Black Kings, who called their leader, J.T., to decide what to do. Fortunately for the researcher, J.T. decided that he would allow Sudhir Venkatesh to study his gang, and the two men became close friends during the research. However, Venkatesh rapidly abandoned the idea of using questionnaires and instead carried out a participant observation study. It allowed him to get something of an insider's into one of the most deprived and crime-prone African-American housing projects on the Southside of Chicago. The Black Kings was a major gang that received most of its income from dealing in crack cocaine and other drugs. Venkatesh was not fully open with J.T. about the purpose of the research, letting him believe that he would write his biography. However he sometimes shared information with J.T., who occasionally used it to demand money from people who had told the researcher about their earnings. Venkatesh did not report the many illegal activities he witnessed, including drug dealing, violence and police corruption, believing that it

was more important to protect his sources than to report law-breaking.

Venkatesh got involved in the activities of the gang to some extent, on one occasion even kicking somebody during a fight. He also took up J.T.'s offer to be 'gang leader for a day' – as J.T. wanted him to appreciate that decision-making wasn't always easy for a gang leader. Venkatesh ended up sympathising with the residents, not only those who were the victims of the drug gangs, but also those who were members of the gangs. As well as showing the violence, he reveals a complex economic system and close-knit community, and he found that in some respects the Black Kings made a positive contribution to the community. He also found evidence of corruption in the police force.

Venkatesh is dismissive of the research of sociologists who rely more on quantitative data, arguing that they simply cannot get close to understanding life in poor neighbourhoods.

Questions

1. Demonstrate an understanding of the evidence which shows that Venkatesh may have 'gone native' during his research.

2. Interpret and describe the practical problems faced by the researcher in carrying out his study.

3. Analyse the ethical issues involved in the conduct of this research.

4. For each ethical issue identified, evaluate the choices and justifications made by the researcher.

5. Venkatesh was only allowed by J.T. to study some aspects of life in the projects. Evaluate whether this makes his research invalid.

FOCUS GROUPS

Focus groups are one of the more common types of research now used in sociology. These groups consist of a group of people who are gathered together by the researcher and asked to discuss a particular issue. In many ways, focus groups can be seen as an informal group interview. The researcher leads with an introduction and then allows the group to discuss the particular issue.

The researcher should ensure that the discussion does not drift too far away from the desired research topic.

Focus groups can be very useful.

> They can provide insights into complex problems, although the researcher must be very careful not to 'lead' the group in any particular direction.

> They allow the participants to tease out responses from one another and allow the researcher to observe interaction.

> They can allow issues to be probed in depth, however, because responses and meanings are jointly constructed by those taking part, it is possible that some of the interviewees may be unduly influenced by more dominant members of the group.

An example of the use of focus groups is Carol Fuller's research into girls and their ambitions in British education (see Topic 1, Chapter 4). Another example is Themina Basit's study (2013) of the influence of parental attitudes on the education of British Asian pupils (see Topic 1, Chapter 3).

Politicians often use focus groups to help devise policies they think will be popular. They hope that because people have had a chance to discuss them, the policies will be seen as reasonable. Is this a good use of focus groups or should politicians work out what policies would work best for themselves?

OBSERVATION AND PARTICIPANT OBSERVATION IN THE EDUCATIONAL CONTEXT

The uses of observational methods

Observational methods have been widely used in studying education, particularly non-participant observation. This is largely because it is difficult for researchers – who are older than pupils at schools or colleges – to blend in and act as students. However, young researchers (such as Paul Willis in his 1977 study of the 'lads' – see Topic 1, Chapter 1) may be able to 'hang around' with those they are studying and participate to some extent in activities outside the classroom. Most observation in schools is carried out in a fairly informal way. For example, David Hargreaves (1967), in a pioneering study, observed teachers and pupils in secondary school without using a formal structure.

Some sociologists have conducted structured observation using the Flanders Interaction Analysis categories that classify interaction in classrooms into one of 10 types, so

that researchers can time the frequency and length of different types of interaction. For example, interaction might involve a teacher asking a directed question, a pupil answering a question or pupils working on their own. Unlike most types of observation and participant observation, this type of observation tends to be favoured by those sympathetic to positivist views on methodology – as the data can be quantified, statistical patterns analysed and the research can be replicated and checked for reliability.

Although many of the general practical, ethical and theoretical issues of observational research apply to education, there are also some specific issues that relate to an educational context.

Practical issues

Like other research methods in education, there may be issues of access resulting from the requirement to obtain permission to carry out research. This is particularly problematic given that you may need to get permission from many different sources (such as teachers, pupils, parents, head teachers or even local authorities). Furthermore, the role of the observer is problematic in schools since the researcher is likely to be older than the children being observed. It is difficult for the researcher to blend in and to be accepted by all the groups involved, so observation in educational settings may require lengthy planning. Observational research is likely to be time-consuming and therefore expensive, and there are practical issues about when and how field notes are recorded. Video recording can overcome this problem, but it makes getting consent from everyone involved that much more difficult. One way to counteract these problems is to use structured observation, which makes it easier to record large amounts of standardised data. However, this risks losing some depth and thereby creating theoretical problems.

Ethical issues

The covert observation of children by adults is unlikely to be seen as ethically acceptable, and this is one reason why it is very rarely done. Indeed the presence of strangers in schools is tightly regulated and it may be necessary to get a Disclosure and Barring Service (DBS) check before it is regarded as ethically acceptable for researchers to even be in the school. Researchers may also face ethical dilemmas if they become aware of rule-breaking behaviour by children and they may have to put confidentiality above disclosure. If such behaviour is discussed in the research report, it is important to guarantee anonymity. Indeed the careers and reputations of individual teachers and managers, and the reputation of schools, may be harmed (or enhanced) if the research is unsuccessful in maintaining anonymity.

Theoretical issues

The validity of observational research in education may be compromised by the Hawthorne effect. This is where the presence of the researcher strongly influences the behaviour of those being observed. It may be impossible for researchers to blend into the background so they are particularly likely to influence the behaviour of teachers being observed, who may see the observer as being like an inspector. For example, Hargreaves (1967) noticed that some teachers appeared to change their lessons when he was present. Talking to some of the pupils, he was told that their teachers acted quite differently from normal when they were being observed.

Both teachers and pupils may act unnaturally and be guarded in their behaviour with the observer present. This is partly because both can be subject to unwelcome scrutiny by those in authority (for example, inspections and lesson observations) and they can be wary with outsiders present. Furthermore, the characteristics of the researcher, such as their age or ethnic group, might affect the results and the willingness and ability of the participants to act naturally.

On the other hand, observation could be seen as more valid than other research methods as it does involve actual behaviour in real social settings (classrooms, staffrooms playgrounds, and so on). There is simply no other way of seeing what really goes on in schools, colleges and universities, and for this reason it is generally supported as a highly desirable research method by interpretivist sociologists.

(For a discussion of qualitative interviewing in an educational context, see Chapter 5.)

FOCUS ON SKILLS: REVIEW OF *EDUCATING YORKSHIRE*

New series *Educating Yorkshire* aired at 9pm last night on Channel 4. A follow on from the previous successes of the Bafta nominated *Educating Essex* in 2011.

As advertised this honest and more than occasionally funny, fly-on-the-wall documentary shows a typical northern school.

New head teacher, Mr Mitchell is our guide over the course of the new term at Thornhill Community Academy near Dewsbury.

Within minutes a year 10 pupil, Bailey, has been caught smoking and we are treated to an example of Mr Mitchell's new brand of discipline, a full day in isolation. When asked, "What is isolation?" Bailey replied, "Death. Two boards and a wall and work". Sounds effective.

The series has been put together from over 2,000 hours of video footage in order to give a non-judgemental example of typical school life.

In some senses it is much like your usual natural history or wildlife programme, as you might find on The National Geographic. There are warring tribes such as school cliques and even watering hole scraps set in the school toilets.

Channel 4 is a veritable David Attenborough, merely observing nature, never interfering.

Source: Holman, J. (2013) 'Educating Yorkshire, Review', *The Yorkshire Times*, 6 September

Questions

1. **Explain**. What do you understand by the term 'fly-on-the-wall documentary'?

2. **Apply**. How can the idea of this type of documentary be applied to observational research?

3. **Analyse** the similarities and differences between this documentary and a wildlife programme.

4. **Evaluate** the view that an edited version of 2,000 hours of video footage can be objective and non-judgemental.

5. **Apply** your answer to question 4 to sociological observation and participant observation studies.

CHECK YOUR UNDERSTANDING

1. Explain the difference between covert and overt observation.

2. Explain the difference between participant and non-participant observation.

3. Explain two advantages and two disadvantages of being overt when conducting observational research.

4. Describe the way that a sociological researcher gained access to observe a social group in any one study mentioned in this chapter.

5. Give one example of a participant and one example of a non-participant observational study of education.

6. Give two reasons why a positivist would see participant observation as unscientific.

7. Give two reasons why an interpretivist would see participant observation as one of the most valid research methods.

8. Provide a definition of a focus group.

9. Briefly outline why unstructured interviews can be seen as a qualitative method of research.

10. With reference to any one observational study of education, explain an ethical, practical and theoretical issue specific to the study.

TAKE IT FURTHER

Carry out these two pieces of observation:

> Go to your local library. Spend one hour watching how people behave. Write down as accurate a description as you can.

> Spend an evening at home 'observing' your family. Write down as accurate a description of home behaviour that evening as you can.

Which study is likely to be more biased? Why? Does this make it any less accurate? Are you able to get greater depth studying your family? Why? Do you think it would make a difference if you operated in a covert rather than an overt way with your family?

2.5 ASKING QUESTIONS: QUESTIONNAIRES AND INTERVIEWS

LEARNING OBJECTIVES

> Understand the principles of using questionnaires and interviews in sociological research (AO1).

> Apply this understanding to researching in the context of education (AO2).

> Analyse and evaluate the strengths and weaknesses of questionnaires and interviews both in a general and in an educational context (AO3).

INTRODUCING THE DEBATE

How many times have you been asked questions in the last month? Who by? Have they been written or oral questions, and has anyone recorded your answers, or not? Asking and answering questions is a very common feature of social life and it is fundamental to much sociological research. This sort of research is based upon the assumption that people will be able to tell others about what they think or do in a way that produces worthwhile data. But of course you can't necessarily take everything that people say at face value. They might not tell the truth, they might not really know the answer or they might be influenced by the question, the questioner or how the question is phrased. Would a sociologist be able to rely on all the answers you give to questions? This chapter will help you decide how valuable questioning is for sociologists.

QUESTIONNAIRES

Questionnaires are used for reaching:

> a large number of people, because the forms can be handed out or distributed without much, if any, input from the researcher in the process of asking the questions

> a widely dispersed group of people, as they can be posted out, emailed or distributed through an online system such as *SurveyMonkey*.

Self-completion questionnaires are also less time-consuming for researchers than interviewing, as they do not require the researcher to go and talk to people in person.

Anonymous questionnaires are also very useful if the researcher wishes to ask potentially embarrassing questions about such things as sexual activities or illegal acts, or wishes to avoid influencing the answers through their presence. People are sometimes more likely to tell the truth if they can do so anonymously than if they have to face an interviewer.

Questionnaires – particularly those using closed questions – are a favourite method used by positivist sociologists (see Chapter 2), as they can be used in large numbers and the answers can be codified and subjected to statistical tests.

Producing questionnaires and types of question

All sociological questionnaires relate to concepts/and or theories that sociologists use to make sense of the world. For example, they might relate to theories such as cultural or material explanations of (the concept of) differential achievement (see Topic 1, Chapters 2–4). The theories and concepts have to be broken down into a series of questions that will allow the sociologist to collect data they think are relevant. In this process, concepts such as educational achievement are put into operation, or **operationalised**.

UNDERSTAND THE CONCEPT

In research, we need to use concepts such as ill health, sexual deviance and educational failure, but in a way that is valid and reliable. By this, we mean that the concepts are accurately measured (valid), and that each time we use them, we are sure that every respondent understands the concept in the same way (reliable).

When concepts are used in research, sociologists say that they are **operationalising** them. So, if there a piece of research is conducted in order to find out the levels of ill health among retired people, the concept of 'ill health' will need to be operationalised. The problem when operationalising a concept is how to ensure that it is accurately and reliably measured.

Ideas that are discussed in sociology, such as 'sexual deviance', 'educational failure', or 'ill health', are all quite vague. Take educational failure – does this mean not having A-level qualifications? Perhaps it means having 'low' grades at GCSE (whatever the concept 'low grades' means)? Or only having one or two GCSEs? You can see that a concept as apparently simple as 'educational failure' is actually capable of having different meanings to different people.

Sociologists have had to find a way around this problem when they ask people questions about the concepts. For example, if you were to ask somebody if they 'suffered from ill health', the reply would depend upon the individual definition of ill health and different people might (and in fact we know they *do*) use very different definitions of ill health.

There are many different types of questionnaire. They vary in the way in which they expect the person to answer the questions set. At one extreme are closed questionnaires, which have a series of questions with a choice of answers – all the respondent has to do is tick the box next to the most appropriate answer. At the other extreme are open questionnaires, which leave a space for the respondents' response. Some questionnaires contain a mixture of both open and closed questions.

Some of the advantages and disadvantages of these different types of question are summarised in Table 2.5.1.

Administering questionnaires

There are several different ways to administer questionnaires, each of which has particular advantages and disadvantages. They can be administered to respondents by a face-to-face interviewer (so they become a structured interview), by post, over the phone or through the internet. These different approaches can affect the **response rate**, the chances of the respondents being unduly influenced by the process (interviewer bias, which will be explored later in this chapter) and how practical it is to use questionnaires. Some of the advantages and disadvantages of the different ways of administering questionnaires are summarised in Table 2.5.2.

Type of question	Description	Advantages	Disadvantages
Closed	Respondents are given a restricted range of options to choose from, for example, agree, disagree, yes, no. Or they might use a ratings scale – rating something from 1 to 10.	This type makes it easy to produce statistical data and to analyse the answers. Positivists see the answers as social facts. It is good for testing existing theories and producing reliable data that can be checked.	There is no opportunity for respondents to clarify concepts or qualify views. It is generally poor for collecting information about feelings, meanings or motives. Not favoured by interpretivists.
Open-ended	Respondents are asked the question and then given a space in which to write whatever response they choose.	This type can produce more in-depth data and it is better for discovering complex feelings, meanings or motives. It is preferred to fixed-choice questions by interpretivists.	Answers need to be interpreted to understand the data, which makes it less objective. It is difficult and time-consuming to produce statistical data from the results. Less favoured than fixed-choice questions by positivists.

Table 2.5.1 *The advantages and disadvantages of closed and open-ended questions*

The advantages of questionnaires

Practical advantages

Questionnaires are a highly practical way to collect data. It is relatively easy to collect large amounts of data from a sizeable sample of people quite quickly. In the case of questionnaires that are not administered by individuals (for example, postal questionnaires), there is no need for a researcher to be present and therefore there is little personal involvement by researchers. Access to the subjects can be relatively easy. You can contact them in a number of ways and most people might be more willing to participate in a simple questionnaire than to agree to an in-depth interview or to be observed. If the questionnaire has fixed-choice questions, it can be very easy to analyse the data using computer programs in order to look for correlations and to see how strong statistical relationships are between different variables (for example, class and educational achievement).

Ethical advantages

There are no great ethical issues concerning the use of questionnaires. It can be quite easy to keep the identity of respondents secret (for example, they don't write their names on paper questionnaires that they hand back) and there is no way of conducting questionnaires covertly, so by filling them in, respondents are, in effect, giving consent. As in any research, it is important to be sensitive and not to harm respondents. However, because it is

UNDERSTAND THE CONCEPT

A **response rate** refers to the proportion of questionnaires that are returned or answered. It is important because you can never be sure whether those who do not return a questionnaire or refuse to take part are a typical of the population as a whole in some significant way. If they are, this can skew the results making them unrepresentative, so that any generalisations based on them are likely to be unreliable. For example, if anti-school pupils are less likely to return a questionnaire than pro-school pupils, then the results of questionnaire research on attitudes to school are likely to exaggerate how positive attitudes are towards school among pupils as a whole.

easy for respondents to decline, questionnaires are quite unlikely to have a negative effect compared to other research methods.

Theoretical advantages

Because the data from fixed-choice questions can be analysed statistically, positivists tend to favour this type of research method. Because everyone gets the same

Method of administering questionnaire	Main advantages	Main disadvantages
Face-to-face	A relatively high response rate. The interviewer can clarify questions if necessary.	The interviewer may influence responses (interviewer bias). It is time-consuming and therefore potentially expensive.
Telephone	Relatively cheap, and easy to access a geographically dispersed sample. There can be no interviewer bias resulting from seeing the interviewer.	The response rate may be low and this method is limited to questioning those with telephones. Respondents may be influenced by the voice of the interviewer.
Postal	Relatively cheap, and easy to access a geographically dispersed sample.	The response rate tends to be very low and those who do respond may be atypical of the population as a whole.
Internet	Very inexpensive and quick to send to a widely dispersed sample.	The response rate is likely to be low and limited to those with internet access.

Table 2.5.2 *Methods of a dministering questionnaires and their advantages/disadvantages*

questionnaire, they are responding to the same stimulus, and therefore differences in answers should reflect real differences between people. Once you have written a questionnaire, it can be reused and repeated in research which replicates the original data collection. You can therefore check the reliability of the results. Reliability is further enhanced by the ability to use large samples and, if you get people to cooperate and participate, to get results from a representative sample of the population. The sample need not be located in one geographical area (as they need to be in observational studies) and because a representative sample is usually possible, you may be able to generalise from the findings. Positivists believe that you can reveal not just correlations, but also causal relationships (and perhaps even laws) by analysing statistical data in a scientific way. From this point of view, questionnaires can be very useful both in producing new theories that can emerge from the statistical analysis and, more typically, testing theories that the questionnaires are being devised to evaluate. Although questionnaires are particularly favoured by those who see sociology as scientific, most sociologists would agree that they can be very useful for collecting straightforward factual data (such as the age or sex of members of social groups) where there is little interpretation required.

The disadvantages of questionnaires

Practical and ethical disadvantages
Questionnaires are probably the most straightforward of all research methods and therefore more practical than the other main methods. Certainly the practicalities of finding a sample, writing the questionnaire, and getting respondents to fill them in and return them present

challenges, but no more so than devising other research methods. Questionnaire research has to respect ethical guidelines, like any other research, but the ethics can be carefully considered in advance during the process of writing a questionnaire, so there are no particular ethical issues which are unique to questionnaires.

Theoretical disadvantages
Theoretical problems with questionnaires are often highlighted by interpretivists.

> They argue that even when people give different responses to questions they might not reflect real differences. Although the same questions are given to all individuals who take part, they might be interpreted differently. This means that the respondents are giving answers to different questions in terms of their understanding of them.

> The use of questionnaires assumes that the researcher knows what is important before they start the research. Many interpretivists argue that this means that the researcher is not trying to understand the social world from the point of view of those who live in it. Instead, they are imposing onto the social world their own priorities and preconceptions about how it works.

> It is difficult to develop new hypotheses from this sort of research because you can only get the information that you ask for. The operationalisation of concepts also distorts social worlds by shaping concepts in line with the researchers' rather than the respondents' meanings. For example, questions on religious or spiritual beliefs in a questionnaire might not get to the heart of what religion or spirituality means to a particular individual.

> The validity of the findings can be undermined by respondents who deliberately lie or who have a faulty memory. Even if respondents try to give honest answers when asked about their behaviour, they might not truly understand why they behave in particular ways. Sometimes an outsider, perhaps doing a combination of observation and interviewing, can gain a better understanding of a person's motives than that person themselves can give in answering simple questionnaire questions.

> Most of the theoretical problems with questionnaires stem from the fact that, in carrying them out, researchers are distant from their subjects, making it difficult to understand the social world from the subject's viewpoint.

> Interaction cannot be easily understood through questionnaires, so they don't really tell you about social life as it is actually lived.

Despite these disadvantages, questionnaires are frequently used in sociological research, both because of their immense practicality and because nearly all sociologists accept that they can be useful for collecting simple information.

INTERVIEWS

Structured and unstructured interviews

Interviews can be defined as one or more researchers asking questions to one or more respondents.

Interviews can have different degrees of structure depending on the extent to which the questions are pre-determined or emerge during the interview. Unsurprisingly, interpretivists favour more unstructured interviews (which give more leeway to the respondents), whereas positivists tend to favour more structured interviews (which are much more like questionnaires with the questions asked by a person rather than handed out on paper, or sent in emails). Researchers can compromise between these two extremes by using a partly structured interview, where they may have some prepared questions but think of others as they go along, or they may have a list of topics to cover but no fixed questions. The advantages and disadvantages of the different types of interview are summarised in table 2.5.3.

Degree of structure in interview	Advantages	Disadvantages
Structured – pre-set questions are asked in the same order without variation.	Favoured by quantitative researchers because it is easier to replicate and compare results, and there is less chance of interviewer bias.	There is no opportunity to probe deeper, so it is hard to discover what is important to the respondents. There is less chance of discovering new hypotheses than in some other types of research.
Partly structured — there is list of topics to be covered, for example, or there are some fixed questions.	Provides some opportunity for respondents to lead the interviews while ensuring the main topics are covered.	They lack the specific advantages of both structured and unstructured interviews.
Unstructured – there are few or no fixed questions; the interview is more like a conversation.	Favoured by qualitative researchers, because they allow respondents to direct the interview and provide more opportunity for developing new hypotheses than structured interviews.	They are hard to replicate, time-consuming, it is difficult to compare interviews and they may go off-track. You might need to **code** the answers if you want to base statistics on them, which takes time and requires interpretation.

Table 2.5.3 *Degrees of structure in interviews and their advantages/disadvantages*

FOCUS ON SKILLS: PARENTS AND MATHEMATICALLY GIFTED CHILDREN

A study by Brenda Bicknell (2014) examined the role of parents in contributing to the education of their mathematically gifted children. The study was conducted in New Zealand. The researcher identified 15 mathematically gifted children and decided to use unstructured questionnaires addressed to the parents, along with unstructured interviews with them, and they also examined secondary sources on school policies relating to gifted children. They interviewed the parents while their children were in their final year at primary school and after their children had moved on to secondary schools. For each question, the parent was asked to strongly agree, agree, disagree or strongly disagree. The answers were then scored so that each parent (or couple) was rated in terms of how far they acted as 'Motivator', 'Resource provider', 'Monitor', 'Maths content advisor' and 'Maths learning counsellor'. There were 23 questions in total, some examples of which are given below, along with an indication of which parental characteristics they were trying to measure.

Questionnaire

Participants were asked to respond to the following statements with Strongly agree, Agree, Disagree or Strongly disagree.

1. When my child says he/she is having trouble learning mathematics, I tell him/her not to worry about it because everybody has problems with mathematics. (Motivator question)

2. At home, I encourage my child to work hard on mathematics problems even though the problems are difficult. (Motivator question)

3. I try hard to have a nice learning environment at home for my child to do mathematics. (Resource provider question)

4. I often buy mathematics related books for my child. (Resource provider question)

5. I check my child's homework regularly. (Monitor question)

6. I always try to monitor the amount of time my child spends on mathematics at home. (Monitor question)

7. I feel I can help my child solve problems from mathematics class. (Maths content advisor question)

8. I often discuss with my child how mathematics is used in our everyday life. (Maths content advisor question)

9. I don't know strategies for helping my child overcome weaknesses in mathematics. (Maths learning counsellor question)

10. I always try to figure out good approaches for helping my child learn different mathematics topics. (Maths learning counsellor question)

Source: Bicknell (2014)

Questions

1. **Explain**. Based on the questions, explain what you understand by each of the categories 'Motivator', 'Resource provider', 'Monitor', 'Maths content advisor' and 'Maths learning counsellor'.

2. **Assess** how the concept of operationalisation is applied in this study. What was being operationalised and how?

3. **Analyse** the reasons why a positivist would approve of the use of this questionnaire to study this particular topic.

4. **Analyse** the reasons why an interpretivist would claim that the unstructured interviews with parents would be more useful.

5. **Evaluate** the strengths and weaknesses of this research by suggesting three strengths and three weaknesses for studying this specific topic.

133

UNDERSTAND THE CONCEPT

In any research where respondents can say or write what they like (for example, in unstructured interviews or questionnaires with open-ended questions), it is difficult to analyse the data. People can go off at all sorts of tangents and write (or talk) about a wide variety of things, some of which may not be relevant to the research. If you want to analyse the data systematically or produce statistics (as positivists might), you will need to decide on a number of categories into which you can place the answers. This process is known as **coding**.

Coding

To illustrate the idea of coding, suppose you asked an open-ended question on a questionnaire or in an interview asking school pupils to explain the things that they like most about their school. Some might talk about the teachers, or a specific teacher, friends, particular lessons, different activities or things that you might not have thought of (maybe the smell of the school or the plants in the school garden). In order to produce statistics, the researcher will have to devise a set of categories that include all the different answers and allow researchers to put them in one category or another. Interpretivists tend to be in favour of more unstructured questions, while positivists would prefer to be able to produce statistics, so by having open questions and coding them you can take elements from both approaches. However, interpretivists might see this as imposing the researcher's own categories on the data and not being true to what the individual said, while positivists might see it as relying too much upon the interpretation of the individual researcher.

Coding is therefore always open to question but it does allow you to make sense of a mass of unstructured data. Whether coding answers or not, the researcher has to do some interpretation of this type of information in order to write up results that will make sense to the audience who reads them. Coding may be a relatively reliable way to do this.

Do you think the coding of answers distorts the results of questionnaire research, and is there a better way of interpreting the answers to open-ended questions?

Interviewing styles

As well as different types of interview, there are also different styles of interviewing, which sometimes reflect different theoretical viewpoints. Most interviewers use a non-directive form of interviewing: the interviewer offers no opinions of their own and does not express approval or disapproval of the responses of those being interviewed. Most sociologists regard this as being the most objective way to interview people (particularly those such as positivists, who want sociology to be scientific). It is thought that this style of interviewing reduces the chance of **interviewer bias**, in which the responses are influenced by the presence of the interviewer. If respondents are unaware of the opinions of the interviewer, it is more difficult for them to give the answers they think the interviewer wants to hear.

UNDERSTAND THE CONCEPT

Interviewer bias occurs when the interviewer affects the responses given by the respondents, so that they are different from the answers that would be given with another interviewer present. It can come about in quite a number of ways and some possible sources of interviewer bias are unavoidable, though the chances of some types occurring can be minimised with careful planning.

However, some interviewers advocate quite different styles. The interpretivist sociologist Howard Becker (1970) advocates more aggressive interviewing in which the statements of the interviewees are challenged. He believes that this can lead to getting closer to people's real opinions. For example, in interviewing Chicago school teachers he used this style to uncover some racist feelings among the teachers, which he believed they would otherwise have kept hidden. The interview in this case can become a little like an interrogation.

BUILD CONNECTIONS

The aggressive interviewing style is linked with early attempts to uncover factors that influence labelling in classrooms (see Topic 1, Chapter 2). Teachers are not expected to discriminate against pupils on the basis of class, ethnicity, religion, sexuality or other such social characteristics, but that doesn't mean that they never do so. They are unlikely to admit their prejudices in a straightforward interview or questionnaire, because such prejudices are not generally seen as socially acceptable and, if known, might even threaten the teacher's job or career. Interpretivist sociologists such as Becker therefore had to devise methods that were quite unlike the scientific approach a positivist might use. Doing so allowed them to probe beneath what people might say in a straightforward interview.

An interesting variation on interviewing style is suggested by the feminist interviewer Ann Oakley (1981), an advocate of collaborative interviewing. In this style, the researcher befriends, advises and tries to help the interviewee: they collaborate with them. In this model, valid data emerges from the development of a relationship between the interviewer and the interviewee. The interviewee becomes fully involved in the research and even checks the research findings to see whether they correspond to their true feelings. Oakley sees this as the most valid and ethical type of interviewing: valid because she thinks more truthful data will result, and ethical because the researcher is not simply exploiting the interviewee for information to help further their own career – the interviewee benefits too.

Interviewer bias

Interviewer bias can result from the following factors.

> *The social characteristics of the interviewer.* The ethnicity, age, sex, physical appearance, accent and even the clothing haircut of the interviewer will have some influence on how the interviewee perceives them and could therefore affect interviewee responses. Based on such characteristics, the interviewee may make assumptions about the type of responses they think the interviewer would like to hear, and change their answers accordingly (even if they don't do this consciously). These factors can also affect how open the interviewee is. For this reason, the

possibility of interviewer bias in face-to-face interviews is unavoidable.

> *Leading the interviewee.* The interviewer may consciously or unconsciously direct the interviewee towards certain answers. They may ask leading questions in unstructured interviews (such as 'you don't like school, do you?') or their tone of voice and other forms of non-verbal communication (frowns, smiles, arm movements, and so on) may be interpreted as suggesting approval or disapproval of certain interviewee answers. This type of bias can be avoided to some extent by careful, well-trained interviewers.

> *Misunderstandings.* The interviewer is likely to influence the course of the interview if they misunderstand what the interviewee is trying to say, either forcing them to explain themselves more, or perhaps directing the conversation in a particular direction. This is less likely if the researcher and interviewee have similar characteristics; for example, if they are a similar age.

Can you ever completely eradicate interviewer bias? Can you rely solely on interview data when conducting sociological research?

Individual or group interviews

A final choice that interviewers have to make is whether to interview individuals or to interview a group of several people together. Table 2.5.4 shows that there are different advantages and disadvantages for each type of interview and demonstrates that there is no perfect way to conduct an interview.

The advantages and disadvantages of interviews

Type of interview	Advantages	Disadvantages
Individual	This type prevents respondents from being influenced by other interviewees and it is generally less time-consuming than group interviews.	There is no opportunity to observe the interaction of different people (which makes an individual interview less like normal social life).
Group	The interviewer can observe interaction, and it encourages deeper thought about issues and more developed answers. It is closer to normal social life than more formal interviews.	Respondents may be influenced by the desire to conform to the views of others (especially dominant people in the group interview). They may therefore not say what they really feel.

Table 2.5.4 *Advantages and disadvantages of individual and group interviews*

The main advantages of interviews – practical, ethical and theoretical

As discussed above, there are specific advantages associated with particular types of interview (as shown in Tables 2.5.2–4), and the advantages and disadvantages vary according to the type of interview being discussed. At a practical level, interviews are a very flexible research method and so they are used by a variety of sociologists who have different theoretical approaches to methodology.

Ethically, it is hard to conduct interviews in secret, but it may be important to guarantee anonymity. Interviews are not really the ideal method for positivists or interpretivists, but are useful to both. For example, quantitative researchers, such as positivists, prefer interviews to participant observation – because larger samples can be used, statistical data can be produced with the coding of answers, and the research can be replicated to increase reliability. On the other hand, qualitative researchers, such as interpretivists, prefer interviews to questionnaires because concepts can be clarified, and there is more opportunity for respondents to express ideas in their own way, say what is important to them and explore issues in depth, than there is in a questionnaire.

However, perhaps the main advantages of interviews for sociologists of all types is their practicality and flexibility. Interviews can examine past, present or future behaviour, peoples' feelings, opinions and attitudes, or simple factual information. They can be as in-depth or as superficial as the researcher wants. They are also very useful for studying groups who might not return questionnaires or consent to participant observation (for example, Laurie Taylor (1984) studied professional criminals using interviews). But there are a few sociologists who are particularly keen on interviewing. To feminists such as Ann Oakley (1981), interviews have theoretical advantages because they provide space and time for critical reflection, collaboration and interaction between interviewer and interviewee. This means that interviewees can check the interpretations of the researcher, and the personal relationship between the two can develop in a non-exploitative way.

The main disadvantages of interviews

Despite their undoubted strengths and practicality, there are some significant disadvantages to interviews as a research method. In terms of ethics, it is important to handle with care interviews on sensitive issues that might psychologically affect the interviewees. For example, interviews asking respondents to recall traumatic events should perhaps be avoided unless they are essential to the research and the researcher has the appropriate training.

Theoretically, as with questionnaires, the validity of interview data may be affected by respondents being untruthful. Even where people wish to tell the truth, their answers can be affected by having faulty memory or not fully understanding their own behaviour. People may also have reinterpreted past events in the light of later experience, so they may not give the real reasons for their behaviour at the time. The presence of the researcher may also influence answers (interviewer bias). This can happen in a variety of ways. For example, interviewers may consciously or unconsciously lead respondents towards preferred answers. Another possibility is that social factors such as ethnicity may influence the sort of answers members of different social groups are willing to give to the person asking the questions.

For these reasons, the findings of interview research should always be approached with some caution. However, despite their imperfections, the practicality and flexibility of interviews makes them attractive to researchers using different theoretical perspectives, and they are widely used. Hammersley and Gomm (2004) believe that interview data should be handled carefully but that it remains useful when combined with other methods.

136

FOCUS ON RESEARCH: STEPHEN FROSH *ET AL.* (2002) AND THE YOUTH LIFESTYLES STUDY

Stephen Frosh et al. (2002)

Stephen Frosh wanted to find out how boys in the early years of secondary school arrived at an idea of what masculinity means to them and how this impacted upon their behaviour and their learning. Frosh undertook two main types of qualitative research: group interviews/focus groups and informal interviews. In total, 78 boys were interviewed.

Each interviewer was given a list of topics and possible questions to guide them through the interview. This is a perfect example of qualitative, semi-structured interviewing methods. All the answers were recorded and then transcribed, and the researchers looked for the key themes that emerged.

General self-description

› Could you tell me three things you think are important about yourself?

Ethnicity

› What ethnic group do you think you belong to?

› Do you see some boys as belonging to a different ethnic group to you? How would you describe their background? Do you go around with boys from this/these backgrounds? Why/why not? Do you do the same things with them as boys from your 'own' ethnic background?

› Can you imagine having a girlfriend from a different ethnic group?

› Do you think boys are treated differently because of where their parents come from? Is your ethnic background important to you? What difference does it make being a boy from this background? Are you pleased you are from this background?

› Have you ever thought you'd not like to be?

› Are there things you dislike about boys from other ethnic and cultural backgrounds?

› Are there things you admire about boys from other ethnic and cultural backgrounds?

Source: Frosh *et al. (2002)*

Youth Lifestyles Survey

The following questions were taken from a quantitative study into bullying by young people. It was part of a Home Office national survey and was completed by 4,800 people between the ages of 12 and 30.

Would you say that students are bullied by other students …

a a lot   **b** a little   **c** or not at all?

In the last 12 MONTHS, have you been bullied by other students?

a Yes   **b** No

If yes … how often has this happened in the last 12 months?

a Every day   **e** Once a month

b A few times a week   **f** Less often than this

c Once or twice a week   **g** It varies

d Once every two weeks

In the last 12 months, have other students made you give them money or your personal possessions?

a Yes   **b** No

Source: Youth Lifestyles Survey, Home Office (1998–1999)

Questions

1. Compare the questions in the two extracts.

2. What are the advantages and disadvantages of each type of questioning?

3. Which type of questioning do you think is more time-consuming? Why?

4. Which type of questioning do you think is likely to lead to greater reliability? Explain your answer.

5. Which type of questioning do you think is likely to lead to greater validity? Explain your answer.

6. Explain how bias might possibly creep into this form of research interview.

QUESTIONNAIRES IN THE CONTEXT OF EDUCATION

Questionnaire research has been used in a wide variety of contexts, including studying:

› the impact of parental attitudes to achievement (for example, J.W.B. Douglas, 1964)

› the impact of class on cultural capital and achievement (for example, Alice Sullivan, 2001)

› the choice of Higher educational institution (Reay *et al.*, 2005).

Alice Sullivan (2001) collected data from 465 pupils in four schools using questionnaires. She asked questions about:

› the involvement of the children in cultural activities (for example, reading books, attending theatres and concerts)

› the parents' own educational achievements.

Her conclusion was that parental income helps to boost the educational performance of children independent of cultural factors.

Practical issues

In some ways, questionnaire research is relatively easy to conduct in educational settings, because the existence of sampling frames such as lists of pupils and staff makes it possible to choose random samples. It is also relatively easy to access large numbers of suitable respondents concentrated in particular places (for example, schools). If you want greater geographical dispersal of the sample, you can include schools from different areas. Once you have consent from the school, you are likely to get quite a high response rate, especially if you hand the questionnaires out in class – you have in effect a captive audience. It may be more difficult to get questionnaires back from parents though. Questionnaires make it possible to gather large amounts of straightforward information relatively quickly and cheaply in educational settings. However, researchers are limited in the questions that they can ask to young children and older children with poor literacy skills, and schools may be unhappy with researchers asking questions on sensitive subjects.

Ethical issues

The main ethical problem when researching is maintaining the anonymity of respondents, particularly if the questionnaires deal with sensitive issues. It is also important that schools are kept anonymous because they would be very unhappy with any research which damaged their reputation, and it might even lead to job losses in the school if the school became less popular. There may also be a problem with getting truly informed consent from young children and ensuring that you get consent from everyone you need to, especially if you are distributing a large number of questionnaires.

Theoretical issues

Apart from the general theoretical issues of questionnaires, a particular problem might be the influence of peer groups within education, which may influence the types of answer which pupils give. As a small, relatively enclosed community, it may be difficult to prevent discussion among pupils of the questionnaires and the responses they think appropriate, which could distort the findings. Children may be particularly prone to deliberately making up misleading answers 'for a laugh', which could undermine the validity of questionnaire findings. Parents and teachers filling in questionnaires may tend to provide socially acceptable answers rather than saying what they truly think.

THE USE OF INTERVIEWS IN EDUCATIONAL CONTEXTS

Interviews have been used to study a wide range of educational topics. For example, Paul Willis (1977) used group interviews with the 'lads' who formed an anti-school subculture to understand their attitudes towards school, other pupils, teachers and careers (see Topic 1, Chapter 1). Stephen Frosh *et al.* (2002; see Focus on Research) used interviews with 78 boys in secondary school to collect data on their attitudes towards masculinity and how this affected their educational progress.

Practical issues

Like the use of questionnaires, interviewing children in schools requires consent from head teachers and parents. This may limit access and those in authority may wish to restrict the scope of the interview. Interviewers may also be required to undergo a DBS check, which you don't need in order to send out questionnaires to children. Interviews with children must be carefully designed because children have less developed language skills than adults and may not be able to concentrate for as long. Questions therefore need to be phrased in simple language and interviews should be kept short. However, interviews are generally a practical research method and it is possible to question children on a very wide range of issues. If interviews are unstructured, you have considerable opportunity to explain anything the children do not understand. Interviewing parents and teachers is more straightforward in some ways, but finding the right time and place to conduct interviews and getting interviewees to agree to take part can cause problems.

Ethical issues

Interviews with children must be carefully designed so that they do not cause distress or fatigue. They should therefore be short and avoid issues that may be sensitive to the children. Furthermore, the confidentiality of interviews needs to be assured, although if the interview reveals evidence of abuse, interviewers have a duty to report it, thus compromising confidentiality. Interviewers are in a difficult moral position if they are unsure whether something reported to them is an example of abuse they should report. They could do a good deal of harm if a parent or teacher ends up being investigated when they have done nothing wrong, but on the other hand the risks of not reporting abusive behaviour might be greater.

Theoretical issues

The validity of interview responses may be affected by the way in which the interview is conducted and by interviewer bias. Interviewees may see the interviewer as an authority figure, like a teacher, and therefore be unwilling to give full and frank answers. In group interviews, there is a risk of the responses being influenced by peer group pressure, although they may also be useful for drawing out the shared values that individual pupils might be reluctant to express (for example, Paul Willis's study). Children change quite rapidly as they pass through school, and it may be difficult for them to look back at past events and to give a clear

explanation of why they behaved in a particular way at that time. The responses of teachers in interviews may be affected by the considerable professional scrutiny they are under (for example, lesson observations, inspections and performance reviews). This may make them cautious and guarded in interviews and less likely to open up to outsiders than some other groups.

Pupils and students are often given questionnaires about their education. Evaluate the view that in-depth interviews with pupils or students would be much more effective than questionnaires in helping education managers to improve the education they were offering.

CONCLUSIONS

Whatever their limitations, questionnaires and interviews are certainly among the most frequently used types of research in educational settings. There is no doubt that they have proved immensely valuable in producing both qualitative and quantitative data for researchers, and it is probably true that the majority of studies use at least one of these methods. While neither method is perfect, much sociological research could not be carried out without using one or other of them. There is a limit to what can be observed, and to the issues that you can conduct experiments on. Furthermore, it is impossible to rely upon secondary sources on many issues because the information may simply not exist. Nevertheless, as we shall see in the next chapter, secondary sources can be very valuable for sociologists studying the topic of education and indeed those studying many other topics as well.

CHECK YOUR UNDERSTANDING

1. Explain what is meant by operationalising concepts.

2. Suggest one advantage and one disadvantage of using open as opposed to closed questions in a questionnaire.

3. Suggest one advantage and one disadvantage of using emails rather than distributing questionnaires directly to individuals.

4. Explain what is meant by the coding of answers.

5. Identify and explain four reasons why interpretivists would criticise questionnaires with closed questions as a research method for studying the labelling of pupils in schools.

6. Explain three ways in which interviewer bias can take place.

7. Explain what is meant by a semi-structured interview and give two examples of ways in which interviews can be semi-structured.

8. Identify and explain one advantage and one disadvantage of using groups as opposed to individual interviews.

9. Suggest two reasons why the validity of data from interviews with head teachers might be questionable.

10. Identify and explain three reasons why it might be useful to combine interviews and questionnaires for studying ideas about masculinity amongst male pupils.

TAKE IT FURTHER

In pairs or groups, devise a short questionnaire of around 10 questions to find out why students at your school or college chose to continue their education by studying A-levels. Also, devise an unstructured interview by identifying six issues you think you should cover in an interview on the same topic.

Now give the questionnaire to three people and conduct short unstructured interviews with three people on the same topic. Analyse and write up the findings in a short report. Compare the data you got from each source. What were the strengths and weaknesses of each? How reliable and valid was each type of data? Reach a conclusion about which of these methods you would choose if you were going to conduct a larger-scale study of this topic using just one method.

2.6 SECONDARY SOURCES OF DATA

LEARNING OBJECTIVES

> Understand the principles of using secondary sources in sociological research (AO1).

> Apply this understanding to researching in the context of education (AO2).

> Analyse and evaluate the strengths and weaknesses of secondary sources both in a general and in an educational context (AO3).

INTRODUCING THE DEBATE

Not all research uses primary sources – that is, where the sociologist collects original data, for example, by observing people in real life, sending out questionnaires or carrying out interviews. Many sociologists prefer to use material collected and published by other people. This material is known as secondary data.

Secondary data consists of a very wide range of material collected by organisations and individuals for their own purposes. They may be quantitative, qualitative, or a mixture, and may be personal or produced for large organisations. Thus they can range from official government statistics to personal material such as diaries or Facebook posts or tweets. This data includes written material, sound and visual images. Such material can be from the present day or it can be historical data. Finally, and most commonly, secondary sources include the work of sociologists, which is read, analysed and commented on by other sociologists (although this chapter will focus on other types of secondary sources).

Secondary sources are invaluable to sociologists. References to the work of other sociologists feature in nearly all sociological research, and most also make some use of other existing sources of data.

WHY SOCIOLOGISTS USE SECONDARY SOURCES

Some of the main reasons for using secondary sources include the following points.

> The information required already exists as secondary data, so this saves time and money conducting expensive primary research.

> Many secondary sources include data that is beyond the means of sociologists to collect because of the scale or scope (e.g. census data).

> Secondary sources allow the study of societies in the past for which it is impossible to produce primary sources because possible respondents are too elderly or are no longer alive.

> The researcher is unable for financial or other reasons to visit places to collect data at first hand.

> The subject of the research concerns illegal activities and it is unsafe for the researcher to collect primary data.

> Data needs to be collected about groups who are unwilling to provide accounts of their activities – for example, extreme religious sects or the very rich, who may not want their activities to be open to study.

PROBLEMS AND LIMITATIONS OF SECONDARY SOURCES

Whenever sociologists use a secondary source, they must be aware that the person who first created the source did so for a specific reason, and this could well create bias. A diary, for example, gives a very one-sided view of what happened and one that is most likely to be sympathetic. Official statistics may have been constructed to shed a positive light on the activities of the government – for example, so that they can claim they are improving the economy. They may not include the data that sociologists are interested in and the data may have been collected without the rigour that sociologists would like. They may use categories or concepts that do not fit with sociological theories. Furthermore, the categories used may change, making comparisons over time difficult. For example, the government has changed definitions of poverty and unemployment, and exams change from time to time, making comparisons in levels of achievement problematic (for example, from O Level to GCSE). Even the work of previous sociologists may contain errors and biases and use concepts that later sociologists may not see as relevant and useful.

TYPES OF SECONDARY DATA

Sociologists commonly use all these types of secondary data:

> previous sociological research

> official publications, including statistics and reports

> diaries and letters

> novels and other works of fiction

> oral history and family histories

> the media

> documents relating to businesses, charities and pressure groups

> the content of the internet.

Previous studies as a starting point

Whenever sociologists undertake a study, the first thing they do is carry out a **literature search**. The sociologist can then see the ways in which the topic has been researched before, the conclusions reached and the theoretical issues thrown up.

UNDERSTAND THE CONCEPT

A **literature search** involves a search of the internet and/or libraries to look up the available sociological research on the topic of interest. It is easy to use search engines to find relevant journal articles, and references contained in books can provide useful clues about sources that are likely to be valuable. With the increasing digitalisation of academic research (for example, in online journals), literature searches are become quicker and, arguably, more thorough.

Armed with this information, the researcher can then construct the new research study to explore a different 'angle' on the problem, check the reliability of previous findings or simply avoid the mistakes made earlier. There are sometimes methodological errors in published research, as well as possible bias in the research findings, so they should always be used with caution. However, at least the methods used to collect the data are likely to be explicit and therefore open to scrutiny. Sometimes research can be replicated and repeated to highlight changes over time. Sociologists may also simply compile data from a wide variety of sources in order to produce a more comprehensive picture than that provided by any one study, or they may combine the findings of several studies in a **meta-analysis**. Often sociologists do not want to carry out a new research project, but prefer instead to examine previous research in great detail in order to find a new interpretation of the original research results. Secondary data then provides all the information that is needed.

UNDERSTAND THE CONCEPT

Meta-analysis involves the analysis of a range of existing studies. Rather than collecting their own original data, researchers compile all the studies on a relevant topic and analyse what the overall weight of evidence suggests. Very often a single study will have a sample which is too small to be able to produce decisive conclusions, but if there have been 10 or 20 studies in the same field, the combined sample might make it possible to make a much more reliable judgement. Sometimes studies are not exactly the same and therefore not strictly comparable, and this can create problems for meta-analysis. Nevertheless, it can be a very useful technique because it avoids reliance upon a single study, which could produce unrepresentative results.

Government statistics and reports

Government statistics cover a wide range of topics, including births, deaths, population size and migration (demography); crime; unemployment; educational achievement and participation; divorce; and so on. The government also conducts statistical surveys such as the Labour Force Survey. Since 1801 it has also carried out a **census** every decade.

Some sociologists admit that government statistics can be unreliable, but believe it is still possible to produce reliable and valid statistics. For example, they believe that reliable crime statistics can be produced if surveys are conducted to supplement the information collected by the police. An example of this is the Crime Survey for England and Wales, an annual social survey using questionnaires to ask households if they have been victims of crime.

UNDERSTAND THE CONCEPT

A **census** is an official enumeration of the population and of certain statistics relating to them. In the UK it happens every 10 years. A census form is distributed to every household and is supposed to provide comprehensive demographic information. You can be prosecuted for not filling in the census but some people still avoid completing it. Furthermore, you cannot guarantee that people give accurate answers. In the 2001 census, for example, thousands of people stated that their religion was Jedi Warrior, suggesting that some respondents deliberately mislead.

UNDERSTAND THE CONCEPT

By **social facts**, Durkheim meant objective, real features of society, particularly those which could be measured. For example, he saw rates of suicide, the religious beliefs of individuals, and statistics on marriage and on the economy as social facts. As a positivist he looked for patterns which linked social facts (correlations) in the search for causal explanations. As we will see below though, some interpretivists question the idea of social facts.

Interpretivist views of official statistics

From the interpretivist point of view, official statistics are not facts but merely an interpretation produced by government agencies. It is therefore impossible to produce objective, reliable and valid statistics. Interpretivists argue that all data requires classification and interpretation. For example, in crime statistics, the police, the Crown Prosecution Service, and courts all have considerable discretion in determining whether a crime has taken place and whether a particular individual has committed the crime. Some interpretivists regard all statistics on crime and deviance as invalid. They see them as simply the product of the categorisation procedures used to produce them (categorising some things as crimes but not others, or some events as suicides and others as accidental deaths). For example, Maxwell Atkinson (1978) sees suicide statistics as the product of coroners' assumptions about the sort of people who commit suicide. He states that whether a death is an accident, a murder or a suicide is often a matter of opinion and coroners use their 'common sense' to arrive at conclusions.

Such statistical sources are invaluable because they are easily accessible and much more thorough than any data sociologists could produce. The census is the only survey that tries to include the whole of the population, and participation is legally compulsory. However, not all government statistics are generally accepted as valid and reliable and there are a number of different sociological perspectives on them. These different perspectives are discussed below.

Positivist views of official statistics

Some positivists, such as Émile Durkheim (1970), regard official statistics as both valid and reliable. For example, he used suicide statistics, which he regarded as **social facts**, to investigate the causes of suicide. However, many official statistics are highly unreliable – for example, many crimes are not reported to, or are not recorded by, the police.

Do you agree with the interpretivist view of statistics? Are statistics facts, interpretations or something in-between? Does it depend on the type of statistic?

Radical views of official statistics

There is another view of official statistics, supported by radical sociologists such as Marxists, feminists and anti-racists, who are critical of inequality in society. They all agree that government statistics are systematically distorted by the powerful. For example, they believe that governments deliberately define poverty in such a way as to minimise the amount that is reported, thereby hiding the negative effects of capitalism. Similarly, the crimes of the powerful, such as those committed by big corporations, rarely appear in the statistics, but the crimes of the poor are frequently recorded. The statistics may exaggerate criminality of minority ethnic groups, since they are more likely to be picked on and arrested by the police than others, while crimes against women by men, such as domestic violence, are not taken seriously enough and rarely appear in the statistics.

BUILD CONNECTIONS

As the previous discussion implies, crime statistics are a crucial source in the sociology of crime and deviance. This is not just because they are interesting from a methodological point of view, but also because they are very important in understanding trends in crime and power in the criminal justice system (depending on your point of view). Some sociologists studying the topic of crime are just as interested in activities that are not classified as crimes but still do great harm (such as activities which contribute to climate change) as they are in what is currently defined as illegal. Radical criminologists often argue that laws themselves discriminate in favour of the most powerful groups.

Conclusions

Some statistics may be relatively reliable and valid. For example, death statistics are highly reliable since the vast majority of deaths are likely to be recorded, and they are valid since it is easy to classify whether someone is alive or not. Similarly, statistics on exam results are likely to be accurate (though whether they measure performance accurately is another matter). Some statistics are much less

reliable and valid, for example, crime statistics, because there is a large 'dark figure' of unrecorded crime and there is often considerable room for personal opinion in determining whether crime has taken place. Sociologists should therefore always be aware of possible sources of distortion or bias in official statistics. Official statistics are nevertheless very useful, even if they are imperfect, because they are often the best available data on a topic. They can often allow comparisons over time and provide data that sociologists would not have the time and money to collect (for example, census data).

Corporate criminals are less likely than working-class criminals to come to justice and radical sociologists believe the crimes of corporations are under-recorded.

Reports and government inquiries

The civil service and other linked organisations will often produce official reports that investigate important problems or social issues. However, although they draw together much information on these issues, they are constrained by their 'remit', which states the limits of their investigations. The government and other powerful bodies are therefore sometimes able to exclude discussion of issues that they do not want to become the centre of public attention. Government discussions on issues related to drugs, for example, are usually carefully controlled so that the legalisation of drugs is simply not discussed. The Chilcot Inquiry into the Iraq War was announced in 2009 but had still not reported at the start of 2015.

FOCUS ON SKILLS: THE EQUALITY AND HUMAN RIGHTS COMMISSION: *HOW FAIR IS BRITAIN?*

In 2010 the Equality and Human Rights Commission (EHRC) launched the study called How *Fair Is Britain*? The aim of the study was to try and identify whether there were equal opportunities in Britain or whether factors such as gender, class, ethnicity and age meant that some individuals had much greater opportunities than others. The study covered a wide range of issues including health, justice, employment and power, and also examined education. The Commission general did not carry out original research to produce the report but relied instead on existing research. For example, the chapter of the report on education used seven different sources, including the Youth Cohort's study, Office for National Statistics opinion surveys, data from the Higher Education Statistics Agency and from the Department for Education, and the Labour Force Survey.

One section covered participation in continuing education by adults. It used data produced by the following question in the Labour Force Survey:

'During the last 12 months have you participated in any of the following activities with the intention of improving your knowledge or skills in any area, including hobbies?

1. Lesson or course, either practical or theoretical including classroom instruction or lessons?

2. Courses conducted through open and distance education?

3. Seminars or workshops?

4. Guided on the job training?

5. None of these?

It then looked at the relationship between class, gender, ethnicity and age, and participation in lifelong learning. Other parts of the section on education compiled data on issues such as access to the internet, qualifications achieved both at school and in higher education, bullying and permanent exclusions from school.

Source: EHRC (2010)

Questions

1. **Explain**. Suggest why the Equality and Human Rights Commission decided to rely largely on existing studies in order to examine fairness in education.

2. **Analyse** the strengths and weaknesses of the question used on adult continuing education.

3. **Evaluate** the range of issues considered in the report. Can you think of any other inequalities in education that might also be important?

4. **Evaluate** Could this research have been improved by relying more upon primary sources? Suggest what additional primary research could have been collected to supplement the largely secondary sources used by the commission.

Qualitative secondary sources

Qualitative sources and documents

Sociologists don't just use quantitative secondary sources, they often also use qualitative secondary sources. These are any sources with a non-statistical content. Very often these sources take the form of various types of document: physical or digital material containing some data and/or images of interest to sociologists.

These may be public documents produced by organisations rather than individuals, for example, transcripts of proceedings in Parliament, statements issued by companies, or the content of publicly accessible websites. Alternatively they may be private documents produced by individuals, for example, emails, paintings, private photographs, diaries and letters. Public documents are generally intended to be available to the general public whereas private documents are not. Documents may also be contemporary or historical.

One source of data that researchers might use are the transcripts of prime minister's question time in the House of Commons. What use might this source be? How much would it tell you about party politics? Are there any other qualitative secondary sources you could use in addition to give a fuller picture of the workings of parliament?

Historical sources

Historical sources are vital for studying long-term social changes. Sociologists have made use of a great deal of classical sociology in order to explore how contemporary societies have developed. For example, Peter Laslett (1972, 1977) used parish records to show that industrialisation led to an increase in extended family households in Britain. Similarly Max Weber (1958) used religious tracts to study the relationship between religious belief and the development of capitalism.

A major problem with all historical sources is that only some have survived and there is no guarantee that these are representative. There tend to be few surviving documents produced by individuals, and very often the data that sociologists would like is not available. For example, the survival of diaries is likely to be haphazard and the people who take the trouble to keep a diary may be unusual. Qualitative sources reflect the subjective views of those who produced them. Sometimes this is still useful – for example, in Weber's work it was useful to know the ways in which members of religions thought, but the content of this type of source is not always so useful in providing accurate descriptions of society.

Life documents

Life documents are private documents created by individuals that record subjective states. They include diaries, letters, photos, biographies, memoirs, suicide notes, films, pictures, and so on.

They were used by early sociologists such as Thomas and Znaniecki (1919), who used letters and statements to study Polish peasants who had emigrated to the USA.

However, Plummer (1982) argues that personal documents are rarely used by contemporary sociologists, because surviving documents may not be representative. Furthermore, they tend to be highly subjective – the same events discussed in a document such as a diary might be described very differently by someone else involved. The content may also be influenced by the identity of the person or people intended to read the document (except in documents intended to remain private).Today there is also the problem that relatively few people keep diaries or write letters, but there has been a growth in material available on the internet.

Nevertheless, Plummer believes that life documents are still very useful because they allow insights into people's subjective states, and from an interpretivist point of view they can reveal the personal meanings and self-concepts of individuals that they see as shaping behaviour.

Novels and autobiographies

Novels can give an insight into the attitudes and behaviour of particular groups, especially if the author is drawn from one of those groups. They can help a sociologist to understand how the author views the social world around them. However, they are fiction and will exaggerate actions and values for the sake of the story. Also, writing books is typically a middle- or upper-class activity, which may limit the insight that can be gained about lower social classes. The same applies to some extent to autobiographies, but these do at least claim to be non-fiction. However, the authors may well be influenced by the type of audience they have in mind when writing, they may sensationalise events to encourage sales and they may be influenced by a desire to give a positive impression of themselves.

The media and content analysis

One of the most important sources of secondary data is the mass media. A huge amount of material is available from newspapers, the internet, magazines and television. In fact, so much material is available that one of the major problems with using the mass media as secondary data lies with the selection of material: on exactly what grounds are items included or excluded? Sociologists also have to be careful about bias within the media. Many newspapers, for example, support a particular political party, while magazines are often aimed at a specific audience. For these reasons, the content is likely to be biased towards a particular viewpoint. However, this can make the media useful as an object of study in its own right. A good deal of research is focused on analysing biases within the media.

For example, the Glasgow Media Group, one of the best-known research groups on the media in Britain, has analysed the bias in the reporting of a wide range of issues, including the economy, strikes, wars and coverage of the Palestinian–Israeli conflict in the Middle East. In their coverage of the latter issue (Philo and Berry, 2004), they found that TV news tends to give the impression that Palestinian and Israeli deaths are on a par, whereas in reality many more Palestinians have been killed in recent years than Israelis in the ongoing conflict. The news provides little background for the audience, so, for example, many people do not understand that Palestinian lands are being occupied and settled by the Israelis.

Research on the mass media tends to use one or more types of content analysis (an analysis of the content of the media). Content analysis can be either quantitative or qualitative, or a mixture of both. It could be as simple as counting the number of times a word is used in particular sources, or as complex as trying to understand the meaning behind the coverage of a particular theme.

Content analysis tends to be a relatively cheap research method, and media material is easily accessible so there are few problems with sampling or representativeness. There are also likely to be few ethical problems since the content of the media is freely available to the public. The main problem with analysing the media as a secondary source is the interpretation of the material. Table 2.6.1 describes some of the main types of content analysis, gives some examples of each and identifies some of the main advantages and disadvantages of these approaches.

The internet as a secondary source

Increasingly the internet is being used as a secondary source in a wide range of studies. Clearly, a vast range of both qualitative and quantitative data is available on the internet, and much of it can be accessed with unprecedented ease, often at no cost. Sometimes the internet is a convenient way of accessing information that might previously have been accessed in a physical rather than virtual form (for example, government reports) but there is also a mass of information that is produced specifically for the virtual world.

Type of content analysis	Description/example	Advantages	Disadvantages
Formal content analysis	Content is classified and counted. For example, Best (1993) counted gender roles of boys and girls in children's books.	Provides objective statistical data which positivists regard as social facts, allowing patterns to be uncovered.	The classification of data may be somewhat subjective and does not directly reveal the meaning behind the content.
Thematic analysis	Examines the message behind the portrayal of a particular topic. For example, Soothill and Walby (1991) studied rape coverage in newspapers.	Makes it possible to examine the messages behind media coverage in order to look for ideological bias.	Messages are open to interpretation. The audience may not interpret the content in the same way as the researchers.
Textual analysis	Involves the detailed analysis of small pieces of text. For example, the Glasgow Media Group (Beharrell, 1974) looked at the words used to describe managers and strikers.	Provides an in-depth interpretation of the content of the media.	Does not provide an overall analysis of the media content and is therefore rather subjective.

Table 2.6.1 *Types of content analysis and their advantages/disadvantages*

As discussed at the start of the chapter, this includes the content of social media. Wikis, blogs and webpages produced by organisations, media companies and governments can all be useful sources of data, either about the social world or for analysis in its own right. However, the open nature of the internet brings particular problems.

Stuart Stein (2002) points out that, unlike with published sources, there are no editorial or review processes designed to ensure the reliability and validity of the data. Consequently, data needs to be used with caution, particularly in relation to the identity, credibility and authority of the author(s).

FOCUS ON RESEARCH: THE INTERNET AS A SECONDARY SOURCE ON SEX WORK

Teela Sanders (2005) discusses some of the advantages and disadvantages of using the internet for research in the context of her own study of sex work (Sanders, 2004). Sanders used some traditional methods in her study: she observed interactions in the foyers of brothels and massage parlours, carried out 56 in-depth interviews with sex workers, and spoke informally to over 200 women. However, she also used the internet as a source of information.

Sanders argues that internet research can sometimes provide access to information that would not otherwise be available, especially in relation to secretive or illicit activities. She was able to gather ethnographic information about the sex industry using the website *Punternet*. The site provided message boards, 'field reports' from clients of sex workers, and generally facilitated the exchange of information between sex workers, and between workers and their clients. Sanders was able to carry out what she calls virtual observations using the site.

Before the advent of the internet, Sanders argues, it would not have been possible to observe the community of sex workers in the same way, because it was the internet that allowed geographically dispersed sex workers and their clients to communicate together as a virtual community in the first place. She says: "Previously, buyers and sellers of sex communicated only on a private and individual basis, whereas now ... these interactions have entered into the public domain"

(Sanders, 2005). Furthermore, she says that: "Through the internet the researcher can now be privy to other aspects of sexual behaviour that have been hidden and largely clandestine."

Conducting such research can raise ethical issues, since it may be impossible to gain consent from those who post messages on websites. However, since the contributors use pseudonyms there is little problem in maintaining anonymity. Where content is available publicly, ethics committees usually consider that informed consent is not necessary.

As well as being a source of information about the world described in the webpages on the internet, the cyber world can be considered a social setting in its own right.

Source: Haralambos and Holborn (2013)

Questions

1. Explain what Sanders means by the idea of virtual observation.

2. Suggest at least two types of information on sex work that might not be accessible using primary research but which could be accessed using the internet as a secondary source.

3. Suggest at least two reasons why Sanders thought that she needed to carry out primary research as well as using secondary sources.

4. Evaluate Sanders's arguments that the ethical issues raised by this type of research are not too serious because most people use pseudonyms and the information is in the public domain.

5. Evaluate the view that the cyber world should be seen as a social setting in its own right.

6. Suggest at least two ways in which internet content can be used to research attitudes to education.

Why do you think Wikipedia is usually frowned on as a source for undergraduate essays and academic research? Do you agree that it should not be used as a source of information? Is Wikipedia of any use or interest to sociologists?

Conclusions

Despite the problems described above, qualitative secondary sources continue to be used because of their relative accessibility, cheapness and ability to produce insights into personal life and historical processes that could not otherwise be studied. So long as the material is used critically, it can be invaluable in sociological research.

SECONDARY SOURCES IN THE CONTEXT OF EDUCATION

As in the study of other areas of social life, secondary sources are widely used in the study of education.

The use of official statistics

Official statistics are often used in the study of education, particularly statistics about levels of attainment and subject choice. The Department for Education (DfE) produces masses of statistics every year of potential interest to sociologists. These include statistics on truancy, school exclusions, and transitions to work and higher education. Statistics are particularly useful for examining longer-term trends and making comparisons between social groups, for example, males and females.

Practical issues

Official statistics are an easily accessible and plentiful source of information on education. However, the information required by sociological researchers is not always available. For example, data on achievement is usually broken down into the performance of males and females, but data on class backgrounds or the ethnicity of pupils and their achievement is less often available. Where particular statistics are not produced as a matter of course – for example, statistics on ethnicity and achievement – then sociologists have to rely upon occasional survey research carried out by other bodies. For example, data on ethnicity tends to be taken from the Youth Cohort Study. This makes comparisons over time more difficult and, because the data is based upon a sample, is not as reliable as data produced by every school.

The categories used for ethnic groups can vary between sets of statistics, making comparisons problematic. Official statistics do not always use the categories that sociologists use. For example, official definitions of social class do not always match sociological definitions. Therefore, sociologists sometimes have to use indirect indicators of class (such as eligibility for free school meals).

Ethical issues

There are no real ethical issues in using official statistics, since they are publicly available and using them is unlikely to cause harm. However, statistics produced by individual schools or local authorities may not be intended for publication, so there could be ethical issues about using them in published work.

Theoretical issues

Official statistics tend to be comprehensive, since state-funded organisations are often required to produce them. They are also generally reliable, since the government imposes definitions and categories on educational institutions and stipulates that they are produced using standardised procedures. However, the validity of statistics may be open to question. Schools may deliberately manipulate data in order to secure funding, improve their chances of a favourable inspection report or achieve success in league tables. For example, they may not accurately records absences or lateness, they may exclude pupils or fail to enter pupils for exams to improve league table performance, or they may appeal against exam results to influence the figures which appear in league tables.

School league tables are a particularly contentious issue. Schools that are able to be selective or to attract more middle-class pupils tend to do better by virtue of their intake. The Labour government of 1997–2010 introduced **Contextual Value-Added (CVA) tables**, which took account of the background of the pupils in judging school performance. Statistics on the progress made by pupils between different stages in their education are still produced, but there is no account taken of the social characteristics of the pupils. Furthermore, schools are generally ranked in terms of their crude exam performance, not in terms of how much they have improved the performance of the pupils. Schools are also inspected and grades are awarded. However, these grades are contentious, and schools often dispute their accuracy; only four grades are available, so they are quite a crude measure.

UNDERSTAND THE CONCEPT

Schools routinely give predicted grades for students in exams, and base these upon government statistics on average performance by pupils given how well they have done in previous exams. For example, GCSE grades are used to predict what, on average, a pupil or student should get in A-levels they are studying. Of course they might do better or worse than predicted, which will affect how well the school is seen as doing and provide a value-added score that tries to measure how much the school or college has helped improve educational attainment. Value-added scores provide a better measure of school success than crude scores of achievement (which are greatly affected by the sorts of pupil/student the institution can attract), but even they fail to take account of the background of the pupils (for example, their class background, whether they get free school meals, the sort of area they live in, or their gender). **Contextual value-added tables** do take these sorts of factor into account and therefore provide the best indication of how successful a school or college is.

Qualitative secondary sources in education

Sociologists can make use of a wide range of public documents relating to education, such as inspection reports, school policies and publicity brochures, and the minutes of governors' meetings. These can be very useful in studying how policies are made and implemented, and can be compared with primary research examining what actually happens in schools. Sociologists also sometimes make use of personal documents such as written work, school reports on individual pupils, text messages or even notes passed in class.

Practical issues

Public documents tend to be easily available to researchers and are relatively cheap and quick to access. However, personal documents are not available in such large quantities nor are they necessarily easy to access. The availability of such documents is patchy and researchers may not be granted access to them readily. Therefore relatively little research has been done using these sources.

It can therefore be difficult to base a complete study on secondary sources, especially qualitative ones, but they can be very useful in conjunction with primary research. For example, in a study of the introduction of markets into education by Stephen Ball *et al.* (1994), extensive use was made of documents such as admissions policies, marketing material and interviews with parents, in order to understand how the education market worked. They also helped researchers to understand the social policy context in which interaction takes place within schools.

Ethical issues

There are no major ethical issues with using public documents since they are already in the public domain and others can easily access them.

When private documents are used, ethical issues become more significant. The researcher may need to seek informed consent from those who produced the documents. If they fail to do so, then the research could be considered unethical (for example, Hey picking private documents out of bins). Some documents, such as school reports, could be considered to be confidential and researchers should try to maintain the anonymity of the pupils to whom they refer.

Theoretical issues

The validity of public documents may be open to question. For example, some educationalists would not accept that inspection reports provide a valid description and assessment of the school. School publicity material is likely to put a positive gloss on the image and the performance of the school. Indeed many schools and colleges employ experts in marketing for this very purpose. Documents produced for the government by schools may be manipulated to maximise funding or increase the likelihood of positive inspection reports. Schools are generally very concerned about inspection and they can try to suppress information that might affect their grading.

Private documents have the potential to provide valid information on the subjective viewpoints of those involved in education. However, if they are intended to be read by someone else, they may be written in a way that has the audience in mind rather than being a completely valid account. So it is always important for the researcher to consider why the document was produced to in order try to assess its validity.

Conclusions

As in other areas of social life, secondary sources are widely used to study education. Statistical data is very important to schools, colleges and universities because it affects their funding, public image and recruitment. Educational statistics provide valuable information for sociologists, but they should not always be taken at face value.

Qualitative secondary sources are used less frequently but they can sometimes prove invaluable. Public documents provide some useful information. Private documents may provide valuable and original insights, but some ingenuity may be required by researchers to gain access to them.

CHECK YOUR UNDERSTANDING

1. Identify four reasons why sociologists sometimes use secondary sources.

2. Explain three practical problems that can arise when sociologists use secondary sources.

3. Outline three competing views on the usefulness of official statistics for sociologists.

4. Identify two types of statistical data that sociologists might use from the census.

5. Describe how secondary sources have been used in any one sociological study of education.

6. Give an example of one public document and one private document containing qualitative data that might be used by a sociologist.

7. Explain what is meant by meta-analysis.

8. Briefly explain three ways in which the content of the mass media can be analysed.

9. Briefly explain one advantage and one disadvantage of using personal diaries in sociological research.

10. Evaluate the usefulness of GCSE school league tables in studying differential achievement, by identifying three advantages and three disadvantages of this source of data.

TAKE IT FURTHER

Collect the prospectuses of various universities, colleges or schools (including your own school or college). Look at the photographs in each. How do they portray their students? From your own experience of education, do you think this is an accurate portrayal? What motives might there be for the particular images presented? Are there any negative photographs or comments in the text about the educational institution? In what ways might this sort of data be useful to sociologists?

APPLY YOUR LEARNING

AS LEVEL

Methods in Context

1   Read **Item A** and answer the question that follows.

ITEM A

Ethnicity and differential educational achievement

There is considerable evidence to show that pupils from some ethnic-minority backgrounds fall behind in school, particularly during the secondary phase. These include Black, Pakistani and Bangladeshi pupils. By contrast, Indian and Chinese pupils do better than the average. There are also class and gender differences in achievement within all of these groups, just as there are among White pupils. One explanation for these patterns of achievement lies in the school itself and the processes at work there. For example, Black pupils are more likely to be excluded from school than members of other ethnic groups. Other factors within school include peer groups and subcultures. For example, Sewell found that a minority of Black boys joined 'rebel' subcultures. However, he also found that some teachers labelled all Black boys as rebels, regardless of the facts. One method used to study differential educational achievement is participant observation. This involves the researcher joining in with the activities of the group whose behaviour he/she wishes to understand, either openly (overt) or without revealing that he/she is a researcher (covert).

Applying material from **Item A** and your knowledge, evaluate the strengths and limitations of using participant observation to investigate educational achievement among ethnic-minority pupils.   [20 marks]

Research Methods

1   Outline **two** problems of using biographies and autobiographies in sociological research.   [4 marks]

2   Evaluate the uses and limitations of official statistics in sociological research.   [16 marks]

A LEVEL

Methods in Context

1 Read **Item B** and answer the question that follows.

ITEM B

Parental involvement and educational achievement

› Research indicates that parental involvement in children's education from an early age has a significant effect on educational achievement, and continues to do so into adolescence and adulthood.

› The attitudes and aspirations of parents and of children themselves predict later educational achievement. Moreover, international evidence suggests that parents with high aspirations are also more involved in their children's education.

› One method that could be used to study this topic is unstructured interviews. 'Unstructured' means that the interview does not involve working through a pre-set list of questions in a fixed sequence, but more closely resembles a natural conversation.

Applying material from **Item B** and your knowledge, evaluate the strengths and limitations of using unstructured interviews to investigate the impact of parental involvement on children's educational achievement. [20 marks]

Theory and Methods

1 Outline and explain what is meant by 'validity' and 'reliability' in social research. [10 marks]

You can find example answers and accompanying teachers' comments for this topic at www.collins.co.uk/AQAAlevelSociology.

3 CULTURE AND IDENTITY

3.1 CONCEPTIONS OF CULTURE

> Understand different meanings of the word culture and different types of culture (AO1).

> Understand different theories of culture (AO1).

> Apply this understanding to examples from Britain and from different cultures (AO2).

> Analyse the differences between competing theories of culture (AO3).

> Evaluate competing theories of culture (AO3).

INTRODUCING THE DEBATE

The idea of being 'cultured' suggests being a cut above other people who lack culture. However, in the sociological sense, everybody has a culture, otherwise you wouldn't be able to live as a member of a society. Talking about somebody being cultured suggests instead that they have an understanding of highly valued aspects of a culture, such as art, literature, theatre or highly regarded music. But culture in a broader sense is much more than this, and who is to say that one type of culture is better than any other? Is it just a question of rich and powerful people asserting that the culture they like is better than the culture of less powerful groups? This chapter looks at different types of culture and examines sociological theories which attempt to explain both differences in culture and the reasons why some cultures are valued more than others.

GETTING YOU THINKING

Shirbit culture

The Shirbit culture believes that the human body is ugly and that its natural tendency is to feebleness and disease. The Shirbit therefore indulge in rituals and ceremonies designed to avoid this, and consequently every household has a shrine devoted to the body. The rituals associated with the shrine are private and secret. Adults never discuss the rituals and children are told only enough for them to be successfully initiated. The focal point of the shrine is a box built into the wall in which are kept charms and magical potions for the face and body.

These are obtained from the medicine men who write down the ingredients in an ancient and secret language which is only understood by the herbalist who prepares the potion. These potions are kept in the charm-box for many years. Beneath the charm-box is a small font. Every day, twice a day, every member of the family enters the shrine room in succession and bows his or her head before the charm-box, mingles different sorts of holy water in the font and proceeds with a brief rite of ablution.

The Shirbit have an almost pathological horror of and fascination with the mouth, the condition of which is believed to have a supernatural influence on all social relationships. Were it not for the rituals of the mouth, they believe that their teeth would fall out, their friends would desert them and their lovers would reject them. Finally, men and women indulge in barbaric acts of self-mutilation. Men engage in a daily body ritual of scraping and lacerating their faces with a sharp instrument, while women bake their heads in a small oven once a month.

Based on Levine (1956)

Feral children

Feral or 'wild' children are those who, for whatever reason, are not brought up entirely, or at all, by humans. One example is the case of Oxana Malaya. She was born in 1983 and at the age of 8 she was found in the Ukraine living in a kennel at the back of her house and spending her time with wild dogs. Although she had been raised by her parents until she was 3, the parents were alcoholics who were incapable of looking after her. She therefore moved into the kennel and started associating with the wild dogs which roamed the streets, rather than with humans. As a result she had developed a number of dog-like habits such as growling, sniffing her food and crouching like a dog. Her sense of smell and her sight were very acute. When she was found, Oxana could not talk and she ran around on all fours. She was taken to live in a home for the mentally disabled and only lost her dog-like habits slowly. Even at 23, she would still bark occasionally, though by this time she had learnt to count (though not to add up) and she could speak, though with little or no tone or inflection in her voice. She continued to have learning difficulties but found work outside the home milking cows.

Based on Grice (2006)

Feral children like Oxana are sometimes brought up by animals.

Questions

1. Make a list of the ways in which Oxana Malaya behaved differently to most 8 year olds when she was found.

2. What kind of skills do you think she would have that other 8-year-old children would not have?

3. Why do you think she continued to have some learning difficulties?

4. What does the first extract on Shirbit culture tell us about the behaviour of human beings?

5. Which aspects of Shirbit behaviour seem alien to you?

6. In what ways might Shirbit behaviour be thought to resemble British culture?

DEFINING CULTURE

The concept of 'culture' has been interpreted and used in a number of ways by both sociologists and non-sociologists. For this reason, defining precisely what is meant by culture is not a straightforward process. Christopher Jencks (1993) identifies several ways of defining culture but perhaps the most general one is that of culture 'as the whole way of life of a society'. From this point of view, culture involves shared beliefs, **values**, **norms**, **customs**, language, symbols, history and knowledge that make up the way of life of a social group or society. All of these features influence the ways in which members of a society live their lives. For example, culture is partly composed of symbols that people use to convey meaning. As Abbott (1998) notes, language is the most obvious set of symbols through which members of society share meanings – without language, communication between people would be much more limited. Culture also includes the material objects produced by a particular social group, such as furniture, houses, paintings, tools and so on.

UNDERSTAND THE CONCEPT

Values are widely accepted beliefs that something is worthwhile and desirable. They don't have to be supported by everyone, but they do have to be accepted by most people and be assumed to be 'normal' in most groups in a society. For example, most societies place a high value on human life – although during wartime this value may be suspended. Other British values might include a belief in hard work, good hygiene, democracy, free speech, justice, romantic love and family life.

Norms are values put into practice. They are rules of behaviour that relate to specific social situations, and they govern all aspects of human behaviour. For example, norms govern the way we prepare and eat food, our toilet behaviour and so on. Norms are based on wider values – for example, norms governing toilet behaviour are based upon the value attached to good hygiene.

Customs are traditional and regular norms of behaviour associated with specific social situations, events and anniversaries, which are often accompanied by rituals and ceremonies. For example, in Britain it is the social custom to mourn for the dead at funerals, and this usually involves an elaborate set of ritualistic norms and a ceremony. It is also generally expected that people will wear black at funerals in Britain. Turning up in a pink tuxedo would be regarded as deviant, or norm-breaking, behaviour.

CULTURE AS THE WHOLE WAY OF LIFE

One way of seeing the idea of culture as a way of life is to define it in terms of the non-natural aspects of human societies, including the non-biological features of humans. Marshall (1998) suggests that culture is everything 'in human society which is socially rather than biologically transmitted'. Culture, therefore, refers to all that is learned from others in society. At birth, people join a social world with a culture already in existence. Children learn how things are done; that is, they learn cultural rules in order to take their place successfully in society. This teaching and learning process is known as socialisation and will be explored in greater depth in Chapter 2.

Would you say there is such a thing as the British way of life? If so, what is it? If not, why not?

CULTURE AND SOCIETY

At this stage, it is useful to stress that culture is not the same as society. As Giddens (1997) notes: "no cultures could exist without societies. But equally, no societies could exist without culture. Without culture no one can be 'human' at all."

Society is made up of all the formal and informal social institutions that people create by coming together and interacting with each other. These include marriage and the family, the peer group (see Chapter 2), education, government (sometimes referred to as the State), mass media, religion and the workplace. Culture shapes how those institutions work by setting behavioural rules (norms) and by shaping expectations about the **status** an individual should have and the social **roles** people should play in those institutions. For example, culture is responsible for shaping how we should behave as mothers, fathers, sons, daughters, teachers, students, police officers, doctors, and so on.

UNDERSTAND THE CONCEPT

All members of society are given a social position or **status** by their culture. Sociologists distinguish between 'ascribed' statuses and 'achieved' statuses. Ascribed statuses are fixed at birth, usually by inheritance or biology. For example, gender and race are fixed characteristics (which may result in women and minority ethnic groups occupying low-status roles in some societies). Achieved statuses are those over which individuals have control. In Western societies, such status is normally attained through education, jobs and sometimes marriage.

Society expects those of a certain status to behave in a particular way. A set of norms is imposed on the status. These are collectively known as a **role**. For example, the role of 'doctor' is accompanied by cultural expectations about patient confidentiality and professional behaviour.

CULTURE AND IDENTITY

Identity, like culture, is also not a straightforward concept. It generally refers to our 'sense of self', which means our subjective feelings, how we see ourselves and, very importantly, how we think other people see and judge us. Identity is therefore made up of two components – how we see ourselves and how others see us. It involves some choice on our part – we often actively identify with aspects of our culture with regard to particular groups or activities, such as a football team, a friendship network, or a fashion or trend. However, our identity is partly imposed on us by our culture. We are born into particular cultural positions or statuses – we do not choose our social class, gender, ethnic group, age, religious background or initial nationality. Social forces like these shape our identity.

Most sociologists suggest that culture and identity are closely related. Culture is what links the individual and their sense of self to society, because who we think we are is related to what society – in the shape of cultural values and norms – says we should do and be. Richard Jenkins (1996) argues that identity is partly negotiable – we generally try to persuade others to think of us in a positive light. We put on a performance to impress others but we can't entirely control how others see us and our identity may become damaged or change without us wishing it to. Jenkins uses the example of becoming a pensioner: a similar example would be turning 18. Although you might be the same person the day before your 18th birthday, your identity changes from that of a child to an adult regardless of your wishes. This may also change the way that you see yourself.

Kath Woodward (2000) argues that identity is always partly formed by our individual decision-making (or what sociologists call agency) and partly affected by the structures of society that surround us. We are linked to our roles and positions in society structures through our identities and symbols, and images may be used to remind us of those identities and connect us to them. For example, adverts may portray people with particular identities (such as housewives, football supporters, teenagers or heterosexuals) and by doing this they remind us of our position in society and reaffirm those identities. However, Woodward believes that in modern Britain there is perhaps more uncertainty about identity than ever before. A number of factors have caused this including the decline of traditional working-class jobs in industry, the increasing employment of women outside the home, uncertainty about national identity in a multicultural society, and the growth of consumer society, which gives everybody more choice about how they present themselves and the identity they adopt. For example, there is a wide range of clothing styles, and people can even change their identity by working out at the gym, getting tattoos or having cosmetic surgery. Consumer society encourages these choices, partly because they provide opportunities for businesses to make money out of those who want to improve their identity.

Can you really choose your own identity or do people around you and your position in society determine who you are?

High culture

It is important to acknowledge alternative and narrower ways in which the concept of culture has been used by sociologists. Haralambos and Holborn define high culture as 'cultural creations that have a particularly high status' (Haralambos and Holborn, 2013, p. 727). They are creations which are seen, at least by some people, as the pinnacle of human creativity and therefore as aesthetically superior to other cultural products and leisure activities. These cultural products are usually established historically and include classical music, opera, ballet, art (in the form of traditional paintings and sculpture), Shakespeare, great literature and poetry, and so on. As we shall see in Chapter 3, high culture is an important part of the identity of parts of the economic and political elite in the UK – that is, the upper class. However, the view that high culture is superior to other forms of culture is controversial.

Folk culture

Folk culture refers to traditional cultural products and activities that originate with ordinary people and are rooted in pre-industrial societies. They have been passed down, usually by word of mouth, over the generations, and, in Britain, include Morris dancing, folk singing and traditional storytelling. These activities do not claim to be art or high culture – rather they claim to tell authentic stories about real lives and experiences.

Low culture

Low culture refers to the culture of lower-ranked groups in society (those without high status or much power) and implies that the culture it describes has little worth or value (in contrast to high culture). Mass culture is sometimes seen as a form of low culture. The same could be said of folk culture, although the term 'folk culture' has more positive connotations than the term 'low culture'.

Can you think of contemporary examples of folk culture? Does it make sense to talk about folk culture in a society where the mass media are so important?

Mass or popular culture

Mass or popular culture refers to the products of the mass media in modern capitalist societies, such as television programmes, films, popular fiction, magazines and comics, and popular music. Some sociologists have argued that this type of culture is manufactured for mass consumption rather than created for its own sake, and consequently has little or no artistic merit compared with the products of high culture. For example, in 1957 the American critic of mass culture Dwight McDonald attacked mass culture for threatening to undermine high culture. Because it was much easier to understand and enjoy, it stopped people taking the trouble to try to understand more worthwhile culture and he even claimed that it turned adults into children by getting them to consume child-like products. Modern examples include superhero films such as *Spiderman*, which originally appeared in comics but are now watched by adults as well as children. Others have suggested that mass culture can be a corrupting influence on young people – for example, hip hop or rap music might encourage violence or sexist attitudes computer games have also been accused of encouraging violence.

FOCUS ON SKILLS: UNDERSTANDING, ANALYSIS, EVALUATION

a.

b.

c.

d.

e.

f.

Questions

1. **Understanding.** What different types of culture would you understand to be represented by these different photographs?

2. **Analyse** the images and rank them in hierarchical order. Place the ones you think are the most valued by society at the top and those least valued at the bottom.

3. **Analyse** the criteria you used to judge 'value'.

4. **Evaluate.** Is it possible to make objective judgements about whether one type of culture is better than another?

THEORETICAL PERSPECTIVES ON CULTURE

Different theoretical approaches have been developed in order to explain both why societies develop particular cultures and why some cultures are ranked more highly than others. Theories of culture are often closely bound up with the general theories of human behaviour and/or of society which are proposed by these theories.

Sociobiology

Sociobiologists generally believe that culture is the product of biology or nature. This contrasts with the sociological point of view that culture is the product of social learning or nurture. For example, Morris (1968) argued that biology shapes culture, because sharing culture is based on the inbuilt or genetic need to continue the life of the social group over time – the need to survive.

On the other hand, sociologists argue that if human behaviour is influenced by biology at all, it is only at a reflex or physical level, for example when we feel hungry. They argue that culture determines *what* is eaten – for example, in Britain, we culturally disapprove of cannibalism and eating certain creatures such as dogs, horses and insects. We also express some cultural anxieties about overeating (obesity) and not eating enough (dieting and eating disorders). Even *when* and *how* we eat are shaped by cultural rules – think, for example, about what time you have 'dinner'. Indeed sociologists argue that many aspects of social life that are taken to be natural are in fact produced by society or are **social constructs**. An example is gender differences. Sociologists view the differences between male and female as a product of society, not as something in-built in male and female bodies (see Chapter 4).

UNDERSTAND THE CONCEPT

A **social construct** is a belief, characteristic or set of behaviours that is produced by society rather than by nature. Examples might include the values and behaviours associated with masculinity and femininity, motherly love, God, and believing it is rude to burp in public. Sociologists sometimes question whether things which appear very natural indeed, such as smiling, are anything other than social constructs.

Culture as a system – functionalism

The founder of functionalism, Emile Durkheim (1858–1917) (see Topic 1, Chapter 1) believed that society and culture were more important than the individual. This

belief was based on a simple observation: society exists before the individual is born into it and continues relatively undisturbed after the death of the individual.

Durkheim (1893) noted that all societies are characterised by social order rather than chaos or anarchy. People's behaviour is generally patterned and predictable. Durkheim argued that this was because society's members were united by a value consensus, meaning that they shared the same cultural values, goals and norms. Like other functionalists, Durkheim saw culture as the cement that bonds individuals together in the form of society and allows people to interact successfully with each other.

Culture in pre-industrial societies

Durkheim argued that the function of the social institutions that make up society – the family, religion, education, and so on – was to socialise individuals into the value consensus. He noted that in traditional pre-industrial societies, socialisation agencies such as religion were extremely powerful cultural influences over individual behaviour. Consequently, in these societies, individual identity was secondary to cultural conformity. In other words, people went along with what society demanded; they rarely spoke out or complained. These societies therefore demonstrated high levels of solidarity or social belonging because people felt very similar to each other. Social order was a natural outcome of these processes. He thought that this sort of culture produced mechanical solidarity – a strong bond between people based on their similarity to one another.

Culture in modern societies

Durkheim notes, however, that industrial societies are much more complex. The social changes that occurred during the 18th and 19th centuries, such as industrialisation and urbanisation, have the potential to undermine value consensus and cultural conformity because we experience a great deal more choice in our beliefs and actions; we have more opportunity to be individuals. As a result, we become less like each other. This is potentially disruptive, because people may become confused about what values, beliefs, rules, and so on, they should live by, and could come into conflict with each other. Durkheim called this '**anomie**'.

Despite this, Durkheim believed that social order would still be generally maintained (although in a weaker form than previously), because social institutions continue to socialise people into a shared culture – in particular, the cultural goals that achievement, competition and hard work are all important, and that people should be prepared to take their place in the specialised division of labour (the way the economy organises work into specialist jobs).

UNDERSTAND THE CONCEPT

Anomie occurs when the norms and values of society become unclear so people are no longer sure what is considered right or wrong or how to behave. This can occur during periods when society is changing rapidly. For example, during a revolution or a civil war (such as the war in Syria in 2015), people may be unclear who is in charge and how society is going to change. Economic change can have this effect too, so during the industrial revolution, or big slumps such as that after the banking crisis of 2008, anomie can occur.

This specialised division of labour reinforces social order because it results in people being dependent upon each other for society's survival and continuation. Jobs do not exist in isolation from each other – teachers need supermarket workers, sewage workers, plumbers, bus drivers, and vice versa. Durkheim thought that culture in this type of society was based upon organic solidarity – people were bound together by their dependence on each other – but that this was weaker than organic solidarity in which people were very similar to one another.

Criticising Durkheim

Durkheim has been criticised for exaggerating cultural consensus and hence social order. Social conflict between groups within the same society is generally neglected. Interpretivist sociologists are critical of Durkheim because he sees people as less important than society and culture, as if their actions and choices are shaped solely by social and cultural forces, and by socialisation. There is little acknowledgement that people play an active role in shaping culture. He may also exaggerate the degree to which culture is shared in countries, such as Britain, where there are diverse social classes and ethnic groups. Nevertheless, his theory does help to explain why shared cultures are important and why most societies do not break apart easily.

Culture as a system – Marxism

Marxism focuses on the economic organisation of modern societies, particularly the fact that societies such as the UK are capitalist societies characterised by class inequalities of wealth, income and power. Social class refers to the amount of economic power – wealth – that social groups have or do not have. Karl Marx (1818–83) saw capitalist societies as characterised by class inequality and conflict. One group, the bourgeoisie, owned and controlled the **means of production** and exploited the labour power of another group, the proletariat or working class, in order to make even greater wealth.

UNDERSTAND THE CONCEPT

According to Marx the **means of production** consists of all the crucial things that are needed to grow or manufacture products to sell or to provide services. These include land, machinery, buildings such as warehouses and factories, capital (money used to finance production) and labour power – the ability of people to work. The working class (or proletariat) can only sell their labour power. They need the bourgeoisie (ruling class) to employ them, because only the bourgeoisie have the means to create products and services of value to sell.

Culture as ideology

Marx noted that the bourgeoisie, in order to protect their interests, used their wealth to acquire political and cultural power. As Marx and Engels (1974) stated: "the ideas of the ruling class are in every epoch the ruling ideas, that is the class which is the ruling material force of society, is at the same time its ruling intellectual force." In other words, cultural ideas and values are dominated by ruling-class ideas and values. Marx called this ruling-class culture 'ideology'. He argued that social institutions such as religion, education, the mass media and even the family, functioned to socialise society's members – especially its working-class members – to accept ruling-class culture, and consequently to see their own low status and lack of opportunity as 'normal', 'natural' and a product of their own shortcomings. How these agencies do this in practice will be explored further in Chapter 2.

Neo-Marxism

Some neo-Marxists (new Marxists) have questioned the idea of culture as simply being ideology. For example, the Italian Marxist Antonio Gramsci (1971) suggested that individuals in capitalist societies possessed dual consciousness. In part, they saw the world through the ideology of the ruling class, for example they might feel that they were not clever or hard-working enough to enjoy high wages but that the 'captains of industry', the so-called 'wealth creators', deserved to be rich. On the other hand, their everyday experience of low wages, poor working conditions and their own exploitation, helped them to see through ideology and to realise that society was not fair. For this reason, ruling-class control over ideas is never complete and there is always the possibility that the ideology they promote will be challenged by some members of the working class (for example, through trade unions). Neo-Marxists (and indeed some Marxists) therefore acknowledge that not everyone will accept ruling-class ideology to the same extent, and there may be differences in the values and beliefs of those from different social classes. Although some aspects of culture will be shared, others will not, and different classes will have different cultures.

BUILD CONNECTIONS

These ideas can be closely linked to Marxist and neo-Marxist theories of education. Think about how they compare with the Marxist ideas of Bowles and Gintis, and the neo-Marxist ideas of Paul Willis discussed in Topic 1, Chapter 5.

The Frankfurt School

A distinctive neo-Marxist approach to culture was developed by the Frankfurt School, who combined ideas from Karl Marx's work with ideas from psychology (Jenks, 1993). The Frankfurt School originated in Germany in the 1930s as a response to the rise of Fascism. Some its early followers had to flee Nazi Germany and moved to the USA. The Frankfurt School were alarmed by what they saw as the mass indoctrination of the population into following fascist ideas, leading to a mass culture. They saw this as partly the result of techniques used in the mass media and partly the way children were raised. Max Adorno (Adorno *et al.*, 1950), a founder of the school, believed that over-strict fathers led to children developing an authoritarian personality (they liked to control others and had little empathy), which left them with a lack of sympathy for the Jewish and other victims of Nazi oppression. While personality was a result of upbringing, racist prejudices were a product of culture.

Herbert Marcuse (1964), a French follower of the school, further explored the idea that societies developed a mass culture in the 1960s. He thought that mass communication, and particularly advertising, was dumbing-down culture and creating a *One Dimensional Man* who thought only about material possessions. This created a type of mass culture in which political alternatives to the status quo were never considered and thought-provoking art was undermined by popular culture.

The Frankfurt school have a certain amount in common with more conservative critics of mass culture such as MacDonald (see above). However, they see it as preventing radical and progressive change which could challenge the position of the ruling class, and they are more concerned with its threat to radical culture (which challenges the status quo) than to high culture. Like some other neo-Marxist approaches to culture, the Frankfurt school might underestimate the extent to which ruling-class culture is already challenged in the media and elsewhere.

Criticising Marx

Marx's theory may be guilty of overemphasising social class as the main source of conflict in modern societies. There is evidence that gender, religion, ethnicity and nationalism may also be important causes of inequality. Feminist theories see culture as a product of male dominance (or patriarchy) rather than ruling-class dominance. They claim that the contribution of women to social life is consistently devalued in patriarchal societies, whatever their class background. (Feminist views on culture and identity are discussed in detail in Chapter 4.) Marxism also assumes that the working class are the passive victims, or puppets, of ruling-class culture and ideology. However, neo-Marxism recognises this limitation and suggests that the working class may be aware of inequality and exploitation. Marx predicted that capitalism would eventually be overthrown as the working class came to realise they were being exploited. However, there is little sign of this in Britain or most capitalist societies, which instead seem to have become consumer societies (see Chapter 7).

How far do you agree with Marxists that people are taken in by ruling-class ideology? For example, do you think people on benefits are all scroungers and the rich have all worked hard for their money? Do different classes think differently about issues like this?

INTERACTIONIST THEORIES OF CULTURE

Everyday interaction and culture

Functionalists and Marxists relate culture to the overall structure of society. They link it to the major institutions of society (such as the economy, religion and the state) and they focus on society as a whole. Interactionists (sometimes known as symbolic interactionists) are much more concerned with the details of social life, pariculary everyday interaction when people come together at the same place. While they don't deny that there are wider structures (such as class structures) and important institutions (such as the state) they stress that, at least to some extent, culture is produced from the bottom-up at least as much as from the top-down. Culture is not just a product of shared norms and values or the beliefs of the ruling class, but is also produced by individuals as they interact. This approach is sometimes called micro sociology (it looks at the small-scale) rather than macro sociology (big-scale sociology which looks at society as a whole). The emphasis is on social action (the decisions and actions of individuals in social settings) rather than on social structure (how society is put together).

Unlike functionalists and many Marxists, interactionists stress that there is potential for individuals to change the culture of society by acting differently. The founder of interactionism was the American social psychologist George Herbert Mead (1934) whose work was interpreted and applied to sociology by Herbert Blumer (1969). Mead and Blumer argued that social structures largely consisted of roles (such as the mother, father, customer, student, government minister, and so on). These roles had norms associated with them, about, for example, how a good mother or father should act. However, these roles were not like a straightjacket, completely determining how people should behave. Instead, they were flexible and open to interpretation and change. For example, many individuals might not be able to live up to the ideal of being a good mother or father, and different groups have different ideas about how mothers and fathers should behave. Additionally, over time, roles might change as people interpret them differently: in the 1950s, it was widely assumed that being a good mother required that you stay at home to look after your child or children, but in the 21st century this is not always expected and a 'good mother' is quite likely to go out to work even when her children are quite young. As roles changed, so the culture of society changed. To interactionists, culture is more open to change than it appears in functionalist and Marxist theory.

Erving Goffman and the interaction order

One of the most influential interactionists was Erving Goffman, who developed the idea of the interaction order (1983). He saw the interaction order as any environment in which two or more people are physically in the same place and have the potential to interact with one another. It therefore includes public spaces like streets, shops and places of work, and private places such as homes. It can involve long-standing relationships or passing relationships but, despite these differences, Goffman sees all of these interactions as part of a distinctive domain in social life, and, as such, as an important part of a society's culture. Goffman points out that some sociologists see what goes on in the interaction order as simply the effects of wider structures and relationships (like class, gender, age and ethnic divisions) but Goffman argues that the interaction order is a distinctive sphere of social life in its own right, with its own rules that exist independently of other social divisions.

Unlike other areas of social life, the immediate presence of other people means that movements of the body, facial expressions and the expression of emotions and moods through movement and speech are very important. The interaction order also requires people to collaborate and coordinate their movements and actions. Individuals need to understand and characterise the other individuals with whom they come into contact in order to anticipate and understand their actions.

Sometimes they will know the person well and can define them as a particular *individual* (Goffman calls this individual identification). Often, however, they don't know the person personally and must understand them in terms of the category to which they belong (which Goffman calls categoric identification). Categoric identification might be based on age, class, gender, ethnicity, appearance or other factors, such as the way a person moves and the way he or she talks. The culture of a society influences the way these categorisations are made, but this culture is itself built up through everyday encounters with different people.

Goffman (1972) applied his general ideas to studying everyday interaction in Western societies in a range of settings, including between people walking down a street. He was interested in how people are able to walk down busy streets in Western cities without constantly bumping into each other. He found that the culture of these societies had informal rules governing this type of situation. These involved avoiding staring at strangers or trying to interact meaningfully. He called this civil inattention and deemed it important in the context of urban settings, where people were unlikely to know one another. Despite the rules about staring, it *is* considered polite to glance briefly at others to check whether you know them, whether they might be hostile and threatening, and in order to coordinate movements to avoid collisions. Small-scale societies did not have these rules, partly because they were not necessary.

Evaluation of interactionist theories of culture

interactionist theories of culture have been widely criticised for neglecting wider structural features of society, such as those explored by functionalists and Marxists. Marxists and feminists suggest that they tend to ignore or neglect class and gender inequalities and differences in power. Most interactionists, however, are aware of power inequalities and of the significance of institutions and structures (such as the economic system) but they choose to concentrate on studying day-to-day interaction, which they see as equally important. For example, interactionists see labelling in schools and the formation of subcultures as affecting educational achievement as well as class inequalities in society as a whole (see Topic 1, Chapter 5). They also see culture as being created, at least to some extent, from the bottom up, rather than being entirely imposed from above. They therefore recognise that humans have a degree of agency which is not always recognised by structural theories (see Topic 1, Chapter 5 for definitions of structure and agency).

POSTMODERN THEORIES OF CULTURE

Modern and postmodern societies

Theories of postmodernism suggest that since the 1980s societies have begun to change and have gone from being modern to being postmodern. From this point of view, modern societies (which developed from the early 17th century onwards) had clear dividing lines between social groups (such as men and women, different social classes, ethnic groups and age groups) and between different types of culture (for example, high culture, folk culture and popular or mass culture). Sociologists such as Stephen Crook, Jan Pakulski and Malcolm Waters (1992) believe that these dividing lines started to break down from the late 1970s.

For example, it has become harder to decide what class a person is in, and the behaviour of different age groups is no longer as different as it used to be. Retired people may now take part in adventurous activities and people may carry on working into their 70s or beyond. In terms of culture, high culture, such as classical music, is now mixed into popular culture, including adverts. Furthermore, some popular culture is taken seriously: the work of singers such as Bob Dylan (who started out as a folk singer) are studied in university courses and popular films are analysed in media and cultural studies degrees. According to Crook, Pakulski and Waters, this is partly due to the growth of consumer culture, which offers endless choices in terms of the lifestyles that people wish to have. For example, it is possible to buy food from all around the world. In major cities you can eat food typical of many different nationalities and ethnic groups, and both online and in shopping malls there is an extremely wide choice of fashion. This allows people to construct their own sense of identity, mixing and matching different cultures, which may have little in common, to create an individual sense of identity.

Postmodernism and popular culture

Dominic Strinati (1995) provides a very clear explanation of how some of these changes might apply to popular culture (although he himself is a little sceptical of some of the claims of postmodernism). He makes the following points.

1. Societies today are increasingly dominated by the mass media, so that the difference between reality and media images becomes unclear. For example, people might begin to see soap opera characters as real rather than simply roles in fiction.

2. There is more and more emphasis on style as opposed to substance. For example, people are more concerned about designer labels than the actual quality of clothing.

3. Art and popular culture are becoming mixed together. For example, the pop artist Andy Warhol produced a print which reproduced 30 images of Leonardo da Vinci's *Mona Lisa*.

4. Social life is speeding up. New ideas spread rapidly around the world (because of global communication) and old aspects of culture are mixed in with the new. For example, theme parks might have areas devoted to periods in history and new buildings often have features borrowed from the architectural styles of the past.

According to postmodernists, the differences between different types of culture may no longer apply. The boundaries between them are blurred and some types of culture are no longer automatically seen as superior to other types. Old social divisions are becoming less and less significant and people can largely choose what sort of person they want to be, and what kind of identity they want to have.

Criticisms of postmodernism

Having outlined how postmodernism can be applied to popular culture, Dominic Strinati suggests some possible criticisms of it. He questions whether the mass media really has taken over reality, arguing that most people can tell the difference between fact and fiction. He suggests that social divisions, such as those between class, ethnic, and age groups and between males and females, have not disappeared and still influence cultures and identities. For example, he agrees with Marxists that your class is likely to affect your ability to consume the new products that are available, so some people have much more opportunity to choose their identity than others. Some people may be able to go shopping for designer clothes, but not everybody can. He accepts that the clear-cut dividing line between popular culture and high culture and art has become a little blurred, but he still believes that the culture of those in elite positions in society is valued more than the culture of the working class or poor. For example, high-status qualifications are still more likely to focus on high culture rather than on popular culture.

CULTURAL DIVERSITY AND SUBCULTURES

Postmodernists argue that culture has become increasingly diverse, but there may be some truth in the functionalist and Marxist accounts which see some aspects of culture as widely shared. For example, on the whole, people live in families, see education as a good thing, believe in democracy, are polite and respect the law. Shared culture also helps us to make sense of the world. However, both theories are probably guilty of overstating this sharing of culture (although Marxists accept there are some class differences) and, as a result, fail to note the extent to which modern societies are characterised by cultural diversity.

Although the cultures of modern societies may seem to be dominated by cultural agreement, in reality such cultures have always been fragmented into competing subcultures, even before postmodernists argued that culture was becoming more diverse. Subcultures may be based on social class, age, religion, ethnicity or taste (such as tastes in fashion or music) that subscribe to the values and norms of mainstream society in most respects, but they may also subscribe to cultural values, norms and customs that are unique to them. Some of these subcultures may even be regarded as deviant by wider society or by those who wield power. These groups will be explored further in Chapters 3–6.

FOCUS ON RESEARCH: CLASSICAL MUSIC, HIGH CULTURE AND EDUCATION

Music education has seen a huge revival in deprived areas.

In recent years, there has been a worldwide explosion of music education programmes bringing classical music to children in deprived areas, following the model of El Sistema, a Venezuelan music education project. In the UK these 'In Harmony El Sistema' programmes have been set up in Stirling, Newcastle, Norwich and Liverpool, and in several other cities. However, in the UK more generally, classical music is overwhelmingly played and listened to by the middle and upper classes. Does this gap between classical music's usual suspects and its new recruits matter?

To answer this question, we need to examine the links between classical music and class. Prevailing explanations for the dominance of the middle classes in classical music tend to be economic, suggesting that inequalities are simply a question of access. Therefore, if we give all children access to instruments, good quality teaching, and clear progression routes, then class will no longer be an issue.

However, this study also found that the reasons that both children and adults give for choosing not to play a musical instrument is that they were not interested in learning, or that they have lost interest.

It suggests that the benefits of classical music may not be evenly shared, but instead may be more easily accessible to those who already fit into a middle-class world. In order to shift these ongoing inequalities, I would suggest that we need to change the musical practice itself by letting the music evolve and change more. While some music conservatoires are still following the same formula they did a hundred years ago, others are changing their practices by getting students to play with musicians from other genres, improvise, and learn how to use music technology.

Questions

1. What do you understand by the phrase 'the benefits of classical music may not be evenly shared, but instead may be more easily accessible to those who already fit into a middle-class world'?

2. Could you apply the arguments here to other types of high culture that are valued in the education system?

3. Using the information here and your own ideas, analyse possible reasons why the culture of working-class pupils may lead to them not enjoying learning to play classical music.

4. Analyse why the authors think that improvising, using music technology and including other genres might encourage a wider range of pupils to learn instruments.

5. Evaluate whether this study seems to support or contradict the following theories of culture:
   › functionalism
   › Marxism
   › postmodernism.

Source: Bull (2014)

GLOBAL CULTURE

Cultural diversity has also been influenced by globalisation. Only 30 or so years ago, our culture was local and familiar. Travelling abroad was not a common activity; most of the products we consumed were produced in the UK and, although we watched Hollywood films and listened to American singers, there was also a reasonably healthy British entertainment industry focused on pop music and television. Today, however, it can be argued that globalisation is now a profound influence on how we live our cultural lives. As Marsh and Keating (2006) note:

"The British are increasingly a globalised people. We appear willing to travel far and wide. We increasingly eat and drink the foods and beverages that our European or even North American neighbours consume. We drive similar, if not identical cars, albeit on the other side of the road. Moreover, our consumption patterns are increasingly influenced and shaped by the growth of global media and advertising. I can now sit in my hotel room in the USA or Egypt, and watch my favourite Premier League side lose yet again. Our world, that is to say the affluent Western world, is the world of Levi's, a world of Gap, a world of Coca-Cola, McDonald's, H&M, a world of Oil of Ulay." (p.431)

Some sociologists, especially postmodernists, argue that globalisation is good for us because it offers us more choice in terms of constructing our identities and lifestyles. Consequently, postmodernists argue that both our personal identities and our cultural identity are now influenced in a positive way by a range of cultures from around the world. However, others see globalisation as potentially harmful, both for economic reasons (it could make some people in poorer countries more vulnerable to poverty) and for cultural reasons (it could undermine local cultures and lead to a mass culture dominated by the USA, for example, Coca-Cola and Hollywood films). See Chapter 7 for a more detailed discussion of globalisation and culture.

CONCLUSIONS

The debate about culture involves a number of key questions.

1. Is nature responsible for culture, or is culture the product of learning? This will be explored in Chapter 2.

2. Are society and culture integrated into a unified shared whole, or is society characterised by subcultural diversity and possible conflict? This will be explored in Chapters 3 to 6.

3. How have globalisation and the development of consumer society affected culture and identity? This is examined in Chapter 7.

4. Are human beings cultural robots who react passively to the demands of cultural and social forces beyond their control, or are they the masters/mistresses of their own destinies?

Sociologists influenced by different perspectives have taken different positions on these types of issue. Interpretivists are critical of both functionalism and Marxism for ignoring the role of human agency in the construction of culture and identity. They argue that culture is actively created by people via social interaction. They argue that culture is not static: it is constantly evolving, as people interpret the actions of others around them and make their own choices about their behaviour. Postmodernists too tend to emphasise the importance of individual choices. Some postmodernists go even further than interactionists in suggesting that choices are no longer even influenced very much by the social groups in which people belong. Interactionists tend to see people's identities as likely to be shaped by those around them, and therefore they see membership of particular social groups as having considerable influence upon the choices that people make.

CHECK YOUR UNDERSTANDING

1. Explain what is meant by the terms 'folk culture', 'high culture' and 'popular culture'.

2. Identify two differences between popular culture and high culture.

3. Explain the difference between self-identity and social identity.

4. Explain what is meant by the terms 'status' and 'role'.

5. Explain how Durkheim sees culture developing in industrial societies.

6. Explain the Marxist term 'ruling-class ideology'.

7. Analyse the differences between Marxist and postmodern theories of culture by identifying and explaining two differences between them.

8. Analyse the differences between Marxist and functionalist theories of culture by identifying and explaining two differences between them.

9. Evaluate sociological approaches by explaining how sociologists criticise them.

10. Evaluate postmodern theories of culture by giving two weaknesses and two strengths.

TAKE IT FURTHER

Obtain the Review pages from a Sunday broadsheet newspaper such as *The Sunday Times*, *The Sunday Telegraph* or *The Observer*. Work out how many column inches or pages are dedicated to specific cultural activities, such as literature (book reviews), films, popular and classical music. Does this evidence suggest that these newspapers distinguish between high culture and popular culture?

3.2 THE PROCESS OF SOCIALISATION

INTRODUCING THE DEBATE

Socialisation is seen by many as a crucial if fairly straightforward aspect of society. It involves an individual learning the culture of a society from childhood in order to be able to live successfully in that society, communicating effectively with others and avoiding unnecessary conflict. Socialisation is a necessary part of all societies, and parents and families are usually crucial in the early stages of this process. However, have you ever thought about whether the way in which socialisation takes place has been changing?

For example, does the development of new technology have an impact on the role of different agencies in socialisation? Furthermore, should it be assumed that socialisation is a one-way process in which the knowledgeable, older members of society impart their knowledge and understanding to younger members of society? In reality, socialisation continues throughout life and it is not always a one-way process. People actively participate in learning the culture of their society and don't always simply accept what they are told.

SOCIALISATION AND THE TRANSMISSION OF CULTURE

At birth, we are faced with a social world that already exists. Joining this world involves rapidly learning 'how things are done' in it. Only by learning the cultural rules of a society can a human interact with other humans. Culture needs to be passed on from generation to generation in order to ensure that it is shared. Shared culture allows society's members to communicate and cooperate. The process of learning culture is known as socialisation. This involves learning the norms and values of a culture so that ways of thinking, behaving and seeing things are taken for granted or **internalised**.

UNDERSTAND THE CONCEPT

Internalisation involves something from outside the individual (for example, social norms) becoming internal to the individual. If there is full internalisation, then particular ways of thinking and acting become second nature – you do them without thinking and they seem natural.

The primary agency of socialisation has always been the family, but some argue pressures on parenting may be reducing the effectiveness of this particular child-rearing institution. Secondary agencies of socialisation, such as the mass media, may be increasing in importance. Some commentators, notably Postman (1982) and Palmer (2007), have expressed anxiety at the quality of the socialisation experienced by children viewing television, reading teenage magazines and surfing the internet.

Socialisation, culture and subculture

Although the first few years of a person's life are crucial in learning how to behave, it is important to understand that socialisation is a life-long process. This is because humans are social animals who live in complex and sophisticated societies based on detailed rules and traditions. For this reason, we have a great deal more to learn than other animals over the course of our lifetime. This learning process is therefore a continuous process, which really only ends at death.

For socialisation to be effective, it should not be experienced as forced or as an imposition. The individual should not feel that they are being subjected to a form of brainwashing. Such feelings run the risk of rejection, dissent and rebellion. Instead, as Paul Taylor (1997) notes, socialisation should be organised in such a way 'that the ways of thinking, behaving and perceiving things that are accepted by culture come to appear normal, natural and inevitable'. As Marsh and Keating (2006) argue, effective socialisation should happen to children without them even noticing it.

Stages of socialisation – primary and secondary socialisation

The main agent of primary socialisation is the family. The first few years of socialisation in the family are crucial to a person's development, having a profound effect upon all later social learning. Close social relationships with other people are essential in order for children to learn to interact and to communicate. These processes allow children to become aware of themselves as 'social beings'. They recognise that they occupy particular social roles – such as son, daughter, brother, sister – and that they are capable of social action that has consequences for others.

As this process develops, children acquire uniquely human skills; they learn that love, sadness and humour are appropriate emotional responses in certain situations, and they acquire the ability to smile, laugh, cry, and so on. The socialisation process results in children acquiring most of the skills necessary to empathise with others. Consequently, the helpless infant becomes a self-aware, competent, skilled and knowledgeable member of society. Children learn to function as good and useful citizens in their community.

Secondary socialisation takes place outside the home, for example, when children start in the education system. Although the culture of society may be largely internalised in the early years of life, it continues indefinitely. This is partly because the culture of society continues to change over time, and because, as adults, individuals continue to encounter new situations and to become involved with different subcultures.

SOCIALISATION AND IDENTITY

Baumeister (1986) notes that family socialisation provides children with an identity. A very young child has no life apart from its role in the family, and so a child will believe that the family will love and care for it so long as it does what it is supposed to do. Many children successfully learn what they are supposed to do through imitative play. Social roles, particularly the significant roles played by parents, provide children with blueprints for action – examples and illustrations of how to behave that they can then copy. Play activities may involve imitating parents by playing 'house' or 'mummies and daddies' – this too encourages empathy, as they gradually learn what it might feel like to be a father or mother.

SOCIALISATION AND SOCIAL CONTROL

Morgan (1996) suggests that a great deal of socialisation is concerned with social control and encouraging conformity. This can be illustrated in a number of ways.

> Parents often use sanctions to reinforce and reward socially approved behaviour, and to discipline and punish 'naughty', or deviant, behaviour. Positive sanctions might include praise, sweets or new toys, while negative sanctions include smacking, 'grounding' and especially the threat to withdraw love.

Both positive and negative sanctions are employed by parents to encourage conformity.

169

> Sanctions encourage the development of a conscience in the child. It is culturally expected that a child will eventually know the difference between 'good' and 'bad' behaviour, and that guilt will act as a deterrent, preventing deviant behaviour. Socialisation is seen to be successful when the child realises that the costs in terms of parental punishment outweigh the benefits of deviant actions, and so exercises self-control. This is the first step to independent action, that is, actions not shaped solely by parents.

> Morgan suggests that the function of toilet training is to instil in the child some sense of control over their bodily functions so that the child is accepted into wider society as a 'civilised' being. Similarly, children will be taught 'civilised' norms, such as politeness and table manners. At the same time, they will learn to avoid uncivilised behaviours, such as swearing, and vulgar behaviours, such as burping, picking their nose and breaking wind in public.

> Children internalise cultural expectations of what being a boy or a girl entails, and generally conform to traditional feminine and masculine gender roles. Durkin (1995) notes that most children can categorise themselves correctly and consistently as a boy or a girl between the ages of 2 and 3 years of age. The reasons for this will be explored more fully in Topic 4.

Socialisation changes over time within particular societies. Norbert Elias (1978) argues that the process of socialisation has grown more influential throughout history, so that culture exerts a greater civilising influence over our behaviour now than in any other historical age. He points out that in the Middle Ages there were fewer cultural constraints on individual behaviour. Burping, breaking wind, spitting and picking one's nose in public were regarded as perfectly normal forms of behaviour. For example, in medieval times, people blew their noses with their fingers, but by the end of the 17th century the upper classes at least could afford and thought it polite to use handkerchiefs.

Elias refers to this as the *Civilising Process* and he believes that it came about as people became more and more dependent on one another. It became more essential that people got along. From the 13th century, books about manners were produced, first for people at court and later for the wider population, setting out what standards of behaviour were acceptable. The books assumed that 'good manners' could be learned through practice and through imitating others (including parents) who set a good example. Since then, informal rules about what is 'civilised behaviour' have become increasingly restrictive.

Over time, what is considered 'civilised' by society has changed.

PERSPECTIVES ON SOCIALISATION

Functionalists and socialisation

The family

Functionalists such as Parsons (1951) see the family as a 'personality factory' – the child is seen as a 'blank slate' at birth and the function of parents, especially the nurturing mother, is to train and mould the passive child in the image of society. The child is to be filled up with shared cultural values and norms, so that it assumes that cultural values are somehow naturally its own values. This ensures that the child subscribes to value consensus and so feels a strong sense of belonging to society. Parsons puts particular emphasis on identification with adults, particularly adults of the same sex. Because children identify with them, they want to become like them, so they can fill similar social roles when they grow up as those filled by their same-sex parent.

Education

Functionalists see education systems as an essential part of secondary socialisation, because education transmits shared cultural values, thus producing conformity and consensus. Durkheim believed that subjects such as History, Language and Religious Education link the individual to society, past and present, by encouraging a sense of pride in the historical and religious achievements of their nation, which reinforces their sense of belonging to society.

Parsons argued that the main function of education was to act as a social bridge between the family unit and wider society – he called it a focal socialising agency. It helps children make the transition from being judged as particular individuals (based on **particularistic** values) to being judged impartially according to general social rules (**universalistic** values).

UNDERSTAND THE CONCEPT

In the family, parents are likely to view each child as a unique individual. They may treat children differently because they know them so well and can try to tailor their child-rearing to particular personalities. However these **particularistic** values are not expected to be applied in schools or the legal system, where someone is not judged according to who they are, but according to what they have done (for example, whether they have broken the law or answered an exam question well). In these cases, they are being judged in terms of **universalistic** values, which are applied in the same way to everyone (at least in theory). Education socialises children into important values such as achievement, competition and honesty – functionalists see the transmission of these values as essential in preparing young people for the world of work.

Religion

Functionalists also see religion as playing an important role in secondary socialisation. According to Durkheim (1912), the major function of religion is to socialise society's members into value consensus by investing certain values with a sacred quality, that is, by infusing them with religious symbolism and special significance. These values consequently become 'moral codes' – beliefs that society agrees to revere and socialise children into. Such codes regulate our social behaviour with regard to crime, sexual behaviour and obligation to others. The Ten Commandments are a good example of a set of moral codes that have influenced both formal controls such as the law (for example, 'thou shalt not kill', 'thou shalt not steal'), as well as informal controls such as moral disapproval (for example, 'thou shalt not commit adultery').

Evaluation of the functionalist view of secondary socialisation

Critics of functionalism, such as Alvin Gouldner (1970), attack it for underestimating the amount of conflict that occurs in socialisation. He says, "you would never guess from reading functionalist texts on socialisation that training children can be a continual, room-to-room-battle, invariably exhausting to the parents and repellent to the children". Functionalists are also criticised for exaggerating the extent to which people conform to their socialisation and ignoring the extent to which people might rebel against it. Parsons has been accused of seeing children as the passive recipients of socialisation from parents and schools, neglecting the role of peer groups and the active involvement of children in the process (Fine, 2006).

Marxist perspectives on socialisation

The family

Marxists are critical of the functionalist view that children are socialised into shared cultural values and norms that are a benefit to society as a whole. Instead, they see socialisation as being linked to the interests of particular social classes, particularly the ruling class. Zaretsky (1976), for example, argues that the family is used by the capitalist class to instil values, such as obedience and respect for authority, that are useful to the capitalist ruling class. Such values ensure that individuals can be exploited later in life by the ruling class, because ordinary people will have learned that power, authority and inequality should be viewed as normal and natural.

Education

In contrast to functionalist theorists, Marxists, such as Althusser (1971), argue that education as an agency of socialisation is dominated by a hidden curriculum – a ruling-class ideology that encourages conformity and an unquestioning acceptance of the organisation of capitalism.

Althusser claimed that few students are allowed to access educational knowledge that challenges the existence of capitalism. It is claimed that when the national curriculum was introduced in England and Wales in 1988, critical subjects such as Sociology and Politics were deliberately excluded from mainstream education because the ruling class believed that socialisation into ideas commonly taught by these subjects might lead to students becoming too critical of capitalist inequality.

Marxists also claim that schools socialise pupils into uncritical acceptance of hierarchy, obedience and failure. In particular, working-class pupils are socialised to see their failure as their own fault and as deserved rather than being caused by capitalism's need for a relatively uneducated manual labour force.

FOCUS ON RESEARCH: JULIA BRANNEN AND ELLEN HEPTINSTALL (2003)

Children may offer practical help in order to show their appreciation for everything their parents do for them.

This study of nearly 1,000 London 10- to 12-year-olds focused on how children view care, parental responsibility and family life. A questionnaire survey was conducted with the children, as well as 63 in-depth interview-based case studies from four different types of family: two-parent, lone-mother, stepfather and foster-care.

The researchers found that children saw the process of family life, especially parental unconditional love and care, as far more important than family structure. Furthermore, the children emerged as active contributors to family life. They showed considerable ability to understand other people's feelings and

circumstances. Some expressed a strong appreciation of what their parents had done for them and wanted to reciprocate by being caring, as well as offering practical help. One girl wrote on her questionnaire: "It gives me a chance to do something for my parents instead of them doing things for me."

The research suggests that children are active co-participants in care and co-constructors in family life. They make a contribution to family life while also trying to fulfil their increasingly onerous responsibilities at school. In this context, it is not surprising that children also think adults should listen to them more than they do at present.

Source: Brannen and Heptinstall (2003)

Questions

1. Analyse the strengths of the research methods used in this research. (For example, think about the benefits of using several methods together).

2. Analyse the weaknesses of the research methods used in this study. (For example, think about the validity and reliability of the different methods).

3. Analyse whether the findings support the view that socialisation is a two-way rather than a one-way process. (Consider how active children are in the process of socialisation).

Religion

Marxists, on the other hand, describe religion as an ideological apparatus that serves to reflect ruling-class ideas and interests. According to Marxists, religion socialises the working class into three sets of false ideas.

> It promotes the idea that material success is a sign of God's favour, whereas poverty is interpreted as a result of wickedness, sin and immorality.

> Religious teachings and the emphasis on blind faith serve to distract the poor and powerless from the true extent of their exploitation by the ruling class.

> Religion makes exploitation, poverty and inequality bearable by promising a reward in the afterlife for those who accept, without question, their suffering or poverty in the here and now.

Evaluation of Marxist perspectives on socialisation

Some criticisms of Marxist views on socialisation tend to echo criticisms of functionalist views. Like functionalists, many Marxist tend to see children as the passive victims of socialisation, neglecting or ignoring any active part that they might play in the process. They also tend to assume that children and older age groups simply accept the way that they are socialised and do not resist or rebel against it. Although Marxists recognise that socialisation might not be reproducing the culture of society as a whole, but rather the culture that favours the interests of the ruling class, they still see it as being effective and one-dimensional, appearing to believe that everyone is indoctrinated into capitalist ideology.

However, these criticisms cannot be so easily applied to some neo-Marxist (new Marxist) approaches. For example, Paul Willis (1977) discussed how working-class pupils in a secondary school developed a counter-school culture which rejected some aspects of what they were taught by teachers and actively created their own culture (see Topic 1, Chapter 1). In this case, the peer group (see below) of the pupils was important in their socialisation, as were their teachers and the educational institution they attended. Neo-Marxists tend to emphasise that socialisation does not work perfectly to indoctrinate the working class into accepting ruling-class beliefs, and the working class – and indeed members of all classes – can to some extent be socialised into beliefs which may reject ruling-class ideology. Nevertheless, neo-Marxist views have themselves been criticised by sociologists supporting other perspectives. Post modernists tend to reject the view that class differences are still very significant in the way that socialisation operates, arguing that people have more and more individual choice about the cultures they accept or reject. Feminists, on the other hand, agree with Marxists that socialisation can be a form of indoctrination, but they see it as indoctrination into patriarchal ideology rather than capitalist ideology.

Can you suggest some ways in which feminists might argue that there is gender bias in the socialisation process? Who tends to do most of the child care? Are boys and girls socialised in the same way? If not, what are the consequences?

Interpretivist perspectives on socialisation

Interpretivist perspectives on socialisation reject the idea that socialisation is just a passive process. Interpretivist approaches are concerned with the interpretation of meaning – they examine the meanings that individuals and social groups attach to the social world around them and to each other. They do not see individuals as reacting passively to events; instead they argue that individuals interpret these events themselves before they react. As individuals are active in the way they make sense of the world, they are also active in developing identities and in taking part in socialisation.

BUILD CONNECTIONS

Interpretivist approaches are not just important in terms of substantive topics, they are also very important in relation to research methods. They are generally seen as offering an alternative approach to more scientific methods, such as those advocated by positivists (see Topic 2, Chapter 2 on methodology).

The interactionist Gerald Handel (2006), emphasises that socialisation is not a one-way process but requires social interaction. From birth, children begin to learn skills that enable them to take an active part in socialisation.

> First, they develop the ability to communicate using symbols such as words in order to express what they want to their carers.

> Second, they develop the ability for empathy; that is, the ability to understand how things might feel from another person's point of view. This allows children to understand the viewpoint of others as they interact with them, and this can sometimes enable them to get the response they want from adults.

> Third, and most importantly, they develop a sense of **self**. This means that they can imagine themselves through the eyes of others and start to regulate their own conduct and evaluate their behaviour from another person's point of view. They can therefore actively choose how to behave in order to give a good impression of themselves or to get what they want.

The ability to communicate, have empathy, and have a sense of self develop further during play where children must take account of the views of others but, at the same time, can try to shape what happens through their own actions.

UNDERSTAND THE CONCEPT

A sense of **self** (sometimes known as self-concept) refers to the idea that we can think about who we are and imagine how others see us. We are able to reflect on our own behaviour, be critical of it and try to change it, or congratulate ourselves and resolve to continue to behave in the same way. Our sense of self is very much tied up with our sense of personal identity, but it is also shaped by our social identity and how we think other people see us.

Handel argues that parents have considerable freedom in how they socialise their children, so that children from different backgrounds may be brought up differently. For example, he uses research to show that in both the USA and Italy, working-class children are brought up to be more obedient than middle-class children, with middle-class children expected to use their initiative more. He also emphasises that children can socialise each other in peer groups, and are not just shaped by parents, education, religion and other institutions.

Evaluation of the interpretivist approach to socialisation

The interpretivist approach certainly makes much more allowance than Marxism or functionalism for the active role that children and adults play in socialisation, and acknowledges that it is not always a smooth process and can involve conflict between different people. However, the perspective is quite generalised and it can be argued that the interpretivist approach underestimates the role of institutions such as families, religion, education and the mass media in influencing socialisation. Furthermore, it tends to look at socialisation on a small scale and ignores the wider influence of power in society. Thus, compared to Marxism, it takes relatively little account of class inequality, and, compared to feminism, it tends to ignore gender inequality (see Chapter 4 for more discussion of feminist views).

THE PEER GROUP

The discussion of socialisation so far has focused on situations where a particular group, such as parents, teachers and religious leaders, have some power and authority to socialise people with less power and authority. However, socialisation can also take place in the interaction between individuals with similar amounts of power or similar status such as friendship networks, school subcultures or groups of work friends; that is in peer groups.

Handel distinguishes between socialisation agents, those such as teachers and parents who may be actively seeking to socialise others, and peer groups. He suggests that peer groups among children operate differently than those for adults because:

> the children play a part in making the rules rather than following those passed down to them by other people

> they are more concerned with immediate gratification (enjoying yourself now) than with making a long-term adjustment to society.

They may also have different values and standards from adults, which can lead to conflict between the peer group and adults.

Thus, for example, teenagers may feel a tension between parental controls and their desire for more responsibility and independence, and so come into conflict with their parents. A common cause for this conflict may be the teenager's choice of friendships – and especially their choice of boyfriend or girlfriend.

Peer pressure

In general, teenagers may feel a great deal of peer pressure to fit in with their friends, and this may lead to radical changes in their identity during their teenage years in terms of their image and behaviour. Some teenagers may feel that they have to engage in 'deviant' behaviour, such as drug-taking, delinquency and under-age sex, in order to be accepted by their peers. Friendship networks may put considerable pressure on teenagers to conform; they may use negative sanctions such as gossip and bullying to control the behaviour of their fellow teenagers.

Do you believe that teenagers are vulnerable to peer pressure? Can they select the peer groups they choose to associate with and are they able to resist peer pressure when it occurs?

Peer groups and young adulthood

Some sociologists, most notably Sue Heath (2004), have suggested that friendship networks are becoming increasingly important as agents of socialisation in the period known as 'young adulthood'. This period is characterised by movement in and out of a variety of independent living arrangements – for example, a student may move between living in a hall of residence, flatsharing and going home to stay with parents. It is also marked out as the period when a person is most likely to be single. Cote (2000) suggests that in young adulthood, peer groups or friendship networks eventually become more important than relationships with parents as a source of knowledge about how to live one's life.

Occupational peer groups

The workplace is another important source of peer-group relationships. Our experience at work teaches us not only skills and work discipline, but also the informal rules that underpin work, that is, the tricks of the trade. We may also be influenced by our membership of more formal work-based organisations to behave in particular ways.

For example, membership of a trade union may produce a collectivist outlook, in which the person puts the interest of the group before their individual interests, whereas membership of a professional organisation, such as the Law Society or the British Medical Association, will make clear how a professional person should behave in practice.

The importance of peer groups helps to demonstrate that individuals can play an active role in their own socialisation either through interaction in small groups or through joining together with peers in order to exercise some power, for example, by joining trade unions.

THE MASS MEDIA AS AN AGENT OF SECONDARY SOCIALISATION

Many sociologists argue that the mass media – newspapers, magazines, television, films, pop music, computer games, the internet, and so on – comprise one of the most significant socialisation agencies today, in terms of their influence over values and norms (and especially those of young people). Many people use the mass media to make sense of the world around them. The media offer a window onto the wider world and provide much of the information required to make sense of events that have a bearing on our everyday lives. The media may also provide us with role models and designs for living, that is, images and ideas that we use to fashion our identities. It is therefore important that all points of view are presented to us in an objective and neutral fashion, because the media may have the power to structure how and what we think.

Marxist sociologists are critical of the mass media because they argue that it is mainly responsible for indoctrination into the values of capitalism. Some see the mass media as helping to create a harmful mass culture. Sociologists such as Marcuse suggested that popular culture, especially television and advertising, has had a negative effect on culture because, as Marsh and Keating note, "popular culture is a false culture devised and packaged by capitalism to keep the masses content." Its function is to encourage 'false needs' (for example, the acquisition of non-essential consumer goods) and to discourage any serious or critical thought, especially that relating to the inequalities caused by the organisation of capitalism.

This theme has been taken up by modern commentators such as Steve Barnett, who argues that media output in the UK that once encouraged a critical outlook, such as quality drama, documentaries and serious news coverage, has gone into decline and is being increasingly replaced with dumbed-down light entertainment – reality shows, soap operas and the like – which focuses on transmitting superficial, mindless entertainment (Barnett and Curry,

1994). Such critics argue that we are being socialised into not being able to think for ourselves.

These critics argue that different people interpret media messages in different ways and audiences do not always passively accept what is being fed to them. This view is sometimes called the 'active audience model' and it sees audiences as selective and, at times, critical. From this point of view, the idea that the audience can be manipulated does not recognise the ways in which they actively and critically use the media to enhance their lives and identities.

More sophisticated recent approaches based partly on Marxist ideas (for example, Philo, Miller and Happer, 2015) counter these criticisms by arguing that the media do have a strong influence in socialising audiences. For example, in studies of audience attitudes to benefit claimants, most of the sample were well aware that the media often portrayed claimants as 'scroungers' and most of those in the study were strongly affected by this view. Only a minority of the sample, who had direct experience of claiming benefits, either themselves or via close friends and family, were likely to be little influenced by the coverage and to reject the idea that most claimants were lazy and a burden on the taxpayer. Not everybody accepts media messages, but messages which are constantly repeated do have considerable influence.

However, the role of the media in socialisation may be changing with the development of social media, which allows members of peer groups to communicate with one another. The messages of the media are no longer simply passed from media professionals to audiences. This may also mean that power is less concentrated in the hands of media companies, which can have some negative effects. For example, peer pressure can be exerted through cyber-bullying.

CONCLUSIONS

Many accounts of socialisation discuss this process as if it is a relatively straightforward, positive and, hence, unproblematic one. However, not all adults acquire the skills necessary to nurture children towards adulthood; as a result, such poor parenting may, unfortunately, result in neglect or child abuse.

Other commentators suggest that childhood socialisation is not as effective today as it was in the past. Postman (1982) suggests that childhood is a much shorter period today compared with 50 years ago and bemoans children's loss of innocence, which he sees as the result of overexposure to sex and violence in the media. Palmer (2007) also notes the negative influence of television and computer games, and argues that parents all too often use these as a substitute for spending quality time interacting with children. She believes that, as a result, children today are less likely to be socialised into important moral codes of behaviour. Phillips (1997) argues that children have too many rights today and claims that they have used these to resist parental power, so undermining socialisation. She suggests that the antisocial behaviour associated with young people today is a direct result of parents being too content not to take responsibility for their children's upbringing. These themes are explored further in Topic 4, Chapter 6.

Socialisation, particularly socialisation by those of high status or in authority, always involves the exercise of power to some degree. People, both children and adults, could always be socialised differently and how they are socialised might benefit some groups more than others. These issues are evident in Marxist views of the media and will be explored in the next three chapters.

Finally, some accounts of socialisation portray it as a one-way process – for example, with the child as a vessel waiting to be filled with the wisdom of its parents. However, interpretivist sociologists point out that socialisation is a two-way process, and that parenting itself is a learning process. Where peer groups are involved in socialisation, this is as much about group interaction as the exercise of power by some people over others.

FOCUS ON RESEARCH: SCHOOL HOLIDAYS INCREASE THE RISK OF CYBER-BULLYING

Many teenagers spend longer online during holidays, as they often stay home during the day and go to bed much later.

Teenagers are at risk of cyber-bullying during the summer holidays as they spend more time online, a charity has warned.

Almost a quarter of 12 to 16-year-olds spend more than five hours a day online during the school holidays, while averaging just over an hour during term time.

Some 20 per cent admitted interacting with strangers online — and 25 per cent said they had witnessed cyber-bullying.

For the report, The Online Behavioural Habits of Young People Today, 1,000 children aged between eight and 16 were questioned, along with 1,500 parents.

Teachers fear that cyber-bullying is a growing issue, and a study by the NSPCC suggested that more than 40 per cent of children can expect to be victims.

Emma-Jane Cross, founder of BeatBullying, said: "What's most worrying is the number of teens who accept being bullied online as part of life, and the fact that many are unaware who they can speak to when they witness bullying online."

"The summer holidays can be a wonderful break for children and families, but the sheer number of hours that some teenagers spend online every day puts them at risk of cyber-bullying. It's vital that parents speak to their children about how to enjoy the Internet safely." Children are most likely to use the internet in their bedrooms, with experts saying this increases the likelihood of getting into difficulties on the web.

Source: Buchanan, R. 'School holidays increase the risk of cyber-bullying', *The Times*, 26 July 2013

Questions

1. Identify and summarise the evidence in this article which suggests that cyber-bullying is a serious problem.

2. Analyse the similarities and differences between face-to-face bullying in a peer group and online bullying. (Use your own knowledge of social media sites and teenage peer groups to do this.)

3. Evaluate the view that online communities/ networks are another type of peer group in which everybody plays an active role in their own socialisation. (Again you can draw on your own experience here and think about whether or not there are passive and active members of online communities/networks.)

4. On the basis of the evidence here and your own knowledge, evaluate the view that online peer groups are taking over part of the role of parents in socialising children. (Do you think the influence of parents is being eroded because of the way social media groups can seep into home life?)

CHECK YOUR UNDERSTANDING

1. Identify six skills that children acquire during primary socialisation.

2. Identify three ways in which socialisation might have negative consequences for some children.

3. Define the term 'peer group'.

4. Define the term 'self' or 'self-concept'.

5. Define the term 'primary socialisation'.

6. Outline and explain one example which suggests that children may play an active role in the process of socialisation.

7. Outline and explain the ways in which children learn to differentiate between 'right' and 'wrong' during primary socialisation.

8. Explain what Parsons means when he describes the family as a 'personality factory'.

9. Compare Marxist and functionalist views on the role of education as an agency of secondary socialisation.

10. Outline and evaluate the view that the peer group is becoming increasingly important as an agent of socialisation.

TAKE IT FURTHER

Using this chapter, design a questionnaire as a class that focuses on what parents think is important in bringing about effective primary socialisation and whether parents share the concerns of commentators such as Postman, Palmer and Phillips that parenting is becoming less effective.

Aim to get at least ten parents to fill in the questionnaire and compile the results as a class.

a. How far do the results reflect the sociological views discussed in this chapter?

b. Evaluate your research methods. How successful were they in obtaining the type of data you wanted?

c. How far could you rely upon this data?

d. How could they have been improved?

3.3 IDENTITY AND SOCIAL CLASS

LEARNING OBJECTIVES

> Understand different ways of defining social class (AO1).

> Understand the identities associated with particular social classes (AO1).

> Apply this understanding to examples from Britain and from different cultures (AO2).

> Analyse the reasons for differences in culture and identity between social classes (AO3).

> Evaluate the claim that social class is no longer an important source of identity in Britain (AO3).

INTRODUCING THE DEBATE

It has often been thought that Britain is a society obsessed with class, and that this was reflected in many aspects of life from leisure activities to voting patterns. Many sociologists in earlier decades saw class as the single most important source of identity and cultural differences, but more recently some have questioned whether it retains much significance at all. Others argue that if you scratch beneath the surface, class is still very influential, and even if we don't think about it as much as we once did it still shapes the way we think of ourselves and others, and the sort of lifestyles we lead.

DEFINING SOCIAL CLASS

Social class can be a difficult concept to define. This is because a person's subjective sense of class identity, that is, what they think they are, may differ from objective attempts to categorise their social class.

Objectively, social class refers to the economic differences between social groups. Some sociologists see wealth as the key to defining social class, but others put more emphasis on income, which is often closely linked to occupation. However, culture is also linked to social class so some definitions of social class take culture and identity into consideration as well. The following are some influential ways of defining class.

1. Karl Marx and Frederick Engels (Marx and Engels, 1848) saw class in terms of differences in wealth or, more specifically, ownership of the means of production – the things required to produce wealth. These consisted of land, raw materials, machinery, labour power (workers) and capital (money used to finance production). From a Marxist point of view, society is essentially divided between a capitalist ruling class (the bourgeoisie) and the rest (the proletariat) who do not own the means of production and therefore have to work for the bourgeoisie. Marx and Engels did recognise some other classes, however, such as landowners and the **petite bourgeoisie** – the self-employed and those with small businesses.

UNDERSTAND THE CONCEPT

The **petite bourgeoisie** ('little' bourgeoisie) are those who have some capital, so they don't have to work for others, but not enough to employ large numbers of workers so that they can live off the profits made by those workers. They are self-employed and own their own tools (some electricians or hairdressers, for example) or they run small businesses such as corner shops. Their identity may be distinctive both from the ruling class and the working class.

2. A more complex view of class is developed by those who see it in terms of income, status and the way that these are linked to different occupations. In government statistics on class, occupations are seen as the main source of income and status.

The government categorises people into one of nine social classes, using an occupational scale known as the National Statistics Socio-Economic Classification (NS-SEC), which is reproduced in Table 3.3.1. The NS-SEC differentiates between different jobs on the basis of employment relations (whether people are employers, self-employed or employees, and how much authority they exercise over others) and market conditions (how much they earn, their promotion opportunities, job security, and so on). Sociologists have observed that groups of people who share similar socio-economic status also share similar educational backgrounds and experiences, lifestyles and outlooks. There is also evidence that there are distinct inequalities between social classes in terms of **life chances**, such as infant mortality, life expectancy, the educational achievement of their children and the distribution of wealth and poverty.

UNDERSTAND THE CONCEPT

Life chances can be defined as the odds on those from different backgrounds gaining or achieving things which are socially desirable, such as high-status well-paid jobs, comfortable housing, good health, a long life or high-level educational qualifications. These are often closely linked to class. Lower classes don't lack opportunities completely, but the odds are stacked against them compared to higher classes.

3. A recent attempt to distinguish classes partly according to economic differences and partly according to social and cultural differences has involved joint research between the BBC and sociologists at Manchester University (Savage *et al.*, 2013). It is based on the ideas of the French sociologist Pierre Bourdieu (1984) who distinguished three types of capital.

› economic capital consisting of income and wealth, measured in the survey through questions on such things as jobs, savings, and home ownership

› social capital involving social contacts, measured through questions on friendships with people from different occupations

› culture, measured through questions on leisure activities and interests – distinctions were made between highbrow culture (or high culture) and lowbrow culture (popular or low culture).

How would you categorise your own class background in terms of the three ways of defining and distinguishing classes discussed here? In the light of your answer and other knowledge, evaluate which of the three provides the best way of defining class. (You can think about whether they seem to fit with opportunities and identities in Britain today.)

Despite the disagreements between sociologists about the precise number of classes, and how they should be measured, it is generally possible to distinguish three or four broad social-class identities that exist in the UK today: the upper class (the very wealthy), the middle class (with well-paid, skilled and high-status employment) and the working class (with regular but less skilled and less high-status jobs). In the view of some people, there is also an underclass of those largely reliant on benefits.

179

1.1	*Employers & managers in large organisations –* Company directors, managers of corporations, police inspectors, bank managers, senior civil servants, military officers
1.2	*Higher professionals –* Doctors, barristers and solicitors, university lecturers, librarians, social workers, teachers
2	*Lower managerial & professional occupations –* Nurses and physiotherapists, journalists, actors and musicians, prison officers, police, soldiers (NCO and below)
3	*Intermediate occupations –* Clerks, driving instructors, computer operators
4	*Small employers & own account workers –* Publicans, playgroup leaders, farmers, taxi drivers, window cleaners, painters and decorators
5	*Lower supervisory, craft & related occupations –* Printers, plumbers, butchers, bus inspectors, TV engineers, train drivers
6	*Semi-routine occupations –* Shop assistants, traffic wardens, cooks, bus drivers, hairdressers, postal workers
7	*Routine occupations –* Waiters, road sweepers, cleaners, couriers, building labourers, refuse collectors
8	*Never worked/long-term unemployed*

Table 3.3.1 *The National Statistics Socio-Economic Classification (NS-SEC) occupational scale*
Source: National Statistics Socio-economic Classification (2010)

This class scheme produced a seven-class model, as shown in Table 3.3.2.

Class	Percentage of British population	Characteristics
Elite	6%	Very high economic capital (especially savings), high social capital, very high highbrow cultural capital
Established middle class	25%	High economic capital, high status of mean contacts, high highbrow and emerging cultural capital
Technical middle class	6%	High economic capital, very high mean status of social contacts, but relatively few contacts reported, moderate cultural capital
New affluent workers	15%	Moderately good economic capital, moderately poor mean score of social contacts, though high range, moderate highbrow but good emerging cultural capital
Traditional working class	14%	Moderately poor economic capital, though with reasonable house price, few social contacts, low highbrow and emerging cultural capital
Emergent service workers	19%	Moderately poor economic capital, though with reasonable household income, moderate social contacts, high emerging (but low highbrow) cultural capital
Precariat	15%	Poor economic capital, and the lowest scores on every other criterion

Table 3.3.2 *The seven-class model*
Source: Savage et al. (2013)

180

FOCUS ON RESEARCH: SOCIAL CLASS AND CULTURE

	Professional executive class	Intermediate class	Working class
More than 5 hrs TV per weekday	8	22	33
Once a year or less to cinema	33	52	62
Read no books last year	8	13	27
Go frequently to night clubs	21	20	23
Go several times a year to opera	10	4	3
Never go to museums	15	33	50
Never go to musicals	19	35	60
Sometimes go to opera	10	4	3
Never go to orchestral concerts	42	64	80
Go to pub at least once a week	29	29	30
Soap opera, favourite TV programme	10	16	22
Sport, favourite TV programme	12	13	12
News/current affairs, favourite TV programme	24	19	14
Who-dunnits, favourite book	32	30	30
Modern literature, least favourite book	26	39	56
Like classical music	43	31	25
Like urban (including hip-hop, R&B) music	17	17	19

Table 3.3.3 *Levels of participation and taste in selected activities, by class (percentages)*
Source: Bennett *et al.* (2009)

Using a three-class model, Tony Bennett and colleagues carried out a survey using a sample of 1,788 people to study the relationship between class, culture and taste. They found that there continued to be a strong relationship between class and culture. The highest class was strongly associated with participation in high culture, while the lowest class (the working class) participated very little in high culture. The highest class also tended to be cultural omnivores – they sampled a full range of culture including popular culture, although few listened to Country and Western music and they watched little reality TV. Tastes also varied between classes; for example, the highest class was more likely to eat in French restaurants, while the lowest class ate fish and chips more often.

Questions

1. Identify three examples of high culture and three examples of popular culture from table 3.3.3

2. Assess the extent to which the cultures of the three classes are distinct and the extent to which they overlap.

3. Explain what you think the researchers mean by 'cultural omnivores'.

4. Suggest three reasons for differences in the cultural preferences of the different classes. (You could think about factors related to subcultures, socialisation, occupation and levels of income.)

5. On the basis of this research, evaluate the view that there are no longer distinct class cultures. (Does the research support this claim or not?)

UPPER-CLASS IDENTITY

Ken Roberts (2011) sees the upper class as consisting of two groups. The old upper class is made up of the aristocracy who got their wealth originally from the ownership of land. The new upper class started to form in the 19th century and made much of their wealth from mining and industry. However, these two groups are now fully integrated and they also increasingly include finance capitalists who have made their money from banking and related occupations. According to Roberts, the upper class develop a common identity and, to some extent, culture through the operation of what is sometimes called 'the establishment'. They tend to meet each other at social events such as the Oxford and Cambridge Boat Race, the Lord Mayor's Banquet, pheasant shoots and the Chelsea Flower Show. Often they are members of the same exclusive London clubs. There are close connections between different families in the upper class due to high rates of inter-marriage. Many members of the upper class share a similar educational background, having attended top public (independent) schools such as Eton and Harrow, and many have attended elite universities such as Oxford and Cambridge. These types of institutions mould the ideas and outlooks of their students so that they quickly realise their common upper-class interests. They are likely to promote the values of conservatism, especially respect for tradition, as well as hostility towards socialist ideals. Moreover, these schools and universities produce 'old-boy' or 'old school-tie' networks made up of people who share the same cultural values and assets, and who use these contacts to further each other's adult careers and influence.

There is some evidence that the value system of the upper class differs from that of other social classes. John Scott (1991) notes that the conservative values of tradition and the acceptance of privilege, hierarchy and authority are regarded as particularly important aspects of upper-class identity. Upper-class tastes and activities generally focus on higher cultural pursuits, such as classical music, theatre, opera and ballet. Other leisure activities revolve around exclusive social events that provide a distinctive upper-class lifestyle, such as debutantes' balls, hunting, shooting and sports such as polo and rowing.

The upper class, therefore, is a self-selecting and exclusive elite relatively closed to outsiders, which is known as 'social closure'. This is reinforced by parents encouraging their children to choose partners from other upper-class families and by the practice of sending children away to boarding schools.

Some people who are not from upper class backgrounds can gain wealth quickly, for example, through winning the lottery. Can such people really be considered part of the upper class? If not, why not? Are their children likely to become upper class?

THE MIDDLE CLASS

The term 'middle class' is used in a broad way to describe non-manual workers, those who do not work 'with their hands'. They tend to rely more upon their education and intellectual abilities, as opposed to physical ability and experience in making things, like manual workers. This slightly crude distinction is often used to distinguish the middle and working class.

Savage's research (1995) describes four distinct types of middle-class groups and therefore identities.

> *Professionals such as doctors and lawyers* – Savage claims that this group subscribes to an intellectual identity gained from a long and successful education. He claims that they value cultural assets or capital such as knowledge, qualifications, achievement, experience of higher education and altruism (they often see themselves as serving a higher purpose – namely, society).

> *Managers* are generally less qualified than professionals and are more likely to have worked their way up in a company from the shop or office floor. Savage suggests that this group generally defines its status and identity in terms of its standard of living and leisure pursuits. Managerial middle-class identity is less secure today compared with the past because of factors such as globalisation, economic recession, mergers and takeovers.

> *Self-employed owners of small businesses* – Roberts notes that this group has traditionally been very individualistic. Surveys suggest that they believe that people should be independent and stand on their own two feet rather than rely on the welfare state. They also have great faith in hard work and discipline – believing firmly that success in life is a result of effort and application rather than luck.

> *White-collar or clerical workers* – Clerks and secretaries, for example, have traditionally been seen as having a middle-class identity, despite often being the children of manual workers, because their pay and working

conditions were superior to manual workers. However, the introduction of technology such as computers has led to their pay and status going into decline, and it is suggested that they now have more in common with the working class. However, surveys of clerical workers indicate that they still see themselves as middle class. They rarely mix with manual workers, and spend their leisure time and money in quite different ways.

Despite these differences in material circumstances, sociologists such as Roberts argue that these different groups do share some values, such as an emphasis on career success. A general middle-class identity can be seen to exist, mainly focused on the home. The middle class values home ownership; they are more likely than other social groups to have mortgages, own their own home and live in the suburbs. They are generally a commuting class.

Members of the middle class generally encourage their children to do well in education. Many are keen on private education, although their children often do exceptionally well within the state sector. Middle-class parents often move home to get their children into the catchment area for the best state primary and secondary schools. Their children dominate the top streams of state schools, get the best GCSE results, are more likely to stay on and do A-levels, and dominate the university sector.

FOCUS ON SKILLS: I'M IN THE TECHNICAL MIDDLE CLASS... GET ME OUT OF HERE!

Glastonbury Festival – just one of many places in Britain where class identity is irrelevant?

The class system is dead, except in BBC dramas and university sociology departments. Yesterday the BBC joined forces with the sociologists to modernise old social divisions. Their 'Great British Class Survey', analysing data from 161,000 people, came up with seven different categories.

This all proves that in modern Britain class is utterly fluid to the point of being meaningless. Contrary to the myths peddled by politicians, lack of social mobility is not a significant problem. Eighty per cent of children born in households below the poverty line are no longer poor when they grow up. Almost everyone moves between two or more categories during their lifetime. The only exception is a small group within the Precariat whose poor education holds them back, yet even their prospects are much better than those of manual labourers 60 years ago.

It's pointless to divide people up — the rise of service industries, from banking to coffee shops via web design and personal fitness, means that job classifications no longer denote income levels. And a huge expansion in home ownership starting in the Thatcher years has broken the link between property-owning and privilege. Posh accents are irrelevant — everyone can speak Estuary now, including the Chancellor.

Education has also dissolved the class system — a university degree has increased opportunity for many more people but it is no longer a predictor of financial security. A young academic with two post-graduate degrees is defined as Precariat by this survey because his income is low and he rents his home. But the owner of a nail bar is one of the New Affluent because she eats out at trendy restaurants and lives in a smart urban apartment. Yet both grew up in households with average income, have friends who are teachers and IT workers and organise their social lives through Facebook.

Neither can be defined by abstract notions of class. It's a shame that sociologists are still bound by it.

Source: Kirkby, J. 'I'm in the Technical Middle Class... get me out of here', *The Times*, 4 Apriial 2013

Questions

1. **Outline** the arguments put forward to suggest that class is no longer significant.

2. **Explain** what is meant by the claim that a rise in home ownership 'has broken the link between property-owning and privilege'.

3. **Explain** what is meant by 'service industries'.

4. **Evaluate.** Using the evidence and arguments in this chapter, evaluate the arguments put forward in the article. What evidence is there in the chapter to contradict these claims?

The middle class generally believes in the concept of meritocracy – that high position and status can be achieved by ability or effort. It is said that the middle class is more willing than other social groups to 'defer gratification' (for example, financial rewards or pleasure) in the pursuit of education. In other words, they are more willing to make sacrifices while qualifications are achieved.

However, despite some similarities there are undoubtedly a range of significant differences in the middle class. As well as those differences already mentioned, those who are employed by the state (in health, education and government) may have different cultures and identities to those employed in private businesses. Their income comes from different sources and this may influence their attitudes and values.

THE WORKING CLASS

The traditional working class

Sociological evidence suggests that those engaged in traditional manual work, especially in industries such as mining and factory work – the working class, had a very strong sense of their economic or social-class position. This traditional working-class identity was dominant for most of the 20th century and is still very influential in some parts of the UK today.

Manual workers, probably more than any other group of workers, identified very strongly with each other. This was partly due to the dangerous nature of some manual jobs (such as mining) but was also due to the collective nature of their jobs; for example, factories were often made up of thousands of workers controlled by a minority of supervisors, managers and employers. This led to a strong sense that the world was divided into 'them', the bosses (capital), who were only interested in exploiting the workers and making profits, and 'us', the worker on the shop floor (labour). Consequently, relations between management and labour until the 1980s were often characterised by mistrust and hostility. Many workers belonged to trade unions, which represented workers' interests and engaged in industrial action when it was thought that such interests were being threatened by management.

BUILD CONNECTIONS

Working-class culture has been linked with attitudes to education by some researchers who have used differences in middle-class and working-class subcultures to explain differences in educational achievement. How clear cut these distinctions are and how important they are in explaining achievement is disputed. They are discussed in Topic 1, Chapter 2.

There is evidence that the traditional working class had a strong political identity and saw the Labour Party as representing its natural interests against those of the employers. At general elections until the 1970s, the Labour Party could therefore count on the loyal support of about 80 per cent of the working-class electorate. Trade-union support for Labour reinforced this political allegiance.

Such workers also had a strong sense of their class identity because they often lived in close-knit communities made up of extended kinship networks. Adult children often lived close to their parents and saw them on a regular basis. Mutual support was offered by a range of relatives, especially in terms of childcare, financial help and finding work.

The decline of traditional working-class identity

More recently, some researchers have claimed that traditional working-class identity is less important today because of the decline in manual work over the last 30 years. The numbers employed in traditional heavy industries, such as mining and shipbuilding, have fallen rapidly since the 1970s and 1980s. Consequently, manual workers now make up well under half the total workforce, so the economic basis for class identity and solidarity has weakened. However, research by Robert McKenzie et al. (2006) among redundant steelworkers, and Darren Theil (2007) among building workers, has found that a sense of belonging to the working class still exists in some groups of workers and they also retain quite a strong sense of solidarity with workmates or former workmates. The ex-steelworkers in the study by McKenzie et al. also saw society as strongly divided between a disadvantaged working class and a powerful ruling class. In recent years, this awareness of class inequality has continued to be widely expressed in the form of hostility to bankers and other groups among the very rich, particularly those who find ways to pay little tax.

Nevertheless, it may be dangerous to generalise about the working class as a whole. As early as the 1960s, researchers identified a new sort of working-class identity, mainly found in the South East, which saw work as a means to an end, that is, a wage, rather than as a source of community, status and identity (Goldthorpe et al., 1968). This working-class identity now tends to be found in the newer types of high-tech manufacturing industries. This new working class has no heightened sense of class injustice or political loyalty. They believe in individualism (putting themselves and their immediate families first), rather than collective or community action. They define themselves through their families, their lifestyle and their standard of living, rather than through their work. They vote for whichever political party furthers their individual financial interests. These workers had not become middle class, but they had changed their identities and differentiated themselves from the rest of the working class. However, Mike Savage (2005) argues that the distinctiveness of a new working class can be exaggerated, and that most of this group still see society as sharply divided between 'us' (the disadvantaged workers) and 'them' (the rich).

'Chavs'

Social groups cannot always maintain the identity they would like to have; sometimes a negative identity can be imposed on them whether they like it or not. Recent research has suggested that a very negative identity – that of the 'Chav' – has been imposed on parts of the working class (particularly the young working class) by the media. Beverley Skeggs (2015) has researched the way that reality TV and game shows frequently portray the working class as immoral, lazy and uncultured. Programmes such as *Snog Marry Avoid*, *Wife Swap* and *The Jeremy Kyle Show* position the viewer as someone of higher class who should sneer at the primitive behaviour and tastes of their inferiors. While members of the working class might try to distance themselves from such identities, it might be difficult to do so, particularly if they are seen by others as members of an even lower class – the underclass.

The underclass

Another type of working-class identity may be held by those who exist at the margins of society. A number of commentators, most notably Murray (1994) and Mount (2004), have identified a supposed 'new' form of working-class identity organised around dependency upon state benefits. This is the so-called urban underclass allegedly found on run-down council estates and in the depressed inner cities. He sees this group as consisting of individuals such as the long-term unemployed, single parents, drug addicts and criminals. Murray suggests that the culture and identity of this underclass revolve around being work-shy, feckless, anti-authority, anti-education, immoral and welfare-dependent. It is suggested, too, that the children of the underclass are being socialised by their inadequate parents into a culture of idleness, failure and criminality.

Unemployment, poverty and identity

Not everyone agrees that this so-called deviant underclass exists. Studies of the poor and long-term unemployed carried out by Jordan (1992) suggest that those living in poverty share the same ideas about work and family as everyone else. Surveys also show that the unemployed want to work in order to gain the respect of their loved ones and

to regain their dignity. Surveys indicate that unemployment often brings with it negative self-image or identity, shame, guilt, low self-esteem, insecurity and poor mental and physical health. These are not feelings or effects that people choose to have. Furthermore, most unemployed people do not enjoy a high standard of living. They often lack basics, are in debt and feel guilty because their children go without at crucial times such as birthdays and Christmas.

Jordan also notes that most people do not choose to be unemployed or poor, or to be dependent on welfare benefits. Rather, it is often the fault of global recession, government policies and the fact that capitalist companies find it more profitable to close down factories in the UK and instead exploit workers in the developing world. The unemployed and poor are therefore excluded by society, rather than choosing this lifestyle.

Simon Charlesworth's study of working-class people on a run-down council estate in Rotherham in 2000 suggests that those at the bottom end of the working class are often misunderstood by other social classes because they experience negative self-identity and low self-esteem. He argues that their negative experience of education results in them devaluing themselves, restricting their ambitions to 'being disappointed' in life and hence turning to drink, drugs or antisocial behaviour as a form of compensation. But their response is a rational one to the economic decay of their area. It is often only through such behaviour that they can manage to make ends meet, cope with psychological problems and continual disappointment, and continue to survive in such a hostile and unforgiving environment.

There are undoubtedly some groups at the bottom of the class structure who are poor, disadvantaged and unable to participate in society in the same way as those with secure employment. However, whether they have a distinctive identity and lifestyle is more debatable because they have a great deal in common with low-paid groups in the working class.

THE DECLINE OF SOCIAL CLASS AS A SOURCE OF IDENTITY

In recent years, some sociologists have argued that class has ceased to be the main factor in creating identity. Postmodernists such as Crook, Pakulski and Waters (1992) argue that class identity has fragmented into numerous separate identities – young people, in particular, have more choice today as to how they construct their identity. For example, a young male might experiment with identity by taking ideas from femininity (make-up, accessories), global culture (a t-shirt celebrating an

185

American band), a media role model (copying their hero's hairstyle or attitude) and consumption (wearing designer shades or labelled clothing). It is argued, therefore, that social class as a source of identity is no longer recognised by the young, and hybrid identities (where different identities are fused together) are increasingly the norm.

However, there is some evidence that postmodern ideas may be exaggerated. A Guardian/ICM poll conducted in October 2007 showed that 89 per cent of the sample, including the majority of 18 to 24 year olds who took part, believed that social class was still a significant influence on their lives.

Postmodernists also ignore the fact that, for many, consumption – that is, the ability to buy designer labels and so on – depends on having a job and an income. Poverty is going to limit any desire to pursue a postmodern lifestyle. In other words, consumption – what we buy – depends ultimately on social class and, as the research by Bennett et al. discussed earlier shows, even our culture and tastes are still strongly influenced by social class.

Harriet Bradley (1996) takes a more balanced position on the relationship between class and identity. She accepts that class has become a weaker source of identity in contemporary Britain, even though there is very significant class inequality and polarisation between the rich (who are getting richer) and the poor. Class is therefore still important, but other sources of identity, including gender, ethnicity and age, are increasingly important as sources of identity so that no single source of identity dominates. Bradley therefore argues that fractured identities (identities made up of different pieces or fragments) are typical today, whereas a single overarching identity associated with class was more typical in the past. Some of the other important sources of identity are examined in Chapters 4–6.

CHECK YOUR UNDERSTANDING

1. Identify six types of inequality or difference that can be linked to social class.

2. Identify three ways to define social class.

3. Define the term 'cultural capital'.

4. Define the term 'social closure'.

5. Define the term 'life chances'.

6. Outline and explain one example which suggests that some groups still have a strong class identity.

7. Outline and explain the ways in which the upper class develop a strong identity.

8. Explain what Murray meant by the 'underclass'.

9. Analyse and explain the similarities and differences between working-class and middle-class culture and identity.

10. Outline and evaluate the view that class identity is no longer important in Britain today.

TAKE IT FURTHER

Take the BBC class calculator test at http://www.bbc.co.uk/news/magazine-22000973

You may need to ask your parent(s)/guardian(s) to answer some of the questions. What class do you come out as? What are the characteristics of this class? Do you agree with the results and why? Follow this up by looking at this news article which discusses the class model (www.bbc.co.uk/news/uk-22007058) and a page on how you identify the classes (www.bbc.co.uk/science/0/22001963). What do you think are the strengths and weaknesses of this way of looking at class?

3.4 IDENTITY, GENDER AND SEXUALITY

LEARNING OBJECTIVES

> Understand the meaning of sex and gender (AO1).

> Understand the identities associated with masculinity, femininity and different sexualities (AO1).

> Apply this understanding to different cultures within the UK (AO2).

> Analyse the reasons for differences in culture and identity between those of different genders and sexualities (AO3).

> Evaluate the extent of change in gender identities and sexual identities in recent decades in Britain (AO3).

INTRODUCING THE DEBATE

Your identity as female or male, and as heterosexual, homosexual or bisexual, is commonly thought to be the result of your biology. However, sociologists have challenged these assumptions and looked at the ways in which masculinity, femininity and different sexualities may be socially constructed. It is fairly obvious that the role of males and females in British society have changed in recent decades, as have attitudes towards those who are not heterosexual. This strongly suggests that the identities associated with gender and sexuality are not simply the product of biology but are connected to the sort of society you live in at a particular point in time. This chapter examines changing gender and sexual identities in Britain.

GENDER-ROLE SOCIALISATION

When examining the source of our identities as males and females, sociologists distinguish between the concepts of **sex** and **gender**.

Gender expectations are transmitted to the next generation through gender-role socialisation. Sociologists believe that gender differences between males and females are largely the result of society's expectations. Sociologists therefore argue that masculinity and femininity are **socially constructed** rather than being the product of biology.

UNDERSTAND THE CONCEPT

The term **sex** refers to the biological differences between males and females, for example, chromosomes, hormones, menstruation and genitalia. The concept of **gender**, however, refers to the cultural expectations that society associates with 'masculinity' and 'femininity'. Men and women are expected to conform to expectations about 'masculine' and 'feminine' behaviour. Such expectations are not fixed – they change over time and are often different in other cultures.

Something can be said to be **socially constructed** if it is a product of society and not a product of the natural world. Often things which may be taken to be natural are instead seen by sociologists as a product of society, including the differences in behaviour between men and women and beliefs about that behaviour. For example, the idea that males are naturally aggressive is seen by many sociologists as a social construct, as is the idea that women are naturally more emotional than men.

The idea that gender is a social construction has been strongly supported by feminist sociologists. There are different types of feminist, including **radical feminists** and **liberal feminists**, but all agree that ideas about gender stem from male domination of society or **patriarchy**.

UNDERSTAND THE CONCEPT

Feminists agree that women are disadvantaged and exploited in existing society and that this should be changed. **Radical feminists** see the exploitation of women as the most significant type of exploitation and inequality in society and they tend to argue that although there may have been many changes in society, these have been superficial and limited, and society continues to be very much dominated by men. They see revolutionary change as necessary to overthrow patriarchy. **Liberal feminists** tend to accept that women have made significant progress in countries such as Britain, although they think there is a long way to go before equality is achieved. They see gradual change as the solution.

Patriarchy is the central concept in feminist theory. Literally it means 'rule by the father' but it is used more generally to refer to systems or societies that are dominated by men and run in the interests of men.

The influential feminist writer Judith Butler (1999) further argues that gender is just a performance. Her theory of performativity suggests that practising or performing a

gender role is vital to becoming masculine or feminine. From this point of view, it is not something which comes naturally. After many repetitions of acting in a 'feminine' or 'masculine' way, the body becomes programmed to act out the roles of man and woman; to walk, talk or behave like a member of one sex or another. However, Butler believes it is possible to undermine gender roles by 'subversive body acts' involving acting in ways which are not seen as 'normal' for a particular sex (for example, men dressing as and walking like women or vice versa).

Do you agree that if men and women all started acting differently this would undermine traditional gender differences and identities? Would the power of men (patriarchy) prevent the changes from happening?

THE FAMILY AND GENDER-ROLE SOCIALISATION

Sociologists note that from an early age infants and children are trained to conform to social expectations about their gender. Much of this training goes on in the family during primary socialisation. Oakley (1982) identifies four processes central to the construction of gender identity.

1 *Manipulation* refers to the ways in which parents encourage and reward or discourage behaviour on the basis of whether it is appropriate for the child's sex.

2 *Canalisation* refers to the ways in which parents direct children's interests towards toys and play activities that are seen as normal for their sex.

3 *Domestic activities* – Daughters may have cultural expectations about their future responsibilities that are reinforced by parents insisting they help with housework.

4 *Verbal appellations* – Parents may reinforce cultural expectations by referring to daughters and sons using stereotypical feminine and masculine descriptions such as 'pretty' and 'handsome'.

Gender codes
Gender-role socialisation therefore involves the learning of gender codes, which generally result in social conformity

to expectations about appropriate gender behaviour. These include:

> *colour codes* – for example, dressing boys in blue and girls in pink (although the association of these colours with boys and girls is historically quite new)

> *appearance codes* – for example, we learn what dress, hairstyles, cosmetics and jewellery are appropriate for males and females

> *toy codes* – for example, gender-specific toys give us clues about our expected future gender roles, that is, girls get dolls for mothering while boys may receive aggressive toys

> *play codes* – for example, boys may be expected to play boisterously whereas girls may be expected to play in more docile or decorous ways

> *control codes* – boys and girls are subjected to different types of social control, especially when they reach their teenage years, with girls often being interrogated more closely about their social lives, boyfriends, and so on, than boys.

Statham (1986) found that by the age of 5, most children have acquired a clear gender identity. They know what gender they belong to and they have a clear idea of what constitutes appropriate behaviour for that gender.

BUILD CONNECTIONS

The discussion of conjugal roles in the family (see Topic 4, Chapter 5) shows that, despite changes, there are still significant gender differences in who does what around the home. Mothers and fathers may still therefore act as role models, contributing to sons and daughters adoption of different gender identities.

THE MASS MEDIA AND TRADITIONAL GENDER-ROLE SOCIALISATION

Billington *et al.* (1998) argue that the mass media have traditionally portrayed masculinity as dominant and femininity as subordinate, so that women have generally been represented on television in a narrow range of social roles, whereas men have been shown performing the full range of social and occupational roles. Women have rarely been shown in high-status occupational roles; rather they have tended to be overrepresented in domestic settings – as busy housewives, contented mothers, eager consumers, and so on. Women have often been presented as sexual objects to be enjoyed by men.

The most extreme media version of this is pornography, which has become more accessible for children with the development of digital technology. A National Union of Teachers report (Coughlan, 2013) found evidence of increased sexualisation of images of women in the media, for example, in pop music videos and even in video games. Research clearly shows that the media tend to emphasise the importance of appearance and attractiveness for girls and women. For example, research by Tebbel (2000) found that there are more than ten times more adverts and articles about weight loss in women's magazines than in men's magazines.

REFINING GENDER-ROLE SOCIALISATION

The idea of gender-role socialisation has been refined in two main ways.

> The experiences of men and women vary greatly. There are huge differences in the experience of socialisation because of factors such as ethnicity, social class and age. Most accounts of gender socialisation ignore these differences (although Connolly's research discussed below is an exception). For example, there is evidence that socialisation into gender roles in Asian families may be more traditional and hegemonic than is found in other ethnic groups. See Chapter 5 for further evidence of these processes.

> It is assumed that women passively accept the traditional gender identity imposed on them. Gender-role socialisation neglects the choices that people have in developing an identity and the fact that many women and men resist attempts to make them conform to hegemonic gender stereotypes.

These criticisms are taken into account in more sophisticated research into the development of identities. For example, Paul Connolly (1998) studied the formation of identity among 5- and 6-year-olds in an ethnically mixed inner-city primary school. He found that children brought their own expectations about masculinity and femininity into school, and these did not always fit with those of their teachers and peer groups. Gender also interacted with ethnicity in identity formation, and some of the black girls were willing to challenge the idea that boys would be dominant in school.

Hegemonic definitions of masculinity and femininity

R. Connell (1995, 2009) argues that there is no single version of masculinity or femininity in societies such as modern Britain. Instead, there are several different ways of being male and being female. Nevertheless, there is still a dominant or **hegemonic** type of masculinity and a traditional set of ideas about how men and women are supposed to behave in the UK has dominated our culture until fairly recently.

> ## UNDERSTAND THE CONCEPT
>
> **Hegemony** means political and social dominance so that a particular set of ideas are dominant in a particular society. Hegemony never involves complete control. It might require negotiation or compromise with less powerful groups and their ideas, but it still allows one group to keep most of the power and to have the biggest influence on how people think.

Hegemonic masculinity in Britain today is the masculinity of white, middle-class men. It values rationality, control, power, toughness and dominance, and looks down on weakness and anything which is seen as being effeminate (behaviour or mannerisms seen as typical of women). From this point of view, openly displaying emotion and affection are seen as more feminine behaviours. Hegemonic masculinity still sees traditional gender roles as normal (if a little more flexible than in the past) with men still seen as the primary breadwinners and women as the primary carers. Hegemonic masculinity still assumes that men should be the head of the household. However, hegemonic masculinity is not the only type of masculinity; there are variations on it and new alternatives are emerging.

SOCIAL CHANGE AND MASCULINE IDENTITY IN THE 21ST CENTURY

R. Connell argues that masculinity today is experiencing change. There now exist, in addition to the hegemonic type of masculinity, other alternative types of masculinity. They are not as high status as hegemonic forms, but they are at least becoming more acceptable. Gay masculinity is one example. Another is a sensitive and non-competitive form of masculinity sometimes associated with men who have become vegetarians or who support the environmental movement. Other sociologists have identified a range of new emerging types of masculinity.

> Some sociologists suggest that a 'new man' has emerged in recent decades who is more in touch with his feminine and emotional feelings, and who shares childcare and housework with his female partner. However, others have suggested that this is merely a creation of the advertising industry and that surveys show that although men have increased their share of domestic and childcare tasks, true equality within the home is still a long way off.

> Mort (1996) has highlighted the emergence of metrosexual men. These are heterosexual males who are concerned with image and consequently invest in personal grooming products such as hair conditioners and skincare products. David Beckham is often cited as a prime example of metrosexual man.

> Mac an Ghaill (1996) claims that hegemonic masculinity may be experiencing a 'crisis of masculinity' because of the decline of traditional industries and the resulting unemployment. Work is central to the identity of traditional men, and unemployment can therefore lead to a loss of self-esteem and status as well as a loss of identification with others. Younger males may see their futures as bleak and so view schooling and qualifications as irrelevant to their needs. This may reinforce educational failure as they seek alternative sources of status in activities in which they can stress their masculinity, such as delinquency and gang violence.

However, although masculinity has undergone some change, it would be a mistake to exaggerate these trends. Collier (2002), for example, notes that women are still objectified in an explicitly sexual fashion in parts of the media, and there is a whole media industry devoted to encouraging women to perfect their figures, make-up and sexual desirability for the benefit of men.

SOCIAL CHANGE AND FEMININE IDENTITY

Today, female achievement at all levels of the examination system outstrips that of males (although a significant number of working-class females continue to underachieve). This success is partly the result of educational changes, including a national curriculum that aimed to prevent the gender stereotyping of subject choice. However, the main cause is probably the profound changes that the economy has experienced in the last 25 years. Changes in demand for British goods and the globalisation of the economy have led to changes in the labour market, particularly a decline in traditional industries such as mining, iron and steel, heavy engineering, and so on (which mainly employed men). While demand for men's jobs fell, there was a corresponding expansion in the service sector of the economy, that is, white-collar and professional jobs in financial and government services, managers of retail outlets in new shopping centres, and so on. Most of these new jobs were gender-neutral; there was no clear preference for men or women filling the roles.

Wilkinson (1994) argues that the feminisation of the economy and the workplace has led to a revolution in women's ambitions. Wilkinson argues that family commitments no longer have priority in many women's lives; careers and economic independence are now the defining feature of young women's identity and self-esteem. Younger women and girls are encouraged to think along these lines because they are likely to experience the positive role model of a mother who enjoys a career rather than just a part-time job. Some young women choose voluntary childlessness and a career as an alternative to getting married and having children.

Natasha Walter (2010), however, argues that while opportunities for women have increased dramatically, and women do have much greater independence to form their own identities than in the past, new forms of sexism are creating problems for women. In her book, *Living Dolls: The Return of Sexism* she suggests that a new hypersexual culture places a very strong emphasis upon women's appearance and puts great pressure on women to conform. While women no longer need to base their identities around mother and wife roles, patriarchal culture demands that they base their identities primarily around their heterosexual attractiveness. Even female politicians are frequently seen in terms of their perceived sexual attractiveness (or lack of attractiveness).

Consumption, leisure and feminine identity

Increasing economic independence means that women are now viewed as significant consumers. There are signs that mass-media products are increasingly being targeted at single women. This means that young women today are also likely to see consumption and leisure as key factors in their identity. Such processes have supposedly led to the emergence of 'girl power' and 'ladettes', who are increasingly adopting male forms of behaviour, such as drinking and smoking heavily, and being sexually aggressive. However, writers such as Whelehan (2000) see it as questionable whether these consumer freedoms really allow women to choose their own identities, or merely pressurise young women to conform to patriarchal identities that are both sexualised and sexist.

IDENTITY AND SEXUALITY

Biology versus culture

Theories of sexuality can be divided into those which see sexuality as a product of biology, and those which see it as a social construction (Cronin, 1997). There is a widespread belief that the sexuality of individuals is biological – that we are born gay, straight or bisexual. In recent times, this view has been supported by the idea that there is a 'gay gene'. However, some sociologists have disputed this and have seen sexual preference as more a matter of choice than

as something that is biologically determined. Ann Cronin argues that the idea of heterosexuality or homosexuality being something you *are* rather than something you *choose* only really developed in the 17th century, at the time when a distinctive homosexual social identity became established. This suggests that, in important respects, sexuality can be seen as a social construct, much like gender.

IDENTITY AND HOMOSEXUALITY

In the UK, heterosexuality has been traditionally defined as the dominant and ideal form of sexuality because of its links to reproduction. This is known as **heteronormativity**.

> **UNDERSTAND THE CONCEPT**
>
> **Heteronormativity** is the acceptance in a culture that heterosexual relationships are the norm and all other types of sexual relationship are abnormal and deviant because they break norms of behaviour. Heteronormativity portrays heterosexuality as superior to all other forms of sexuality.

In contrast, homosexuality was seen in the early part of the 20th century as a form of abnormal sexuality. Some saw it as a type of mental illness brought about by factors such as too much mothering and the lack of a strong father figure. In the UK, homosexual activity between men was made illegal in the 19th century and was punishable by imprisonment. Many homosexual men were subjected to electric shock treatment in the 1950s and 1960s in an attempt to 'cure' them of their condition.

These repressive attempts to control homosexuality made it exceptionally difficult for gay men to 'come out' and publicly declare their homosexuality. However, in the 1950s, cultural attitudes towards homosexuality began to shift, and homosexual acts between consenting adults over the age of 21 years were decriminalised in the 1960s. By the 1970s, homosexuality was no longer defined as a psychiatric condition by doctors. In 2001, the age of consent for homosexual activity was lowered to 16, the same as that for heterosexual activity. In 2005, Civil Partnerships for same-sex couples were introduced and in 2014, the first same-sex marriages took place under new legislation. In 1999, the first laws prohibiting discrimination on the basis of sexuality were introduced and these were extended further in the Equality Act of 2010.

191

FOCUS ON SKILLS: A BRUTAL CHOICE – CHANGE SEX OR KILL YOURSELF

Conchita Wurst - the Austrian winner of the 2014 Eurovision Song Contest

They're used to the vilification. Now transgender people have had enough and are poised to demand their civil rights.

A month before the self-styled 'bearded lady' Conchita Wurst was hailed queen of a tolerant, rainbow Europe, Britain had a milder revolutionary moment. Emma Laslett, a student of French at Lincoln College, Oxford, competed in the semi-final of *Mastermind* (specialist subject, coincidentally, Eurovision 1981 to the present day).

It takes nerve to enter that unblinking spotlight, but immeasurably more for Emma, a transgender woman who does not, as she says, easily 'pass' as female. Comments online were of the 'Gawd, there's a bloke in a frock on *Mastermind*' variety. But Emma says this is just the 'background radiation' of her life.

In an otherwise mindful world, transgender people are just about the last group it is permissible to mock. 'We are', as Emma says, 'the punchline to every joke.' From Shakespeare to *Little Britain* cross-dressing is seen as hilarious.

In Britain tolerance of gays and lesbians is now almost universal: to my kids a person's sexuality is no more remarkable than hair colour. So why are transgender people still vilified, far more likely to be beaten up or even murdered, and ostracised at work (if they can find a job at all)?

Perhaps because they make up 0.5 per cent of the population, a tiny minority, easy to cast out as freaks. But in a school of 1,000 pupils that means five children will feel that their biological sex and the gender they

identify with do not correspond. Emma says she felt female from 15, but at an all-boys school told no one — 'I got very good at repression' – until at 19, depressed and self-harming, she felt she must either change or kill herself. Helped by a girlfriend she 'transitioned' into a woman without warning her Oxford circle, to a stunned but mainly positive response. Relief was immediate: 'It's like you've been wearing a really itchy suit your entire life and didn't know until now you could take it off.'

A tortured childhood is the norm for those such as Emma. In America, parents are pressing for children who 'persistently and insistently' identify with a different gender to play in opposite-sex sports teams. In Britain, there is a furore about prescribing drugs that temporarily block the onset of puberty to gender-confused children as young as ten. It sounds like meddling medical insanity until you read how postponing dreaded secondary sexual characteristics reduces the horrific suicide rate.

Transgender people are fed up too with our prurient obsession with what's in their pants.

And they have a point. For years we fixated about what gays do in bed until we got over ourselves and saw them as people. The ultimate liberation for Emma would be appearing on cosy, middle-England *Mastermind* and no one remarking on anything but her score.

Source: Turner, J. 'A brutal choice: change sex or kill yourself', *The Times*, 31 May 2014

Questions

1. **Understanding**. What does the author mean by saying that 'The ultimate liberation for Emma would be appearing on cosy, middle-England *Mastermind* and no one remarking on anything but her score'?

2. **Analysis.** Using your sociological understanding of gender, analyse the reasons why transgender people often find life in contemporary Britain difficult.

3. **Explain** how transgender people demonstrate that 'sex' and 'gender' are not always matched to one another.

4. **Evaluate** the claim that 'transgender people are just about the last group it seems permissible to mock'.

As Taylor (1997) notes, female homosexuals, that is, lesbians, have always had a much lower social profile than gay men. As we have seen, the law generally criminalised gay men until the 1960s, but not lesbians. Changes in the law, changing cultural attitudes towards homosexuality, and the feminisation of education and the economy benefited lesbian women. Many sought to bring about greater social change for women in general by becoming involved in the radical feminist movement, which sees political and sexual separateness from men as a necessity if patriarchy is to be overcome.

FOCUS ON RESEARCH: EDMUND COLEMAN-FOUNTAIN (2015)

Many gay and lesbian young people no longer feel they have to be in private or go to a gay bar/club to express their sexuality.

Coleman-Fountain conducted research in North-East England in which he carried out in-depth interviews with 14 young gay men and 5 lesbians all aged between 16 and 21. He was interested in the effects that changes in the law and changes in attitude had had on the identities of young gay men and young lesbian women. He found that the young people had a somewhat contradictory attitude towards their identities. They welcomed what they saw as a new-found freedom to express their sexuality in many public places – for example, by kissing or holding hands – without having to be in a private place or in a gay/lesbian bar or club. However, they still felt there were places where this was impossible, such as the Bigg Market in Newcastle – an area with many pubs, which is still seen as being quite 'rough' and macho

Many gay and lesbian interviewees said that they just wanted to be accepted as 'normal people' who were 'like anyone else'. Some of the gay men tried to avoid being seen as 'camp' so they could fit in with the heterosexual population. Many did not want their identity to be based exclusively on their sexuality – they just wanted being gay to be seen as one of their identities, among many others. However, they also had a sense of pride in their difference from others and many did not want to lose this sense of pride. Coleman-Fountain says, "In hindsight it seems to me that some of the more interesting material involved participants trying to justify still going to the gay scene when it was the 'mainstream' they really thought they ought to be a part of. Sometimes this was because they felt that 'straight' bars were not welcoming, but at others it was about a shared sense of identity. Despite many emphasising their sameness to heterosexuals (and others suggesting that sexuality is more complicated than 'straight' and lesbian/gay), they saw the value of a sociality based on difference."

Based on Coleman-Fountain (2015)

Questions

1. Outline the ways in which the interviewees took pride in their sexuality.

2. Explain why they still 'wanted to be accepted as 'normal'' despite their pride in their identity.

3. Evaluate the extent to which this evidence suggests that gay and lesbian identities are now accepted by 'straight' society.

Homosexuality, leisure and consumption

By the 1970s, a distinct gay subculture could be seen to have emerged in British culture, offering a positive gay identity. Much of the gay subculture that emerged focused on leisure and consumption – the 'pink pound' or spending power of gay professionals was targeted by gay bars, clubs and restaurants in areas such as Manchester's Canal Street. At the same time, gay culture became politicised as gays sought to assert their identity. Organisations such as Stonewall actively sought changes in the law in order that homosexuals could enjoy the same rights as heterosexuals.

Furthermore, in cities such as London, Brighton and Manchester, Gay Pride marches sought to increase the visibility and social acceptability of gay people. These strategies, aided by the increasing number of celebrities and politicians coming out as gay, and sympathetic portrayals of gay subcultures in some TV programmes and films, have undoubtedly made it easier for gay people to be open about their sexuality. More recently, campaigns for equal rights have been extended in the lesbian, gay, bisexual and transgender movement (LGBT). However, it should also be acknowledged that prejudice and discrimination have certainly not disappeared completely. Homophobic attacks on gay people are still relatively common, which suggests that this type of sexuality is not totally accepted by all sections of the community. Research by Michel Dorais (2004) found that many young men who attempted suicide did so because they struggled with their own sexual identity in a homophobic society. Most of the men in the study were either gay or were regarded as effeminate by other people and therefore they did not conform to hegemonic ideals of masculinity.

Consider the extent to which different social groups tend to have different attitudes towards gay and lesbian identities. Which social groups do you think are most likely to be hostile and why might that be?

IDENTITY AND HETEROSEXUALITY

Heterosexuality is also, to some degree, the product of culture rather than biology and this can be illustrated by examining the way that definitions of sexual attractiveness have changed over the course of the last 100 years in Western societies. Studies of 18th- and 19th-century paintings suggest that the ideal of feminine beauty in

this period stressed plump women, while even in the 1950s, female sexual icons such as Marilyn Monroe were much bigger women than the waif-like supermodels and celebrities favoured by the fashion industry and championed by the media in the early 21st century.

Some feminist sociologists have suggested that these types of media representations of femininity may be responsible for eating disorders in modern societies. Hunt (2001) argues that "the media recognise society's obsession with looking slim and perpetuate the idea that slimness equals success, health, happiness and popularity" (p. 5). Although images of an ideal male body are increasingly being portrayed in the media, there is little sign that this is having the equivalent effect upon males.

Another clue that suggests that heterosexuality is socially constructed rather than being the product of biology is the double standard that exists with regard to comparable male and female sexual behaviour. There is an assumption that males and females have different sexual identities. Males are supposed to be promiscuous predators (they supposedly want to have sex with as many women as possible), whereas females are supposed to be passive and more interested in love than sex. Because of this, women's sexual identity carries risks. Lees (1986) found that they may be subjected to being labelled a 'slag' or a 'slapper' by both men and other women if they are promiscuous.

CHECK YOUR UNDERSTANDING

1. Identify four processes involved in gender-role socialisation and give an example of each.

2. Identify two types of evidence which demonstrate that some individuals express pride in gay or lesbian identities.

3. Identify two types of evidence that those with LGBT identities may still suffer discrimination and/or prejudice.

4. Define the terms 'gender' and 'sex'.

5. Define the term 'hegemonic masculinity'.

6. Outline and explain one argument which suggests that sexuality may be socially constructed.

7. Outline and explain two ways in which identities associated with femininity may be changing.

8. Outline two changes in the position of women in society in the last 50 years and explain how they may have affected identities associated with femininity.

9. Outline and evaluate the view that there are several different types of masculinity and femininity in modern Britain.

10. Outline and evaluate the view that sexual and gender identities develop through the passive acceptance of socialisation.

TAKE IT FURTHER

Visit the website www.feminist.com. Access their 'Resources' page and pick an article that relates to some aspect of femininity. Summarise the article and discuss what it tells us about changing gender identities.

3.5 IDENTITY, ETHNICITY AND NATIONALITY

3.5

LEARNING OBJECTIVES

> Understand the meaning of ethnicity, nationality and identity (AO1).

> Understand the identities associated with different ethnicities and nationalities (AO1).

> Apply this understanding to examples from the UK (AO2).

> Analyse the reasons for differences in culture and identity between those of different nationalities and ethnicities (AO3).

> Evaluate the extent of, and reasons for, change in ethnic and national identities in recent decades in the UK (AO3).

INTRODUCING THE DEBATE

Since the rise of nation-states over recent centuries, states have often encouraged their citizens to identify with their nation and to be loyal and patriotic. Such sentiments not only help to foster a sense of community, but can also be useful when you need to mobilise the population, for example, in times of war. Yet people don't always identify with the nation that they are a citizen of; they may also feel loyalty to their ethnic group. Ethnicity is concerned with a sense of common origin and a shared culture. With increased migration in a globalising world, ethnicity and nationality do not always fit together and most nation-states include sizable minority ethnic groups. Sociologists are interested therefore in how ethnic identities are developed, maintained and sometimes weakened, and how they relate to national identities. In multicultural societies, ethnic and national identities are becoming increasingly complex.

ETHNICITY AS CULTURAL DISTINCTIVENESS

Ethnic identity is often quite complex. For example, UK citizens of Chinese extraction are likely to share a common language (Cantonese or perhaps Mandarin) and a common heritage (their Chinese background). However, they may well not subscribe to an exclusively Chinese identity. It is likely that their ethnic (Chinese) identity will overlap with a national (British) identity, and quite possibly also with a regional identity, based on the part of the UK where they live.

Despite these difficulties, sociologists note that significant numbers of people in the UK share an ethnic identity, that is, they recognise that they share cultural characteristics, and that their ethnicity is distinctive compared to the majority White and 'Anglo-Saxon' culture. These characteristics include:

> *Common descent* – This may be represented by colour or other racial characteristics. Modood's (1997) research, for example, suggests that being Black is an important source of identity for young African Caribbeans.

> *Geographical origins* – Links with a country of origin are important, and ethnic identity may involve seeing oneself as 'Pakistani' or 'Indian' or 'Irish' first and foremost.

> *History* – Members of minority ethnic cultures may share a sense of struggle and oppression, which originates in particular historical contexts, such as slavery, colonialism or persecution. For example, Jewish identity may be partially shaped by events, notably the Holocaust during the Second World War, while some African Caribbeans may feel that the fact that they are descendants of slaves is central to their identity.

> *Language* – Members of particular groups may speak the language(s) of their country of origin at home; for example, older-generation Chinese people may speak in Cantonese, while young British Pakistani Muslims may talk to each other in a combination of Urdu and English.

> *Religion* – This is the most important influence for some minority ethnic groups; for example, some Pakistanis will see themselves first and foremost as Muslim.

> *Traditions and rituals* – These may be religious or cultural, such as the Notting Hill Carnival, which is held annually in the UK to celebrate African Caribbean culture.

> *Racism* – Prejudice and discrimination may be experienced and can take several forms, for example name-calling, police harassment, violence, and so on.

ETHNIC MINORITIES

In Britain, ethnicity is mainly associated with minority groups from the former British colonies on the Indian subcontinent, in the Caribbean and in Africa. However, this kind of categorisation can be a problem because it emphasises skin colour rather than common cultural characteristics. In doing so, it ignores significant White minority ethnic groups resident in the UK, such as Jews, gypsies, Eastern Europeans and Irish people.

Ethnic identity and primary socialisation

Singh Ghuman (1999) suggests that the first generation of Asian parents to arrive in the UK in the 1950s and 1960s were concerned to transmit the following key values to their children during primary socialisation in the family.

> Children should be obedient, loyal to and respectful of their elders and the community around them. Social conformity was demanded.

> Parents were considered to know best the interests of their children regardless of the child's age.

> The choice of marriage partner was thought to be best left to parents.

> Religious training was considered very important because it reinforced respect for family and stressed humility rather than self-pride and assertiveness.

> The role of the mother tongue was seen as crucial in maintaining links between generations. Children therefore tended to be bilingual, and were often able to use both the mother language, for example Urdu, Punjabi, Gujarati or Hindi, and English interchangeably.

Many of these family socialisation practices are still the norm in the early 21st century. For example, Singh Ghuman found that Asian families – whether Hindu, Muslim or Sikh – socialise children into a pattern of duty, obligation and loyalty to the extended family community, as well as religious commitment, which, in most cases, they accept. The concept of corporate or family honour (*izzat*) is particularly important in Muslim kinship relations. Consequently, even when they leave home, children will often continue to live near their parents and visit them regularly.

Sometimes primary socialisation (in the family) and secondary socialisation (outside the family) might be contradictory for some young members of minority ethnic groups in Britain. Can you give some possible examples of this? Evaluate the effects this may have on the development of identity.

Ethnic identity, marriage and family life

Evidence suggests continuing strong support for arranged marriages across all Asian groups, even among the young. Hennink *et al.* (1999) found in their study that 75 per cent of Sikh and 85 per cent of Muslim teenage girls expected an arranged marriage. Singh Ghuman notes that this is the product of successful socialisation into a collectivist family culture that stresses obedience, loyalty to and respect for elders. Brah (1993) notes that the majority of Asian adolescents felt confident that they would not be forced into a marriage they did not want. Arranged marriage, then, was regarded as a joint undertaking, with scope for negotiation.

Further evidence of traditional attitudes to family life among British Bangladeshis was found in a study of Bethnal Green, by Dench, Gavron and Young (2006).

They found that there were very few single-parent families in this community, very few people living alone and very low divorce rates. However, Ghazala Bhatti (1999) did find that there was conflict between generations in a minority of Asian families stemming from some adolescent boys wanting to marry a girl of English descent.

Ethnic identity and religion

Religion has a profound influence as an agency of socialisation in shaping the ethnic identity of young Asians. Modood (1997) questioned two generations of Asians, African Caribbeans and Whites about the statement: "Religion is very important to how I live my life". He found that those most in favour of religion were the Pakistani and Bangladeshi samples: 82 per cent of the age 50+ sample and 67 per cent of the 16 to 34 year age group valued the importance of Islam in their lives. About one third of young Indians saw their religion as important. The lowest figure was for young Whites – only 5 per cent saw religion as important compared with 18 per cent of young African Caribbeans.

Modood (1997) notes that the centrality of religion in Asian communities – and therefore in shaping their ethnic identity – can be illustrated by the fact that very few Asians marry across religious or **caste** lines, and that most of their children will be socialised into a religious value system. Singh Ghuman notes that the mosque is the centre for the religious, educational and political activities of Muslim communities and these religious institutions often exert a strong influence on the way parents rear and educate their children. Religious identities may be linked to the 'radicalisation' of a small number of British Muslims who have joined radical organisations associated with terrorism or have chosen to fight in the civil war in Syria in the 2010s. This seems to support Bradley's (1997) claim that the strength of different ethnic and national identities depends very much on how they are mobilised, or made to seem important in political and cultural battles over identity.

UNDERSTAND THE CONCEPT

Caste is a form of division in traditional Indian Hindu society in which people are born into groups of different status based upon their supposed religious purity. In theory the caste system has been abolished but it may still affect the way that individuals and families are viewed by other individuals and families.

African Caribbean identity

Modood (1997) found that skin colour is an important source of identity to many young African Caribbeans. Some African Caribbean youth stress their Black identity because of their experience of racial prejudice and discrimination from White society. Black pride and power may be celebrated, especially if Black youth perceives itself to be deliberately excluded from jobs or stereotyped by White people – in particular, by symbols of White authority, such as teachers and the police.

African Caribbean identity and peer-group pressure

The African Caribbean sociologist Tony Sewell (1996) argues that peer-group pressure is extremely influential in shaping ethnic identity among disaffected African Caribbean youth in British inner cities and that this is probably partly responsible for educational underachievement and the high levels of unemployment found in this group.

He argues that African Caribbean male identity is focused on being a hyper-male and 'gangsta' in the eyes of their peers. This, he claims, often compensates for the lack of a father figure in the lives of many of these teenagers, many of whom live in one-parent families headed by their mothers. Furthermore, Sewell notes that this street identity is partly shaped by media agencies such as advertising and MTV, which encourage young African Caribbean males to subscribe to a consumer culture that views material things such as clothing, trainers and jewellery ('bling') as more important than education.

Mixed-race identity

Recently, sociologists have observed that intermarriage, especially between Whites and African Caribbeans, has risen considerably. As a result, more mixed-race children are being born. Tizard and Phoenix (1993) found that 60 per cent of the mixed-race children in their sample were proud of their mixed parentage, but they noted that "it is still not an easy ride to be of mixed Black and White parentage in our society because of racism from both White and Black populations".

FOCUS ON SKILLS: SCARED THEIR BOYS WILL GO TO SYRIA, SCARED TO GO TO THE POLICE

Certain religious traditions coexist uneasily with the secular values of many modern societies.

"There are British Muslim girls who believe they will go to paradise if they marry a jihadist," Souad Talsi tells me frankly. "Being married to a man who becomes a martyr gives her status. That dangerous view is reinforced by mothers who have been absorbed by a blanket fundamentalist Muslim mentality that has no bearing on the beliefs and cultures of their country or parents."

Thirty years ago Talsi, 53, a British Moroccan, founded the Al-Hasaniya Centre on Golborne Road in North Kensington, London. It supports women of the local Arabic-speaking community.

Increasingly the growing threat of young people going to Syria is influencing Talsi's work and that of her staff. She is deeply troubled by the numbers of young British men and women leaving for Syria. "Having helped support mothers of Moroccan and Arabic background to integrate better, we now face this strange challenge of trying to integrate British-born and English-speaking children who seem to have lost their identity," she says.

"Girls are raised with the very traditional and strict values that belonged to their parents' countries back in the Sixties and Seventies," explains Esma Dukali, 36, the centre's manager and a British-born daughter of Moroccan migrants. "The countries themselves have moved on, but families living here haven't necessarily. Even though they're British, it's difficult for these young women to reconcile their cultural upbringings with modern Western society and they're confused about who they are. They turn to religion as a common connection, which is why there is more emphasis on religion now. Girls are being enticed into fighting a religious war under the umbrella of religious authority, which they believe gives them permission over everything else."

"In cases where the mother hasn't integrated, daughters are vulnerable," agrees Talsi.

Talsi says: "Youngsters are exposed to graphic images of how Muslims are suffering. Gaza is a potent example which has had an impact on young people concerned with human rights. I tell young people if they want to make a difference then make it through the ballot box or by volunteering for a charity or doing a meaningful job. 9/11 changed the shape of our society. There is mistrust, and a balance needs to be struck.

"These young people don't have a distinct identity," she continues. "They're lumped together as Muslim and as a result are losing sight of their individual cultural heritage. A Moroccan in West London is very different from a Pakistani in Birmingham or a Saudi in Knightsbridge. Islam is part of an identity, but not everything. Syria has given them a warped sense of purpose. Part of our work is to give them a positive one."

Source: Brinkworth, L, 'Scared their boys will go to Syria, scared to go to the police' *The Times*, 20 January 2015

Questions

1. **Understanding**. Explain what you think Souad Talsi means by her claim that some of the young women she sees have 'lost their identity'.

2. **Analyse** different factors that Talsi suggests have led to some young Muslims turning to religion for their main source of identity.

3. **Evaluate** the explanations given here for some young Muslims travelling to Syria by considering whether Islamophobia (hostility, hatred or racism based on religious/cultural differences towards Islam/Islamic people) could be another factor persuading people to do this.

4. **Evaluate** the view that emphasising non-religious identities could reduce the risk of young British Muslims travelling to Syria.

Hybrid or dual identities

There is considerable evidence that ethnic identities are evolving and modern hybrid forms are now developing among Britain's younger ethnic-minority citizens. Johal (1998) focused on second- and third-generation British Asians. He found that they have a dual identity, in that they inherit an Asian identity and adopt a British one. This results in Asian youth adopting a 'White mask' in order to interact with White peers at school or college, but emphasising their cultural difference whenever they feel it is necessary. He notes that many British Asians adopt 'hybrid identities'. They select aspects of British, Asian and global culture relating to fashion, music and food in order to construct their identity. For example, many young British Asians like Bhangra music – a mixture of Punjabi music married to Western rhythms.

White European identities

There has been increasing sociological interest in White European ethnic groups living in Britain with increased migration from this area as more countries join the European Union. Poland joined the EU in 2004 and a significant number of Polish people moved to Britain. Most were in their twenties, and they came to seek work. They joined an established Polish community in Britain who arrived as refugees around the time of the Second World War.

Agnieszka Bielewska (2011) carried out ethnographic research into these two groups of Poles in Manchester. She found that most members of the longer-established community had strong, Polish, ethnic identities. They often ate Polish food and tended to live close to other ethnic Poles. By contrast, most of the newer migrants were not closely integrated into established Polish communities. They mixed largely with people of a similar age from a variety of ethnic backgrounds and their lifestyle generally was little different to that of non-Polish people. They did however shop at Polish shops. Bielewska suggests that the differences are partly explained through globalisation. The newer migrants could maintain links with those in Poland through digital technology, and many thought they might return to Poland to live. More generally, Bielewska suggests that the younger group constructed their identity more as individuals than as members of an ethnic group. Their identities were based partly on loyalty to brands and consumption. This suggests that ethnic identities might become less strong as consumer lifestyles become ever more important (see Chapter 7).

NATIONAL IDENTITY

National identity can be defined as the feeling of being part of a larger community in the form of a nation, which gives a sense of purpose and meaning to people's lives as well as a sense of belonging.

National identity is not necessarily the same thing as nationality. The latter concept is a formal, legal category that derives from belonging to a 'nation-state', that is, a country recognised by other countries as exercising authority and power over a geographical territory. Nationality is symbolised by legal rights, such as being able to carry a passport, being able to marry legally or vote at a particular age. It also involves certain duties, such as obeying the law of the land. The crime of 'treason', that is, betraying one's country, is seen as one of the most heinous crimes one can commit.

It is important to recognise that the legal status of being British – having formal British nationality – does not necessarily mean that people will subscribe to a British identity. Many citizens of the UK, defined as British by law, identify with 'nations within the nation', that is, they see themselves primarily as English, Scottish, Welsh or Irish. Moreover, many British subjects may see their national identity as primarily tied up with their country or region of origin, and so see themselves as African Caribbean, Punjabi, Bengali, Pakistani, and so on. Others may subscribe first and foremost to identities deriving from their religious affiliations, such as Muslim or Jewish.

British national identity

The British are essentially a 'mongrel nation', that is, a mix of social and immigrant groups that have settled in Britain since before Roman times. As Guibernau and Goldblatt (2000) note, no case can be made for a single, original, authentic group of Britons. They note that until the 1707 Act of Union that linked Scotland to England and Wales there was no such thing as a British national identity. People identified more with the regions in which they lived than with a loyalty to the British nation-state.

However, Guibernau and Goldblatt argue that a sense of British identity was gradually created around five key themes.

> *Geography* – The fact that Britain consists of islands gave it a clear sense of boundaries that made it distinct from Europe. A result of this is that very few British people have identified themselves as European.

> *Religion* – Protestantism is the dominant religious identity in Britain. Many people who do not attend church on a regular basis still identify themselves as Church of England. In times of national celebration, such as royal weddings and Remembrance Sunday, religion plays a central role. In the courts, people still swear to tell the truth using the Bible, and the National Anthem asks God to look after the Queen.

> *War* – Wars have reinforced the sense of 'them' versus 'us' and especially the British themes of self-sacrifice, perseverance, fair play, heroism and putting up with exceptional hardship. This Britishness is associated with historical events such as the London Blitz and Dunkirk. Public ceremonies and celebrations marking events such as the end of the Second World War symbolise both individual sacrifice for the nation and the preservation of the British way of life.

> *The British Empire* – Britain's success as an imperial power in the 18th and 19th centuries brought economic success and a sense of pride and achievement in what was perceived as British superiority over other cultures and races.

> *Monarchy* – The cultural symbols of British nationality, in particular the anthem *God Save the Queen* and the Union Flag (known as the 'Union Jack') are designed to place the monarchy at the heart of British identity. The outpouring of grief after the death of Diana, Princess of Wales, in 1997 illustrated very clearly how deeply many of the British feel about such symbols.

National identity and socialisation

Schudson (1994) points out that the British people are socialised into a British identity in several ways.

> *A common language* – English is seen as central to our cultural identity.

> *Education* – The teaching of History, English literature and Religion in British schools tends to promote national identity. For example, Shakespeare is often proudly described as the world's greatest playwright, while traditional History teaching often focuses on Britain's positive achievements at the expense of negative British activities such as slavery, massacres and exploitation. The Education Reform Act (1988) stresses Christian worship in schools, despite the fact that the UK is a multicultural society.

> *National rituals* – Royal and state occasions are used to reinforce the British way of life, and the public are invited to take part, usually via television, in events such as the Cenotaph ceremony on Remembrance Sunday. Rituals unite us in Britishness.

Think about how other uniquely British rituals, for example, royal weddings and funerals, the Queen's televised Christmas speech, and even Bonfire Night, reinforce national identity in individual British citizens.

> *Symbols* – These include styles of dress, uniforms, passports, styles of music, national anthems, and particularly, flags. The Union Jack is symbolic of Britishness, especially of the British Empire, the Queen and Parliament. It often indicates tradition and patriotism, especially during wartime or at sporting events.

> *The mass media* – Television, magazines and newspapers encourage people to identify with national symbols such as the Royal Family by taking a keen interest in their activities. The media also play a key role in reinforcing our sense of national identity by talking up British achievement. In times of war, the media focus on 'our boys', while sporting events such as the Olympic Games are reported almost as quasi-wars against other nations.

> *The mass production of fashion and taste* – Britishness can also be embodied in particular foods, such as fish and chips, consumer goods such as the Rolls-Royce car, and retail outlets such as Marks and Spencer.

Consider how different ethnic, religious and national identities have been mobilised in Britain in recent years. Which have become more prominent and which less? How can you explain these changes?

The decline of British identity?

Waters (1995) suggests that British identity may be under threat in the 21st century for four reasons, outlined below.

Celtic identities

Celtic identities especially Welsh and Scottish identity, has always been a powerful source of identity in those countries, and has recently been given political and legal legitimacy in the form of a Scottish Parliament and a Welsh Assembly, which have the power to introduce legislation on a wide range of issues. Scottish National identity figured prominently in the campaign for a Yes vote in the 2014 referendum for Scottish independence, in which the campaign for Scottish independence was only narrowly defeated, and in the electoral success of the Scottish National Party in the 2015 general election. In 2012, the British Social Attitudes Survey found that, when forced to choose, 69 per cent of people in Scotland identified themselves as Scottish and just 20 per cent as British. On the other hand, in England just 29 per cent identified themselves as English, even fewer (18 per cent) saw themselves as British, but a very large proportion (44 per cent) saw themselves as equally English and British.

Globalisation

Globalisation is becoming more significant as transnational companies and international financial markets increasingly dominate world trade. British identity may be diluted, as some British companies and products are taken over by foreign companies, while others close down their factories in the UK and move production to the cheaper developing countries. There are also concerns that American culture is taking over the British high street, as companies such as McDonald's and Starbucks expand

their British operations. Moreover, television programmes, films and music are increasingly being produced for the international market. There are fears that these largely American products may erode Britishness and create a single commercialised culture offering superficial mass entertainment.

BUILD CONNECTIONS

The decline of traditional sources of identity (such as British nationality) and the increasingly diverse range of influences on identity as a result of globalisation, can be linked to postmodern theories of culture, which were addressed in Chapter 1.

FOCUS ON RESEARCH: MARK URBAN (1999) AND ENGLISH IDENTITY

The British monarchy and the Notting Hill Carnival – two different aspects of English identity?

Urban's research confirms that people's sense of English identity differs according to factors such as region, ethnicity and age. He showed two videos of national images to focus groups around the country and facilitated group interviews discussing the content. Both concentrated on English themes: one on the traditional defiance towards outsiders, the other on love of personal freedom. The 'traditional' video contained shots of war, the monarchy and emphasised teamwork. This video drew a very positive response from older audiences, especially those outside London. The 'liberal' tape featured images of innovation, freedom and tolerance, along with pictures of Shakespeare, the Notting Hill Carnival, great British inventions and Lenny Henry. Many people in London identified with these images, but people in the provinces were less convinced that these images represented Englishness and were less likely to identify with the images of race and multiculturalism.

Questions

1. How did the contents of the two videos represent Englishness?

2. Analyse the reasons why responses to these images varied by social group. (You can think about factors such as experience of ethnic diversity in their daily lives and the ethnic mix of the country at the time when different age groups were growing up.)

3. Evaluate whether there could be alternative ways of representing Englishness (think about what Englishness means to you). What does this suggest about problems in devising this type of research?

4. Evaluate the validity of the data produced using focus groups on this topic. For example, could the responses of some individuals become distorted by the format? Are there advantages in having a group discussing the issues?

Multiculturalism

The multicultural nature of British society seems to be having an effect on our sense of British or national identity. The survey by Modood (1997) of ethnic-minority groups found that most of his second-generation sample thought of themselves as mostly – but not entirely – culturally and socially British. A survey conducted in March 2005 by ICM found that only 39 per cent of minorities saw themselves as 'fully British'. Modood (2005) found that Asians and African Caribbeans did not feel comfortable with a 'British' identity: they felt that the majority of White people did not accept them as British because of their colour and cultural background. See Chapter 3 for more on multiculturalism.

English identity

Concerns have also been expressed about English identity. Research by Curtice and Heath (2000) suggests that the group who identify themselves as 'English'

rather than 'British' has increased from 7 per cent of the population in 1996 to 17 per cent in 1999 (that is, more than 6 million adults). This group are known as 'Little Englanders', with 37 per cent of this total openly admitting to being racially prejudiced.

A new form of Britishness?

Despite these trends, there are positive signs that a new sense of 'Britishness' is slowly emerging in the field of popular culture, especially in the worlds of food, fashion and music. It is illustrated with the news that chicken tikka masala, a hybrid of Indian spices and English gravy, has now replaced fish and chips as the UK's most popular food, and in the multicultural nature of the British Olympic team at London 2012. In other words, a new form of Britishness may be emerging, shaped both by 'traditional' British values and institutions, and by values and institutions that originate in the increasingly multicultural and globalised nature of UK society.

CHECK YOUR UNDERSTANDING

1. Identify seven factors which contribute to a person's ethnic identity.

2. Identify four norms or values which are passed down the generations in many Asian families.

3. Explain one way in which national identity is sometimes linked to ethnic identity and one way in which it is sometimes not linked to it.

4. Explain what is meant by 'dual' or 'hybrid' identity with regard to both ethnic and national identities.

5. Explain two factors which have made British identity less strong than some other national identities.

6. Explain four ways in which people are socialised into British identity.

7. Analyse how British identity has been challenged in recent years.

8. Analyse the reasons why English identity is not as distinctive as Scottish or Welsh identity.

9. Evaluate the view that British national identity is in decline. (Look for arguments for and against this view.)

10. Do minority ethnic groups retain strong ethnic identities in Britain today? (Think about whether ethnicity, nationality or another source of identity seems most important.)

TAKE IT FURTHER

Visit the tourist board websites of England, Wales and Scotland. List 10 characteristics, images or symbols that are used to represent identities for each of these countries. What differences are there between the countries? Consider how far the representations are stereotypes and how far they represent real differences in identity.

3.6 IDENTITY, AGE AND DISABILITY

LEARNING OBJECTIVES

> Understand the nature of age and disability as social phenomena (AO1).

> Understand the identities associated with different age groups and disabilities (AO1).

> Apply this understanding to examples from Britain (AO2).

> Analyse the reasons for differences in identity between those of different ages and physical abilities/disabilities (AO3).

> Evaluate the extent of, and reasons for change in age-related and disability-related identities in recent decades in Britain (AO3).

INTRODUCING THE DEBATE

Both age and physical disability tend to be thought of as biological issues that are primarily concerned with physical capacity. Mental illness is sometimes seen in a similar way, although in relation to the functioning of the brain rather than the body. However, sociologists have tended to argue that neither age nor disability can be understood outside of the social context in which people live, and they generally claim that society plays a key role in producing the identities of different age groups and those with different capacities. Societal expectations and failures to accommodate the needs of different groups may push the disabled and different age groups towards identities that reflect prejudice as much as the capacities of individuals. However, there is evidence that older people and the disabled are becoming less willing to accept society's expectations and are challenging the boundaries that have restricted their social roles in the past.

AGE AND IDENTITY

We have seen in previous topics that personal and social identity are shaped by social factors such as social class, gender, ethnicity and globalisation. However, it is also a fact that the UK segregates its members by age, so that how young or how old people are has a significant influence on their identity. Marsh and Keating (2006, p. 358) note that age both enables us and constrains us: "Our age may influence where we shop, what we buy and even how we pay for our goods. Our age may affect the types of books we read, the music we listen to, the television programmes we watch, the leisure activities we engage in. Our everyday lives are shaped by the way our age is understood and expressed in the society we live in."

Biology and age

Biology obviously has some influence on the way that society divides people by age. Babies, infants and children are not physically or psychologically developed enough to perform adult tasks, while the ageing process may mean that the elderly may not be as physically or as mentally effective as they were when younger. However, sociologists point out that there are enough cultural differences across different societies and even across subcultural groups within the UK to suggest that age differences – and therefore, identities – are socially or culturally constructed rather than just the result of biological differences. It is sometimes assumed that there is a predictable **life cycle** based on biological age, in which people pass through set stages in a particular order (for example, childhood, adolescence, young adulthood, childrearing, retirement, old age and death). But some sociologists believe that such a life cycle is no longer the norm and it is better to think in terms of the **life course** – a less predictable passage through life where social and cultural expectations allow individuals a great deal more flexibility in how they negotiate the different stages of their lives (Green, 2015).

UNDERSTAND THE CONCEPT

The **life cycle** refers to the different stages of life which it is seen as normal for people to pass through. It is also assumed that some stages are likely to precede others (for example, adulthood being followed by marriage which is followed by having children). It is assumed to be fairly standard in most societies and linked to biological age, physical maturity and capacity.

The term **life course** refers to the changes which individuals experience as they age and their lives and identities change, but the idea of life course does not imply that there are necessarily fixed or standard stages in everybody's lives. Not everyone has the same experiences at different stages in life.

The social and cultural construction of age

This can be illustrated by comparing traditional pre-industrial societies with modern industrial societies such as the UK. In many traditional societies, people often do not have a precise age because births are not registered. People may not even know their birth date and so may not celebrate birthdays. In these traditional societies, people's identities in terms of their age generally go through three major stages.

> *Children* – This age group is regarded as dependent upon older groups for protection and survival.

> *Adults* – Children, usually at puberty, go through a rite of passage or initiation ceremony, in which they are instructed in adult ways. Boys may learn how to be warriors or hunters and have to go through several tests of skill and/or strength. Girls are instructed on sexual matters so that they can become wives and mothers, sometimes shortly after puberty. An important difference between traditional and modern societies is that adolescence – the teenage years – is often not recognised as a distinct period by the former.

> *Elders* – As people get older in tribal societies, they often acquire greater status and power because they are regarded as having greater experience and wisdom than those who are younger. It is often taken for granted that young people should defer to their elders.

Age and modern industrial societies

In modern Western societies such as the UK, the state insists that all births are registered. It is taken for granted that people know their birth dates and that they celebrate birthdays. Bradley (1996) identifies five generational major stages in age identity in the UK. Generations are age groups that live through the same historical and social events, and whose common identity and attitudes are cemented by similar experiences of consuming cultural goods such as fashion, music, films, television programmes, and so on.

Childhood

This is regarded as a special innocent time in which children are supposed to be cosseted and protected by their parents. The parents are supported in this enterprise by the state, which has introduced laws, for example various Children Acts, in order to regulate the quality of parenting. The state has also introduced legislation in order to set out guidelines for what is acceptable behaviour for children; for example, the state has decided that schooling should be compulsory between the ages of 5 years and 18 years, and that 10 years should be the lowest age that a child can be held responsible for a criminal offence and 16 the youngest age at which they can legally consent to sexual intercourse.

The experience of childhood is central to understanding age as a social construct. Some childhood experts, notably Aries (1962), argue that the experience of childhood identity has changed considerably over the last 500 years. Other commentators, such as Postman (1982), argue that the nature of childhood continues to change even today.

Sociologists have examined childhood in the context of family life, particularly in terms of the changing relationships between children and adults, and especially parents. Some have argued that there has been a loss of innocence in childhood (partly because of access to adult images in the media), others that childhood is being extended as time spent in compulsory education keeps increasing. These themes of childhood identity are explored further in Topic 4, Chapter 7.

Adolescence or youth

This is the period between puberty and the achievement of full adult status. Until the late 1960s, adulthood in the UK was usually celebrated at 21 years, but since the last part of the 20th century, 18 years has become more common. This is the age at which the state confers legal adulthood via being able to vote, to marry or leave home without parental consent, and to sit on a jury.

In the 1950s, adolescence or youth was recognised as a unique age group for the first time. Before this period, adolescence was generally regarded as part of adulthood because the majority of youth prior to the Second World War left school in their early teens and started work. They were not recognised as a separate social category because they were generally indistinguishable from their parents in terms of their values, tastes, behaviour, dress, and so on. No specific teenage market existed for fashion, cosmetics and mass media such as films and popular music.

The postwar period saw the emergence of a **youth culture** based on specific teenage fashions, hairstyles and tastes in music, such as rock and roll, which the older generation found both shocking and threatening. This culture was the product of an increase in young people's spending power brought about by full employment in the 1950s. Capitalist entrepreneurs reacted to this lucrative new market by developing products specifically for youth, such as comics and magazines for teenagers, pop music, fashion and cosmetics.

UNDERSTAND THE CONCEPT

Youth culture is a set of values and norms of behaviour relating to fashion, dress, hairstyle, lifestyle, and so on, subscribed to by some young people, and that may be seen as deviant by mainstream culture.

Studies of the mass media have focused on how youth is demonised. Cohen (1980) was the first sociologist to observe how newspapers tend to sensationalise and exaggerate the behaviour of groups of young people in order to create newsworthiness and to sell papers. His study described how fights between two sets of youths in 1964 – labelled 'mods' and 'rockers' – produced a **moral panic,** or social anxiety about young people in general, and **folk devils**, with young people being blamed for the moral decline of the nation. According to Cohen, this generally illustrates how young people are seen as a 'social problem' by the older generation. Contemporary studies of the mass media's portrayal of teenagers, particularly Thornton (1995) and Savage (2007), suggest that teenagers are more frequently condemned than praised by the mass media.

UNDERSTAND THE CONCEPT

Moral panics are waves of anxiety felt by members of society about the behaviour of social groups, which are usually caused by media sensationalism and exaggeration.

Folk devils are groups stereotyped by the media as deviants during moral panics. There have been moral panics over such diverse folk devils as dangerous dogs, Islamic extremists, various groups of immigrants, paedophiles, muggers, punks and welfare 'scroungers'. The extent to which the concern is justified, if at all, can vary, but moral panics are usually linked to deep-seated fears about a decline in morality and/or threats to identity or social order.

However, studies of young people suggest that the generation gap (the notion that teenagers and parents are in conflict because of differing sets of values) implied by moral panics is exaggerated. There is little evidence that youth identity is significantly different in terms of what young people value compared with their parents. Few young people have become involved with those youth subcultures defined as deviant by the media, such as teddy-boys (1950s), mods and rockers (1960s), skinheads (early 1970s), punks (late 1970s) or ecstasy-using ravers (1980s/1990s). Most young people are generally conformist – they get on well with their parents and place a high value on traditional goals such as getting married, having children and buying a house.

Young adulthood

This type of age identity is focused on the period between leaving the parental home and middle age. Pilcher (1996) points out that this age group has rarely been researched and so we have little information about this significant group of people. Jones and Wallace (1992) suggest that modern societies such as the UK have private and public 'markers' that signify the beginning of adult status. For example, private markers might include a first sexual encounter or first cigarette, while public markers include the right to vote or the granting of a bank loan. Pilcher concludes that adult identity revolves around living with a sexual partner, having children, having a job and maintaining a home. Hockey and James (1993) see it as bound up with having freedom and independence from parents, having control over material resources and having responsibilities.

Mid-life

There is some disagreement as to when middle age begins. Brooks-Gunn and Kirsch (1984) set it as low as 35 years, whereas others have suggested it might be as high as 50 years. There are physical indicators of middle age, such as greying hair, the appearance of the 'middle-aged spread' and, in women, the menopause, as well as social indicators, such as children leaving home to go to university or having more money for leisure pursuits. There may even be emotional or psychological indicators – the mid-life crisis, for example.

Old age

This period, when a person may retire and receive a state pension, currently legally begins between the ages of 65 and 68 in the UK, depending on a person's date of birth. The 2010-15 Coalition Government introduced staged adjustments upwards in the state pension age (previously 60 for women and 65 for men) to reflect increased life expectancy and the consequent increased cost of state pensions. Pilcher argues that because of increasing life expectancy and differences in generational attitudes, tastes and behaviour, we should differentiate between the 'young old' (aged 65 to 74), the 'middle-aged old' (aged between 75 and 84 years) and the 'old old' (aged 85+). However, in contrast to traditional societies, the elderly in the UK are not accorded a great deal of respect or status, because work is the major source of status in industrial societies. Loss of work due to retirement can result in a significant decline in self-esteem, social contact with others and income, as well as a consequent rise in loneliness, poverty, depression and poor health in general.

Age and discrimination

The low status associated with elderly identity in UK society is not helped by the fact that people are often stereotyped and discriminated against because of their age. This is known as ageism. Johnson and Bytheway (1993) define it as the "offensive exercise of power through reference to age" and suggest that it has three integral elements.

> Ageism is often institutionalised, in that it is embedded in organisational and legal practices; for example, people aged over 70 years are excluded from jury service.

> Ageism is often expressed through the stereotypical prejudices that underpin everyday interaction, in that people often assume without question that a person's competency is limited by their age; for example, they may be deemed too old to carry out a particular task.

> Ageism can involve the well-meaning assumption that the very old are vulnerable and depend on younger and fitter adults for care and protection.

There is evidence therefore that old age as a stage in the life course is largely negatively perceived. This is reflected in everyday descriptions of elderly people as being 'past it' or 'over the hill' or having 'one foot in the grave'. Pilcher notes that old people are often described in derogatory or condescending ways, such as 'old fogey', 'old biddy', 'old bat' or 'sweet little old lady/man'. Pilcher points out that such stereotypes tend to marginalise old people and to label them as inferior.

Arber and Ginn (1993) suggest that ageism is reinforced and perpetuated by institutional practices. It is often the case that workers who are made redundant in their mid-40s experience age barriers in finding new jobs. Bradley notes that old people may be seen as less suitable for employment because they are assumed to be "physically slow, lacking in dynamism and not very adaptable to change". However, the Employment Equality (Age) Regulations Act came into force in late 2006, providing protection against age discrimination in employment and education. The Equality Act (2010) further strengthened these protections against age discrimination and added new regulations covering discrimination in the provision of goods and services.

Ginn and Arber note too that the increasing number of the elderly – in 2002, for the first time, people aged 60 years and over formed a larger part of the population than children aged under 16 years – has led to rising fears about the costs to society. For example, the rising costs of pensions and of the increased use of health and welfare services have led to media reports portraying the elderly as a 'burden' on taxpayers.

Ageism and the mass media

Ageism is often reflected through mass media representations of youth and old age. Advertising reinforces the view that the appearance of youth is central to looking good and that ageing should be resisted at all costs. As a result, adverts for anti-ageing creams, hair dyes to conceal greyness and cosmetic surgery are common on television and in women's magazines. Ageism (combined with sexism) may also be reflected through the underrepresentation of middle-aged and elderly women as news presenters and hosts of light-entertainment shows. Sontag (1978) suggests that there is a double standard on ageing, especially in television, according to which women are required to be youthful throughout their media careers but men are not. The newscaster Moira Stuart claimed to be a victim of this type of ageism at the BBC in 2007 when she was 'retired' by the corporation at the age of 58, while male counterparts such as David Dimbleby (still presenting *Question Time* in 2015 at 76) are allowed to carry on beyond retirement age. In a wide-ranging review of the portrayal of old age in the world's media, Milner, Van Norman and Milner (2012) found that the elderly are largely portrayed negatively and stereotypically, but in adverts selling products to older people there are much more positive images of them as 'super seniors' – presumably because such portrayals make the target audience more likely to buy the products.

Compare the discrimination against the old and against those under 18 in Britain today. Using examples, explain which group you think is more disadvantaged by discrimination?

De-standardisation of the life course

While some sociologists question the idea of a life cycle closely linked to age, using the term 'life course' to indicate that individuals are less likely to follow a standard pattern, others go further and argue that there has been a de-standardisation of the life course.

Some go further and argue that there has been a de-standardisation of the life course. By this they mean that people are increasingly able to act in ways which a particular culture has not traditionally seen as appropriate for a particular age group. Brückner and Mayer (2005), for example, claim that how people behave at different ages

has become unpredictable and less bound by convention. People may choose to stay single, get married late in life, have children when they are older, enjoy adventure sports when they are elderly, or go clubbing at any age. Lorraine Green (2015) agrees that some changes have taken place in the life course, but thinks that these can be exaggerated. For example, there are still some biological constraints on people's choices in life (for example, about when to have children) and most people do continue to 'act their age' even if a minority do not. Nevertheless, improving life expectancy and health among older age groups does offer the potential for more choices for older members of the population.

DISABILITY AND IDENTITY

The medical model of disability

Best (2005) notes that, traditionally, disability was seen "in terms of a person's inability to fully participate in various activities that the rest of us take for granted, such as washing yourself, cleaning the floor, walking and driving, shopping... and generally looking after oneself."

This definition reflected the medical model of disability, which assumed that disability is a personal tragedy and that the disabled deserve our pity. In terms of the disabled identity, it was also assumed that the disabled are dependent on the able-bodied and are unable to function effectively without constant help. In other words, disabled people were labelled by the medical model as inferior because it was assumed that to be disabled was to be abnormal, and that normalisation could only occur with a medical cure or round-the-clock care.

The social model of disability

This medical interpretation of the disabled identity began to change in the 1980s with the appearance of the social model of disability. This view was developed by disabled people themselves, who argued that biological disability was less important than social disability. As Oliver (1996) argues "it is society which disables physically impaired people" because the disabled are excluded from full participation in society by stereotypical attitudes held by able-bodied people. As Best notes: "Society generates forms of discrimination and exclusion that disabled people have to cope with. The problem is to be found in the social constructions of prejudice that surround disability and not in the bodies of disabled people."

FOCUS ON SKILLS: DO YOU WANT TO LIVE FOR EVER?

Fauja Singh completes a marathon – the world's oldest marathon runner, he retired from the sport at the age of 101.

Rejuvenation biotechnologies, tissue engineering, cellular restoration, 'electronic medicine', testosterone injections and stem-cell facelifts in your lunch hour – the battle against growing old, experts argue, is a war that's already being won.

Age defiance is a staggeringly lucrative industry. Last year the global anti-ageing market generated more than £150 billion. By 2018 it will hit £216 billion. A new tribe is taking advantage of sophisticated scientific breakthroughs.

Peter Thiel, co-founder of PayPal and a Facebook board member, is a supporter of SENS, a research foundation specialising in rejuvenation treatments.

SENS is run by Aubrey de Grey, a Cambridge PhD graduate and gerontologist who believes that the first person to live to 150 is already alive today.

"Rejuvenation biotechnologies are, very simply, medicines that restore the structure of the body to how it was in early adulthood, and thereby restore it to maximum physical and mental performance," explains de Grey, who also co-founded Methuselah – a foundation whose aim, through tissue engineering and regenerative medicine, is to create a world by 2030 in which 90-year-olds can be as healthy as 50-year-olds.

This notion that, like the painting in Dorian Gray's attic, we can reverse ageing, has become an obsession for scientists. So much so that Dr David Sinclair, a professor of genetics at Harvard

Medical School, has taken matters into his own hands. Every day he swallows capsules that he believes trick cells into thinking they are young again. "We're talking not just slowing down ageing, but reversing it," he says.

In research published last year in the journal *Cell*, Sinclair described how mice were given a naturally occurring molecule called nicotinamide adenine dinucleotide, or NAD, which reduces in the body as we age and makes cells less efficient. By increasing the amount of NAD, in just one week of treatment, two-year-old mice tissue resembled that of six-month-old mice. In human years, that is akin to a 60-year-old's cells becoming more like a 20-year-old's.

"In ten years, there will be medicines available that you will start taking when you're 30 and will prevent diseases of ageing," he predicts. He wields terms like 'reprogramming' as though reading the script for the latest sci-fi movie. He even talks about body-part replacement – the idea that we will be able to grow our own skin, even our own livers.

"We will be able to live not just a little bit longer, but a lot longer, and to look younger as well. We are on the verge of a number of separate medical breakthroughs that together will allow us to live to 150. These technologies will definitely be available."

Source: McMahon, M. 'Do you want to live forever?', *The Times*, 30 November 2014

Questions

1. **Explain** why new medical approaches to dealing with old age are radically different from those based on cosmetic surgery.

2. **Explain** how the idea of de-standardisation of the life course can be applied to the changes discussed in this article.

3. **Analyse** what effects rejuvenating medicine would have on the social and cultural construction of age if it were to become scientific reality.

4. **Evaluate** the view that it would be desirable for individuals and for society if everybody could live to be 150 or older.

Disability as a social construct

Disability activists and sociologists have suggested that most of the UK population are impaired in some way but are rarely classified as 'disabled'. They argue that there are degrees of difference in disability or impairment; for example, the author of this chapter is impaired in that his eyesight is extremely poor without glasses or contact lenses. However, he is not socially labelled as 'disabled' because society does not define short-sightedness as a problem and so does not produce a social environment in which people who wear glasses or contact lenses are handicapped. However, people who have to use wheelchairs *are* handicapped by society's failure to provide a social environment in which they can be as mobile as able-bodied people.

The disabled identity and independence

The disabled movement is also very critical of the concept of 'independence' as an aspect of normality. The negative social reaction to disability is often based on the view that the disabled are dependent and constantly in need of help. Marsh and Keating (2006) point out that very few of us are really independent: "In modern societies, we are, of course, interdependent: we cannot manage to feed and clothe ourselves without relying on a vast network of other people and organisations. Similarly, we are all dependent on many aids for mobility and communication. Few of us could function without telephones, transport, ladders, tools and so on, and many of us cannot function at all without glasses, or medication, or other aids." Marsh and Keating go on to ask why some mobility aids, such as wheelchairs and white sticks, attract such a negative social reaction in comparison.

The disabled identity and capitalism

Marxists such as Finkelstein (1980) have suggested that our negative cultural attitudes towards the disabled may be the product of capitalism's emphasis on work as a source of identity, status and power. He suggests that in pre-industrial societies, the idea that disabled people should be segregated and treated differently simply did not exist. However, industrialisation was responsible for a dramatic shift in cultural attitudes because capitalist society required a healthy and fit workforce to generate profits for the capitalist class. In this context, the disabled become an economic burden for society and are defined as abnormal and as a social problem.

Learned helplessness

Watson (1998) argues that the perception of disabled people is based upon stereotypical ideas about dependency and helplessness, and these can have a negative effect on how disabled people perceive themselves and their abilities. Disabled people may respond to the constant assumption that they are helpless and dependent by developing low social esteem and worth. A classic study illustrating this self-fulfilling prophecy is Scott's 1969 study of blind people. After observing the interaction between medical professionals and blind people in the USA, Scott argued that the blind developed a 'blind personality' because they internalised the experts' view that they should be experiencing psychological problems in adjusting to their loss of sight. Part of this process also involved '**learned helplessness**', that is, that they should rely on sighted people for help.

Mass media representations of the disabled

A number of studies indicate that disability is represented in a negative fashion by the mass media. Longmore (1987) suggests that disabled people tend to be represented on television as evil, as monsters, as inhuman, as dependent on others, as maladjusted, as the objects of pity or charity, or as dangerous and deviant. If the disabled are portrayed as courageous, this is often contrasted with the tragedy of their situation. These stereotypes reinforce cultural stereotypes, and consequently prejudice and discrimination. As Cumberbatch and Negrine (1992) argue, media representations of the disabled rarely present them as "a person, an individual, who happens also to have a disability". Wood (2012) argues that this is partly the result of disabled people rarely being employed in the media, but where they are employed, stereotypical images are more likely to be challenged. For example, the BBC sitcom *The Office* was produced by a disabled person and includes a disabled character, while highlighting problems for disabled people in employment. The BBC soap opera *EastEnders* character Donna Yates is also wheelchair-bound, but the scriptwriters focus very little on her disability and portray her in the same way as every other character.

It should be acknowledged that, recently, more positive images of the disabled have become more widely available in the media, for example, in the coverage of the London Paralympic Games in 2012, although sporting events involving disabled participants have not featured very prominently in British sports coverage since the 2012 games.

Prejudice and discrimination

Stereotypes and prejudices about the disabled affect their quality of life in several ways.

> The disabled may find themselves segregated from able-bodied society – for example, in special schools – which consequently makes it more difficult for them to be 'normal' and to integrate into society.

> Prejudice may be translated into discrimination in the field of employment, as employers may be reluctant to take on a disabled person. The disabled therefore may be more likely to be on welfare benefits and to experience poverty.

> Brown (1994) argues that people with disabilities may be seen as either 'innocents or perverts'. Anderson and Kitchin (2000) found that a number of myths about disability and sex existed among professionals who worked in family planning clinics in Northern Ireland; for example, it was believed that the disabled should be discouraged from having sex because they were not responsible enough to cope with sexual relationships.

> Kallianes and Rubenfeld (1997) argue that women with disabilities are often discriminated against. It is assumed by professionals that such women should not be having sex and that they are likely to make unsuitable mothers. There have been a number of cases in which disabled women have been forcibly sterilised or have had their children taken into care.

Watch an episode of Channel 4's *The Undateables*. How does it aim to dispel stereotypes of the disabled? Is it successful?

The disabled identity and resistance

The social model of disability argues that more positive disabled identities should be promoted, stressing independence, choice and autonomy for disabled people. It proposes that the state should invest in a disabled-friendly social environment and should address prejudice and discrimination against the disabled.

Recent sociological studies suggest that the disabled identity may now be underpinned by the social model of disability, and that disabled people are more likely to resist those definitions of disability that stress dependence and helplessness. Antle (2004) found that children with disabilities do not qualitatively differ in how they see themselves compared with children without disabilities.

FOCUS ON RESEARCH: STEREOTYPING, SEXUALITY AND DISABILITY

Anderson and Kitchin found that many health professionals held a range of misconceptions about the sexuality of disabled people.

Anderson and Kitchin studied the attitudes of health professionals working in family planning clinics in Northern Ireland. This survey research involved sending a short questionnaire to every family planning clinic in the country. It found that many of them subscribed to cultural myths about the sexual behaviour of disabled people. For example, professionals tended to believe that:

> disabled people were unable to take part in sexual activities

> disabled people were sexually irresponsible and therefore needed to have their sexual appetite and behaviour controlled by professionals

> some disabled people were unable to sustain long-term relationships

> some disabled people lacked a sex drive.

There was little information produced specifically for the disabled and even access to some centres was problematic for wheelchair users and those with mobility problems.

Based on Best (2005)

Questions

1. Analyse whether the beliefs held by health professionals in Northern Ireland support the medical or social model of disability?

2. Analyse how these beliefs might undermine integration and encourage learned helplessness among the disabled.

3. Evaluate the reliability and validity of the research methods used in this study. (You could consider the problem of non-response and how far you could trust the answers provided.)

4. What are the strengths of this research method?

Olney and Kim (2001) argue that the disabled people in their study felt positive about their disability despite their awareness that people without disabilities evaluated them negatively. They rejected the medical labels and had a very positive self-image. Such positive self-images are likely to be further encouraged by the greater prominence of disabled people in the media – for example, the TV presenter Ade Adepitan.

The disabled identity – recent developments

Critiques of the social model of disability have recently appeared. These acknowledge that prejudice and discrimination need to be addressed and that the social environment in which we live is not always conducive to the disabled. However, they argue that we cannot ignore the fact that physical and biological factors such as pain, mental impairment, and so on, *do* have a negative impact on how disabled people experience social life and can make it unpleasant and difficult. The disabled identity therefore probably consists not only of coping both with the limitations caused by the physical impairment of the body and mind, but also the limitations of a social environment shaped by negative and stereotypical attitudes towards disability.

Evaluate the view that most problems associated with disability are a product of society and not of the disability itself.

CONCLUSIONS

Sociologists argue that age and generation are products of the culture of the society to which we belong. As Marsh and Keating (2006) observe, different cultures attach different cultural meanings and values to different age groups. These shape our behaviour in terms of how we respond to others of the same generation and how we treat people in other age groups. Although these expectations may be becoming less rigid, they still have important effects on people's lives. It is also important to note that how particular age groups or generations are treated will often be shaped by influences such as gender, social class and ethnicity. For example, being an elderly, African Caribbean woman may be a quite different experience from being an elderly, white, middle-class man.

Societal expectations around the disabled may also be becoming less rigid. This is reflected both in the way media stereotypes have been challenged, and in the greater awareness of the ways a disabling society can restrict opportunities. However, there is still a way to go before the societal limitations for the disabled can be eradicated, and until then further campaigning will be necessary to make significant progress.

CHECK YOUR UNDERSTANDING

1. Explain the terms 'life course' and 'life cycle'.

2. Explain 'ageism' and 'learned helplessness'.

3. Identify and briefly explain two ways in which people may be disabled by society.

4. Identify and briefly explain an example of research that suggests that the media tends to portray the elderly in stereotypical ways, and another piece of research which shows that the disabled are portrayed stereotypically.

5. Identify and explain two changes in youth identity over the last 50 years.

6. Analyse the main differences between the biological and the social models of disability.

7. Evaluate the view that there has been a de-standardisation of the life course.

8. Evaluate the view that disability is primarily a product of society rather than physical or mental (in)capacity.

TAKE IT FURTHER

Visit the sites www.ageuk.org.uk and www.cpa.org.uk. Identify 10 positive aspects of the portrayal of the elderly on each site. Compare these images with two TV dramas (e.g. soap operas) by watching a single episode of each. Are the programmes portraying the elderly in a positive light? (Use any appropriate method of content analysis.)

3.7 IDENTITY, PRODUCTION, CONSUMPTION AND GLOBALISATION

LEARNING OBJECTIVES

› Understand the meaning of production, consumption and globalisation in the context of identity (AO1).

› Understand how identities are shaped by consumption choices and how social identity affects consumption and lifestyle (AO1).

› Apply this understanding to examples from Britain and elsewhere (AO2).

› Analyse the extent to which individuals can choose and shape their social identities (AO3).

› Analyse the effects of globalisation on identity (AO3).

› Evaluate the importance of production, consumption and globalisation in the formation of identity (AO3).

INTRODUCING THE DEBATE

In previous decades it was widely assumed that your identity was closely linked to your position in society and that this position was in turn closely linked to your background. As discussed in Chapter 3, social class was seen as a key to people's identities, and social class was connected to the type of work that individuals did. Identity was therefore seen as being linked to production – what you produced through your work. However, in recent decades a number of sociologists have argued that consumption – what you buy rather than what you make – is an increasingly important source of identity. In addition, it is claimed that people

increasingly define themselves in terms of their leisure activities – what they do for fun rather than what they do for work. Globalisation has made it easier for people to buy products from around the world, relate to cultures from other countries or even emigrate to start a new life and adopt a new lifestyle. All this suggests that identity is increasingly chosen rather than simply inherited from your family, from the place where you live, or from your starting position in society. But not all sociologists agree that there is so much choice, and this chapter explores the different views on how the construction of identity is changing in society today.

IDENTITY AND PRODUCTION

Work, class, identity and leisure

In early research, Stanley Parker (1976) argued that work, identity and leisure were very closely connected. He conducted interviews with workers in a number of professions and looked at existing sociological research. He concluded that there were three relationships between work and leisure.

In the extension pattern, identity and leisure activities were very closely associated with work. There was no clear dividing line between work and leisure. This was typical of those who had satisfying and high-status work, as managers and professionals, for example. Their identity largely came from their jobs and in their leisure time they might entertain clients or do activities linked to their work; a social worker, for example, might run a youth club.

The neutrality pattern involved occupations where individuals had medium to low levels of autonomy or control over their work, as clerical or semi-skilled manual workers, for example. In this case, work was not closely connected to leisure and identity, and leisure frequently focused around family activities.

In the opposition pattern, leisure was an escape from work. This was typical of those in heavy manual jobs (such as coal mining, fishing or working in a steel factory) and working-class jobs where there was a strong sense of identity associated with the occupation, and people often lived in occupational communities close to their work base. Because of the dangers and harshness of the work, they wanted to forget about it during leisure time. Drinking alcohol in pubs or working men's clubs was typical of the leisure activities in this pattern.

Parker was heavily criticised by other sociologists for ignoring the influence of factors other than work in shaping identity and leisure activities. He paid no attention to ethnicity, gender or age, and his work has been seen as quite **deterministic** – it assumes leisure patterns are entirely determined by work patterns, leaving people little agency or choice over their leisure or identities.

UNDERSTAND THE CONCEPT

In a **deterministic** theory, human behaviour is seen as being determined by external factors, and individuals have little or no opportunity to choose to act in different ways. Deterministic theories are often criticised for denying human agency, that is, the ability to choose how to behave, and by doing so, to affect the course of events.

Scraton and Bramham (2001) criticise Parker for a limited view of the nature of work. Feminists point out that not all work is paid work; in particular, the unpaid work involved in housework and childcare (which is still predominantly done by women) is ignored in much of the discussion. Yet the long hours spent on unpaid work by women severely restrict opportunity for leisure, and typically men have more spare time than women to engage in the leisure pursuits of their choice.

Pierre Bourdieu: social class and leisure

Pierre Bourdieu (1984) argues that social class is directly linked to culture and therefore to identity and leisure. Social class itself is partly shaped by occupation (although also by ownership of wealth). As discussed in Chapter 3, Bourdieu believes that the highest class engages in highbrow culture (such as opera, theatre and classical music), the middle classes are preoccupied with middlebrow culture (such as easy listening music and popular novels), and the working class are more concerned with mass or popular culture (for example, pop music). Research by Bennett et al. (2009) suggests that there is some connection between class and culture, although other factors are important as well, and the highest classes tend to be cultural omnivores who enjoy many different types of culture and not just highbrow culture.

A pluralist view on leisure

Ken Roberts (1986) takes a much broader view of leisure than Stanley Parker. While he accepts that work has some influence on leisure and identity, he sees leisure activities as being largely a matter of choice. He adopts a **pluralist** view of society, arguing that there are many different groups in contemporary societies. One single social division, such as social class, does not dominate people's identities and leisure choices. His research on men in Liverpool suggested that there was little connection between the work that people did and their leisure pursuits, and in any case a considerable proportion of the population were not in employment. Certain leisure pursuits were found in all occupational groups, particularly watching television, drinking alcohol, gambling and having sex. Some pursuits, such as going to the theatre, were predominantly middle class, but since they take up such a small proportion of all leisure time this did not have a strong effect on overall patterns of leisure. The stage in the life cycle had some effect upon leisure patterns; for example, choices might be affected by whether people had children or not, or whether they were retired.

UNDERSTAND THE CONCEPT

Pluralism is a theory of modern societies which argues that there are many different groupings in society. Class is one important grouping, but others are also very important, including ethnicity, age, gender, sexuality, stage in the life cycle and personal interests (for example, hobbies). Pluralists believe that no one group is dominant in society.

Leisure and capitalism

John Clarke and Chas Critcher (1985) question the pluralist view put forward by Ken Roberts. They believe that leisure activities are largely shaped by capitalist society, and they support a neo-Marxist approach to the sociology of leisure. They argue that capitalism shapes not only the nature of work but also the nature of leisure, and individuals are manipulated in capitalist society to take part in certain sorts of leisure activities.

The state, they claim, tries to encourage people to take part in healthy leisure pursuits that are not a threat to stability and order in society. This includes active involvement in sport, partly because it helps to keep the workforce healthy and to save the state money on healthcare.

Most leisure, however, is run by private businesses and is increasingly commercialised. An increasing proportion of consumer spending goes on leisure in Britain, most of it organised by large corporations, including those in the film, brewing and gambling industries. People's choices are restricted by the limited options made available to most of the population; for example, only a small range of films are shown at mainstream cinemas.

From this point of view, people's identities are manipulated in favour of a mass, consumer market for particular goods and services. However, Clarke and Critcher do accept that there are some groups who try to resist the commercialisation of leisure and the manipulation of identities in line with mass culture. For example, the Campaign for Real Ale (CAMRA) has challenged the dominance of the big brewers and has succeeded in encouraging many more small breweries to open. Another example is the existence of independent cinemas in some cities, which choose to show alternative films from outside the mainstream, some of which may express anti-capitalist views.

A problem with the exclusive emphasis upon capitalism and class differences is that it ignores other social divisions such as gender, which will be discussed later in this chapter.

Does evidence and your own experience suggest that leisure is a matter of personal choice, or is it manipulated by big business or shaped by class and other social factors?

Modern and postmodern leisure

Many more recent theories of leisure and identity have been influenced by theories of postmodernity. To some extent they hark back to Ken Roberts's pluralist theory but they link their theories to the idea that there has been a fundamental change in society. They argue that society has moved from modernity (when class differences were central to society) to postmodernity, where there is much more choice over identity, and indeed leisure pursuits. One supporter of postmodern theories is Rojek (1995). He identifies four main differences between modern and postmodern leisure.

> The modernist view of leisure is that work and leisure are contrasted as two separate parts of life, but with postmodernity they come together. For example, more and more people work in leisure industries, people can experience fun and enjoyment at work, and they can even see going to work as a leisure activity.

> Leisure is less planned and purposeful in postmodern society. People are less likely to pursue leisure activities for particular purposes, but to take part in them just for the sake of it, for fun.

> In postmodernism, peoples' leisure choices are no longer shaped by their position in society in terms of class, age or gender. For example, older people might continue to go to night clubs and rock concerts, and young people might engage in more sedate pursuits associated in modern thinking with older age groups (crown green bowling or knitting, for example).

> Postmodernism breaks down a whole series of barriers between areas of social life. Societies become more pluralistic in the lifestyles and identities of their members, and less rigid in terms of who can adopt particular identities. **Identity politics** becomes more important for people. They can pick and choose who to be and are not even limited by their biological make-up. For example, white people can choose to listen to and identify with the music of black people, men can dress as women, and vice versa. Leisure plays a central role in identity politics.

In short, in modern societies leisure reflects who you are, but in postmodernism your leisure increasingly creates your identity – you become who you are through your leisure.

On the whole, Rojek welcomes the tendency towards more postmodern patterns of leisure. He believes that people experience greater choice and freedom than in modern leisure.

Gender, ethnicity and leisure

The postmodern view of leisure is criticised by Scraton and Bramham. They argue that it fails to take account of continued social divisions, including gender divisions.

Leisure itself remains gendered – it is different for males and females. For example, they point out that video games and virtual reality technology are mostly enjoyed by men, and most games involve aggression and violence. Sex tourism to countries such as Thailand is almost exclusively male-orientated, although it is young women who are exploited through it.

Racism is another important feature of society that restricts leisure choices. Scraton and Bramham quote research which suggests that racism is endemic in many sports, making it difficult for ethnic-minority men and women to fulfil their potential.

IDENTITY AND CONSUMPTION

Consumer society

Many of the views expressed in the preceding section saw relations involved in production as dominant in shaping leisure (although the views of Ken Roberts are an exception). However, increasingly some sociologists have argued that it is consumption that is important in shaping identity and leisure activities. Instead of having identities shaped through work, they claim identities are shaped through choices about what to consume, and particularly through shopping.

To some sociologists, changes in the nature of leisure are strongly associated with the growth of consumer society and consumer culture. In a consumer society, identity is primarily determined by what is consumed (bought and used) rather than by membership of particular social groups, such as social classes.

Celia Lury (2011) discusses the growth of consumer culture, which she sees as having the following characteristics:

> there has been a rapid increase in the range of products available to buy in countries such as the UK

> shopping has become a more and more important leisure pursuit

> there are more opportunities to consume both in person and online

> credit is relatively easily available, for example through credit cards, in order to fund consumption

> branding and advertising are present in nearly all areas of social life

> consumption is even becoming linked to illnesses such as 'binge shopping'

> people are bombarded with choices about the goods and services that they consume and are almost forced to think about how their own choices relate to those of others, particularly celebrities.

With an increasing sociological interest in consumption, the effects of consumption on identity have been discussed more and more, but the sociology of consumption has a long history which predates the recent growth of consumer society.

Conspicuous consumption

One of the earliest ideas about the relationship between consumption, identity and leisure was that there was a link between class and leisure. Thornstein Veblen, in *The Theory of the Leisure Class* (1899), introduced the idea of conspicuous consumption. In the late 19th century, very few people had disposable income to spend on consumption over and above what was necessary to meet basic needs (such as housing, clothing and food). The only people who did have spare money were the very wealthy, and they consumed in order to show off their wealth and status in society by buying ostentatious or showy goods – such as jewellery – which very few other people could afford. It was this practice that Veblen called conspicuous consumption.

Consumption and personal identity

As the 20th century progressed and living standards rose, more people became able to afford at least some consumption beyond the essentials. Some sociologists therefore began to argue that consumption of non-necessities was no longer confined to a small minority but instead could be used by a wide variety of individuals, and not just the very rich.

Walter Susman (1973) argued that by the 1970s people were no longer particularly concerned with demonstrating their position in society or their social class, but increasingly wanted to express their personal taste. No longer driven by a desire to be seen as respectable and to have 'good taste', they wanted to express themselves as individuals and show their unique characteristics rather than their membership of particular social groups. Susman claimed that each individual became a 'performing self' by buying material goods which showed what kind of person they were.

Similarly, Helga Dittmar (2007) argues that buying material possessions helps to cement a particular identity. What we own – for example, clothes, mobile phones, houses and music collections – becomes an 'extension of the self', helping to consolidate our individual identities. From this point of view, we can improve or alter our identity simply by acquiring new objects.

Evaluate the ideas that consumption is used to display wealth, demonstrate respectability, express personal identity or to strengthen our sense of identity through owning particular items. How important are each of these in Britain today?

Zygmunt Bauman: the limits to choice in consumer culture

On the surface, a society in which everyone can choose their identity through something as simple as shopping sounds very attractive. It implies that nobody has to be excluded and everyone effectively ends up as a winner. Zygmunt Bauman (1988, 1997) accepts that consumption has become perhaps the central feature of contemporary society, but he doesn't see it in quite such a positive light as some sociologists. He points out that, much as in any other type of society, there are always winners and losers in consumer society. Most obviously, the winners are those who can afford to consume and the losers are those who cannot, but there are other reasons apart from money that might prevent some people from taking a full part in consumer society.

Bauman broadly divides consumers into two groups:

1. The 'seduced' are those who are financially secure, usually in well-paid regular work, knowledgeable about consumption and physically able to

take part in it. They have been seduced by the attractions of consumer society. They enjoy consumption and they are seen by companies as attractive customers.

2. The 'repressed' may also be attracted to consumption, and in particular shopping, but they only have a limited ability to shop and consume. This may be because they have low income and cannot easily get hold of cheap credit, or they lack the knowledge of consumer trends to know what to buy. Or perhaps a disability or old age may be preventing them from taking advantage of all the goods and services available. The repressed might include those on low wages, those in insecure work, recent migrants and the chronically sick.

Although the seduced obviously do better in consumer society, the term 'seduced' suggests that they have been taken in by the producers and are encouraged to consume more than they really need to. However, it is the repressed who are the real victims of consumer society, because they have a devalued identity. If they are not able to buy the 'right' products or services, they won't be fully accepted by others in their peer groups. For example, young people unable to afford an up-to-date mobile phone might be excluded from particular youth cultures. It is not the product or service that is important in itself, it is the fact that they cannot project the image they need to through consuming that is important.

Bauman has been criticised for over-simplifying the difference between the seduced and the repressed, and failing to accept that there might be a range of different relationships to consumption in society (Hetherington and Harvard, 2014). He also doesn't acknowledge that some people reject consumer society altogether; for example, supporters of the green movement try to consume as little as possible to prevent damage to the environment.

Freedom and constraint

Different views of consumer society imply that individuals have either a great deal of freedom to create their own identities, or are very limited or constrained in the identities that they can attain. Lury believes that you can exaggerate the amount of choice in consumer society. A great deal of consumption is routine and is linked to your identity and position in different social groups. It is not only a matter of money but also of taste, which is shaped by belonging to a particular class, ethnic group, age group, and so on. Identities based upon group membership are still important and it is only some groups (for example, the affluent young) who really attach primary importance to what people consume. Nevertheless, Lury does believe that more people are able to consume than

in the past as a result of generally rising living standards, and there is more freedom to use consumption to influence your identity, at least to some extent.

FOCUS ON RESEARCH: THE 24-HOUR CITY

Nightlife in Leeds

Two recent research projects by Rowe and Lynch (2012) in Sydney, Australia, and by Bramham and Spink (2009) in Leeds, UK (cited in Scraton and Watson, 2015) have looked at leisure and consumption in 24-hour cities that have global connections. Both Sydney and Leeds are known to have a lively nightlife with plenty of clubs and alcohol consumption. Shopping is also important in both cities. People work, live and play in the two cities and there are plenty of opportunities for developing different identities and lifestyles. Often the boundaries between work and leisure are blurred, with many people having jobs in leisure industries. However, both sets of researchers have found that not everyone has equal opportunities to take part fully in the leisure activities of the two cities. There is an increasing divide between the young and the old, and also between those with relatively high levels of

pay and those with poorly-paid jobs. The disabled and members of some minority ethnic groups too often find it difficult to enjoy the opportunities for leisure offered by the two cities. So while there are opportunities for self-expression and the creation of new and varied identities, both Leeds and Sydney are also places where there is exclusion and sometimes conflict between different social groups.

Based on Scraton and Watson (2015)

Questions

1. Suggest two ways in which work and leisure might be blurred within cities such as Sydney and Leeds.

2. Analyse possible reasons why older people, the disabled, some ethnic minorities and those on low income might find it difficult to take full advantage of the leisure activities available in the cities.

3. Analyse the kind of identity that young and well-off residents of Leeds and Sydney might be able to create through their participation in leisure.

4. Evaluate the view that only a minority are likely to be able to develop new identities through consumption and leisure in cities such as Sydney and Leeds.

GLOBALISATION, CONSUMPTION AND IDENTITY

Globalisation

Anthony Giddens defines globalisation as "the intensification of worldwide social relations which link distant localities in such a way that local happenings are shaped by events occurring many miles away and vice versa" (Giddens, 1990, p. 64). According to theorists of globalisation the world has become a smaller place, national boundaries have become less important and

different parts of the globe are closely interconnected in many different ways.

Daniel O'Byrne (2015) points out that these connections are:

> economic (for example, through increased worldwide trade and the growth of transnational companies operating in many states)

> political (for example, through the growth in importance of global political movements such as human rights movements)

⟩ cultural (for example, through the increased familiarity of people with music from around the world).

Globalisation may be a macro (large scale, affecting whole societies) change in social life, but it has major effects on a micro (small scale, affecting individuals or small social groups) scale, affecting individuals as well, and it can have important effects on their consumption and identities.

BUILD CONNECTIONS

Globalisation is also discussed in relation to education, and increased opportunities to study outside your own country may affect identity (see Topic 1, Chapter 6).

Identity and different responses to globalisation

Stuart Hall (1992) points out that because of globalisation, individuals are no longer tied as they once were to identities based upon the area in which they live, but can incorporate elements of identity from a variety of very different cultures. Hall called this a 'cultural supermarket effect' in which people can in theory pick their clothing style, way of speaking, lifestyle, musical tastes, and so on from any group they choose. Mass communications and cheap air travel make these sorts of choices possible. According to Hall, there have been three main reactions to this situation.

1. Some majority ethnic groups have reaffirmed their ethnic or national identity as a reaction to globalisation and as a defence against a sense that their identity is under threat. In a British context, Andrew Pilkington (2002) identifies a group who fit into this category; a group he describes as 'Little Englanders'. They tend to see England in terms of quite a narrow sense of identity. For example, the Conservative MP John Townsend argued that most people would prefer England to stay as an 'an English-speaking white country'. Little Englanders tend to be strongly opposed to large-scale immigration and to policies of multiculturalism that encourage the appreciation and valuing of different cultures.

2. A second reaction identified by Hall involves members of ethnic-minority groups reacting in a similar way, emphasising their culture of origin and expressing much stronger pride in that identity than the national identity of the country in which they

live. Pilkington sees those British Muslims with a very strong Islamic identity as fitting into this category.

3. Hall's third group consists of those who construct new identities that don't fit neatly into previously existing categories. Pilkington uses the concept of hybrid identities in this context. These are identities produced by combining two or more established identities. Examples include Black British or British Asian identities. Through hybrid identities, different cultures can be fused together. One example is Bhangra music, which started in the 1980s and combines Punjabi and Bengali music with house and hip-hop.

Zygmunt Bauman: unstable identities

The ideas of Hall and Pilkington suggest that there is a wider range of identities, in response to globalisation and that some new identities develop, but they also suggest that people still have a strong sense of identity. Zygmunt Bauman (1996, 1998, 2012) goes further, suggesting that globalisation undermines a strong sense of identity. According to Bauman, in the past identity was like a pilgrimage: people had a clear identity that they were aiming for in their lives, and they set out to achieve it (for example, by getting a professional job) in the same way that a pilgrim sets out on a journey to get to a specific holy place.

However, in a globalised world that changes rapidly, even if you achieve the identity you want, it may not last for long, as social changes can undermine it (for example, if your job is replaced by technology). People are therefore much more likely to sample different identities without committing to a single one. This is typical of consumer society and Bauman compares it to people flitting between different TV

A globalised world has shaken previously stable sources of identity.

channels or continually trying out new products in a shopping mall or supermarket where there is endless choice. Bauman says: "In our fluid world, committing oneself to a single identity for life, or even ... a very long time to come, is a risky business. Identities are for wearing and showing, not for storing and keeping" (1998, p. 89). To Bauman, globalisation and the growth of consumer society help to make this possible.

> New technology allows people to create new identities, using social media. You can reinvent yourself online without even having to leave your own house.

> Identity involves identifying with people similar to yourself, and globalised consumer society allows you to identify with a never-ending range of new fashions and consumer trends. Sometimes this can be linked to particular brands.

However, Bauman (2011) also points out that there are growing inequalities in a globalised world, so not everyone can afford to participate fully (or sometimes at all) in consumer society. For example, not everyone can afford the time or money to play around with online identities. The rich have more chance to try out different identities than the poor.

CONCLUSIONS

It may be impossible to generalise about the effects of globalisation and consumption on identities. The effects vary from place to place and from one social group to another. But most theorists agree that there is now a greater variety of identities than in the past, and, at least for the better-off, there is more chance to change identity. However, as the Focus on Skills feature above shows, some sociologists, such as Naomi Klein (2000), believe that globalisation and consumer culture can also undermine differences in identity through the branding used by major corporations in order to develop identification with brands such as Coca-Cola, McDonald's and Nike. Such brands can shape identities around the world and undermine local identities. Nevertheless, this still leaves room for some new identities that are opposed to the power of global corporations. These identities are associated with anti-globalisation, human rights and global justice movements. They offer an alternative to strong nationalist or ethnic identities on the one hand, and unstable or fragmented identities on the other, and the possibility of creating new global identities based on sets of values rather than on membership of particular social groups or brand loyalty.

FOCUS ON SKILLS: NAOMI KLEIN – A CRITICAL VIEW OF GLOBALISATION AND BRANDING

The McDonald's 'golden arches' are instantly recognisable across the globe.

In *No Logo* (2000) Naomi Klein offers a radical critique of global or transnational corporations.

By the 1980s, corporations were discovering that rather than promoting the product as a brand, it was possible to promote the company, or the logo of the company,

as a brand in its own right. Once the company itself and its logo were sufficiently well established in the minds of the public, the company could diversify and sell a wider variety of products through their association with the logo. In Britain, for example, Richard Branson's Virgin company has used its logo not just to promote its original products (records and music shops) but also to sell cola, mobile phones, airline and rail services, financial services, etc. Particular symbols such as the swoosh symbol of Nike, the golden arches of McDonald's and the Coca-Cola logos have become globally recognisable and powerful marketing tools for promoting the respective businesses. Once they are established worldwide, they become a superbrand.

For consumers, it is increasingly the logo that it is important for them to buy rather than the product it relates to. Often, logos are associated with particular lifestyles. For example, Nike has tried to associate the swoosh with the ideals of sport.

Corporations are willing to extend advertising and marketing into virtually every area of social life. They sponsor television programmes, sporting events, rock music tours, and are increasingly involved in sponsoring education and advertising in schools and universities. Corporations also try to make use of every trend in youth culture to make their products seem more 'cool'. Nike is so focused on borrowing style from black street culture that it has invented a word to describe the practice: bro-ing.

Klein's work suggests a world in which branding by multinational corporations has become the dominant cultural force across the globe. Nevertheless, Klein does not believe corporations are totally dominant. As well as exploring the rise of branding and the power of corporations she also examines the rise of social movements opposing corporations. One reaction against corporate branding is culture jamming. The term was coined by a group in San Francisco in 1984 and referred to their practice of visually changing an advertisement in order to reveal what they saw as the real meaning of the ad. For example, Joe Camel (advertising Camel cigarettes) became Joe Chemo.

Source: Haralambos and Holborn (2013)

Questions

1. **Interpretation.** Explain what Klein means by the 'superbrand'.

2. **Application.** Identify a superbrand which is not mentioned here and suggest the lifestyle it is associated with.

3. **Analyse** how branding could lead to the creation of global identities which cut across other social divisions such as class, gender and ethnicity.

4. **Evaluate** how far identities associated with brands have replaced other sources of identity. (You could think about how far groups choose brands based upon class or ethnic background rather than identifying with the brand itself.)

5. **Evaluate** whether opponents of superbrands have succeeded in undermining brand identities. (Have critics of McDonald's managed to undermine its reputation?)

CHECK YOUR UNDERSTANDING

1. Explain the term 'consumption'.

2. Explain what is meant by 'globalisation'.

3. Explain the terms 'the seduced' and 'the repressed'.

4. Explain 'conspicuous consumption'.

5. Identify and briefly explain two characteristics of consumer society.

6. Identify and briefly explain two ways in which some people have responded to globalisation in constructing their identities.

7. Identify and explain two ways in which gender still influences leisure.

8. Analyse the main differences between the pluralist view of the relationship between work and leisure and the view of Stanley Parker.

9. Evaluate the view that work no longer has much influence on leisure.

10. Evaluate the view that most people can now construct their own identity with few restraints.

TAKE IT FURTHER

Interview a small sample of your classmates about the branded goods they buy. Ask them what they think the brands say about the sort of person they are. Search for some advertising produced by any two of these brands (for example, by looking for TV adverts on YouTube). Does there seem to be a link between the brand image of the product and the reasons why people are choosing those brands? Do the brand choices of your classmates simply reflect factors such as their age, ethnicity or social class, or is there more to it than this?

APPLY YOUR LEARNING

AS LEVEL

1   Define the term 'culture'. [2 marks]

2   Using **one** example, briefly explain how sexuality can act as a master status. [2 marks]

3   Outline **three** reasons why people today may be less likely than in the past to identify with a particular social class. [6 marks]

4   Outline and explain **two** ways in which disabled rights campaigners have sought to promote a positive identity for disabled people. [10 marks]

5   Read **Item A** below and answer the question that follows.

ITEM A

Functionalist views of culture

According to functionalist sociologists, everything in society performs a function, including culture. In the view of functionalists such as Emile Durkheim, the key feature of society is that it is orderly and harmonious. Despite the fact that different individuals may have competing or conflicting interests, they are still able to live together and cooperate with one another.

Durkheim argues that this is because of the existence of a shared culture or 'value consensus'. This shared culture binds individuals together by giving them a sense of belonging and a set of common goals which they can achieve through cooperation. This helps to safeguard individuals and society from anomie.

Applying material from **Item A** and your knowledge, evaluate the strengths and weaknesses of the functionalist view of culture. [20 marks]

A-LEVEL

1 Outline and explain **two** reasons for the alleged 'crisis of masculinity' in the contemporary UK. [10 marks]

2 Read **Item B** below and answer the question that follows.

ITEM B

National identity as a social construct

National identity involves, first, a belief in the existence of a social group called a 'nation' and, second, the feeling of being part of this nation. 'Nations' might seem easy to define, and nationalists tend to see them as fixed, permanent and real, but in fact they are social constructs. Definitions of what a particular nation is or should be, and what its 'national character' is – for example, what a 'true Brit' or a 'real Aussie' is – are often contested and sometimes even fought over.

Applying material from **Item B** and your knowledge, analyse **two** ways in which British identity can be seen as contested or fought over. [10 marks]

3 Read **Item C** below and answer the question that follows.

ITEM C

Old age and social identity

There is evidence that old age as a stage in the life course is largely negatively perceived. This is reflected in everyday descriptions of elderly people as being 'past it' or 'over the hill' or having 'one foot in the grave'. Old people are often described in derogatory or condescending ways such as 'old fogey', 'old biddy', 'old bat' or 'sweet little old lady/man'. Such stereotypes tend to marginalise old people and to label them as inferior.

Applying material from **Item C** and your knowledge, evaluate explanations for the negative social identity often associated with old age in the UK today. [20 marks]

You can find example answers and accompanying teachers' comments for this topic at www.collins.co.uk/AQAAlevelSociology.

4 FAMILIES AND HOUSEHOLDS

AQA Specification	Chapters
Candidates should examine:	
The relationship of the family to the social structure and social change with particular reference to the economy.	Chapter 1 (pages 224–241) covers this topic but examples to illustrate particular theories can be found elsewhere, especially in Chapters 2 (pages 242–250) and 5 (pages 282–291).
The relationship of the family to the social structure and social change with particular reference to state policies.	Chapter 2 (pages 242–250) covers this topic, with further examples in Chapter 4 (pages 265–281).
Demographic trends in the United Kingdom since 1900: birth rates, death rates, family size, life expectancy, ageing population, and migration and globalisation.	Chapter 3 (pages 251–264) covers this topic and is also useful to an understanding of the concept of diversity focused on in Chapter 4 (pages 265–281).
Changing patterns of marriage, cohabitation, separation, divorce, childbearing and the life course, including the sociology of personal life, and the diversity of contemporary family and household structures.	Chapter 4 (pages 265–281) covers this topic.
Gender roles, domestic labour and power relationships within the family in contemporary society.	Chapter 5 (pages 282–291) covers this topic.
The nature of childhood, and changes in the status of children in the family and society.	Chapter 6 (pages 292–304) covers this topic.

4.1 THE FAMILY, SOCIAL STRUCTURE AND SOCIAL CHANGE

LEARNING OBJECTIVES

> Demonstrate knowledge and understanding of theoretical perspectives on the relationship between the family and social structure, particularly the economy (AO1).

> Apply and compare theoretical perspectives on the family and evidence from sociological studies of the family to the relationship between the family and social change (AO2).

> Analyse how different theoretical perspectives contribute to the view that there is a relationship between the family and social structure (AO3).

> Evaluate the functionalist explanation of the family and its relationship to social change by contrasting it with critical theories of the family (AO3).

INTRODUCING THE DEBATE

The problem with studying the family is that we all think we are experts – not surprisingly, given that most of us are born into families and socialised into family roles and responsibilities. For many of us, the family is the cornerstone of our social world, a place to which we can retreat and where we can take refuge from the stresses of the outside world. It is the place in which we are loved for who we are, rather than for what we are. This topic deals with sociological theories of the family that have contributed in some way to our understanding of family life in the 21st century.

GETTING YOU THINKING

Technology and increasingly unsociable eating habits are often invoked as contributing to the disintegration of traditional family life.

According to the 21st Century Family Life Survey of 2006 which was commissioned by First magazine, the traditional nuclear family is in meltdown because of a decline in morality and an increase in the number of children born outside marriage, especially to single mothers. Of the 1,736 mothers surveyed, 90 per cent felt that family life was breaking down. They were particularly worried that the parent–child relationship was in danger of disintegrating because families no longer sat down together for meals and parents were increasingly fighting with their children because they

believed that they spent too long playing computer games or watching television. Fifty per cent of the mothers also blamed higher levels of sexual imagery in the media, drug use, violence and bad language for family decline. Two-thirds of those surveyed blamed the government for not doing enough to protect the nuclear family and suggested that politicians are more interested in looking after single mums and single-sex parents.

Questions

1   Identify five family-orientated reasons why according to the 21st Century Family Life Survey the 'traditional nuclear family is in meltdown'.

2   What four other reasons were blamed for family decline by 50 per cent of mothers?

3   Who or what did two-thirds of the mothers see as the main cause of family decline?

4   What, in your opinion, are the major causes of teenage pregnancy?

5   Why do you think some people claim that teenage pregnancy is undermining the traditional family?

FAMILY CONCEPTS

It is useful to begin our exploration of the relationship between the family, **kinship** and social structure by examining some of the common terms used in theoretical perspectives on the family.

UNDERSTAND THE CONCEPT

Kinship is a concept that generally refers to the system of family relationships between people in a society or cultural group who are biologically related by blood and descent or have attained the status of relatives via marriage, cohabitation, adoption or fostering. Kin normally enjoy legal rights, such as those relating to the inheritance of property. Moreover, they may feel obliged to offer other kin material and emotional support.

The most common family type experienced by the majority of people in the UK is the 'nuclear family'. Traditionally, this has been defined as a two-generational

social group – two parents and one or more children – who share a common residence. In addition to the nuclear family, evidence suggests that some kinship groupings constitute 'extended families'. This means that, in addition to the nuclear family grouping, kin such as grandparents, uncles, cousins and so on may share common residence or proximity and/or mutual support.

Finally, the concept of 'household' is central to an understanding of family. All families that share a common residence are households. However, there are also household set-ups that are not families. For example, a single person who lives alone, a couple of friends who share a flat, students who share a house or a kitchen in a student hall of residence, and elderly people who live in sheltered housing are all examples of non-family households.

THE FUNCTIONALIST THEORY OF THE FAMILY

The functionalist theory of the family sees the nuclear family as functioning for the greater good of society because, as the cornerstone of society, it makes a massive contribution to the maintenance of social order

225

and stability. Moreover, the nuclear family also plays a major role in the construction and maintenance of an effective economy.

Functionalists argue that the nuclear family also benefits the individuals who comprise it. Both adults and children benefit from the emotional wellbeing and satisfaction associated with marriage and family life. The nuclear family also provides social support, identity and security. Consequently, family members are happy to take their place in society as responsible and well-behaved citizens. Overall, then, functionalists see the family as extremely important and serving a purpose: its existence is both beneficial and necessary for the smooth running of society and the personal development of individuals.

G.P. Murdock

A good example of a functionalist thinker is George Peter Murdock (1949) who compared the family set-ups of over 250 societies worldwide. On the basis of this global study, he concluded that the nuclear family was universal – it existed in every known society and therefore must be a social institution which functioned for the good of society. He defined the nuclear family as: "a social group characterised by common residence [which] includes adults of both sexes, at least two of whom maintain a socially approved sexual relationship, and one or more children, own or adopted, of the sexually cohabiting adults".

Murdock argued that this global nuclear unit performed four functions essential to the continued existence and smooth running of all societies. However, these functions benefit family members too, therefore reinforcing their commitment to one another.

1. *Reproductive* – All societies require new members to ensure their physical survival. However, Murdock noted that his global study clearly showed that childbearing generally occurs within a marital and family context in most cultures. He claimed that children therefore were symbolic of a couple's emotional commitment to one another. In that sense, having children functioned to stabilise both the marital relationship and family life.

2. *Sexual* – Murdock argued that the nuclear family functions to regulate sexual behaviour and therefore functions for the good of both the individual and society. With regard to individuals, marital sex creates a powerful emotional bond between a couple, which encourages both fidelity (faithfulness) and the life-long commitment of the individual to family life. In many societies,

breaking the marital contract either through divorce or adultery is still regarded with strong moral disapproval.

Moreover, sex within marriage contributes to social order and stability because society is agreed that marriage is a social goal that all members of society should strive to attain. The institution of marriage is regarded as something that others should respect and not undermine.

3. *Educational* – This function refers to the **primary socialisation** that occurs within the family. Murdock argued that culture needs to be transmitted to the next generation because without culture, social life, and therefore social order, is not possible. A major function of parenting, therefore, is to teach children the dominant values, norms, customs, rituals, traditions and so on of a society. For example, parents civilise their children by teaching them language, toilet behaviour, manners, respect for others, empathy and the avoidance of behaviour and language that might offend other members of society. This is also beneficial to the individual child who grows up to be a well-integrated citizen and avoids bringing shame and dishonour on their family.

UNDERSTAND THE CONCEPT

Primary socialisation is the process by which parents and other significant family members teach children the culture of the society in which they live. The goal is to produce individuals who are civilised. That is, they have the social skills to interact and empathise successfully with others and to avoid behaviour that is regarded as anti-social. What is learned during primary socialisation is usually reinforced by agents of secondary socialisation, such as schools, the workplace and the mass media.

4. *Economic* – Children are dependent on their parents or adult carers for their health and wellbeing for a significant number of years. Murdock argued that parents therefore show their commitment to the care, protection and maintenance of their children by becoming productive workers. Parents use their wages to provide housing, food, clothing, and so on for their dependent children. This economic function also benefits society, which generally agrees that family members should take their place in the economy

as specialised workers, thereby contributing to the effective organisation of both the economy and society.

However, a number of criticisms of Murdock's theory can be identified.

> Murdock's definition of the nuclear family is very **ethnocentric** and reflective of a particular time and place. It is based on his own experience of the American family as it was in the 1940s.

UNDERSTAND THE CONCEPT

The concept of **ethnocentricity** is mainly used to criticise theories which not only reflect the dominant culture of a society but are seen to impose the values of that culture on other social groups or time periods. Talcott Parsons' model of the family (1965) reflects the American middle-class culture of the 1950s – it cannot be imposed on family life, say, in Britain in 2015.

> Murdock's theory is also very dated. It fails to take account of a number of distinct modern trends that have challenged the effectiveness of the family functions identified. For example:

  – *Reproduction* – the size of families has declined because women's attitudes to marriage, family and child-rearing have changed; for example, women may regard getting married and having children as optional in the 21st century, compared with previous generations who saw it as obligatory

  – *Sexual* – the decline of religious belief and the subsequent relaxation of social attitudes mean that sex before and outside of marriage is now the norm; moreover, families based on alternative sexualities such as homosexuality and lesbianism have become more socially acceptable.

  – *Socialisation* – there are concerns that the mass media, especially television, computer games and social network sites, as well as the peer group, have become more influential than parents and families as agents of socialisation, and that these alternative sources may be fuelling social problems such as crime, anti-social behaviour, teenage pregnancy and so on.

> Murdock's emphasis on two parents, and particularly on heterosexual marriage, is politically conservative: he is clearly saying that there are 'right' and 'wrong' ways to organise family life.

Families are no longer confined to traditional models centred on heterosexual marriage.

Functionalism and social change

Functionalist sociologists, such as Parsons, have attempted to trace the historical development of the family in order to explain why the nuclear family form has been so dominant. Parsons' theory of the family focused on examining how the social and economic change associated with the industrial revolution shaped family structures and relationships.

Parsons argued that pre-industrial societies were largely organised into relatively small farming communities. Land and other economic resources were commonly owned or rented by extended families. For example, it was not uncommon to live with and work alongside cousins on the land. Duty and obligation to the family and community were the key values of pre-industrial societies. Individuality was subordinated to the needs of the extended family group.

In return for this commitment, the extended family network generally performed the following functions for its members.

> The extended family functioned as a unit of production to supply the food, shelter and clothing required for the group to survive. They would trade with other family groups for those things they could not produce themselves.

> The family equipped its members with the basic skills and education they needed to take their place in the family division of labour. However, this socialisation rarely extended to literacy and numeracy.

> The family functioned to maintain the health of its members, in the absence of a system of universal health care. However, the high infant mortality rates and low life expectancy of the pre-industrial period suggest that this was probably a constant struggle.

> The family functioned to provide welfare for its members. For example, those family members who did make it into old age would be cared for, in exchange for services such as looking after very young children.

The effects of industrialisation

Parsons argued that the extended family was effective for the needs of pre-industrial society but was no longer practical in terms of what was required by the industrial revolution and the manufacturing economy that developed from it.

He argued that the extended family had to evolve into the smaller, more streamlined and mobile nuclear unit, in order to function in a way that effectively met the needs of an industrial-capitalist society. He argued then that the industrial revolution brought about five fundamental social changes to the family.

1. The new industrial economy demanded a more **geographically mobile** workforce. The responsibilities and duties that underpinned extended families (for example, a strong sense of obligation to remain near to extended kin and to defer to elder kin) did not suit these modern economic demands. Most people in the UK in the 18th century had lived in rural communities for generations. However, manufacturers were building their factories and mills in urban areas.

UNDERSTAND THE CONCEPT

Geographical mobility refers to the physical movement of people and families around the country, usually in search of work. If you go away to another city to do a university degree, you will experience geographical mobility.

Parsons argues that because of mechanised farming (which resulted in many of the rural poor losing their land) nuclear families broke away from their extended families and moved to the towns and cities to take advantage of the wage-labour opportunities in the new factories and textile mills brought about by the industrial revolution. Major **urbanisation** occurred between 1700 and 1830 as the proportion of the UK population living in cities and towns increased from 15 per cent to 34 per cent.

UNDERSTAND THE CONCEPT

Urbanisation refers to the movement of people who had previously lived in the countryside to the towns and cities, usually to find work in factories, mills, and so on.

2. Another social change brought about by industrialisation was the opportunity to improve oneself materially. This is known as social mobility. Parsons noted that in order to be effective, industrial societies needed to allocate people to an occupational role in the specialised division of labour that best suited their ability and talent. Parsons believed that the nuclear family was better suited to the more achievement-orientated society produced by the industrial revolution because this leaner type of family was **relatively isolated** from its kinship network. Members of nuclear families were consequently more independent as individuals and less prone to the sorts of pressures from extended kin and community that might have made them less adventurous in their social ambitions and choice of jobs.

UNDERSTAND THE CONCEPT

The concept of **relative isolation** suggests that family members no longer live in the same close-knit, rural communities in which they would see each other every day. Members of extended kinship networks are now more likely to live in nuclear units separated by geographical distance. They are isolated in the sense that they have less frequent physical contact with extended kin and therefore their behaviour is less likely to be influenced or shaped by other kin.

3. The 18th and 19th centuries also saw the emergence of specialised agencies that gradually took over many of the functions of the pre-industrial extended family. Parsons referred to this development as 'structural differentiation'. A key difference between rural extended families and urban nuclear families was that the latter had experienced a separation between home and workplace. They had become wage earners in the factory system and were no longer in a position to grow or rear their own food, build

their own homes, make their own clothing, and so on. Members of urban nuclear families therefore became dependent on outside agencies – businesses – which evolved to meet many of these needs. For example, processed canned food was mass-produced in factories and sold in stores that eventually developed into supermarket chains. In this sense, Parsons saw the nuclear family as largely losing its production function.

The state also eventually took over the functions of education, health, welfare and justice during the course of the 19th and 20th centuries although, as Chambers (2012) notes, many nuclear families continued to 'opt in' to provide care or financial support to extended kin.

4. Parsons suggests this process of structural differentiation meant that the nuclear family could focus on reproducing and rearing the next generation in more effective ways to meet the needs of modern society, particularly the need for social order and stability. Consequently, Parsons claimed that the nuclear family specialised in two essential functions that were beneficial both for society and for the adults and children that made up the nuclear family unit: (a) the primary socialisation of children and (b) the stabilisation of adult personalities.

Primary socialisation of children

Parsons believed that the family was the main centre of primary socialisation – the teaching and learning of the attitudes, values, behavioural norms and traditions that mainly occurs during childhood and prepares a child to take their place as an adult in a particular culture or society.

Parsons believed that personalities are 'made not born' – a child could only become a responsible and effective social adult if parents made sure that they were socialised into the shared norms and values (Parsons called this 'value consensus') of the society to which they belonged. He therefore saw nuclear families as 'personality factories', churning out young citizens committed to the rules, patterns of behaviour and belief systems that make positive involvement in social life and good citizenship possible. In this sense, Parsons saw the family as a crucial bridge connecting the individual child/adult to wider society. He also saw mothers, in particular, as playing the major role in this process of nurturing and socialisation in families.

What evidence would you use to challenge Parsons' idea that primary socialisation is successful in churning out young citizens committed to the rules of society?

Stabilisation of adult personality

Parsons argued that the second major specialised function of the family is to relieve the stresses of modern-day living for its adult members. Modern-day workplaces can be very hectic and competitive places.

Members of a nuclear family no longer have extended kin easily available for advice and guidance to help them cope with modern-day living. However, Parsons saw this as an opportunity for spouses and children in the nuclear family to positively reinforce their relationships.

Parsons claimed that the nuclear family could act as a 'warm bath' – he suggested that immersion in family life could relieve the pressures of work and contemporary society just as a warm bath soothes and relaxes the body. Steel and Kidd (2001) note that the family does this by providing "in the home a warm, loving, stable environment where the individual adults can be themselves and even 'let themselves go' in a childish and undignified way", for example, by playing with their children.

This emotional support and security, and the opportunity to engage in play with children, acts as a safety valve. It prevents stress from overwhelming adult family members and, as a result, it both stabilises the adult personality by de-stressing the individual and strengthens social stability in wider society.

Parsons saw marriage in particular as essential to the health, happiness and stability of adults in modern societies. Parsons therefore viewed the family as a positive and beneficial place for all its members – as 'home sweet home', as a 'haven in a heartless world' and a place in which people could be their natural selves.

What evidence might you use to challenge Parsons's idea that the family successfully stabilises the adult personality?

Parsons argued that this new nuclear unit provided the husband and wife with very clear and distinct social roles. He claimed that the male should be the 'instrumental leader' – this means that the father and husband is responsible for the economic welfare and living standards of the family group and the protection of other family members. He is the wage earner and consequently the head of the household.

Parsons claimed that the female is best suited to being the 'expressive leader' – this means that the mother and wife should be primarily responsible for the socialisation of children and, in particular, the emotional care and support of family members.

Parsons argued that this sexual division of labour is 'natural' because it is based on biological differences.

For example, many people believe that women have 'maternal instincts' which make them best suited to be the emotional caretakers of both children and their spouses. However, Parsons did see the relationship between husbands and wives as complementary, with each equally contributing to the maintenance of the family but in a qualitatively different way.

FOCUS ON RESEARCH: INDUSTRIALISATION AND THE NUCLEAR FAMILY

Anderson's (1971) study of Preston in 1851 found that extended family units persisted long after the onset of industrialisation.

Historians have suggested that Parsons' nostalgic view of a fit between the family and industrialisation is a simplistic and selective interpretation of the available evidence.

Peter Laslett (1972) looked at English parish church records from the pre-industrial period and found that the isolated nuclear family predates the industrial revolution by many years. In fact, Laslett found that only 10 per cent of households in the pre-industrial era in England contained extended kin. In other words, most pre-industrial families were not extended as Parsons claimed.

Laslett notes that nuclear families in this pre-industrial period were probably due to late marriage, early death due to the constant presence of disease such as the plague, and the practice of sending children away to become servants or apprentices. Laslett speculates that one of the reasons industrialisation took off so quickly in Britain was because nuclear families already existed. People with small families could move quickly to those parts of the country in which there was a demand for factory and mill workers.

However, Laslett's data has been criticised by functionalists as unreliable because the parish records he used are one-dimensional. They tell us how many people lived in a particular household but they do not give sociologists any real insight into the quality of family life, that is, how people actually experienced the family or the meaning they attached to family life. For example, people may have lived in nuclear units but may have felt a strong sense of duty or obligation to extended kin, who they may have worked alongside every day just as Parsons describes.

Michael Anderson's study (1971) of the industrial town of Preston in 1851, using census statistics, also contradicts Parsons' view that, after industrialisation, the extended unit was replaced by the nuclear family. Anderson found that a large number of households in Preston were shared by extended kin. These probably functioned as a mutual economic support system in a town in which unemployment and poverty were common. In other words, people who came to Preston probably sought out relatives in order to pool their low wages to help share the cost of the high rents and to help out with extended kin who were sick, disabled or elderly.

Questions

1. Identify two major criticisms of Parsons using historical evidence gathered by Laslett and Anderson.

2. Identify three reasons why sociologists use secondary sources such as parish church records or census data.

3. Analyse the reasons why sociologists who are interested in qualitative data might be critical of Laslett's methodology.

4. Outline and evaluate the functionalist theory of how the family has evolved historically.

Why can Parsons' view of the relationship between men and women in families be criticised as patriarchal?

In conclusion, then, Parsons argued that extended families, with their emphasis on tradition, hindered progress and modernity. In contrast, he argued that the nuclear family unit was superior because it was more adaptable to the needs of modern industrial societies. Only the modern nuclear family could effectively provide the dutiful citizens happy to share culture and a stable social life and the achievement-orientated and geographically mobile workforce required if modern industrial economies were to be successful.

Evaluating the functionalist theory of the family

Functionalism has attracted so much criticism that some sociologists view it as a discredited theory. However, it does have strengths. It was the first theory to point out that in *almost* all societies throughout the world we can see the two-generation nuclear family with adults of both sexes and dependent children. Furthermore, despite the growing diversity in family types, many people still desire to live in the kind of nuclear households outlined by Parsons. Finally, many social policy initiatives aimed at regulating family life, especially those emanating from Conservative politicians and governments, have their origin in functionalist theories of the family.

However, the functionalist theory of the family has been criticised for a number of reasons.

Fletcher (1988), a British functionalist, argues that Parsons was wrong to suggest that the family had lost its functions. He argues that the family performs three unique and crucial functions that no other social institution can carry out. These include: satisfying the long-term sexual and emotional needs of parents; raising children in a stable environment; and the provision of a home to which all family members return after work, school and so on.

Moreover, Fletcher argues that the family continues to perform the functions that Parsons believes it lost to the state and that the role of social policy is to make parenting and family life more effective by providing social, economic and educational supports, such as postnatal care, free health care from the cradle to the grave, and compulsory education.

Fletcher accepts that the nuclear family has largely lost its economic function of production, although many family-based companies continue to exist successfully.

However, he argues that the family functions as a major unit of economic **consumption** because the modern home-centred nuclear family spends a great proportion of its income on family- or home-orientated consumer goods, such as the family car, garden equipment, the latest electrical appliances for the kitchen and leisure use, and toys.

UNDERSTAND THE CONCEPT

Consumption refers to the spending of money on goods and services. A successful economy needs to market its goods and services competitively in ways that attract consumers to spend their money on them.

The consumption function of the family therefore motivates its members, as workers, to earn as much as possible. It also motivates capitalist entrepreneurs and businesses to produce and market what families want. In other words, the nuclear family is essential to a successful economy.

Parsons failed to consider the impact of **global migration** on family life in the USA and other industrial nations. This migration has resulted in a diversity of family types existing alongside each other. The nuclear family is therefore no longer as dominant as it once was.

UNDERSTAND THE CONCEPT

Global migration refers to the movement of people around the world. The UK has experienced a good deal of immigration from India, Pakistan, the Caribbean, Africa and Eastern Europe over the past sixty years. Many British people have also migrated, particularly to Western Europe and America.

Interpretivist sociologists argue that Parsons' theory of the family is inadequate because it paints a picture of children as 'empty vessels' being pumped full of culture by their parents. They claim Parsons fails to realise that this is an 'over-socialised' view of children because, in reality, socialisation is a two-way interaction. It can also involve children socialising and modifying their parents' behaviour, for example, by taking part in family decision-making with regard to consumer spending and influencing their parents' taste in fashion, music, television viewing, use of social media sites, and so on.

Parsons presents a very positive picture of relationships within the nuclear family, but evidence suggests that living in such a unit can sometimes be very dysfunctional or harmful to its members. As Cheal (2002) notes, functional relationships can easily slip into damaging relationships, and love can often turn into hate in moments of intense emotion. He states that "we have to face the paradox that families are contexts of love and nurturance, but they are also contexts of violence and murder" (Cheal 2002, p. 8). In other words, there is a dark side to family life that functionalism rarely acknowledges.

> An examination of the official criminal statistics paints a very negative picture of family life. Most recorded murders, assaults and child abuse, sexual or otherwise, take place within the family unit. There are three domestic killings of women each fortnight on average in the UK, accounting for about 40 per cent of all female murders.

> On average, nearly four children a week die at the hands of their parents and in the UK, usually the father or the step-father. The 'Baby P' affair that hit the headlines in 2007–08 and focused on the killing of 17-month-old Peter Connelly by his mother's boyfriend was one of 200 child murders in that same period.

> Child abuse is a major social problem in the UK. Radford et al. (2011), in a study carried out on behalf of the NSPCC, found that 1 in 20 children had been sexually abused in the UK, while 1 in 14 children in the UK had been physically abused.

> The official crime statistics suggest that violence by men against their female partners accounts for about a third of all reported violence. Nearly one in four women has been assaulted by a partner at some time in her life – one in eight repeatedly so. Stanko's (2000) survey found that one incident of domestic violence is reported by women to the police every minute in the UK.

Functionalist community and kinship studies

Young and Willmott in their study 'Family and Kinship in East London' (1957) disagree with the Parsonian view that industrialisation brought about the death of the extended family. Young and Wilmott argue that the movement towards the nuclear unit was not as quick as Parsons implies. They suggest that it was more gradual in nature and that urban communities dominated by extended families existed well into the 20th century. Their empirical research conducted in the 1950s in the Bethnal Green area of the East End of London showed that extended families still existed in very large numbers in this period.

An extended family unit in the 1950s

Young and Willmott argue that the extended family unit only went into decline in the 1960s, when working-class communities were rehoused in new towns and on council estates after extensive slum clearance. Moreover, the welfare state and full employment of the 1950s undermined the need for a mutual economic support system. Bright, young working-class men also made the most of the opportunities and qualifications made available by the 1944 Education Act and were less likely to follow their fathers into manual work. Their social mobility into white-collar and professional jobs often meant geographical mobility. In moving away from traditional working-class areas and their parents to progress their careers, they consequently experienced less frequent contact with kin.

In 1975, Young and Wilmott published a major piece of research on the family, 'The Symmetrical Family', based on over 2,500 interviews with people across London. This research generally confirmed that the nuclear family, which they called the **symmetrical** family, had become the universal norm in Britain in the late 20th century.

UNDERSTAND THE CONCEPT

Symmetrical means balanced or in equilibrium, while **asymmetrical** means uneven or unequal. Young and Wilmott used the concept of symmetry to mean that the roles of men and women in the family were each as important as the other. In contrast, patriarchal families are asymmetrical because the male role dominates the female role.

Young and Wilmott identified a number of features which characterise their symmetrical family:

> it is composed of two parents plus their children; in other words, it is nuclear in structure

> it is 'privatised' – the family has infrequent contact with extended kin and neighbours

> women are no longer full-time housewives, they are often in part-time or full-time paid work

> it is often dual-career – both spouses' income is essential to their standard of living

> it is egalitarian – men and women have more economic equality and this has led to the adoption of 'joint conjugal roles': domestic tasks, childcare, decision-making and leisure time are more likely to be shared rather than segregated into male and female activities

> it is home-centred – the family spends much of its leisure time in the home; for example, the television became the focal point of family interaction from the 1960s on, while DIY became a central leisure activity for many men

> it is child-centred – the proportion of family income spent on children's happiness is high.

Young and Wilmott's analysis therefore generally agrees with that of Parsons. The family has experienced a gradual 'march of progress' from a pre-industrial patriarchal unit, first to an extended unit in which men and women occupied very different roles and performed very different functions, and then to a nuclear unit based on equality and independence from kin. Young and Wilmott claim that the symmetrical family is now dominant across the UK and is found in both middle-class and working-class communities.

However, the study has not escaped criticism. Feminists have questioned the notions of symmetry and equality between spouses. Young and Wilmott have also been accused of over-focusing on harmonious families and ignoring the very real problems of domestic violence and child abuse, which are more common than their research acknowledges.

A study by Harris, Charles and Davies (2006) has explored the social change of the last 40 years by examining changes in family life in Swansea using a 1000-household survey of individuals randomly selected from the electoral register and interviewed in 2002. Harris et al. take a postmodernist position. They consider that the social and economic changes that have occurred in the later parts of the 20th century have produced a type of nuclear family that differs in some important respects from the isolated and privatised models proposed by Parsons and by Young and Wilmott.

They note that in the 21st century people are more individualistic than they were 40 years ago. As a result, they suggest that there has been a decline in both family and community obligations. People no longer cooperate with one another because family or community tells them it is the right thing to do. People now cooperate with each other because something – an advantage or a personal service – can be gained from dealing with others. Moreover, this decline in community spirit means that modern society is becoming de-institutionalised – this means that the traditional ways in which people used to do things are being abandoned as 'the present is privileged over the past'. This rise in individualisation and de-institutionalisation has implications for the dominance of the nuclear family. For example, people no longer feel obliged to enter the institution of marriage because there are now other choices – singlehood and cohabitation. They also point to the rise in the number of people who will never found their own nuclear families because they have opted never to have children. Another trend is that grown-up children in the early stages of adulthood may elect to cut or downgrade ties with their parents in their pursuit of individualistic goals.

Harris et al. argue that their research suggests that the idea that the nuclear family is 'isolated' or 'privatised' may not be totally valid. Their data showed that although there has been a decline in sibling contact in adulthood (between adult brothers and sisters), this is only true of parents and grown-up children when those children are single or are in childless relationships. Once children are born to grown-up children, these new parents renegotiate their relationships with their own parents, who are now grandparents, and the extended mutually-supportive family re-emerges. For example, it may be mutually beneficial for grandparents to babysit children in the holidays, thus strengthening the qualitative nature of the relationship between them and their grandchildren, and releasing the parents to go out to work. These supports may be reciprocated as grandparents proceed into old age.

Harris et al. therefore seem to support the idea put forward by Litwak (1965) that sociologists need to view the nuclear family not as an isolated 'group' in its own right, but as part of a collection of households and nuclear family groups that still have the potential to become extended families, albeit in a modified form compared with those described by Young and Wilmott.

BUILD CONNECTIONS

According to the founding father of functionalism, Emile Durkheim, increasing individualisation and its subsequent negative effect on community is the major cause of crime in modern industrial societies. He notes that pre-industrial societies are composed of powerful communities that do not tolerate individuality and punish crime and deviance severely. Consequently, crime is low in such societies. However, he also notes that modern industrial societies are more tolerant of difference and individuality but that this has had the effect of weakening community and bringing about 'anomie' or moral confusion. When people are confused about morality, they are often unsure what the rules are or they are not afraid to break them, therefore increasing the potential for crime.

THE MARXIST THEORY OF THE FAMILY

Marxists are very critical of the functionalist view that the modern nuclear family has evolved in order to benefit wider society. Instead, Marxists generally see the nuclear family as serving the interests of the ruling class because it mainly promotes capitalist or ruling-class ideology aimed at discouraging working-class criticism of capitalism or the inequalities that this economic system tends to generate.

Friedrich Engels

Engels claimed that the monogamous nuclear family only became popular after the industrial revolution because the ruling class encouraged it in order to protect the property and wealth they had accumulated. Engels claimed that monogamous marriage, in particular, was useful to the ruling class because it conferred legitimacy on children and therefore members of the bourgeoisie were able to ensure that their fortunes were inherited by their direct descendants. However, Engels' speculation is not based on any convincing historical evidence.

Eli Zaretsky

Eli Zaretsky's (1976) ideas on the family challenge those of the functionalist Talcott Parsons who insisted that the nuclear family was positive for society and its members because it promoted social order and stability. In contrast, Zaretsky claims that the modern nuclear family mainly benefits capitalism and the ruling class at the expense of other members of society. This can be illustrated in three ways.

1. Zaretsky sees the family as a crucial agent in the socialisation of children, and therefore future workers

and citizens, into capitalist ideology, that is, values and norms that advocate the view that capitalist societies are organised in a fair and just way. He argues that a working-class child's experience of socialisation usually involves learning obedience, conformity, showing respect for those in authority, and so on. Consequently, such children grow up to become conformist citizens and passive workers who accept inequality and exploitation as part of the 'natural' state of things. Marxists therefore suggest that the family is partially responsible for the suppression of ideas that might challenge the current organisation of the capitalist system.

Is it entirely true that children grow up to become conformist citizens and passive workers? Which types of social behaviour might challenge this idea?

2. Zaretsky is very critical of Parsons' 'stabilisation of adult personality' argument. In contrast, he argues that the role of the family is more sinister because its real function is to help workers manage their resentment of the capitalist workplace that generally oppresses and exploits them. Zaretsky notes that the nuclear family dampens such feelings because the worker who has a family is unlikely to engage in actions that threaten their income and therefore their family's standard of living. There is evidence that companies such as Ford would only employ married men with families in the 1980s because these types of men were more reluctant than single men to take strike action since they felt that their main responsibility was to their wives and children rather than to their fellow workers.

3. Zaretsky argues that the nuclear family is an essential component of capitalism because it is the major unit of consumption of manufactured goods and services, and therefore it is essential to the success and especially the profitability of the capitalist system. Moreover, the pursuit of consumerism and materialism may have the added bonus for the ruling class of distracting workers from the organisation of capitalism. For example, Marxists argue that parents are encouraged to teach their children that the main route to happiness and status lies in consumerism and the acquisition of material possessions. Consequently, the inequalities in wealth and income produced by capitalism often go unchallenged by a generation fixated on the acquisition of the latest designer labels and gadgets.

Evaluating Marxist theories of the family

In terms of strengths, Marxist sociologists have questioned the notion that the nuclear family is always good for society, and have drawn sociological attention to the possibility that powerful interests may be shaping family life in the UK. For example, there is little doubt that the nuclear family is deliberately targeted by advertisers as a unit of consumption and that the family is essential to the health of the capitalist economy.

However, Marxists such as Zaretsky rarely consider that some working-class parents may resist ruling-class ideology by teaching their children values and norms that are the product of working-class culture, and thus empower their children with knowledge of capitalist inequality and exploitation. Another possibility is that working-class parents may be well aware of the pitfalls of capitalism, such as inequalities in wealth, but feel that the standard of living provided by capitalism is so comfortable that they are willing to dismiss inequality as a lesser evil.

Marxism is a structural theory and, like functionalism, it fails to consider how individual men, women and children experience and interpret their family set-up and its relationship to other social institutions. Consequently, Marxism may be guilty of neglecting the very real emotional and social satisfaction that people get from being members of a family. The Marxist tendency to write off such satisfaction as the product of capitalist ideology is both simplistic and too patronising.

FEMINIST THEORIES OF THE FAMILY

Feminists are highly critical of the functionalist theory of the nuclear family because they believe that the nuclear family has harmful effects for women and that it is generally responsible for patriarchy (see Topic 1, Chapter 4) and the inequalities that patriarchy generates between men and women.

However, it is important to understand that there are four broad types of feminism, which emphasise different aspects of patriarchy and which, consequently, have different views on what social change is required with regard to families in order to improve women's position in society. These categories of feminism – Marxist, radical, liberal and difference – are quite crude because, as Bradley (2013) points out, not all writers or studies fit neatly into one of the four types.

However, Bradley suggests they are worth persevering with because each identified approach does display a distinct 'take' on gender.

Marxist feminism

Marxist feminists, like all feminists, see patriarchal oppression by men as central to women's experience, but they do not see this oppression as the main source of social inequality. Like Marxism in general, they see social-class relationships as the major cause of inequality. From a Marxist–feminist perspective, all labour – paid and domestic – is exploited by the ruling class. Gender oppression is therefore part and parcel of the general oppression of the working class.

Moreover, Marxist feminists view patriarchy as a deliberate ideology constructed by the ruling class and designed to reproduce and justify gender exploitation because this benefits the organisation of capitalist society. However, and this is where they part company with conventional Marxists, all men – whether they are working-class or bourgeois – also benefit from the influence of this patriarchal ideology.

Most Marxist–feminist analysis has focused on the contribution of domestic labour – such as housework and childcare – to capitalist economies. They point out that such work is unpaid but has great value. For example, Margaret Benston (1972) suggests that the nuclear family, and especially women's nurturing role within it, is important to capitalism because it produces and rears the future workforce at little cost to the capitalist state.

Marxist feminists link class and gender exploitation.

Is it true that there is little cost to the state in terms of women and families rearing children?

Women's unpaid domestic labour – housework as well as sexual services – also ensures that the male workforce is fit and healthy for work and consequently productive. In other words, the housework role (which involves feeding the male worker, shopping to meet his needs, bringing up his children and making sure he has a clean and relaxing environment to return home to every day) contributes to the effectiveness of male labour and the value of the work he produces for his employer.

For example, in 2014, it was estimated by the Office of National Statistics (ONS) that laundry and ironing in the home was worth an estimated £97.2 billion in 2012, while unpaid childcare was estimated to be worth £343 billion in 2010 – three times higher than the contribution to the economy made by the financial sector. Marxist feminists argue that women's work is being exploited by the ruling class because the wage received by the male worker only includes payment for his labour – it does not include payment for the domestic labour of his female partner, which makes an essential contribution both to his value as a worker and to the capitalist economy.

Marxist feminists such as Ansley (1972) also suggest that capitalism has stripped male workers of dignity, power and control at work. Surveys of factory workers suggest that many are bored by the tedious nature of their work. Many are **alienated**, meaning that they cannot identify with or bring themselves to care about the product they are producing. They feel powerless and, consequently, feel that their masculinity is being challenged.

UNDERSTAND THE CONCEPT

Alienation is a concept which Marxists in particular suggest is now becoming a common characteristic of how workers feel about their jobs. It refers to the lack of satisfaction, identification and control that workers experience on a daily basis, and the fact that they work merely for a wage rather than for job satisfaction.

However, Ansley argues that this male frustration and alienation is often absorbed by the family and particularly by the female partner. She suggests that the crisis of masculinity and powerlessness that men experience today leads to problems such as domestic violence and child abuse as men attempt to assert power, control and

authority in the home. Wives therefore act as safety valves for capitalism because these men are not directing their anger at the real cause of their problems – the nature and organisation of capitalism itself.

Evaluating Marxist feminism

On the positive side, Marxist feminists have shown how gender roles within the family may be created and perpetuated by the requirements of capitalist society, rather than being 'natural' as functionalists argue.

However, like Marxists, they see the family as performing predetermined functions for the good of capitalist society rather than for society as a whole. They therefore insist that the nuclear family only benefits the ruling class and men. This view can be criticised because it ignores the day-to-day experiences and interpretations of women who choose to live in such families because they enjoy and benefit from the experience from being a mother, wife, partner and so on.

Moreover, the Marxist–feminist model of the family is still largely based upon the rather dated model of the nuclear family as working husband and economically dependent full-time housewife. Many families no longer fit into this category because modern families are extremely diverse in their organisation and structure. Many nuclear families are dual-career and consequently women may now have the economic and cultural power to resist any attempt to allocate them to exclusively domestic and maternal roles.

Radical feminism

Radical feminists argue that it is not capitalism that exploits women but men. They suggest that patriarchy – the system of male domination in society – existed well before capitalism appeared in the 18th century. Men have always controlled women and this will not change by establishing socialist or communist systems. Moreover, radical feminists argue that patriarchy benefits all men. Radical feminism is thus a 'woman-centred' approach – it sees gender as the primary source of social inequality.

Radical feminists such as Millett (1970) and Firestone (1971) take this analysis one step further when they argue that men and women constitute separate and often conflicting 'sex classes' and it is the interaction between these classes, especially in marriage and the family, that is responsible for the most important and long-standing form of inequality that exists in human societies – gender inequality.

Radical feminists reject the functionalist idea that "the family is a cooperative unit founded on common interests and mutual support between husband and wife" (Chambers, p. 29). Instead they have focused on how the nuclear family functions mainly to benefit heterosexual men. It does this by teaching children patriarchal ideology and especially the idea that the sexual division of labour is 'natural' and unchangeable via gender role socialisation.

Furthermore, radical feminist thinkers have drawn attention to a range of ways in which the patriarchal nuclear family has oppressed or exploited women. For example, Firestone claims that "love … is the pivot of women's oppression today", while Delphy and Leonard (1992) claim that husbands exploit their wives despite genuinely loving them. Delphy and Leonard argue that a woman's role within a marriage is to 'flatter' her husband and to provide emotional support for him. In contrast, men rarely perform this function for women. These claims have led to critics accusing radical feminism of 'man-hating'.

Do you agree that husbands exploit their wives or that they expect their wives to flatter them or provide them with emotional support?

Other radical feminists have examined why the nuclear family is often the site of violence against women and children. Redfern and Aune (2013) conclude that male violence against women takes many different forms, including female genital mutilation, acid throwing, forced marriage, marital rape, honour violence, domestic violence, and psychological bullying. Radical feminists working in these fields point out that such violence is often the product of a patriarchal set of ideas that see women as second-class citizens and are deeply rooted in a society's history and culture. The family is the means by which that patriarchal history and culture is reinforced and transmitted to the next generation.

Many radical feminists are pessimistic about the possibility that patriarchal gender relations can be transformed while current family set-ups continue to exist. They believe that the patriarchal and monogamous nuclear family must be abolished, or at the very least radically altered, and that alternative ways of living, such as female-only communes, must be encouraged. Firestone, for example, argues that women should use new **reproductive technologies**, such as in vitro fertilisation (IVF), to exclude men from families because she believes women's dependence on men derives from their childbearing and child-rearing functions. Greer (2000) also argues in favour of all-female households or **matrifocal families**.

UNDERSTAND THE CONCEPT

Reproductive technology refers to scientific developments in the last 30 years to help men and women, who may for example be experiencing fertility problems, to have children. Firestone is keen on IVF that involves the egg of the female being fertilised by sperm outside the body in a laboratory. This is attractive to some radical feminists because it involves no direct physical contact with a man.

In **matrifocal families**, women are the head of the family. Fathers may or may not be present, but if they are they occupy a secondary role. Matrifocal families are thought to be common in African Caribbean communities in the UK.

Evaluating radical feminism

Radical feminist theories of the family have dated fairly significantly, because they fail to account for recent economic and social changes, such as the educational success of young females, women's use of divorce, and many women's rejection of domestic labour as their exclusive responsibility.

Radical feminist sociologists also portray women as passively accepting their lot. However, Somerville and Hakim both argue that they probably exaggerate the exploitation of women in the family and that most women still value relationships with men. The bulk of male–female relationships are based on mutual love and respect rather than exploitation, domination and subordination.

Radical feminists also ignore those accounts of family life in which females experience motherhood as fulfilling and rewarding, or they dismiss this experience as less rewarding than having a career. Hakim argues that this is condescending. Many women choose to be mothers and gain great satisfaction from this role. As an option, it should be judged no differently from any other.

Finally, like other structural theories, radical feminism is guilty of overemphasising the nuclear family and neglecting the rich diversity of other family types in modern society.

Liberal feminism

Liberal feminism has also been called 'equal rights' feminism because, as Bradley notes, it differs from both Marxist feminism and radical feminism in its conception of the family. Liberal feminists do not see gender inequality in the family as the product of a system or structure, as Marxists do, nor do they see it as a consequence of one dominant sex class deliberately oppressing another, as in the radical feminist perspective.

FOCUS ON SKILLS: FEMINIST EXPLANATIONS OF DOMESTIC VIOLENCE

Feminist scholars link domestic violence to the reassertion of a threatened masculine identity.

Feminists argue that gender role socialisation carried out by parents in the family, the adolescent peer group, the tabloid media and lads' magazines socialise young males in the UK into 'masculine' values that revolve around risk-taking behaviour, toughness, aggression, proving oneself, and so on. As a result of this socialisation, some boys and men may see violence as a legitimate problem-solving device. Socialisation into femininity, on the other hand, involves learning to be passive and subordinate, which may be a reason why some women tolerate domestic violence.

Fiona Brookman (2000) carried out in-depth interviews with violent men who had attacked and killed their female partners. She also examined documentary sources such as police murder files and official statistics. She concluded that in British culture, the dominant version of masculinity places high value on control over others, particularly women. When men feel they are losing control over what they perceive as their female property, they may resort to violence as a means of re-asserting their masculine identity. Brookman found that in 80 per cent of the cases she investigated in

which a wife or girlfriend had been murdered by their male partner, the female was in the process of leaving or was suspected of being sexually unfaithful. In most cases, the male felt compelled to act violently because his masculinity had been compromised.

Men may be undergoing a 'crisis of masculinity'. Working women and male unemployment have challenged men's status as head of the household and breadwinner. Men's traditional source of identity – work – is no longer guaranteed. Some women may be demanding more authority in the home and insisting that unemployed men play a greater domestic role – some men may see this domestic responsibility as threatening their masculinity. Some men therefore may use violence to reassert their masculinity and status within the family unit.

Questions

1. **Identify** the three agencies of socialisation that are seen as responsible for indoctrinating boys and young men into masculine ideology.

2. **Analyse** how the masculine values learned during socialisation might lead to domestic violence.

3. **Explain** how the concept of a 'crisis in masculinity' might assist sociological understanding of the causes of domestic violence.

4. **Evaluate** whether Brookman's research can be seen as providing a reliable and valid picture of the relationship between murder and masculinity.

5. **Outline** and **evaluate**, using the information in this article and from elsewhere, the strengths and weaknesses of feminist theories of domestic violence.

From the liberal feminist perspective of sociologists such as Oakley (1981), gender inequality in the family is simply a product of discrimination by individuals and those who run institutions (rather than being embedded in the social structure of society) and this discrimination is largely based on ignorance, prejudice and a mistaken view of the biogenetic differences between males and females. Bryson (1999) notes that this viewpoint has resulted in liberal feminism being labelled 'common-sense' feminism, while Bradley suggests that, for some, this perspective was the 'acceptable

face of feminism' because Marxist feminism and radical feminism were judged as going too far in their critiques of capitalism and men respectively.

Oakley has attempted to pin down the source of gender discrimination and the patriarchal inequality that has traditionally characterised male–female relationships in the family and most other social institutions. One aspect of family life that has received a lot of attention is the process of gender role socialisation. This important process involves boys and girls learning about and internalising 'differences' in gendered behaviour. Oakley has suggested that this may be a major source of patriarchal discrimination because the ideological consequence of girls being 'persuaded' to accept that their main responsibilities are going to be family-bound prevents them from competing on an equal playing field with men, both for well-paid jobs and for positions of power.

However, liberal feminists do acknowledge that the last 50 years have seen massive social change in both society and the family, which has challenged traditional definitions of masculinity and femininity, and therefore the patriarchal domination of men. For example, Somerville (2000) points out that women now have much more choice about whether to marry, whether they take paid work when married and whether they stay married. She also notes that there is now greater equality within marriage and greater sharing of the responsibility for paid and unpaid work and childcare.

This evolutionary change has come about for a variety of economic, social and legal reasons, which include those listed here.

> *Economic and social changes* – Helen Wilkinson notes that the economy has undergone tremendous change in the last 50 years because of recession and globalisation. The UK economy has evolved from being dominated by heavy industry and manufacturing in factories (types of work dominated by men) to being a service economy in which financial, retail and public sector jobs dominate. The rise of the **service sector** was accompanied by the feminisation of the British workforce, as many of the new service jobs available were taken up by women. This has led to women acquiring economic power; they are now more likely to earn their own wage, rather than being dependent on their husband's or partner's wage.

UNDERSTAND THE CONCEPT

Traditionally, economists have divided the economy up into three sectors. The primary sector is concerned with the obtaining of natural resources – mining coal or iron, drilling for oil, fishing, and so on. The secondary sector is made up of manufacturing industry, such as factories, textile and steel mills, refineries, breweries, and so on. The tertiary or **service sector** of the economy generally deals with the transfer and creation of information and services rather than goods. It includes jobs in the financial sector, retail, government services and personal services.

Moreover, Wilkinson argues that these economic changes have led to a dramatic cultural change in women's attitudes, which she calls a **'genderquake'**. She notes that women today have a radically different attitude towards family responsibilities, education and careers compared with their grandmothers. They are no longer content to see their lives as defined simply by marriage, family and children. They are now more likely to aspire to university, careers and economic independence.

UNDERSTAND THE CONCEPT

It is important to understand why Wilkinson called such change a **'genderquake'**. This was because, in her view, this change had a seismic (huge earthquake-like) effect on women's attitudes and therefore on the relationship between men and women.

> *Political, legal and social policy changes* – Oakley notes that changes in the economy and social attitudes have led to political and legal changes that have also challenged patriarchal practices in both the family and the workplace, thus improving opportunities for women. For example, the Equality Act 2010 reinforced the view that discrimination against women in all walks of life is illegal. This Act is policed by the Equality and Human Rights Commission. Such changes have strengthened women's position in the family because they now contribute a wage and can demand in return more say in family decision-making and a fairer distribution of domestic and childcare tasks.

In addition, women have benefited from a wide range of other social policies. They now have much improved maternity rights and pensions compared with the past. There is also some evidence that women have benefited more from changes in the divorce laws than men in that two-thirds of divorces today are initiated by women.

Moreover, women today have improved **reproductive rights** compared with earlier generations because of the availability of the contraceptive pill on the NHS.

Reproductive rights are the rights that women have over their bodies. Until 1962, women did not really have reproductive rights. Access to the contraceptive pill on the NHS transformed this situation. The pill allows women to control whether they want to get pregnant, how many children they want to have and when they want to have them. Control over reproductive rights was also reinforced by the 1967 Abortion Act which introduced free abortions on the NHS.

However, these changes do not mean that liberal feminists are fully happy about the degree of social change in women's favour or that they believe that patriarchy is in terminal decline. They acknowledge there is still a long way to go in terms of women's position in the family. Equality in terms of domestic roles is still a long way off and domestic violence is still a problem. However, liberal feminists do believe that gentle persuasion and consciousness-raising will eventually convince men (and other women) that the elimination of patriarchal discrimination, and the consequent equal opportunities that will result for both men and women in all social institutions, will work for the benefit of all society.

Evaluating liberal feminism

Although liberal feminist theory is useful in explaining the improved position of women in the family, workplace, and education, there have been a number of criticisms advanced against it.

It is a rather cosy view, reflecting the experiences of white, middle-class professional groups of women. The experiences of women in poorer sections of society may not be so positive, especially in terms of their roles within the family unit or of economic equality with male partners.

Corsaro (2011) is critical of gender role socialisation arguments. He argues that there is little research on parent–child interaction in the home, and there is no real and convincing evidence and analysis of how toys are used or symbolically valued. He claims that much of the sociological research on gendered play that does exist assumes rather than proves that gendered play – such as when a little girl plays with dolls – leads to a gendered experience of childhood or to gendered outcomes, in which girls expect to become mothers and boys to become breadwinners. He argues that no sociological research has definitively established such a link.

Difference feminism

Difference feminists are critical of the three previous feminist perspectives because they tend to assume that all women are members of a single unified group who share common interests and are all equally exploited. Difference feminism emphasises that women are not one single, united group but rather have a variety of experiences of patriarchy and often have very different goals and interests. Some examples are given below.

> Black difference feminists stress the importance of racial/ethnic differences between women. For example, some ethnic-minority women may have less power and status in families, compared with women from other minorities or the ethnic majority. As a result, patriarchal inequalities may be less important than those brought about by racial discrimination and prejudice.

> Some ethnic-minority women who live in societies that practice equal opportunities and in which institutional forms of patriarchy have been challenged may find that they are unable to make the most of such opportunities because patriarchal control of family life by men is a 'natural' outcome of the religious or cultural belief system that dominates their everyday life.

> Other difference feminists have emphasised differences in class, age or nationality. For example, middle-class women may have economic, cultural and social capital (see Topic 1, Chapter 2) which enables them to challenge patriarchal structures and, consequently, be less likely to be exploited by men than working-class women who lack these advantages.

> Difference feminism also recognises that there is increasing family diversity today and women may not be equally exploited in all family types. For example, many women are lone parents and therefore cannot be exploited by a cohabiting man.

> Calhoun (2003) points out women in lesbian families cannot be exploited by men.

Difference feminists therefore suggest that not all women are equally exploited in the family. Some are more exploited than others.

CONCLUSIONS

The functionalist theory of the family has proved extremely influential but Marxist and feminist sociologists have generally taken issue with its view that the nuclear family is good – or functional – not only for society but also for its members. These sociologists have also discovered that while the majority of society probably experiences a positive, loving and supportive family environment, a significant minority of women and children experience the family as a dangerous and harmful place in which violence, abuse and neglect is commonplace. The consequence of such experiences may be death, great emotional trauma, psychological damage, the thousands of children on 'at risk' registers or in care, and homelessness as young people attempt to escape the everyday cruelty they experience at the hands of a family member.

CHECK YOUR UNDERSTANDING

1. Identify four functions that Parsons claimed were carried out by the pre-industrial extended family.

2. Define what Parsons means by 'structural differentiation'.

3. Define what Young and Wilmott mean by the 'symmetrical family'.

4. Outline and explain what functionalists such as Parsons mean when they describe the family as 'functional'.

5. Define what is meant by the 'dark side of the family'.

6. Analyse and explain why the symmetrical family became the dominant family form of the 20th century, according to Young and Wilmott.

7. Outline and evaluate the view that the nuclear family functions for the good of society and family members.

8. Identify three reasons why Marxists believe that the nuclear family functions to benefit capitalism.

9. Identify the four types of feminism mentioned in this chapter and discuss the similarities and differences between them.

10. Analyse and explain the types of power acquired by women since the 1960s and their impact on patriarchy.

11. Outline and evaluate why feminists believe that the family oppresses and exploits women.

TAKE IT FURTHER

Interview your grandparents and/or great-grandparents about their experience of family life between the 1950s and 1960s. Think about how their recollections might support or challenge the sociological studies mentioned in this chapter. Compare your own experience of family life to theirs.

Summarise the main issues and concerns of feminist organisations with regard to the family by consulting websites such as www.thefword.org.uk and www.fawcettsociety.org.uk.

4.2 THE FAMILY AND SOCIAL POLICY

LEARNING OBJECTIVES

> Demonstrate knowledge and understanding of family social policy and how it has impacted on the relationship between the family and social structure (AO1).

> Apply New Right ideas to the relationship between social policy and the family (AO2).

> Analyse the effects of social policy on family life in the UK (AO3).

> Evaluate theoretical explanations of the relationship between the family and government social policies (AO3).

INTRODUCING THE DEBATE

A social or state policy is any attempt by the government to deal with a social problem, such as poverty, unemployment and homelessness, or to ensure that social needs such as jobs, benefits and a happy family life are achieved. A social policy therefore is usually aimed at changing, improving or regulating social conditions. For example, the British state insists that children should be protected from harm and consequently it has social policies in place to ensure this. Such policies are often enforced by Acts of Parliament, which means that they are established in law.

The family is a fertile area for social policies because it is such an important social institution. There are therefore social policies that attempt to regulate many areas of family life. There are health policies that ensure family members are supported by a complex system of health care from the cradle to the grave. There are social policies that aim to protect children from poor or abusive parenting, or to ensure that every family in the UK has some sort of roof over its head. There are economic social policies that help families with the high cost of childcare and provide financial support through periods of ill health, unemployment and poverty so that family members, especially children, do not experience sustained hardship.

Despite these very positive efforts, New Right sociologists claim that the government is doing too little to protect the family. However, it is important to understand that these critics are talking about a particular type of family: the traditional heterosexual nuclear family, underpinned by a sexual division of labour in which the man is the primary breadwinner and the woman is the primary caregiver.

New Right sociologists argue that the nuclear family has been neglected by government social policies over the past 30 years in favour of family diversity. In their view, social policy has actively and positively promoted other family types, which New Right sociologists such as Charles Murray and Patricia Morgan dismiss as morally inferior and potentially deviant. Furthermore, the New Right claim that state policy has created a set of social problems that are undermining morality, family life and social order in general. In contrast, feminist sociologists, such as Leonard, Barrett and McIntosh amongst others, argue that the New Right have exaggerated the effects of state policies on the quality of family life.

THE NEW RIGHT

The New Right is comprised of a group of American and British sociologists, politicians, think tanks and pressure groups united by their approach to government social policies, especially those on which the **welfare state** has been constructed.

UNDERSTAND THE CONCEPT

The **welfare state** is a collection of social policies introduced between 1944 and 1948, which brought about the NHS, the extension of schooling, the social security system, an increase in social housing, and a commitment to full employment. These policies were based on a shared belief that citizens should have the right to be free of five social evils – poverty, ignorance, disease, squalor and idleness – and that people should have the right to welfare where the only criterion for help was that of being in need.

The New Right approach to the family

In the UK over the last 50 years, public debate about the family has focused on the changing nature of family life and its impact on society. This debate has often been dominated by New Right thinkers, who take the view that the traditional nuclear family and the moral character of the young are under attack or threatened by government social policies. These commentators often assume that there was once a 'golden age' of the family, in which husbands and wives were strongly committed to each other for life, and children were brought up to respect their parents and social institutions such as the law.

New Right views on the family often reflect and transmit a dominant **familial ideology**. This ideology is transmitted by sections of the media and advertising, politicians, religious leaders, and pressure groups such as the Family Education Trust, The Institute for the Study of Civil Society and the Institute of Economic Affairs.

UNDERSTAND THE CONCEPT

Familial ideology is set of dominant ideas that promotes a particular set of family features and virtues as the ideal, aspirational type of family. This 'perfect' model is a nuclear family firmly grounded in heterosexual marriage, in which the father is the head of the household responsible for the family wage while the mother focuses on her nurturing and caretaking responsibilities. Children are brought up to have a keen sense of morality and to respect both their parents and those in authority.

The New Right emphasise that the nuclear family plays a very important role in shaping the moral order of society. This is achieved by making sure that the next generation is socialised into values such as discipline, respect, civility and responsibility. Parenting based on these principles is seen as producing order and stability and is therefore regarded by the New Right as a key feature of a 'morally healthy' family, and consequently a 'socially healthy' society. In this sense, the New Right are clearly influenced by the functionalist ideas of Murdock and Parsons (see Chapter 1).

The threat to the nuclear family

The New Right today see the traditional nuclear family as under threat and in decline. They suggest that this is one of the main causes of wider moral decay in society as evidenced by crime, anti-social behaviour and welfare dependency. Such sociologists often claim that feminism has turned the 'natural' order of things, and especially women's role within the family, upside down.

Many New Right thinkers see the emergence of feminism and government social policies in the 1960s and early 1970s as the beginning of a sustained attack on traditional family values. They are therefore critical of several government social policies, such as those discussed below.

The *1967 Abortion Act* legalised abortion in the UK and made it available through the National Health Service. It is often argued by New Right writers that some young women use abortion as a form of contraception, thus undermining the sanctity of family life and childbearing.

Although abortion has been legal in the UK for nearly 50 years, there are still those who are against it.

The *1967 Sexual Offences Act* partially decriminalised male homosexuality in England and Wales. The age of consent was set at 21 by the 1967 Act. This was reduced to 18 in 1994 and 16 in 2000.

Since 2000, a number of social policies favouring gay rights have become established in law, despite opposition from the New Right, some of which are listed below. In 2005, the first same-sex civil partnerships recognised by the law took place. In 2014, the Coalition government legalised same-sex marriage, which gave gay and lesbian couples the same rights and responsibilities as heterosexual couples who opt for a civil marriage. The *2002 Adoption and Children Act* allowed same-sex couples the right to apply to adopt a child. The *Human Fertilisation and Embryology Act*, which came into force in 2009, legally recognised lesbians and their partners as parents in cases of in-vitro fertilisation or assisted/ self-insemination.

However, New Right sociologists such as Patricia Morgan argue that gay families are unnatural because children can only be the outcome of what she describes as the natural loving sexual union of a man and woman. She further suggests that the motivation of lesbians and gay men for children is questionable. She claims that they only desire children to acquire the benefits of a life that imitates heterosexuality: children are merely prizes to be shown off to other gay couples. She claims that children brought up in homosexual families, whether they are adopted or the outcome of IVF or surrogacy, are not the outcome of love. They are trophy children, who may suffer bullying and stigma because of their association with their gay parents.

In your opinion, do children need fathers? Do you agree with Morgan's view that gay couples only want children as trophies?

The *1975 Sex Discrimination Act* (which outlawed discrimination against women by employers in the workplace) and the *1970 Equal Pay Act* (which made it illegal for employers to pay women less than men employed in the same jobs) 'encouraged' women, especially mothers, to enter the workforce in large numbers. New Right thinkers have claimed that these social policies distracted women from their 'natural' calling as mothers. Consequently, society has seen a rise in fertile women choosing to be childless because they see their paid career as more important than motherhood. Moreover, some New Right thinkers suggest that these social policies have led to generations of children being 'damaged' by **maternal deprivation**.

UNDERSTAND THE CONCEPT

Maternal deprivation is a term coined by the psychologist John Bowlby who claimed that an emotional and psychological bond existed between a mother and newly-born child. He argued that if that maternal bond was broken (because the mother returned to work, for instance) the child would feel deprived of maternal love and experience psychological problems that might be acted out, for example, through crime and delinquency. Feminist sociologists claim that there is no convincing scientific evidence that maternal deprivation occurs and argue that this is yet another patriarchal ideology.

The contraceptive pill was made freely available through the NHS in the 1960s and through Family Planning clinics in the 1970s. It is claimed that this social policy has weakened the family because contraception separates sex from reproduction. The New Right claim that the pill encourages sexual freedom and promiscuity. Furthermore, contraception is perceived by the New Right as a threat to existing marriages and families because the existence of the contraceptive pill undermines marital fidelity and encourages immorality in the shape of extra-marital affairs.

The *1969 Divorce Reform Act* reduced the previously high cost of divorce and made the legal process of getting a divorce a great deal simpler. However, the New Right argue that the Divorce Reform Act has resulted in people no longer taking marriage seriously. This theme will be revisited in Chapter 4.

The welfare state, notably the benefit system, is disliked by New Right sociologists because they argue that it has relieved families of responsibility for their own welfare. In particular, an over-generous welfare system is seen by the New Right as responsible for the rise in one-parent families. Morgan is very critical of the welfare state's policies towards such families. She argues that two-thirds of the average income of one-parent families comes from benefits and tax credits. She argues that this is a major problem because the willingness of the state to pay for the upbringing of children in these families is undermining 'self-supporting family structures'. In other words, people in these families are being discouraged from supporting themselves and their children because the payment of benefits encourages them to stay at home rather than to actively look for work.

Butler (2010) also argues that strong and durable families are important to the stability of society as 'broken families' are more likely to produce children who will break the law, be unemployed and/or be dependent on benefits. Murray argues that one-parent families are more likely than other family types to produce crime, hooliganism, drug abuse and educational failure. The New Right claim that the lack of positive male role models – fathers – in such families means that mothers lose control over their children when they reach adolescence, arguing that teenage boys are more influenced by deviant role models, such as other boys or men who may be engaged in delinquent or criminal activities.

STATE POLICY ON THE FAMILY SINCE 1997

An examination of a selection of government policies towards the family since 1997 may be useful in evaluating these New Right claims.

The Labour Government 1997–2010
Lewis (2007) points out that before 1997, UK governments, unlike their European counterparts, did not explicitly formulate or foster family policy. They did not have government departments or ministers exclusively devoted to the upkeep of the family. However, Labour reversed this trend by appointing a Minister for Children in 2003, and in 2007 it formed the new Department for Children, Schools and Families (which became the Department for Education in 2010) led by a Secretary of State who sat in the Cabinet.

Finch (2003) argues that Labour's election victory in 1997 marked a change in family social policy from a 'familistic' regime, which exclusively promoted the nuclear family ideal, towards a more 'individualistic' outlook, which aimed to extend the right for both mothers and fathers, regardless of whether they were married or not, or living in nuclear families or one-parent families, to gain better access to jobs and training.

Lewis argues that the Labour government of 1997–2010 took the idea of 'social investment in children' more seriously than previous governments by appointing a Children's Commissioner to look after their interests, and setting goals to eradicate child poverty. Furthermore, Labour generally ceased to condemn single mothers as a moral problem or threat, and recognised that family life reflected a rich diversity of family types in addition to the nuclear family. Labour also recognised that there are few families in the 21st century in which the breadwinner is exclusively male. It recognised that most families rely on two incomes and most women work (albeit often part time).

Labour introduced a Child Tax Credit (in addition to Child Benefit) in 2003 for all families that pay income tax, which Finch argues recognised children as individuals in their own right. This is paid to the main carer of the children, usually the mother. Finch notes that this decision "addresses 'purse and wallet' concerns that money paid directly to the mother is more likely to be spent on children, whereas money paid to the father will be spent on himself" (p. 15).

However, Labour's very explicit family policy attracted New Right criticism that it undermined family privacy and that Labour was constructing a 'nanny state' that interfered excessively in family life. Morgan (2007) argues that the Labour government's family policy undermined both marriage and the traditional family because it was biased towards single parents, dual-career families and gay people, at the expense of single-earner, two-parent nuclear families. She suggests that, contrary to what Labour believed, their family policy actually replaced individual choice with increased state control in citizens' private lives.

Despite these New Right criticisms, Labour's family policies have been praised in some quarters. For example, Judge (2012) points out that between 1999 and 2011 the

number of children in poverty was reduced by 900,000, while another 900,000 were prevented from falling into poverty in the same period.

Bradshaw (2012) also claims that the Labour government's family policy was successful because child neglect and abuse fell and subjective child wellbeing, especially with regard to 'happiness with family', improved in international league tables.

FOCUS ON SKILLS: EARLY CHILDHOOD UNDER LABOUR

Child wellbeing improved under the last Labour Government.

Perhaps the simplest way to sum up what we have found is to consider the early experiences of a hypothetical child born in 2009 compared to that of his sister born in 1997. The child born later could expect to spend twice as long at home with his mother in the first year if she had worked before birth. Whether she had worked or not, and whatever her occupational background, he was more likely to be breastfed in his first few days and also more likely to still be breastfeeding six months later. His chances of attending a formal childcare setting before the age of three were higher, and from age three onwards he was now almost certain to access early education. The childcare and early education settings would very likely have been of better quality than those his sister attended, structured around a play-based curriculum and with more chance of contact with a trained graduate professional. If he spent his first few years at home or with a childminder or part-time working parent, he would have had access to more local play

sessions, art and singing groups and toy libraries, especially if he lived in a disadvantaged area. His mother would have had more support, with easier access both to networks of other parents and to more formal advice and information. He would have been a little less likely to experience harsh parenting and a little more likely to have a more stimulating home environment. His household would have been better off financially and considerably less likely to live below the poverty line.

In terms of outcomes, our younger child was less likely to have been born at low birthweight than his sister and less likely to die in his first year. His cognitive and social development at age five were likely to have been considerably higher, but his chances of being overweight had not changed. In both health outcomes and cognitive and social development, the gap between our child and babies his age but from different social backgrounds had narrowed.

Source: Stewart (2013)

Questions

1. **Identify** the qualitative differences that the boy born in 2009 could expect compared with his sister born in 1997.

2. **Identify** and **explain** why the boy's health was likely to be better than his sister's.

3. **Outline** and **evaluate** which of the Labour Government policies narrowed the gap between children from working-class backgrounds and children from more affluent homes.

Coalition family policy 2010–2015

A Coalition government composed of Conservatives and Liberal Democrats was in power between 2010 and 2015, led by Prime Minister David Cameron. One of Cameron's first tasks was to abolish the Department for Children, Schools and Families, and to replace it with the Department for Education. Responsibility for children and families now lay with the Parliamentary Under-Secretary of State for Children and Families. However, this Under-Secretary does not sit in the Cabinet.

When the Coalition took power in 2010, it stated that society should be more 'family-friendly' because 'strong and stable families of all kinds are the bedrock of a strong and stable society'. Two pieces of Coalition social and economic policy and legislation are worthy of examination.

How might David Cameron's reorganisation of family responsibilities be interpreted?

The Troubled Families Programme

From 2011, members of the Coalition government started to express anxiety about the quality of family life in the UK, and especially so-called 'broken families', which many Conservatives blamed for the 2011 London riots.

BUILD CONNECTIONS

The 2011 London riots took place over two days and involved widespread looting and arson. They are sometimes called the 'BlackBerry®' riots because of the alleged use of this type of mobile phone by the rioters and looters to coordinate their actions and to avoid the police. About 3,100 people were arrested. Sociologists are particularly interested in riots and their causes. Some commentators see them simply as a criminal act motivated by opportunity and greed, while Marxist sociologists see them as political uprisings caused by deeper structural influences such as inequalities in wealth and income brought about by the capitalist system. Others point to poor police–community relations, which sometimes break down entirely because of perceived police racism. In the case of these riots, the shooting of an ethnic-minority young man, Mark Duggan, seems to have triggered and fuelled the unrest.

In 2006, the New Right think tank The Centre for Social Justice (CSJ) produced a report called *Breakdown Britain*, which stressed that Coalition social policies should focus on 'family breakdown'. This report, which was heavily influenced by Charles Murray's notion of an **underclass**, claimed that family breakdown was underpinned by:

> 'dissolution' – because divorce was too easy to obtain

> 'dysfunction' – because parents were not taking responsibility for the behaviour of their children

> 'dad-lessness' – because too many fathers were losing contact with their children and/or were refusing to take responsibility for them.

UNDERSTAND THE CONCEPT

The concept of an **underclass** was used by the New Right sociologist Charles Murray to describe a social group that is workshy and dependent on over-generous welfare benefits, which allegedly act as a disincentive to search for a job. This underclass supposedly socialises its children into deviant social values and behaviour.

These ideas culminated in a significant piece of Coalition family social policy introduced in 2012, the Troubled Families Programme, which identified 120,000 households who:

> are involved in crime and anti-social behaviour

> have children who persistently truant from school

> have adults who have never worked or who are long-term employed and are therefore welfare dependent,

> are a high cost to the public purse in terms of what they claim from the state and other problems such as poor health.

It is estimated that the 'chaotic lifestyles' and 'multiple problems' of such families cost the taxpayer £9 billion annually.

In 2014, the government claimed that this programme, which aims to 'turn around the lives' of people in 'troubled families' within three years by reducing their criminal activity, getting them jobs and getting their kids regularly into school, was showing signs of success. However, the programme has been criticised on a number of counts.

› Historians note that it presents a misleading and empirically inaccurate picture of a British past filled with 'happy untroubled families'. However, historical evidence suggests that every generation over the last 200 years has expressed concerns and moral panic about so-called 'troubled' or 'problem' families.

› Data suggests that three-quarters of troubled families who have supposedly been 'turned around' are still committing crime, being excluded from school and are without jobs.

› Levitas (2012) argues that the language used by the New Right is punitive and vindictive. She notes that it blames and labels the behaviour of poor families, and fails to appreciate that poor families are often unemployed and in poverty through no fault of their own. She argues that poor families are often the victims of government economic policies and global factors over which they have no control. Therefore, blaming so-called troubled families deflects the blame away from more powerful causes of family poverty.

Look at the available evidence and evaluate whether 'troubled families' are just another name for the 'underclass' as described by Charles Murray.

FOCUS ON SKILLS: TROUBLED FAMILIES

Many ascribed the 2011 London riots to a small number of troubled families.

The Coalition Prime Minister David Cameron said in 2011: "I ... think we need to make Britain a genuinely hostile place for fathers who go AWOL. It's high time runaway dads were stigmatised, and the full force of shame was heaped upon them. They should be looked at like drink drivers, people who are beyond the pale."

After the 2011 London riots, he argued that the unrest was not caused by poverty but instead by 'a slow-motion moral collapse' in behaviour that originated in families whose members believed they did not have to work or take responsibility for themselves because the 'state will always bail them out'. Moreover, the Prime Minister made it very clear who he and other New Right policy-makers specifically blamed for the 2011 riots when he said:

"I want to talk about troubled families. Let me be clear what I mean by this phrase. Officialdom might call them 'families with multiple disadvantages'. Some in the press might call them 'neighbours from hell'. Whatever you call them, we've known for years that a relatively small number of families are the source of a large proportion of the problems in society. Drug addiction. Alcohol abuse. Crime. A culture of disruption and irresponsibility that cascades through generations." (Cabinet Office, 2011)

Questions

1. **Identify** the reasons why David Cameron is concerned about absent fathers.

2. **Explain** how David Cameron's reaction to the 2011 riots supports the view that he is sympathetic to New Right attitudes towards family social policy.

3. **Outline** and **evaluate** the view that 'multiple disadvantages' are not self-inflicted but instead are the product of local and global influences that are beyond the influence of the individual.

The effect of Coalition economic policy on family policy

The financial crisis of 2008–9 led the Coalition government to implement an economic policy based on 'austerity' and focused on cutting public spending, in an attempt to reduce the national debt or deficit and to increase economic growth. Most critics agree that this austerity policy has had a negative impact on family social policy in the following ways:

› Bradshaw (2013) claims that, by 2015, cuts in public spending have had a disproportionately large impact on the poorest and most vulnerable families with children, and resulted in a rise in child poverty.

> Reed (2012) predicted that, by 2015, austerity measures would result in 120,000 more workless families, 25,000 more families with a mother suffering from depression and 40,000 more families living in overcrowded or poor-quality accommodation.

> The United Nations Children's Fund (UNICEF) noted that the Coalition's performance on child poverty was disappointing compared to 18 other wealthy countries that have actually cut child poverty despite the recession. For example, in 2013, child poverty rose by 1.6 per cent in the UK while in Poland it fell by almost 8 per cent.

New Right criticism of Coalition family policy

Despite the fact that the 2010–2015 Coalition government was led by a Conservative Prime Minister, and Conservative politicians took most of the leading roles in the Cabinet, the New Right have generally expressed dismay at the Coalition's family policies, especially its failure to deal with family breakdown. The CJS actually awarded the Coalition 4 marks out of a possible 10 for dealing with this issue. The CSJ wanted the Coalition government to do more to strengthen marriage and family life.

Evaluating state policy

Both the Labour and Coalition Governments have been criticised by the New Right for undermining the traditional nuclear family unit, and especially the traditional sexual division of labour – father as the main breadwinner and mother as the main carer. However, feminist critics of the New Right, such as Leonard, argue that familial and patriarchal ideologies still shape most state policy on the family. The nuclear family is still the most likely outcome of such policies, as illustrated by the following examples.

> Over the past 30 years, tax and welfare policies have generally favoured and encouraged the heterosexual married couple rather than cohabiting couples, single parents and same-sex couples. Graham Allan (1985) suggests that these policies have actively discouraged cohabitation and one-parent families, which challenges Morgan's assertions that family social policies have undermined marriage.

> Policies such as the payment of Child Benefit to the mother, and the government's reluctance to fund free universal nursery provision, have reinforced the idea that women should still take prime responsibility for childcare. Moreover, despite changes to maternity and paternity leave, it is still overwhelmingly the mother of the child who elects to take time out of the workplace and consequently falls behind others, especially men, in terms of pay and promotion opportunities.

> Policies such as 'care in the community', in which the state in the 1980s encouraged families to take responsibility for the elderly and long-term sick and disabled, have not been reversed by subsequent governments. Moreover, it is often the female members of the family who carry the burden of this care, which means they are less likely to work full time and are more likely to be economically dependent upon a male. The traditional sexual division of labour, in which women act as emotional and physical caretakers and men as breadwinners, is therefore reinforced.

The introduction of community care in the 1980s resulted in many women caring for elderly relatives at home.

> Mothers are still most often awarded custody of children after divorce because the courts still see women as most suited to child-rearing.

> Fox Harding (1996) argues that the best council housing is still often allocated to married couples with children, while the worst housing on problem estates is allocated to one-parent families. Both private and council housing in the UK are still mainly designed with the nuclear family in mind.

> The New Right is arguably correct in its assertion that intervention in family life has increased since 1997, but this has occurred in order to ensure that the family unit did not overwhelm the rights of the individuals within it. For example, laws regarding domestic violence and marital rape aim to protect women, while child protection legislation and successive Children's Acts aim to improve the rights of children. There is no doubt that such legislation has undermined traditional male dominance in families, but many people believe that improved rights for women and children strengthen the family rather than weaken it.

> Barrett and McIntosh (1982) argue that familial ideology is anti-social because it dismisses alternative family types as irrelevant, inferior and even deviant.

Moreover, it views the nuclear family as a private institution, and this may have led to the general neglect of the problem of child abuse. There is some evidence that social workers have in the past preferred to take children out of a problem family only as a last resort. Such inaction has contributed to a series of abuse-related child deaths. Barrett and McIntosh argue that familial ideology may have over-idealised the nuclear family – consequently New Right sociologists often fail to acknowledge that divorce and one-parent families may be 'lesser evils' than living in dysfunctional nuclear families.

> Donzelot (1979) in 'The Policing of Families' notes that familial ideology is part of a wider process of surveillance and social control operated by the state. He argues that family social policies are mainly targeted at 'controlling' problem social groups, such as the so-called underclass, and preventing and/or solving wider social problems, such as juvenile delinquency and crime. In this sense, families are used in order to keep potentially problematic individuals under surveillance. Family social policy is therefore focused on keeping families intact, supporting parents and producing children who are psychologically well-adjusted and who will conform to cultural expectations, because this prevents problems such as crime spiralling out of control.

CONCLUSIONS

New Right politicians strongly believe that the family – and therefore family ideology – is in decline, and that this is the source of all our social problems. However, critics note that it may simply be the case that the family and ideas about how it should be organised are evolving rather than deteriorating, as society realises that the traditional family denies women and children the same rights as men.

CHECK YOUR UNDERSTANDING

1. Identify the four central beliefs of New Right sociologists with regard to social policy in general.

2. Identify four social policies introduced in the 1960s or 1970s that threaten the nuclear family, according to the New Right.

3. Define and briefly explain 'familial ideology'.

4. Define what the Coalition government meant by 'troubled families'.

5. Explain how the New Right view feminist ideas.

6. Outline and explain why New Right sociologists see the welfare state as undermining both family life and morality in the UK.

7. Outline and analyse whether the Labour government's social policies were good or bad for the family.

8. Explain and analyse the Coalition government's record regarding marriage and family policies.

9. Outline and evaluate the relationship between the nuclear family and social policy.

TAKE IT FURTHER

Observe the media and other institutions for signs of familial ideology. You could, for example:

> study television commercials at different times of the day

> examine the content of specific types of programmes, such as soap operas or situation comedies

> analyse the content of women's magazines

> visit family-orientated stores, such as Mothercare, Boots and BHS, to see whether familial ideology is apparent in their organisation, packaging, marketing, and so on.

250

4.3 DEMOGRAPHIC TRENDS AND FAMILY LIFE

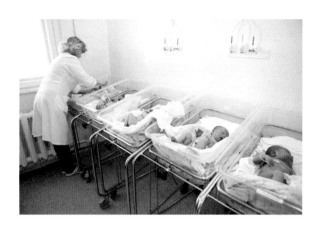

LEARNING OBJECTIVES

> Demonstrate knowledge and understanding of changing patterns in birth and fertility rates, death rates, life expectancy, the ageing of the population, migration and globalisation and their effect on family size and diversity (AO1).

> Apply theories of the family and evidence from sociological studies of the family to explanations of these changing patterns and the concept of family diversity (AO2).

> Evaluate sociological ideas that demographic trends since 1900 have produced a diversity of family structures and internal family dynamics (AO3).

INTRODUCING THE DEBATE

The study of demography is focused on how the number of births and deaths, and the number of people entering and leaving the country (migration), all affect the size, sex and age structure of the population. Sociologists argue that demographic changes over the past 100 years have had a major influence on British family life and, in particular, have contributed to the rich diversity of family types and living arrangements found in the UK today.

THE POPULATION OF THE UK

The population of the United Kingdom has grown throughout the last century or so but at a declining rate. For example, between 1901 and 1911, the growth rate averaged 1 per cent per year, but this has now fallen to about 0.25 per cent per year. The population of the UK has therefore grown steadily from 38 million in 1901 to 64.1 million in 2013. Population projections suggest that it will reach 70 million in 2027 and 73.3 million by 2037.

The rate of population change over time depends upon four demographic factors:

> the birth rate – this refers to the number of live births per 1000 of the population per year

> the fertility rate – this refers to the number of live births per 1000 women aged 15–44 per year

> the death rate – this refers to the number of deaths per 1000 of the population per year

> migration – this refers to the number of people entering the UK (immigrating) and the number of people leaving the UK (emigrating).

Reasons for population growth

Up to the 1950s and 1960s, natural change (more births than deaths) was the main reason for population growth in the UK. Since the 1980s, net migration (immigration exceeding emigration) has been the main factor. For example, in the 1950s, natural change accounted for 98 per cent of population change and net migration for only 2 per cent. However, Cangiano (2014) estimates that between 1991 and 2012, net migration accounted for 54 per cent of the increase in the UK population.

Changes in the birth rate

Birth rates in the UK have been in decline for some time. For example, in 1901 there were 1,093,000 births but in 2013 only 698,512 babies were born.

An examination of the birth rate over the course of the last century suggests that this decline has not been straightforward because it has been punctuated by a number of 'baby booms', for example, immediately after the First and Second World Wars, and in the periods 1957–1966 and 1986–1992. Since 2001, the birth rate has steadily risen. In 2012, the number of births was the highest since 1971.

Explanations for the decline in birth rate between 1900 and 2000

The decline in the birth rate in the first 60 years of the 20th century was mainly caused by a major decline in the infant mortality rate (that is, the number of children dying at birth or in their first year of life per 1000 births). The decline in child death rates actually began in the 19th century as a direct result of improvements in public health services. Various factors combined to ensure that by the 1920s most children born would survive into adulthood: the provision of services such as sanitation and clean water supplies; improved knowledge and education about hygiene; and improvements in living standards, especially diet and nutrition.

What other reasons might explain the high birth rates of the 19th century?

There is some evidence that women's attitudes to childbearing underwent significant change in the later part of the 20th century. Wilkinson (1994) coined the phrase 'genderquake' to describe the radical difference in attitudes towards family life, childbearing, education and careers between the generation of young women brought up since the 1980s and previous generations of women. One consequence of this genderquake is that women no longer automatically see childbearing as a priority. There are probably several reasons for this genderquake in female attitudes.

> The feminisation of the economy and workforce in the 1960s and 1970s (see Chapter 5) has probably led to young women becoming more career-orientated and postponing marriage, childbearing and family life.

> Feminist ideas about the role of women that challenged traditional and patriarchal ideas about marriage, childbearing and the sanctity of family life became very popular in the 1970s.

> Feminist ideas, particularly those based on academic research, had a great deal of influence on social policymakers, and led to social policies such as the Equal Pay Act, the Equal Opportunities Act and the introduction of more female-friendly teaching practices in schools, which led to a significant rise in the number of females entering university. Social policy also led to the contraceptive pill becoming more widely available on the NHS. Surveys indicate that childbearing, marriage and family life are well down the list of priorities for female graduates.

BUILD CONNECTIONS

The attitudes of women towards family life and having children are very influenced by their experience of the education system. There is some evidence that girls who do not do very well in education are more likely to fall pregnant and to become single mothers. In contrast, the more success a woman experiences in the education system, the more likely she is to postpone marriage and childbearing until her late 30s. Well-qualified women are also more likely to choose to be child-free. See Topic 3, Chapter 4 for more on this.

During the 20th century, childhood became commercialised, which meant that having babies and raising children became a very expensive business. For example, it was estimated in 2014 by the Centre of Economic and Business Research that the average cost of raising a child until the age of 21 in the UK was £227,000, and that parents spend 28 per cent of their income on their offspring. Parents today may therefore choose to have fewer children for financial reasons.

The decline of religious beliefs and practices – secularisation – among the bulk of the population that characterised the second half of the 20th century in the UK, led to a decline in **conservative** attitudes about the morality of personal behaviour. More **liberal** ideas emerged after the 1960s, which resulted in the gradual acceptance of practices such as contraception, abortion, homosexuality and divorce. Most importantly, the view that marriage, children and family life were the only authentic ways in which a woman could derive satisfaction from life went into decline.

UNDERSTAND THE CONCEPT

Conservative attitudes tend to be very traditional. Conservatives generally want to keep things the way they always have been. Conservatives are therefore not keen on change. **Liberals**, on the other hand, tend to believe that society is in need of change and that traditional ways of thinking often lead to discrimination and inequality. Liberals tend to believe that people need to be more tolerant of one another and that people should be afforded the same opportunities regardless of social background.

Some sociologists argue that the decline of community, as symbolised by the decline of the extended family and close-knit urban neighbourhoods in the 1960s and 1970s, also contributed to a change in women's attitudes towards family life. The rise of the geographically and socially mobile nuclear family meant that younger women had less contact with influential extended kin and neighbours, who might have pressurised them into marriage and childbearing. As a consequence, traditional ideas about family honour and shame which might have resulted in the labelling of a woman's decision not to have children as 'unnatural' and 'shameful' in the past also went into decline.

Postmodernists suggest that there is evidence that as men and women were more exposed to consumerism, materialism and leisure in the late 20th century, they consequently became more individualistic and selfish. Beck and Beck-Gernsheim (1995) suggest that in late capitalist society there are simply more choices available to young women and that they are choosing freedom and independence rather than restricting themselves to childbearing and parenthood.

Sociologists therefore argue that these influences on the birth rate have had the knock-on effect of causing a decline in fertility rates as women chose to have fewer children, often at a later stage of their lives compared with their own mothers and grandmothers, while some chose not to have children at all in order to make the most of the opportunities that modern society now offers them.

Changes in the fertility rate

The general fertility rate (GFR) generally refers to the number of children that women of childbearing age, 15–44, have in any one year. Fertility rates for England and Wales have generally declined over the past 100 years: in 1900 the fertility rate was 115, had dropped to only 57 in 1999, and recovered to 64 by 2010.

Since 2009, the government has preferred to use another way of looking at fertility. This is the Total Fertility Rate (TFR) – the number of children that are born to an average woman during her childbearing life. Hicks and Allen (1999) note that in 1900 the TFR was equivalent to a completed family size of 3.5 children. In 2001, the UK's TFR was only 1.63, although this gradually increased to 1.8 in 2005 and 1.94 in 2012. However, the consequence of the fall in fertility rates is that families today are significantly smaller than those of the past.

Explanations for the general decline in fertility rates

There are two main reasons why fertility rates fell towards the end of the 20th century.

> *Reliable birth control*, particularly the contraceptive pill, which became widely available through the NHS in 1961, gave women far greater control over reproduction. They could now make decisions about when to have children, how many to have and so on. Between 1962 and 1969, the number of women using the pill rose from an estimated 50,000 to around one million. However, the real revolution in reproductive power for women came in 1974 when the government gave family planning clinics permission to prescribe the pill for single women. In 2014, about 2 million women were using the pill. It is estimated that at least 70 per cent of women have used it at some stage in their lives.

> *The feminisation of the economy:* economic change has had a profound effect on women's attitudes and practices with regard to childbearing and the TFR. In particular, some women are choosing to have children at a much later period in their lives and to have fewer of them, because they are prioritising careers and economic independence. The evidence with regard to fertility rates clearly shows that women are having children at an older age than they were 30 years ago.

Age group	Under 20	20–24	25–29	30–34	35–39	Over 40
1971	82.6	285.7	247.2	109.6	45.2	12.7
2001	44.2	108.8	159.9	178.9	86.5	16.3
2010	40.6	137.3	199.2	202.5	115.8	27.7
2012	33.8	132.5	202.4	216.2	114.8	29.9

Table 4.3.1 *Live births by age of mother – in thousands*
Source: ONS (2012)

In general, fertility rates for women aged 30 and above have increased, while those for women aged below 30 have declined. We can clearly see this in Table 4.3.1.

Babies born to women aged 24 years and under constituted 47 per cent of all births in 1971 but by 2012 this had fallen to 23 per cent of all births. In contrast, the number of babies born to women aged over 30 constituted only 21 per cent of all births in 1971 but by 2012 this age group was responsible for 49 per cent of all births.

The average age of married women giving birth has increased by six years since 1971 to nearly 30 in 2012.

The highest rate of fertility is found in the age group 30–34, while 2012 ONS figures showed a 154 per cent increase in births among women aged from 35–39 between 1971 and 2012. Moreover, the number of children born to women aged 40 and over has more than doubled in the last 30 years.

There has been a rise in fertility in recent years. This has mainly been credited to the increase in the number of immigrants coming to live in the UK. The proportion of births to mothers born outside the UK has increased every year since 1990 when it was only 11.6 per cent. Babies born to mothers from overseas – Poland, Pakistan and India were the three most common countries of birth – accounted for 26.5 per cent of all births in 2013. The TFR for women born outside the UK was 2.19 in 2013, compared with 1.79 for women born in the UK. This suggests that the families of women born outside the UK are larger than those of British-born women.

The ONS argue that, in any given year in the UK, the proportion of births to women born outside the UK is higher than the proportion of births among women born in the UK. This is because the foreign-born women are aged 25–34, the age when they are most likely to have recently immigrated into the UK, and also the time during which fertility is highest.

THE EFFECTS OF BIRTH AND FERTILITY RATES ON THE FAMILY

Despite the changes in birth and fertility rates documented so far, the nuclear family continues to be important. In 2013, about 38 per cent of families in the UK (4.7 million) were composed of traditional nuclear families – two parents plus children. However, 7.7 million families in the UK were made up of couples, or couples who have non-dependent children living with them. It is important to understand that these couples can also be interpreted as nuclear units. This is because many are either empty-nest nuclear families – their children may recently have left home – or they may be planning to have children in the future. When these couples are added to the mix, two-thirds of families can probably be defined as nuclear, post-nuclear or potentially nuclear families.

However, changes in birth and fertility rates have had several effects on family life in the UK.

> Families have declined in size. In 2013, 47 per cent of nuclear families had one child, while only 14 per cent of nuclear families had more than two children.

> There has been a significant decline in the number of women aged 24 or under who are having children. There has been a major increase in older mothers.

> There is some evidence that declining fertility rates are linked to the decline of the full-time mother role and the growth of dual-career families, in which couples combine paid work with family life and childcare. Over 60 per cent of couples with children now combine jobs and family life. There are generally two types of dual-earner families:

> > Some professional couples are extremely committed to their careers but make the decision to have a child once their careers are established. These couples are probably partly responsible for the doubling in the

number of women aged 40 or over having babies in the last 20 years. These couples can probably also afford professional childcare services such as nannies, au-pairs and private nurseries.

> The other more common type of dual-earner family is composed of a man who earns the major share of the family income, and a woman who works part time. In this situation, it is likely to be the mother who takes major responsibility for childcare and the upkeep of the home.

Voluntary childlessness

Women's control over their own fertility has seen an increasing number of women voluntarily choosing to reject childbearing altogether. The Family Policy Studies Centre found that in 2000, one in five women aged 40 had not had children compared with one in ten in 1980. This figure is predicted to rise to one in four by 2018. Some studies also note that one in three female graduates have opted not to have children. The ONS notes that a greater percentage of British women remain child-free at the end of their childbearing years compared with the rest of Europe.

Hakim (2010) argues that voluntary childlessness is a relatively new lifestyle choice, which could only have been brought about by the contraception revolution. However, attitudes in favour of procreation are still quite powerful – deciding not to have children can still attract social disapproval especially from parents who wish to be grandparents. There may also be social pressure from relatives, friends and colleagues because, as Hakim notes, a woman's fertility status is still very much considered public property.

Gillespie (2003) identifies two motivational factors for voluntary childlessness.

> There may be a 'pull' factor in that some women will be attracted by the pull of being child-free, especially the increased freedom and better relationships with partners that it affords. A number of studies indicate that couples are happier without children. Wallander (2001) notes that married couples without children have more disposable income than households with children.

> There may be a 'push' away from motherhood. Park (2005) found that women who were motivated by this factor tended to see parenting as conflicting with their careers or leisure interests. These women claimed to be disinterested in children and often rejected the notion of a maternal instinct.

Voluntary childlessness may have negative implications as child-free women and couples reach old age. Child-free couples may have less social support and emotional ties in old age. However, other studies contradict this by stating that single child-free people fare better than married couples because they are more likely to be actively engaged with family and friends.

THE DEATH RATE

Generally the number of births in the UK exceeds the number of deaths. In 1901, 632,000 deaths were officially registered in the UK, which at that time had a population of approximately 38 million. The annual number of deaths therefore represented approximately 1.7 per cent of the population.

The 20th century saw both a substantial growth of the UK population and a correspondingly steady rise in the number of deaths.

However, the last 60 years have seen a steady decline in the death rate, that is the number of deaths per thousand people. For example, the period 1983–2013 saw a 13 per cent fall. Only 576,000 deaths occurred in Britain in 2013, despite a population of approximately 64 million. This means that the total number of deaths only represented about 0.9 per cent of the population. The 2014 death rate stood at 9.34 deaths per 1000 people in the population.

Life expectancy

In 1851, life expectancy at birth in England and Wales was 40 years for males and 44 years for females. Just 150 years later, in modern-day industrialised Britain, life expectancy has nearly doubled from Victorian levels: male children born in 2013 will, on average, live for 78.7 years while females will, on average, live for 82.6 years. Around one in three babies born in 2013 will live to be 100 years old.

It is estimated by the ONS that in 2013, a female aged 65 years will live for another 20.7 years compared with males who have on average another 18.2 years of life. In 2013, there were more women aged 90 years and over (372,290) than men (141,160).

Explanations for the fall in the death rate and the rise in life expectancy

The decrease in death rates and the corresponding increase in life expectancy, according to McKeown (1976), are the result of six factors.

1. Rising wages lifted many people out of poverty and improved their standard of living, and particularly their diets, in the early part of the 20th century.

255

FOCUS ON RESEARCH: WOMEN WHO CHOOSE CHILDLESSNESS FAIL TO MATCH THE STEREOTYPES

Highly qualified women are more likely to choose to remain childless.

Women who choose to be childless are far from the stereotypes of work-driven careerists, self-centred individualists or 'ultra feminists' who scorn family life, according to research supported by the Joseph Rowntree Foundation. The new study suggests – on the contrary – that they and their partners hold conventional views about relationships and parenting and that their careers are rarely central to their sense of personal fulfilment. Highly qualified women are more likely to remain childless but career identity did not emerge as central to personal identity or personal fulfilment for the majority of voluntarily childless people.

However, a series of in-depth interviews with 45 voluntarily childless women and with some of their partners reveals a high degree of caution about assuming the responsibilities of being a parent. Parenthood is clearly identified with unwanted disruption and change in their lives as well as a heightened risk of financial insecurity. The study found that relatively few interviewees of either sex had made an early, irrevocable decision not to have children. Their choice of childlessness had come about slowly in the context of their work, personal health, relationships and other life events.

The researchers placed the way that women and men explained their childless status in five broad categories:

› **People who were certain that they did not want children:** nearly a third of those interviewed said they had made a firm decision and had never wavered in their resolve.

› **People who were certain now that they did not want children:** four women and one man had experienced some wavering, but felt they had 'come out on the other side' with a clear decision not to start a family.

› **People who accepted childlessness:** six women in their 40s, some of whom were single, described how they had once thought they would have children, but had since changed their view.

› **People who were ambivalent:** eight women and three men voiced mixed feelings about being childless and were still not clear that a firm decision had been taken against having children.

› **People who felt the decision had been taken for them:** this small group included women who had encountered fertility problems but not sought treatment and others who maintained that their childlessness was determined by factors outside their control.

The study found little evidence to suggest that a child-free lifestyle resulted from 'alternative' values or self-centredness. Many of those interviewed played an important part in extended family networks – supporting brothers and sisters who did have children, or caring for older parents. Yet the respondents had, variously, concluded that it would be undesirable, difficult or impossible to make parenthood part of their own lives.

Source: McAllister and Clarke (1998)

Questions

1. Why can this survey be described as a qualitative piece of research?

2. What evidence in this research supports the view that voluntary childlessness is the result of alternative values or selfishness?

3. Analyse how parenthood is viewed by the childless people who took part in this survey.

4. Using the article and other sources of knowledge, assess the view that the growing number of women who do not want children are undermining the nuclear family unit.

2. Public health policy, especially the introduction of clean piped water into people's homes and sewage and sanitation systems in the 19th century, prevented the sorts of infectious diseases that had killed previous generations.

3. The provision of social housing for the poor – council flats and homes with good ventilation – contributed to the near eradication of tuberculosis in the late 20th century.

4. Maternity care services were improved in the early part of the 20th century and health visitors were introduced to visit and assist women who had just become mothers.

5. The introduction of the welfare state after the Second World War resulted in poorer sections of society being provided with a range of social and economic services and supports, such as free school meals, sickness and disability benefit, old age pensions, housing benefits, income support, and so on.

6. The creation of the National Health Service (NHS) in 1948 resulted in the provision of better and free health care. For example, in 1958, the NHS began to vaccinate everybody under the age of 15 to prevent diseases such as polio and diphtheria, and in 2000 a national flu vaccination programme was introduced for all those aged over 65. Advances in drug technology and surgery now mean that more people than ever are likely to survive bouts of cancer, heart disease and other life-threatening diseases, or to live longer even if they have these diseases. Furthermore, numerous NHS preventative health campaigns have raised awareness of health-threatening behaviour and persuaded people to change their lifestyles with regard to smoking, drinking, diet, exercise, and so on.

The ageing population

In the UK today, there are increasing numbers of people aged 65 and over and declining numbers of children under 16. The number of older people is high because when they were born women had larger families, and those aged over 60 years today are now likely to live for much longer periods compared with the elderly of the past.

In 1821, there were very large numbers of young people but very few of them survived into old age. In contrast, the 2011 Census shows that there are fewer young people today – only 5.5 per cent of the population is aged under 10 years compared with 27 per cent in 1821.

The UK saw an acceleration in this ageing process in the late 20th century – the number of people aged under 16 declined by 18 per cent between 1971 and 2004, while the number of people aged over 65 increased by 29 per cent in the same period. The 2011 Census clearly shows that the proportion of people aged over 50 in the UK (34.8 per cent) is higher than the number of teenagers (23.9 per cent). The number of those aged over 80 years has increased nearly fivefold from 1 per cent in 1821 to 4.7 per cent in 2011. Between 2005 and 2013, the number of people aged 85+ increased by 30 per cent.

However, Chambers (2012) notes that it is important to understand the following points.

› The elderly population of the UK is not a uniform group – there are differences in the experience of ageing because of a variety of factors, including social class, gender, sexual orientation, location, migration and the degree of family support.

› The elderly are often stereotyped as part of a culture of decline, as "unproductive, infirm and dependent while the reverse is often the case" (p. 112). Chambers argues that many elderly people remain independent until death. They are active players in family life and they often remain in paid work after reaching retirement age. For example, 50 per cent of the elderly reported to the ONS that they enjoyed 'good health' in 2011. Furthermore, the ONS also reported that 16 per cent of 65–74 year olds were still economically active.

› The elderly are often interpreted as an economic liability to both family members and the state, but Chambers argues that there is a strong case for seeing the elderly as a resource rather than as a burden.

There are three major reasons why Britain is experiencing an ageing population:

1. the decline in the death rate, especially the infant mortality rate

2. the rise in life expectancy, which is due to a variety of factors including improved living standards, the welfare state and a health care system that has been reasonably successful at keeping people active, healthy and alive for many years post-parenting and post-retirement

3. the decline in the fertility rate and especially the fact that women are choosing to have children later on in their lives.

THE EFFECTS OF AN AGEING POPULATION ON FAMILIES AND HOUSEHOLDS

Elderly couple households

An ageing population means that the number of elderly couples living independently in their own households as either married or cohabiting spouses has increased from 52.6 per cent of the elderly population in 2001 to 56.8 per cent in 2011.

There is some evidence that, as couples survive into their 70s, health problems are more likely to appear, but such couples are likely to remain in their own home. Only 3.7 per cent of the elderly lived in sheltered housing or residential homes in 2011 and the majority of those in the latter type of institution were aged over 85.

However, studies do suggest that as ill health and disability become a problem for one member of the couple, the other is likely to become the primary carer (albeit with support from family, neighbours and social services). The 2011 Census results indicate that almost 1.3 million people aged over 65 are caring for other relatives, and especially their spouse. The majority of these older carers are women.

Elderly one-person households

The ageing of the population has led to a significant increase in the number of one-person households over state pension age as a proportion of all households. In 2013, 14 per cent of all households and 47 per cent of all one-person households were of this type, a total of 3.6 million households.

Of those aged 65 and over who live alone, 68 per cent are female. This is because there are more women than men aged over 65 in the population. Moreover, it is also the case that, on average, women live longer than men and they tend to marry men older than themselves. In 2013, there were 1.7 million widowed women aged 65 or over living alone in the UK. This was three times the number of widowers. Chambers refers to this trend as the 'feminisation of later life'.

However, it is important to note that these households vary quite significantly in their experiences of 'being alone'. The elderly as a group covers a broad range of ages – 65 to 90 plus – and this means they may not necessarily share the same values and outlook. The 'young-elderly' are very likely to be healthy and to lead active and independent lives. They may be actively interacting with other members of their kinship network. In contrast, the 'elderly-elderly', those aged 80 and over, are generally more likely to be experiencing chronic illness and disability. They may be housebound and consequently very dependent on family members, social services and neighbours for support. They are also more likely to be in residential care.

Chambers notes that family support for single-person households may be less available in the future because of the following factors.

> High levels of geographical mobility mean that elderly relatives live further away from their adult children than they did 50 years ago. Extended family ties may be weaker as a consequence.

> Families are getting smaller – couples are increasingly choosing to have only one child. This reduces the options with regard to family support when people get older: previous generations who had 3–5 children were likely to receive better support.

> Some women are choosing not to have children, so there may be no next generation to offer them support in old age.

> Same-sex couples and gay and lesbian single-person households are less likely than heterosexual couples to have children and consequently have no younger generational support.

Extended families

It was generally thought until fairly recently that the extended family residing under the same roof was in terminal decline. Wall (1998) found that in the 1950s, 40 per cent of the elderly had been taken in by their relatives, but this had dropped to only 5 per cent by the mid-1990s.

However, there are signs that the extended family in which adult children are caring for an aged parent either in the same or an attached residence (a 'granny flat'), may be experiencing a revival. In 2010, it was estimated by Lloyds TSB Insurance that there were 500,000 three-generation households in the UK. Victor (2010) estimated that 10 per cent of those aged over 65 now live in this type of family.

This growth in the number of extended families may be the result of economic pressures – parents and their adult children may not have the economic resources to pay for private residential care homes. Children may feel obliged to take in their parents, especially as old age can be socially isolating and lonely. Furthermore, living alone can be potentially dangerous for the elderly because of limited mobility or declining mental functions.

Lievesley (2013) also notes that extended families containing elderly relatives are much more likely in British Asian communities. For example, using the 2011 Census, Soule et al. found that 42 per cent of Asian men and

68 per cent of Asian women aged 85 and over lived in multigenerational extended households, compared with only 12 per cent of White men and 19 per cent of White women in the same age group.

Extended ties and residential proximity

There is evidence that working-class families in particular still see great virtue in regularly maintaining extended kin relationships. Research by Victor *et al.* (2005) found that 77 per cent of older people saw their relatives on a weekly basis, while only one in ten saw their relatives less than once a year. Hoban *et al.* (2011) found that 78 per cent of their sample saw their adult children at least once a week. Chambers noted that an increased number of the elderly are using communication technologies such as telephone, email, Skype™ and Facebook™ to keep in contact with their extended kin.

However, despite these very positive contacts, it is important to be aware that caring for the elderly may have some negative consequences for families and their members, as the following list of possible effects indicates.

> Feminist sociologists have noted that females, especially daughters, tend to take on a disproportionate responsibility for the care of elderly parents compared with men and particularly sons. Healey and Yarrow (1997) studied parents living with children in old age and found that most of their sample had moved into their daughter's household. The 2011 Census also showed that 58 per cent of carers of the elderly in families are female and this rises to 60 per cent for those who are caring for 50 hours or more per week.

> Feminist sociologists point out that women's disproportionate responsibility for caring for elderly relatives leads to economic inequality between the sexes. Women are more likely than men to give up work in order to care for elderly relatives. Caring responsibilities mean that women are excluded from the full-time labour market. This means that women carers are likely to be economically dependent on men.

> There is also evidence that caring for elderly relatives can create financial hardship, and even poverty, for the family, especially if one of the spouses has had to give up work. Caring itself brings with it additional capital costs – for example, investing in assistive equipment such as stair-lifts, special baths or showers – and higher living costs for items such as heating, laundry and transport.

> From an interactionist perspective, it can be argued that, if an elderly dependent relative moves in with a nuclear family, the quality of family relationships may be profoundly altered. For example, female carers may be stressed and emotionally affected by caring for a physically or mentally deteriorating parent, and this may undermine a happy marriage by creating conflict. The female carer may feel resentful at having to give up a career and her economic independence and/or feel that her partner should be doing more to assist. The working spouse may feel neglected or resentful because career opportunities that may involve the family relocating to another part of the UK, or holidays abroad, may be impossible because of caring commitments.

> Moreover, from an interactionist perspective, the quality of parent–child relationships may also be negatively affected as the grandparent's health deteriorates. Children and teenagers may feel that their everyday contact with their parents and their quality of life are undermined by their parents' need to put a grandparent first; for example, parents may not be able to afford to buy children the things that they want or they may not be able to find the time to go on a family holiday.

Beanpole families

Brannen (2003) notes that the ageing of the population, the increasing tendency of women to pursue both higher education and a career, the consequent decline in fertility and the availability of divorce has led to the recent emergence of four-generational families – families that include great-grandparents and great-grandchildren.

Brannen calls such family set-ups 'beanpole families' because such families are less likely to experience horizontal intragenerational ties, that is, they have fewer aunts, uncles and cousins. This is because for the last 20 years or so, families have been having fewer children: children today have fewer relatives compared with previous generations of children.

Brannen argues that family members are now more likely to experience vertical intergenerational ties, that is, closer ties with grandparents and great-grandparents. She argues that the 'pivot generation' – the generation sandwiched between older and younger members of the family – is increasingly in demand to provide for the needs of both elderly parents and grandchildren. For example, 20 per cent of people in their fifties and sixties currently care for an elderly person, while 10 per cent care for both an elderly person and a grandchild. Such services are based on the assumption of 'reciprocity': the provision of babysitting services, for example, might be balanced by the assumption that daughters will assist mothers in their old age.

Grandparenting

Chambers notes that there is a growing recognition that families benefit from the presence of grandparents and that the interaction between grandparents and grandchildren is more qualitative compared with the past. This is because grandparents today live longer. They are more healthy and active compared with previous generations. Consequently they make a significant contribution to the parenting and socialisation process.

A study carried out by the insurance company RIAS in 2012 estimated that 5.8 million grandparents currently look after their grandchildren regularly for an average of 10 hours a week, and this represents 47 per cent of the nation's grandparents aged over 50. This amounts to a saving of nearly £11 billion in childcare costs over the course of a year.

Ben-Galim and Silim (2013) found that grandmothers are putting in a greater number of informal childcare hours than grandfathers, and play a crucial role in helping families with childcare. Statham (2011) found that in families in which the mother is in work or education, 71 per cent receive some level of childcare from grandparents, and 35 per cent rely on grandparents as the main providers of childcare.

FOCUS ON SKILLS: RELATIONSHIPS BETWEEN GRANDPARENTS AND TEENAGE GRANDCHILDREN

The grandparent–grandchild relationship shifts with age, from childcare, outings and play to mutual support.

Ross *et al.* (2005) explored the relationship between grandparents and teenage grandchildren, looking at the ways teenagers and their grandparents relate to each other, how they care and provide support and how the relationship changes over time.

Seventy-five young people (aged 10–19) and 73 older people (aged early 50s to late 80s) participated in the study. The majority of participants were unrelated and were interviewed individually or in small groups. A few interviews were held jointly with a related grandparent–grandchild pair.

Ross *et al.* (2005) found that grandparents spoke positively about becoming and being a grandparent. When grandchildren were younger, time was spent on outings and playing together, or with the grandparents teaching skills and providing childcare. As grandchildren grew older, the relationships were more likely to revolve around talking, and giving advice and support. Grandparents often provided financial support to assist their grandchildren, from pocket money to school fees.

Both generations studied in Ross *et al.* (2006) described how grandparents usually played a key role in 'listening' to grandchildren. Many young people said they could share problems and concerns with their grandparents and that their grandparents would sometimes act as go-betweens in the family, particularly when there were disagreements between themselves and their parents.

Ross *et al.* also found that grandparents provided a bridge to the past by acting as sources of family history, heritage and traditions: storytellers who kept grandchildren aware of their own family experiences and their culture. They were also active in keeping wider sets of relatives connected.

It was also apparent that the direction of care and support altered during teenage years, with some taking greater responsibility for their grandparents. They sometimes helped their grandparents who had health issues by providing emotional and practical support for the other grandparent of the pair.

Based on Ross *et al.* (2005)

Questions

1. **Understanding**. What sorts of material support did grandparents in the study offer their grandchildren?

2. **Interpretation**. In what ways do children benefit from having regular contact and interaction with their grandparents?

3. **Analyse** how the relationship between grandparents and grandchildren changes over time.

4. **Evaluate** the strengths and weaknesses of grandparents living with a nuclear family as part of a multigenerational extended family.

The economic consequences of an ageing population for the family

The ageing population has tremendous implications in terms of the costs to the state, society and the family because the state pension system is currently funded on a 'pay as you go' basis: the contributions of the current workforce pay for state pensions, rather than any accumulated reserve of previous contributions. Population ageing means that there will be greater numbers of elderly dependents in the future but fewer workers to support them, and consequently an increase in what economists call the 'burden of dependency'. This means that there will be a greater tax burden on a shrinking number of future workers in order to pay for the pensions of a fast-growing number of future elderly people.

Rutherford argues that future governments therefore are going to have problems in funding both pensions and the NHS. It is generally agreed that the increase in the elderly population, and in particular the number of people aged 85 and over, will put greater pressure on the NHS and care home capacity. It may therefore be very likely that families in the future will be asked or instructed by law to make a greater contribution to the cost and care of ageing relatives.

What effects on family life might result from families being legally compelled to look after elderly relatives?

MIGRATION

Migration is central to population growth in the UK because of the decline of the birth and fertility rates and the ageing of the population. In 2013, the ONS reported that the UK population will grow by 9.6 million over the next 25 years. Of this increase, 57 per cent will be 'natural', meaning that there will be more births than deaths. The other 43 per cent of the increase will be the product of migration. However, it is important to understand that both of these factors – birth and migration – interact with one another because migrants are more likely than the host population to be of childbearing age. They also tend to have higher fertility rates than the host population. Consequently, the ONS estimate that 29 per cent of the natural increase in the British population between 2012 and 2037 will be the result of migration.

Historically, the population of Great Britain was made up of people from a White British ethnic background. The pattern of migration since the 1950s has produced a number of distinct minority ethnic groups within the general population. The 2011 Census showed that the majority of the population of England and Wales was White (86 per cent) although only 80 per cent were born in the UK.

The remaining 14 per cent of the population belonged to other ethnic groups: Asians (Pakistani, Indian and Bangladeshi) make up 6.8 per cent; Black (African Caribbean and African) make up 3.4 per cent; Chinese make up 0.7 per cent; Arab make up 0.4 per cent, and others make up 0.6 per cent. The 2011 Census also indicates that 2.2 per cent of people in England and Wales were mixed-race (up from 1.27 per cent in 2001), while 12 per cent of households had partners or household members of different ethnic groups, three percentage points up from 2001.

Immigrants to the UK in the past 30 years have tended to be both relatively young and fertile. For example, the 2011 Census shows that of the foreign-born individuals who had arrived in England and Wales in the previous 10 years, 95 per cent were aged 45 years or under and this has had the effect of pushing up both the birth and fertility rates since 2005.

Factors influencing migration

Legislation and border controls

Legal migration is affected by laws governing the rights of people to move to other countries, while illegal migration is affected by the attempts of governments to control access to their territory. For example, the UK has limited immigration from the Caribbean and the Asian subcontinent through Acts such as the 1962 and 1968 Commonwealth Immigration Acts. The 1999 Immigration and Asylum Act made it tougher for asylum seekers to settle in Britain. However, Britain is a member of the European Union (EU), which allows the free movement of people within its boundaries.

Globalisation

Globalisation involves a process by which national boundaries become less important and interconnections between different parts of the globe become more important. With the development of mass communications such as satellite television and the internet, awareness and understanding of other countries and cultures has increased. Rapid, cheap and safe transport systems such as jet air travel have made movement around the globe affordable and easier than in the past. These factors have increased the total amount of migration in the world. The world has also seen an increase in global crime such as people-trafficking.

Push factors

These types of factors push people out of particular societies. People may come to Britain because they are fleeing persecution, torture, religious repression, war, and so on. They may also be pushed out of their societies because of poverty.

Pull factors

These types of factors, which are mainly economic, make Britain attractive to would-be migrants. A high proportion of migrants state that they moved to Britain because of the following factors

> Migrants are attracted by job opportunities in the UK, which are more numerous than in the societies in which they were brought up. For example, after 2004, there was a high rate of migration to the UK from Poland because Britain's economy was booming, while the Polish economy was less strong. However, since the 2008/09 credit crunch and subsequent recession, many of these migrants have returned to Poland.

> Migrants may be studying for educational qualifications at UK universities or colleges. In 2007, more than a quarter of immigrants came to the UK for this reason. Many leave after achieving their goal.

> Many migrants come to Britain to join partners, family members or friends.

CULTURAL DIVERSITY IN BRITISH FAMILY LIFE

Asian family life in the UK

The main research into Asian families (specifically people who come from Pakistani, Indian and Bangladeshi backgrounds) has been carried out by Richard Berthoud who discovered the following facts about Asian family life in Britain.

> The majority of people in Pakistani and Bangladeshi communities live in nuclear families. This is because the housing stock in the UK is mainly designed with the nuclear family in mind. However, about 33 per cent of Asian families – mainly Sikhs and East African Asians – live in extended multigenerational families. East African Asian extended families are likely to contain more than one generation (that is, they are likely to be vertical extended families), while Sikh extended units are organised around brothers and their wives and children (that is, they are likely to be horizontal extended families). For example, a study by Victor et al. (2014) interviewed 110 Asian families living in the south of England and found that 90 per cent of Asian people in her study lived in multigenerational families, with two or three generations under the same roof.

> Asian people tend to be more traditional in their family values than White people. For example, marriage is

highly valued in most Asian cultures and there is little cohabitation or divorce (although the latter may indicate more empty-shell marriages – see Chapter 4). Marriage in Asian families – whether Muslim, Hindu or Sikh – is mainly arranged (that is, negotiated with children rather than forced) and there is little intermarriage with other religions or cultures. There is also evidence that Bangladeshi and Pakistani women marry at a younger age than White women, and that Indian women have more children at younger ages.

> There is some evidence that attitudes to the family role of women differ between Asian groups. For example, Muslim families (that is, Bangladeshi and Pakistani Asians) are more likely to encourage segregation between males and females. Females may not be permitted to have contact with unrelated men, which means they are largely confined to motherhood and housework or they may work in family businesses.

> Relationships between Asian parents and their children are also very different from those in White families. Asian children tend to respect religious and cultural traditions, and they feel a strong sense of duty to their families, especially to their elders. They are very aware that bad behaviour can bring 'dishonour' to their families. For example, many Asian children are happy to go along with the tradition of arranged marriage so long as they can negotiate with their parents with regard to their future partner. However, as Asian teenagers come into more contact with British culture and their British peers, there is more potential for generational conflict between parents and children, as the latter may indulge in peer group behaviour such as drinking alcohol, taking drugs, and so on.

> Asian families, and South Asian families in particular, feel a strong sense of duty and obligation to assist extended kin in economic and social ways. This is important because Bangladeshi and Pakistani families in the UK are more likely to be living in poverty than Indian and White families. Such obligations are often global in character because they extend to sending money to relatives abroad on a regular basis and travelling half way around the world to nurse sick or dying relatives.

However, a study by Victor et al. found that older people from Pakistani and Bangladeshi communities in England were uncertain about whether they could depend on their children to follow tradition and look after them, because children were increasingly geographically mobile and more likely to move away from their parents. Moreover, they perceived a change in young Asian people's cultural attitudes. Examples were cited of 'neglectful' children and people being put into residential homes by their families. There was a general feeling that children were not as respectful compared with 'back home' or the past. Moreover, although there were global ties to Bangladesh and Pakistan, these were weakening as parents and other relatives in their home country died, although new global links were being made as their children moved to the USA, Europe and other countries.

African Caribbean families in the UK

There is evidence from the work of Berthoud that African Caribbeans may have different family experiences compared with the majority population. Berthoud's research has observed that the average African Caribbean family is likely to have the following characteristics.

> Only 39 per cent of British-born African Caribbean adults under the age of 60 are in a formal marriage, compared with 60 per cent of White adults.

> African Caribbean communities have a higher proportion of one-parent families compared with White communities – over 50 per cent of African Caribbean families with children are one-parent families. The main reason for the high number of one-parent families according to Chamberlain and Gulbourne (1999) is the increasing trend of African Caribbean mothers choosing to live independently from their children's father. Among 20-year-old African Caribbean mothers, 66 per cent remain single compared with only 11 per cent of their White peers, while at the age of 25 these figures are 48 per cent and 7 per cent respectively.

Many African Caribbean mothers choose to live independently from their child's father.

These trends indicate that African Caribbean women are avoiding settling down with the African Caribbean fathers of their children. Berthoud (2003) suggests that the attitudes of young African Caribbean women are characterised by 'modern individualism' – they are choosing to bring up children alone for two reasons.

> Firstly, African Caribbean women are more likely to be employed than African Caribbean men. The latter experience extremely high rates of unemployment. Berthoud argues that pregnant African Caribbean women probably rationally weigh up the costs and benefits of living with the fathers of their children and conclude that African Caribbean men are unreliable as a source of family income and are potentially a financial burden. Surveys indicate that such women prefer to be economically independent of men.

> Secondly, Chamberlain and Goulborne's study of African Caribbean mothers in Leeds noted that African Caribbean single mothers are often supported by an extended kinship network when bringing up children. Interestingly, African Caribbean definitions of kinship often extend to **'fictive kin'**, including family friends and neighbours as 'aunts' and 'uncles'.

UNDERSTAND THE CONCEPT

Some sociologists have suggested that some families regard people who are not related to them by blood, marriage or adoption as kin. It is argued that the relationship between family kin and these so-called **fictive kin** – usually close friends and neighbours – is no different from any other family relationship in terms of obligation and duty to one another.

Dual-heritage or mixed-race families

Research by Lucinda Platt (2009) indicates that African Caribbeans are more likely than any other ethnic minority group to intermarry with members of another ethnic group, especially White people. The number of mixed-race partnerships means that only a minority of African Caribbean men and women are actually married to fellow African Caribbeans, and only one-quarter of African Caribbean children live with two Black parents.

Ali (2002) notes that such marriages result in inter-ethnic families and mixed-race (sometimes called 'dual-heritage') children. Platt found that the number of mixed-race children has grown considerably in recent years. For example, over the past 14 years the number of children of Caribbean heritage with one White parent has risen from 39 per cent to 49 per cent. Young people aged 18 and under are six times more likely to be mixed-race than people aged 30 and over.

In contrast, mixed-race marriages tend to be lower among other ethnic-minority groups. For example, 35 per cent of Chinese, 11 per cent of Indians and only 4 per cent of Pakistanis are in mixed-race marriages.

Some sociologists have suggested that these types of families have their own unique problems, such as facing prejudice and discrimination from both White and Black communities.

Mixed race marriages and inter-ethnic families are increasingly common in the UK.

CONCLUSIONS

Demographic changes in the number of births and deaths, the fertility rate and migration have had a fairly profound effect on the structure and internal organisation of families in the modern UK. Sociologists have examined demographic changes and concluded that family life is not static – rather it is in a constant state of change and flux. Demographic changes reflect the greater choices available to people, especially women. It is the job of sociologists to document this diversity and to explain how these demographic changes are producing new forms of family and household. The next chapter also focuses on family diversity and how this has been affected by changes in marriage and divorce rates.

CHECK YOUR UNDERSTANDING

1. Identify three reasons why birth rates have generally declined over the past 100 years.

2. Why did the infant mortality rate fall between 1900 and 1950?

3. Identify four reasons why women's attitudes towards childbearing changed in the latter half of the 20th century.

4. How does the 'general fertility rate' differ from the 'total fertility rate'?

5. What explanation is usually cited for the rise in fertility rate in the UK in the last ten years?

6. Why are some women choosing to be voluntarily childless?

7. What have been the effects for the family of the decline in both the birth and fertility rates?

8. In what ways has the function of grandparenting changed in the past 30 years?

9. What are the implications of an ageing population for society, the family and women?

10. What is a beanpole family?

11. Explain and illustrate, using either Asian or African Caribbean families, what is meant by cultural diversity.

12. What is an inter-ethnic or dual-heritage family?

TAKE IT FURTHER

Design a research tool that allows you to gather quantitative and qualitative information about your classmates' relationships with their elderly relatives. Do your findings confirm or challenge previous sociological research?

4.4 MARRIAGE, DIVORCE AND FAMILY DIVERSITY

LEARNING OBJECTIVES

> Demonstrate knowledge and understanding of changing patterns in marriage, cohabitation, separation, divorce, and childbearing outside of marriage, and their effect on family diversity (AO1).

> Apply theories of the family and evidence from sociological studies of the family to explanations of these changing patterns and the concept of family diversity (AO2).

> Evaluate New Right ideas that changing patterns in marriage, cohabitation and divorce are symptoms of family decline (AO3).

INTRODUCING THE DEBATE

Fifty years ago, most people in the UK got married at a reasonably young age. Most people remained married for most of their life. Divorce was relatively rare. Cohabitation was regarded as immoral and consequently few couples practised it. Most people lived in the traditional nuclear family – mum, dad, plus two or three kids – and dad went out to work while mum spent most of her time in the home.

In 2015, this picture of family life has dramatically changed. There seems to have been a significant decline in marriage. Divorce and cohabitation are common. There

are few traditional nuclear families left in which the father is the breadwinner and the mother is the full-time housewife. There are now lots of different types of family structures with very different internal organisations compared with the past. This chapter explores how marriage and divorce have evolved over the past 50 years and how these changes have led to the emergence of new types of family. Some sociologists do not like these changes and see them as symptoms of social decline. In contrast, others, especially feminists and postmodernists, view these changes in a very positive light.

MARRIAGE

Sociological studies of global cultures suggest that marriage is a universal institution practised by most societies, although the forms that it takes and its functions may differ across societies. In the UK, monogamy is

practised; legally men and women can only be married to one wife or husband at any one time. Being married to more than one wife or husband at the same time – bigamy – is illegal in the UK. However, serial monogamy is increasingly becoming the marital norm in the UK. This means it is quite common for people to marry more than once during their lifetime because of divorce (and/or in some cases the death of their spouse).

Studies of other societies have discovered that polygamy – marriage to more than one partner at the same time – is a common global phenomenon. There are two types.

Polygyny is the term used when a religion or culture allows a man to take more than one wife. Khan (2014) estimates that there may be as many as 20,000 polygynous Muslim marriages in the UK. Technically, polygyny is against the law in the UK. However, no Muslim man has ever been prosecuted for it.

Polyandry is the term used when cultures allow a woman to take more than one husband. It is less common than polygyny but Starkweather and Hames (2012) have identified nearly 80 cultural groups worldwide that practise it.

Patterns of marriage in the UK

In 1972, a record number of 480,000 couples were married in the UK. However, since then, the annual number of marriages in England and Wales has gone into steep decline. In 2009, a record low of only 231,490 couples got married.

The General Marriage Rate (GMR) refers to the number of men and women who get married in any given year per 1,000 men and women aged 16 and over who are unmarried (single, divorced or widowed). Table 4.4.1 clearly shows this decline in marriage.

	Females	Males
1862	50.0	58.7
1900	44.9	53.7
1950	51.7	66.1
1970	59.5	77.5
1990	36.1	42.1
2000	25.9	30.1
2009	19.2	21.3
2011	19.8	22.0

Table 4.4.1 *GMR: England and Wales 1862–2011*
Source: ONS (2014)

Despite some booms in marriage, the marriage rate for both women and men has generally been on a downward spiral between 1862 and 2009. For example, the female marriage rate actually rose to 59.5 in 1970 (compared

with 44.9 in 1900) but had fallen by two-thirds in 2009 to 19.2. The marriage rate for men has experienced a similar trajectory – it rose to 77.5 in 1970 (compared with 53.7 in 1900) but it had fallen steeply to 21.3 by 2009. There has been a slight recovery between 2009 and 2011 but it is probably too early to categorically state that this is the end of the 40-year decline experienced in the period 1970–2009.

Other trends in marriage rates

The mean age at first marriage in 1972 was 24.9 for men and 22.9 for women. However, the last 40 years has seen a significant rise in the age at which people are getting married for the first time. In 2012, the average age had increased to 32.4 for male first marriage and 30.3 for female first marriage.

Women tend to marry at a slightly younger age than men. This pattern reflects the fact that men generally tend to marry women younger than themselves.

Office for National Statistics (ONS) research (2013) suggests that there may be a social-class divide in marriage. In 2012, 66.3 per cent of people in social class 1 – such as professionals – were married, in contrast to 44.5 per cent of people in social class 7 – such as unskilled manual workers.

Sarah Corse et al. (2013) found in the USA that the decline of full-time factory jobs and the rise in unstable casual employment means that working-class men and women are now less likely to get and stay married and have children within marriage. Consequently, marriage is increasingly becoming a middle-class institution.

There are also some ethnic variations in marriage.

> Research by Berthoud (2000) suggests that three-quarters of Pakistani and Bangladeshi women are married by the age of 25, compared with just over half of White women. This probably reflects powerful expectations, both cultural and religious, in the **British Asian** communities.

UNDERSTAND THE CONCEPT

When the concept '**British Asian**' is used by British sociologists, it generally refers to people born in the UK whose parents or grandparents originally came from the Indian subcontinent – for example, India, Pakistan or Bangladesh. Chinese people are usually categorised as a separate social group.

> British African Caribbeans are the group least likely to get married – only 39 per cent of African Caribbean adults under the age of 60 were in a formal marriage, compared with 60 per cent of White adults in 2011.

> Approximately 8 per cent of married couples in the UK today are made up of people from different ethnic backgrounds, according to ONS figures, compared with just 2 per cent in 2001. Nearly 30 per cent of married African Caribbean men and 47 per cent of married non-Caribbean Black men are married to White women, while 20 per cent of African Caribbean women and 34 per cent of other Black women are married to White or mixed-race men.

> People from South Asian backgrounds were the least likely of minority ethnic groups to marry outside their ethnic or religious group.

Why are Asian people less likely to marry outside their ethnic or religious groups?

THE DEBATE ABOUT MARRIAGE

The fall in marriage rates over the past 40 years has provoked a keen debate between New Right commentators and feminists. New Right commentators such as Patricia Morgan (2000) have expressed concerns about the decline in marriage. Morgan argues that marriage is centrally important to society, morality and social order because it involves unique attachments, obligations and mutual expectations that legally and ethically regulate and limit people's behaviour.

Morgan is concerned about the decline of marriage because, in her view, marriage contributes to social stability. She argues that married people make better lovers, parents, workers and citizens because marriage reinforces and promotes the sharing of the same legal and social duties and obligations to the community. In this sense, marriage helps bind the individual to society.

Moreover, Morgan argues that marriage and the social/community obligations that accompany it are good for

both the health and wealth of the married couple. For example, she claims that married men are more likely to be employed than unmarried or cohabiting men, and earn 10 to 20 per cent more because their commitment to the social obligations underpinning marriage motivates them to work harder than any other male group. An analysis of marriage statistics by the ONS in 2007 supports this view. It concludes that marriage is good for the health of couples and that married people live longer than single or divorced people.

New Right thinkers such as Morgan argue that marriage is in decline because social policies, particularly those related to the welfare state, have put people off marriage. Rector (2014) argues that the welfare state damaged marriage because the benefits system has encouraged single parenthood, at the expense of married parenthood, by reducing the financial need for marriage. He notes that less educated mothers in particular have increasingly become married to the welfare state and to the taxpayer rather than to the fathers of their children. This is because if such mothers get married, the rules which underpin the benefit system actually reduce the amount of money they receive from the state. He argues that welfare has become a substitute for a husband. He notes that welfare benefits create a destructive feedback loop: they promote the decline of marriage, which generates a need for more welfare.

Other New Right thinkers see secularisation – the decline of religious belief and practice, especially among Christians – as partly responsible for the decline in marriage rates. It is argued that people are now less likely to get married in church 'before God' and consequently they are less likely to take their 'sacred' wedding vows seriously. For example, in 2012, only 30 per cent of weddings were held in places of worship. Moreover, traditional ideas rooted in religion – such as the notion of a 'life-long commitment to one person', or the idea that adultery and divorce are shameful forms of behaviour and deserving of moral condemnation – are now regarded as old fashioned and redundant in a secular society.

What limitations on conduct are imposed by marriage? How do weddings and marriages in general contribute to the stability of families, communities and societies?

THE CRITIQUE OF THE NEW RIGHT POSITION ON MARRIAGE

New Right views are not shared by feminist thinkers who argue that the decline in marriage rates in the UK over the past 40 years reflect a positive change in the nature of marriage.

Changes in attitude

Feminists argue that the 1970s saw a cultural and attitudinal shift towards the idea of marriage as a personal and intimate relationship that needs to be achieved and sustained, rather than merely a status conferred by a legal ceremony. Feminists claim that this led to changes in the nature of marriage, in that patriarchal marriage has been replaced by a more companionate and egalitarian form of marriage.

Changes in significance

Marriage appears now to be regarded as the primary rite of passage – the most important decision in a person's life – and one that requires great emotional commitment. For this reason, it may appear to be in decline, because men and women are willing to delay marriage. The majority of people still get married but rather than falling into it at an earlier age, they may now be working towards it because it occupies a much more elevated position compared with the past.

A number of feminist studies have explored the attitudes, expectations and experiences of married couples and consequently confirmed this cultural shift in attitudes towards marriage. For example, Askham's (1984) research into married couples highlighted how both spouses saw compromise and negotiation as essential to their marital success. They both saw marriage as worthy of significant emotional and practical effort, while they saw 'taking each other for granted' as potentially destructive of the relationship.

From this perspective, then, the decline in marriage rates in this period and the rise in divorce are not negative trends. They indicate that people, and especially women, are less carefree about marriage. People now see marriage as a serious individual choice, and consequently are more careful in their choice of partner and more willing to make the personal sacrifices necessary to make the marriage work. As a result, the institution of marriage has become stronger rather than weaker.

British Social Attitude (BSA) surveys indicate that most people, whether single, divorced or cohabiting, still see marriage as a desirable life-goal, especially if the couple have children.

Surveys indicate that few people believe that either the freedom associated with living alone or cohabitation are better than being married to someone. Marriage is still considered by both married and unmarried people to be the 'gold standard' – there is nothing that more effectively gives public expression of overall and complete commitment to another person than marriage and the wedding ceremony.

Around 40 per cent of all marriages are remarriages (in which one or both partners have been divorced). Approximately 100,000 marriages a year are second, third or even fourth attempts at marital happiness. Men remarry more often than women. This is probably because taking responsibility for children reduces women's opportunities in the repartnering market. Whatever the reasons for remarriage, the fact that it occurs so often indicates that marriage is still popular as a social institution despite people's previous negative experience of it.

Changes in the cost of marriage

It is important to consider the possibility that there may be practical economic reasons for the decline of marriage. Marriage is an expensive option, especially for the poor.

Rates of marriage are tied to the economic fortunes of society.

Recession and austerity have been the norm in western societies for some time now and may account for the 7.5 per cent decline in marriage rates for social class 7 since 2001. People may elect to cohabit and save money for the two biggest events in their life – getting married in a traditional but expensive wedding ceremony and buying their first home.

In conclusion, there is a danger that concerns about the decline of marriage have been exaggerated by the New Right. Despite the decrease in the overall number of people marrying over the last 40 years, married couples are still the main type of partnership for men and women in the UK. In 2012, 67 per cent of families were headed by a married couple and at any one time around 21 million people are firmly ensconced in the institution of marriage. About 4.5 million divorcees lived in the UK in 2013 but many of these will remarry. Based on marriage, divorce and mortality (death) rates, the ONS estimated in 2010 that the percentage of marriages ending in divorce was 42 per cent. This was actually down from the 45 per cent estimated in 2005. It also means that 58 per cent of marriages are probably successful. It is therefore overly dramatic to suggest declining marriage figures are a rejection of a tradition that is, on the balance of evidence, very much alive.

ARRANGED MARRIAGES

In the UK, heterosexual marriage is generally a matter of chance, in that people normally follow cultural expectations about courting and romance. A person might date a number of people. Eventually it will become clear that one of these relationships will result in the emotional and physical compatibility from which feelings of love and a proposal of marriage can emerge.

However, not all subcultures in the UK invest in love marriage. A significant majority of Asian people – Muslims, Hindus and Sikhs – as well as Orthodox Jews still practice arranged marriage. It is important to note that such marriages do not mean parents forcing a child into wedlock against their will. Instead, an arranged marriage usually involves mutual discussion about a proposed match. No decision can usually be agreed unless both the potential bride and groom consent.

Robert Epstein (2011) explored the strength of arranged marriages by interviewing more than 100 Indian, Pakistani and Orthodox Jewish couples and compared the results against 30 years of research into love marriages. His research concluded that arranged marriages tend to grow more stable as time goes on, while love marriages

are more likely to deteriorate. He found that those in arranged marriages tended to feel more in love the longer they spent together, while those in regular marriages felt less in love over time.

Epstein claims arranged marriages are generally more successful than love marriages because those who arrange such marriages carefully check for compatibility in terms of beliefs, values, interests and goals. He claims that the couple have more confidence in one another and consequently are more likely to commit to one another for life. This also means that they positively attempt to work out any difficulties that might appear in the marriage. Moreover, extended kin are well-placed to advise and guide. In contrast, Epstein argues that those who marry for love are blinded by passion and lust, and consequently fail to think seriously about issues of compatibility. When the marriage hits difficulties, they are less likely to consult extended kin for advice and more likely to believe that relationship problems mean their romantic dreams and marriage have come to an end.

FORCED MARRIAGE

Despite the emphasis on choice and consent in most arranged marriages, there is evidence that forced marriages continue to exist in the UK, to the extent that the government set up a Forced Marriage Unit (FMU) in 2005. Forced marriage is defined by the unit as "a marriage conducted without the valid consent of both parties where duress (emotional pressure in addition to physical abuse) is a factor".

The UK forced marriage statistics for 2013 show that there were 1,302 forced marriages, although the FMU estimates that there are actually 8,000 forced marriages a year in the UK. It is very difficult to assess the real degree of this problem: victims are reluctant to come forward because they are often unwilling to report their parents to the authorities. They may be reluctant to bring shame upon themselves or their families by not fulfilling what they see as a family duty, and they may be fearful of the consequences – failure to obey may result in 'honour crimes' such as abduction, acid attacks, mutilation and even murder. For example, 2,823 honour-based incidents were reported to the police in 2010.

FOCUS ON SKILLS: ARRANGED MARRIAGES

Arranged marriages are common in Indian society.

Sardar (2009) notes that arranged marriages are very popular among young British Asians. He notes that this very traditional arrangement has been modernised, in that both parties are free to accept or reject the choice of marriage partner made by their parents. He argues that young British-born Asians are attracted to the notion of arranged marriages for two main reasons.

Firstly, many young Asian women do not want to go through the 'humiliation' of the 'dating game' with its associated pressures of learning the feminine charms – looking attractive and sexy – necessary to attract a man, because it is demeaning. Moreover, rejection can often be cruel and hurtful. In contrast, many young Asians see the modern version of arranged marriages as more dignified because being introduced to a man or woman thought suitable by caring relatives means that both prospective partners are meeting as equals and are both committed to the concept of a life-long relationship.

Secondly, there is usually tremendous family support. Sardar notes that whole families are welcome at Asian speed dating events. He argues that an arranged marriage is a social act because marriage is regarded by Asian families as much too important to be left to the would-be bride and groom. The extended family therefore play a vital role in bringing two people together and that role continues throughout the whole course of the marriage. Sardar notes that kin is always ready to share and ease the burdens of marriage and to provide a safety net of support and encouragement so that people can get through the hard times.

However, the evidence suggests that these 'hard times' are few and far between because, as Epstein notes, the love in arranged marriages tends to grow so that, ten years on, the affection couples felt for one another in arranged marriages is typically twice as strong compared with love marriages.

Partners in love marriages also know that marriages do not have to last forever because of the easy access to divorce. In contrast, in Asian arranged marriages, commitment is planned. Couples get married knowing that they will not leave and are therefore more determined to make it work.

However, some critics of arranged marriages remain unconvinced that they are better than love marriages. They suggest that arranged marriages may lack physical and emotional chemistry and stultify into empty-shell marriages in which partners are afraid to leave one another because they do not want to bring shame and dishonour on their extended families. Women, in particular, who experience unhappiness and leave their husbands may be shunned by their community.

Questions

1. **Identify** the ways in which arranged marriage has been modernised.

2. **Identify** three reasons why arranged marriages are still very popular among young British Asians.

3. **Analyse** the ways in which love marriages are supposedly inferior to arranged marriages, according to the article.

4. **Outline and assess** the view that arranged marriages are more successful than love marriages because they are the result of planning.

SAME-SEX MARRIAGE

The Marriage (Same Sex Couples) Act 2013 legalised marriage for same-sex couples in England and Wales, either in a civil ceremony or on religious premises if the religious organisation is in agreement. The arguments in favour of the Act claimed that the system previously in place for gay couples who wanted to legally validate their relationships – civil partnerships – did not have the same status and confer the same legal rights as heterosexual marriage. However, the most significant argument in favour of same-sex marriage was a civil rights or equal opportunities one. It was argued that it is not right that a couple who love one another and want to publicly confirm and formalise that love should be denied the right to marry.

Despite the Act becoming law, strong objections have been raised to same-sex marriages. First, there were religious objections, which have resulted in two legal definitions of marriage – those marriages which are recognised by the state and those recognised by the Church of England, and other religious groups which exclude same-sex marriage.

Morgan objects to same-sex marriage because she argues that it indicates a rejection of Christian values and consciousness, and a general moral decline. She argues that an alternative secular ideology, with a focus on sexual and family diversity, has come to culturally dominate western societies. She claims that this ideology, which is encouraged by government social policy, seeks to undermine the moral authority of religious institutions and the traditional nuclear family and to stigmatise those who object to same-sex marriage as narrow-minded and prejudiced bigots.

In your opinion, what are the strengths and weaknesses of the school of thought opposed to gay marriage?

COHABITATION

Cohabitation is defined by the ONS as living with a partner, but not being married to or in a civil partnership with them. A constant source of concern to New Right sociologists such as Morgan is the significant rise in the number of couples cohabiting during the last decade. ONS statistics for 2012 indicated that there were 5.9 million people cohabiting in the UK, which means that the number of individuals cohabiting has doubled since 1996. The total number of cohabiting couples in 2012 was composed of just over 2.9 million opposite-sex cohabiting couples and 69,000 same-sex couples. These figures indicate that cohabitation is one of the fastest growing types of household in the UK.

Childbearing inside and outside of marriage
ONS data states that in 2012, 39 per cent of opposite-sex cohabiting couples had dependent children, compared with 38 per cent of married couples. Dependent children are defined as those living with their parent(s) aged under 16, or aged 16 to 18 and in full-time education. Another way of looking at this is to examine the proportion of children born out of wedlock. In 1938, only

4 per cent of babies had unmarried parents but in 2012 this had risen to 47.5 per cent, according to the ONS. The New Right have suggested that these statistics are yet another nail in the coffin of the nuclear family.

However, this is not a black and white picture for a number of reasons. Firstly, most cohabiting couples are in the most fertile age groups for childbearing. This may be the main reason why there are more cohabiting couples with only one child than married couples with one child in 2012. Secondly, married couples with dependent children have more children on average than cohabiting couples, as shown in Figure 4.4.1. This suggests that childbearing may be leading cohabiting couples into marriage.

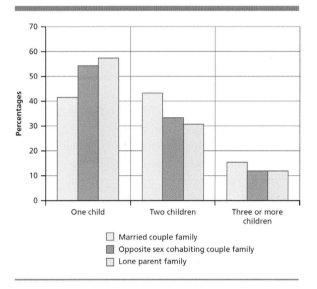

Figure 4.4.1 *Families with dependent children by family type and number of dependent children, UK, 2012*
Source: ONS (2012)

The debate about cohabitation
New Right commentators claim that the rise in cohabitation is responsible for the decline in marriage rates and the traditional nuclear family. Many New Right commentators even argue that cohabitation is replacing marriage. They tend to see this as particularly problematic because they claim that cohabitation is less stable than marriage. For example, Morgan refers to cohabitation as 'marriage-lite' because she claims evidence suggests that cohabiting couples are less happy and less fulfilled than married couples, more likely to be abusive, unfaithful, stressed and depressed, and therefore more likely to split up. In 2007, ONS data analysed by Murphy suggested that children whose parents live together but are not married get worse results at school, leave education earlier and have a higher risk of developing a serious illness.

However, Beaujouan and Ni Bhrolchain's (2011) study of cohabitation is generally critical of this New Right position. They argue that cohabitation has become a normal part of the life-course in the UK. For example, they note that about two-thirds of people aged 25–44 have cohabited at some point in their lives. Cohabitation therefore is no longer seen as socially deviant or immoral, probably because of secularisation.

Beaujouan and Ni Bhrolchain are particularly doubtful that marriage is in decline because of cohabitation. Instead, they argue that cohabitation is delaying marriage because it is seen by couples as a test of compatibility for marriage. They note that the vast majority of marriages – 80 per cent in recent years – are now preceded by a spell of cohabitation; in 1980–84 the figure was only 30 per cent. Indeed they note that "marriage without first living together is now as unusual as premarital cohabitation was in the 1970s", because living with a partner before first marriage has been a majority practice since the early 1990s. Cohabitation is regarded as a 'trial run' for marriage rather than as an alternative to it.

Beaujouan and Ni Bhrolchain's research found that at the tenth anniversary of moving in together, half of cohabiting couples had married each other, just under four in ten had separated and just over one in ten were still living together. In this sense, cohabitation is not a long-term arrangement for many couples in Britain but it can be viewed as an increasingly popular option for couples who want their future marriages to succeed. Moreover, Beaujouan and Ni Bhrolchain also point out that surveys and official statistics indicate that marriage rather than cohabitation is still the main cultural goal for most people in the UK. For example, 84 per cent of women are married by their 40th birthday.

Beaujouan and Ni Bhrolchain also suggest that cohabitation may be responsible for the decline in marriages ending in divorce by their fifth anniversary because it 'screens out' weaker relationships which without cohabitation might have immediately progressed to marriage.

Finally, there are also some practical reasons for the rise in cohabitation.

1. People may be separated from a previous partner and awaiting a divorce. Once the two-year official separation period is over, they may intend to marry a new partner. In the meantime, they may cohabit with that new partner. In 2005, for example, 23 per cent of cohabiting men were separated from a previous partner, while 36 per cent were divorced.

2. Barlow and Duncan (2000) found that the importance of a lavish wedding was such that if only a modest one was within financial reach, the couple would choose cohabitation over marriage.

FOCUS ON RESEARCH: COHABITATION – TESTING COMMITMENT

Many young couples consider cohabitation a serious and permanent relationship milestone.

Jamieson et al. (2002) looked at the meaning of marriage, cohabitation and commitment for young adults in the age group 20–29 in the first year of the 21st century. They wanted to see whether it was possible for a couple to enter into cohabitation with different levels and understandings of commitment. Jamieson et al. identified three approaches that couples might adopt. Firstly, they might view living together as the beginning of a permanent partnership. Secondly, they might see cohabitation as a way of testing out whether a permanent relationship is viable – bet-hedging, as it has been described. Or, thirdly, they might drift into cohabitation with very little thought for the future, seeing it as a pragmatic arrangement that carries with it little or no burden of expectations.

Jamieson et al.'s study was based on a sample of 202 randomly selected men and women aged 20–29. The sample was stratified equally between the 20–24 and 25–29 age groups, and between men and women. Among the sample, 93 members were in a relationship, while the other 109 were single. Respondents in couples were almost equally divided between the married and cohabiting. Younger couples were more likely to be cohabiting while older couples were more likely to be married. They interviewed 137 out of the 186 people in couples – a response rate of 74 per cent.

The study used a structured questionnaire to ask a series of questions of couples aimed at finding out their level of commitment to one another. When possible, both partners of a couple were surveyed at the same time. Self-completion questions were used when the possibility of partners influencing each other's answers was not desired, or when the topic might force disclosure of sensitive information or initiate disagreement between the couple. As a follow-up to the survey, intensive interviews were conducted with 16 single people and 25 couples aged 25–29 of which 17 were married.

The study concluded that there was no simple relationship between cohabitation and lack of commitment. The majority of couples in the study chose to describe how they began living together as a serious and permanent commitment. Most expected the cohabitation to evolve into marriage at some stage. Few of the couples saw cohabitation as 'hedging their bets'.

Adapted from Jamieson *et al.* (2002)

Questions

1. Identify the aim of this study.

2. Explain why some sociologists prefer to use representative samples.

3. Explain why the study might be criticised for using structured questionnaires.

4. Explain why surveying both people in a couple at the same time might be unreliable.

5. Outline and evaluate how the findings of the study challenge New Right ideas about cohabitation.

MARITAL BREAKDOWN

Types of marital breakdown
Marital breakdown can take three different forms: divorce, separation and empty-shell marriages.

1. *Divorce* refers to the legal ending of a marriage. Before the Divorce Reform Act of 1969, one partner had to prove the 'fault' or 'guilt' of the other – for matrimonial 'offences' such as adultery, desertion and cruelty – in order to obtain a divorce. This was usually very costly and complex because it involved a type of trial with a judge, barristers and so on. The Divorce Reform Act added a new rule. Divorce can also be granted on the grounds of irretrievable (that is, permanent) breakdown, once the couple have completed the legal formality of two years of separation or five years of separation if one spouse objects. This is a cheaper option and does not involve the need for a public hearing.

   However, 'quickie' divorces are also available, in which, one spouse can sue the other on grounds such as adultery and unreasonable behaviour. This type of divorce does involve going before a judge and proving fault. They tend therefore to be very expensive and used by celebrities.

   Since 1984, couples have been able to petition for divorce after the first anniversary of their marriage. The legal separation can begin 12 months after the wedding.

2. *Separation* is where couples agree to live apart after the breakdown of a marriage. In the past, when divorce was too difficult or expensive to obtain, separation was often the only solution. Some people, especially those with strong religious beliefs, may prefer this option, although their ex-partner can obtain a divorce after five years despite their objections.

3. *Empty-shell marriages* are those in which husband and wife stay together in name only. There may no longer be any love or intimacy between them. Today, such marriages are likely to end in separation or divorce, although this type of relationship may persist for the sake of children or for religious or economic reasons.

Trends in divorce
Three distinct major trends in divorce can be observed since 1938.

> In 1938, there were only 6,000 divorces granted in the UK but this figure had increased almost tenfold by 1970 to 58,239. In 1993, the number of divorces peaked at 165,000.

> Apart from some fluctuations, the general trend in divorce between 1994 and 2012 has been downwards, with 118,140 divorces in 2012.

> The period 2010–2012 saw a fluctuation in divorce rates – up in 2010, down in 2011 and up to 118,140 in 2012. However, the 2012 figure is still 20 per cent lower than it was in 2002. The ONS optimistically states that there are now signs that for those marrying since 2000 the proportion of those marriages ending in divorce is actually in decline.

The ONS identified a number of additional statistical facts in 2012.

> The younger a couple are when they get married, the more likely it is that the marriage will end in divorce. For example, divorce is highest in the 25–29 age group – these people are more likely to have married in their late teens or early 20s.

> It is expected that 34 per cent of marriages will end in divorce by the 20th wedding anniversary. An additional 6 per cent of marriages are expected to have ended by the 20th wedding anniversary because one of the spouses has died. Therefore 60 per cent of marriages are expected to survive to their 20th anniversary.

> 'Silver splitters' – the number of people aged over 60 who are divorcing – have risen by 45 per cent since 2002.

Another way to look at these trends is to look at the divorce rate. This refers to the number of divorces per 1,000 married people. The divorce rate reached a height of 14.2 in 1994 but has fallen to 10.8 in 2012, a fifth lower than its level in 2002.

Why did divorce increase so dramatically between 1972 and 1993?

Changes in the law
There is no doubt that the Divorce Reform Act, especially the 'irretrievable breakdown' option, made divorce both easier and cheaper. For example, there were 74,000 divorces in 1971 but this climbed to 119,000 in 1972 when the Act became law. The number of divorces continued to climb steeply thereafter until 1993. It is highly likely that many couples who had been in empty-shell marriages or who could not afford to divorce after separating before 1972 took the opportunity of the new rule to escape from their unhappy marriages.

However, sociologists argue that there other influences in addition to the Divorce Reform Act.

Changes in attitudes
Sociologists note that legal changes often reflect other changes in society, especially changes in attitudes. In particular, they argue that social expectations about marriage changed dramatically in this period. This can be illustrated in a number of ways.

> Functionalist sociologists argue that high divorce rates are evidence that marriage is more valued today and that people are demanding higher standards of marital behaviour from their partners. Couples are no longer prepared to put up with unhappy, empty-shell marriages or to take their relationships for granted. People want more from their marriage than just companionship – they are increasingly demanding emotional and sexual compatibility and equality in decision-making and domestic tasks. Functionalists argue that some people are willing to go through a number of partners to achieve these goals.

> Feminists note that women's expectations of marriage have radically changed since the 1970s compared with previous generations. In 2012, 65 per cent of divorce petitions were initiated by wives. Thornes and Collard (1979) argued that this trend supports the view that women expect far more from marriage than men and, in particular, that they value friendship in marriage and emotional gratification more than men do. Women may be using divorce to escape particular marriages when their husbands fail to live up to their high expectations. In 2012, 54 per cent of women-initiated divorces were on the grounds of the husband's unreasonable behaviour, which supports this feminist perspective.

> Before the 1970s, if women were unhappily married and/or trapped in empty-shell marriages, it would have been difficult for them to escape the marriage because they were likely to be highly dependent on their husband's wages. The entry of women into the labour force in large numbers resulted in an independent wage and more choice available to women when it came to the ending of a marriage.

> Hart (1976) notes that increasing divorce rates may also be a reaction to the frustration that many working wives feel if they continue to be seen by their husband as responsible for the bulk of housework and childcare.

> Similarly, increased divorce may be the outcome of tensions resulting from women taking over the traditional male role of breadwinner in some households, especially if the male is unemployed.

The secularisation of society
This period also saw some profound attitudinal change as divorce was no longer associated with stigma and shame. This was partly due to a general decline in religious beliefs and practices, or secularisation.

The declining influence of the extended family
There was probably a decline in the social controls exerted by extended kin and close-knit communities,

which traditionally had put pressure on couples to stay together in order to avoid the 'wicked' and 'shameful' labels associated with divorce. Consequently, in a society dominated by privatised nuclear families, the view that divorce can lead to greater happiness for the individual became more acceptable. This view was even more likely if divorce involved escaping from an abusive relationship or if an unhappy marriage was causing emotional damage to children. However, it is important to recognise that such attitudes were not necessarily a sign of a casual attitude towards divorce. Most people experienced divorce (and continue to do so) as an emotional and traumatic event, equivalent to bereavement. They are normally also very aware of the severe impact it may have on children.

The postmodernist theory of divorce

The postmodernist sociologists Beck and Beck-Gernsheim (1995) argue that increasing divorce rates are the product of a rapidly changing and postmodern world, in which the traditional rules and rituals of love, romance and relationships no longer apply. They argue that the postmodern world is characterised by three important social influences.

> *Individualisation* – People are under less pressure to conform to traditional collective goals set by members of the extended family, religion or culture. They now have the freedom to pursue individual goals. This makes them more selfish.

> *Conflict* – Beck and Beck-Gernsheim note that there is now more potential for conflict between men and women because there is a natural clash of interest between the selflessness required by marriage and the selfishness encouraged by individualisation. They argue that men and women are more likely to enter a marriage wanting different things. For example, one partner may be focused on their career while the other may want children. In a highly individualistic postmodern society, Beck and Beck-Gernsheim argue that this potential conflict – 'the chaos of love' – means that all too often marriage becomes a battleground in which selfishness triumphs over selflessness.

> *Choice* – Cultural and economic changes mean that people have a greater range of lifestyle choices and living arrangements available to them. As a result, there is now greater family diversity – people can choose to get married or cohabit and, most importantly, if they feel that the marriage is not working out they can choose to divorce. In the postmodern world, divorce is merely another lifestyle choice.

In your opinion, what are the strengths and weaknesses of the postmodern theory of divorce?

The decline of divorce

The ONS point out that, since 2000, the percentage of marriages ending in divorce appears to be falling. This recent decrease may be related to the following two factors.

> The age at which people first marry has been increasing, and research has shown that those marrying when they are older have a lower risk of divorce.

> Cohabitation has increased in recent years and the evidence suggests that this may be functioning to prevent fragile relationships from progressing to marriage and consequently to divorce.

It can be safely concluded that New Right fears about divorce have been exaggerated. This conclusion is based on four observations.

1. It may be true that about 40 per cent of all marriages will end in divorce but 60 per cent are successful.

2. Over 75 per cent of children are living with both natural parents who are legally married.

3. According to the ONS, the average marriage in the UK lasts 32 years.

4. Two-fifths of all marriages are remarriages (in which one or both partners have been divorced). Divorce does not mean that people are becoming anti-marriage. It simply means that they want to escape one particular marriage. Remarriage rates suggest that people are not put off by a previous marriage going wrong.

This final observation does suggest that eventually monogamy (one partner for life) will be replaced by serial monogamy (a series of long-term relationships resulting in cohabitation and/or marriage). However, as the Marriage Foundation think tank concludes, marriage is far from becoming an obsolete institution, as the New Right fear, and, ironically, cohabitation is probably the reason why it has become stronger in recent years and why divorce is no longer the massive problem that it was 20 years ago.

Divorce and family diversity

One-parent families

In 1961, only 2 per cent of all UK households were made up of one-parent (sometimes called single-parent) households. However, by 2012, the ONS estimated that there were approximately 2 million such families with dependent children in Britain, making up about a quarter of all families in the UK. About 24 per cent of people under the age of 19 lived in a one-parent family in 2012, that is, approximately 3 million children.

Kiernan and Holmes (2010) found that rates of one parenthood vary according to ethnicity. Their research found that lone parenthood was most common among Black and mixed-race mothers, particularly in deprived urban areas in the major cities of the UK.

In 2012, 91 per cent of one-parent families were headed by women, and 49 per cent of single mothers had had their children within marriage but were since separated, divorced or widowed. It is culturally expected in the UK, because of familial ideology (which is often reinforced by family courts), that women should take on the main caring responsibilities for any children when relationships break down.

However, Haskey (2002) also identified a fast-growing group of female single parents made up of those who have never married or cohabited. Contrary to popular belief, this group is not composed of teenagers, who actually make up less than 2 per cent of single parents. Instead, Haskey notes that an increasing number of middle-class career women are electing to have children in their late 30s and early 40s, and such women are choosing to bring these children up alone.

One parent families face many challenges, including balancing professional and family life.

In contrast, New Right sociologists suggest that there is a large group of single mothers who have never married or cohabited, who are long-term unemployed, less educated and attracted to lone motherhood by the 'perverse incentive' of being able to claim welfare benefits. Certainly 2013 statistics suggest that approximately 650,000 single parents are currently

not in work, and are therefore dependent on state financial support.

The New Right and one-parent families

New Right sociologists typically see the lone-parent family as an inherently second-rate and imperfect, 'broken' or 'fractured' family type. They argue that such families are caused by adults who put their own selfish needs before those of their children, and by the state's willingness to pay out billions of pounds in benefits to people who live in this type of family.

They are particularly critical of families headed by lone mothers, arguing that children from such families lack self-discipline and can be emotionally disturbed by the lack of a firm father figure in their lives.

Flouri and Buchanan's (2002) study of 17,000 children from families that had experienced separation and divorce found that in families where fathers were still involved with their children, the children were more successful in gaining educational qualifications and continued to seek out educational opportunities in adult life. They were less likely to get into trouble with the police and less likely to become homeless. Such children also grew up to enjoy more stable and satisfying relationships with their adult partners. However, Buchanan found that if conflict between parents continued after divorce, children could become vulnerable to mental health problems.

The Centre for Social Justice report 'Fractured Families' (2013), reported that a child being brought up in a one-parent family headed by a lone mother is 'more likely to:

> grow up in poorer housing

> experience behavioural problems

> perform less well in school and gain fewer educational qualifications

> need more medical treatment

> leave school and home when young

> become sexually active, pregnant or a parent at an early age

> report more depressive symptoms and higher levels of smoking, drinking and other drug use during adolescence and adulthood' (p. 53).

The New Right believe that in communities where there is a shortage of father involvement, the presence of other positive male role models, such as male primary school teachers, is vital. However, they point out that one in four English primary schools have no full-time qualified male teachers – this affects over 360,000 boys. In areas with high levels of one-parent families, only one-third of primary schools had male teachers. It is suggested that this lack of positive role models for boys may be responsible for their underachievement, compared with the success of girls.

The critique of the New Right stance on one-parent families

A number of crucial weaknesses can be observed with regard to the New Right perspective on one-parent families.

> A study of the impact of family breakdown on children's wellbeing conducted by Mooney *et al.* (2009) suggests that parental conflict is more important than parental separation as an influence in producing negative outcomes in children. They contrasted couple families experiencing high levels of conflict with one-parent families and found that children in the former were more likely to have emotional or behavioural problems than children in the latter.

> Ford and Millar (1998) argue that the 'perverse incentive' argument is also flawed when the quality of life of lone parents is examined. Many experience poverty, debt and material hardship despite being paid state benefits. Ford and Millar's survey found that many single mothers attempted to protect their children from poverty by spending less on themselves.

> Ford and Millar suggest that New Right analyses strongly imply that the poverty that single mothers experience is the result of 'choosing' this lifestyle. However, they argue that the New Right have misinterpreted this relationship. Their survey of single mothers suggests that poverty is a major cause of single parenthood. Single women from poor socio-economic backgrounds living on council estates with higher than average rates of unemployment are more likely than others to become single mothers. Motherhood is regarded as a desired and valued goal by these women because it is a realistic alternative to their poor economic prospects. Surveys of such women

suggest that children are a great source of love and pride, and most lone parents put family life at the top of things they regard as important.

> Feminist sociologists maintain that the one-parent family is unfairly discriminated against because of familial ideology, which emphasises the nuclear family ideal. This ideal leads to the negative labelling of one-parent families by teachers, social workers, housing departments, police and the courts. Consequently, housing officers may allot them a council house or flat on a problem estate because they label such families a problem. This may produce a self-fulfilling prophecy as their children go to failing inner-city schools, come into contact with children who are delinquent or criminal, and are criminalised by a police force which may label everyone who lives on a 'problem' estate as potentially criminal through the use of frequent stop and search policing.

> New Right sociologists rarely consider that single parenthood may be preferable to the domestic violence that is inflicted by some husbands on their wives and children. Single parenthood is rarely a permanent state. It lasts about five years on average and most single parents remarry and form another type of nuclear family in which a father is present – the step-family (also known as the reconstituted or blended family). Moreover, critics note that the New Right are dishonest in that they are not targeting or criticising all one-parent families. The reality is that they are focused on poor families. They rarely make the same criticisms of the thousands of middle-class one-parent families that exist in the UK. In this sense, the New Right's critique of one-parent families is ethnocentric. Finally, it is rarely reported that the majority of one-parent families bring up their children successfully to be relatively well-adjusted and law-abiding citizens and workers.

RECONSTITUTED FAMILIES

Step-families or reconstituted families are one of the fastest growing types of family in the UK. The main causes of this family form are divorce and remarriage. For example, in 2009, 19.1 per cent of marriages involved the remarriage of one partner, while 15.8 per cent involved the remarriage of both partners. However, it should also be noted that cohabiting couples may have children from previous relationships living with them. In 2013, the ONS estimated that 8 per cent of families in England and Wales – about 540,000 in all – were step-families, and that one in three people in the UK is now a step-parent, stepchild, adult stepchild, step-sibling or step-grandparent.

In 2010, 78 per cent of step-families consisted of a natural mother, her offspring and a stepfather. However, 18 per cent of step-families had a natural father, his children and a stepmother, while 4 per cent of step-families included children from both relationships.

Couples who have remarried often choose to have more children with their new partner. These 'new' children become the half-brothers and sisters of the stepchildren. For example, in 2001, it was estimated that 57 per cent of married couples in step-families have their own children. Some American sociologists distinguish between reconstituted families and blended families – the former merely include stepchildren, while the latter contain stepchildren plus half-brothers and sisters.

Reconstituted families are unique because children are also likely to have close ties with their other natural parent. An increasing number of children experience co-parenting, where they spend half their week with their mother and stepfather and the other half with their father. Some family experts see co-parenting as a characteristic of bi-nuclear families – two separate households following a divorce or separation are really one family system as far as children are concerned.

De'Ath and Slater's (1992) study of step-parenting identified a number of challenges facing reconstituted families.

> Children may find themselves pulled in two directions, especially if the relationship between their natural parents continues to be strained. They may feel they are being disloyal to their natural parent if they are seen to like or get on with the step-parent. Martin (2013) notes that the stepmother with good intentions may become a target for the children's resentment about the amount of change in their lives and their natural mother's unhappiness. In the children's minds, she is transformed into the 'wicked' step-mother who is the cause of all their problems.

> Strained relations between step-parents and children may therefore be the norm in these families, especially if the step-child is unwilling to accept the newcomer as a 'mother' or 'father', or is unwilling to accept disciplinary action from the step-parent. Martin argues that such conflict is normal in the first few years of step-family life.

> The step-parent may resent children from the previous relationship because he or she sees them as a symbol of love or a sexual relationship with another person. This could lead to physical abuse of such children. A significant number of children have been killed or injured by male step-parents in the UK.

Reconstituted families may be further complicated if the new couple decide to have children of their own, which may create the potential for envy and conflict among existing children. Some fathers may cut themselves off from children who are the product of a previous relationship because they want to start afresh with a 'new' family, or they may attempt to compensate for a new baby by lavishing time and money on older children living with their mother. The appearance of a new baby may also complicate relations with the ex-partner and the grandparents of the other children.

SINGLEHOOD

One of the most dramatic post-war changes in Britain has been the increase in single-person households. In 2013, 7.7 million people, or 13 per cent of the UK population, lived alone. This is nearly four times higher than it was 40 years ago. However, this reflects a common trend across Europe where the average proportion of single households is 14 per cent.

The single-person household is now the biggest category of household in the UK, in that it makes up 30 per cent of all households in England and Wales. This means that there are almost twice as many single-person households than there are traditional nuclear families containing two parents and dependent children.

About 4.1 million of these households are aged between 16 and 64. The majority of these single households – 58 per cent – were male as males are more likely than females never to marry. However, for those aged 65 and over, the pattern is reversed: the majority – 68 per cent – of people living alone at this age are women. This reflects women's superior life expectancy and the fact that husbands are typically older than wives. The ONS estimate that there are about 1.7 million widows living alone in the UK – this is three times higher than the number of widowers.

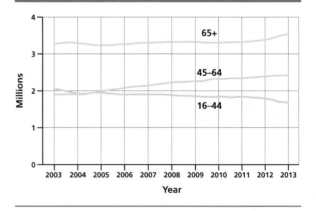

Figure 4.4.2 People living alone: by age-group, 2003 to 2013

The statistics also highlight how trends on living alone have changed between 2003 and 2013. The biggest change is among the middle-aged: those aged between 45 and 64 have experienced a 28 per cent increase in living alone, which is probably due to rising divorce rates.

There has been a 19 per cent fall in the number of younger people living alone. There is evidence that young people are living in the parental home for much longer periods compared with the past because they cannot afford to enter the housing market. The rise in youth unemployment has probably also contributed to the decision to stay in the family home. However, studies also show that there has been an increase in young professional adults who elect to share flats or houses with others.

There are also ethnic variations in living alone. For example, 16 per cent of Whites were living alone in 2011 compared with only 7 per cent of British Indians and 4 per cent of British Pakistanis. The ONS speculates that these variations probably relate to cultural, religious and economic differences. For example, the emphasis on extended kin obligations in working-class Asian communities may result in young people failing to consider the possibility of leaving the family home for long periods. However, 23 per cent of African Caribbeans and 16 per cent of mixed-race individuals were also living alone in 2011.

There are a number of explanations for the increase in single-person households among younger age groups.

> More women are gaining financial independence and choosing singlehood as a creative option before they elect eventually to settle down, although some are opting for voluntary childlessness in favour of their career.

> Trends in marriage suggest that people are marrying later and have other priorities, such as going to university and developing their careers.

> The increase in divorce creates both one-parent families and single-person households.

However, it is also important to note that for many young people, singlehood is only a temporary phase before they establish a couple relationship and a nuclear family.

One in ten people in Britain today has made what is seen as a growing, and increasingly acceptable, lifestyle choice known as LAT ('living apart together'), in which couples who regard themselves as firmly committed to one another have separate homes through choice or circumstance. Duncan *et al.* (2013) surveyed 572 people who don't live with their partners and found LATs are predominantly young – of the 572, 61 per cent were under 35. The researchers conclude that up to a quarter of people documented as single in fact have a partner living elsewhere. They identified three reasons for choosing to live apart but together: 30 per cent were LATs from choice, where one or both partners wanted to live apart; 19 per cent were LATS because of 'constraints', meaning that they wanted to share a home but circumstances such as unsuitable accommodation made it impossible or extremely difficult; and 12 per cent were 'situational', meaning that they regarded their lifestyle choice as the best possible choice considering their circumstances.

THE LIFE-COURSE

Postmodernist sociologists argue that sociological studies of the family should focus on the 'life-courses' of individuals rather than 'the family'. In other words, sociologists should examine the ways in which lives evolve and change as people experience personal events or **rites of passage** such as marriage, the birth of a child, divorce or the death of a partner.

UNDERSTAND THE CONCEPT

In many cultures, the most important stages of life – birth, puberty, marriage and death – are often marked by ceremonies in which the community or family comes together to celebrate or mourn. These ceremonies (for example, the funeral) are **rites of passage** – they symbolically acknowledge movement along the life-course.

Tamara Hareven (2000) notes that the life-course is made up of several stages: birth; early childhood (being a baby); infancy (being a toddler); childhood (beginning with compulsory schooling); adolescence (being a teenager); young adulthood (18–29); adulthood (30–50); middle age (51–64); old age (beginning with retirement); and death.

Hareven notes that a life-course might affect the structure and dynamics of family life in a number of ways. For example, a child might experience a settled nuclear family from early childhood to adolescence but a one-parent family thereafter because his or her parents separate and divorce. This might lead to a dual-parenting arrangement, or the child may no longer have any contact with the father. As adolescence develops, the child may experience the reconstituted or step-family (in which relationships might be tense). Figure 4.4.3 shows how someone might live in up to eight types of household before they reach 30.

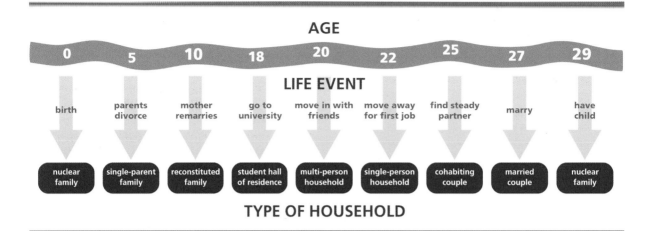

Figure 4.4.3 *How an individual can live in eight types of household before the age of 30*

As people progress through the life-course stages into middle and old age, family life continues to evolve. For example, when children leave home, parents have to cope with the concept of the empty-nest household. They are no longer distracted by children and may have to learn to live with one another again. Some older people may elect to divorce at this stage. Many of them will derive emotional satisfaction from being grandparents and be hands-on with helping out their adult children with childcare. However, many of these decisions and choices may be shaped by events such as death, sickness and disability, and by influences such as wealth, poverty, ethnicity and geography. Some people will decide to continue as a single-person household after the death of their partner. Others may elect to live with their children or enter a residential home or sheltered accommodation.

Life-course analysis therefore focuses on the diversity of family practices that occur during the life-course. Postmodernists, such as Stacey, argue that family life is not about living in a static and unchanging ideal type of family structure. Families and households are not concrete things that people should strive to attain, as argued by functionalist and New Right sociologists. Instead, family life is in a continual state of flux and change. There is therefore no such thing as the perfect family, because interactions between family members and the family dynamics that result are unique to that group of people. If every experience of family is different, there can be no universal criteria by which 'families' can be judged as right or wrong. Postmodernists argue that sociologists need to focus on what family members regard as important (as opposed to what sociologists think is important) in order to find out how family dynamics give meaning to people's lives.

Pahl and Spencer (2001) also argue that the concept of 'family' is no longer useful to describe personal relationships in the 21st century. They suggest that people

no longer feel they have to maintain relationships with other kin out of duty or obligation. Instead, people are now more likely to subscribe to 'personal communities', which are made up of a combination of those relatives and fictive kin, such as friends, who are valued for their friendship and social support.

Weeks *et al.* (2001) suggest that the concept of the 'family' is being used by non-heterosexuals to denote something broader than the traditional heterosexual version. Weeks *et al.* note that the gay model of the family often refers to kin-like networks of relationships mainly based on friendships rather than blood or children. As Weeks *et al.* note "these have a cultural and symbolic meaning for the people who participate or feel a sense of belonging in and through them" (p. 19).

The sociology of personal life

Smart (2007) recommends using the term 'personal life' instead of 'family' because the latter concept is too often associated with value judgements about 'ideal' or 'normal' family types. Smart argues that the concept of 'personal life' is more neutral and flexible because it goes beyond marriage and biological kin to include newer types of relationships, such as post-divorce relationships, same-sex relationships, relationships created by new reproductive technologies, relationships in which people commit to each other but live apart open relationships and friendships.

In which ways might personal lives be affected by new forms of media such as social networking sites?

The idea that sociologists should focus on the life-course is not a new one. Robert and Rhona Rapoport (1976) argued that the life-cycle was the main cause of family diversity in modern societies, rather than social change or declining morality. In addition to life-cycle diversity, they identified five other types of diversity in family and household structures and relationships.

> *Structural diversity* simply refers to variations in family size or organisation. For example, most families, are nuclear but some are one-parent, extended, reconstituted, blended and bi-nuclear.

> *Domestic diversity* – there will be variations in the way men and women divide and manage childcare and housework.

> *Cultural diversity* – this refers to the impact of global migration on family structures and dynamics, as outlined in Chapter 3.

> *Class diversity* – this refers to social-class variations in the quality of family relationships and lifestyles. For example, upper-class family life may be very different from that experienced by middle-class or working-class families.

> *Cohort diversity* – a cohort is a group of people born over the same period of time (for example, the baby boomer generation born between 1946 and 1964). Cohorts or generations often have a qualitatively

different experience of family life compared with their parents' generation because of the influence of wider social and historical events, such as whether the economy is doing well or badly, changes in the law, global migration, racism, and so on. Family life, especially children's experience of it, in 2015 may be very different from that experienced in 1955 because of consumerism and access to media technology such as games consoles, mobile phones and the internet.

CONCLUSIONS

There is no doubt that marriage and therefore family life have undergone considerable change. Cohabitation and divorce, once regarded as immoral forms of behaviour, have now become part of everyday life and no longer attract the moral disapproval they did in the past. The evidence also clearly shows that the notion of an ideal family type should be abandoned because family diversity is now the norm. The postmodernist view that sociologists should look at the life-course in order to understand the diversity of family types and internal dynamics in just one individual's life is a convincing one.

CHECK YOUR UNDERSTANDING

1. Identify the difference between monogamy and polygamy.

2. Identify the three causes of the decline of marriage according to Patricia Morgan.

3. Define what is meant by the 'general marriage rate', and describe what happened to it between 1970 and 2009.

4. Define 'the reconstituted family'.

5. Define 'the life-course'.

6. Outline and explain the popularity of cohabitation.

7. Explain why wives are more likely than husbands to initiate divorce.

8. Explain why postmodernists believe it is more useful to study 'the life-course' and 'personal life' than families.

9. Analyse and explain why more people are living alone.

10. Outline and evaluate the view that the rise in divorce in the later part of the 20th century indicates that marriages were becoming stronger.

TAKE IT FURTHER

Carry out a mini-survey across three different age groups (for example, 15–20, 25–30, and 35–40), investigating experiences of and attitudes towards marriage, cohabitation, one-parent families, step-families, co-parenting, teenage pregnancy, and so on. Does your survey demonstrate the dominance of one family type or family diversity?

4.5 DOMESTIC LABOUR, POWER RELATIONSHIPS AND THE FAMILY

LEARNING OBJECTIVES

> Demonstrate knowledge and understanding of gender roles, domestic labour and power relationships within the family in contemporary society (AO1).

> Apply and analyse theories of the family and evidence from sociological studies of the family to gender roles, domestic labour and power relationships within the family (AO2).

> Evaluate sociological explanations of gender roles, domestic labour and power relationships within the family in contemporary society (AO3).

INTRODUCING THE DEBATE

The functionalist sociologist Talcott Parsons argued that the nuclear family was evenly balanced with regard to power relationships. Although the roles of husband and wife were fundamentally different in terms of their contribution to domestic labour, Parsons claimed that they both played an equally important role in the maintenance of the family unit.

In the late 20th century, sociologists such as Young and Wilmott continued this theme and claimed that gender roles within marriage were positively evolving in the direction of equality in domestic labour. This was allegedly due to women increasingly taking on economic responsibilities in the form of paid work outside the home and men responding by getting more involved in childcare and housework. The family was therefore portrayed as an egalitarian institution in which husbands and wives shared domestic chores, parenting and decision-making.

In contrast to this optimism, feminists have generally been sceptical about the claim that modern marriage is characterised by equality. Fifty years ago, Betty Friedan argued that women were enslaved by marriage and domesticity, and particularly housework, which she noted was not regarded as 'real' work because it was both unpaid and, consequently, under-valued. Feminists today, such as Ann Oakley, generally agree that equality in domestic life is still not the norm. As Oakley said in 2014, "what people say is more egalitarian than what they do".

This chapter investigates how domestic labour is organised by couples today, in order to see which of these two points of view has the most validity. It looks at both quantitative and qualitative studies of marriage and the domestic division of labour in the UK.

THE DISTRIBUTION OF DOMESTIC LABOUR IN THE HOME

In their study of working-class families in the East End of London in the 1950s, Young and Wilmott observed that **conjugal roles** and the **domestic division of labour** in working-class families were clearly segregated. Men were primarily wage earners and were responsible for very few domestic tasks around the home. It was rare for a father to attend the birth of his child or to be involved with the day-to-day care of his children. Men regarded themselves as the head of the household – they exercised this social power on the basis of their superior earning power and, consequently, were responsible for family discipline and decision-making. Furthermore, they spent their leisure time with other men rather than their spouses. In contrast, few females worked outside the home and, consequently, they were often economically dependent on their husband, who would allocate 'housekeeping' money. The wife was usually exclusively responsible for all aspects of housework and childcare. Wives generally exercised little power over decision-making and were sometimes the victims of their spouse's physical power in the form of domestic violence. Power relations in the home therefore were generally unequal.

UNDERSTAND THE CONCEPT

Conjugal roles are the domestic roles or tasks that spouses are primarily responsible for within their married or cohabiting relationship. The **domestic division of labour** refers to the way the couple divides up these domestic tasks.

However, on the basis of research they conducted in the 1970s, Young and Wilmott claimed that men and women's attitudes towards the distribution of labour in the home had undergone a radical change so that in both middle-class and working-class households, conjugal roles were more likely to be jointly shared. They argued that this trend towards joint conjugal roles meant that marriage in the 1970s was likely to be **egalitarian**.

UNDERSTAND THE CONCEPT

Egalitarian marriage essentially means that power within the marriage is equally distributed, rather than being exclusively in the hands of the male (patriarchal).

Young and Wilmott claimed that this change in the nature of conjugal roles and the distribution of power in the family was caused by four major social changes that had occurred during the 1950s and 1960s.

> Slum clearance programmes had relocated many working-class families to council estates and, in the process, had fragmented many extended families. Isolation from extended kin meant that couples were forced to rely on each other for social support and companionship.

> Greater educational and job opportunities led to larger numbers of working-class people experiencing geographical mobility, which also caused isolation from extended kin.

> Women started going out to work in greater numbers than ever before and began making a significant economic contribution to the standard of living of their family. Families could afford to buy goods (such as televisions) and labour-saving devices (such as vacuum cleaners), which made the home a more attractive place to be for both husband and wife.

In the 1950s and 1960s, going out to work gave women more economic independence than they would have ever known before.

> Women acquired more power in a variety of ways, such as over their own fertility because of access to contraception, and economic power through working and no longer being exclusively dependent on money from their husbands. These powers meant that women could put pressure on men to do more at home.

Young and Wilmott concluded that these changes had resulted in a new family form – the symmetrical family (a type of nuclear unit) – in which men and women play similar roles to one another. In this type of family, both spouses were involved in paid work and therefore made a joint contribution to the family income and bills, while housework and childcare tasks were more fairly distributed. Decision-making was shared and spouses enjoyed spending leisure time together.

The feminist response to Young and Wilmott

The feminist sociologist Ann Oakley (1974) responded to Young and Wilmott's ideas that marriage was becoming increasingly egalitarian with her own academic study of domestic work. As Chambers (2012) notes, until Oakley's study appeared housework had not been considered worthy of study by male sociologists because it was regarded as an everyday private activity. Chambers notes that "the domestic sphere of labour had been marginalised and rendered invisible" (p. 30) by **malestream sociology**.

UNDERSTAND THE CONCEPT

Malestream sociology refers to the notion that male sociologists dominated sociological research and often defined what was 'worthy' of study. This generally reflected male rather than female concerns and issues.

The idea that equality is a central characteristic of marriage was strongly opposed by Oakley, who rejected the notion of a symmetrical family. She argued that patriarchy was still very much a major characteristic of modern nuclear families and that women still occupied a subordinate and dependent role within the family and in wider society.

Oakley interviewed 40 housewives living in suburban London and found some quantitative evidence of husbands helping in the home but little evidence of symmetry or equality. Only 15 per cent of husbands had a high level of participation in housework, but even this group saw housework as 'her work' rather than something to be jointly shared.

Oakley's research was carried out over 40 years ago but recent research suggests that her view may still hold true. Contemporary feminist sociologists suggest that there is little hard evidence in the 21st century for equality in marriage with regard to domestic labour, despite the fact that many women are now engaged in paid work and working long hours outside the home. The gender revolution in the home so celebrated by Young and Wilmott seems to have fizzled out, as can be clearly seen in recent studies of the distribution of domestic labour.

Research by Craig (2007) found that women do between one-third and one-half more housework than men. She argues that this inequality begins when a couple move in together and before they have children. She calls this aspect of domestic inequality the 'partnership penalty'. Her research found that when couples marry, the wife's unpaid domestic labour rises in volume whilst the husband does less housework compared with when he was single. She also discovered a 'mother penalty' – the decision to have a baby results in the mother being financially worse-off across her lifetime, compared to men in general and child-free women.

Ben-Galim and Thompson (2013) found that eight out of ten married women carried out more household chores than men, while only one married man in ten did the same amount of cleaning and washing as his wife. They concluded that patterns of housework have changed only slightly since the 1980s, as illustrated by their findings that more than eight out of ten women born in 1958 said they did more laundry and ironing than their partner, compared with seven out of ten women born in 1970. These figures suggest an incomplete gender revolution.

A survey conducted by Mumsnet in 2014 questioned nearly 1,000 working mothers and found that women did double the housework of men despite doing a full day at work. Moreover, when it came to major events such as Christmas, 81 per cent of the women surveyed said they were mainly responsible for organising events.

Another survey of 1,000 men and women by the BBC in 2014 argued that modern marriage was characterised by 'chore wars' rather than equality and symmetry. It found evidence of consistent conflict between partners over domestic chores. Two-thirds of those aged between 18 and 34 admitted that they regularly argued with their partners over housework. Women were particularly frustrated with their partners over how little they did around the home or about the male standard of cleanliness, which many felt did not achieve their standards.

The quantitative evidence regarding the domestic division of labour clearly supports the feminist argument that women today are experiencing a 'second shift' or 'dual burden' with regard to housework. They therefore have two jobs – one paid and one unpaid – and experience the double burden of trying to be effective at both.

Sociological studies have also noted that the distinction between work and leisure or free time is less clear-cut for married women. For example, Green (1996) found that wives usually interpret leisure time as time free from both paid work and family commitments, whereas husbands saw all time outside paid work as their leisure time. In Green's study, women felt they were on call with regard to domestic duties, and especially childcare, 24 hours a day.

However, although the gender revolution in terms of domestic labour has some way to go, there may be good news in favour of equality occurring at some future date.

Men today are doing a great deal more around the home compared with their fathers and grandfathers. For example, Kan *et al.* (2009) found that the time spent by British men on domestic work had risen from 90 minutes per day in the 1960s to 148 minutes per day by 2004. Crompton (1997) argues that as women's earning power increases relative to men's, so men do more in the home. In 2015, women's earnings still remain unequal at about three-quarters of those of men. However, Crompton's analysis concludes that if female earnings were to improve then so too will the division of labour in the home. Research does also indicate that men are more likely to be involved in childcare rather than housework.

MEN AND CHILDCARE

Fisher *et al.* (1999) argued that British fathers' care of infants and young children rose 800 per cent between 1975 and 1997, from 15 minutes to two hours on the average working day, while Smith (2009) found that fathers in nuclear families carry out an average of 25 per cent of the family's childcare-related activities during the week, and one-third at weekends. Maume (2008) found that in families in which mothers worked, more than one father in four took emergency time off work to care for their sick child.

However, sociologists need to be cautious in their interpretation of this data because it does not say a great deal about the quality of the relationship between the father and the child. For example, Craig found that often men only engage in childcare when the mother is nearby, while most of the time fathers spent with their children was spent playing with them or talking to them. Craig noted that women's time with children was mainly spent practically servicing them: feeding, clothing, cleaning them, and so on. Women often found it difficult to find the time for the sorts of quality interaction with children enjoyed by men because they were more likely to be looking after children while undertaking other tasks such as preparing meals.

The majority of time that fathers spend with their children is spent playing and talking.

DECISION-MAKING IN FAMILIES

An important aspect of equality and symmetry for Young and Wilmott was the spouses' sharing of family decision-making, which in traditional patriarchal families with segregated roles had always been dominated by men. Some sociologists have therefore focused on the distribution of power within marriages with regard to decision-making and argue that true equality, in terms of the domestic division of labour, can only occur if decision-making or power is shared equally between a couple.

Stephen Edgell's classic (1980) study of professional couples found that decision-making in nuclear families could be allocated to three broad categories.

> Very important decisions – these generally were economic or financial decisions involving finance, a change of job or moving house. Edgell found that these decisions were either taken by the husband alone or taken jointly but with the husband having the final say. Edgell concluded that the husband's power mainly derived from his superior earning power.

> Important decisions – these decisions focused on the quality of family life or children's lives, such as those about children's schooling (for example, whether to choose private or state schools) or where to go on holiday. These were normally taken jointly but seldom by the wife alone, probably because such decisions were likely to involve a substantial economic investment.

> Less important decisions – these decisions focused on the everyday minutiae of family life such as shopping for food, domestic items and children's clothing, and were usually made exclusively by the wife.

Why do you think less important decisions were made exclusively by the wife?

Hardill *et al.* (1997) repeated Edgell's research over a decade later and found few signs of change. She discovered that middle-class wives generally deferred to their husbands in major decisions involving where to live, the size of the mortgage, buying cars, etc. They concluded that the men in their sample were able to demand that the interests of their wives and families should be subordinated to the man's career because he was the major breadwinner. However, Gillian Leighton's (1992) research did discover that the power to influence and make family decisions changed when males became unemployed. In her study of professional couples, working wives often took over responsibility for bills and initiated cutbacks in spending.

Vogler and Pahl (2001) also found that decision making was shaped by income. In their study, only one-fifth of households were egalitarian decision-making units. Most household decision-making was controlled by men because they earned the higher incomes.

EMOTION WORK

As well as the practical aspects of domestic labour, some sociologists, such as Duncombe and Marsden (1995) argue that any measurement of equality within households must take account of 'emotion work'. This involves thinking about the emotional wellbeing and happiness of other members of the household and acting in ways which will be of emotional benefit to others. This might include:

› sustaining the relationship between fathers and children

› complimenting family members for their achievements

› smoothing over arguments between family members

› buying presents and cards for birthdays so that the family keeps in touch with close relatives and extended kin

› hugging family members and reassuring them of love

› planning and organising social events that others will enjoy.

Duncombe and Marsden argue that women take the major responsibility for the emotional wellbeing of their partners and children, in addition to paid work and responsibility for housework and childcare. In this sense, women actually work a 'triple shift'. Gabb (2008) argues that the activities that women routinely do, such as feeding the family, not only serve a pragmatic purpose, but they also perform a symbolic function, with mothers literally constructing a sense of family community and sense of belonging. The message of women's work in the family is essentially emotional. It is a practical way of confirming love and care and reinforces family bonds.

However, feminists point out that most family members generally benefit from women's emotion work but women themselves rarely do. Hochschild (2003) argues that mothers are rarely thanked for this work because what they do is gender bound – it is seen by other family members as part of their gendered duty. For example, if the father provides childcare, it is often interpreted by him as a gift to the mother; if the mother provides it, it is seen as her job.

Duncombe and Marsden carried out in-depth interviews with 40 couples and found that women felt that their male partners were lacking in terms of 'emotional participation': men found it difficult to express their feelings, to tell their partners how they felt about them, to relate emotionally to their children and to show gratitude for the work women did in the home. This increases the burden on

women because women feel they should attempt to compensate and please all parties in the family.

This triple shift and the inequality in the exchange of emotion associated with it often leads to the neglect of women's wellbeing, which can have negative consequences for women's happiness and their mental and physical health. A number of studies of marriage confirm this inequality in the exchange of emotion.

For example, Bernard's classic study of marriage (1982) found that the men in her study were more satisfied with their marriage than their wives, many of whom expressed emotional loneliness. Moreover, these men had no idea that their wives were so unhappy.

Loscocco and Walzer (2013) reviewed sociological and psychological studies of contemporary marriage and made the following findings.

› Women often express unhappiness and see problems in their marriage more than men do.

› Women are more likely to initiate divorce proceedings and are more than three times as likely as their former husbands to have strongly wanted the divorce. Bittman and Pixley (1997) suggest that inequality in the distribution of childcare, housework tasks and emotion work is the major cause of divorce in UK society.

› Once-married men are more likely to say that they want to marry again than once-married women.

Loscocco and Walzer also note that women find it exhausting to be the one who maintains the emotional temperature of a relationship and who keeps the ties to family and community going. This creates resentment, which can lead to marital tension and divorce.

LESBIAN COUPLES AND GENDER SCRIPTS

Gillian Dunne (1999) argues that the traditional division of domestic labour continues today because of what she calls deeply ingrained 'gender scripts' – these are the traditional or conventional social expectations or norms that set out the different gender roles that heterosexual men and women in relationships are expected to play. Such expectations are normally embodied in familial and patriarchal ideology.

In her study of 37 cohabiting lesbian couples with dependent children, Dunne found that such gender scripts do not operate to the same extent. Many of the characteristics of the traditional domestic division of labour do not exist in the lesbian family or household. For example, Dunne found evidence of symmetry and egalitarianism in her sample of lesbian households – both partners gave equal importance to each other's careers and viewed childcare positively. However, she did find that where one partner did much more paid work than the other, the time that each partner spent on domestic work was likely to be unequal.

Dunne's point about paid work was confirmed by Carrington (1999) who carried out an ethnographic study of gay and lesbian couples. He found that there was tension in these relationships about inequalities in the distribution of household tasks which was no different from that experienced by heterosexual couples. Carrington remained unconvinced that the domestic arrangements of lesbian and gay couples were somehow an example of equality that heterosexuals should aspire to imitate.

BUILD CONNECTIONS

Research by Croft (2014) suggests that the parental sharing of housework and childcare plays a key role in shaping the gender attitudes as well as the educational and career aspirations of children, especially daughters. The research found that fathers who were regularly involved with housework and childcare were more likely to raise daughters who aspired to higher education and careers such as accountancy and medicine than fathers who subscribed to traditional ideas about domestic labour. Croft notes "talking the talk about equality is important, but our findings suggest that it is crucial that dads 'walk the walk' as well – because their daughters clearly are watching".

EXPLANATIONS FOR INEQUALITIES IN DOMESTIC LABOUR AND POWER

Biology

Functionalists see the sexual division of labour in the home as brought about primarily by biological differences between the sexes. Parsons, for example, argued that women are 'naturally' suited to the caring of the young because of the fact that they physically bear children, while Murdock cited the greater physical strength of the male as the reason why men were able to dominate economic life.

What criticisms do you think feminist sociologists would make of the functionalist view that biological differences are the main cause of inequalities in power between men and women in families?

Familial and patriarchal ideology

Both feminist and postmodernist sociologists have long blamed familial ideology – the dominant idea that there is an ideal way to organise family life – for inequalities in power in the home. Bernardes (1999) argues that this ideology is essentially patriarchal in outlook, in that masculinity and fatherhood are still primarily associated with paid work, the breadwinner role, and the avoidance of domestic labour and responsibility for childcare, despite recent social, economic and cultural changes. This familial ideology also shapes cultural expectations about femininity, which is still primarily associated with motherhood and home-making despite the feminisation of the economy and workforce.

Leonard (2000) also argues that patriarchal ideology underpins dominant ideas about both paid work and domestic labour, and suggests that men resist change because the persistence of an unequal division of labour suits them. Oakley (2014) agrees and notes that "men are a privileged group and there is no reason they should give up their privilege unless they are forced to do so. Most of the change in men's behaviour has come about because the women they are involved with have put pressure on them to change. Men haven't, en masse, decided that housework is a good thing to do". The reinforcement of familial ideology in all walks of life is central to the continuation of this inequality.

O'Brien and Shamilt (2003) argue that ideological beliefs about masculine and feminine roles have discouraged men from participating in or taking responsibility for what this ideology regards as 'women's work'. This can particularly be seen in situations in which men have more time to do housework than their wives because they are unemployed or because the wife has a better paid and more demanding job than her husband. McKee and Bell (1986) argued that unemployed men in their study felt emasculated because paid work was central to their sense of self-esteem and masculine power. They therefore actively resisted increased involvement in housework because they interpreted it as 'women's work' and viewed it as degrading. They felt demeaned as men because they were being kept by their wives. Ramos (2003) found that in families where the man is not in paid work and his partner works full time, male domestic labour only just matches that of his partner.

The ideology of motherhood and fatherhood

Chambers argues that there is an ideology of motherhood organised around the idea of 'putting children's needs first'. She says "the mother is perceived as the core of the family, as its emotional stabiliser that keeps the whole family together." Data from the BSA survey (2012) supports Chambers' observations. Among the British population, 26 per cent still believed that most women should prioritise their caring role over having a job, while 45 per cent believed that the role of housewife was just as fulfilling as the role of worker; 30 per cent believed that preschool children suffer if their mother works.

Familial ideology therefore expects women to take on jobs that are compatible with family commitments. It also results in large numbers of mothers feeling guilty about working full time. Some actually give up work altogether because they believe that their absence somehow damages their children. Leonard argues that women who continue to see housework and childcare as an essential part of being a 'good wife and mother' are more likely to be satisfied with an unequal domestic division of labour than women who reject such roles.

FOCUS ON SKILLS: DON'T DARE CALL ME A HOUSEWIFE... I'M THE DOMESTIC CEO

Galstaun is the finance director, executive and travel agent for her Surrey family.

Natasha Galstaun, 43, runs a formidably tight domestic ship. "My husband has a busy job, so I run the household completely," she says. "He pays the mortgage but I look after everything else, from the bills, to childcare, to any DIY. I book all our holidays and social life and cook from scratch every night."

Galstaun, who lives in Surrey, quit her job as an interior designer in July to be a more hands-on parent to Sacha, 4, and Felix, 2. But, whatever you do, do not call her a housewife — or stay-at-home mother or home-maker, for that matter. Like many forty- and fifty-something women these days she sees herself more as a "domestic chief executive officer".

Mum is typically now the head accountant, financial adviser, executive decision maker, school liaison officer, chief administration expert and party planner. Also relatively new are the roles of family travel agent (with its accompanying hours on TripAdvisor and Sky-scanner), chauffeur and "playdate" co-ordinator: no self-respecting domestic CEO would leave her children to their own devices when they could be on team-building exercises. If the family firm's finances are good, she may turn human resources manager, delegating chores and childcare to staff. Nannies and tutors around exam time are also the norm. She also retains the traditional duties of cook, cleaner, decorator

and occasional nurse – regardless of whether she works full-time. "Housewife" no longer quite cuts it.

Research reveals the extent to which women in this age bracket now rule the roost: 93% of those surveyed claimed to make all or most of their family's financial decisions; 92% to be the one who chooses large home appliances; and 85% to decide where the clan goes on holiday. However, Gaby Hinsliff, a former newspaper political editor and author of *Half A Wife*, a guide to cracking the life-work balance, argues that "running a home is nothing like being a CEO, bar the hours. As a CEO, when you tell someone to do something they do it, without howling or telling you you're the worst CEO in the world. You don't get woken up by an employee at 2am asking for a drink. You also get to concentrate on the high-level fun stuff, whereas being a mum is the opposite. You have to do all the boring stuff for everyone else. It's more like being an intern – unpaid and you have to make a lot of hot drinks for ungrateful people."

Source: Hornak, F. 'Don't dare call me a housewife... I'm the domestic CEO', *The Times*, 25 November 2012

Questions

1. **Identify** what percentage of women claimed to make all or most of the family's financial decisions, according to research cited in the article.

2. **Identify** the responsibilities that Natasha Galstaun and the research featured claim that mothers are now responsible for in addition to being a 'cook, cleaner, decorator and nurse'.

3. **Analyse** how the content in the article challenges the studies cited throughout this chapter on decision-making, emotion work, marriage and fatherhood.

4. **Evaluate** the view that mothers are the Chief Executive Officers (CEOs) of families.

Miller (2010) points out that the responsibilities and practices associated with fatherhood are not as clear-cut or as morally regulated as those of motherhood. However, there is an ideology of fatherhood that is mainly associated with concepts such as 'breadwinner', family provider, head of the household, unemotional disciplinarian, and the notion that absent fathers are negative.

Warin *et al.* (1999), in their study of 95 families in Rochdale, found that fathers, mothers and teenage children overwhelmingly subscribed to the view that the male should be the breadwinner, despite changes in employment and family life. The majority of the sample believed that mothers should dominate childcare because they were the experts in parenting.

Gender socialisation of children

Some studies suggest that the socialisation of children is also shaped by familial ideology, so that when they grow up to be adults they are more likely to subscribe to traditional ideas about gender roles. Van Egmond *et al.* (2010) argue that the gender identity of children is firmly in place by the age of eight, and that children consequently have a very clear idea which jobs in the home belong to which sex. The normality of this everyday experience means that they are unlikely to challenge this inequality when they are older.

Social policy

Williams (2004) argues that state policy encourages female economic dependence on men (and therefore, inequalities in domestic labour and power). The lack of universal free childcare is regarded as an obstacle to gender equality, as is the expense of childcare in the UK which, according to Schober and Scott (2012), is higher than anywhere else in Europe.

Relative resources theory

This theory argues that the main cause of gender inequality in the home is economic. It is argued that men have a comparative economic advantage over women in terms of labour market characteristics and, therefore, human capital.

In terms of labour market characteristics, men generally enjoy access to a greater range of jobs, have greater job security, do not have their careers interrupted by children and earn higher pay. This means that the human capital of men – their work-related skills, knowledge and experience – is allegedly worth more than that of women. This gives men superior bargaining power in the home and, consequently, they choose to dominate decision-making and to elect not to share domestic labour and childcare.

Breene and Cook (2014) argue that the mass movement of women into the economy in the 1970s and the resulting increase in dual-earner couples led to women acquiring more economic power. They began to obtain 'relative economic resources' to their husbands and consequently they were in a better position to bargain with their partners about the allocation of domestic labour. Changes in the divorce law also increased women's bargaining power, in terms of the distribution of housework and childcare. Breene and Cook note that the increasing divorce rate seen in the 1970s and 1980s may have been women's response to men's reluctance or failure to change their domestic behaviour.

Empirical evidence has indeed shown that double income couples demonstrate a more egalitarian distribution of tasks. Harkness (2005) demonstrated that the burden of housework is more evenly split in families where women earn an amount that is equal to or greater than their partners, although this might have been because these families are able 'buy back' time through hired help such as cleaners, childminders and nannies. Sigle-Rushton (2010) also showed that the divorce rate is lower when fathers actively engage in housework and childcare, regardless of their wives' employment status.

However, this theory is weakened by the following facts.

> Households in which there is 50–50 equality are rare. In households where children are present, women generally put in twice as many housework hours as their partner even when they are earning a similar wage.

> It is predominantly women who take time off to look after sick children even if they have an equivalent occupational status and pay scale to their male partners.

> Full-time employed women increase their contribution to domestic chores when their partner loses their job. This is difficult to explain from the relative resources perspective.

Feminism

Marxist feminism

Marxist feminists argue that domestic labour performed by women serves the needs of capitalism, in that it maintains the present workforce and reproduces future labour power. Cox and Federici (2010) argue that under capitalism women have assumed the role of breeders, housewives and consumers of the goods manufactured by capitalism's factories. These ideas are explored in detail in Chapter 1.

Does the evidence presented in this chapter generally support the Marxist-feminist view that women have assumed the role of breeders, housewives and consumers in UK capitalist society?

Radical feminism

Radical feminists such as Delphy (1984) believe that "the first oppression is the oppression of women by men – women are an exploited class". The housewife role is therefore created by patriarchy (which existed well before capitalism appeared) and is geared to the service of men and their interests. This idea is also explored in Chapter 1.

Radical feminists argue that domestic violence is often used by men to threaten, control and punish women who complain about their exploitation in the home, or who fail to live up to the expectations of men with regard to being a 'good' partner, housewife or mother. Radical feminists therefore argue that as long as men have the capacity to threaten to commit such violence, there can never be equality within marriage.

Some criticisms of feminist theories

Feminist theories often fail to explain why women's roles vary across different cultures. For example, the mother/housewife role does not exist in all societies.

Catherine Hakim (1996) also suggests that feminists underestimate women's ability to make rational choices. She argues that some women choose to give more commitment to family and children, and so have less commitment to work than men have. Hakim demonstrates that part-time female workers in Germany, the UK and the USA are twice as 'traditional' as full-time women workers in their opinions about family gender roles. She argues that women generally feel they have two main choices in life.

› Half of women choose the 'employment career'. They aspire to well-paid jobs and will juggle the dual burden of paid work and a disproportionate share of housework and childcare if they get married and have children.

› Half of women choose the 'marriage career' – their main commitment is to their marriage and raising children. If they do paid work, it will be part-time work that fits around their domestic commitments. Hakim argues that marriage is seen to confer certain advantages for wives. As Chapman (2004) notes, these include "gaining social status through a husband's work, freedom from full-time employment, economic security and a chance to invest fully in the upbringing of children" (p. 91). Hakim argues that these women are more than happy to support their husband's careers by taking on the bulk of the domestic work and aren't interested in wielding equal power in the home.

Hakim therefore argues that feminism may be guilty of devaluing the role of mother/housewife as 'second-class'. For many women, housework and childcare, like paid work, have real and positive meaning. Such work may be invested with meaning for women because it is 'work done for love' and it demonstrates their commitment to their families.

She also claims that feminists probably underestimate the degree of power that women actually enjoy. The fact that many women divorce their husbands indicates that they have the power to leave a relationship if they are unhappy with it.

FOCUS ON SKILLS: STAY-AT-HOME MOTHERS – 'WE DON'T CARE ABOUT HAVING IT ALL'

They're young, smart, educated – and all they want is to stay at home and have babies. Meet the women for whom caring matters more than a career.

Twenty years ago being a housewife and mother would have been seen as the ultimate failure for a woman in her twenties. Women boasted about careers, not cupcakes. A good degree, a satisfying job and financial independence were the ultimate goals. If they thought about babies at all it was in terms of alien life forms and how to avoid them. Staying at home was something they did when they had a hangover.

Fastforward to Generation Y – the women who are in their twenties today – and there is a significant change happening. In 2009 a YouGov poll for the Conservative Centre for Policy Studies found that only 12 per cent of mothers surveyed wanted to work full-time, while a staggering 31 per cent didn't want to work at all. The author of the report, Cristina Odone, claimed: "Instead of finding satisfaction in full-time work, most women realise themselves in other roles as carers, partners, community members and above all mothers."

Justine Roberts, co-founder of parenting site Mumsnet, agrees that some women, having found it impossible to fulfil the fantasy of Having It All, are now choosing to make a career out of motherhood. She says, "Smart, energetic women are devoting themselves to motherhood in the same way that they used to approach their careers: setting targets, thinking creatively and filling time efficiently." But she strikes a word of warning. "If more educated and capable women are choosing not to enter the workplace, we will be in danger of losing some of the economic power that our mothers fought very hard to gain in the first place."

Emily Petley, 23, has two sons aged 3 and 1 – "I realise most 23-year-olds are probably out chasing their dream job, travelling the world and aiming for the big things in life, but

I'm more content staying at home and raising our family – and what's wrong with that? It seems strange to me that women have to defend themselves for staying at home".

Source: Harris, S. 'Stay-at-home mothers: 'We don't care about having it all", The Times, 10 July 2010

Questions

1. **Identify** what the 2009 YouGov poll concluded about women in their twenties.

2. **Analyse** how the information given in this article supports Hakim's rational choice theory.

3. **Evaluate** the impact on both society and women of young women choosing to have babies instead of embarking on careers.

4. **Outline** and **evaluate** the arguments for and against the view that the Generation Y women featured in this article are representative of young women today.

CONCLUSIONS

March of Progress sociologists, such as Young and Wilmott, were keen to trumpet a gender role revolution in family life in the 1970s. They genuinely believed that equality in the distribution of domestic labour, and consequently power, was a very real possibility and that egalitarian marriage and the symmetrical family were going to be the universal norm in the UK. However, as feminist sociologists predicted, the evidence suggests that although men are doing a great deal more around the home than they were 50 years ago, the majority of all types of domestic labour apart from DIY is still done by women. Moreover, the evidence strongly indicates that there is still a large section of society, both men and women, that believes that domestic labour – especially childcare – should be the responsibility of women. Feminist and postmodernist sociologists argue that this fact suggests that familial and patriarchal forms of ideology are still very powerful. They therefore conclude that the distribution of domestic labour and power in families is likely to be unequal for some generations to come.

CHECK YOUR UNDERSTANDING

1. Why was Oakley critical of malestream sociology's attitude towards domestic labour.

2. Identify the main conclusions that can be drawn about family symmetry and equality from quantitative studies of domestic labour.

3. Define the 'dual burden'.

4. Define what Hakim means when she claims that gender inequality is the result of women making rational choices.

5. Define what is meant by 'emotion work'.

6. Outline and explain Loscocco and Walzer's ideas about the advantages and disadvantages of marriage for both men and women.

7. Analyse the reasons why men are able to dominate decision-making within marriage.

8. Explain how attitudes towards gender roles, and especially motherhood and fatherhood, may be shaped by ideology.

9. Explain relative resources theory.

10. Outline and evaluate the view that there has been an incomplete revolution in gender equality in the distribution of domestic labour in British households.

TAKE IT FURTHER

Design a household task survey and ask couples separately who is mainly responsible for the task, and whether they think that their partner does enough around the home. Also, ask a set of parents to keep a diary over a week documenting the time spent on child-related activities.

4.6 THE SOCIAL CONSTRUCTION OF CHILDHOOD

LEARNING OBJECTIVES

> Demonstrate knowledge and understanding of the nature of childhood and changes in the status of children in the family (AO1).

> Apply and analyse theories of childhood and evidence from sociological studies of childhood to the changing nature of childhood (AO2).

> Evaluate sociological explanations of childhood (AO3).

INTRODUCING THE DEBATE

There are two broad ways of looking at childhood. Childhood refers to a number of distinct biological and psychological stages of human life – being a baby from birth to 18 months, an infant between 18 months and 4 years, a child from 5 to 12 years, and an adolescent from 13 to 17 years.

However, the sociological view of childhood is very different to that of the biological approach. It argues that childhood is constructed by society. In other words, how children are treated (for example, whether they are regarded as fundamentally different from adults) in any particular society is dependent on the dominant social attitudes, laws and social policies of that society. For example, the United Nations Convention on the Rights of the Child states that a child "means every human being below the age of 18 years". This was ratified by the UK government in 1991, which means that they agree to be legally bound by it. Child protection laws also define children as anyone under

the age of 18 years, while criminal law in the UK states that the age of criminal responsibility in England and Wales is 10 years old, while in Scotland it is 12 years.

The consensus in the UK today is that childhood is a very special period in people's lives and requires special attention and treatment. However, the social construction argument suggests that this version of childhood is a very recent social invention. Moreover, sociologists point out that childhood today is shaped by a variety of social factors, which means that the treatment of children and childhood differs across the social groups that live in the UK. Sociologists argue therefore that there is probably no universal experience of childhood in Britain. Moreover, the global picture suggests that in many countries childhood as experienced by British children does not exist. Instead, childhood in these societies is often a risky, dangerous and harmful social condition.

CHILDHOOD IN PRE-INDUSTRIAL SOCIETY

The social historian Philippe Aries (1962) suggested that what children experience today as childhood is a recent social invention or construction. As Clarke (2003) notes, "this view holds that sometime between 1600 and the twentieth century the idea of childhood was 'invented' and what we now think of as childhood would not have made sense to our ancestors" (p. 3).

Aries argued that as soon as children were no longer physically dependent on their parents, that is, around the age of seven, they were treated no differently from adults. Childhood did not extend beyond this age. He argues that children in medieval societies were treated as 'miniature adults' who took part in the same work and play activities as grown-ups. They certainly did not enjoy the special and unique treatment in terms of protection, responsibilities and rights to which UK society believes children are entitled today. He says that this is because the concept of age in medieval societies, and its interpretation, were very different from how they are viewed today. In pre-industrial societies, people did not generally know their date of birth or their exact age. The registration of births – a legal obligation today – did not exist.

Aries argues that this uncertainty about age meant that people did not see individuals in terms of their chronological age but rather in terms of their physical appearance, abilities and habits. Consequently, if a seven-year-old had a distinct personality – if they could perform physical tasks and converse with older people – then they were regarded as little different from their adult peers. It was therefore perfectly normal for such mini-adults to be working alongside their older peers in agricultural work, or for royal or aristocratic seven-year-olds to be fully participating in formal ceremonies or to find themselves engaged to be married.

Aries based his ideas about the medieval experience of childhood on an analysis of representations of children in medieval paintings. He claimed that there was no qualitative difference in the way children and adults were portrayed. Clarke notes that Aries suggests that medieval artists saw children as 'reduced' versions of adults. Paintings showed infants wearing baby clothes which were generally the same for boys and girls, but artists portrayed those aged seven years and above as wearing smaller versions of adult clothes and having the same physiques, albeit miniaturised, as their adult peers. They were often portrayed with serious adult-like expressions on their faces. There were rarely any of the stylised features that are often associated with paintings of children today, such as innocence, dependency, large eyes, small hands, and smiling faces. Children were very rarely painted playing.

The familiar distinction between childhood and adulthood has not always been with us. Medieval paintings illustrate much greater continuity between infants and adults.

Why might some sociologists criticise Aries' research methodology?

Aries argues that the medieval concept of childhood first began to resemble today's version of childhood towards the end of the 17th century. He notes that paintings of children during this period start to specifically show them as children rather than mini-adults. He suggests that the main reason for this was a steady decrease in the infant mortality rate, which meant that it became more likely that children would survive childhood. Consequently, parents began treating them with more interest and affection, and a distinct culture of childhood started to emerge: certain styles of clothes were seen as exclusive to children, and games and toys were invented and manufactured specifically for children.

However, Aries argues that the biggest impact was a profound social change, especially among the middle class, in terms of people's everyday lifestyles. Up to the 17th century, Aries claims that it was normal for people to spend most of their time in the community with their friends, neighbours and so on, but during the course of the century, everyday life based on privacy became more dominant as a lifestyle. This meant that people increasingly chose to spend most of their time at home with their close kin, which Aries argues coincided with more attention being paid to children. Clarke suggests that a middle-class model or ideology of the family became popular in this era, based on the idea of the self-contained family led by a strong father organised around the 'proper' upbringing of children. Aries claimed that child-rearing gradually became the central purpose of family life in industrial societies, although this was not fully achieved until the second half of the 19th century.

What are the strengths and weaknesses of using historical sources to investigate social life in the past?

Critique of Aries

Pollock (1983) criticises Aries for using a limited and highly selective set of sources and evidence: paintings. She argues that such sources were generally unrepresentative of medieval society as they were mainly commissioned by wealthy elites whose approach to children and childhood may not have been typical of wider society, especially the peasant class. Moreover, a piece of art may only reflect the artist's subjective experience, or their desire to follow an artistic trend. Pollock argues that sociologists need to examine qualitative data that focuses on actual child–parent relationships rather than images. These can be found in diaries, autobiographies and other first-hand accounts from these historical periods.

Wilson (1980) argues that Aries makes the mistake of being ethnocentric and is therefore guilty of applying modern standards to past societies. It may be that these societies had different standards of childhood – they may have loved their children in ways that people in modern societies might not understand.

Despite these criticisms, Aries' work has been very influential. Most historians agree that modern society has experienced a massive change in sentiment about children. It is generally accepted that childhood was experienced and imagined quite differently in the medieval period. Aries clearly showed that childhood is not just a natural category that is experienced in the same way at all times and in all societies – rather it is an ever-shifting social concept or invention.

CHILDHOOD AND INDUSTRIALISATION

It is very important to understand that the changes in childhood that Aries documented took some time to filter down to ordinary families from the upper- and middle-class experience. Aries acknowledges that industrialisation did not lead to a radical change in the way that working-class children were treated. An examination of British society in the industrial 18th and 19th centuries suggests that the concept of childhood as it is known today was still evolving. Many children's lives were characterised by poverty, hard labour and exploitation.

During the early industrial period, working-class children were often found working in factories, mines and mills, which had an adverse effect on their health. Children were frequently killed or injured at work and exposed to toxic substances, which shortened their lives. Despite the risks, children's labour was often regarded as an economic necessity by parents in order to stave off poverty and the threat of the workhouse. In the absence of a welfare state, children could also help to support their parents when they were too old or sick to work.

Social attitudes towards children started to radically change in the middle of the 19th century. Factory Acts were passed that excluded children from the mines and from certain types of mill and factory work, and reduced the number of hours of paid work they could do. Many 19th-century campaigners were concerned about the number of children who had become pickpockets, beggars and prostitutes, and consequently legislation was passed by Parliament to get them off the streets and away from predatory adults. In 1867, Thomas Barnardo opened his first Children's Home, while 1889 saw the setting up of the National Society for the Prevention of Cruelty to Children (NSPCC).

Mass education for those aged 5–12 was introduced in 1870 and became compulsory in 1880, which meant that school was a common childhood experience by the beginning of the 20th century. However, some working-class parents continued to resist these moves to protect and educate children because their family income and standard of living were very dependent on their children's wages. Nevertheless, as Clarke notes, by the end of the nineteenth century, "while the lives of most children were still dominated by poverty, ignorance and illness, the idea of child-centredness as a key focus for policy development had firmly taken root" (pp. 9–10).

Most sociologists now accept the validity of Aries' argument that the separation of the status and identity of childhood from other life-stages is a modern social construction. Chapman (2004), for example, notes that "it was not until the nineteenth century that childhood became socially constructed as a significant life transition that required, in middle-class families at least, particular forms of nurturing, supervision, discipline and even different kind of clothes, play and dedicated space in houses. Instead of children bringing economic advantage to households through gainful employment, they now represented a significant cost to parents and for longer periods of time" (pp. 25–6). Chambers too argues that the idea of a 'protected or sheltered childhood' became very popular in the late 19th century. This was reflected in social policy, which sought to regulate child labour and to establish compulsory schooling. Heywood (2001) stresses that although progress was made in the protection of children, inequalities between classes, regions and ethnic groups persisted.

A CHILD-CENTRED 20TH CENTURY

The 20th century saw the emergence of a child-centred society in which treating children's needs became a priority and childhood was seen as a very distinct and separate category from adulthood. Chambers argues that children came to be seen as sacred and were perceived by society as "special people with unique needs who need separate forms of treatment as well as protection from the dangers and corrupting influences of the adult world" (p. 80). Today, children are cherished for their sentimental value. They now occupy a central place in the emotional life of the home, in the sense that having and rearing children is seen as symbolic of commitment and family stability.

Cunningham (2006) notes that this child-centred society has three major features:

> childhood (which legally extends to the age of 18) is regarded as the opposite of adulthood – children are viewed as innocent, vulnerable, dependent and in need of adult protection from potential 'threats' such as bad parenting, neglect and exploitation

> the social worlds of adults and children are physically and symbolically separated; for example, children occupy social spaces such as the home and schools, in which they are expected to engage in play and learning, and are excluded from adult spaces such as the workplace, the public house and so on

> childhood is associated with certain rights; for example, the right to 'happiness', to be 'safe', to be healthy, and for children to enjoy their childhood.

CHILDREN AND THE STATE

The state has also contributed to the social construction of childhood as a sacred and special period in the life-course. The 20th century saw a massive increase in state interference in family life, which was justified by the need to protect children and childhood. Wells (2009) notes that the government of childhood is almost entirely organised

around saving children from internal threats (for example, neglectful or abusive parents) and external threats (such as germs and viruses, media representations of violence, pornography, exploitation by employers, and so on). In this sense, the state aims to takes responsibility for the emotional, physical, intellectual and spiritual development of the child so that it grows up to be a normal law-abiding citizen. As Chambers notes, this is the state taking on the role of the 'good parent'.

Social policy aimed at safeguarding children has taken a variety of forms.

> The NHS today oversees children's health in a variety of ways: via antenatal, maternity and post natal care; the mass vaccination of children; through family GPs and consultants (paediatricians) who specialise in children's illnesses; and in specialist children's hospitals.

> The state shapes and supervises the secondary socialisation of children through compulsory state education, which lasts from the age of 4 to 18.

> A major role of social services and social workers is to police those families in which children are thought to be at risk of neglect or abuse.

> Laws exclude children from activities which may harm them. For example, children are not allowed to buy alcohol, smoke, have sex or marry without their parents' permission until they reach a certain age.

> Laws and punishments have been put into place to deter physical and sexual abuse, as well as neglect (the most common type of mistreatment of children).

> The state takes some economic responsibility for children by paying Child Benefit and Child Tax Credit to parents.

> The 1991 Child Support Act protects children's welfare in the event of parental separation and divorce, emphasising that the prime concern of the family courts should be the best interests of the child.

> The 2004 Children's Act appointed a Children's Commissioner whose job is to raise awareness of the best interests of children, especially those in care and with difficulties in their lives.

> The Labour Government of 1997–2010 made a commitment to reduce child poverty, which the Coalition Government of 2010–2015 also adopted. This aimed to improve the educational and job opportunities of the parents of poorer children, in order to free children from the effects of family poverty.

FOCUS ON SKILLS: CHILDHOOD IN BRITAIN

In recent years, child poverty has risen dramatically.

The UNICEF report 'Child well-being in rich countries: a comparative over view', published in 2013, suggests that the British experience of childhood today may be far from ideal. The UK was ranked 16th out of 29 countries in terms of children's wellbeing, which is measured using five dimensions of children's lives – material wellbeing, health and safety, education, behaviours, and housing and environment. Children were also asked about their subjective wellbeing. Eighty-six per cent of British

children reported a high level of life satisfaction but the UK was marked down because of a rise in the number of children whose childhoods were being undermined by poverty, high infant mortality (compared with other European nations), poor participation in further education, poor housing standards, and high rates of alcohol abuse and pregnancy among teenagers. The UNICEF report concluded that the state had to do more to ensure that every child had the right to develop to their full potential. According to UNICEF, this is not currently the case in the UK.

Questions

1. **Identify** the five dimensions that were used by UNICEF to judge the global experience of childhood.

2. **Analyse** the reasons why UNICEF was only able to rank the UK 16th out of 29 countries.

3. **Evaluate** the role of the British state in explaining why the experience of childhood was ranked so low in the UK.

State family policy and the law are therefore central today in defining and shaping parental responsibility towards children. The state sets out the duties of parents and gives them rights over children's bodies and time. However, what children are allowed to do according to the law can sometimes be contradictory. For example, adolescent children can have sex at the age of 16 but cannot marry without the permission of their parents or see a film with an 18 certificate. Furthermore, some critics argue that the state does not always protect children. Some governments seem to be very reluctant to legislate with regard to parental violence – smacking children. It is banned in 30 countries, including Scotland but is acceptable in England and Wales, the USA, Canada and Australia.

What are the arguments for and against the parental smacking of children?

CHILDHOOD AS A RELATIVE EXPERIENCE

Sociologists generally accept that childhood is a social construction but they also point out that this

concept of social construction is not straightforward in the 21st century. This is because there are significant variations on children's experience of childhood, due to influences such as gender role socialisation, social class, culture, ethnicity, religion, region and globalisation. Therefore, an important aspect of the social construction argument is the understanding that childhood is not a fixed, universal experience. Rather it is a **relative** experience – it can be experienced positively and negatively, and, most importantly, not all cultures construct it as a sacred and special experience. In some parts of the world, childhood is a dangerous and risky period of a person's life, which often involves early death and suffering.

UNDERSTAND THE CONCEPT

Relativity refers to the notion that people's experience of social life is not the same: it is not fixed or absolute. It often differs according to their social class, ethnicity, gender, global location, and so on.

Gender

Experiences of childhood in the UK may differ according to gender. Evidence from feminist studies such as Sharpe (1976), Oakley (1985) and Fine (2010) show that boys and girls are socialised into a set of behaviours based on cultural expectations about masculinity and femininity. Consequently, girls have a qualitatively different experience of childhood in terms of bedroom decoration, the toys they receive, the nature of their play activities, the chores they do around the home, and their interaction with their parents compared with boys. This gendered socialisation, according to feminist analysis, is mainly designed to teach them the feminine skills and attitudes needed to perform the adult role of home-maker and mother. McRobbie (2000) also suggests that girls' experience of childhood may differ from boys because parents see them as in need of greater protection from the outside world. This means that they are subjected to stricter social controls from parents, compared with boys, when they reach adolescence, and consequently spend more time in the family home than their brothers.

In contrast, boys' experience of childhood involves what Chapman calls 'toning down their emotionality and familial intimacy' so that they effectively acquire the masculine skills and attitudes required for their adult roles as wage-worker and breadwinner. Boys are rarely seen to be in need of protection from external threats and consequently spend a lot of their childhood outside the home socialising with their peers. Evidence from McHale *et al.*'s study (2003) suggests that where families have limited budgets, they are more likely to invest in activities that enhance development for their sons than for their daughters.

Compare your own experience of childhood with that of the opposite sex. Can you see similarities and differences?

Social class

Experiences of childhood in Britain may vary according to social class. Upper-class children may find that they spend most of their formative years in private boarding schools. Middle-class children may be encouraged from an early age to aim for university and a professional career, and they are likely to receive considerable economic and cultural support from their parents. Recent research on middle-class parenting by Lareau (2011) found that social class influences patterns of family life and childhood. She found that the experience of middle-class childhood was socially constructed by

parents who were engaged in a 'concerted cultivation' of children. This involved such parents enrolling children at a young age in a range of specific cultural, artistic and sporting activities and courses. In addition, these children would be encouraged to join libraries, and parents would take them on visits to museums, art galleries and sites of historical interest.

In contrast, Lareau found that working-class parents emphasised the 'natural growth' of their children – they did not cultivate their children's special talents. Instead they believed that as long as they provided their children with love, food and safety, their children would grow up to be healthy and well-rounded individuals.

Donzelot (1979) argues that poor families and their children are more likely to be controlled and regulated by the state. For example, the state monitors the quality of both parenting and childhood through the use of health visitors, social workers and 'at risk' registers. The function of such surveillance is to prevent the forming of deviant attitudes and delinquent behaviour.

BUILD CONNECTIONS

A study of middle-class childhood by Vincent and Ball (2007) found that British middle-class parents raise 'renaissance children' – these children are provided with a range of expensive enrichment activities organised around sport and creative pursuits such as music, art and drama. This positively contributes to the children's educational and occupational success because this middle-class experience of childhood results in the child's acquisition of cultural capital – a set of values and knowledge that confers advantages on children in educational environments. Vincent and to Ball conclude that the renaissance child is equipped with the skills to make better choices than the working-class child. They are able to realise their abilities or potential and to become the self-developing project their parents had aspired for them to be.

Nelson (2010) has identified a new kind of upper middle-class parenting emerging among the wealthy in the USA. He argues that rich parents excessively interfere in the lives of their children in terms of guidance and shaping their experience of childhood. Nelson notes that many of these 'helicopter parents', as he calls them – because they hover around their children – construct detailed schedules outlining how their children should live their daily lives. Nelson claims that such attention is stifling development and producing spoilt and immature children, and, eventually, adults who feel they are entitled to do whatever they wish and are ill-equipped to deal with the real world. There are signs that a similar parenting culture might be emerging in the UK.

Working-class childhood may be made more difficult by the experience of poverty. For example, research by Jefferis *et al.* (2002) found that, by the age of seven, children who experienced poverty had significantly fallen behind children from middle-class backgrounds in terms of maths, reading and other ability tests. Poverty also increases the chance of illness during childhood. The Child Poverty Action Group also notes that children from low-income families often do not experience childhood activities and events that most others take for granted, such as going on school trips, inviting friends around for tea or spending holidays away from home.

Ethnicity and religion

In a multicultural country such as Britain, experience of childhood may differ across ethnic and religious groups. For example, there is evidence that Muslim, Hindu and Sikh children generally feel a stronger sense of obligation and duty to their parents than White children. These children generally shared their parents' view that it was important not to bring shame on the family.

Ghumann (2003) found that religion had a big impact on the childhood experience of Asians. For example, many Muslim children spent their Saturday mornings at the mosque learning the Qur'an. Shaw (2000), who carried out an ethnographic study of British Pakistani Muslims in Oxford, found that young people were internalising Islamic values and family traditions. The study also found that female children were treated in more traditional ways than their brothers. Ghumann argued that generational conflict between Asian parents and children exists, especially over fashion, dating and marriage, but it is often resolved through compromise.

However, it is important to realise that children in the White majority group may also have their childhood partially constructed by religious beliefs and values. For example, if a child is born into a Roman Catholic or a 'born again' Pentecostal or Baptist household, church-going is likely to be a feature of their childhood. Consider too the Jehovah's Witness child whose religion forbids the celebration of Christmas or birthdays.

It is also likely that racism has direct and indirect effects on the childhood of ethnic-minority children and that many children from all ethnic groups are implicated, whether as victims, perpetrators or witnesses. O'Brien *et al.* (2000)

found that 'race' and gender often interact to have a negative impact on the experience of childhood, with Asian girls in particular not being allowed out on their own compared with young Asian males because of the parents' belief that they were more vulnerable to racist attacks and abuse. Chahal and Julienne (1999) found that parents whose children had suffered racist harassment or attacks did not allow them the freedom to move about the neighbourhood by themselves.

GLOBAL EXPERIENCES

In many less developed nations, the experience of childhood is extremely different from that of the industrialised world. Children in such countries are constantly at risk of early death as a result of poverty and a lack of basic health care. For example, UNICEF notes that measles kills over 500,000 children a year in Africa, while malaria kills over one million children a year, most under the age of five.

Moreover, children in these countries are less likely to have access to education. According to UNESCO, 67.4 million children do not attend school in the developing world, while an estimated 122 million children aged 18 and under cannot read or write. Two-thirds of these are thought to be girls, who face more challenges than boys in receiving an education because of cultural and religious discrimination and **social stigma**. Often, girls' education is seen as secondary to childcare, looking after the sick and elderly, and other household responsibilities.

UNDERSTAND THE CONCEPT

Social stigma is the social disapproval that an individual or group may receive from society when their behaviour is thought to be deviant or immoral. The stigma is the negative label that is attached to the person or group and which marks them out for disgrace, prejudice and discriminatory treatment.

Children in developing societies may find themselves occupying roles as workers, much like British children did in the 18th and 19th centuries. Punch (2002) found that children in Bolivia as young as five were put to work looking after animals, tending the fields and so on. According to the International Labour Organisation (ILO), about one in five of the world's 1.5 billion children are involved in paid work. Many of them – 126 million – are engaged in hazardous work that has adverse effects on physical or mental health or moral development. Many of them are working more than 30 hours per week for exploitative rates of pay, for example, in sweat shops producing goods for Western markets – in 2008 it was discovered by the BBC that children as young as eight were earning 60 pence a day working for suppliers to Primark.

Many children in developing nations find employment making products for Western markets. They often do so for very low wages and face exploitation by employers.

War also shapes childhood because they not only kill a disproportionate number of children but they also increase the likelihood of children becoming orphans, refugees, hostages, slaves and soldiers. In 1995, UNICEF reported that in the previous decade approximately 2 million children had been killed in wars around the world – this figure exceeded the number of soldiers killed in the same period. In 2013, it was reported that over 11,000 Syrian children had been killed in the civil war. In just 50 days, 490 children were killed in the Israeli bombing of Gaza in 2014. In Afghanistan, almost 35,000 children have been the victims of land mines since 1979. In Nigeria, in April 2014, the Islamist group Boko Haram kidnapped over 300 girls and sold them into slavery.

Thousands of children, some as young as ten, are serving as child soldiers around the world. They are used as fighters, cooks, suicide bombers and human shields. Girls are often used for sexual purposes. Singer (2006) observes that African states have been at the epicentre of the child soldier phenomenon, although children have also fought in wars in Palestine, Iran, Iraq, Afghanistan and Sri Lanka. In Northern Uganda, as many as 14,000 children have been abducted to serve as soldiers in the Lord's Resistance Army, while during the civil war in Sierra Leone in the 1990s, many children were drugged and brainwashed by rebel militias and forced to kill and

maim civilians and government soldiers. Children who objected were killed.

A child soldier in Somalia

In many countries, street children are not regarded as special or as in need of protection. UNICEF estimates that 100 million children are growing up on urban streets around the world. There are estimated to be 11 million street children in India and 400,000 street children in Bangladesh (of which nearly 10 per cent have been forced into prostitution in order to survive). Charities estimate that there are 1.9 million children in Mexico sleeping rough on the streets and 240,000 of these have been abandoned by their parents.

Research how the Taliban seek to control the childhood of boys and girls in Afghanistan and Pakistan.

CHILD ABUSE

Despite the emphasis on saving children in child-centred societies, some children's experiences of childhood may be extremely damaging. Different types of child abuse have been identified in recent years in the UK, such as neglect, and physical, sexual and emotional abuse. The NSPCC points out that each week at least one child will die as a result of an adult's cruelty, usually a parent or step-parent, while 30,000 children are on child protection registers because they are at risk of abuse from family members. Moreover, the negative emotional and social effects of divorce on children have been documented in several surveys. It is a fact, then, that not all children experience their childhood as happy, positive, secure and safe – for many childhood is exploitative, abusive and sometimes very dangerous.

THEORETICAL APPROACHES TO CHILDHOOD

In addition to the social constructionist argument outlined above, there are three other sociological approaches to childhood. Both agree with the view that childhood is socially constructed. However, they differ in their perception of what role children themselves play in the social construction of their childhoods.

The conventional approach

Many functionalists and New Right thinkers tend to subscribe to what has been termed a 'conventional' approach to childhood. They highlight the role of parenting and suggest that primary socialisation is the key to a successful and happy childhood. Successful parenting and therefore happy childhoods involve parents socialising their children into positive social values such as working hard, showing respect to others, always demonstrating good manners, and so on. Good parents, from this perspective, should exercise sensible control and discipline over their children's behaviour, and seek to ensure that negative outside influences do not undermine their children's upbringing, and that children are kept safe from threats to their innocence.

Why do you think that some sociologists are critical of the idea of socialisation?

The conventional approach to childhood has always assumed that successful child-rearing requires two parents of the opposite sex, and that there is a 'right' way to bring up a child. Consequently, its adherents tend to see the experience of childhood as being potentially undermined by 'deviant family' units such as single-parent or gay families. Some argue that 'working mothers' are denying their children qualitative family interaction because they are too busy and that this may be the cause of what the conventional approach sees as the decline of civilised childhood, in which children always respected their elders.

Melanie Phillips' book *All Must Have Prizes* (1997) is typical of this conventional approach to childhood. She argues that the culture of parenting in the UK has broken down and the 'innocence' of childhood has been undermined by two trends.

› Good parenting has been distorted by liberal ideas and state policies, which have given too many rights and powers to children. Phillips argues that children should be socialised into a healthy respect for parental authority. However, she argues that children's rights have undermined this process, and parents are increasingly criticised and penalised for resorting to sanctions such as smacking.

› The media and the peer group have become more influential than parents. Phillips sees the media – magazines aimed at young girls, pop music videos and television – as a particular problem, because they encourage children to envisage themselves as sexual beings at a much younger age.

These trends mean that the period of childhood has been shortened – it is no longer a sacred and innocent period lasting up to the age of 13 or 14. Phillips complains that adulthood and particularly **sexualisation** encroaches upon the experiences of children a great deal earlier than in the past, and consequently the innocence of childhood is allegedly being lost. She argues that many children do not have the emotional maturity to cope with the rights and choices that they have today, or with sexualisation. The result, she believes, is an increase in social problems such as suicide, eating disorders, self-harm, teenage pregnancy, depression, and drug or alcohol abuse.

UNDERSTAND THE CONCEPT

Sexualisation refers to the imposing of adult models of sexual behaviour, dress and so on onto children at too early an age. For example, media and advertising images may encourage young girls to see themselves primarily in terms of their physical attraction to the opposite sex, preventing them from innocently enjoying their childhood.

How valid do you think the 'early sexualisation' argument is?

Postman (1982) also sees childhood as under threat because television exposes children to the adult world too soon. Postman argues that childhood, as a period of innocent happiness, is being lost, for two reasons.

Firstly, the popularity of television means that there are no more secrets from children. Television gives them unlimited access to the adult world. They are exposed to the 'real world' of sex, disaster, death and suffering.

Secondly, 'social blurring' has occurred so there is little distinction between adults and children. Children's games are disappearing – they are often playing the same computer games as adults – and consequently children seem less childlike today. They speak, dress and behave in more adult ways, while adults' fashion choices are starting to reflect their children's and youth in general. Over time, nearly all the traditional features that mark the transition to adulthood – getting a job, religious confirmation, leaving home, getting married – no longer apply in any clear way. The fact that children are spending more time living at home and are economically dependent on their parents for longer periods compared with the past have compounded this problem.

However, Postman's analysis has been heavily criticised. His arguments do not appear to be based on solid evidence, while recent studies indicate that adults are actually taking more and more control of their children's lives. For example, David Brooks (2001) diagnoses parents today as being obsessed with safety, and ever more concerned with defining boundaries for their children and widening the controls and safety net around them.

Sue Palmer in *Toxic Childhood* (2007) argues that adults are benefiting enormously from living in a wealthier society in which electronic technologies have enriched their lives. However, the same technologies are harming children because, all too often, parents are using them as an alternative to traditional parenting practices. Instead of spending quality time with their children and reading them stories, Palmer claims parents are too happy to use television, electronic games and junk food to keep them quiet. Children are therefore deprived of traditional childhood and family life, and she claims that "every year children become more distractible, impulsive and self-obsessed – less able to learn, to enjoy life, to thrive socially" because of these trends.

Another trend that has alarmed some sociologists is the rise of children as consumers. It is estimated that children aged between 7 and 11 are worth about £20 million a year as consumers. Advertisers have therefore targeted children in order to encourage 'pester power' – the power of children to train or manipulate their parents to spend money on consumer goods that will shape and increase the status of their children in the eyes of their peers. Two related sociological concerns have arisen out of this trend.

> Commentators often hark back to a so-called 'golden age' of childhood; they see their own childhood as being much less pressurised and complex, and suggest that the shift into a more consumer-orientated society has resulted in children cynically manipulating their parents with regard to consumer goods. Pugh (2002), for example, suggests that parental spending on children is 'consumption as compensation' – parents who are 'cash-rich but time poor' alleviate their guilt about not spending time with their children by buying them whatever consumer goods they desire.

> There is some evidence that some parents are using their children as symbols of conspicuous consumption. For example, it is suggested that some parents deliberately spend large amounts of money on children's parties or presents in order to symbolically mark themselves out as having more wealth and status than others.

However, there is evidence that the conventional approach to childhood may be wrong about the dangers of consumerism. Many parents seem to be using it as a strategy to keep their children safe. Evans and Chandler (2006) found that many parents justified their consumption of children's products on the basis that the world had become a much riskier place for children and that spending money on consumer goods meant that children spent more time in the home. Items such as DVDs and computer games were therefore justified as 'safer leisure options'.

Feminism

Walter argues that ideas appeared in the 1990s which suggested that females should celebrate their sexuality and that women could be empowered by their bodies. However, Walter argues that this association of empowerment with sexuality, which was mainly driven by the media, has had a negative effect on society and, in particular, on the childhood experience of girls and their aspirations as they enter adult society. Walter argues that a hyper-sexual culture underpinned by the media's obsession with celebrities such as the Kardashians and with the objectification of women's bodies now dominates British society and, to some extent, the way that girls are socialised within families. She argues that parents and families are unwittingly endorsing such a culture through their choice of toys and dress for girls.

Social action theory and childhood

The conventional approach has been criticised by social action sociologists who have focused on researching how children see and interpret the world around them, and how children's decisions and social actions can help to socially construct their unique experience of childhood.

Social action approaches to childhood suggest that functionalist and New Right arguments wrongly assume that children are simply empty vessels waiting to be passively filled with values, parental wisdom, appropriate behaviours, and so on. Family life is presented in the conventional approach as a one-way process in which parenting and socialisation aim to transform children into good citizens. However, social action theory argues that socialisation is actually a two-way process to which children actively contribute.

There are three big themes in the social action approach to childhood and family life.

> Social action theory criticises the conventional view of childhood for ignoring the idea that children are social actors who actively contribute to the social construction of their childhood. For example, research by Morrow (1998) found that children can be constructive and reflective contributors to family life. Most of the children in Morrow's study had a pragmatic view of their family role – they did not want to make decisions for themselves but they did want a say in what happened to them.

> Chambers therefore argues that sociologists need to examine how children themselves see childhood. They should no longer be treated as the passive recipients of parental care and socialisation. She notes that they "need to be acknowledged as moral and social practitioners of family life in their own right" (p. 92).

> Children should have the right to make an active contribution to both their childhood and family life in general. For example, Valentine (1999) argues that children and adults often fight over the 'right to independence'. She notes that children can influence the process of acquiring this right by behaving in particular ways – by manipulating their parents' judgements or by convincing one parent that they are competent and responsible in order to secure the right to more independence and freedom.

Childhood therefore is not a static and universal experience; children contest it every step of the way. They generally want more rights as they get older. However, social action theory acknowledges that this can lead to tension and conflict, which can be illustrated in four ways.

> Children often want the right to more independence but this potentially conflicts with the state's desire to construct a legal framework within which children can be protected. The notion that children can be totally free to make their own decisions may be illusory.

> There is tension between the idea of children being active agents of their own behaviour and the need for parents to protect children from external threats such as bullying. Evans and Chandler found that peer pressure was an important aspect of children's rationale for putting pressure on their parents to buy them consumer goods. The children in their study were very aware of what clothing and designer labels were approved by their peers and which were not. Moreover, they were very aware of the possibility of the teasing, name-calling and

bullying that might result if they did not conform or fit in because they lacked these items.

> Some sociologists, such as Giddens, also argue that childhood is becoming more individualised because of children's influence over economic consumption and a corresponding decline in the traditional relationship between parents and children, especially a decline in obedience. Because of this individualisation, the growing autonomy of children in the future may mean that families experience difficulties in fitting children into society and that more social problems involving children are likely to appear.

> Chambers identifies a tension between parents and children caused by children's use of new media. She notes that since 2000 there has been a revolution in the range of new media gadgets being used in the family home, which has prompted a renegotiation of relations between children and parents. Livingstone (2009) notes the rise of a youth-centred media and 'screen rich bedroom culture'. Most parents believe that a very important part of a good childhood is that children should have the right to their own personal space, that is, their own bedroom in the family household. Adolescents now spend significant amounts of leisure time in the privacy of their own bedrooms using new media such as gaming consoles and laptops in a solitary way. Livingstone notes that children communicate more with the virtual outside world than with adult members of their own family. Parents often have to text their children or contact them via Facebook™ to gain their attention at meal times.

Some sociologists argue that children's newfound freedom to actively engage with new media has resulted in a fragmentation of family life and childhood. It is argued that children have disengaged from family life. Van Rompaey and Roe (2001) argue that children's active use of new media has led to a new type of family interaction which they call 'living together but separately'. However, there may be tension and conflict between children and parents as parents feel obliged to restrict access to phones, computers, the internet and computer games because of their fear that children may witness harmful violence or sexual content, be sexually groomed online or experience cyber-bullying. Moreover, conflict between parents and children often arises when parents are perceived as invading their children's personal territory in order to investigate their activities. Parents want to know what their children are doing because they want to protect them. However, children are not keen on their parents knowing what they are doing because they want their autonomy.

Drotner *et al.* (2008) argue that children's use of new media has led to childhood becoming privatised, as adolescents are separated from adult and family life. However, others argue that increased use of new media by older children has led to greater teen autonomy and choice, and the enhancement of peer group relations.

POSTMODERNISM AND CHILDHOOD

Postmodern theory suggests that the status of children may be changing because of the emergence of new kinds of intimate relationships and new versions of the family. Giddens (1992) argues that late modernity has seen a transformation of intimacy, which has led to more democratic relationships in families. Children are now gaining the right to determine and regulate their association with parents. Chambers argues that in families where children are involved in decision-making, "parents now have to be answerable to them and to offer them respect in order to be respected" (p. 82).

FOCUS ON SKILLS: TOO MUCH TV CAN CAUSE EMOTIONAL TURMOIL FOR CHILDREN

Young children who spend hours each day in front of the television or playing computer games are more likely to suffer from a range of emotional problems and to be overweight, according to two studies into the impact of excessive screen time. One study found that the more TV children watched, the more likely they were to suffer from difficult family relationships, one of the primary causes of unhappiness. The study examined data from more than 3,604 children from eight different countries aged between two and six, collected over several years, making it one of the biggest of its kind. Their screen time ranged from less than 30 minutes to more than three hours a day. It found that for every extra hour of screen time, there was a 30 per cent increase in emotional problems for girls and a 20 per cent increase for boys.

"Watching television appeared to be associated with poorer outcomes more than playing electronic games or using computers," said Trina Hinkley, the lead researcher from Deakin University in Australia. "The risk of emotional problems and poorer family functioning

increased with each additional hour." However, it was still not clear what the relationship between screen time and emotional problems was, and further research would be required to establish the reasons, she said.

Government-commissioned research published last year found that older children who spent less than an hour a day playing computer games were almost three times more likely to say they were happy and enjoyed life than those who spent longer on screens.

British children spend disproportionately large amounts of time in front of screens, compared with those in other Western European countries. In the UK, 62 per cent of 11-year-olds, 71 per cent of 13-year-olds and 68 per cent of 15-year-olds report watching more than two hours of TV a day on weekdays. In Switzerland the figure is less than 35 per cent in all three groups.

Source: Bennett, R. 'Too much TV can cause emotional turmoil for children', *The Times* 18 March 2014

Questions

1. **Identify** what percentage of British children spend more than two hours a day watching television compared with Swiss children.

2. **Identify** the impact on older children if they spend less than one hour a day playing video games.

3. **Analyse** and explain how the research by Hinkley supports the findings of Postman and Palmer.

4. **Evaluate** the arguments for and against the view that children's use of television and new media has led to them becoming disengaged from family life.

Chapman notes that the experiences of children at home are clearly also very varied because of new versions of the family that exist today. He argues that the experiences of children in gay and lesbian households, or those who have experienced their parents' divorce, live in single-parent, reconstituted or step-families, or who have to care for adults, and so on, cannot be directly compared with those of children who live in conventional two-parent nuclear families. Indeed, he points out that even if children did all live in the same type of household, their experiences of childhood would still be shaped by a variety of factors, such as their parents' occupation, social class, education, ethnicity, religion, and so on.

Finally, postmodern sociologists note that the Western approach to childhood is increasingly becoming globalised and being exported to other societies such as China.

However, critics suggest the following points.

> The Western model of childhood may not be objectively better than the models of childhood that preceded it or that still exist within the developing world.

> The interests of children may not be the same everywhere. For example, it might be more positive for children to spend their time in paid work rather than in full-time education if the society and the families

that live in it are constantly in a state of poverty. It is suggested that the Western value judgement that children are in need of protection from exploitation and need to be removed from such situations is not very useful in this context.

> Developing societies in Africa, Asia and Latin America may not have the level of economic development necessary for children's health, education and happiness to be the norm. Western norms of childhood may therefore not be relevant or useful in the context of these societies.

CONCLUSIONS

This chapter has shown that childhood as a crucial part of the life-course is more than just a biological experience. It is also very much a social experience, moulded by the societies to which people belong. In this sense, it is both a recent social invention and a social construction. Moreover, it is also important to understand that children are not just passive recipients of parental childcare – they actively contribute to the construction of their own childhoods. Finally, postmodernists have questioned whether the Western model of childhood is the only standard of childhood worth pursuing.

CHECK YOUR UNDERSTANDING

1. Identify three ways children were treated in pre-industrial society according to Aries.

2. Identify four ways in which the state has helped to socially construct childhood in the UK.

3. Define the concept of 'social construction'.

4. Define what is meant by 'renaissance children'.

5. Define what Palmer means by 'toxic childhood'.

6. Explain the conventional approach to childhood.

7. Outline and explain, using only examples from the UK experience of childhood, the idea that childhood is a relative concept.

8. Explain why the UK was not a child-centred society until the 20th century.

9. Analyse and explain the reasons why some claim that childhood is under threat today.

10. Outline and evaluate the social action view that children actively contribute to the social construction of their own childhoods.

TAKE IT FURTHER

In order to document the changing experience of and attitudes towards childhood, design a survey asking three generations about their experience of being a child.

APPLY YOUR LEARNING

AS LEVEL

1 Define the term 'symmetrical family'. [2 marks]

2 Using **one** example, briefly explain what is meant by 'maternal deprivation'. [2 marks]

3 Outline **three** different forms that marital breakdown can take. [6 marks]

4 Outline and explain **two** reasons why women who are victims of domestic violence may nevertheless choose to stay with their partner. [10 marks]

5 Read **Item A** below and answer the question that follows.

ITEM A

Families in 21st century Britain

Family life in Britain has changed dramatically over the last fifty years. The 'traditional' nuclear family of bread-winning father and stay-at-home mother is relatively uncommon and there are far more one-parent and reconstituted families.

Some social commentators talk about a 'breakdown' in family life while others insist that family diversity should not be equated with a breakdown of family life, insisting that families evolve and adapt as society changes.

Applying material from **Item A** and your knowledge, evaluate the view that families continue to be the bedrock of (British) society, performing a wide range of functions throughout life. [20 marks]

A-LEVEL

1 Outline and explain **two** reasons for the growth in single-person households in the UK in recent decades.   [10 marks]

2 Read **Item B** below and answer the question that follows.

ITEM B

Step-Parenting and blended families

As divorce has increased, so too has the number of reconstituted or 'blended' families. When families blend, they are likely to have to cope with a number of tensions not present in unblended families. The 'wicked stepmother' of fairytale fame may well be a caricature, but nevertheless hints at the challenges involved when people take on parenting responsibilities for children to whom they are not related.

Applying material from **Item B** and your knowledge, analyse **two** sources of potential conflict in blended families.   [10 marks]

3 Read **Item C** below and answer the question that follows.

ITEM C

Postmodernism and family norms

Demographic changes in the number of births and deaths, the fertility rate and migration seem to have undermined the traditionalist view that the nuclear family is the most common type of family in the UK. In contrast, these demographic changes tend to support the postmodernist view that family diversity is now the norm and that family life is not static – rather it is in a constant state of change and flux.

Applying material from **Item C** and your knowledge, evaluate the postmodernist view that demographic change has produced family diversity.   [20 marks]

You can find example answers and accompanying teachers' comments for this topic at www.collins.co.uk/AQAAlevelSociology.

5 HEALTH

AQA Specification	Chapters
Candidates should examine:	
The social construction of health, illness, disability and the body, and models of health and illness.	Chapter 1 (pages 308–322) covers this topic, but examples to illustrate particular theories can be found elsewhere, especially Chapters 3 (pages 336–345) and 5 (pages 358–367).
The unequal social distribution of health chances in the United Kingdom by social class, ethnicity and region.	Chapter 2 (pages 323–335) covers this topic, but examples to illustrate particular theories can also be found in Chapter 4 (pages 346–357).
The unequal social distribution of health chances in the United Kingdom by gender.	Chapter 3 (pages 336–345) covers this topic but examples to illustrate particular theories can also be found in Chapters 4 to 6 (pages 336–368).
Inequalities in the provision of, and access to, health care in contemporary society.	Chapter 4 (pages 346–357) covers this topic.
The nature and social distribution of mental illness.	Chapter 5 (pages 358–367) covers this topic but examples to illustrate particular theories can also be found in Chapters 1 to 3 (pages 308–345).
The role of medicine, the health professions and the globalised health industry.	Chapter 6 (pages 368–380) covers this topic but examples to illustrate particular theories can also be found in Chapter 4 (pages 346–357).

5.1 DEFINING HEALTH, ILLNESS AND DISABILITY

INTRODUCING THE DEBATE

For most of us, most of the time, we simply don't think about our health. After all, being healthy is just the natural state of things. It is only when we 'don't feel ourselves' that we begin to think about our bodies and why the discomfort we may be experiencing is not normal. If it is serious enough we may visit our GP who will confirm whether we are ill and what the problem is. However, definitions of 'health', 'illness' and 'disability' are not straightforward. In fact, they vary considerably within the UK because British society is made up of a mixture of very different subcultures and communities who may subscribe to very different ideas about what constitutes and causes 'good health', 'illness' and 'disability'. There may even be differences within households. For example, what some members of a family may consider to be 'illness', other family members may think of as the normal aches and pains of being elderly, of 'growing up' or of 'that time of the month'. This chapter investigates the ways in which health, illness and disability are defined in the UK, and the implications of these definitions for society and individuals who are defined as 'ill' or 'disabled'.

GETTING YOU THINKING

1

2

3

Look at the five photos on this page and then answer the following questions.

1. Examine images 1 to 3. In what ways might these people differ in their view of what constitutes good health?

2. Consider the following six physical and mental conditions: a severe hangover, throwing up during pregnancy, feeling very sad, hyperactivity, Tourette's and cirrhosis of the liver. Which of these, in your opinion, counts as a legitimate illness? Justify your reasoning.

3. In your opinion, can any of the conditions you decided were illnesses in question 2 be blamed on the sufferer? Why?

4. Look at images 3 to 5. What messages are these individuals sending out to the rest of us via their bodies?

4

5

5. List as many types of disability as you can. Explain why each type qualifies as a disability.

6. Think about the television coverage of telethons and the Paralympics. In your opinion, does this TV coverage stereotype disabled people in any way?

DEFINITIONS OF HEALTH AND ILLNESS

Sociologists have observed that people in Western societies such as the UK take for granted the 'normal' state of their bodies until this 'normality' is disrupted in some way. In other words, they equate 'normal' with 'healthy' and 'abnormal' with feeling 'ill', 'poorly' and 'unwell'. However, sociologists such as Herzlich (1973) and Blaxter (1990) point out that there is no universal agreement within such societies about what 'good health' or 'illness' mean, what these conditions should feel like and how they should be recognised and acted upon, despite the existence of health care systems which employ medical experts. In fact, many studies have discovered that there is often a disparity between how medical professionals define 'health' and 'illness' and the **lay definitions** of these conditions.

UNDERSTAND THE CONCEPT

Lay definitions, in this context, are definitions held by ordinary members of society rather than those who are health professionals or scientists.

Defining health

Sociologists argue that health as a concept is socially constructed – it is a product of several social influences. This can be illustrated in several ways.

Sociologists have carried out a number of surveys in order to uncover the influence of lay definitions of health. Pill and Scott's (1982) study of a group of working-class mothers with young children stressed the absence of

309

Illness but also emphasised the functional nature of good health – this means they saw being healthy as allowing them to effectively carry out and cope with their everyday routine. Illness obviously disrupted this function.

Blaxter carried out a national survey into health and lifestyle using questionnaires and found that young people tend to define health in terms of physical fitness, but as people get older, they come to define health in functional terms, for example, being able to cope with everyday tasks. She found examples of older people with serious arthritis who nevertheless defined themselves as healthy, because they were still able to carry out a range of routine activities. The evidence therefore suggests that as people age, their definitions of health expand to accept greater levels of physical discomfort and pain.

Blaxter concludes that from a lay perspective "health can be defined negatively as the absence of illness, functionally as the ability to cope with everyday activities or positively, as fitness and well-being" (p. 42, Scambler).

Definitions of health and illness often change over time. The social construction of what counts as good health is dynamic rather than static. For example, in the 1960s, the notion of good health rarely extended to people adopting preventative behaviour in order to avoid disease or to live longer. Heavy smoking and drinking were the norm. However, good health today is more likely to be perceived by large sections of UK society as inextricably linked to the adoption of preventative behaviour, such as healthy diets, sensible drinking habits, non-smoking, vitamin intake, fitness and exercise, healthy sexual relationships, and so on.

The National Health Service (NHS) now takes a more active role in promoting good health and therefore has contributed significantly to the social construction of health today. A good example of the success of these health promotional initiatives have been various anti-smoking campaigns, which have encouraged significant numbers of people, especially men, to give up smoking and which have contributed to a dramatic reduction in lung cancer compared with pre-1970s levels.

Sociologists such as Nettleton (1995) note that definitions of good health are increasingly being socially constructed and dominated by global commercial interests, such as the pharmaceutical industry. It is argued by Scambler (2008) that the human body has been targeted by capitalist entrepreneurs who aim to influence the social construction of health by redefining it as a process of:

> ❭ 'self-surveillance' – people are encouraged to constantly monitor their weight, calorie intake, blood pressure, appearance and so on

> ❭ 'body maintenance' – members of society are increasingly encouraged to materially invest in their bodies (and their health) by spending money on consumer items and services that will prevent their bodies from 'deteriorating' too quickly, such as diets, fitness videos, health club/gym membership, jogging outfits, and so on.

Dumit (2012) argues that the global pharmaceutical industry has managed to convince people that they are potentially at risk from illness and ageing, and that they need to financially invest in precautions in the form of vitamin pills, protein shakes, energy boosters, anti-ageing creams, and so on.

These commercial influences have largely succeeded in adding yet another dimension to people's definition of **health**. This is the notion that the body can and should be what Scambler calls "a representation of happiness and success" (p. 42).

How valid is Scambler's view in terms of your experience of self-surveillance and body maintenance?

Defining illness and disease

Sociologists generally define illness (also known as **morbidity**) as the subjective experience of feeling unwell. However, it is important to understand that members of society do not experience or feel symptoms in the same way. For example, some people may choose to ignore the symptoms of illness and carry on as 'normal', others may continue to go to work but self-medicate, some will take time off work or college and a minority will choose to seek advice from their GP.

UNDERSTAND THE CONCEPT

Morbidity refers to a person's experience of illness. The morbidity rate is used to measure the frequency of diseases in the population and is based on the number of visits people make to their GP in any given year.

Sociologists are also interested in **disease** because this medical condition is responsible for most long-term or chronic **illness** and disability, as well as death (also known as mortality). Disease (as opposed to illness) is an objective medical reality. It normally refers to a biological abnormality caused by the body being attacked by germs, viruses, cancerous cells and so on, which can be scientifically observed and diagnosed by doctors using tests.

Illness therefore refers to how people experience symptoms whereas diseases are clinical conditions defined by medical professionals. Blaxter has pointed out that it is possible to have an illness without a disease and a disease without an illness. For example, women in early pregnancy often experience nausea or morning sickness but they are not suffering from a disease, while people who are medically diagnosed with the disease of HIV/AIDS may not experience any feelings of being unwell because antiretroviral drugs prevent HIV from reproducing itself or targeting healthy cells.

UNDERSTANDING THE CONCEPT

Health refers to a person's perception of wellbeing based on their everyday experience of their body.

Illness refers to people's perception of feeling unwell because the wellbeing of their body has deteriorated compared with the everyday norm.

Disease refers to a change in the body's biological condition brought about by identifiable causes observed and diagnosed by medical professionals.

THE SOCIAL PROCESS OF RECOGNISING AND TREATING ILLNESS

There is strong evidence that many people do not consult their doctor for symptoms of disease that would respond to medical treatment. Epsom's (1978) research of 3,160 people found that 57 per cent of them showed physical signs of disease and would have benefited from seeing their GP. Scambler concludes that despite concerns expressed by GPs and A&E hospital departments that many people visit them for trivial and unnecessary reasons, a significant **clinical iceberg** of unreported symptoms exists in the UK. He argues that a substantial number of people are enduring avoidable pain and discomfort and that consequently the NHS is treating "only the tip of the sum total of ill-health".

UNDERSTAND THE CONCEPT

The **clinical iceberg** refers to the figure of unreported and unrecorded illness that exists in society. Only a minority of ill people feel the need to consult their GP – most self-medicate by taking medicines bought over the counter.

Sociologists such as Jylha (2009) have attempted to map out the social process of becoming ill in order to understand why this clinical iceberg of unreported health problems exists. They argue that the process of being recognised and diagnosed as ill is also a 'social construction' – this means that a person's chances of being recognised, diagnosed and treated as sick are more likely to be influenced by social factors than by biological factors. Scambler too argues that whether or not people consult their doctor depends on how they, and others, define health and how this shapes their response to the symptoms of their illness. However, this response is also shaped by social factors such as subcultural influences, the moral aspects of sickness and health, the competing definitions of health, and the growing influence of complementary medicine.

Subcultural influences

Ethnicity

There is some evidence of subcultural differences in terms of how symptoms are interpreted by some ethnic groups, especially with regard to the experience and reporting of pain. Krause (1989) found that Hindu and Sikh Punjabis living in Bedford often visited the doctors with chest pains. However, doctors rarely found anything wrong with them. Krause found that these ethnic minority subcultures called this pain 'sinking heart' (*dil ghirda hai*). Claiming it was caused by the deep emotional upset of public shame. Krause found no evidence of any other subculture responding to emotional distress or disgrace in this way.

Age

Blaxter found that as people age, they gradually redefine health and accept greater levels of pain. The elderly may therefore not respond to pain or discomforting symptoms by consulting a doctor if they believe they can cope with their everyday routine.

The elderly tend to accept greater levels of pain as their definition of health changes.

Gender

Graham (2002) suggests that dominant definitions of masculinity in the UK stress men's toughness and their ability to cope with pain. Consequently, some men may be less likely to define themselves as ill or as needing medical attention. On the other hand, socialisation into feminine roles requires girls and women to recognise that being a woman may require regular medical check-ups, such as smear tests, because of the nature of their biology.

Social class

Blaxter's research also showed that working-class people were far more likely to accept higher levels of illness than middle-class people. Blaxter describes working-class people as 'fatalistic'– that is, they accept poor health and pain as 'one of those things' and tolerate a higher level of discomfort before they consider themselves ill enough to visit the doctor.

Recognition and knowledge of illness

Jylha argues that differences in culture, age, gender and class overlap in influencing people's decision to see a doctor, but this decision also depends on the ill person having sufficient knowledge to recognise their symptoms as signs of illness. Jylha notes that recognition and knowledge about illness depend on a range of factors.

> Some people may not recognise their symptoms as a problem because they associate particular types of illness with other social groups. For example, a person in their thirties who develops early stage Alzheimer's may associate such an illness with the elderly and fail to seek help.

> People often fail to recognise that an illness is sufficiently serious to seek medical treatment. For example, stomach cancer is a major killer of young men. However, evidence suggests they do not visit the doctor once symptoms show themselves. Instead they tend to dismiss the early symptoms as part and parcel of their heavy drinking, fast-food lifestyle.

> Some victims of disease may feel socially embarrassed by their symptoms and consequently fail to seek medical treatment.

> Some may view health and illness in terms of costs and benefits. For example, a person may feel that seeking medical help is a cost that infringes on the benefits of going to work and earning a wage, because it might mean taking time off work to go into hospital.

The moral dimension of seeking medical help

There is often a moral dimension to defining health and illness, and this too may affect a person's decision to seek medical help. Some illnesses are seen as contentious, either because the ill person's lifestyle is seen by the media or society as contributing to their medical condition or because there is no consensus among doctors that the condition actually exists. For example, people who develop medical problems because of alcoholism, heavy smoking, over-eating, and sexual disease are increasingly negatively judged and blamed for their illnesses by the media, politicians and society. People who fit into these categories may be reluctant to seek help because of the stigma attached to their behaviour. It is also argued by some doctors that diseases such as myalgic encephalomyelitis (ME), Chronic Fatigue Syndrome and Gulf War Syndrome do not actually exist. Again, people who present symptoms of these diseases may be fearful of being labelled as idle rather than ill, and consequently reluctant to consult with doctors.

Which sorts of people are more likely to be negatively judged for, and even blamed for, their illnesses by the media, politicians and society?

The sick role: sickness as deviance

The moral dimension of sickness was explored by the functionalist sociologist Talcott Parsons (1975) who argued that being sick was potentially a form of deviance because it prevents a person undertaking their normal social functions. He believed that if workers used sickness as an excuse not to work then this could become a threat to the smooth running of the economy and, therefore, society and social order. However, he believed that society controls this potential deviance through a social system of duties and obligations known as 'the sick role'.

This role involves patients having to convince doctors that they are genuinely ill by conforming to certain rules of behaviour, for example, by submitting themselves to the care of doctors and by exempting themselves from leisure-based activity. If they do so, doctors legitimate their illness and this entitles the worker to be officially excused from work. The sociological validity of Parsons's ideas are explored more fully in Chapter 6.

Competing definitions of health

The biomedical model: medical definitions of health and illness

Doctors use a particular 'scientific' model of health and illness in order to decide whether someone really is ill or not. This is known as the biomedical model, and it is the basis of all Western medicine. The elements of this model include the following points.

> The body is an organic machine that occasionally breaks down.

> Illness is always seen to be caused by an identifiable and visible physical reason (for example, viruses, bacteria, cell damage). The notion that illness might be caused by magic, religion or witchcraft is dismissed as unscientific.

> Illnesses and their causes can only be observed, diagnosed or identified, classified and measured using objective and rational scientific methods.

> Only trained medical professionals should treat illness and disease in a medical environment such as a clinic or hospital.

> Doctors prefer to take the 'allopathic' approach – this means that if there is a cure for the problem, then it will almost always be through the use of drugs or surgery, rather than, for example, in changing social relationships or people's spiritual lives.

At its simplest, this model presents the human body as a type of machine and, just as with a machine, parts can go wrong and need repairing. Over time, the body 'wears out' just as a machine does and one day it will eventually stop working completely. The doctor is the equivalent of a 'body mechanic or technician' – their role is to restore the functions of the body by solving the problem of what is wrong. This is why this contemporary biomedical model is sometimes referred to as the 'biomechanical' model.

Biomedicine claims that doctors are good for society and that the good health and long life expectancy of the nation are the result of medical science. The biomedical/biomechanical model is the current dominant way of defining health and illness and the lay definitions examined earlier accept it as superior. It underpins most of the medical practices found in the NHS. However, other models of health exist which challenge this model and offer alternative definitions of health.

Traditional and non-Western definitions of health and illness

The biomedical model contrasts markedly with concepts of illness in traditional and non-Western societies, where illness is seen as the result of a wider range of factors than just the body itself.

In some traditional societies these factors could include witchcraft – where the blame for the illness lies in the bad wishes of others – or possibly the 'will of God'. For example, in the Ndembu tribe of Zambia, illness is blamed on sorcerers, witches or the spirits of ancestors. Some

non-Western societies have more complex models of health, in which the body and the mind are seen to be completely linked. Any understanding of the body, and therefore of illness and disease, must be linked to the person's mental and spiritual state. These models believe that the body and mind need to be treated together. The traditional Indian Ayurvedic model of health does just this. It believes that health problems happen because the mind, body and spirit are out of balance. Practitioners claim that certain combinations of Ayurvedic medicine will help to increase energy and wellbeing, balance mind, body and spirit, decrease stress, and possibly prevent and cure diseases such as cancer. These practices are offered as part of the Indian Health Service.

Complementary medicine

In recent years, there has been a major growth in medicines or therapies that usually lie outside the official health sector. These include:

> *alternative medicine* – medical practices that are very different from the orthodox ones used in the NHS; people use these methods as an alternative to official clinical practices

> *complementary medicine* – an approach that uses both biomedical and non-orthodox practices; for example, acupuncture is available on the NHS

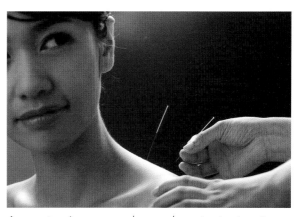

Acupuncture is a very popular complementary treatment.

> *holistic medicine* – both alternative and complementary medicines can be holistic, that is, they aim to integrate the body and the mind or spirit; for example, acupuncture aims to restore balance on an emotional, spiritual and physical level.

Reasons for emergence of alternative/complementary approaches

Giddens (1991) argues that the late 20th century – which he characterises as **'late modernity'** – saw the development of new ways of thinking and acting in contemporary society, particularly with regard to illness and the role of medical science. Leonti and Casu (2013) suggest the increased popularity of alternative approaches to health has been caused by the globalisation of ideas, which has accelerated the interchange between local and global medical treatments via international trade, satellite television and the internet.

UNDERSTAND THE CONCEPT

Late modernity is a term used to describe contemporary society, where there is a greater stress placed on consumption and choice. This compares with modernity in the late 19th and the 20th centuries, which stressed the importance of work status and conformity to social rules.

BUILD CONNECTIONS

Globalisation refers to the increasing interdependence of the different societies that make up the world. What happens in one society often has global repercussions because societies are economically, culturally and politically linked. Most areas of the Sociology specification require application of this concept. For example, globalisation has led to more emphasis on the teaching of information technology in British schools, to a realisation that many domestic crime problems are linked to global crime phenomenon, such as the international drugs trade, and that health care systems are highly dependent on global migration for the recruitment of skilled staff.

These new ways of thinking, according to Hardey (1998), have led to some people becoming disillusioned with medical science because they believe that it has created many harmful effects, such as addiction. Hunt and Lightly (1999) note that people find it hard to accept that orthodox medicine sometimes fails. The social expectations associated with conventional medicine are too high and when it fails to deliver cures, people in frustration experiment with alternative types of treatment.

A second relevant feature of late modernity, according to Hardey, has been the growth in self-expression and individual choice. For example, some people turn to alternative global therapies because they reject aspects of scientific practice for religious or philosophical reasons, while others belong to counter-cultures that prefer to experiment with more holistic approaches.

Postmodernists argue that the growing acceptance of alternative therapies is producing a significant change, as medical practitioners are now starting to see the benefits of some alternatives, such as acupuncture and chiropracty, and are integrating these into the NHS as 'complementary medicines and therapies'. Consequently it is claimed that this has led to a decline in the general public's uncritical acceptance of orthodox medicine and the power and authority of doctors.

Criticisms of the biomedical model

Foucault (1973) is critical of the biomedical model and describes the way that doctors view their patients (like machines in need of repair) as the medical gaze. By this he means that the patient is not seen as a person in themselves, but simply as an example of a particular 'category of ill health', such as an example of pneumonia, or cancer or heart disease. The person and their social context are often overlooked. Foucault suggests that this is because medicine as a science has only focused on the functioning of the body and excluded all other factors.

Trowler (1996) claims that the NHS, which is underpinned by the biomedical model, is too focused on the expensive business of curing people when it should be focused on the cheaper option of preventing people from becoming ill in the first place, for example, through health promotion campaigns. Only about 4 per cent of the NHS budget is spent on health promotion. Trowler argues that the NHS does little to promote good health. It is a National Sickness Service rather than a National Health Service.

McKeown (1979) questions the view that biomedicine is responsible for the good health experienced by the UK population today. He argues that mortality rates were reduced and life expectancy increased by public health services (for example, clean water and sanitation) and better living standards – better paid jobs led to better diet and nutrition, which led to greater physical resistance to disease. Better housing, especially council housing, reduced overcrowding and the possibility of airborne disease such as tuberculosis. McKeown argues that these public health measures and improvements in the general standard of living significantly reduced the death rates of infants and adults in the first forty years of the 20th century before the introduction of the biomedical-dominated NHS in 1948.

Some postmodernist sociologists have expressed concern about the increasing tendency of the biomedical approach to define a greater range of personal and social problems, not previously thought to have anything to do with health or medicine, as medical problems. According to Conrad (2004) and Davies (2006) this 'medicalisation of social life' has resulted in conditions such as pregnancy, childbirth, obesity, shyness, children's misbehaviour, depression and men's impotency being redefined as serious medical problems that only doctors can solve. Actor Stephen Fry explored the medicalisation of mental illness in the 2006 documentary *Stephen Fry: The Secret Life of the Manic Depressive*.

Conrad suggests that this medicalisation has also been driven by the global pharmaceutical industry's search for new markets and consumers, with many products now being advertised as necessities if people are to protect themselves from the risks associated with ill health and ageing.

Finally, Illich (2002) questions the biomedical idea that the medical profession is good for society. He identifies a number of harms (which he groups together and calls '**clinical iatrogenesis**') – premature deaths, injuries, reducing people to vegetative states, and so on – that he claims are the product of the biomedical approach to health and illness. These include negligent acts by:

> hospital staff, including doctors, surgeons, nurses and administrators; for example, mistakes made during operations, misdiagnosis of disease, prescribing the wrong drugs, deaths from hospital infections such as MRSA, or neglect of patient's needs

> Drug companies; for example, deaths and medical problems caused by the side effects of drugs or long-term addiction to them.

UNDERSTAND THE CONCEPT

Clinical iatrogenesis is the inadvertent and preventable induction of disease or health complications by the medical profession. This could include addiction to prescribed drugs, side effects caused by drug treatments and mistakes made during surgery.

In the USA, it is estimated that clinical iatrogenesis is the third leading cause of death. Emslie's (2002) research on the NHS found that over 400,000 patients suffer potentially preventable harmful events each year. Moreover, there are over 34,000 avoidable deaths every year in the NHS attributed to 'medical mistakes'. Emslie found that claims for clinical negligence against the NHS average over £400 million a year, while outstanding claims amount to several billion pounds.

THE SOCIAL CONSTRUCTION OF THE BODY

Once sociologists began to view health and illness as socially-constructed concepts, the next step was to study the (human) body. For most people, the body is

something natural which is largely shaped by biology, especially genetics, and, to a lesser extent, by lifestyle. This is confirmed by the biomedical model of health and illness, which generally regards the human body as a biological object, the study of which is best left to medical experts.

The body and embodiment

However, sociologists argue that how people understand the body is also socially constructed, and they use the term 'embodiment' to refer to the sociological notion of the body as both a social and physical thing. Specifically, embodiment means that body shapes are heavily influenced by a range of social factors, for example, exercise, diet, quality of housing, types of employment and income. Most of these factors are, in turn, influenced by social class, ethnicity, gender and age. In other words, how the human body as a thing or object is presented, gazed at and evaluated by others is a product of the society in which that body exists. The social construction of the body has been illustrated by sociologists in several ways.

Despite the fact that people exist in 'bodies' that, *objectively,* are different shapes, heights, colours and physical abilities, they are also *subjectively valued* as attractive or ugly, young or old, short or tall, weak or strong. Feminist sociologists argue that these subjective judgements originate in the fact that most societies are patriarchal and that some cultural industries such as the mass media, fashion and pornography are able to shape and dominate cultural beliefs about the body and especially the female form.

The social constructionist argument also stresses that the types of bodies which are considered attractive or ugly, normal or abnormal, and so on has varied over time and across societies. For example, in affluent Western societies, slimness is currently highly valued, as seen in the use of size-zero models in the fashion industry, while obesity in both men and women attracts disapproval. However, historically in most Western societies, up to the beginning of the 20th century, the ideal body shape for a woman was a 'full figure', while in middle-aged men a large stomach indicated that they were financially successful in life. These societies generally dismissed thin and ill-nourished bodies as indicative of poverty and failure.

How is the female body constructed in UK society today? Is the male body presented, gazed at and evaluated in the same way?

FOCUS ON SKILLS: THOUSANDS OF PATIENTS KILLED BY DRUG AND EQUIPMENT ERRORS

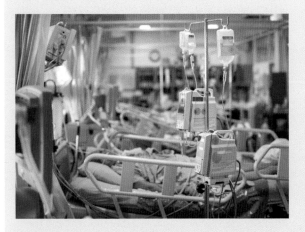

Thousands of patients are killed or seriously injured because of mistakes caused by the poor design of drugs packets and confusing medical equipment, according to a report for the head of the NHS. Medical equipment with the 'off' switch next to key controls, and medicines with similar names and packaging cause errors that would never occur in industries such as aviation which take safety more seriously, experts say. Temporary staff often fail to get to grips with machines in a way that standardisation should make impossible. Jeremy Hunt, the health secretary, has repeatedly said the health service must aspire to airline standards of safety.

Official figures show at least 8,000 patients a year are killed or severely harmed needlessly by drug errors. Jane Reid, a nursing academic, who has written a report on the human factors of safety, said many cases could be avoided with better design. Professor Reid said: "Humans are fallible, they have attention blindness. We don't see what we're not expecting to see. At times of high stress, distraction is a real challenge. I think this has just been put in the too-difficult box. I find it staggering if you think about the purchasing power of the NHS. Staff should not use a piece of equipment unless they've been trained, but you have agency staff who move from one place to another and they may be working with one type of machine one day and another the next, so the potential for errors is quite significant."

Martin Bromiley, who launched the Clinical Human Factors Group after his wife died after an avoidable error during an operation, said: "Hospitals are full of error-prone environments and opportunities for things to go wrong". He said that 'look-alike, sound-alike medication' makes it much more likely that rushed staff will give patients the wrong drugs, particularly if there are no consistent rules about which types are stored where. "The NHS will buy drugs in similar packaging which do very different things, and just say to clinicians, 'Be very careful not to make a mistake'."

Doctors are often blamed for mistakes such as the death of 18-year-old Wayne Jowett, after a cancer drug was wrongly injected into his spine. Professor Reid said it made no sense that intravenous drips had not been redesigned to make this impossible, when even cash machines are standardised.

Soure: Smyth, C. 'Thousands of patients killed by drug and equipment errors' *The Times*, 24 December 2014

Questions

1. **Identify** how many people are killed or injured by errors in the NHS every year according to this article.

2. **Explain** the possible reasons why the report for the head of the NHS identifies significantly fewer deaths due to human error than the number of deaths reported by Emslie. (Use Illich's summary below to guide you.)

3. **Analyse** why the health industry's record on safety is compared unfavourably in the article to that of the aviation industry.

4. **Evaluate** the biomedical view that the medical profession is good for society. (Think about the arguments both for and against this; for example, think of the positive things achieved by the NHS since 1948 but balance your response with some discussion of the negative effects too, such as iatrogenesis.)

The sociological perspective of the body, applied to medicine, goes further than this. According to Foucault (1981), modern science has had an extensive impact on how societies see and understand the body. Foucault noted that the biomedical model is based on extensive scientific studies over a long period of time by experts who have developed measurements of body activity and shape, which establish what is normal (healthy) and abnormal (unhealthy).

A good example of this is the Body Mass Index (BMI), which is a standardised measure of obesity. Those who are above the appropriate height/weight ratio are officially defined as obese. Other well-known examples of standardised scientific measures which distinguish the healthy body from the unhealthy body are blood pressure, cholesterol, blood sugars and heart beat rhythm tests. Foucault is not saying that these are wrong or should not be used, but he does suggest that these tests formalise the distinction between normal bodies and abnormal bodies. This is, he says, part of a much bigger change in society: experts are justified in, first, gathering detailed private information (the process of surveillance) and, second, using that information so that the state can direct and justify appropriate ways to behave, for example, by instructing people not to smoke cigarettes, to eat more fruit and vegetables, to cut down on fatty foods, to limit alcohol consumption, and so on.

Turner (1992) describes this as a process of 'regulating bodies'. He notes that those who deviate from normality in terms of their body behaviour may be constrained through legislation, medical advice or social pressure to change that behaviour in order to conform to the general body norm. He suggests that entire populations are regulated on the basis of medical evidence to behave in certain ways. Examples of this are the use of inoculation and vaccination that children are expected to have in more affluent societies to protect them from specific diseases, and legislation to reduce public smoking.

Some sociologists note that in late modernity, the body has become an especially important 'site' for making statements about oneself. Giddens argues that in contemporary society, individual identity has come to be something which people 'work at'. People today often use their bodies to consciously construct an image which they want to present to others as their real 'selves'. Giddens calls this '**reflexive mobilisation**'. Shilling (2003) found that people are increasingly seeing their bodies as 'unfinished products', or projects for improvement. Bodies are no longer seen as something that people just have, and that should be accepted as they are. Increasingly, he argues, people wish to alter their bodies in order to express their individuality or to achieve some desired state.

UNDERSTAND THE CONCEPT

Reflexive mobilisation refers to the process whereby an individual thinks about how they present themselves to the social world. They are actively engaged in constructing their identity by mobilising or using their bodies, for example by getting a highly visible tattoo.

What sorts of treatments and activities do people who see their bodies as projects seek in order to express their individuality?

However, as Fox and Ward (2008) have pointed out, this ability to remake the body is not necessarily as empowering as people hope it might be. Those who treat their bodies as a project may be the unwitting victims of commercial exploitation. There are great profits to be made by the media, global pharmaceutical companies and private cosmetic surgeons in shaping desire and providing the means to reconstruct bodies into the desired images. Such commercial interests may also be responsible for shaping those desires in the first place.

DISABILITY

Another area where ideas about health and the body overlap is the topic of disability. According to Friedson (1965), the commonsense perception of disability is that disabled people have some physical or mental impediment that prevents them from operating 'normally' – for example loss of limb, paralysis, a physically degenerative disease such as motor neurone disease, blindness or Down's syndrome. Best (2005) notes that disability is defined as the inability to fully take part in activities that the majority take for granted, such as washing or dressing oneself, walking, driving, and so on.

This view of disability is established in the law. Under the Equality Act 2010 people are disabled if they have a physical or mental impairment that has a 'substantial' and 'long-term' negative effect on their ability to do normal daily activities. 'Substantial' means more than minor or trivial, like not being able to work or get dressed without help. 'Long-term' means this condition has lasted 12 months or more.

The biomedical approach to disability

These commonsense and legal definitions of disability originate with the biomedical model of disability which assumes that there exists an ideal normal and healthy body, and therefore disability is abnormal because physical and mental impairments reduce a person's ability to lead a normal life. The biomedical model tends to define disability as a form of long-term chronic illness. Moreover, it works on the assumption that disability leads to dependence on others – doctors and carers (who are often family members). Disability is often presented by the biomedical model as a 'tragedy' and, consequently, the idea that the disabled deserve society's pity and charity is strongly embedded in culture and media representations. It is also often assumed that the disabled person has to be 'helped' to come to terms with the physical and psychological problems that they allegedly face.

Friedson identified that our commonsense definition of disability is an impediment that prevents a person from operating 'normally'.

The social construction approach to disability

Oliver (1996) is critical of the biomedical approach to disability because it assumes that there exists a clear definition of the normal body, and a normal range of activities associated with it. Oliver argues there is no such thing as a 'normal' body. He points out that not everyone is able to do everything as well as others – for example, run, catch or throw – yet society does not describe those who are less able as being disabled. Society accepts these differences as part of the normal range of human abilities. Tom Shakespeare (2013) suggests that bodies should be viewed as part of a continuum, with fit, able-bodied people at one end of the continuum and the severely disabled at the other end. In between these two extremes, Shakespeare points out that there is a range of abilities and impairments.

According to both Oliver and Shakespeare, it is how the lack of some of these abilities and impairments are interpreted by society that is important. This is because people who lack some abilities and/or are in some way

impaired are defined by society as a social problem, as being in some way deviant. Consequently, the individual who lacks the ability or who has the impairment is labelled as 'inferior' compared with an able-bodied individual. In this sense, Shakespeare and Oliver argue that these people are not disabled by their bodies but by society's reactions to their bodies.

The social constructionist approach to disability, then, focuses on how the individual is disabled by society rather than by their physical or mental impairment. It sees disability as a social construction – a product of society – and is very critical of the biomedical model for failing to recognise the social barriers that prevent the disabled from participating in the same social activities as the able-bodied. Oliver refers to these social barriers, which are made up of prejudicial attitudes and stereotypes about the disabled as well as a range of discriminatory actions, as '**disablism**'.

UNDERSTANDING THE CONCEPT

Disablism describes the social barriers that arise when an able-bodied person views someone with an impairment – such that they may be hindered in performing some ordinary tasks – with prejudice and treats them in a discriminatory way.

The origins of disability

If disability is a socially-constructed concept, how did it come about? According to Finkelstein (1980), the modern idea of the dependent disabled person is largely the result of industrialisation and the introduction of machinery. People with impairments were excluded from this type of work and came to be viewed as a burden. The rise of the medical profession in the early 19th century led to them becoming labelled as sick and in need of care.

Oliver (1990) takes Finkelstein's analysis further, by suggesting that the medical profession not only imposes the label of sickness, abnormality and dependency on people with impairments, but also helps to construct the dominant way in which able-bodied people view and treat people with impairments. Oliver notes that people are encouraged to see the impaired individual in terms of their personal misfortune, facing problems very specific to them, rather than as members of a wider minority group which shares a common experience of inequality and discrimination. According to Oliver, this draws attention away from the fact that impairment is turned into disability by the wider economic, physical and social environment that discriminates against disabled people.

Stigma and disability

Stigma is an important term in helping sociologists to understand how people with disabilities are excluded from social activities. The concept was first used in sociology by Erving Goffman (1963), who suggested that certain groups of people are defined as 'discredited' because they possess characteristics that are seen as 'negative'.

UNDERSTAND THE CONCEPT

Stigma refers to the situation in which some people have a label placed upon them because they have a social or physical characteristic which is seen as different from – and possibly inferior to – the norm.

People with impairments are different from the able-bodied norm and, consequently, they are often subjected to stigma (or disablism) in the form of social prejudice and active discrimination. This makes it difficult for them to lead the sorts of independent and active lifestyles led by their able-bodied peers.

How do you react to people with disability? Do you treat them differently from other people? If you do, why is this?

Types of disablism

Prejudice

Social constructionists argue that the last civil rights battle (now that women, ethnic minority people and gay people have made progress towards equal rights) is the one currently being fought by people with impairments. It is argued that this group are unable to enjoy the same opportunities as able-bodied people – they do not share the same civil or human rights. This is because they face constant prejudice and discrimination.

Sociologists note that myths, negative stereotypes and stigma about disability are held by able-bodied people and act as cultural barriers, contributing to their lack of status and the consequent inequalities that people with impairments experience on a daily basis. These notions, which many people with impairments reject, include the following points.

> A person's disability defines who they are as an individual. This means that people with impairments are often labelled according to their condition or limitations. It is assumed that they cannot carry out particular tasks. As a result of this, some able-bodied people may find it awkward to interact with and have normal social relations with the physically or mentally impaired. For example, during interaction with a person in a wheelchair, the able-bodied may be embarrassed by the impairment and ignore or seek not to mention the 'obvious' disability. They may also spend most of the time conversing and interacting with the carer rather than the person in the wheelchair. Research by Aiden and McCarthy (2014) reported that two thirds of the British public feel uncomfortable talking to disabled people, while one fifth of 18–34-year-old males admit that they have actually avoided talking to a disabled person, because they were unsure how to communicate with them.

> People with disabilities are brave, courageous, superhuman and inspirational for living with their disability. George Covington, a writer who is blind, notes, "We're seen as inspirational, and inspiration sells like hotcakes. My disability isn't a burden: having to be so damned inspirational is" (quoted on www.togetherwerock.com).

> People with disabilities are special and should be treated differently.

> Disability is an unending burden. Aiden and McCarthy's research found that over a third of able-bodied people believed that disabled people were not as productive as everyone else, while 13 per cent think of disabled people as "getting in the way most or some of the time" (p.7).

> Disabled people are always going to be dependent on help from the able-bodied. Aiden and McCarthy found that 76 per cent of their able-bodied sample believed that disabled people were in need of constant care.

> Disabled people are better off in the company of other disabled people.

> Adult disabled people are not capable of loving, physical sexual relationships.

> Disabled people share the same needs, interests and opinions.

> People with disabilities cannot lead a full and productive life.

There is some evidence that some of these prejudicial social attitudes held by the able-bodied are rooted in negative media representations of the disabled. Longmore (1987) found that disabled people tend to be represented on television either as evil, dangerous and monster-like or as objects of pity or charity. Cumberbatch and Negrine (1992) argue that media representations of the disabled rarely present them as 'people who just happen to have a disability', whereas until fairly recently events such as the Paralympics were ignored altogether by television or impaired athletes were treated as 'heroic' in terms of their success in overcoming their physical disadvantages.

Discrimination

It is claimed by Oliver (2009) that a number of different types of discrimination are practised against the physically and mentally impaired, which result in them being disabled by society. These include the following points.

> There is a general failure to consider and include the needs of the impaired when designing and building the physical environment. The social constructionist argument highlights how the inaccessible nature of the physical environment disables the physically impaired; for example, the lack of ramps and lifts for access to buildings, the design of shopping aisles, unsuitable public transport systems and the lack of disabled toilet facilities. Much of society's social space has been designed with the able-bodied in mind. However, there are signs that this is changing and that physical environments such as new shopping centres and schools are now being designed with the impaired in mind.

> There is evidence that employers are reluctant to employ people with impairments: they are six times more likely to be refused job interviews. As a result, people with impairments are disabled in that they are more likely than able-bodied people to be excluded from well-paid jobs and therefore to be economically disadvantaged. It is a fact that people with impairments are more likely to be unemployed, and to occupy lower-paid jobs if employed. Consequently they are more likely to be living in poverty.

> The government has been accused of discriminating against people with impairments and disabling them by introducing 'work capability assessment' for those receiving Employment and Support Allowance (ESA). Disability charities have criticised these 'fitness for work' tests as unfair to those with impairments because they are allegedly finding such people fit for work when they are not. Benefits are cut off if that person is seen to be not actively seeking work – so the impaired are being disabled by society by being thrown further into poverty.

Aiden and McCarthy's research data showed that 28 per cent of disabled people reported being stared at, while 35 per cent had been talked to in a patronising way. Moreover, 20 per cent reported that people treated them as if they

were a nuisance, while 40 per cent felt that able-bodied people did not understand their needs. Finally, nearly a third of the sample suggested that the general public needed to change their attitudes towards the disabled.

There is evidence that people with impairments are disabled by bullying, such as 'hate crimes', both in care homes and in wider society. In 2011, it was estimated that 8 in 10 children with impairments had been the victims of bullying by able-bodied children. According to the official criminal statistics, there were 1,985 recorded incidents of disability hate crime in the UK in 2013–14.

The concept of 'master status'

When people with impairments are negatively labelled, the label becomes what Goffman calls a 'master status'. This means that the label completely dominates the way the person is treated, and any other positive attributes that they have may be seen as less important. For example, the person who is unable to walk unaided is simply seen as 'wheelchair-bound' rather than as an intelligent, articulate man or woman with a personality.

Goffman points out that individuals with impairments may come to accept and internalise this master status and see themselves solely in terms of their dependent disabled status. In other words, they may respond to the constant assumption that they are helpless and dependent by developing low social esteem and worth. A self-fulfilling prophecy therefore results. Some people with physical and mental impairments may become disabled in terms of their mind-set as a result of being constantly treated and judged in terms of their impairment rather than as an individual.

Scott's (1969) study of blind people illustrates this self-fulfilling prophecy very well. After observing the interaction between medical professionals and blind people in the USA, Scott argued that the blind developed a 'blind personality' because they internalised the experts' view that they should be experiencing psychological problems in adjusting to their loss of sight. Part of this process also involved 'learned helplessness' – they should learn to rely on sighted people for help. In other words, they became helpless and dependent because the experts expected that behaviour.

The disabled identity and resistance

Recent sociological studies suggest that people with impairments are more likely to resist those definitions and labels that stress their dependence and helplessness. For example, Olney and Kim (2001) argue that the impaired people in their study felt positive about their bodies despite their awareness that the able-bodied evaluated them negatively. They generally rejected medical and

FOCUS ON SKILLS: THE VILLAGE BY VIC FINKELSTEIN

Imagine a world in which wheelchair-users and able-bodied people live completely segregated lives. The wheelchair-users develop their own society to meet their needs and construct a village which in its design and everyday activity reflects the fact that everybody uses a wheelchair. Able-bodied people do not often visit the village and the wheelchair-users control all aspects of their lives. They make the goods that they sell in their shops with special aids, they work the machines that clean the street, run their own schools, banks, post offices, and the transport system of the village, and so on. For the villagers, being in a wheelchair is normal because everybody else they meet is also in a wheelchair. They see wheelchair-users on television and hear them on the radio. Able-bodied people, however, are rarely seen and little understood.

The wheelchair-users design the buildings in the village to suit their physical situation. Because everyone is always in wheelchairs there is no need to have ceilings at 9 feet 6 inches high or door heights at 7 feet 2 inches. Soon it becomes standard practice to build doors to a height of 5 feet and ceilings to a height of 7 feet 4 inches. Everyone is happy in the village because all the buildings and environment are truly in tune with the needs of the wheelchair-users.

One day a few able-bodied people, through no choice of their own, came to live in this village. Naturally, one of the first things they noticed was the heights of the doors and ceilings – by constantly knocking their heads on the door frames. Soon all the able-bodied members of the village were marked by the dark bruises on their foreheads and the painful back problems they had developed by constantly having to bend down. They went to see the village doctors, who were, naturally, also wheelchair-users. The doctors produced learned reports which said their problems were caused by the handicap of their physical size. This handicap caused a disadvantage which made them disabled in this society. Special aids were designed by the wheelchair-user doctors for the able-bodied disabled members of the village. All the able-bodied were given special toughened helmets (provided free by the village) to wear at all times.

However, the able-bodied disabled caused many problems. When they sought jobs no one would employ them because of prejudice and discrimination and they consequently fell into poverty. Charities were created by the wheelchair-users to collect money for the able-bodied poor and many shops and pubs had an upturned helmet placed on the counters for customers to leave their small change. Painted on the helmets were the words "Help the able-bodied disabled". Later, when the able-bodied were sitting together and discussing their problems they realised that they were never consulted by the wheelchair-users about the way the village was designed and run. They realised that there were solutions to their problems which had never occurred to the wheelchair-users because the wheelchair-users never looked at the problems in the same way as the able-bodied.

Based on Finkelstein (1975)

Questions

1. **Identify** and briefly **explain** four aspects of the village's design that enabled people in wheelchairs to lead a normal life.

2. **Identify** and briefly **explain** three problems that the able-bodied face when they come to live in the village.

3. **Analyse** the response of both the wheelchair-users and the able-bodied to the problems of the latter. Compare these to the real world.

4. **Outline** and **evaluate** the view that disability is a social construction. (Think about both sides of the argument – the biomedical view that disability makes it difficult to live a normal life, and the view that the impaired are disabled by society.)

media labels of their condition and consequently had a very positive self-image.

The social model of disability argues that more positive disabled identities should be promoted, stressing independence, choice and autonomy for people with impairments. They believe that the state should invest in an impaired-friendly social environment and should more actively address the prejudice and discrimination that results in disablism. People with impairments are directly addressing politicians by setting up self-help groups, such as the Black Triangle Campaign, in order to challenge the types of disabled stereotyping documented in this chapter.

Critiques of the social model of disability

Critiques of the social model of disability have recently appeared. These argue that sociologists cannot ignore that physical and biological factors such as pain, mental impairment and being bedbound do impact negatively on how some people with impairments experience social life and can make that life unpleasant and difficult. In other words, not all people with impairments can lead active and independent lifestyles and this has nothing to do with labels, stereotypes or the physical

environment. This group of people is quite simply disabled by their impairment.

CONCLUSIONS

This chapter has demonstrated that defining health and illness is not straightforward. How people define health and illness, and how they respond to symptoms differs according to a range of social influences. The medical profession's main approach to health, illness and disease is scientific but this has been challenged for a number of convincing reasons by sociologists and alternative health practitioners. Furthermore, some sociologists have argued that, to understand how society views health and illness, research should focus on how the human body has come to be seen as a health project in recent years by people wishing to project a healthy identity. Finally, no examination of the body can ignore the debate about disability and what constitutes a 'normal' body. Disabled sociologists have raised interesting questions as to whether people are disabled by their impairment or whether they are disabled by society's prejudices and actions.

CHECK YOUR UNDERSTANDING

1. Define the concept of 'morbidity'.

2. Define the term 'disablism'.

3. Define the term 'reflexive mobilisation'.

4. Identify the main features of the biomedical model of health.

5. Identify three reasons why the clinical iceberg of unreported and unrecorded illness exists.

6. Outline and explain how definitions of health held by lay people are influenced by social factors.

7. Outline and explain the relationship between impairment and stigma.

8. Explain what Parsons means by 'the sick role.'

9. Outline and evaluate the similarities and differences between the biomedical and social constructionist explanations of health and illness.

10. Outline and evaluate, using perspectives on the body and disability as examples, the view that no universal definition of the normal human body exists.

TAKE IT FURTHER

Select a small sample of people, ideally from different generations, and ask them to rate their degree of sympathy on a scale of 1 to 5 for people with the following 'illnesses': hangover, headache (not caused by a hangover), impotence, cirrhosis of the liver (caused by drinking too much alcohol), anorexia, heart disease, breast cancer, lung cancer caused by smoking, sexually transmitted disease.

Do your results show any different attitudes to illness and disease amongst people? What explanations can you suggest for your findings?

5.2 HEALTH INEQUALITIES: CLASS, ETHNICITY AND REGION

LEARNING OBJECTIVES

› Demonstrate knowledge and understanding of the unequal social distribution of health chances in the United Kingdom by region, social class and ethnicity (AO1).

› Demonstrate knowledge and understanding of the different theories which aim to explain why regional, social class and ethnic inequalities in mortality and morbidity exist (AO1).

› Analyse and apply the evidence collected by sociological surveys of health to the range of sociological theories that aim to explain health inequality (AO2).

› Evaluate sociological explanations in order to make judgements and draw conclusions about the main causes of differences in mortality and morbidity across regions, social classes and ethnic groups (AO3).

INTRODUCING THE DEBATE

This chapter focuses on epidemiology – the study of the social distribution and causes of illness, disease and other factors related to health. The chances of an early death, of a serious long-term illness and of a disability are closely related to social class, income, area of residence and ethnic group.

But why should this be? Health, illness and disability are generally thought of as linked to our genes – that

is, they are caused by biology. Yet sociologists argue that research indicates it is the interaction of our social experiences with our biological make-up that determines our health. Some might argue that the more important of these two factors is the social rather than the biological. In this chapter, we will explore the major social determinants of our health: geographical region, social class, and ethnicity.

GEOGRAPHICAL OR REGIONAL INEQUALITIES IN HEALTH AND ILLNESS

Ellis and Fry (2010) identified a number of regional inequalities in health using statistics gathered by the Office for National Statistics (ONS) They included the following points.

> There is a clear north-south divide with regard to life expectancy in the UK. The chances of dying before the age of 75 are a fifth higher in the north of England compared with the south. For example, men in Blackpool and women in Hartlepool now live on average 10.5 and 9.6 years fewer than their counterparts in Kensington and Chelsea.

> The death rate in the north-east was 1,041 per 100,000 population in 2009 compared with 849 for the south-west and 852 for the south-east (Buchan et al, 2011).

> Infant mortality rates are highest in the West Midlands where the rate per 1,000 live births was 6.4 in 2009. Yorkshire and Humberside reported a similar rate of 6.1. The infant mortality rate in the south-east is only 3.9.

Whyte et al. (2012) found that premature death rates in Scotland have been the worst in Europe since the late 1970s. For example, mortality in the 15–44 age group among women in 2009 was 46 per cent higher in Scotland than in England and Wales, while for men in that group it was 54 per cent higher. Moreover, the mortality rate for stomach cancer, lung cancer and heart disease in Glasgow is almost twice as high compared with the south of England.

Life expectancy at birth is also lower in Scotland. For example, between 2010 and 2012, newborn boys in Glasgow had a life expectancy of 72.6 years, while for girls it was 78.5 years. In contrast, the UK average for boys and girls is 78.9 years and 82.7 years respectively. A World Health Organisation (WHO) study in 2008 found that a child born in one deprived Glasgow suburb can expect a life 28 years shorter than another living only 13 kilometres away in a more affluent area.

The idea of regional inequality is closely linked to both class and ethnic inequalities because the regions that suffer the worst health tend to have greater proportions of people from working-class and ethnic-minority backgrounds. For example, the north of the UK has greater numbers of manual routine workers whereas middle-class professional and managerial workers are more likely to be found in the south-east.

SOCIAL CLASS INEQUALITIES IN HEALTH AND ILLNESS

BUILD CONNECTIONS

Social class is a very important differentiator in terms of income, wealth, education and life expectancy, and therefore cuts across all areas of the specification. It is also a controversial concept because some sociologists argue that other sources of inequality such as gender and ethnicity are just as important, while postmodernists suggest that it has declined in importance. However, Marxists argue it is more relevant than ever in all areas of social life.

Mortality

In 2008, the death rate among men aged 25–64 and women aged 25–59 was twice as high for those in unskilled jobs as for those in higher professional classes. Over the last 25 years, life expectancy has risen for both men and women in all social classes but it has risen faster for those in the higher social classes. The life expectancy gap between those in higher and lower social classes has actually widened in the past 35 years.

The ONS (2007) notes that in the period from 2002 to 2005 there were significant social-class gaps in life expectancy.

> Men in professional occupations had a life expectancy at birth of 80.0 years, compared with 72.7 years for those in unskilled manual occupations. For women this was 85.1 years and 78.1 years respectively.

> Life expectancy at age 65 varied by occupation, with professional men aged 65 expected to live to 83.3 years on average, and unskilled manual working men expected to live to 79.1 years.

> Deaths from heart disease and lung cancer (the two most common causes of death for people aged 35 to 64) were twice as high in people from manual backgrounds compared with non-manual backgrounds. For example, the death rate from cancer was 60 per cent higher in Liverpool compared with Dorset in the south of England.

> Although infant death rates in general have fallen by around a fifth over the last decade, infant deaths were still 35 per cent more common among those from manual backgrounds than among those from non-manual backgrounds.

FOCUS ON SKILLS: BABIES BORN ON RIGHT SIDE OF NORTH-SOUTH DIVIDE LIVE YEARS LONGER

A baby boy born in the Home Counties today can expect to live about eight years longer than a new arrival in the north-west according to official figures. Girls born in part of Buckinghamshire are likely to live the longest along with boys arriving in south Cambridgeshire. Girls born in the Chiltern district of Buckinghamshire, which is home to prosperous Amersham and Chesham, can expect to live to 86 years and four months, more than six years longer than a girl born in Manchester, according to figures from the Office for National Statistics. A boy born in south Cambridgeshire, described several years ago as one of the best places to live in England and Wales, is likely to live to 83 years, eight years and seven months longer than a boy arriving in Blackpool.

Official life expectancy figures showed a stark north–south divide caused partially by migration of healthy individuals from poorer to more affluent areas. The rise in life expectancy for the newborn is being driven by falling death rates among the over-65s owing to sweeping advances in medical science, better nutrition, improved public health and the decline in heavy industry. Dr Andrew Goddard, of the Royal College of Physicians, said better medical care and improvements in public health had helped increased longevity. He said: "We have seen many changes in public health such as the decline in smoking, a ban on

smoking in public and the perception that smoking is no longer acceptable". Advances in medical science had also helped to increase life expectancy as people can now survive diseases and illnesses such as cancer and heart attacks from which they previously would have died.

Most of the regional differences we now see are owing to public health reasons such as levels of smoking, obesity and alcohol use. He said the difference between the north and south remains stark. "We know health is directly related to economic status. We know that the divide between deprived people and the well off remains stubborn." David Buck, senior fellow in public health at the King's Fund, warned of inequality for those living longer: "People may be surviving longer but for those living longer they are surviving with more multiple chronic conditions. That is a real challenge for the NHS".

Source: Richard Ford, The Times, 20 November 2014

Questions

1. **Identify** and summarise the evidence in this article which suggests that there is a north–south divide in life expectancy.

2. **Analyse** the reasons why falling death rates among people aged 65 and over are partly responsible for the rise in life expectancy for newborns. (There are at least five reasons highlighted by the article.)

3. **Evaluation**. On the basis of the evidence here and your own knowledge, evaluate the view that regional health inequalities are directly related to economic status. (As a starting point, think about whether people in the north of England behave in unhealthy ways that are different from the behaviour of people in the south, or whether these regional inequalities are caused by factors beyond the control of people in the north.)

Measuring social class

The social class of an individual in the UK is objectively determined by sociologists using their occupation. Sociologists and the Office for National Statistics (ONS) use the National Statistics Socio-Economic Classification which divides the UK population into eight social classes, based on factors such as whether their jobs involve the exercise of power over others and their earnings. Those who are in manual or blue-collar work have traditionally been seen as working class while those in non-manual – managerial, professional and white-collar – jobs have traditionally been categorised as middle class.

Morbidity

Although death rates have fallen and life expectancy has increased, there is little evidence that the population is experiencing better health than 20 years ago. In fact, there has actually been a small increase in self-reported long-standing illness, and differences between the social classes are still quite clear. General Household Survey data in 2006 showed that of those suffering from chronic illness or disability, 52 per cent came from unskilled occupations compared with only 33 per cent from professional backgrounds.

However, this type of measurement comes from a very subjective source – as Bartley and Blane (2008) note "the more physically demanding nature of manual occupations might mean that illness is less easily tolerated and recognised earlier".

Longitudinal studies of health may be more reliable because they are based on samples of the whole population. The British Regional Heart Survey (BRHS) of middle-aged men drawn from general practices in 24 British towns recruited between 1978 and 1980 reported in 2013 that manual workers were still twice as likely as non-manual workers to experience coronary problems and to develop cancer compared with 35 years ago. The link between region, neighbourhood, social class and chronic illness was also highlighted in the BRHS finding that older men aged 60–79 have their chances of developing cardiac problems further increased by living in deprived neighbourhoods.

UNDERSTAND THE CONCEPT

A **longitudinal study** is a survey that has been carried out over a considerable number of years on the same group of people.

Why do you think longitudinal studies produce more valid data than one-off social surveys?

Occupational classification	% of working population	Examples
1 Higher managerial and professional	11.0	Company directors, senior civil servants, doctors, barristers, clergy, architects
2 Lower managerial and professional	23.5	Nurses, journalists, teachers, police officers, musicians
3 Intermediate	14.0	Secretaries, clerks, computer operators, driving instructors
4 Small employers and self-accountable workers	9.9	Taxi drivers, window cleaners, publicans, decorators
5 Lower supervisory, craft and related	9.8	Train drivers, plumbers, printers, TV engineers
6 Semi-routine	18.6	Traffic wardens, shop assistants, hairdressers, call-centre workers
7 Routine	12.7	Cleaners, couriers, road sweepers, labourers
8 Long-term unemployed or the never-worked		

Table 5.2.1 *The National Statistics Socio-Economic Classification (NS-SEC)*
Source: ONS

ETHNIC-MINORITY INEQUALITIES IN HEALTH AND ILLNESS

The UK is a **multicultural society** and there is evidence that some ethnic-minority groups experience inequalities in health and illness.

UNDERSTAND THE CONCEPT

Multicultural society refers to the coexistence of different ethnic groups in British society who are entitled to practise their unique cultural and religious norms while sharing the same rights of citizenship and abiding by the same laws.

Surprisingly, there is only limited information available on ethnicity and illness. This is partly because of the complex make-up of ethnic groups in the UK and the difficulty of making generalisations across these groupings. However, the statistics that do exist suggest that:

> most ethnic-minority groups have higher mortality rates than the white majority – life expectancy in ethnic-minority populations is very similar to that experienced by White working-class people, especially if they live in the north of the UK

> people from African Caribbean, Indian, Pakistani and Bangladeshi backgrounds are all more likely to experience and die from tuberculosis, liver cancer or diabetes compared with the White population, however, apart from liver cancer, all ethnic-minority groups have lower levels of death from cancer than the White population

> British people of Indian and Pakistani origin are more likely to die from heart disease compared with all other ethnic groups in the UK

> people of African Caribbean origin are much more likely to suffer from sickle cell disease

> members of minority ethnic groups are more likely to define themselves as having poor health than the majority population, according to Sproston and Mindell (2006) – for example, just under 50 per cent of members of ethnic-minority groups described themselves as having fair or poor health, compared with just under 30 per cent of the majority population

> Indians and African Caribbeans are more likely to experience mental illness, especially schizophrenia, compared with other ethnic groups.

Although ethnicity may be important in its own right as a source of possible explanations for health inequalities between ethnic-minority subcultures and the White population, sociologists have noted that there is considerable overlap between region or neighbourhood, social class and ethnicity. For example, the majority of ethnic-minority people in the UK are employed in routine manual work and therefore can be categorised as working class. Furthermore, the majority of ethnic minorities in the UK, outside of London, live in the north and are most likely to be found in economically - and socially - deprived regions and neighbourhoods. Those ethnic-minority groups living in London, according to Jivraj and Khan (2013), were, like their White working-class peers, most likely to be found living in neighbourhoods that experienced worse health than those boroughs mainly occupied by the middle class.

EXPLANATIONS FOR DIFFERENCES IN INEQUALITIES IN HEALTH

The artefact approach
An artefact is something observed in a scientific investigation that is not naturally present, but occurs as a result of the investigative procedure. Illsley (1986) argues that the link between class and health is not real. Rather it is a statistical illusion caused by the fact that the number of unskilled manual workers has declined so much since the 1960s that their numbers are now too small to be used as the basis for comparisons with other social classes.

However, Acheson (1998) showed that, even when semi-skilled and unskilled manual workers (social classes IV and V) were grouped together, in the 1980s death rates were 53 per cent higher among men in classes IV and V, compared with those in classes I and II.

Social selection
Saunders claims that social class does not cause ill health, but that ill health may be a significant reason why some people occupy lower social-class positions. For example, if a person is chronically ill (has a long-term illness) or is disabled, it is usually difficult for them to obtain a secure, well-paid job; they are less likely to be socially selected by employers because they are too much of a risk in terms of carrying out a job continuously and effectively. In contrast, the fit and healthy are more likely to be socially selected and therefore upwardly mobile in terms of jobs, income and consequently social class.

However, there are two problems with the social selection approach. First, most chronic diseases tend to present later in life, well into adulthood and after most careers have been decided upon. The association with chronic illness and lower social-class position is therefore not proven. Second, countless studies of health differences suggest that poor health is linked to either the cultural or economic disadvantages associated with occupying a lower social-class position in society. In other words, it is not ill health that causes a person to be working class, rather it is either the working-class lifestyle or the working-class experience of economic inequality that brings about poor health and lower life expectancy.

Cultural or behavioural explanations

Cultural explanations of health inequalities (also known as behavioural approaches) stress that differences in health are best understood as the result of the lifestyles and cultural choices made by some individuals or groups in the population. It is suggested that working-class people prefer less healthy lifestyles and that they tend to make the wrong choices with regard to smoking, alcohol consumption, unhealthy foods and exercise compared with the middle class. In other words, working-class culture encourages more risky behaviour, which is damaging to health. Middle-class people benefit from a more health-conscious culture and are better educated about diet and the avoidance of risky behavioural choices.

Diet

Roberts *et al.* (2013) note that the diet of the working class is not as healthy as the diet of the middle class. For example, manual workers have higher sugar and salt consumption than professionals, and they eat more fatty fried food, especially fast foods and processed convenience food. In contrast, middle-class people are nearly twice as likely as working-class people to eat five or more portions of fruit and vegetables per day.

Middle-class families are almost twice as likely to reach the '5 A Day' target for fruit and vegetables.

Leung and Stanner (2012) identify a number of dietary differences that allegedly originate in the cultures of ethnic minorities that may contribute to the poor health of ethnic-minority groups. They claim that South Asians are less likely to reach the '5 A Day' target for fruit and vegetables compared with the rest of the UK population. They also claim that some ethnic minorities, especially women, are at risk of low iron status and vitamin D deficiency because of fasting, dietary restrictions and dress codes (which block out the sun's rays). Donin *et al* (2010) have highlighted the higher levels of fats – especially ghee – and carbohydrates, and the lack of vitamin D in Asian diets, which encourage obesity. Donin also found that obesity in both Asian and African Caribbean children was caused by **acculturation**, particularly consumption of fast foods.

UNDERSTAND THE CONCEPT

Acculturation refers to the influence of a majority culture on ethnic-minority subcultures. For example, in the UK, younger members of an ethnic-minority subculture may be influenced by their White peers or the mass media to adopt aspects of British culture in terms of dress, behaviour, taste in food and music, and so on. This may sometimes bring them into conflict with their parent culture.

How does Donin's observation about acculturation and fast foods support the culturalist case?

Smoking

The ONS reported in 2013 that working-class people were more likely to smoke than middle-class people. In 1998, one third of those in manual work smoked. This had declined to 26 per cent in 2010. However, in contrast only 15 per cent of those employed in non-manual work smoked in 2010. Moreover, 7 per cent of manual workers reported heavy smoking compared with only 3 per cent of non-manual workers. Those in managerial and professional households were the most likely never to have smoked cigarettes.

There is evidence that smoking among some ethnic-minority groups may be slightly higher than that reported by the White working class. The Health Survey for England (2004) found that 40 per cent of Bangladeshi men, 29 per cent of Pakistani men, but only 25 per cent of Black Caribbean men and 20 per cent of Indian men regularly smoked. However, rates of chewing tobacco, which is almost unknown among the White population, is a cause of concern according to Erens *et al.* (2001).

There are also regional variations in rates of smoking. About 20 per cent of people in England smoked in 2010, although this rises to 24 per cent of men in Yorkshire and Humber and 23 per cent of men in the north-west. In Wales and Scotland, 25 per cent of people were regular smokers in 2010.

Alcohol

It has been assumed that alcohol consumption is much higher among the semi-skilled, unskilled and unemployed working class compared with the middle class. There is some evidence that the working class are more likely to 'binge-drink'. For example, Fone *et al.* (2013) carried out a survey of 58,000 people across Wales between 2003 and 2007 and found that residents of deprived neighbourhoods were more likely to binge-drink compared with residents of the least deprived areas of Wales. However, overall, the evidence regarding alcohol consumption and social class is mixed. A number of studies indicate that the higher the social class of a person, the more likely they are to drink frequently. For example, Ling *et al.* (2012), using in-depth individual and group interviews with middle-aged white-collar workers, found that their sample associated 'problem' drinking with others, particularly those living in deprived areas. However, Ling *et al.* concluded that these middle-class workers frequently drank to relieve stress at levels harmful to health but did not define themselves as having a problem.

Leisure and lifestyle

It is argued that the middle class are more knowledgeable about health and this results in them taking up a wider range of physical exercise compared with the working class and ethnic-minority groups. Roberts *et al.* note that the Active People Survey (2012), an annual survey of participation in sport and physical activity in England, found that 43 per cent of their middle-class sample took part in sport for at least 30 minutes once a week or more compared to 27 per cent of their working-class sample. Middle-class people are more likely to exercise via activities such as jogging and cycling. They are actively involved in a wider range of sporting activities, such as golf and tennis, than working-class people. They are more likely to use sports centres and belong to fitness clubs. These activities reduce levels of stress and help maintain a higher standard of health. As a result, middle-class people are generally fitter and experience better health than working-class people.

In adulthood, being overweight is a measure of possible ill health, with obesity a risk factor for many chronic diseases. There is a noticeable social-class gradient in obesity, which is greater for women than men.

Knowledge and take-up of health services

It is argued that the middle class use the NHS more effectively because they are more aware of available health services, such as immunisation, antenatal surveillance and contraception, and how to make more efficient use of them. They are also more likely to complain about inadequate health facilities and services and therefore get access to better health care. In contrast, it is argued that working-class people and ethnic minorities are more likely to lack the appropriate knowledge or information about health services and healthy behaviour. For example, it is claimed that Asian women are less likely to visit ante- and postnatal clinics and consequently the Asian infant mortality rate is higher than the rest of the population.

However, Bartley and Blane note that long-term studies following people's behaviour and changes in their health have shown that cultural behaviour only accounts for about a quarter to a third of the class differences in illness and premature death. Moreover, studies have shown that even when behaviour has been changed, the results in terms of overall health outcomes have been disappointing.

The cultural approach has also been criticised for failing to recognise the economic context in which health behaviour occurs; a healthy diet or the ability to exercise by joining a gym may be shaped by cost. Middle-class people can afford to invest in their health while others may be 'forced' by their economic circumstances into an unhealthy lifestyle. The culturalist perspective also does not explain why even middle-class people who live in the north experience worse health than their southern counterparts.

Materialist explanations

Materialist explanations of health inequalities tend to focus on the unequal economic and social organisation of UK society. They see a direct relationship between differences in patterns of health, sickness and disease, and the distribution of income and wealth. Materialists tend to accept that the behavioural differences identified by the culturalist perspective contribute to poor health but claim that unhealthy behaviour is more influenced by economic factors and, in particular, by exposure to the hazards associated with living in poverty.

The role of poverty

The impact of poverty on those who live in deprived areas is seen as central to explaining the higher mortality and morbidity rates of working-class White and ethnic-minority people. People often have little or no control over the causes of poverty. For example, workers may be forced into long-term unemployment and therefore poverty in the UK because of global capitalist priorities such as shifting production to countries in which labour costs are cheaper.

It is thought that moving the production of goods abroad may be contributing to long-term unemployment in the UK.

Materialists identify a number of characteristics of poverty that contribute to the reasons why working-class people suffer worse health than middle-class people.

A sizeable percentage of the working class are in jobs but they often earn below the average income because they are paid the minimum wage and/or are on zero hour contracts. The austerity measures which were put into place by the Coalition government (2010–2015) resulted in a 6 per cent fall in wages, while food prices rose by 12 per cent in the same period.

Research by Shaw, Dorling and Davey Smith (2006) found that 40 per cent of people in ethnic-minority communities in the UK were living in poverty compared with only 20 per cent of the White community. This is unsurprising because the evidence suggests that ethnic minorities are over-concentrated in low-paid semi-skilled and unskilled jobs, while White people are twice as likely to be found in better-paid skilled manual jobs.

Many sections of the working class are claiming benefits such as income support or disability benefit. Between 2010 and 2015, access to these benefits became more difficult because the Coalition government sought to cut welfare spending in the name of austerity.

Sections of the working class are more likely to experience poor housing conditions, such as run-down, damp, vermin-ridden and over-crowded rented accommodation in economically- and socially-deprived areas. These conditions can significantly contribute to poor health. Palmer *et al.* (2005) found that individuals living in council housing were three times more likely to suffer chronic illness and disability than people who owned their own homes.

It is mainly ethnic-minority people who are most likely to experience these poor housing conditions. In the UK, 70 per cent of ethnic-minority people live in council housing in the country's 88 most economically- and socially-deprived areas; 30 per cent of Bangladeshis and 22 per cent of Pakistanis live in accommodation that is officially classed as damp and overcrowded, compared with only 2 per cent of the White population. Alcock (2006) found that poor, damp housing often leads to poor health in ethnic-minority children. This leads to time off school and fewer qualifications, which often leads to low-paid jobs or unemployment, and consequently poverty when they reach adulthood.

Dorling *et al.* (2000) highlight the effects on health of environmental factors found in deprived areas, such as vandalised buildings, dog dirt and pollution from traffic, and social problems such as high levels of crime, drug-dealing, street gangs and anti-social behaviour. Children and youths may lack safe spaces in which to play or congregate. Acheson notes that this may negatively affect the ability of children to exercise because "it's safer to keep the kids in front of the TV than let them go out to play".

Poverty has a direct effect on children. In 2015, the Child Poverty Action Group (CPAG) estimated that 3.5 million children were living in poverty in the UK. The CPAG notes that child poverty is associated with a higher risk of both illness and premature death. They also note that growing up in poverty often means being cold or going hungry. The Faculty of Public Health noted in 2015 that malnutrition was on the increase among poorer children and that conditions such as rickets were becoming more apparent because parents could not afford quality food in their children's diet. Children from poorer families are therefore more likely to suffer chronic illness or disability during childhood than children from more affluent families.

Poverty often has a negative effect on diet and therefore health. This can be illustrated in four ways.

1. Dobson *et al.* (1994) researched 48 poor households, half of which were single-mother families living on the poverty line, to investigate the relationship between poverty and shopping for food. They found that the main influence over choice of food was not health but the need to economise. Working-class mothers could not afford to waste money or food and bought 'unhealthy' foods such as crisps and biscuits for their children's school lunch so they would fit in with the other children. In contrast, middle-class mothers were prepared to experiment with

healthier foods and to waste such foods if their children did not like them. Dobson concluded that poverty meant working-class women had little choice in buying foods that experts would regard as less healthy.

2. Dowler (2008) notes that "if you live for more than six months on the minimum wage or on benefits there is growing evidence you cannot afford to buy the food you need for health … Food is the flexible area that you cut back on when you are on a low income … you buy the kind of food that fills you up most cheaply".

3. The National Food Alliance (NFA) has observed that many deprived areas of the UK, especially inner city areas and council estates, are becoming 'food deserts'. Studies by Shaw (2007) and Rawling (2012) observe that the biggest supermarket chains in the UK have largely withdrawn from the areas where poorer working-class people live. People living in these areas therefore have to rely on corner shops, which have a limited choice of healthy foods and which charge higher prices than supermarkets. Acheson notes that "if the nearest supermarket is miles away or the bus doesn't go there when you can, it can be difficult to buy food which is cheap and healthy".

4. There is also some evidence that fast-food chains target poorer areas. Jamie Oliver's (2012) television series on eating habits in Rotherham, *The Ministry of Food*, suggested that the result of this targeting was that some poor families and young people are over-dependent on fast-food outlets for their meals.

POVERTY, REGION AND HEALTH

Mary Shaw *et al.* 1999 study of regional poverty found that areas with high rates of poverty experienced mortality rates that were twice the national average. For example, Shettleston, an extremely deprived area of Glasgow, has a Standardised Mortality Ratio (SMR) for deaths under 65 of 234 compared with Wokingham, a middle-class town in the south of England, which has an SMR of 65. Shaw estimates that 71 per cent of deaths in Shettleston could have been avoided if the population had been lifted out of poverty. Similarly, Mitchell, Shaw and Dorling (2000) estimated that nearly 12,000 lives a year could be saved each year in the UK if child poverty was reduced.

Marxist explanations

Marxist sociologists agree with materialist explanations that there is a causative link between poverty and health inequality. However, Marxists note that materialists rarely attempt to explain the origin of such poverty. Marxists, on the other hand, argue that poverty and therefore the conditions in which ill health can thrive are caused by the organisation or structure of the capitalist economy.

The distribution of wealth and income

Marxist sociologists argue that poverty and therefore inequalities in health and illness exist because wealth – the money found in shares, savings, land, property, bank accounts, etc. – is concentrated in very few hands. In 2014, the ONS revealed that the wealthiest 1 per cent of the UK population owned as much wealth as the poorest 55 per cent put together. Moreover, 7 per cent of the British population (about 4 million people) controlled about 85 per cent of the country's wealth. These statistics suggest that 93 per cent of the UK population only have 15 per cent of the country's wealth to share between them. Those at the very bottom of society are unlikely to share in any of this wealth. Marxists also point out that these figures probably underestimate the concentration of wealth in fewer hands because they do not include wealth that is diverted into off-shore tax havens in order to evade paying tax.

Social-class inequalities in wealth, poverty and health are also reinforced by income inequality. Between 1997 and 2013, income inequality between the rich and poor in Britain widened until it was at its most unequal since records began at the end of the 19th century. The Resolution Foundation (2014) notes that the top 1 per cent of earners increased their share of income to 10 per cent, while the bottom 50 per cent of earners saw their share reduced from 19 per cent to 18 per cent. No other Western industrialised country, apart from the USA, has experienced this level of inequality.

Marxists therefore argue that the health gap is caused by the wealth gap. Dr John Collee summed this position up when he said in 1992, "there is one piece of health advice which is more effective than all the others. One guaranteed way to live longer, grow taller, avoid chronic illness, have healthier children, increase your quality of life and minimise your risk of premature death. The secret is: be rich!"

FOCUS ON SKILLS: HEALTH – A MATTER OF PERSONAL RESPONSIBILITY?

Steve Field is Chief Inspector of General Practice at the Care Quality Commission. He argues that too many of us neglect our health and this is leading to increasing levels of illness, obesity and early death. He also argues that parents too often feed their children junk food in the name of convenience when they need to act as role models and take control of their children's eating habits by providing sensible and appropriate portion sizes.

Research by the thinktank The King's Fund in 2012 seems to support Field's ideas. It found that the social-class divide in health is widening as better-off people avoid damaging habits such as smoking and eating badly but poorer people do not. In particular, it found that people with no educational qualifications were more than five times as likely as those with degrees to engage in four key damaging behaviours in 2008 – smoking, drinking, physical inactivity and poor diet – compared with three times as likely in 2003.

However, both Field and The King's Fund research have attracted criticism because they imply that the poor are to blame for their plight. Both Field and The King's Fund have been accused of over-simplistic victim-blaming.

Professor Michael Marmot (2010) argues that we need to understand that the behavioural choices we make as individuals are rooted in our social and economic circumstances. People born into more advantageous situations find it easier to adopt healthy lifestyles and give up unhealthy behaviour. He argues that differences in health cannot be attributed to genetic make-up, lack of personal responsibility or difficulties in access to medical care. They are linked to the conditions in which we are born, grow, live, work and age. Childhood deprivation, the stress of poverty, overcrowding, living in a run-down area, feeling powerless at work and being unemployed do not give people the control over their lives that fosters good health and enables them to succeed in making difficult changes in behaviour.

Other health experts such as Dr Ruth Stern argue that the government also needs to do more in terms of adopting policies that promote health, such as controlling the number of fast-food outlets, banning cheap alcohol, introducing regulations to control the advertising of unhealthy foods and using legislation to force manufacturers to cut the amounts of fat, sugar and salt in foods.

Questions

1. **Identify** and summarise the causes of poor health according to the Chief Inspector of General Practice.

2. **Analyse** how The King's Fund research supports the culturalist theory of health inequality.

3. **Evaluate** how the views of Marmot and Stern contribute to the view that behavioural theories of health inequality are guilty of over-simplistic victim-blaming. (Think about how the poor are unable to have any influence over the several factors that Marmot identifies as causes of ill health.)

4. **Outline** and **assess**. Using material from this article and elsewhere, outline and assess the materialist explanation of class explanations in health. (Remember that materialist explanations focused on the role of poverty are closely related to Marxist and psycho-social explanations but are criticised by culturalist or behavioural explanations.)

Social policy

Marxists point out that there are also class inequalities in the exercise of political power that can be seen in the lack of any political will to seriously challenge the existence of poverty in the UK. In fact, many government policies have actually made poverty worse. For example, the Conservative government's free-market social policies in the 1980s led to many traditional heavy industries, such as coal mining and steel production, going into terminal decline. Many areas, especially in the north of England, Scotland and South Wales experienced decline, and consequently many workers became long-term unemployed. Both the Labour government (1997–2010) and the Coalition government (2010–2015) failed in their promises to eradicate child poverty.

The relationship between globalisation and health inequality in the UK

Mass unemployment and, therefore, poverty and ill health among British workers has been exacerbated by economic globalisation – many British businesses have relocated their factories and call-centres to developing countries in order to cut costs and to make even greater profits for their owners and shareholders. This has resulted in a major decline in British manufacturing and greater unemployment, poverty and ill health in urban areas of the UK.

In what other ways might globalisation be responsible for unemployment and poverty in the UK? Think about the causes of the economic crisis of 2008, which triggered the austerity measures the UK is currently experiencing.

Health and the organisation of the workplace

Marxists have drawn particular attention to the number of workers who die or are injured at work – in factories, on building sites, etc. – because their employer breaks health and safety laws. About 500 workers die at work every year and thousands are injured. Industrial diseases due to workers being exposed to toxic conditions and/or substances also contribute to the poor health of thousands of working-class people.

Industries vary in how dangerous they are to their employees: respiratory diseases are common among those working in road and building construction, as a result of the dust inhaled, while various forms of cancer are associated with chemical industries.

Private medicine

Marxists point out that income inequality means the middle class have access to private medical care, so they are less dependent on the NHS and its waiting list. It also gives them access to medical services that may not be available on the NHS. This has a knock-on effect on the NHS because private hospitals employ nurses, consultants and other specialists who have been trained by the NHS, therefore contributing to the shortage of trained staff in NHS hospitals.

Criticism of the Marxist position

There is some evidence that the relationship between capitalism and ill health may not be as straightforward as Marxists argue. Research by Marmot and Shipley (1996) shows very clearly that there is not a simple threshold below which people have shorter lives. There is, instead, a life expectancy gradient, with people in higher socio-economic positions living longer than those in positions slightly lower than themselves. In other words, those in the most senior management jobs live longer, on average, than those in slightly less senior management jobs. This latter group, in turn, will live longer, on average, than people in junior management jobs, and so on. Health inequality is not, therefore, simply caused by poverty, but rather it is related to inequality in general, which affects all social groups except those at the very top.

Davey Smith (2003) argued that one aspect of this general inequality is the control or lack of that people have over their everyday routine at work. He found that workers who exercised little power or control over their jobs and who found their jobs boring were likely to experience worse health than those who enjoyed responsibility and job satisfaction.

Psycho-social explanations

Wilkinson and Pickett (2010) claim that stress and anxiety are the major causes of health inequalities in morbidity and mortality, and these feelings are more prevalent in societies with high levels of income inequality. They suggest that many rich societies are 'dysfunctional' societies because large sections of the population are experiencing low levels of psychological and social wellbeing and high levels of stress and anxiety, as symbolised by high crime and suicide rates.

In contrast, societies with lower levels of income inequality have the psychological effect of producing high levels of social capital: people in such societies experience a strong sense of belonging and feel positively connected to others, increasing their sense of wellbeing and minimising health risks to both mind and body.

The concept of social capital is used to explain social trends in other areas of the specification. For example, there is some evidence that the upper class use social networks and contacts (that is, the old-boy or school-tie network) to gain advantageous access to top jobs in the UK. Middle-class parents may use their social contacts to ensure their children get into the school of their choice.

Wilkinson believes that wellbeing positively correlates to standard of living.

Wilkinson and Pickett's psycho-social approach is almost holistic in its insistence that what happens to the body in terms of illness is the product of the psychological reaction to inequality. They argue that social reactions to inequality in general, such as distrust of and disconnection to a society's wealthy leaders, and the daily experience of living with the consequences of inequality, such as poverty, lead to negative psychological states such as stress and depression. This can undermine body chemistry as the physical body's attempts to cope produce overload and exhaustion. Long-term stress and anxiety can damage the immune system and the ability to fight off infection and disease. Stress can also cause high blood pressure, heart disease and trigger cancer.

Wilkinson (1996) notes that "to feel depressed, cheated, bitter, desperate, vulnerable, frightened, angry, worried about debts or job and housing insecurity; to feel devalued, useless, helpless, uncared for, hopeless, isolated, anxious and a failure; these feelings can dominate people's whole experience of life, colouring their experience of everything else. It is the chronic stress arising from feelings like these which does damage to health. It is the social feelings which matter, not exposure to a supposedly toxic material environment. The material environment is merely the indelible mark and constant reminder of the oppressive fact of one's failure...and one's social exclusion and devaluation as a human being".

They therefore conclude that if health inequalities in mortality and morbidity in the UK are to be reduced, politicians need to acknowledge that material standards, economic growth, psychological and social wellbeing and health differences are all inter connected.

How might sociologists go about proving the link between income inequality, a toxic environment, chronic stress and poor health? What research methods would you recommend they use?

Karlsen and Nazroo (2004) note another problem common in unequal rich societies: racism, which is unique to ethnic minorities. They note that the experience of living in a racist society causes fear, anxiety and stress, which has an additional negative effect on the health levels of minority groups. For example, their research found that those members of ethnic-minority groups who reported racial harassment and violence and who perceived employer discrimination were most likely to report their health as only fair or poor. Wilkinson and Pickett also note that "the prejudice which often attaches to ethnic divisions may increase inequality and its effects" (p. 186).

Critiques of the psycho-social approach
Some sociologists have claimed that Wilkinson and Pickett have been selective in their use of data. For example, it is pointed out that the nations in the south of Europe around the Mediterranean, such as Spain, France and Italy, have lower levels of health inequality than countries such as Norway and Sweden, which experience much narrower social differences in income inequality.

Other sociologists argue that epidemiologists need to adopt a 'life-course' approach. Barker and Clarke (1997), for example, observe that the chances of good or poor health may be influenced by what happened to people in very early childhood or even before they were born.

Finally, neo-materialists such as Scambler and Higgs (2001) point out that Wilkinson and Pickett side-step the issue of why inequalities in income and wealth exist in the first place. From a Marxist perspective, then, the main cause of health inequalities in mortality and morbidity is the economic class-based power that enables the bourgeoisie to shape capitalist society in such a way that they themselves derive the greatest benefit.

CONCLUSIONS

Epidemiologists have uncovered distinct and wide health inequalities in British society related to region, social class and ethnicity. There is not only a north-south divide in mortality and morbidity but also social class and ethnic differences too. All three types of inequality overlap.

Culturalists blame the choices and decisions of the least healthy for these inequalities. However, experts argue that this victim-blaming focus on cultural lifestyle only accounts for a quarter to a third of these inequalities. In contrast, materialists, Marxists and the psycho-social explanation of Wilkinson and Pickett have focused on economic factors beyond the control of those who experience the worst health. All three of these approaches agree that economic inequality has had a huge impact on health. In particular, Wilkinson and Pickett have suggested that the material experience of inequality leads to negative experiences for those at the bottom of society, and these produce psychological strains and negative emotions that increase the potential for physical and mental forms of illness. These are all pertinent possibilities in explaining why health inequalities exist, but you should also be aware that some sociologists blame the organisation and funding of the NHS. This theme will be explored further in Chapter 4.

CHECK YOUR UNDERSTANDING

1. Identify three ways in which the north of England and Scotland differ from the south of England in terms of health inequalities.

2. Identify five poor lifestyle choices supposedly made by people from either working-class or ethnic-minority backgrounds which are responsible for health inequalities according to behaviourist sociologists.

3. Define what is meant by 'epidemiology'.

4. Define what is meant by a 'dysfunctional society'.

5. Explain what is meant by the 'artefact' explanation of health inequality.

6. Outline and explain one problem associated with the social selection theory of health inequality.

7. Outline and explain the ways in which poverty might have a negative effect on diet and therefore health.

8. Explain what Marxists mean when they argue that the health gap is mainly brought about by the wealth gap.

9. Analyse and explain the difference between culturalist and materialist views on why there are inequalities in health.

10. Outline and evaluate the psycho-social view that health inequalities could be reduced by narrowing inequalities in income.

TAKE IT FURTHER

Design a questionnaire survey based on the culturalist theory of health. You should ask between 15 and 20 questions based on diet, smoking, drinking alcohol, taking exercise, and so on. Select a sample of 20 people to fill in your questionnaire. You might wish to divide the sample by parental occupation – use the NS-SEC – to work out the social-class composition of your sample. You could also stratify by ethnicity and age. What differences emerge? Do these support or challenge culturalist ideas?

5.3 GENDER AND HEALTH

LEARNING OBJECTIVES

> Demonstrate knowledge and understanding of the unequal social distribution of health chances in the United Kingdom by gender (AO1).

> Demonstrate knowledge and understanding of the different theories which aim to explain why gender inequalities in mortality and morbidity exist (AO1).

> Analyse and apply the evidence collected by sociological surveys of health to the range of sociological theories that aim to explain gendered health inequality (AO2).

> Evaluate sociological explanations in order to make judgements and draw conclusions about the main causes of differences in mortality and morbidity between men and women (AO3).

INTRODUCING THE DEBATE

In addition to regional, social class and ethnic inequalities in mortality and morbidity, there are also gender differences. An examination of NHS statistics suggests that gender differences in health can be summed up by the phrase 'women get sicker while men die quicker'. However, this is probably an over-simplistic picture because it fails to take account of the fact that gender differences also overlap with social class – for example, middle-class women live longer and get less sick than poorer women; with ethnicity – for example, white women may be more healthy than Asian women;

and with geography – for example, women in Scotland may not live as long as women who live in the affluent London borough of Knightsbridge.

There is a tendency when discussing gender differences to focus on women. There is even a case for arguing that men's health has been neglected by both epidemiologists and sociologists. However, it is important to note that gender refers to both men and women. It is essential that the influence of men's roles and masculinity on health inequalities are examined as much as the influence of women's roles and femininity.

INEQUALITIES IN MORTALITY AND MORBIDITY

Mortality and gender

There appear to be significant differences between men and women in terms of average life expectancy and cause of death. At all ages, and in almost every society globally,

women's death rates are lower than men's. In the UK, a female born in 2014 can expect to live until she is 82.5 years old, while a male born in the same year can expect to reach the age of 79.5. About two-thirds of deaths that occur before the retirement age of 65 years are male. Consequently, 58 per cent of people who survive beyond the age of 65 are female.

The three leading causes of death for each gender are circulatory disease (including heart disease and stroke) followed by cancer and then respiratory diseases (for example, pneumonia). All three causes of death have shown a consistent downward trend for both genders over the last 50 years.

There are gender differences in the type of cancer that people are likely to suffer from. For men, it is lung cancer, followed closely by prostate cancer. Lung cancer is also the biggest killer in women. The most common type of cancer in women is breast cancer (one in nine women are expected to develop it and 80 per cent survive it) followed by cervical cancer. Both of these cancers present early, which means that cancer rates are 70 per cent higher for women compared with men in the 30–34 age-group.

Morbidity and gender

Using official statistics relating to the use of the National Health Service (NHS), a number of observations can be made regarding the relationship between morbidity and gender.

› Women are the main users of health care services in terms of GP visits and hospital admissions for operations.

› Women experience more chronic long-term illness, psychiatric disorders and illness, especially anxiety and depression, and disability.

› Women consult their doctors on average about five times a year compared with three times a year for men.

› Women consume more prescription and non-prescription drugs, especially tranquillisers, sleeping pills and anti-depressants.

› Men are three times more likely to commit suicide.

› Women are more likely to seek advice about preventative care, to self-examine and to take health supplements.

EXPLANATIONS FOR THE LINK BETWEEN GENDER AND HEALTH

Biology

There is some evidence to suggest that women are biologically stronger than men (for instance, female foetuses are less likely to die than male foetuses) and females may possess a greater biological propensity to live longer because their immune system possesses extra T cells (a type of white blood cell essential for human immunity). There is also evidence that, because the hormone oestrogen may protect them, women have a greater resistance to heart disease than men, who are more likely to develop cardiac problems in middle age. This may account for why men suffer more sudden death than women before retirement age.

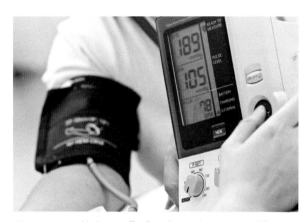

Men are more likely to suffer from heart disease in middle age.

However, this does not mean that females are more immune to general illness. They often suffer from a range of health problems uniquely associated with reproduction and the menopause. Women may suffer more chronic and degenerative ill health because they are more likely to live into their eighties and nineties.

Access to health care services

There have been significant improvements in health care which may have benefited women rather than men with regard to both mortality and morbidity. One of the major killers of women up to the mid-20th century was childbirth. The maternal death rate – the death of women while pregnant or giving birth – was high. However, improvements in antenatal and maternity care in the NHS now mean that death in childbirth is relatively rare.

Another important contributor in reducing female deaths (while also artificially inflating the morbidity statistics) is the use of screening for breast and cervical cancer introduced in 1988. This has resulted in earlier diagnosis and consequently has had a great effect on reducing the female mortality rate. As Scambler (2008) reports, the death rate from breast cancer was about 40 per 100,000 in 1988. Screening increased the diagnoses of breast cancer to a record high of about 120 per 100,000, but the death rate fell to 30 per 100,000.

Luck et al. (2000) argue that NHS screening services have benefited women more than men. They note that testicular and especially prostate cancer, which kills about 10,000 males a year (five times higher than the number of women who die from cervical cancer), have no national screening programmes. Luck et al. suggest health services for females are more focused and holistic in their organisation whereas health services for males are more fragmented and indirect.

Questioning the validity of the statistics

Some sociologists argue that the idea that females suffer more sickness than males is a statistical illusion. There are two reasons given for this.

1. Nettleton argues that the fact women experience more morbidity or illness (and consequently visit the doctor more often) may be distorted by the biological function of their bodies. She notes that the statistics on women's illness have little to do with actual illness and more to do with the maintenance of the female body, with regard to menstruation, contraception, infertility, pregnancy and the menopause. The nature of women's bodies means that such visits cannot be avoided. In other words, the official statistics on illness may not reflect levels of female sickness but instead routine visits caused by the need to be prescribed the pill or to check the progress of pregnancy.

2. Moreover, because women live longer than men they are likely to use health services for a greater number of years. Women are therefore more likely to be consulting doctors because many illnesses and disabilities are a product of the ageing process.

Nettleton suggests that once all these factors are taken into account, females only have a slightly higher morbidity rate than men.

Cultural or behavioural explanations

Some sociologists have examined the role of UK culture in explaining gender differences in morbidity and mortality. UK culture, through the process of **gender role socialisation,** teaches children that specific types of behaviour are expected from girls and boys, so society rather than biology shapes femininity and masculinity. These cultural expectations may have a positive or negative effect with regard to each gender's adoption of healthy and unhealthy behaviour.

UNDERSTAND THE CONCEPT

Gender role socialisation is the process through which male and female children learn their gender roles – how society expects men and women to behave in terms of their masculinity and femininity. This is mainly performed in the family through the allocation of toys, clothing etc., and the encouragement of gender-appropriate behaviour. However, other secondary agencies such as the peer group, the educational system and the mass media often reinforce what parents have taught their children.

There is some evidence that traditional masculine values and norms may stress that seeking help with discomfort and pain is feminine and unmanly. Boys and men may be encouraged by their male role models and peers to shrug off the symptoms of illness in order to be viewed as a 'real man'. They often postpone consultation with doctors, which means that a disease may not be officially diagnosed until it has done significant damage to the body. For example, research by O'Brien et al. (2005) with men from different social-class backgrounds found that men were generally reluctant to concede that they were in physical pain or suffering from emotional distress and in need of medical or psychiatric help. They were loath to admit that they were in any way in pain or vulnerable, anxious or depressed because they interpreted such conditions as signs of femininity, weakness and inferiority.

This may mean that males are less likely to talk to their friends, family or doctors about physical or mental problems. They may therefore have no outlet for nervous tension compared with females, who have been socialised into talking through problems. This male inability and reluctance to communicate may lead to the earlier onset in men of health problems, such as heart disease, that could eventually kill them.

Boys and men are also socialised into being more aggressive and more likely to engage in 'high risk' behaviour, which may have a negative effect upon health and life expectancy. As Scambler (2008) observes, "masculinity, it seems, still needs to be affirmed and continually renegotiated by men's participation in activities such as dangerous sports like hang-gliding, car and motorbike racing, rock climbing and so on" (p. 146). Being willing to take risks that result in more harm and death from violence and road accidents may explain why males make up about 60 per cent of annual road casualties and why road accidents are the biggest killer of males aged 15–25 years. Moreover, men are more likely to drink, smoke and use illegal drugs than women. They may overuse drink in order to cope with anxiety, stress and depression rather than visit the doctor for prescription drugs.

The **Crime Survey for England and Wales** consistently reports that males are three times more likely to be the victim of violent criminal attacks. Studies of territorial street gangs suggest that the deaths and injuries that result from membership of such gangs are often the result of members attempting to live up to some violent hyper-male ideal.

FOCUS ON SKILLS: UNDERSTANDING HOW MEN EXPERIENCE, EXPRESS AND COPE WITH SYMPTOMS OF ILLNESS

The dominant narrative about masculinity in the literature is that men are more reluctant to seek help than women, regardless of their health concerns. Research in the UK suggests that men have a higher threshold for distress before they seek help, and women are more likely to seek help from family and friends than men are. In other research carried out by Rogers *et al.* (2001), while both genders were hesitant to tell their doctors that they were not coping, men were especially reluctant to do so. Men may fear exposing their emotional vulnerabilities by asking for help. With regard to treatment for cancer, Gooden and Winefield found differences between men and women in terms of the language they used. For example, while "women clearly expressed their emotions, men tended to imply emotion". While women focused on nurturing, men preferred to use battle metaphors in discussing cancer.

In terms of help-seeking, we also need to focus on relations between men, professionals and institutions. Some men's relative inability to articulate their distress can also mean their emotional problems remain hidden from professionals. It is possible that professionals are not always successful in decoding the language used by men to refer to their distress, which may be hidden or minimised. And professionals may not look

for emotional distress in men. For example, in the treatment of cancer, there appear to be differences in the way doctors behave towards men and women, with relatively less recognition of distress in men. Moreover, some argue that psychiatric classification systems, such as the Diagnostic and Statistical Manual, lead professionals to overlook male expressions of distress (such as being angry, hostile and violent, substance abuse, blaming others) in favour of female presentations (such as emotional distress, feelings of guilt and unworthiness). Some sociologists argue that mental health classifications thus reinforce social constructions of gender by diagnosing women and ignoring men.

Based on Ridge, Emslie and White (2011)

Questions

1. **Identify** and summarise the evidence in this article that supports the view that socialisation into masculinity may deter males from reporting illness.

2. **Analyse** the role of health professionals in the under-reporting of illness by males.

3. **Analyse.** 'The links between gender and help-seeking are more complex than once thought'. To what extent is this true? (As a starting point, identify the similarities between men and women's reaction to illness.)

4. **Evaluate.** Using the information in the article, evaluate the view that male illness rates are unreliable because men interpret reporting illness, pain and mental distress as undermining their masculinity. (You should clearly distinguish between how men see themselves and how society and professionals, such as health workers, perceive and stereotype men and women.)

FOCUS ON SKILLS: TEENAGE BOYS STRAIN TO MEET BODY IDEALS

Growing numbers of teenage boys are suffering from body image disorders, according to a senior doctor in Scotland who blames the 'deeply worrying' trend on the internet and society's obsession with the perfect body. Dr Jane Morris, chair of the newly established Faculty of Eating Disorders at the Royal College of Psychiatrists in Scotland, said young men have become socialised to think about their bodies in the same way as women have been. The result is that by the time they reach puberty, many feel under pressure to lose weight and 'bulk up', often with protein shakes and other muscle-enhancing supplements that can potentially lead to kidney and liver damage.

Figures on male eating disorders are not officially collated but Morris, who is also an associate of Cambridge University's Newnham College, said reports of young boys suffering from muscle dysmorphia — more commonly known as the Adonis complex — are becoming more common.

She said society's obsession with body image dominates advertising, computer games and gossip magazines. "It's even extended to toys and fictional characters," Morris added. "Batman today is far more bulked up than when he was first created."

Recent research has suggested that insecurity about weight and body image is driving men to obsessive lengths down the gym. As many as 45% of men are believed to suffer from muscle dysmorphia – an obsession with the idea that they are not muscular enough – at some point in their lives.

Charities such as The Only Way Is Up Foundation claim that 70% of girls and 30% of boys aged 11–19 cite their relationship with their body as their 'No. 1 worry'. It says that body insecurity prevents young people from raising their hand in class, expressing an opinion, attending physical education lessons or even from turning up to school or college.

Source: Macaskill, M. 'Teenage boys strain to meet body ideals', *The Sunday Times*, 16 November 2014

Questions

1. **Identify** three health problems mentioned in the article that boys suffer from because of the insecurity they feel about their bodies.

2. **Identify** the reasons why there is a lack of statistics on male eating disorders and male body image disorders.

3. **Analyse** the reasons mentioned in the article why boys are more likely today to experience body image disorders. (Think about the role of the media and computer games.)

4. **Outline** and **evaluate**. Using the information in the article, and from elsewhere, outline and evaluate the view that girls and women are more likely than boys and men to be subjected to social pressures from the mass media to achieve an ideal body. (Think about the statistics cited in the article as well as how boys and girls are socialised into masculinity and femininity respectively, and how cultures expect boys and girls to look and behave.)

The **Crime Survey for England and Wales** is an annual survey carried out by the government that aims to ask people whether they have been victims of crime in the previous year in order to find out how much crime has been committed and reported. It is a valuable tool in finding out the extent of crime in Britain.

In contrast, there is some evidence from 2015 to show that young females are increasingly more likely than males to smoke. Although the trends with regard to smoking by most social groups are downward, there is worrying evidence that girls up to the age of 15 are now more likely than boys to be regular or occasional smokers. Furthermore, there are signs that young females may be more involved in violent crime than ever before. Both these trends are likely to impact on female morbidity and mortality levels in the future.

The same gender socialisation processes may mean that women at a very young age are socialised into expressing their feelings. Women may therefore be more open about their health problems and consequently more willing to take them to a doctor. Similarly, the high take-up of health services by women may be due to the social or cultural expectations that underpin socialisation into the feminine role in UK society. Women may be socialised by their mothers into being more in tune with their bodies and more aware of health issues because the female body is more complex than the male body; females uniquely experience menstruation, oral contraception, pregnancy, childbirth and the menopause.

Weaver et al. (2008) suggest that cultural expectations regarding femininity may mean that women are subjected to social pressures from sources such as the mass media to achieve a physical ideal in terms of slimness. As Hunt observes, it is assumed that slimness equates to happiness in societies such as the UK. Females may therefore adopt healthy forms of behaviour in the pursuit of this ideal. For example, females may be more aware of the calorific, fat and sugar content of foods than men. They are more aware of diets and slimming plans and more likely to eat wholemeal bread, fruit and vegetables once a day, eat probiotic yoghurts, drink semi-skimmed milk and eat less unhealthy foods such as crisps and chips. However, they

are also more likely to adopt starvation diets that can lead to eating disorders such as **bulimia** and anorexia.

UNDERSTAND THE CONCEPT

Bulimia nervosa is a mental health and eating disorder that causes sufferers to binge and purge in order to lose weight, or to maintain an often unhealthy low weight. Sufferers battle to control their weight and restrict what they consume, but then feel compelled to binge eat, consuming excessive amounts of unhealthy and fattening food in a short space of time. This results in feelings of guilt and shame, so the sufferer purges soon after eating to compensate, forcing themselves to vomit or take laxatives in order to rid their body of the food they have just binged on.

Materialist explanations

This explanation focuses on the economic organisation of society, particularly the way that wealth and income is distributed, and the consequent economic inequality, specifically the feminisation of poverty that results from this. It is argued that women's disproportional experience of poverty is the main reason why they suffer more illness.

Materialists argue that poverty has become feminised partly because of inequalities in employment conditions. They note that:

> only 70 per cent of women of working age are in paid employment and 42 per cent of these are employed in low-paid part-time jobs because of their unpaid family roles

> the expense of childcare and lack of free childcare provision in the UK make it difficult for mothers to work full time; consequently, they bring in less income than single or childfree women (in 2015, two-thirds of employed mothers with children aged 12 years and under were in part-time work)

> women are more likely to be lone parents – Gingerbread observed in 2015 that paid work is not a guaranteed route out of poverty for single mothers; for example, the poverty rate for children in families where single mothers work part time is 30 per cent and 22 per cent where they are able to work full time.

There are many explanations offered for the disproportionate poverty experienced by women.

> about 33 per cent of single mothers were claiming benefits in 2014 as their sole income, according to the Policy Exchange (2014)

> the rise in the cost of living, and in particular the costs of food and fuel, results in many lone mothers skipping meals to feed their children, which is undermining their health, according to a study carried out by McHardy in 2013

> only 50 per cent of women from ethnic minorities are employed in the UK – this falls to about 25 per cent for women from Pakistani and Bangladeshi backgrounds

> despite the existence of equal pay and opportunities legislation, women in full-time employment in the UK are paid, on average, 17 per cent less than men.

> lower life-time working opportunities and pay negatively impact on women's income in old age because they may not pay as much into occupational pension schemes and consequently only receive low occupational pensions when they retire – the ONS estimated in 2006 that women's weekly retirement income was 47 per cent less than men's

> as much as 20 per cent of women probably live in households characterised by poverty, according to Palmer et al. (2010).

As the evidence suggests, women, whether they are employed full time or part time, lone mothers or pensioners are likely to be economically worse off than men.

Psycho-social explanations

Wilkinson and Pickett (2010) argue that the negative economic and social conditions in which women are more likely to find themselves, compared with men, can trigger negative psychological states of mind that can lead to poor health. Their idea can be illustrated with regard to obesity.

> Obesity has changed its social distribution over the course of the last century: the rich used to be fat and the poor were thin but this has now reversed in the richer developed world. By the early 1990s, obesity was more common among poorer women than richer women in the UK and UK women are now more likely to be obese compared with men.

> There is a strong relationship between income inequality and obesity in women: the lower the socio-economic status of women, the more likely they are to be obese. Moreover, it could be argued that women in the lowest income bracket may also feel deprived compared with men, whose income on the whole tends to be higher.

Poorer women may express their discontent from these inequalities through comfort eating. Research carried out by Diez Roux et al. (2000) found that women who are chronically stressed because of their experience of income inequality tend to overeat to compensate for that stress, to gain weight and to lead an inactive lifestyle. Moreover, obese women tend to view themselves negatively, reinforcing low self-esteem. Stress is therefore both the cause and the consequence of obesity in poorer women and this undermines their physical and emotional health and well being. Wilkinson and Pickett conclude that if society is to resolve the epidemic of female obesity it needs to lessen inequality. See Chapter 2 for more on Wilkinson and Pickett's research.

Do you agree that obesity is caused by factors beyond the individual's control?

Marxist explanations

Marxist sociologists point out that it is working-class men who suffer the worst mortality rates in modern societies. They argue that the cause of health inequalities lies in the organisation of the capitalist economy. Health is merely one inequality, and it exists alongside inequalities in income, wealth, political power, access to educational qualifications and opportunities for upward social mobility. The bourgeoisie and their children monopolise wealth and income, and consequently wield other types of power because they exploit the labour power of working-class men and women. By paying wages which are only a fraction of what working-class labour is really worth to the bourgeoisie, the latter therefore contribute not only to the poverty experienced by working-class people but also to the related health problems that are a fact of life in most capitalist societies. They also exploit working-class men and create the potential for high mortality rates by controlling the organisation of the workplace and the work process. This latter form of exploitation has repercussions for men's health because it means that:

> the ruling class sees the health of workers as less important than making profit and men's health is therefore adversely affected by the risks and hazards associated with the manual jobs that they do, especially industrial accidents and diseases – male workers are also more likely than female workers to be exposed to toxic chemicals, fumes and radiation, which may cause chronic illness in old age and shorten their life expectancy

> men are more likely to work full time and to work longer and unsociable hours than women – on night-shifts, for example, which can also be harmful to health

> stress may result from the feelings of powerlessness, lack of control and alienation felt by manual workers who work in routine jobs that generate little job satisfaction

> while work is often a central part of a man's identity and he may see his job as defining his masculine status as well as his family role as provider and protector, redundancy and unemployment can therefore have a severe negative effect on a man's physical and mental health and even lead to suicidal thoughts and actions.

A report by The Work Foundation (2014) notes that men are twice as likely as women to suffer mental health problems if they lose their job, with the immediate aftermath being a particularly difficult time. Between 2008 and 2010, there was a steep rise in the number of male suicides. Many of these were directly attributable to unemployment.

BUILD CONNECTIONS

Suicide is a type of deviance in that it is not regarded as a 'normal' type of behaviour. The functionalist Emile Durkheim's study of suicide (1897) is seen as a classic example of positivist and scientific research in action. For more on Durkheim, see Topic 2, Chapters 3 and 6.

Research by Platt (2012) found that middle-aged men aged between 35 and 54 were far more likely to commit suicide than any other group. This group accounts for half of all the 6,000 or so suicides each year, with men on low pay or benefits particularly heavily represented. Platt argues that these middle-aged men are now part of the "buffer generation, not sure whether to be like their older, more traditional, strong, austere fathers or like their younger, more progressive, individualistic sons".

Platt found that men in the lowest social group and living in the most deprived areas were up to ten times more likely to attempt suicide than those in the highest social class. He notes that middle-class men could 'reinvent' their masculinity if they lost their job but working-class men struggled to cope with the impact on their masculinity.

What do you think has been the impact of the feminisation of the economy and workforce on men's health? Justify your answer with specific examples.

Marxist-feminists have suggested that health care systems have focused on improving women's health, especially in terms of maternal care. This is because the capitalist system needs to exploit women's fertility; it needs women to produce the next generation of workers. Women's health may be undermined because they are also exploited in their role as providers of free childcare and as informal carers of the disabled and the elderly.

Feminist explanations

Feminist explanations for health inequalities between men and women tend to focus on the concept of patriarchy, that is, the male domination of social institutions, such as the family and marriage, and the social role played by women in such societies. This can be illustrated by a number of feminist studies of health.

> Bernard (1982, originally 1972) takes the view that women may suffer more ill health because of marriage. In her study, she found that married women were less healthy than single women and full-time housewives were less healthy than women who worked full time. Furthermore, married men were healthier than single men. Bernard concludes that giving up work and becoming a full-time mother-housewife can lead to depression, insomnia and nervous anxiety.

> Oakley (1986) suggests that the patriarchal social expectations which state that women should take primary responsibility for childcare and domestic labour can have a negative effect on women's health. Housework is rarely experienced as fulfilling and the rates of depression in women may be linked to the unpaid, repetitive, unrewarding, often isolating and low-status nature of housework in a society where only paid employment is really respected.

Many women perform a dual role. They have to juggle paid work with the majority of housework and childcare. This is seen by feminists as problematical to women's health. The mother-housewife role is seen to be monotonous and feminist studies suggest there is little or no recognition that this role is important. Society, men and children rarely acknowledge that women do this work. It is argued that the result is that women who perform the dual role have a double burden that results in physical and mental exhaustion, low self-esteem and feelings of worthlessness. From a psycho-social perspective, this may result in depression and stress, which can in turn trigger other health problems. Duncombe and Marsden (1995) point out that many women actually suffer a triple burden – they are low-paid workers, who are mainly responsible for childcare and housework, and for the management of their family's emotions. In many cases, the stress of these responsibilities is increased by having to manage limited household budgets and by having little leisure time (compared with males) in order to relax.

Busfield (2002) argues that the official statistics on gender differences in mental illness may be distorted by stereotypes held by the male-dominated psychiatric profession. She argues that the same symptoms in men and women may be diagnosed and labelled quite differently by doctors. When women demonstrate symptoms of depression, these may be interpreted by male doctors as an inability to cope with children or with housework. In other words, doctors see the cause of women's ill health as a sign of individual emotional weakness rather than the result of patriarchal inequality in the family set-up. Doctors rarely consider the causes of women's illnesses to lie in the patriarchal environment in which women are subjected to inequality in the distribution of housework and childcare, domestic violence etc., or in the ways women are generally treated by society.

Moreover, Busfield argues that anxiety and stress in a man may be diagnosed as symptoms of overwork and rest might be prescribed by the doctor, whereas the same symptoms in women are diagnosed as a 'natural' outcome of a woman's 'weaker' character and treated with drugs. Women are therefore more likely to be diagnosed as depressed or suffering from anxiety than men, and consequently they are more likely to be prescribed drugs such as anti-depressants and admitted to mental health units. The statistical fact that women tend to be sicker than men may have more to do with how the medical profession interprets female symptoms than the result of objective scientific analysis.

Feminists argue that women's health is also harmed by patriarchal assumptions that women should take the main responsibility for birth control. They note that young women are at risk from the clinical iatrogenesis, especially the increased risk of cancer or heart conditions, associated with the contraceptive pill. In the UK, doctors recommended as safe the contraceptive Depo-Provera, which was subsequently found to have damaging side effects for women. Women's increased use of mental health services may mean that iatrogenesis is also brought about by addiction to anti-depressants and sleeping pills.

Criticisms of the social role argument

The feminist analysis of health inequalities between men and women has tended to assume that men and women are located in very distinct and different social roles at work and in the home. It was assumed that what was good for men was bad for women when it came to health. It was also assumed that male health was unproblematic and that men benefit from masculinity. However, this perspective has dated badly and masculinity and femininity are increasingly complex concepts. For example, male dominance has weakened in a variety of fields, such as the economy and the family.

What forms do you think these different versions of masculinity take nowadays?

Feminists have also been criticised for neglecting differences between men based on social class, ethnicity, religion, region, and so on. They tend to assume that all men experience similar levels of health, but as documented in Chapter 2 this is not the case. Similarly, feminists fail to recognise that some women have more economic and cultural power than other women to resist patriarchal influences and poor health. Annandale (1998) argues that women who go out to work enjoy better levels of health than those who do not because work gives women a sense of independence and access to a wider social network. Both of these have the effect of lowering stress levels – and stress is closely related to standards of health. However, research from the USA suggests that one consequence of women having a career is that their life expectancy is lowered to the level of men's.

Postmodern explanations

Some postmodernist sociologists have focused on the role of **embodiment** in bringing about poor health in women. Frost (2001), for example, argues that at a very early age females are encouraged by society, and in particular the mass media, to focus on their bodies in terms of weight and shape. They are encouraged to see their bodies as a project in need of improvement and to fear weight gain. Frost argues that this leads to women interpreting their body image in a very negative way – Frost calls this 'body hatred' – resulting in a loss of self-esteem. Frost notes that health problems, such as the eating disorders anorexia and bulimia, largely originate from these damaging emotions.

UNDERSTAND THE CONCEPT

Embodiment refers to the fact that the body has increasingly become a symbol and site for expressing personal identity; for example, people may have cosmetic surgery, get tattooed, diet, jog, body-build, etc., in an attempt to differentiate themselves and make themselves unique.

CONCLUSIONS

It is clear that there are differences between men and women in terms of life expectancy, but these are now starting to narrow, especially as women adopt elements of the male lifestyle – such as having a career with all of its associated stress – and younger men, in particular, adopt behaviour that previous generations of men may have written off as 'unmanly'. However, there is evidence that older men are still prone to masculine pressures and that this may account for the significant suicide figures for this group.

Some feminist sociologists still argue that females are more prone to poor mental health than males because of patriarchal pressures that question and criticise women's femininity, body weight and shape, intellectual competence, mothering abilities, and capacity for paid work. Scambler, for example, argues that these social pressures on females combine to lower self-esteem and to increase anxiety, tension and depression, and consequently bring about a greater number of health problems compared with males.

CHECK YOUR UNDERSTANDING

1. Identify two reasons why GP statistics may tell sociologists very little about women's illness.

2. Identify four reasons why Marxists believe capitalism is detrimental to men's health.

3. Define what is meant by the 'feminisation of poverty'.

4. Define what is meant by 'embodiment'.

5. Outline and explain one example of how going into paid work may improve women's health.

6. Outline and explain one example of how taking on roles traditionally associated with males may negatively affect women's health.

7. Outline and explain the ways in which masculinity can have a negative effect on men's mortality rates.

8. Explain what Bernard means when she argues that marriage makes women sick.

9. Analyse and explain the similarities and differences between materialist and Marxist theories of gender inequalities in health.

10. Outline and assess sociological explanations of gender differences in health chances.

TAKE IT FURTHER

Organise a group of boys into a focus group and explore the impact of body image on them. Do your results support or challenge the research mentioned in the chapter? Now do the same for girls.

5.4 INEQUALITIES IN ACCESS TO HEALTH CARE IN CONTEMPORARY SOCIETY

> Demonstrate knowledge and understanding of the inequalities in the provision of and access to health care services that exist in contemporary Britain (AO1).

> Demonstrate knowledge and understanding of the different explanations for inequalities that exist in provision of and access to NHS services (AO1).

> Analyse and apply the evidence collected by sociological surveys of health to the range of explanations that aim to explain why inequalities exist across NHS services (AO2).

> Evaluate sociological explanations in order to make judgements and draw conclusions about the reasons why inequalities in the provision of and access to NHS services persist (AO3).

INTRODUCING THE DEBATE

Although the National Health Service (NHS) is free to users, and taxpayers spend over £115 million each day paying for the NHS, some groups in the population have greater access to health care than others. This contradicts the fundamental notion of 'equity' that underpins the NHS – the principle that provision of services should be based solely upon need.

According to this principle, health services for the most disadvantaged groups in the population should not be of poorer quality or less accessible than those serving the more affluent groups in society. Furthermore, if a social group is experiencing poorer health than others, in terms of mortality and morbidity, then more NHS resources should be allocated to that group.

However, sociologists argue that equality of access to health care in the NHS does not exist. This is because some regions and social groups such as the working class seem to experience inequality in both the provision of health care services – such as GPs, nurses, hospital beds – and access to them. For example, referral to cancer screening units is slower for some social groups and regions in the UK than others.

General inequalities in mortality and morbidity across region, social class, ethnicity and gender, and several explanations for those inequalities have already been examined in Chapters 2 and 3. This chapter focuses on how NHS funding and organisation might also be a cause of poor health.

ISSUES OF PROVISION

Graham and Kelly (2004) suggest that the NHS is an important contributor to the health gap because, despite the culturalist stress on lifestyle choice, health care is something which is largely outside the control of the individual. Seddon (2007) argues that not only does the NHS do little to combat inequality, it makes that inequality worse by providing an unfair service. He suggests that those who need it least – the middle class – are utilising its services the most, and consequently benefiting more from its funding.

CHANGES IN THE ORGANISATION OF THE NHS

The NHS was set up in 1948 by the Labour Government after negotiations with the medical profession. The goal of the NHS, as documented by Mays (2008), was to secure equality of access throughout the whole of the UK to a comprehensive and free set of medical services, which would be funded by taxation. However, it has become apparent that although certain types of inequality have been reduced by NHS practices, inequalities in mortality and morbidity still persist and the blame for this cannot be exclusively placed on factors outside the health services, such as poor lifestyle choices, poverty and deprivation.

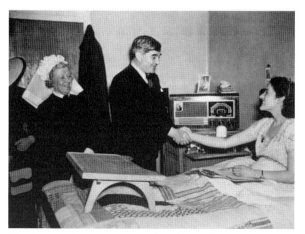

Nye Bevan, who was Minister of Health, is often credited as being the founding father of the NHS.

The inverse care law

In 1971, Dr Julian Tudor Hart found that "in areas with most sickness and death, general practitioners have more work, larger lists, less hospital support, and inherit more clinically ineffective traditions of consultation, than in the healthiest areas; and hospital doctors shoulder heavier case-loads with less staff and equipment, more obsolete buildings, and suffer recurrent crises in the availability of beds and replacement staff. These trends can be summed up as the '**inverse care law**': that the availability of good medical care tends to vary inversely with the need of the population served" (Tudor-Hart, 1971, p.14).

UNDERSTANDING THE CONCEPT

The **inverse care law** means that those who need health spending the most are the least likely to receive it, whereas those who are already healthy receive more funding than they actually need.

Reasons for the inverse care law

Tudor Hart highlighted two reasons for this inverse care law. Firstly, he noted that the allocation of NHS funding needed to be modernised because those areas in greatest need were receiving less money to spend on NHS resources, while areas that had enjoyed relatively good health for decades were receiving considerably greater levels of funding. For example, areas in the south of England were receiving up to £30 million more than they actually needed, while some very deprived districts in the north-east of England were receiving up to £27 million less than they needed. Secondly, Tudor Hart blamed the medical profession because studies clearly showed that doctors from middle-class backgrounds overwhelmingly chose to work in middle-class suburban areas which already had good medical facilities.

In 1974, the Labour Government attempted to address the issue of the inequality of provision by introducing the Resource Allocation Working Party (RAWP) in order to redistribute NHS funding more fairly between different parts of the country on the basis of the size of their populations and their relative need. However, Mays argues that regional inequalities persisted because the size of the NHS budget failed to increase and politicians who represented areas in the south of England, and especially London, which had traditionally received generous NHS funding, were motivated to successfully fight off all attempts to reduce their constituency's funding for fear of losing their seats in Parliament.

Further reform of the NHS occurred between 1982 and 1991 when the Conservative Government of Margaret Thatcher imposed a managerial revolution. At every level of the NHS, managers were appointed who took control of budgets in order to produce more efficient use of resources. In 1991, the Conservative government attempted to create an 'internal market' within the NHS in order to minimise costs while maximising quality of service. The idea was that certain fund holders within the NHS, such as GPs and health authorities, could choose to buy health services on behalf of their patients from any public, private or voluntary provider. Hospitals were encouraged to compete with other hospitals and the private sector to provide services such as surgery.

However, Mays argues that the internal market did little to reduce inequalities in health care provision across regions. In fact, it probably made such inequalities worse by creating a two-tier system of health care. The patients of fundholding GPs were given preferential treatment over patients whose services were purchased by the health authorities, by benefiting from shorter waiting times for operations.

The New Labour Government of 1997–2010 abolished GP fund holding and instead established 481 Primary Care Trusts (PCTs). These PCTs were given budgetary responsibility for delivering health care for communities of about 100,000 people through the funding of GPs and the commissioning of hospital and mental health services from NHS trusts or the private sector. From 1999, Wales, Scotland and Northern Ireland took over responsibility for the NHS in their own territories, although funding still came from the UK government.

Furthermore, the Labour government attempted to reduce inequalities in health provision across regions by introducing 'target-setting', whilst their NHS Plan for England (2000) aimed to significantly increase funding so that more staff could be recruited and more hospital beds provided, especially in those areas of greatest need.

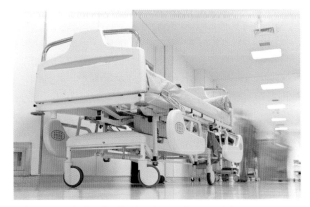

Labour's NHS Plan for England aimed to provide more hospital beds in under-resourced areas.

Mays argues that Labour produced very significant improvements in the NHS between 1997 and 2010. He notes that the NHS in this period was "probably closer to meeting its original goals of a universal comprehensive service free at point of use than it ever has been" (p. 244). Between 1997 and 2010, NHS funding trebled to over £90 billion. Moreover, there was a 26 per cent increase in nurses and a 20 per cent increase in GPs. Access to most medical services improved, waiting times for operations were reduced, more preventative services were introduced, and surveys of patients suggested that they were more satisfied with the service offered by the NHS.

In 2013, the Coalition government introduced the Health and Social Care Act. This Act again reorganised the NHS, replacing PCTs with Clinical Commissioning Groups (CCG, also called GP consortia) responsible for commissioning health care through 'competitive tendering'. Both NHS trusts and private health companies are encouraged to compete with one another to provide health services.

Does the inverse care law still exist today?

Tudor-Hart focused on the distribution of resources and the desire of doctors to work in nice areas as the main causes of the inverse care law in 1971. There is evidence that the inverse care law continues to persist some 40 years after his observations.

The Healthcare Commission (now known as the Care Quality Commission, or CQC) reported in 2004 that although NHS funding had increased nationally, there were still many disparities based on wealth, race and region. Ten PCTs were identified as suffering big funding shortfalls with regard to a need totalling more than

£210 million. Most of these PCTs were situated either in urban parts of northern England that were documented as experiencing high rates of poverty or in severely deprived inner-city areas in Birmingham and parts of Essex. For example, it was estimated that Easington in north-east England, which has 10,000 people claiming incapacity benefits (almost one in five of those of working age), was receiving £26.5 million less than it needed to cover its health needs effectively. Knowsley in Merseyside, one of the most economically deprived areas of the UK, required £30 million more in NHS funds. In contrast, the Commission found that wealthy areas of the UK were over-funded by almost £250 million. For example, the wealthy London borough of Westminster received £66 million more in health care funding than it needed.

Buck and Dixon (2013) observe that the distribution of NHS funding was still dependent on the level of need in a community, as required by the original aims of the NHS. This need is measured now by three inter-related factors:

› the age profile of an area's population

› the level of deprivation that exists within an area

› the level of health inequalities, that is, how an area contrasts with others in terms of mortality and morbidity levels.

Buck and Dixon observe that the practice of under-funding areas with deprivation and over-funding affluent areas is no longer the case for most areas of England in 2012. However, inequitable funding had not totally disappeared. Some PCTs were still receiving funding in 2012–13 that was below the target based on the three principles of need, while a small number of mainly affluent areas, such as Kensington and Chelsea, were still receiving funds that were 20 per cent higher than their real needs. So, although the inverse care law was tackled between 2004 and 2012, it still exists in some parts of the country.

What political reasons can you identify to explain why governments and politicians might be reluctant to tackle the inverse care laws in some areas?

Buck and Dixon suggested that the Coalition's reorganisation of the NHS in addition to the austerity cuts were likely to widen the NHS funding gap between rich and poor, and that, consequently, the inverse care law is still a very valid explanation for regional, social-class and ethnic inequalities in mortality, life expectancy and the social distribution of disease.

Buck and Dixon argued that the 2013 Act had downgraded health inequalities as an aspect of need and that this had resulted in a shifting of funds from deprived areas in the north of England and inner London to better-off areas in the south and east. Moreover, not only were deprived areas receiving a lower overall proportion of total NHS funds, austerity cuts in NHS spending meant that PCTs in deprived areas were struggling to meet local needs.

A number of sociologists have suggested that the concept of the inverse care law should be updated to describe how those in poorer areas are disadvantaged in terms of access to a range of health services. It is suggested that this unequal access can be described as a 'postcode lottery'. Buchan (2011) argues that even when people in the north and the south are born into similar socio-economic groups, health inequalities persist because people in the south, even if they have low incomes, have greater access to resources.

Various studies have clearly shown that areas such as the north of England, Scotland and Wales, and especially communities with high levels of unemployment, poverty, social deprivation, low life expectancy, above-average levels of crime, drug addiction, mental health problems and suicide, as well as large ethnic-minority populations, are more likely to experience:

› fewer and older hospitals that require a greater proportion of funding to either upgrade or maintain their upkeep

› fewer and less adequate specialised facilities in diagnostic testing, such as screening for cancer, and treatments such as kidney dialysis

› fewer hospital beds per head of population

› greater waiting times for cardiac surgery.

Pell et al. (2000) found that the waiting time for cardiac surgery increased in line with deprivation. Their study of over 26,000 heart patients in Scotland found that patients living in the most deprived areas waited roughly three weeks longer for surgery compared with patients from less deprived neighbourhoods. Seddon found that the poor and ethnic minorities were significantly disadvantaged in terms of experiencing longer waiting times for operations in general. He notes that this is not merely inconvenient; the stress of waiting itself actually makes people sicker.

Seddon believes that the increased waiting times for treatment experienced by the poor can cause further deterioration to a patient's health.

Acheson (1998) and Gordon *et al.* (1999) argue that there now exists an 'inverse prevention law', which means that those communities most at risk of ill health tend to experience the least satisfactory access to the full range of preventative health services, such as cancer screening, immunisation programmes, dental check-ups and other health promotion initiatives. In contrast, the middle class take up these services more frequently. Acheson notes that health care is inequitable not just in diagnosis and treatment but also in the prevention and early detection of illness.

GPs and the inverse care law

In 1971, Tudor Hart partly blamed GPs for the inverse care law. Buchan notes that there continue to be fewer GP practices in deprived areas and therefore higher patient-doctor ratios, meaning that there are fewer doctors for those most likely to get ill. The GP Patient Survey (2014) found big discrepancies in the number of GPs employed in different areas. In the fairly affluent areas of north, east and west Devon, there were over 60 full-time GPs per 100,000 patients compared with Slough, which suffers more deprivation but only has 22 full-time GPs per 100,000 patients. Moreover, people living in localities with fewer GPs are reporting that they cannot get GP appointments. Almost a quarter of people in deprived districts of Bradford were concerned that they could not get a consultation with their family doctor when they needed it, compared with only 5 per cent of people in affluent Bath.

Tudor Hart claimed that this is because doctors had a poor sense of public service – they preferred and chose to work in environments that were not deprived. Buchan instead blames the government for not providing enough incentives to encourage doctors to work in deprived neighbourhoods.

However, research has also suggested that regional and class inequalities may be made worse by the quality of the doctor-patient relationship. Research by Stirling *et al.* (2001) and Chew-Graham *et al.* (2002) found that GPs in middle-class areas spent greater amounts of time in consultation with patients who suffered from depression than doctors in working-class areas. Stirling *et al.* noted that the longer the consultation, the more likely psychological distress was to be recognised and treated. Chew-Graham *et al.* noted that doctors who dealt with working-class patients with depression were less likely than doctors with middle-class patients to refer their patients to therapy.

Research by Mercer and Watt (2007) among about 3,000 patients and 26 GPs living and working in areas of high and low deprivation found that working-class patients in high-deprivation areas had a greater number of psychological problems, more long-term illness, more **multi-morbidity** and more chronic health problems. However, they also found that, in contrast with patients in the least deprived areas, poorer patients took longer to get an appointment with their GP and doctor-patient consultations were generally shorter, despite the fact that these patients had more problems to discuss. Patients felt dissatisfied and less enabled to deal with their problems, especially the psychological ones.

UNDERSTANDING THE CONCEPT

Patients who experience **multi-morbidity** are usually the chronically sick and disabled whose conditions may lead to them experiencing a wide range of illnesses.

Le Grand *et al.* (2007) conclude that the GP–patient relationship is the main source of health inequalities in the UK, because access to most specialist services and treatments are controlled by GPs. They suggest that GPs are biased in favour of middle-class patients because their own social-class and ethnic backgrounds mean that they find it easier to respond to such patients. Moreover, because of their education, confidence and ability to express themselves articulately, middle-class patients may be better at persuading GPs of their need for specialist services. As Cooper (2010) notes, the middle-class are more likely to have a voice that is heard, understood and even empathised with by GPs.

FOCUS ON SKILLS: CHUMMY YOUNG DOCTORS ARE BAD FOR YOUR HEALTH

Creating close, personal relationships with patients can affect doctors' objectivity.

Two thirds of young doctors say that they struggle to be objective and truthful with patients they like, according to researchers who warn that 'chummy' medics are blurring the boundaries between personal and professional relationships.

Lesley Fallowfield, from Brighton and Sussex Medical School, said that doctors who had grown up in a 'cyberworld' where formal distinctions have been eroded are particularly likely to blur the line. "If you start off with a chummy, informal introduction, you're already on dangerous ground," she said. Doctors are rightly encouraged to be empathetic with patients, but a sympathetic look or a pat on the arm are enough and doctors should not feel the need "to do the sort of thing you would do if it was your mum or your best friend," Professor Fallowfield said.

"The difficulty, if you hug and kiss patients, if you allow them to call you by your first name, is that quickly the relationship can become confused as a social one rather than a professional one. This becomes a problem for both sides. Doctors become confused, 'I really like this person, how can I bear to tell them that they're going to die?' They find it more difficult to be objective. It can mean patients feel intimidated about complaining, or even mentioning side-effects that could

be very important, 'It doesn't seem fair to go on about it because they're doing their best'." A survey of 338 oncologists under the age of 40 found that 59 per cent said that they found it difficult to be truthful if they liked a patient, and 60 per cent felt that if doctors were too empathetic they could not make objective decisions.

Professor Fallowfield said that this was 'alarming', as were findings that half the doctors had given patients their personal mobile numbers, a fifth had accepted social invitations from patients and 14 per cent had accepted them as friends on Facebook.

"You don't want your doctor to start censoring themselves because they don't want to upset you," she said. "For example, if instead of having a painful conversation about palliative care, you recommend more [fruitless] chemotherapy with all its side effects, you really haven't done well by your patients."

Source: Smyth, C. 'Chummy young doctors are bad for your health', *The Times*, 24 November 2014

Questions

1. **Identify** and summarise the evidence in this article which suggests that the boundaries between professional and personal relationships are becoming blurred for some doctors and their patients.

2. **Analyse** why the researchers believed that growing up in a 'cyber-world' was responsible for the erosion of formal distinctions between doctors and patients.

3. **Evaluation.** On the basis of the evidence here and your own knowledge, evaluate the view that the middle class are more likely to have a voice that will be heard, understood and even empathised with by GPs. (Think about the social characteristics that doctors share with their middle-class patients.)

Evaluating the inverse care law

Blackman and Wistow (2009) note that there is evidence that simply spending more on health care may not be the most cost-effective way of reducing health inequalities. They note that Scotland spends about £2,300 per head on health care compared with England's £1,900, but life

expectancy in Scotland is lower for males. Moreover, life expectancy in the best local authority areas in Scotland only matches England's average life expectancy.

Blackman and Wistow suggest that the strategies that the NHS has adopted to reduce health inequalities may be the wrong ones, in that they are mainly focused on treatment rather than prevention. They suggest that the NHS needs to be more focused on health promotion. They argue that if health promotion campaigns are not employed, it is likely that better NHS care will actually widen health inequalities because many of those in need of treatment will not receive it.

The Labour Government (1997–2010) actually introduced a number of such proactive policies in order to promote health, such as:

> safe sex and contraceptive education in schools

> 'Healthy Living Centres' – these were opened in areas that experienced high levels of poverty and offer services such as counselling and stop smoking programmes

> the 'Healthy Schools' programme, which encouraged schools to raise awareness of health issues and to promote less childhood obesity and better health through healthy eating and lifestyles

> a major advertising campaign focused on the health benefits of physical activity that informed the general public of the risks of poor diet and obesity

> legislation obliging food manufacturers and supermarkets to clearly label the nutritional content of food, and to highlight fat, sugar and salt content.

Blackman and Wistow conclude that as little as 10 per cent of the causes of health inequalities are under the direct influence of the NHS, because factors such as poor educational achievement, poor housing, the environment, and unemployment and lifestyle choices, especially smoking, may be more important. However, other sociologists, such as Tudor Hart and Seddon, argue that NHS funding and provision is just as important as these factors in bringing about health inequalities.

In your view, how do inequalities in funding and the provision of NHS services compare with cultural and material factors in bringing about inequalities in mortality, life expectancy and morbidity?

ISSUES OF DEMAND

Social-class variations

The first half of this chapter clearly shows that there are social-class inequalities in the provision of NHS services. However, there may also be social-class inequalities in demand and access; middle-class people may be more willing to use health services than working class people. For example, the evidence shows that members of the working class are more likely to be ill and to have accidents, but they are actually less likely to attend doctors' surgeries. They are also less likely to take part in any form of screening programme that can discover disease (such as certain forms of cancer) at an early stage. They are, however, more likely to use accident and emergency services – often because health conditions have not been examined earlier and have since become acute. Sociologists argue that the main reasons for this are not that working-class people care less about illness or are ignorant about it, but that there are more barriers to them accessing health care.

> Working-class people may not be able to afford to take time off work as they may lose pay for doing so, and therefore they may be more reluctant to visit the doctor. In contrast, middle-class professionals are less likely to lose pay when they visit GPs and hospitals because they often have flexible working arrangements.

> Working-class people may have to travel a considerable distance to a GP surgery because of the shortage of GP surgeries in poorer areas.

> The middle class are more likely to have access to their own transport, which makes going to the doctor more convenient.

> Some working-class patients may be reluctant to visit their doctor because they feel threatened or patronised by their doctors' middle-class character. They might not feel confident or comfortable enough with their GP or consultant to discuss particular symptoms of illness or the side-effects of treatments, therefore contributing to further illness.

Gender

There are gender inequalities both in the provision of NHS services and in how they are used by men and women. Chapter 3 documents these inequalities in terms of life expectancy, obesity, mental illness and suicide.

Wilkins et al. (2008), who carried out 'The Gender and Access to Health Services Study', observe that there is an increasing recognition among health policy-makers and service planners that an individual's gender is a central determinant of his or her health status. They note a number of significant differences and inequalities in the ways in which men and women experience NHS services.

> Firstly, there are important gender differences in the way cardiac problems are detected and treated by NHS professionals. At the GP stage, heart conditions

are less likely to be diagnosed in women and consequently women are less likely to be referred to specialist care. Even when they are referred, they are less likely to be prescribed some medications.

> Secondly, women tend to seek help for weight issues outside the NHS by joining private slimming programmes such as Weight Watchers. Only a quarter of people who participate in such programmes are male. The NHS needs to be doing more for both genders in terms of weight reduction.

> Thirdly, with regard to depression and anxiety, women are more likely to receive treatment for psychiatric symptoms both in primary care and in the hospital sector, and more women than men are diagnosed each year with minor disorders. They are more also more likely to be prescribed drugs for their condition.

Feminist sociologists argue that women actually under-use the health services, if their use is compared to their actual needs. However, this view has been challenged by those sociologists who suggest that the NHS caters better for the health needs of females than it does for males. For example:

> there is a national strategy for women's mental health but no equivalent for men, although there is a focus on the prevention of young male suicide in the National Suicide Prevention Strategy

> the National Chlamydia Screening Programme has pioneered a strategy for increasing the take-up of services by men – currently the only strategy of its kind in any area of health provision.

Research carried out by the Men's Health Forum (MHF) found that men were unhappy with the service provided by their local GP surgeries. The forum points out that since men are twice as likely as women to work full time and three times as likely to work overtime, it is more difficult for them to see doctors during conventional opening hours. The MHF has suggested that NHS trusts offer health checks in venues frequented by men, such as workplaces and sports clubs. Only 27 per cent of Medical Research Council funding of sex-specific research goes to studies researching men's health.

Ethnicity

There is a lower use of medical services by certain ethnic-minority groups. Culley and Dyson (1993) argue that the way that [health] services are organised is based on indigenous British culture and focused on the needs of the majority White population rather than all ethnic groups. Consequently, the NHS, like other British institutions, has been accused of institutional racism.

This is not deliberate – the NHS was designed and put into operation before the UK became a multicultural society. However, it has failed to adapt to changing times and it has been accused of failing to cater sufficiently for ethnic-minority cultural and religious needs. Moreover, evidence suggests that some members of ethnic-minority groups may find aspects of NHS provision irrelevant, offensive, unhelpful and even threatening, while surveys indicate that Asians are more likely to report higher levels of dissatisfaction about health care compared with White people.

BUILDING CONNECTIONS

Institutional racism has been used to explain certain practices found in several institutions in Britain, such as the police, the judiciary, the immigration service, the mass media and the NHS; when these institutions discriminate against ethnic minority groups, this can result in racial or ethnic disadvantage. This racism is often embedded into institutional practices, is often unintentional and is based on ignorance rather than on the notion that ethnic-minority groups are inferior and deserving of such treatment.

A number of aspects of NHS care have been highlighted as institutionally racist, such as:

> the failure to provide health information in appropriate languages – there is some evidence that the NHS in areas with large ethnic-minority populations are now responding to this criticism by providing translators and pamphlets explaining how services work in minority languages

> the failure to provide amenities to support cultural beliefs in things such as the importance of running water for washing, death rites, prayer in hospital, visiting times, and food in hospital as an automatic inclusion in health service budgets; for example, after death Muslims must follow specific practices with regard to the dead body and funeral practices, which the NHS has been accused of failing to respect

> young Black British men receive worse treatment for mental health problems than white British patients and are more likely to be treated against their will, with drugs rather than psychotherapy, and on locked psychiatric wards – a 2004 report into the treatment of Black people in the mental health care system concluded that psychiatrists and psychiatric nurses generally regard young Black men as more aggressive, alarming, dangerous and difficult to treat

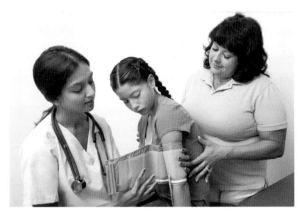

The lack of female health professionals available for medical examinations means that many women from Asian households are reluctant to seek medical help.

> the failure of the NHS to guarantee to women from ethnic minorities that any medical examination will be conducted by a female health professional – the number of female GPs is lowest in those areas with the largest concentration of Asian households and cultural and religious ideas about modesty may mean that many are reluctant to be seen by male doctors.

Studies suggest that these problems persist into the 21st century in Britain's health services. Research by the Maternity Alliance (2004) suggests that women from ethnic minorities are still twice as likely as White women to die in childbirth. The Alliance suggests that ethnic-minority women are more likely to receive substandard NHS care, and Muslim women in particular suffer acute discomfort due to a lack of privacy in hospitals and too few female staff. Moreover, there is a lack of information for women whose first language is not English. The research criticises NHS staff for not understanding how Islamic beliefs can affect women's needs. Many of the women who took part in the research said they had experienced stereotypical and racist comments during the course of their maternity care.

Szczepura (2005) demonstrated how low levels of cultural competence still exist among many GPs and hospital staff, and this contributes to the low uptake of NHS services, negative experiences and poor health outcomes among minority ethnic groups. However, research by Kai *et al.* (2007) suggests that many health professionals lack confidence when dealing with ethnic minorities and this may be impinging on the quality of care such patients receive. When 106 doctors were asked about how they felt when treating people of different ethnicities, many said that they felt anxious because they did not know enough about different cultures and they wanted to avoid causing offence or being perceived as racist. Kai *et al.* concluded that these anxieties hamper the ability of GPs to act flexibly and that they create a 'disabling hesitancy'

that can unintentionally contribute to ethnic disparities in health care.

Salway *et al.* (2014) do suggest there are positive signs that the NHS is now getting to grips with tackling ethnic inequalities in the provision of and access to health care. For example, the Pacesetters programme has funded over 200 projects focused on addressing the health inequalities faced by Black and minority ethnic groups. Other projects have sought to explore and address the low uptake of cervical screening among South Asian women.

However, Salway *et al.* point out that the NHS does not work within a political or economic vacuum. Politicians often insist that the causes of health inequalities lie with 'individual lifestyle choices' rather than inequalities of access to the NHS or institutionally racist health policies. Moreover, they note that even if the NHS were truly equitable in the health services that it provides for all social groups, the poverty and deprivation generally experienced by ethnic minorities in wider society would guarantee the persistence of health inequalities between the majority population and ethnic-minority groups.

Age

The Equality Act 2010 banned age discrimination in the provision of public services such as health. However, there is evidence that health professionals may still discriminate against patients on the grounds of their age. For example, a Macmillan Cancer Support survey in 2012 found that 45 per cent of cancer specialists said that they had dealt with a patient who had been refused treatment on the grounds of age. Lievesley (2009) documents similar ageism for elderly people with dementia, whilst Anderson (2007) suggests that younger people are prioritised by NHS mental health services despite the fact that elderly people have greater need.

Moreover, studies suggest that although direct ageism has been outlawed in the NHS, ageism is now more likely to be indirect and unconscious. For example, Billings (2003), using focus group interviews with NHS staff, found that many of them had observed their fellow professionals being patronising and over-familiar with elderly people, as well as making inappropriate comments about their age. Many reported that they had seen medical staff, particularly doctors, speaking over an elderly person, that is, speaking about them to other doctors and nurses but not including them in the conversation or not keeping them fully informed of their condition. Moreover, there are still concerns about the poor standards of care experienced by the elderly on hospital wards, such as not being fed or washed properly and being treated in undignified and disrespectful ways.

Disability

MENCAP (2004) in their research study 'Treat me right!' document numerous examples of discrimination practised against people with learning disabilities, especially people with Down's Syndrome, by the NHS. MENCAP research found that 75 per cent of GPs receive no training in helping people with learning disabilities, whilst many GPs admitted they felt that a person's disability made it difficult for them to diagnose illness and disease. Moreover, doctors often, consciously or unconsciously, believe that the disabled person's health problem is a result of the disability and that not much can be done about it. This is known as 'diagnostic overshadowing' and can lead to undiagnosed and/or misdiagnosed conditions.

MENCAP also reported that health professionals often did not understand that people with a learning difficulty found it difficult to communicate their symptoms and to understand what they are being told by doctors. Cumela and Martin (2000) found that hospital staff also had low expectations for patients with learning disabilities and were often unresponsive to their needs.

Finally, there is evidence that health professionals make value judgements about the worth of people with disabilities and that this often results in the denial of certain types of treatment and the failure to make life-saving interventions. There is evidence that doctors make negative value judgements about the quality of life of people with profound disabilities and that they often assume it would be in their best interests to die.

THEORETICAL APPROACHES

Some writers have suggested that wider theoretical perspectives may be useful in explaining inequalities in access to NHS services.

Marxism

Marxist writers on health, such as Doyal (1979) and O'Connor (1973), argue that the main function of the NHS is to work on behalf of the capitalist economy to maintain a healthy, hardworking – and therefore productive – workforce. In this sense, the NHS is an agency of social control because it aims to enable workers who are ill or injured to return to work as quickly as possible. According to this Marxist approach, inequalities in health provision are directly related to how productive people are. This explains why there are low levels of expenditure on people with mental illness, people with learning difficulties and the oldest and frailest members of society. These groups are not regarded as productive; spending on them

is regarded as wasteful by the ruling class. The low levels of expenditure on the working class are explained by Marxists by the presence of general social-class divisions throughout society, which dictate that working-class people consistently receive worse treatment across the range of services in housing, education and health.

Marxists also point to the existence of a private medicine sector that exists alongside the NHS and uses its facilities. When the NHS was set up in 1948, the Government was forced to make a deal with the British Medical Association to ensure their cooperation. This deal allowed consultants to keep their private practices and for doctors to treat private patients in NHS hospitals using NHS facilities and nurses.

This means that those who can afford to pay directly for medical services or who have private health insurance – about 11 per cent of the British population – have advantages in terms of provision of services. This increases inequality because private patients:

> can jump NHS waiting lists and receive treatment more quickly than NHS patients

> are able to gain access to a range of medical services that may not be available on the NHS, such as some cancer medicines

> limit the number of hours surgeons can work in the NHS by taking up their time in private practice

> utilise NHS nurses and facilities, so contributing to the shortage of hospital beds and the lengthening of NHS waiting lists.

Without private health insurance, patients may face significantly longer waiting times for treatments and may not be able to access the full range of medical services available.

All of these factors lead to the reinforcement of health inequalities between the rich and the poor.

However, there are a number of problems with the Marxist analysis. It could equally be argued that, rather than being a form of social control, the NHS provides a very powerful alternative message to that of capitalism. The NHS is based on the socialist principle of giving to people in need, irrespective of social class or income, whereas capitalism is based on people choosing to buy services, which depends upon their levels of income. Also, some of the largest areas of NHS expenditure are actually with groups who are not 'productive': the largest group of NHS users are older, retired people.

Pluralist approaches

This approach suggests that the best way to understand any society (or large organisation like the NHS) is to examine the way that power is distributed within it. Pluralist sociologists argue that no one group controls all the power in a society or organisation. Instead, there are numerous ('plural') competing groups who need to adjust to or negotiate with one another.

Pluralist theory explains inequalities in health provision and demand in terms of the differences in power between the various groups that are involved with the NHS. In terms of the provision of services, there is interplay between the various professional groups (consultants, dentists, doctors, nurses, specialists in the care of the elderly, etc.) as well as the managers and politicians, especially those who make up the government of the time. In addition, demands for services come from competing patient groups (for example, the mentally ill, children, older people, cancer patients) and from groups stratified according to ethnicity, age, gender and class. The outcome in terms of provision and use of health services will, therefore, constantly vary according to shifts in power between all of these groups.

Alford (1975) has suggested that both the Marxist and the pluralist approaches are useful, but that combining elements of both produces a better theory. According to Alford there are three groups of interested parties in the health service who operate on different levels and there is conflict both between them and within them.

1. The 'dominant' group consists of the established medical professions who compete with each other for dominance. Whatever the outcome of their struggles, this dominant group – which is made up of organisations such as the General Medical Council, the British Medical Association and the Royal Colleges that represent various groups of medical specialists – exercises the greatest power over NHS decision-making.

2. The 'challenging' group consists of senior health managers and health-service policy planners. This group has significantly increased its power in the NHS at the expense of the dominant group in the last 20 years.

3. The 'repressed' group consists of patients and other consumer groups. Different categories of patients compete for their health needs to be addressed, but they do so within the framework set out by the dominant and challenging groups.

Alford is essentially arguing that the competing interest groups in the health service can be grouped together in terms of the power they hold. Alford is therefore suggesting that the inequalities experienced by patients who are working class, ethnic minorities, elderly and disabled are the direct result of belonging to the least powerful group – patients – in the NHS. In this sense, Alford's theory is a modified version of pluralism. However, Alford incorporates elements of Marxism into his theory because he suggests that the dominant and challenging groups draw their power from their close relationship to the capitalist bourgeoisie. The divisions in health service provision, therefore, reflect the social-class divisions found in wider capitalist society.

CONCLUSIONS

The evidence largely suggests that Tudor Hart's idea about the existence of an inverse care law in the funding and provision of NHS services is still very valid today. Although the NHS has been reorganised at least four times since it was set up, funding in 2015 is not dramatically different to what it was in 1948. Consequently, regions of Britain in which the poor mainly live and in which need for health services is high are generally receiving a lower-quality provision of health services while other healthier areas continue to be over-funded. Moreover, there is also evidence that the way the NHS is organised may be responsible for constructing barriers that prevent groups such as ethnic minorities, the working class, men, the elderly and people with learning disabilities from using NHS services to full effect. Consequently, sociologists argue that the way the NHS works and is funded helps to produce health inequalities, although how influential this is compared with lifestyle or poverty is disputed.

CHECK YOUR UNDERSTANDING

1. Identify three examples of possible institutional racism which might undermine ethnic-minority demand for NHS services.

2. Identify two causes of the 'inverse care law' according to Tudor Hart.

3. Define what is meant by 'pluralism'.

4. Define what is meant by the 'marketisation' of NHS services.

5. Define what is meant by the 'inverse prevention law'.

6. Outline and explain the principles that the NHS was built upon in 1948.

7. Outline and explain how the NHS may discriminate against the elderly.

8. Explain why the middle class use NHS services more frequently than the working class.

9. Analyse and explain gender differences in the provision of NHS services.

10. Outline and evaluate the view that the organisation and funding of the NHS are just as important a cause of health inequalities as lifestyle or poverty.

TAKE IT FURTHER

In order to assess the level of take-up of NHS services among older people, interview a sample of people over the age of 60. Ask them:

> whether they get their 'flu jab' each autumn and why they do or don't

> whether they think older people are treated differently by the NHS than younger people (compare your answers in class)

> whether they feel that the NHS treats them fairly and with respect and dignity.

5.5 THE NATURE AND SOCIAL DISTRIBUTION OF MENTAL ILLNESS

LEARNING OBJECTIVES

> Demonstrate knowledge and understanding of the nature and social distribution of mental illness (AO1).

> Demonstrate knowledge and understanding of the different perspectives on how mental illness is experienced, interpreted and constructed in modern Britain (AO1).

> Analyse and apply the evidence collected by sociological surveys of health to the range of sociological theories that aim to explain mental illness (AO2).

> Evaluate sociological explanations in order to make judgements and draw conclusions about mental illness (AO3).

INTRODUCING THE DEBATE

Mental illness has been the forgotten twin to physical illness, in terms of the attention it has received and the funding provided by the NHS. Mental health has generally been regarded by the medical profession as a low-status field in which to practise. Moreover, Barry and Yuill (2012) point out that the mental health sector and the mentally ill have often been regarded with suspicion and fear by society. This is because mental illness often comes to public attention when the media regard criminal acts committed by someone with a mental health problem as newsworthy. The day-to-day trials and tribulations of the mentally ill are very rarely reported by the media. This is surprising because mental health is a major problem in contemporary British society. About one in seven of the population claim to have experienced mental health problems at some point in their lives. This chapter investigates the extent and social character of mental illness in the UK. Moreover, it will explore: the reasons why some groups seem more prone to mental and emotional distress; competing definitions of mental health; and the very controversial idea that mental illness does not actually exist and is, instead, a product of the imagination of psychiatrists. Finally, it will examine the effects of being labelled mentally ill and how this label shapes the reaction of doctors, hospitals and society to those who suffer from mental health problems.

According to the government publication *Social Trends* 2007 (Self and Zealey 2007), about one in six British people aged 16–74 reported experiencing a (self-diagnosed) neurotic disorder, such as depression, anxiety or a phobia, in the seven days before a national survey on mental health. A higher proportion of women (19 per cent) than men (14 per cent) experienced such a disorder.

However, the mental health charity MIND estimates that of the 300 in every 1,000 people in the UK who experience mental health problems, about 230 of these will visit their GP but only 102 of them will be diagnosed with a mental health problem. Moreover, only 30 of these people will be referred to psychiatrists or counsellors, or admitted to a hospital for treatment.

In your opinion, why are only a third of those who experience mental health problems receiving treatment for their condition?

DEFINING MENTAL ILLNESS

A useful way of approaching mental illness is to adopt Busfield's (2002) typology of psychiatric disorders. She classifies mental health disorders into three broad groups:

> disorders of thought, for example, schizophrenia, psychosis, sociopathy

> disorders of emotion, for example, depression, anxiety, phobias, neuroses

> disorders of behaviour, for example, alcohol and drug dependence.

The sociological analysis of mental health is focused on attempting to understand the ways in which social factors influence and perhaps even shape how mental health and illness is viewed by the general public, mass media, medical profession and those who experience such problems. Sociological analysis is also focused on explaining how society creates social situations that can have a negative impact on an individual's mental health. Sociologists have identified four very distinctive theoretical approaches to mental illness: (i) the biological or biomedical approach; (ii) the social constructionist and labelling approach; (iii) the social causation approach; and (iv) the social realist approach.

THE BIOLOGICAL OR BIOMEDICAL APPROACH

The biological or biomedical approach to mental health sees the causes of illness as situated in the physical or biological body. Some mental illnesses are the result of brain damage, tumours and lesions, faulty genes, or chemical and hormonal imbalances. For example, some types of depression may be caused by a lack of the chemical serotonin in the brain. Drugs are often prescribed to restore the brain's chemical balance. In addition, some mental health disorders may be the result of external factors that damage the biological development of the brain, such as poor diet, pollution or being starved of oxygen. However, only a fraction of mental health disorders are biological in origin.

Psychiatrists have suggested that the main source of mental health disorders may be an emotional trauma that the patient experienced whilst growing up or interacting with others. The biomedical-psychiatric approach generally believes that most symptoms of mental illness can therefore be scientifically diagnosed and categorised. Psychiatrists (as well as counsellors and psychotherapists) have to undertake extensive training so that they can objectively observe patients during face-to-face sessions and psychoanalyse their feelings and actions. On this basis, psychiatrists have classified problematic human behaviour into over 350 psychiatric categories or conditions – such as psychoses, phobias, anxieties, depression – and documented the symptoms of these in the widely-used *Diagnostic and Statistical Manual of Mental Disorders* (DSM). This book allows psychiatrists to follow standardised procedures in terms of identifying symptoms and deciding what treatments to prescribe.

With regard to treatment for mental illness, the biomedical approach has favoured allopathic or cure-orientated treatments focused on the individual. It generally uses counselling, psychotherapy, drugs such as anti-depressants and, in extreme cases, electro-convulsive or shock treatment and even surgery. The biomedical approach may recommend that sufferers from extreme mental health problems such as psychoses, who can pose a threat to others, should be legally **sectioned**, detained and isolated from wider society in secure mental health institutions.

Sometimes the biomedical approach will recommend that an individual suffering from a mental health disorder is 'sectioned', if they pose a risk to the safety of themselves or others.

THE SOCIAL CONSTRUCTIONIST APPROACH

Social constructionist perspectives have been very influential in sociological approaches to mental illness. They start from the argument that behaviour considered normal or mentally ill varies over time and from society to society. For example, in Britain in the medieval period, mentally-ill people were seen as being possessed by devils or as cursed by God. They were often tortured and killed as a result.

Barry and Yuill suggest that in the more enlightened 18th century, mental illness was seen as a crime against reason and rationality. It was consequently stigmatised and associated with danger and violence. Those suffering from mental disorders were perceived as outsiders and deviants, and often shut away from sight in asylums.

Extremes of behaviour have been seen as normal in some societies and as evidence of madness in others. For example, if a person in the UK claimed that he or she was possessed by the spirit of an ancestor, society would probably conclude that person had mental health problems. However, in some American Indian tribes and in some West African religions, it would be a perfectly

reasonable statement that most people would believe to be true. Similarly, there is a very thin line, even in modern societies such as Britain's, between someone defined as 'eccentric' and someone described as suffering from a mental health problem. However, Britain cherishes its eccentrics. Kyaga (2012) also notes how society is willing to tolerate mental health problems in people considered creative geniuses, such as writers and artists.

Michel Foucault

The social constructionist argument has been heavily influenced by the work of the French sociologist, Michel Foucault. He explains the growth in the concept of mental illness by placing it in the context of the changing ways of thinking and acting that developed in the early 18th century. According to Foucault, during the Enlightenment, more traditional ways of thinking based on religious beliefs and emotions were gradually replaced by more rational and intellectually disciplined ways of thinking and acting. These eventually led to the significant scientific and engineering developments that formed the basis of the 'industrial revolution'. Foucault argues that as rationality developed into the normal way of thinking, irrationality began to be perceived as deviant.

Michel Foucault

This shift away from the irrational and towards the rational was illustrated, according to Foucault, by the growth in asylums for those considered mad and irrational. Foucault suggests that putting mad people into asylums both symbolically and literally isolated them from the majority of the population. The asylums symbolised that madness or irrationality was no longer acceptable. Foucault therefore argues that madness or mental illness as we know and treat it today is a relatively modern invention that emerged from the development of modern 'rational' ways of thinking and acting.

Foucault developed his analysis further when he argued that there is no single irrefutable truth that can be agreed upon by everyone. In other words, there is no such thing as normal or abnormal behaviour. However, he pointed out that society – and its institutions and culture – are mainly constructed by those with power, whose main motive is to exert social control over those without power who potentially threaten them.

Foucault saw medicine as an important agency of social control, working alongside other agencies such as the police, courts and prisons to keep problematical people under surveillance, and to regulate, control and punish them for being outsiders. He argued that psychiatrists have constructed a powerful **discourse** – a dominant set of ideas – that allows them to legally define what constitutes abnormal and therefore mentally ill behaviour and to forcefully control that behaviour via legal detention and punitive treatments. For example, once a person has been legally sectioned by the mental health authorities, they often lose all social and civil rights and are subjected to controversial treatments. They can only be released from psychiatrists' care once these mental health experts are convinced the individual has been cured. The authorities are under no obligation to state a release date. As Higgs (2008) notes, those labelled as mentally ill are completely at the mercy of those treating them and can regain their lives only if they agree with their doctors.

UNDERSTAND THE CONCEPT

Foucault defined **discourse** as a system of thoughts composed of ideas, attitudes, beliefs and practices that construct, shape and dominate the worlds to which they refer. For example, scientists conduct experiments in particular ways because they have learned from their training, textbooks and peers – the discourse – that there is a 'right' way to do science.

BUILD CONNECTIONS

Social control is an important concept found in many areas of the Sociology specification, such as Education and Crime and Deviance. There are two types of social control. Formal social controls are usually institutionalised in the form of laws, rules and regulations and are applied by institutions such as the police, courts and prisons, schools, and so on. Informal controls originate in the values and norms of social groups such as families and are normally used to deter or punish poor behaviour.

Anti-psychiatry

Social constructionist sociologists have focused on the relationship between mental illness, psychiatry and power. A good example of this approach to mental health is that undertaken by the leader of the anti-psychiatry movement, Thomas Szasz (1973), who makes a number of important observations.

> Psychiatry and its definitions of mental health and illness are a form of social control. All societies are based on some sort of **consensus** if they are to remain stable. However, there is always a group of people who refuse to abide by the consensus or who cannot conform. These people are often seen and treated as deviants and outsiders. Psychiatric medicine has long been used to explain the actions of these outsiders in terms of mental illness. For example, up to the 1960s, homosexuality was viewed as a mental illness and treated accordingly. The label 'mental illness' is therefore a convenient way to deal with behaviour that people find disruptive, while the role of psychiatry is to control deviance.

UNDERSTAND THE CONCEPT

Consensus refers to the functionalist idea that societies tend to be socially stable because the mass of the population generally subscribe to the same values and norms.

In Russia, homosexuality was declassified as a mental illness in 1999. However, tensions still run high between the authorities and gay rights activists.

> Szasz argues that psychiatry is a fraudulent medical specialism because when someone is experiencing a mental illness – unlike physical illnesses such as cancer – there are usually no clear-cut, objective biological or physical symptoms or evidence that can be observed.

361

Psychiatrists have to rely on what people tell them and their observations. Szasz argues that diagnosis is the result of a deeply subjective and unscientific interpretation of the interaction between the patient and the psychiatric doctor. He argues that mental illness is a myth manufactured by psychiatry to justify its existence. It does not exist as a fact because it has no organic or biological basis.

> Judgements made by psychiatrists may be based on social values and cultural norms rather than on scientific criteria. For example, it can be argued that as homosexuality became more socially acceptable and as the stigma and negative labels attached to homosexuality diminished, the view that homosexuality was a form of mental illness became untenable and was eventually dropped from psychiatric manuals and textbooks.

> Szasz is especially critical of the application of mental health labels to children's behaviour. He points out that children were once defined as simply 'naughty' but nowadays they are more likely to be subjected to psychiatric evaluation, diagnosed with Attention Deficit Hyperactivity Disorder (ADHD) and put on the drug Ritalin. Szasz argues that this is a form of social control and child abuse, rather than a real treatment for a real disease. He asserts that there is no physical biological evidence that ADHD exists.

> Psychiatrists are too willing to 'medicalise social life' and interpret behaviour that is normal, natural, etc. as symptomatic of mental health problems. For example, Szasz suggests that being sad or shy are a normal part of the human psyche. However, American psychiatrists have now categorised these 'conditions' as clinical mental health disorders that can be treated with drugs or therapy. This medicalisation of social life is driven by money. Both the psychiatric profession and the pharmaceutical industry have a vested interest in diagnosing more and more people as suffering from mental health problems.

Szasz' position on psychiatry is supported by an experiment carried out by Katz, (1969) who was interested in whether the process of psychiatric diagnosis was consistently applied to all patients. Katz showed groups of British and American psychiatrists films of interviews with patients and asked them to note down all the symptoms of mental illness they could see and make a diagnosis. However, Katz found clear disagreements in diagnosis between the two groups. The British saw less evidence of mental illness generally and therefore were reluctant to diagnose it. In contrast, one patient was diagnosed as 'schizophrenic' by one third of the Americans, but by none of the British psychiatrists.

In your opinion, why did the British psychiatrists disagree with their American counterparts?

FOCUS ON SKILLS: RESEARCHING ADHD

ADHD: diagnosis of a generation driven to distraction

ADHD is now second only to asthma as the most frequent long-term medical diagnosis of childhood. Recent research shows that its symptoms – which include an inability to concentrate, impulsive behaviour and social awkwardness – mean sufferers struggle to achieve at school and to be happy in their personal lives.

ADHD, which is normally diagnosed from the ages of 3 to 7, is said to affect three times as many boys as girls.

It is also being more commonly diagnosed in adults. In the USA, more than one in seven children receives a diagnosis by the time they turn 18, according to the Centres for Disease Control and Prevention, and two thirds of this number are prescribed medication. According to the NHS, ADHD is the most common behavioural disorder in the UK and it estimates that the condition affects 2–5 per cent of school-age children and young people.

Yet the disorder that keeps parents awake at night with worry and that teachers struggle to cope with does not exist, according to Dr Richard Saul, one of America's leading neurologists. ADHD is not a syndrome on its own but a collection of symptoms caused by more than 20 separate conditions — from poor eyesight and giftedness to depression and bipolar disorder — each requiring its own specific treatment.

Saul says that his conclusion is based on three decades of treating patients who complained of short attention spans and inability to focus. Delving deeper into why they were so easily distracted, he found diverse reasons. One girl who was disruptive in the classroom had myopia and could not see the blackboard properly. She needed spectacles, not drugs. A boy who was inattentive in a mathematics class was simply bored and regained his concentration when he was put in another class with older children. Several of his young patients had undiagnosed hearing conditions. Other children were found to be suffering from Tourette syndrome, obsessive compulsive disorder, autism, fetal alcohol syndrome and learning disabilities.

Too many doctors prescribe ADHD medication with only cursory examination of patients, Saul says, and too many parents accept ADHD diagnoses for their children's behavioural problems since any stigma associated with the condition has faded. Dr Lily Hechtman of McGill University in Montreal and an acknowledged expert on ADHD, says: "Restlessness or

inattention — that's not ADHD. We have to diagnose the condition more carefully".

Based on 'ADHD: Diagnosis of a generation driven to distraction' by Barbara McMahon (*The Times*, 8 January 2014)

Questions

1. **Identify** and describe the symptoms and social distribution of ADHD according to this article.

2. **Evaluate** why parents and schools are happy to accept that ADHD exists as a medical condition.

3. **Outline** and **assess**. On the basis of knowledge taken from the article and your own research, outline and assess the view that ADHD, as an exclusive mental health problem, does not exist. (As a starting point, summarise Szasz's and Richard Saul's ideas on ADHD and consider what the biomedical or psychiatric view would be.)

MENTAL ILLNESS: THE LABELLING OR INTERACTIONIST PERSPECTIVE

Szasz and Katz conclude that some people are labelled mentally ill because their behaviour is negatively interpreted by those in power. However, labelling theory points out that once a person has been labelled as mentally ill there are a number of negative consequences for the person, as it is then assumed that all their behaviour is evidence of their mental state.

A famous study by Rosenhan (1973) illustrates the consequences of labelling. In the early 1970s in the USA, Rosenhan asked eight perfectly 'normal' researchers to enter a number of psychiatric institutions after phoning up and complaining that they were hearing voices. The researchers were under strict instructions to behave completely normally at all times once they had been admitted. However, the doctors and nurses observed this 'normal' behaviour as symptoms of 'abnormality' because they assumed their presence in the hospital was evidence of their mental illness. One researcher who was asked by Rosenhan to write down what they saw was diagnosed as suffering from 'writing behaviour'.

Rosenhan conducted a second study in which doctors in another psychiatric hospital were told that his experiment was to be repeated in their institution. They were asked to identify which of the patients were researchers who were just pretending to be ill. In reality Rosenhan had

sent no researchers into this particular hospital but nevertheless staff identified and labelled some patients who were 'genuinely ill' as pretend patients. This supports Szasz's observations about the unreliability of subjective judgements in defining who is mentally ill.

Erving Goffman (1968) took on a job at an American mental hospital as Assistant Athletic Director in the 1960s and used his position to observe how people who had been labelled as mentally ill were treated by doctors and nurses. His research was a type of participant observation – it was mainly covert in that the patients and hospital authorities did not know he was doing sociological research.

Goffman's research found that, once in a psychiatric institution, people are stripped of all their individuality. He observed that the first stage of this process was to cut off all contact with the outside world. The second stage was to regiment their behaviour. Patients were closely observed by staff at all times, they had little privacy, they were subjected to strict discipline and their personal possessions were taken away. They had to wear official clothing and their day – the time they got up, ate, bathed, took their medicine, went to bed – was timetabled by the doctors. Inmates were expected to show staff continuous signs of respect. According to Goffman's interpretation, mentally ill patients were 'treated like children'. The result of this process – which Goffman called 'the mortification of the self' – was to strip away the self-image or identity the patient had when he or she entered the institution, leaving them bewildered, vulnerable and ready to accept a new role.

Once the old 'mentally ill' self was stripped away, Goffman observed that the total institution then engaged in the reconstruction of the 'self' or personality of the patient by rewarding the patient for conforming to their mentally ill label. Goffman notes that if a patient attempted to reject the label of mental illness, their resistance was interpreted by medical staff as another symptom of the illness, and the patient was often subjected to punishment in the form of further medication or electric shock treatment. On the other hand, the acceptance by the patient of the label 'mentally ill' was interpreted by psychiatrists as the first sign on the road to recovery.

However, Goffman observed that patients developed tricks and strategies in order to cope with their situation. Some patients withdrew into themselves and kept themselves to themselves. Others 'played it cool' by pretending to go along with what the psychiatrists and nurses wanted. A negative by-product of this process was institutionalisation – some patients became over-dependent on the routines of the institution and could no longer live in the outside world.

There is also some evidence that the attitudes of the general public towards the mentally ill are problematic. Survey evidence suggests that many people subscribe to myths and unhelpful images about mental illness. Baker and McPherson (2000) found that 60 per cent of young people admit to using abusive and negative language to describe mentally ill people. Over a quarter of people with mental health problems reported that they had experienced hostility in their community. Media representations of mental illness are also negative. Philo (1999) found that two thirds of media representations disproportionately focus on violence committed by the mentally ill and 40 per cent of tabloid newspaper headlines used derogatory language to describe mental illness. This results in a hostile reaction to the mentally ill among the general public because mass media reports imply that people should fear them. Sympathy for the mentally ill and the severity of their condition is diminished by such media representations.

Goffman concludes, then, that the treatment of the mentally ill by both the medical profession and the general public results in a stigma being attached to them, which has the effect of denying them full acceptance by society. This leaves them with a sense of low self-esteem. Moreover, they are socially excluded and isolated. These experiences of a hostile and discriminatory society may result in some people with mental health problems being reluctant to seek help. This in turn may create further stress and make their mental health problems worse.

How might attitudes towards the mentally ill be improved?

BUILD CONNECTIONS

Symbolic interactionism, which is also known as labelling theory, is an interpretivist theory that opposes the positivist view that people are the puppets of society and that social behaviour is largely shaped by society. Instead, interpretivists argue that people are the architects of society in that they get together in social groups, interact with one another and apply meaning to one another's behaviour. Interactionists are particularly interested in how such interaction can lead to powerful groups labelling and controlling the behaviour of less powerful groups. The theory is important in helping us to understand teacher–pupil relationships in the classroom and police–community relationships.

THE SOCIAL CAUSATION APPROACH

Social causation theories examine how various inequalities in society based on ethnicity, gender and social class produce dangerous levels of stress for some people. As Barry and Yuill (2012) note, "people may be 'tipped' into mental illness, whether it is a woman expected to bring up children on her own and keep down a job or the experience of someone from an ethnic minority group of being racially abused by a neighbour; or the constant soul-destroying grind of poverty and not being able to lead the life that others enjoy" (p.147).

Mental illness and ethnicity

Members of ethnic minorities have significantly different chances of mental illness compared to the majority White population. According to McCrone et al. (2008), women from British Pakistani and Indian households experience more depression than either men or women of White or African Caribbean ethnicity. Nazroo (2001) found that African Caribbean males have particularly high levels of schizophrenia; between three and five times higher than the population as a whole.

Virdee (1997) explains mental illness among ethnic minorities in the UK by arguing that the sorts of pressures and stresses that can cause people to develop mental illness are more likely to be experienced by members of ethnic minorities. This is because they encounter racist and prejudiced attitudes and experience more frequent exposure to stressors such as racial attacks, verbal abuse, and unemployment. Chalal and Julienne (1999) found that being a frequent victim of racism led to people feeling constantly stressed, exhausted and vulnerable. However, Nazroo points out that people of Bangladeshi origin, who are among the most deprived groups in the British population and are also victims of racism, actually have lower levels of mental illness than the general population.

Nazroo also found that young men from African Caribbean backgrounds are far more likely to reach the mental health system via the police, courts and prisons because these institutions are institutionally racist. This is reflected in their assumption that young Black men are more aggressive, threatening and dangerous than young White men. Young Black men in the UK are more likely to be remanded to mental hospitals for psychiatric reports than young White men. They are more likely to be placed in secure wards and to experience harsher, invasive, coercive and punitive forms of treatment, such as being given tranquillisers without their knowledge or consent. They are more likely to have electroconvulsive therapy forced on them than other social groups.

Kelly and Nazroo (2008) conclude as a result of these facts that psychiatry is not only institutionally racist but that it is part of a broader oppressive system which reinforces ethnic disadvantage. However, Lipsedge and Littlemore (1997) challenge the view that psychiatrists are institutionally racist. They argue that the level of schizophrenia among Black patients is a result of psychiatric misdiagnosis. In their view, young Black men are demonstrating paranoia resulting from the racism they have encountered in British society rather than from schizophrenia.

Mental illness and gender

Women are more likely than men to exhibit behaviour defined as mental illness. Overall, women have rates about one third higher than men, but in some specific forms of mental illness the figures are much higher. For example, younger women are at least three times more likely than men to be treated for depression and prescribed anti-depressants, while older women are more likely to be treated for anxiety.

Feminist sociologists such as Brown *et al.* (1995), argue that women are more likely to lead stressful lives because of poverty, debt, unemployment, poor housing conditions and having to combine jobs and the responsibility for childcare. Although most women cope with these situations, some women may be tipped into poor mental health by 'provoking agents' such as marital breakdown, domestic violence and eviction. Women who have more than two children or lack social supports from friends, relatives or neighbours may be more vulnerable to depression and anxiety because of this mixture of potentially stressful social factors.

Ehrenreich and English (1979) and Busfield (1988) are critical of the way that the mental health system has traditionally treated women. They note that Victorian psychiatry defined women as mentally fragile, whereas 20th-century psychiatrists saw unhappiness and depression as a 'normal' part of the female condition. They suggest that sociologists should not trust the mental health statistics with regard to gender because these merely reflect patriarchal psychiatric stereotypes. Chesler (1972) argues that this stereotyping affects diagnosis because it means psychiatrists, when they treat a woman, tend to look for reasons for poor mental health within the individual rather than examining her social environment, which may contain stress triggers such as poverty. Larkin (2011) argues that it is probably a combination of social environmental issues and the psychiatric interpretation of women being more prone to depression and anxiety that has resulted in women showing up in the mental health statistics more often than men.

Scambler (2008) notes that male mental health is invisible in comparison because males tend to express their mental problems in the form of criminal behaviour and attempted suicide, and consequently end up in prison rather than being treated by doctors or mental health institutions. For example, the Social Exclusion Unit estimates that more than 70 per cent of male prisoners have two or more mental disorders (Social Exclusion Unit, 2004, quoting *Psychiatric Morbidity Among Prisoners In England And Wales,* 1998 from the ONS).

Inequality, social class and mental illness

Overall, an examination of the group most likely to suffer from high rates of mental illness shows that the poorest and most excluded are massively over-represented. Many of the women who experience mental illness and members of ethnic minorities suffering from higher levels of depression are part of this group. Social class, gender and ethnicity often intersect.

Link and Phelan (1995) reviewed all the evidence of connections between social class and mental illness over a period of 40 years and concluded that all the research suggests that there is a close relationship between deprivation and low levels of mental health. A government study (ONS, 2004) found that children from the poorest backgrounds were three times more likely to have conduct disorders than those whose parents were in professional occupations.

Myers (1975) has suggested a 'life-course' model, which explains the higher levels of mental illness among the poor. He suggests that poorer people consistently encounter greater social problems over the course of their lives, but do not have access to the educational, social and economic resources that the middle class take for granted to help them overcome these problems. Myers argues that the stress of trying to cope with these problems or life-crises becomes too much for the poor and this is often expressed through mental illness, especially depression.

Putnam (2000) argues that people who have large social networks of friends and relatives experience strong social capital, which protects them from the stress of loneliness and isolation. They are more likely to be happy because they feel they belong to a community. They consequently experience lower levels of stress and are less likely to suffer mental illness.

In contrast, the psycho-social theory of Wilkinson and Pickett (2010) argues that the poor are less likely to have large social networks of friends and relatives. They are more likely to live in urban areas with little sense of community and to be socially isolated. People are more likely to be mutually suspicious of each other because of high crime rates. Anti-social behaviour may mean that people are hostile towards or frightened of others. The poor are also more likely to experience family breakdown and to be in debt.

All of these problems, according to Wilkinson and Pickett, originate in the inequalities in income and wealth that exist in modern societies. They argue that the wider the gap in income, the more physical and mental health problems will be experienced. Britain has a fairly wide gap, so Wilkinson and Pickett argue that the poor in Britain experience high levels of stress and therefore their potential for poor mental health problems, such as depression, is greater than for other social groups.

A similar position is taken by James (1998) who has observed a correlation between an increase in wealth in the UK and higher levels of depression among the population. He blames the media and advertising because it has heightened people's expectations of what life should be about. However, there is a depressing gap between people's reality and their expectations and consequently people focus more on what they haven't achieved than what they have.

James blames the media for creating unrealistic, material expectations of success.

Evaluate whether James is right – do we set our expectations too high?

THE SOCIAL REALIST APPROACH

Social realism is a general term used to describe the approaches of sociologists who, broadly speaking, accept that there are distinctive sets of abnormal behaviour that cause distress to individuals and to those around them. These forms of abnormal behaviour are classified as mental illness. Social realists such as Pilgrim and Rogers (1999) accept that, at different times and in different cultures, there are variations in what is considered mental illness. Nevertheless, they argue that, although mental illness may have different names and may or may not be recognised in different cultures, it does actually exist as a real condition.

Gove (1982) suggests that the vast majority of people who receive treatment for mental illness actually have serious problems before they are treated and so the argument that the label causes the problem is wrong. Furthermore, he argues that the social constructionist view provides no adequate explanation for why some people start to show symptoms of mental illness in the first place. According to Gove, labelling may help to explain some of the responses of others to the mentally ill, but it cannot explain the causes of the illness.

Pilgrim and Rogers point out that people are simultaneously organic biological and social beings. Barry and Yuill suggest therefore that sociologists investigating mental health need to acknowledge the powerful role of culture and environment in shaping mental health but also the importance of medical information and research. They conclude that the causes of mental illness lie in the "complex interweaving of both society and biology". There may be biological processes – for example, chemical changes – at work in shaping mental illness but these processes work within a wider social and environmental context, in which social factors and even labelling may be the cause of that biological change.

CONCLUSIONS

Mental illness is a highly contested issue in sociology. There are arguments over the very definition of the term and how social differences and inequalities in mental illness rates in the population should be explained. However, most of the approaches discussed in this chapter have a valid contribution to make to the debate. The social constructionists have drawn attention to the power of psychiatrists to turn what people say and do into the social problem of mental illness. They have also drawn attention to how psychiatry may be used to exert social control over groups defined as a problem, which

may explain why young African Caribbean males turn up more in the mental health statistics. Very importantly, they have drawn sociological attention to the prejudice, discrimination and harsh treatment that might result from the application of a mental health label and how this may lead to further problems.

The social causation approach has documented the wide variety of social and environmental factors which provoke the stress and other negative emotions that can trigger mental illness and disproportionately affect groups such as women, ethnic minorities and the poor.

Some sociologists have combined both the constructionist and social causation models. Busfield, for example, argues that it is probably true that some groups are much more likely to find their behaviour defined as mental illness, when compared to the behaviour of other groups. However, it is also true that these same groups – ethnic minorities, women and the socially excluded – all suffer high levels of stress and so one would expect them to have higher levels of illness. Both processes therefore reinforce each other.

CHECK YOUR UNDERSTANDING

1. Identify four ways Goffman says patients react to treatment in mental hospitals.

2. Identify the three broad types of psychiatric disorder that exist according to Busfield.

3. Define what is meant by the 'life-course model' of mental illness.

4. Define what is meant by 'social capital'.

5. Outline and explain how the acquisition of social capital may prevent mental illness.

6. Outline and explain the relevance of Rosenhan's experiments to labelling theory.

7. Explain why Szasz concluded that mental illness is a myth.

8. Analyse and explain the social realist perspective on mental health.

9. Outline and evaluate the view that the differences in rates of mental illness are due to labelling.

TAKE IT FURTHER

Conduct a small-scale survey. Using a sample of 20 people:

> ask what the first words are that pop into their minds when you say the words 'mental illness'

> ask them to suggest two reasons why people become mentally ill

> use your imagination to invent scenarios; for example, ask how they would feel if a home for the mentally ill opened in their street

> ask them whether they have used derogatory words such as 'loony'.

Collate your answers – what do they suggest about people's views of mental illness? Do the sociological ideas contained in this chapter ring true?

5.6 THE ROLE OF MEDICINE, THE HEALTH PROFESSIONS AND THE GLOBALISED HEALTH INDUSTRY

LEARNING OBJECTIVES

> Demonstrate knowledge and understanding of the role of medicine, the health professions and the globalised health industry (AO1).

> Demonstrate knowledge and understanding of the different perspectives on the health professions and the globalised health industry (AO1).

> Analyse and apply the evidence collected by sociological surveys of health to the range of sociological theories that aim to explain the links between the role of medicine, the health professions and the globalised health industry (AO2).

> Evaluate sociological explanations in order to make judgements and draw conclusions about the role of the health professions and the globalised health industry (AO3).

INTRODUCING THE DEBATE

This chapter focuses on how the medical profession – doctors covering over 60 specialities – has managed to become one of the most prestigious and well-paid groups in society, while other health professionals such as nurses, midwives, paramedics and health visitors have not managed, as occupational groups, to achieve the same status and power.

In this topic, we have seen a number of references to the fact that the dominant approach to treating disease,

disability and mental illness is focused on biomedicine – the idea that the body is an organic machine under attack from external forces, which can only be repelled by the expertise of medical professionals. Therefore, when we explore the roots of the power and status wielded by doctors, we are also exploring how the biomedical model came to be so dominant.

Finally, this chapter explores some of the links between what goes on in our home-based medical industry or environment – the National Health Service (NHS) – and the wider global world. As we shall see, the NHS would be hard-pressed to operate as effectively as it does without global migration. Rather more worryingly, we will also see that what goes on within our home-grown health service is partly shaped by an extremely powerful global pharmaceutical industry.

DOCTORS AND CONSULTANTS

Hinksman (2015) observes that, in the UK, fully qualified medical practitioners are placed into two categories, doctors and consultants. It is important to understand the difference between these two medical roles.

The term 'doctor' usually applies to a general practitioner (GP). A GP is somebody trained in a broad range of medicine. Doctors work in a variety of settings such as GP surgeries, where they treat people living in the local community, and in hospitals, where they work alongside consultants, nurses and other health care workers. They are responsible for the diagnosis, treatment, care and wellbeing of patients. It is a doctor's responsibility to make the initial diagnosis of a patient, and in many cases doctors can treat the condition themselves. Doctors are permitted to write prescriptions, enabling patients to buy controlled medicines, and can carry out minor procedures and even minor surgery.

When a doctor diagnoses a particular condition and is unable or unequipped to treat it, or if the doctor can't identify the condition, they may refer the patient to a consultant. Consultants have the same basic medical training as doctors but they also have additional training in their specialist field of medicine. For this reason, becoming a consultant often takes longer than becoming a GP.

Consultants are therefore more senior to doctors. Most NHS hospitals divide their wards into different speciality areas and a senior consultant in that speciality will usually be in charge of the ward, overseeing the other consultants and doctors that work there. Most surgery in hospitals is carried out by consultants. An important status difference between consultants and doctors is how they are addressed. While doctors use the title 'Dr' before their name, many consultants are referred to as 'Mr', 'Mrs' or 'Miss'.

A number of sociological theories focus on how doctors have come to dominate the health profession in general.

THE FUNCTIONALIST APPROACH: THE HEALTH PROFESSIONS AS A BENEFIT TO SOCIETY

The first approach to understanding the role of the medical profession developed from the functionalist school of sociology. It seeks to show that there is a functional or beneficial relationship between doctors and society. The first functionalist sociologist to investigate this relationship was Talcott Parsons who invented the concept of the 'sick role'. Parsons was aware that the claim to sickness and disease by citizens and workers had the potential to disrupt both the social order and the effectiveness of the economy. In other words, some members of society might use the excuse of sickness to avoid going to work or to avoid their social responsibilities. From a functionalist perspective, sickness was therefore potentially deviant because it had the potential to create workshy and welfare-dependent subcultures that might undermine consensus and order.

Parsons argues that in order to manage this threat, modern industrial societies such as the UK have constructed the 'sick role', which manages how patients and doctors define, negotiate and overcome sickness. The aim of such a role is to ensure that a person returns as quickly as possible to their occupational and social roles so that social and economic disruption is minimised. Consequently, members of society learn that in order to be legitimately defined as 'sick' they need to consult a doctor, who through diagnosis will confirm that the individual is not malingering.

The patient's adoption of the sick role means that they agree to behave in ways that suggest they want to get better and to return as quickly as possible to their social and occupational responsibilities, for example, by following their doctor's advice, taking prescribed medicines and/or having surgery. In return, the doctor will put the patient's needs first by using their training and expertise to diagnose and treat the patient. If the illness is genuine, doctors have the authority to officially define the patient as 'ill', thus entitling the patient to public sympathy as well as being excused from work or school, or to receive, if chronically ill, welfare benefits. In reality, the adoption of the 'sick role' is simply an aspect of the biomedical model of medicine described in Chapter 1, in which the patient surrenders their body to examination and treatment by doctors.

Criticisms of the 'sick role' concept

The effectiveness of the 'sick role' has been questioned on several counts.

> Only a fraction of those who take time off work for reasons of sickness actually visit the doctor.

> The deviant nature of sickness and malingering may have been exaggerated by Parsons. For example, it was reported that 131 million working days were lost to sickness in 2013. This seems like a large number but actually means that workers in the UK only took an average of 4.4 sick days each in that year (ONS, 2014). This is down from 7 sick days in 1993. Many workers are going to work despite being sick or stressed because of job insecurity. The Trades Union Congress (TUC) General Secretary, Frances O'Grady, noted in 2014 that there is a growing culture of presenteeism in which unwell staff are pressured into coming into work by their employers.

> Some sick people may avoid conformity to the sick role because their illness attracts social stigma and negative labelling – for example, HIV/AIDS or mental illness. Some sick people may therefore conceal their illness from both society and doctors.

> Some illnesses and disabilities are incurable. The sick role may be avoided by some terminally ill patients (for example, those who decide not to have chemotherapy) in order to make the most of a 'normal' life before they die.

> Some sick people may refuse to adopt the sick role and challenge the authority and expertise of their doctors. They may reject conventional medicine and adopt alternative 'natural' treatments. They may even elect to reject the sick role altogether by arranging an assisted suicide, even though this is not legal.

> Marxists argue that the sick role is an ideological tool of the ruling class who need to ensure that workers go to work on a regular basis so that they can be exploited. In this sense, the sick role is merely a means by which doctors exert social control over the workforce on behalf of the ruling class.

The professionalisation of medicine

Another functionalist thinker, Barber (1963), specifically focused on how doctors have managed to convince society that they are beneficial to the community and consequently worthy of high rewards and status.

It is to the advantage of doctors that everybody gets ill, regardless of their social position in society – workers, leaders, prime ministers, the Queen – and that as people get older, they are more likely to develop disease and degenerative illnesses, and to eventually die. Barber argues that it is therefore in the best interests of all members of society to make sure that the medical profession, and consequently the NHS, has the very best people, who maintain the highest standards in providing medical care and in sustaining life expectancy. These people must be skilled and talented but also totally trustworthy because they are dealing with the most vulnerable section of society. Barber argues that doctors in the UK fit this bill and are consequently beneficial to society because they have constructed a professional subculture made up of a number of crucial 'traits' or characteristics which suggest that their main motivation in becoming doctors is **altruistic** – that public service comes before financial rewards or prestige.

UNDERSTAND THE CONCEPT

Altruism refers to the principle and practice of working selflessly for the good of others. Job satisfaction is derived from seeing the benefits for those who are being helped rather than, say, from the money the worker receives.

Barber identifies the following traits or characteristics as central to the social construction of doctors as a medical profession.

> There is a scientific theoretical basis to medical knowledge of which doctors have a full understanding. This allows them to make independent and expert decisions about the cause of illness and the best possible treatment.

> Doctors are trained to the highest possible standards – only the most intelligent can enter the medical profession and succeed. Their competence is tested by examination, there is no favouritism and doctors achieve their position as a result of their ability alone.

> These standards are strengthened by doctors setting up various bodies in order to ring-fence and protect their scientific and medical knowledge from being hijacked by other health professionals. For example, the government has given the General Medical Council (GMC) responsibility for the legal registration or licensing and regulation of all doctors qualified to

practice in the UK. The GMC also regulates medical education, training and standards. Moreover, the expertise of consultants is legitimated by their membership of various Royal Colleges, which lay down the entry and training requirements for particular consultancy disciplines, such as surgery, and which set examinations for their members. Note the 'royal' seal of approval, which confirms the prestige attached to the social position of consultants.

› The medical profession has a strict code of standards and ethics. Doctors deal with people who are weak and susceptible and consequently the GMC has developed a professional and ethical set of rules known as 'Good Medical Practice' that all doctors are legally compelled to follow. The GMC has the legal power to call doctors who are accused of incompetence or deviance before a disciplinary panel. Doctors who are found guilty by this panel of failing to abide by the code of ethics may be 'struck off' the medical register and not allowed to practice again.

BUILD CONNECTIONS

Ethics is the branch of knowledge that deals with moral principles and the study of what people think is right (or wrong) behaviour. Doctors are not the only group whose behaviour is bound by ethics. The British Sociological Association has also constructed a code of ethics that sociologists are expected to follow when conducting sociological research. These rules insist that people who take part in research should be fully informed of the aims of the research and should have given their consent, and that the sociologist must take steps to ensure no harm should come to the research participants.

Barber argues that these characteristics mean that doctors will always put the interests of society and the community first. However, there are a number of criticisms of this position.

› The existence of private medicine and the decision by some doctors to practise in the financially lucrative private field of cosmetic surgery suggests that they are motivated by financial reward rather than public service.

› Foucault's (1976) analysis of medical power (see Chapter 5) suggests that doctors have not gained power and prestige simply because they work for the good of the community. Instead he argues that over

the past two hundred years, doctors have battled to look after their own interests. The best way of doing this is to get control of what is regarded as 'truth' or 'knowledge', and therefore the discourse that defines the best way to do things. Foucault argues that over time doctors have constructed a dominant medical science discourse, through activities such as dissecting bodies and demonstrating to people the ways in which bodies are constructed, in order to establish the biomedical model as the 'truth'. Foucault concludes that medicine has played a major part in constructing the way people think and act in contemporary society with regards to health, because in such societies rational scientific thought is prized above all else. In the process, the medical profession has gained considerable benefits in terms of prestige and financial rewards.

› Jones and Green (2006) focused on whether newly-qualified GPs had different views from older GPs about the nature of professionalism. They claimed that older GPs' perceptions of their role supported Barber's ideas about public service. For example, these GPs perceived their jobs as a vocation, in which they had a duty to their patients and society, and this motivation was as much moral as financial. However, younger GPs described their motivation as wanting 'nice work', meaning good pay, pleasant surroundings, interesting and varied work, and decent patients.

Is it important that the motivations of doctors are different from other jobs such as driving buses or banking?

› Illich (2002) suggests that some doctors do more harm than good and that clinical iatrogenesis is responsible for a large proportion of harm caused and a high number of patient deaths. There is also evidence that doctors have conspired to cover up medical errors and refused to give evidence against one another.

› Some sociologists are critical of the role of the GMC, which is supposed to supervise the profession. It is argued that the GMC frequently covers up or ignores cases of incompetence. Sanctions, such as striking a doctor off the medical register, are used only rarely and then more often for sexual misconduct than for gross medical incompetence.

One reason suggested for this latter point is the existence of the British Medical Association (BMA), the professional association or trade union of doctors. Its function is to protect the bargaining rights and status of doctors and to defend their interests, especially when they come into disciplinary contact with the GMC. It is regarded as a very powerful organisation because it represents all doctors who work for the NHS and negotiates with

the government regarding their salaries and working conditions. The BMA also has a very close and influential relationship with the Department of Health and advises and consults with the government on a wide range of health issues and ethical concerns.

FOCUS ON SKILLS: MEDICS ADMIT THEY DON'T ACT IN PATIENTS' BEST INTERESTS

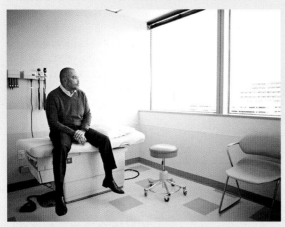

Only one in five doctors says they can always act in their patients' best interests, according to a study that calls for a renewed focus on morality in medicine. Doctors have succumbed to a 'culture of compliance', the experts say, and reasserting the importance of virtue and character could help to prevent more scandals over poor healthcare, such as the one at Stafford Hospital. Doctors at Stafford Hospital failed to protest as patients were neglected to meet financial targets. Up to 1,200 patients are thought to have died over a ten-year period as a result.

More than 90 per cent of doctors say their job makes it hard to treat patients in a way they believe is right, or involves tasks that conflict with their moral values, a survey of 550 doctors and medical students found. Kristján Kristjánsson, deputy director of the Jubilee Centre for Character and Virtues at the University of Birmingham, said that too many professionals were 'embarrassed' about moral questions and patient care suffered as a result. He said he wants virtuous thinking to be included in doctors' training to help them to overcome a 'tickbox' mentality that puts following processes above doing the right thing. "We want to try to replace a culture of compliance with a culture of moral wisdom. Rules are fine as far as they go but you have to see across the board. We think [moral training] is one way that you can forestall further scandals of that

kind. By following these recommendations it is more likely that medical professionals have a firm ethical ground to stand on."

Mark Porter, chairman of the British Medical Association's council, said the problem was overwork rather than moral fibre. "Graduates leave medical school enthusiastic and determined but, over time, rising workloads, insufficient resources and a target-obsessed culture leave many feeling frustrated, exhausted and unable to deliver the quality of care they want to for their patients."

Source: Smyth, C. 'Medics admit they don't act in patients' best interests', *The Times*, 24 January 2015

Questions

1. **Identify** and summarise the evidence in this article that suggests medical professionals do not always act in the best interests of their patients.

2. **Analyse**. Using the work of Illich as your main focus, analyse the view that the health professions – doctors, nurses, midwives – observe a strict code of ethics that work in favour of the patient. (You may remember from Chapter 1 that Illich uses the concept of 'iatrogenesis' to suggest doctors do more harm than good.)

3. **Evaluate**. Using sources such as the Shipman Inquiry (2003), the Francis Inquiry (2013) into deaths at Stafford Hospital, and the Freedom to Speak Up Review (2015) on the treatment of NHS whistleblowers – all available on the internet – evaluate the view that the professional bodies that represent doctors – the BMA and the GMC – are too powerful.

4. **Outline, assess** and **evaluate**. Using material from this article and elsewhere, assess the view that medical professionals are selfless individuals working for the good of the community. Outline this functionalist view in full and evaluate it using other critical perspectives.

THE WEBERIAN APPROACH: PROFESSIONALISATION AS A STRATEGY

The functionalist approach to the medical profession has been heavily criticised by sociologists who describe themselves as Weberian and who argue that the medical profession work in their own self-interest rather than for the benefit or good of the community. This argument has developed from the original writings of Max Weber, an early 20th-century sociologist who argued that all occupational groups are constantly vying with one another to improve their prestige and financial bargaining power. There are a number of different techniques used, but the two main ones are the creation of trade unions (traditionally used by manual workers) and the construction of professional associations (traditionally used by the non-manual middle class).

Parry and Parry (1976) suggest that doctors set up professional organisations such as the BMA, the GMC and the Royal Colleges as part of an **occupational strategy** that aims to control the medical labour market to their advantage. They argue that in pursuit of greater financial rewards, doctors, via both the GMC and BMA, have deliberately acquired the following professional characteristics.

> ❯ The government has given the GMC control over the training and entry requirements necessary to qualify as a doctor. This means that the GMC is able to control the numbers of people qualifying as doctors by constructing a series of specialist educational courses and qualifications. The GMC ensures that the supply of new doctors is deliberately kept quite low in order to ensure scarcity; this means the BMA can demand higher salaries for their services. All doctors have to belong to the BMA in order to practice as GPs or in the NHS. This means that the BMA is in a very powerful bargaining position and has consequently been able to negotiate very high salaries for doctors.

UNDERSTAND THE CONCEPT

Workers attempt to exercise some influence over their employers in terms of their pay, working conditions, etc. They employ **occupational strategies** to do this. For example, if negotiations with employers fail, some trade unions may resort to strategies such as strike action.

In your opinion, is there any contradiction between the notion of public service and high pay?

> ❯ Doctors have managed to convince the government that only their members are qualified to carry out medical diagnosis and treatment. This monopoly is backed by law – it is a criminal offence to impersonate a doctor.

> ❯ Both the GMC and BMA have fought off all attempts to have others impose any control over them. They have demanded clinical freedom, such as the right to prescribe any drug they feel is the best treatment for their patients. They have also resisted any attempts to hand over part of their work to others, such as allowing nurses to prescribe medicines.

> ❯ The BMA has attempted to exclude any competition to doctors' expertise and knowledge. Alternative medicines, such as faith healing, homeopathy, aromatherapy, and so on, have been attacked and discredited by the medical profession, who claim that only scientific medicine and surgery are effective. For example, Cant and Sharma (2002) studied the relationship between the medical profession and the practitioners of chiropracty. (Chiropracty is the manipulation of the spine, joints and muscles in order to realign them.) For over 60 years, chiropractors campaigned to gain legal recognition, which was finally granted by an Act of Parliament in 1994. However, in order to get this recognition, chiropractors effectively had to subordinate themselves to doctors – they are effectively paramedical practitioners who have patients referred to them by doctors.

Parry and Parry argue therefore that doctors are self-seeking individuals who adopt occupational market strategies in order to maximise their earning power. In particular, controlling access to the profession and limiting the number of doctors being trained has been very effective and has resulted in doctors becoming very wealthy, privileged and secure. The medical profession has also managed to prevent other health workers such as nurses and paramedics from taking on more diagnostic responsibilities, so safeguarding their market position. From a Weberian perspective, then, the medical profession is looking after its own interests as well as those of its patients.

In your opinion, do nurses, midwives, paramedics and other health workers deserve similar financial rewards and status to doctors?

This Weberian approach has not escaped criticism. Crinson (2008) notes two challenges.

Firstly, McKinley and Arches (1985) suggest that doctors are losing their traditional dominance within the NHS because they are experiencing a process called **proletarianisation**. This is because in the 1980s the NHS was reorganised so that hospital managers became more powerful in deciding how the funding of health services should be spent. A consequence of this was that managers reduced doctors' control over clinical decision-making. For example, some operations and drugs were deemed too expensive by managers. McKinley and Arches argue that many doctors also experienced some **de-skilling** as the number of paramedical specialists increased and new technology appeared. As a result, managers in particular increasingly viewed doctors as just another group of employees within the NHS.

UNDERSTAND THE CONCEPT

Proletarianisation is the process through which the specialist worker, who had previously been earning high wages for his or her talent, becomes just like any other working-class or proletarian labourer.

De-skilling is the process in which the skills of specialist workers are replaced by machines, or by the breaking down of complicated tasks into a number of routine tasks that can be performed more quickly by cheaper workers.

Secondly, Haug and Lavin (1983) argue that doctors may be undergoing a process they call 'de-professionalisation'. It has been suggested by Dillner (2013) that the knowledge gap between doctors and patients has narrowed because of the internet and the availability of health apps on smartphones. Consequently, there has been a shift in power towards the health consumer as the health market expands to include internet-based and alternative non-medical forms of treatment. Dillner argues that the cultural authority and status of doctors, as well as their monopoly over medical knowledge, are therefore under threat.

However, Elston (2009) believes that de-skilling and de-professionalisation have been exaggerated. She notes that there are three dimensions of professional power and authority within which doctors are found to be exercising influence. These are: (a) economic **autonomy** – the ability to shape salary; (b) political autonomy – the ability to influence government policy on the NHS; (c) clinical autonomy – the right to set standards and to control and regulate the performance of doctors. Elston argues that doctors as a profession have retained their economic and clinical autonomy but have lost some of their ability to influence political and managerial decisions about health.

UNDERSTAND THE CONCEPT

In this context, **autonomy** means freedom from other significant groups such as politicians or hospital managers telling doctors what to do.

Furthermore, Friedson (1994) suggests that the medical profession is still very powerful, as symbolised by what he calls the 'zone of discretion' that is specific to doctors. Friedson argues that the monopoly that doctors enjoy over certain skills means that they have considerable freedom or discretion in how they go about their business compared with other health workers. These discretionary powers allow them to resist the attempts of other health workers, such as nurses, to take on some of their responsibilities.

MARXIST APPROACHES: MEDICINE AS AN IDEOLOGICAL TOOL OF THE RULING CLASS

Marxists, such as Navarro (1977), argue that doctors are agents of the bourgeoisie or ruling class and the high status and salaries that they enjoy are the rewards they receive from the ruling class for playing their part in maintaining economic inequality and exploitation. Doctors work on behalf of the ruling class in a number of ways.

> Marxist writers on health, such as Doyal (1979), argue that doctors and the health service have a 'legitimation' role. This means that they promote ruling-class ideology by persuading the bulk of the population that capitalism 'cares' for them by providing free medical care (when it is actually more interested in exploiting them).

> Doyal and Pennell (1979) argue that doctors mislead the population as to the real cause of their illnesses. The medical profession explains health and illness in

terms of individuals' actions and genetics. Marxists claim that doctors very rarely focus on issues such as poor working conditions, poverty, poor housing and wealth inequalities, which are the true, underlying causes of ill health in capitalist societies. Therefore the only way to improve health is by reducing these economic and social inequalities. For example, Figure 5.6.1 suggests that if inequalities in income can be reduced, this would probably result in a reduction in mental illness among poorer children.

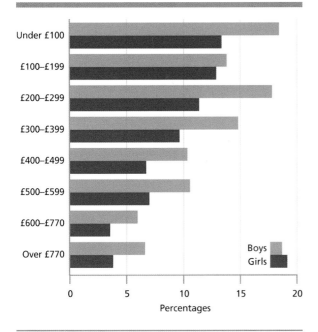

Figure 5.6.1 *Prevalence of mental disorders among children: by gender and gross weekly household income, Great Britain, 2004*
Source: ONS (2005)

> Marxists claim that doctors ensure the health and fitness of the workforce so that workers can go to work on a regular basis and continue to be exploited by the ruling class.

> Doctors control who is defined as ill (see the sick role argument in 'The functionalist approach'), ensuring that workers do not opt out of this system of exploitation.

However, critics point out that Marxism ignores the genuinely beneficial work that doctors do, and that to characterise their work as mainly focused on misleading and controlling the population is inaccurate. Doctors do work primarily in the context of individual problems but many also recognise and acknowledge stress caused by the workplace and the role of poverty. Moreover, the Independent Review into Sickness Absence (IRSA) commissioned by the Coalition government in 2011, was very critical of doctors because they sign off about

300,000 workers a year as long-term sick. The IRSA suggested that at least a fifth of these people should not be signed off or could go back to work sooner than doctors recommended.

Other Marxists, notably McKinley, suggest that Navarro, and Doyal and Pennell, exaggerate the power of doctors. He argues that their professional freedom has been weakened by the state to the extent that doctors too are now exploited by the capitalist bourgeoisie. McKinley argues that their role has been reduced to 'drug pushers', in that they prescribe drugs for all ills and so generate greater profits for the bourgeoisie who own and control the global pharmaceutical companies.

FEMINIST APPROACHES

Feminist analysis of the medical profession has mainly focused on the fact that up to the latter part of the 20th century the profession was male-dominated, supposedly interpreting and treating female health problems in condescending ways that were both patriarchal and socially controlling.

Feminists such as Oakley (1986) and Witz (1992) suggest that, historically, women have always held a key role in healing and traditional health care. For example, so-called 'witches' in the medieval period of European history were often herbal healers who were sought out in rural areas. However, the development of medical science in the 18th and 19th centuries was dominated by men. Women were not legally prevented from entering the medical profession but the values of Victorian Britain and the nature of the educational system, which generally excluded women from higher education, meant that women were strongly discouraged from becoming doctors.

Patriarchal attitudes also affected the treatment of women by the medical profession. For example, Wertz and Wertz (1981) studied the treatment of upper-class women in Victorian Britain and observed that doctors often made links between the female reproductive and sexual organs and a whole range of illnesses, including headaches, sore throats, indigestion and depression. This often resulted in women either having hysterectomies – because male doctors saw the womb (the Greek word for the uterus is hystera) as responsible for any psychological problem experienced by a woman – or being confined for long periods to mental hospitals.

The 'medicalisation' process
Feminist sociologists such as Lupton (1994) also claim that the male-dominated profession of medicine has

375

successfully 'medicalised' a number of female activities or problems. By this, they mean that the normal or natural activities of women (such as childbirth and menopause), or problems faced more often by women (such as anxiety) have been taken over by the medical profession and turned into medical issues or problems. In many cases, this has involved male doctors sidelining health professions such as midwifery, an overwhelmingly female sector of the health service.

Oakley notes that male doctors have extended their power and control over areas such as gynaecology, maternity and childbirth. Her research into pregnancy and childbirth observed that these were treated as 'natural' conditions by midwives up to the 1980s, and consequently there was less, if any, intrusion from doctors. However, since the 1980s, she argues that mothers and male doctors tend to view childbirth very differently. Doctors see pregnancy and giving birth as a 'risk' and therefore as a medical problem, treating women as dependent patients, whereas women regard pregnancy as a 'natural' condition and wish to have some control over how the birth is organised. However, Oakley notes that the pregnant woman is rarely consulted about what is going on in her body. Instead she is subjected by a largely male group of doctors to a series of highly scientific medical interventions, such as scans and obstetric tests, which culminates in a high-tech 'managed' childbirth that may involve early induction, an epidural and a caesarian section. Moreover, it is increasingly doctors rather than midwives – who are actually trained in this skill – who manage and supervise the process of childbirth and who often make the decision to abandon natural childbirth in favour of surgery.

There are signs that this medicalisation of childbirth may be causing real problems. In 2015, an official inquiry into the deaths of up to 30 babies and mothers at the University Hospital of Morecambe Bay between 2004 and 2013 indicated that they may have been the result of a 'turf war' between midwives and doctors. Mothers and babies were put at risk because midwives were not on speaking terms with doctors at the hospital. Midwives gave evidence that, if they called in a doctor to help with a difficult labour, they were made to feel irrelevant and pushed aside.

The official statistics support the view that pregnancy and childbirth have become medicalised. For example, between 1927 and 2006 there was a dramatic shift from home births to hospital births. Only 3 per cent of births are now at home. Caesarian sections have increased from 10 per cent in the 1970s to 25 per cent in 2015, and are as high as 33 per cent in some hospitals. It is consequently not surprising that Oakley reported that 69 per cent of

first-time mothers in her survey felt that they had little control over their childbirth and that male doctors were not interested in their views.

Other feminists argue that the medical profession often reduces female health problems caused by patriarchal influences – such as their subordinate position in society or their dual/triple responsibilities in the family – to stereotypes about females being weaker than men or the notion that women are 'naturally' anxious (see Chapter 3). Furthermore, feminist sociologists claim that symptoms reported to doctors by females are often dismissed as 'women's problems', which are defined by doctors as less serious than other medical problems. There is evidence too that women are more likely than men to be victims of clinical iatrogenesis because of the side effects of contraceptives, anti-depressants and tranquillisers, which are disproportionately prescribed to women.

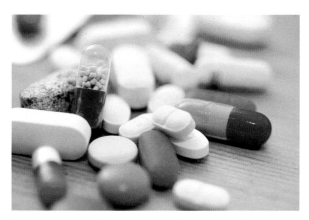

Women are more likely to be prescribed drugs such as contraceptives, anti-depressants and tranquilisers, increasing the risk of clinical iatrogenesis.

However, the feminist position on health professionals has become increasingly dated. The claim that the profession is male-dominated has been severely undermined by the fact that by 2015, 49.8 per cent of GPs, 44.4 per cent of general hospital doctors and 32.3 per cent of consultants and specialists were female. Moreover, since the early 1990s more than half of all new medical students have been female. Compared with the early 1960s, the number of men entering medical schools each year has doubled, but for women the number has increased 10-fold. The number of female doctors is predicted to exceed the number of male doctors by 2017.

Finally, it can be argued that the NHS has focused on the health needs of women at the expense of men. For example, prostate and testicular cancer prevention and screening programmes have not been given the same priority by the NHS as breast or cervical cancer (see Chapter 4).

THE LATE-MODERNITY PERSPECTIVE

The claim to doctors' sole expertise on health matters has been challenged by a wide range of groups. Perhaps the biggest external challenge has come from complementary or alternative medicines, which include homeopathy, herbal remedies, acupuncture and a range of other techniques. Giddens (1991) has argued that this challenge is the result of the development of late-modern society. Two characteristics of late modernity which are particularly relevant to health are discussed below.

1. There has been a decline in conformity and a greater stress on individual desire and choice. This greater individualism has resulted in people looking further afield in terms of their health choices. In particular, people in the UK have been willing to look outside the UK and to utilise the global market in non-western alternative medical remedies. (Alternative forms of medicine and treatment are discussed in detail in Chapter 1).

2. There is a general disillusion, firstly, with the claims of professionals and experts to have a monopoly of knowledge, and, secondly, with the biomedical approach. The particular result for health care and medicine has been a decline in the acceptance that 'doctor knows best' and an increased demand for greater choice beyond the traditional biomedical model in what 'cures' and interventions the ill person should undergo.

Postmodernism

Lyotard (1979) argues that in the postmodern age, meta-narratives, that is, grand explanations or absolute truths, have been rejected in favour of smaller narratives which contain relative truths. In other words, all opinions have value in their view of whatever problem they seek to explain and solve. Medical science is one such meta-narrative, whilst alternative approaches to healing, disease prevention and health promotion are the smaller narratives.

Postmodernists are therefore keen to question medical science as represented by the biomedical model. Gray (1999) notes that postmodern approaches to medicine are concerned with risk rather than benefit, and making sure that patients are well-informed and therefore safe. However, critics such as Cadario (2012) suggest that postmodern scepticism about modern medicine and its insistence that the patient is king has led to a decline in confidence in experts and too much misinformation about health and medicine being made available via the internet. She argues that this postmodernist approach

has created excessive fear of modern medicine and may itself be creating risk as patients shy away from using drugs which would benefit them or try the potentially untested and harmful remedies of alternative medical approaches.

CONTEMPORARY CHALLENGES TO THE MEDICAL PROFESSION AND THE ROLE OF MEDICINE

The NHS has undergone tremendous organisational change since the 1980s. These changes have resulted in the introduction of a bureaucratic managerial culture in an attempt to improve efficiency and cut out wasteful spending. These changes have also meant that the NHS has experienced 'marketisation' – GPs and patients are now offered a greater degree of choice in terms of the treatments available, while hospitals have been encouraged to compete for patients. These changes have had the following consequences for the medical profession.

› Relationships between the key actors in the NHS – the government, managers, doctors and patients – have dramatically changed as a result of modernisation. Doctors have probably seen their power and influence reduced overall, because the state has generally encouraged a 'managerial revolution' in hospitals in order to achieve greater cost-effectiveness and efficiency in the use of resources. This has created tension between managers and doctors. The state has also promoted 'patient-centred care', which demands clearer communication and greater accountability from doctors.

› A number of medical scandals, such as Dr Harold Shipman's mass murder of his patients, and the poor care and high mortality rates (1,200 premature deaths at Stafford Hospital) between 2005 and 2008, have led to a greater examination of patient trust in doctors. There have been calls for more regulation of doctors in the interests of patient safety.

› A number of apparatuses have been put in place by governments since the 1990s in order to manage the performance and accountability of doctors. These suggest that the government is less inclined to trust the medical profession.

› In 1993, the Conservative government introduced performance indicators for the NHS. These were expanded by the Labour government in 1998 to include breast cancer mortality, waiting times for Accident & Emergency, cancelled operations, hospital

377

admissions and complaints against hospitals. League tables were also published, showing which hospitals had the worst mortality rates. NHS England also publishes performance data relating to the mortality rates of the 5,000 surgeons operating in the NHS.

› The Care Quality Commission (CQC) was set up in 2009 to regulate and inspect health services independently of the GMC. It produces interactive maps of 8,000 GP practices so that consumers can compare GP surgeries using a ranking of 1–6 in terms of quality. The latest map showed that the CQC was 'concerned' about 1,200 surgeries in 2014.

› In response to the Francis Report – the inquiry into the Stafford Hospital scandal – the Health Secretary Jeremy Hunt announced an annual national review of 2,000 deaths that aimed to establish just how many lives might be saved with the right care. He argued that this would be used to monitor doctors' performance and that hospitals would be assigned estimates of how many deaths might have been avoided.

To what extent do patients take any notice of league tables? Consider whether league tables make any difference in terms of which hospital you go to.

However, Crinson points out that regardless of these changes, medical professionals still play an important role in perpetuating core beliefs about the role of medicine and especially the idea that doctors know what is in the best interests of their patients. In a review of patient-centred care, which is supposed to address the expressed needs of patients and to involve patients and their families in the decision-making process, Stevenson *et al.* (2000) discovered that patients were not that keen on the idea and that they lacked the will, knowledge, ability and confidence to participate. Most expected and were happy to have their problems solved by their GP. Moreover, the existence of league tables implies that patients can make choices about which hospital they go to for an operation and which surgeon they want to perform it. In reality, that choice is extremely limited. Patients generally have to make do with what exists in their community, whether it is good or bad according to the league table.

There are also signs that the GMC and BMA still exercise considerable influence. When the Francis report recommended that doctors should be legally obliged to own up when medical errors injured or killed patients,

Jeremy Hunt, after taking advice from the GMC and BMA, rejected the idea, claiming it would create a 'culture of fear'.

Finally, Elston (2009) suggests that the medical profession has to undergo change if it is to survive in the 21st century. She claims that there are now two models of the medical profession (see Table 5.6.1): the old model, as described by functionalist and Weberian sociologists, where doctors are an elite group who know what is best for the patient; and a 'new' professionalism, which is being adopted by younger doctors. This new model is more flexible and more focused on improving the interaction between the state, managers, doctors and patients. Most importantly, it stresses accountability and acknowledges that doctors need to do more in the light of recent controversies and scandals if they are to regain the faith and trust of patients, and of society as a whole.

The old professionalism	The new professionalism
Public acceptance of and great trust in medical expertise	Medical expertise still paramount but now set in context of clinical guidelines laid out by the state and NHS managers
Formal qualifications for career entry	Professional development throughout whole career
High status – elite social standing	Acceptance of greater accountability to patients and society
Internal self-regulation and self-discipline based on ethical codes	Continuous surveillance and appraisal based on results and league tables
Doctor-centred – paternalistic	Acceptance and encouragement of patient-centred care

Table 5.6.1 *A comparison of the old versus the new model of professionalism*

THE GLOBALISED HEALTH INDUSTRY

Sociologists have observed that the NHS and the medical profession are partly shaped by three global influences.

1. A significant number of doctors and nurses work in the NHS as a result of global migration. In 2015, 36.8 per cent of doctors working in the NHS came from countries outside of the UK. In 2014,

there were 91,470 nurses from overseas working in the UK – 1 in 7 of the total nursing workforce. It is easier for the UK to recruit from developing societies because the debt and poverty that characterise many of these societies mean they cannot afford to sustain health care systems or pay health professionals a living wage. However, this brain drain to the NHS – the Nursing and Midwifery Council estimates that 15 per cent of nurses have been 'poached' from the developing world – worsens health in the country of origin because these societies then suffer an acute shortage of people with medical knowledge. For example, the UK has on average one doctor for every 520 people but in developing countries the average is one doctor per 17,000 people.

What other global differences are there in medical treatment between modernised countries and less developed ones? Think about the treatment of western volunteers who contracted Ebola in 2015 and people living in Sierra Leone, Liberia and Guinea who contracted the disease.

---

2. The global pharmaceutical industry has a significant effect on the actions of health professionals and how the NHS is funded and organised, because it is responsible for the development, production and marketing of the vast majority of the medications prescribed by NHS doctors. Most drugs are produced by five companies: US companies Johnson & Johnson and Pfizer; Swiss companies Roche and Novartis; and UK giant GlaxoSmithKline. The total revenue earned by the global pharmaceutical industry was nearly one trillion dollars in 2013.

The NHS has no choice but to buy drugs from these multinationals. This affects the NHS and its doctors in two ways:

> the NHS has no influence over what drugs are developed and, very importantly, little influence over the testing of drugs for safety and efficiency – unsurprisingly, there have been a number of drug disasters that have resulted in mass death and injuries since the NHS was set up in 1948; for example, drugs such as thalidomide in the late 1950s, Opren in the 1980s, and Vioxx in 1999

> the NHS has little influence on the price set by pharmaceutical companies, which aim to maximise their profits.

Pharmaceutical companies also target doctors in order to convince them to prescribe their drugs. As Goldacre (2012) points out, doctors spend 40 years on average practising medicine, with little formal education after their initial training. Consequently, they are highly dependent on the information they get from drug companies about the effectiveness of drugs. However, both Abraham (2009) and Goldacre have documented the underhand and fraudulent methods that these global drug companies employ to persuade doctors to use their products, including misrepresenting the benefits and risks of the drugs, paying medical experts to write or speak favourably about the product, suppressing or withholding any negative findings about side-effects, and funding patient groups who believe they would benefit from the drug.

3. Shah (2011) has expressed concern about the increasing global commodification and commercialisation of health care. He notes that global agencies such as the World Bank and the International Monetary Fund are encouraging governments to hand over control of health services to private sector agents which emphasise the biomedical approach to disease, that is, the spending of money on drugs and technology. The World Health Organisation suggests this commodification of health has resulted in less money being spent on preventative measures, such as health promotion, nutrition and other public health services, which prevent disease from occurring in the first place. Moreover, this commodification is the product of narrow self-interest and the search for profit rather than humanitarianism.

CONCLUSIONS

This chapter has demonstrated that there is a strong relationship between doctors and the role of medicine in the form of the biomedical model. As Foucault has noted, doctors have used the biomedical model as the foundation stone to control all aspects of how conventional medicine is organised and practised in the UK. Moreover, in so doing, they have constructed the view that they are a profession that deserves high financial rewards. Functionalists suggest such rewards are deserved for the public service that they perform, whereas Marxists argue that this is a form of blood money for acting as agents of the capitalist system.

What cannot be denied is that doctors have used their medical expertise and power to build up a formidable professional set of intertwining organisations, particularly the GMC and BMA, which successive governments have generally been happy to defer to. However, there are signs that medical power and autonomy are being challenged by a number of increasingly influential factors: the rise of NHS managers; the need to cut NHS spending as part of austerity cuts, the numerous scandals in which doctors have proved less than accountable; the growing popularity of alternative, patient-centred, globally sourced medicines; the power of the global pharmaceutical industry to persuade doctors to adopt their drugs; and finally the growing public disillusion with one of the central tenets of medical power – doctor knows best.

CHECK YOUR UNDERSTANDING

1. Identify three ways in which professionalisation has been used as an occupational strategy by doctors.

2. Identify two reasons why people are becoming disillusioned with the medical profession.

3. Define what is meant by 'altruism'.

4. Define what is meant by 'discourse'.

5. Define what is meant by 'proletarianisation'.

6. Outline and explain how the 'zone of discretion' means that doctors still exert more power than other health workers.

7. Outline and explain why the NHS is dependent on global migration.

8. Explain why Barber believes doctors are good for society.

9. Analyse and explain the influence that the global pharmaceutical industry has over doctors.

10. Outline and evaluate the view that the main function of the health professions is the social control of the population.

TAKE IT FURTHER

Ask a sample of 20 people to identify five characteristics they associate with doctors. Do your results support the points made in this chapter?

Identify a small sample of people who have used some form of 'alternative' healing. Conduct unstructured interviews to uncover their motives in seeking the treatment and the meaning they gave to their experiences.

APPLY YOUR LEARNING

AS LEVEL

1   Define the term 'morbidity'.   [2 marks]

2   Using **one** example, briefly explain what is meant by 'medicalisation'.   [2 marks]

3   Outline **three** features of the biomedical model of health.   [6 marks]

4   Outline and explain **two** causes of ethnic variations in morbidity and mortality.   [10 marks]

5   Read **Item A** below and answer the question that follows.

ITEM A

Health inequalities

While life expectancy in the UK has increased over the last fifty years, significant class inequalities in health have persisted. Sociologists have offered a range of competing explanations for these inequalities, including cultural and behavioural differences; structural and material differences; and differences in health care provisions.

Applying material from **Item A** and your knowledge, evaluate the view that the principal cause of class inequalities in health is differences in behaviour among different classes.   [20 marks]

A-LEVEL

1   Outline and explain **two** reasons for the growth in use of complementary and alternative medicine over recent decades in Britain.   [10 marks]

2   Read **Item B** below and answer the question that follows.

ITEM B

The de-medicalisation of homosexuality

For much of the 20th century, homosexuality was medicalised as a mental illness and a wide range of supposed 'cures' were devised. By the sixties, this view had become widely accepted in the UK, with a 1965 opinion poll finding that 93% of the general public saw it as an illness requiring treatment (Weeks, 1990). However, by the end of the century both the American Psychiatric Association and the World Health Organisation (the two most influential bodies globally in terms of classifications of mental disorder) had stopped viewing homosexuality as a mental illness.

Applying material from **Item B** and your knowledge, analyse **two** reasons for the de-medicalisation of homosexuality in the last quarter of the 20th century.   [10 marks]

3   Read **Item C** below and answer the question that follows.

ITEM C

Gender and health

Because women outlive men in virtually all societies, it is tempting to assume that gender differences in health are a simple product of the biological differences between men and women. However, the extent of the gender gap in life expectancy varies significantly between societies and over time within a society. These variations suggest that social factors must be involved.

Applying material from **Item C** and your knowledge, evaluate the view that gender differences in morbidity and mortality rates are the product of patriarchy.   [20 marks]

You can find example answers and accompanying teachers' comments for this topic at www.collins.co.uk/AQAAlevelSociology.

6 WORK, POVERTY AND WELFARE

AQA Specification	Chapters
Candidates should examine:	
The nature, existence and persistence of poverty in contemporary society.	Definitions and ways of measuring poverty are covered in Chapter 2 (pages 394–403). Competing explanations for the existence and persistence of poverty in Chapter 4 (pages 414–422).
The distribution of poverty, wealth and income between different social groups.	Explanations of the distribution of income and wealth are covered in Chapter 1 (pages 384–393). Chapter 3 (pages 404–413) discusses the distribution of poverty.
Responses and solutions to poverty by the state and by private, voluntary and informal welfare providers in contemporary society.	Chapter 5 (pages 423–434) discusses this.
Organisation and control of the labour process, including the division of labour, the role of technology, skill and de-skilling.	Chapter 6 (pages 435–446) discusses this.
The significance of work and worklessness for people's lives and life chances, including the effects of globalisation.	Chapter 6 (pages 435–446) discusses this.

6.1 WEALTH AND INCOME

LEARNING OBJECTIVES

› Understand how wealth and income are defined and how they differ (AO1).

› Understand how wealth and income are distributed in the UK and how this has changed over time (AO1).

› Analyse the causes of growing economic inequality (AO2).

› Evaluate the effects of growing economic inequality on society (AO3).

INTRODUCING THE DEBATE

For a long time many social commentators felt that, so long as the economy was growing, it didn't really matter how unequal society was in monetary terms since all would share in the benefits from its growing size. This is no longer the case. In recent years, international bodies as diverse as the International Monetary Fund, Oxfam and the Organisation for Economic Cooperation and Development have all issued warnings about the undesirable consequences for both society and for economic growth of rising income inequality.

In a speech delivered in December 2013, Barack Obama, President of the USA, referred to 'a dangerous and growing inequality and lack of upward mobility' as 'the defining challenge of our time'. According to the World Top Incomes Database, the UK is now second only to the USA among the rich nations of the world in terms of the share of national income going to the top 1 per cent.

This chapter will clarify the difference between income (a regular or irregular flow of money over time) and wealth (a stock of things with monetary value) and explore how and why economic inequality has grown since the 1980s. It will also explore sociologists' growing understanding of the links between economic inequality and a host of personal and social problems.

GETTING YOU THINKING

One often hears the claim today that Britain is a very 'materialistic society', where people are preoccupied with material possessions and status is determined by how much you earn and what you own.

The Sunday Times newspaper publishes an annual list of the wealthiest people in Britain: 'The Times Rich List'. Table 6.1.1 is from the 2014 list.

Rank	Wealth (in £billions)	Name(s)	Citizenship
1	£11.9	Sri and Gopi Hinduja	India
2	£10.65	Alisher Usmanov	Russia
3	£10.25	Lakshmi Mittal and family	India
4	£10	Leonard Blavatnik	USA
5	£9.75	Ernesto and Kirsty Bertarelli	Switzerland and UK
6	£9.25	John Fredriksen and family	Cyprus
7	£9	David and Simon Reuben	UK
8	£8.8	Kirsten Rausing and Jörn Rausing	Sweden
9	£8.52	Roman Abramovich	Russia
10	£8.5	Duke of Westminster	UK
11	£7.3	Galen Weston and George G. Weston and family	Canada
12	£6.36	Charlene de Carvalho-Heineken and Michel de Carvalho	Netherlands

Table 6.1.1 *The Times UK Rich List, 2014: The Top 12*
Source: *The Sunday Times* (2014)

Questions

1. The list above is based on 'identifiable wealth', such as land and property, and excludes bank accounts. How do you think this might affect the *validity* of this data?

2. Though resident in the UK, you will notice from column 4 that the majority on this list are citizens of foreign countries. This means that for tax purposes they are classed as 'non-doms' and don't pay UK tax on their foreign earnings.

Who do you think benefits and who loses from these arrangements?

3. The average household wealth of the bottom 10 per cent of the population is less than £12,500 (Equality Trust, 2015). What effects do you think such extreme wealth inequalities might have on society?

4. In judging the personal worth of strangers, how important to you is how much money they have?

WEALTH

Defining wealth

Wealth is defined in economic terms as the ownership of property, shares, savings and other assets – things that have monetary value, such as jewellery or cars. However, there is some debate about exactly what should be included as property and 'assets'. For example, should we include, for those below pension age, their future entitlement to a state pension? The effect of receiving a pension is similar to having savings in the bank, and savings are included.

One solution is to talk about marketable wealth. This is the range of assets that a person is reasonably able to dispose of, if they wish. Marketable wealth would exclude pensions, for those below pension age.

Changes in wealth distribution over time

The data available on changes in the distribution of wealth over time is both less plentiful and less reliable than that on income. Finding out what people *own* is generally harder than finding out what they *earn*. This is because earnings are often on public record, while certain forms of wealth can be hidden. For example, financial assets can be hidden in tax havens (countries that impose minimal or no taxes on foreign holdings). Nevertheless, in general terms we can say that from roughly 1945 to 1980, wealth became more evenly distributed.

This pattern remained fairly stable for the next 20 years, but since 2000, according to the New Economics Foundation (2014), wealth inequality has increased steadily, with a growing concentration of wealth at the top.

Wealth distribution today

Wealth is more unequally distributed than income.

Figure 6.1.1 below, taken from the Equality Trust website, shows how wealth in the UK is distributed in terms of *deciles* (tenths) of the population. The figures relate to households rather than individuals.

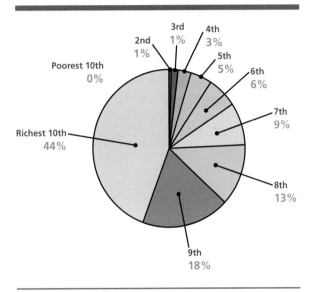

Figure 6.1.1 *How is wealth shared across the UK?*

Source: Equality Trust (2015), based on ONS (2014)

As you can see, the richest 10 per cent of the population owned 44 per cent of all wealth, and the poorest 10 per cent too little to register on the chart! The average wealth of the bottom 10 per cent of households was less than £12,500, while that of the top 9 per cent was £1 million or more. The study revealed that the richest 1 per cent own the same amount as the poorest 55 per cent of the population.

BUILD CONNECTIONS

Wealth can also be understood as 'capital'. In sociology, 'capital' includes not only financial/economic capital, but also less tangible forms of wealth. In relation to differential educational achievement, Bourdieu and Passeron (1990) talk about cultural capital (symbolic goods including attitudes, language and habits) and in relation to health and crime inequalities, Putnam (2000) talks about social capital (social networks and relationships). See also Topic 1, Chapter 2.

INCOME

Defining income

Income can be seen as a flow of money. But income is not the same as earnings. Most people's standard of living depends on what they earn in wages and salaries, or other payments for the work they do. But for some people – particularly those at the top and bottom of the ladder – unearned income is far more important.

> *Earned income* is made up of wages, salaries, bonuses, and so on.

> *Unearned income* is made up of interest from savings, rent from land and property, dividends from shares, and social security payments (such as state pensions and child benefit).

Note that this is a slight simplification of the idea. Some social security benefits, such as the state pension, are based on the 'contributory principle'. That is, people have paid into them over their working lives. In this sense, they are 'earned'.

Changes in income distribution over time

Income inequalities declined steeply from the Second World War to 1980, but then increased rapidly up to 1990. Since then, there has been a more gradual upwards trend of growing income inequality, peaking in 2007/8. Figure 6.1.2 shows the change in household income between 1998/99 and 2008/09.

Note: 1) 'Real' household income means allowing for inflation (a general rise in prices). If prices rise faster than earnings, the real value of your earnings declines. 2) 'Net' household income means income after direct taxes (aka 'disposable income').

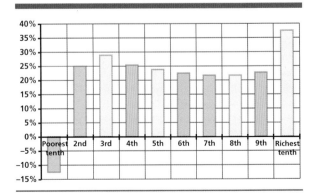

Figure 6.1.2 *Percentage change in real net household income in Great Britain between 1998/99 and 2008/09 (by income deciles)*

Source: DWP (2010)

You might think people's standard of living is a direct reflection of income and wealth. However, most UK households 'live beyond their means' – they have debts outstanding. Average household debt (including mortgages) in November 2013 was £54,197 (The Money Charity, 2014). What do you think are the social implications of this for different groups in society?

Income distribution today

Overall, income is more evenly distributed than wealth, but that does not mean that there is equality. In 2013, according to the Office for National Statistics (ONS), the average net income of adults in the bottom 10 per cent of the population was £8,628, while that of the top 10 per cent was £80,240, almost ten times higher. The overall spread of incomes in the UK in 2013 (by income deciles) is shown in Figure 6.1.3.

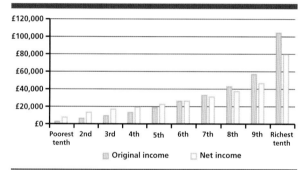

Figure 6.1.3 *What was the spread of incomes in the UK in 2013?*

Source: The Equality Trust (2015)

The chart underplays the full extent of income inequality. According to The World Top Income Database, in 2011 the top 1 per cent in the UK had an average income of £248,480 and the top 0.1 per cent (the top thousandth of the population) an average income of £922,433.

Another way of measuring income inequality is by using a metric known as the Gini coefficient. The Gini coefficient measures income inequality across the whole of society and produces a numerical figure between zero and one. In a society where all income was received by one

person, its value would be one. In a society where incomes were shared equally by all, it would be zero. Typical values in developed societies range between 0.3 and 0.5. The UK Gini coefficient has risen from 0.24 in 1977 to 0.34 in 2012, according to the Equality Trust, making the UK one of the more unequal countries in the developed world.

In 2012, according to inequalitybriefing.org, it would have taken the average worker in the UK 158 years to earn what a FTSE 100 CEO (a boss of one of the top 100 companies listed on the London Stock Exchange) earns in a year. Do you think such pay differentials are necessary or defensible?

REDISTRIBUTION AND THE IMPACT OF TAXATION

Redistribution in the UK is based upon a mixture of taxes and benefits. These include the following systems.

> *Direct taxes* are taken straight from a person's earnings. These tend to be 'progressive': the more a person earns, the more they must pay in tax. Over the last 50 years, direct taxes have been significantly reduced.

> *Indirect taxes* include taxes (such as VAT) which are added to purchases. They tend to be 'regressive': they hit poorer people harder, as they spend a higher proportion of their incomes on necessities. Indirect taxes have increased over the last 20 years.

> *Cash benefits* include payments by the government to lower earners and unemployed people. Depending upon how high these benefits are, they can significantly redistribute income or not.

> *Benefits in kind* are services provided by the state which are freely available, such as education and health services.

What effects do these taxes and benefits have on the distribution of income?

It we look at incomes before taxes and benefits (both cash benefits and benefits in kind), the richest 20 per cent of households had an average income almost 15 times higher than the poorest 20 per cent in 2012/13, according to the ONS. However, after all taxes and benefits are taken into account, the ratio drops to 4 to 1. The tax and benefits systems therefore have an enormous impact on income inequality – they reduce inequalities by about two-thirds – but this still leaves considerable income inequality.

THE DISTRIBUTION OF INCOME BETWEEN DIFFERENT GROUPS

A clearer picture of how economic inequality is distributed throughout society can be gained by looking at the income received by different social groups.

> *Gender* – Men generally earn more than women in the UK, although the gap is shrinking. In 2014, according to the ONS, the pay gap for full-time employees in terms of hourly earnings stood at 9 per cent. However, since more women than men work part time, the gender gap in terms of weekly earnings is higher at 19 per cent. The differences are mainly a result of the fact that, while gender segregation in the job market has declined, men and women are still not spread evenly across the occupational structure.

> *Ethnicity* – There are significant differences in average earnings between ethnic groups. In 2010, according to the Report of the National Equality Panel, median hourly wages ranged from £6.90 for British Bangladeshi men to £12.70 for British Chinese men. These variations mainly reflect differences in educational qualifications and in employment patterns. Also, there is evidence of continuing discrimination in the jobs market, despite its illegality.

> *Age* – Incomes also vary with age. In 2012–13, according to the ONS, the median income before tax of all those below 30 and over 65 was less than £20,000, while that of those between 30 and 65 was over £20,000. These differences reflect the fact that earning capacity tends to increase with age up to retirement.

> *Disability* – Disability tends to impact negatively on income. The median net individual income of disabled men in 2010, according to the Report of the National Equality Panel, was £157 per week, half that for non-disabled men (£316). For women, the corresponding figures were £131 and £198. Even after the impact of disability-related benefits is taken into account, the median income of disabled

working-age adults was still 30 per cent below that of non-disabled adults in 2010. These variations are mainly a product of differences in educational qualifications. In 2010, nearly one third of disabled adults had no educational qualifications, compared to 12 per cent of non-disabled adults. There is also some evidence of employment discrimination, again despite its illegality.

> *Occupational class* – Income is also affected by socio-economic status. The median net individual income of men in higher professional and managerial occupations in 2010 was more than twice that of men in routine occupations. For women, the ratio was 3:1. These variations are mainly a product of differences in qualifications, employment rates and earnings between occupational classes.

INTERSECTIONALITY

While it is possible, as has been demonstrated above, to study the independent effects on economic inequality of gender, ethnicity, age, and so on, the reality is that people's lives are shaped by the interaction of these variables. Thus, being female and black rather than white, or male and disabled rather than non-disabled, for example, means that your income and wealth are likely to differ.

In recent years, sociologists have become increasingly interested in these interactions and have explored them using the concept of **intersectionality**.

UNDERSTAND THE CONCEPT

Intersectionality is the study of interdependent systems of discrimination or disadvantage connected with class, gender, ethnicity, age, and so on. The term was coined in 1989 by a black American feminist, Kimberlé Crenshaw, to draw attention to the fact that women's experiences were not all of a kind. In particular, the experiences of White and African American women were quite different.

EXPLAINING THE GROWTH IN ECONOMIC INEQUALITY

Functionalist, Marxist and Weberian theories of **social stratification** provide an important starting point for trying to understand patterns of economic inequality. However, in order to explain why economic inequality has grown significantly in recent decades, we must look more deeply.

Various social changes have intensified income and wealth inequalities between groups in recent decades. For example, the divide between different kinds of families has been made worse by the concurrent growth of single-parent families (dependent on benefits and/or part-time work) and dual-earner families where both partners are employed. Similarly, the labour market is increasingly polarised between those in secure, well paid, full-time employment and those in poorly paid, insecure work (see Chapter 6). However, such changes alone cannot explain the enormous scale of the economic inequalities that have opened up.

Growing inequality since the 1980s across many of the world's developed economies has given rise to intense political discussion and political protests. These longer-term trends have intensified since the financial crisis of 2007/8, which gave way to economic recession and the adoption of **austerity** programmes by most of the governments of Western Europe and the USA. These programmes focused on reducing budget **deficits** and levels of national **debt**.

An anti-austerity protest in Greece

Austerity policies have given rise to anti-austerity movements and organisations such as the global Occupy movement (originating in the USA), UK Uncut and the *indignados* in Greece and Spain. They have also affected party politics, with the growth of anti-austerity parties such as Syriza in Greece (elected to form a minority government in January 2015), Podemos in Spain and the Green Party in the UK. These movements have not only campaigned against austerity but also against what they see as the unfair application of these policies, which have made economic inequalities even worse.

Kersley and Shaheen (2014) identify six main drivers of growing economic inequality in the UK.

Globalisation
It can be argued that increasing outsourcing of manufacturing and services to newly developing economies has undermined the position of low-skilled workers in richer nations. At the same time, skill-intensive jobs have become more concentrated in the developed economies, generating more opportunities for graduates and a growing divide between the highly skilled and the low skilled.

Technology
Kersley and Shaheen identify two processes here: the growth of new technologies in the workplace (such as computerisation), which require higher levels of skill and are paid better, thus widening the divide in pay between the more and less skilled; and process innovations (such as self-service tills in supermarkets) which have resulted in job losses.

Financialisation
As developed countries have shifted away from industrial capitalism, the effects of **financialisation** have become increasingly evident. This not only affects how financial markets are structured and operated but also influences corporate behaviour and economic policy.

Financialisation occurs when the size and importance of a country's financial sector increases relative to its overall economy. Finance capital (banks, accountancy firms, insurance companies, hedge funds, and so on) become more significant in the economy, while industrial capital becomes less important. In simpler terms, it is to do with the increasing power of organisations that make money from money rather than from making things.

The effect of this can be seen, for example, in the ever-growing price of housing in the UK as the rate of house building has declined. The rising value of capital means that those with money to invest see their income outstripping those dependent on wages and salaries, with the result that the wealth of those at the top accelerates away from those lower down.

Declining trade union membership and labour market liberalisation

Since 1980 in the UK there has been a shift towards more 'flexible' (that is, deregulated) labour and financial markets. This has been associated with declining trades union density (the proportion of employees belonging to trade unions) – which has fallen from around 45 per cent in the early 1980s to around 25 per cent today – and a consequent reduction in the power of trade unions in terms of collective bargaining. The result has been a long-term shift in the 'wage share' of national income from wages and salaries to profits. Lansley and Reed (2013) estimate that the wage share fell from 65 per cent to 60 per cent in the UK between 1970 and 2007.

Government redistribution policies

Government policies, particularly in relation to taxes and benefits, can make a significant contribution to either the widening or the narrowing of economic inequality. Since the late 1970s, income tax has become far less

progressive: top marginal income tax rates have almost halved, from 85 per cent to 45 per cent. At the same time, the taxes that richer people are more likely to pay – such as those on dividends – and corporation tax rates have also declined. Critics of austerity policies claim that these have impacted more severely on poorer people.

Political capture

Kersley and Shaheen claim that democracy has been undermined by the success of those representing the interests of the rich and big business ('**corporate capture**') in 'lobby(ing) governments to fortify and extend policies that protect their privileges' – a concept they call 'political capture'.

At the same time voters have become increasingly disillusioned with party politics and increasing numbers have stopped voting at elections. The fact that it is the young and those on lower incomes who tend not to vote means that politicians are less eager to represent their interests, other things being equal.

Corporate capture is the claim that governments in many rich countries are unduly influenced by large, private companies, through such mechanisms as behind-the-scenes lobbying, the direct funding of political parties, the funding of pro-business think tanks, and 'revolving doors' (the movement of key personnel from government departments into the corporate sector and vice versa). This process has been facilitated by the fact that the press in the UK is overwhelmingly supportive of big business. For example, *The Times* and *The Sun* are owned by Rupert Murdoch; the *Telegraph* and the *Daily Mail* are owned by non-doms (the Barclay brothers and Lord Rothermere respectively).

FOCUS ON RESEARCH: *THE SPIRIT LEVEL*

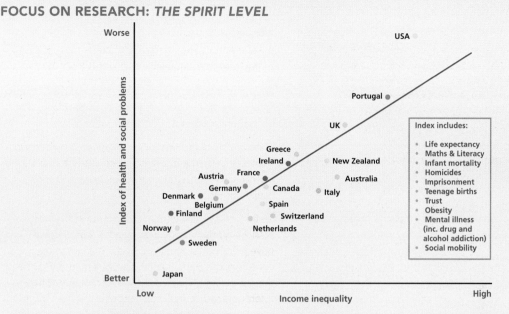

Figure 6.1.4 *Health and social problems are worse in more unequal countries*

Arguments for greater equality are usually framed in moral terms, but a remarkable piece of social research published originally in 2009 argues that the case for more equal societies can be made on empirical grounds.

In their book *The Spirit Level: Why Equality is Better for Everyone*, Richard Wilkinson and Kate Pickett lay out powerful evidence that greater inequality is associated with a wide range of personal and social problems. The research uses mainly secondary quantitative data and represents an example of the value of comparative methods in social research.

The authors compared the severity of health and various social problems across 21 developed countries. In order to increase the reliability of their findings, they also looked at the same measures across different states in the USA. They were careful to use the same data sources for all countries and states for the same reason. Because of the politically sensitive nature of their research topic, the authors took great care to remain neutral in political terms.

In order to present an overview of their findings, Wilkinson and Pickett grouped together the ten measures of health and social problems they looked at into a single index measuring the overall severity of these problems. Figure 6.1.4 identifies the ten components of the index and shows the results of their international comparisons.

Reading along the horizontal axis, the countries are listed from left to right according to the degree of inequality they display. The vertical axis locates each country according to the severity of their health and social problems, with the 'better' countries towards the bottom of the table and the 'worse' towards the top. What the table shows is that "there is a very strong tendency for ill-health and social problems to occur less frequently in the more equal countries" (Wilkinson and Pickett, 2010, pp. 19–20).

Source: Wilkinson and Pickett (2010)

Questions

1. Define what is meant by 'reliability'. Support your definition with an example from the study.

2. In your own words, explain the opening statement: 'Arguments for greater equality are usually framed in moral terms, but a remarkable piece of social research published originally in 2009 argues that the case for more equal societies can be made on empirical grounds'.

3. Using Figure 6.1.4, outline and explain which country comes out best and which worst in this comparison. Remember to explain the criteria that you use to judge the 'best' and the 'worst'.

4. Analyse how the UK compares to the other countries examined in the study.

5. Why is this research 'politically sensitive'?

FOCUS ON SKILLS: TRICKLE-DOWN ECONOMICS

Ed Balls' announcement in 2014 that, if elected, the Labour Party would increase the top rate of income tax from 45p to 50p has resulted in angry business lobbies and Conservative ministers claiming that the move is 'anti-business'. The way they see it, the move would drive away talent and wealth creators and ultimately undermine the recovery.

This is a classic example of trickle-down economics in action. That is, the idea that the rich create economic prosperity that we all gain from. Used to slate virtually any policy that threatens the profits of the mega-rich, trickle-down has a stranglehold on our economic and social policies. It underpins our highly skewed corporate and income tax policies, decisions about public sector spending cuts, weak banking regulation, extortionate executive pay, on-going attacks on workers' rights and much more. Worst of all, the powerful have clung to trickle-down for so long that people are starting to confuse it with common sense.

First, one only needs to look at income growth at the top versus stagnation in median wages to know that wealth has not trickled down. Instead it has amassed at the top. While FTSE 100 CEOs have seen a cumulative 480 per cent pay rise since 1998, income for the average worker has barely budged. The top 10 per cent are now sitting on more wealth (including financial, property and assets) than the entire bottom half of our population. Perhaps even more concerning is that this wealth has flooded out to tax havens – with billions stored safely away from the UK taxman.

Hoarding of wealth only makes it more likely that prosperity will not trickle down. Nobel-prize winning economics Professor Joseph Stiglitz has discussed the rise of 'rent-seeking' – which includes the rich using their wealth to lobby government to ensure policies continue to favour their needs and desires. Furthermore, as the rich get richer, they become increasingly isolated from the rest of us – making them less empathetic and so less supportive of the welfare state.

What about the other promise of trickle-down – that by helping the rich to get richer we will expand jobs and investment and hence boost economic growth?

In reality, the data shows that neither employment nor domestic investment is directly correlated to the top income tax rates. In fact the datasets tend to show oscillation more closely related to the business cycle than to the top tax rate.

A final argument made in support of trickle-down economics is that spending by the rich buoys up consumer demand. The intuition behind this argument goes something like: the rich can afford to buy luxury goods and generally consume more, they can afford to travel and eat out frequently; and all of these activities create jobs which provide incomes for others to spend and so on.

The problem is that consumption patterns show it is the middle class who sustain demand in the economy. This is why, when the recession hit, demand fell sharply even while the rich continued to see increases in income and luxury goods continued to sell. President Obama has put this reality succinctly in recent speeches noting that "growing inequality isn't just morally wrong; it's bad economics. When middle-class families have less to spend, businesses have fewer customers". He concludes that "prosperity needs to come from the 'middle out' rather than the top down".

Source: Shaheen (2014)

Questions

1. **Explain** what is meant by 'trickle-down economics'.

2. **Analyse** how this theory impacted on government policies.

3. **Interpret** what the author means by saying that trickle-down had become 'common sense'.

4. **Identify** the criticisms made of trickle-down theory.

5. **Evaluate** the impact of trickle-down on the distribution of income.

CHECK YOUR UNDERSTANDING

1. Explain the difference between 'wealth' and 'income'.

2. Why might the statistics we have on wealth be less accurate than those on income?

3. What broad changes in wealth and income distribution a) took place between 1950 and 1980 and b) have taken place since 1980?

4. Which is less unevenly distributed across the UK, income or wealth?

5. How many years would it take the average worker to earn what a FTSE 100 CEO earns in one year?

6. Explain what is meant by 'austerity policies'.

7. Identify two examples of anti-austerity organisations.

8. Explain what is meant by 'corporate capture'.

9. Identify two pieces of evidence of corporate capture.

10. Identify three negative social consequences of high levels of economic inequality in society.

TAKE IT FURTHER

In *The Spirit Level*, Wilkinson and Pickett argue that for thousands of years the surest way of improving the quality of human life was through economic growth, thereby raising material living standards. But now, for the first time in history, "economic growth... has, in the rich countries, largely finished its work". If we are to see further improvements in human happiness and wellbeing, while there is still an important role for economic growth in the poor countries, the focus in the rich countries must be on tackling inequality, they argue, particularly given the problem of global warming and the environmental limits to growth.

Organise a debate among your classmates where the proposition to be debated is: 'This house believes that the government should abandon economic growth and instead pursue policies of greater economic equality'.

6.2 DEFINING AND MEASURING POVERTY

LEARNING OBJECTIVES

> Demonstrate knowledge and understanding of the nature and existence of poverty in contemporary society (AO1).

> Demonstrate knowledge and understanding of the different ways in which poverty is defined and measured (AO1).

> Analyse and apply the evidence collected by sociological surveys of poverty to the different ways of defining and measuring poverty in contemporary society (AO2).

> Evaluate the different ways in which poverty is defined and measured by sociologists in order to make judgements and draw conclusions about the extent of poverty in contemporary society (AO3).

INTRODUCING THE DEBATE

Sociological debate about poverty has tended to focus on how poverty should be defined and therefore measured. In the early days of poverty research, researchers preferred to use a budget standards approach, which was a variation on the concept of absolute poverty. The last 30 years or so have seen sociologists favour the relative poverty approach, although since 1997 this has largely been replaced by a focus on social exclusion.

This chapter will investigate the ways in which sociologists have defined and, consequently, measured poverty over the years.

ABSOLUTE POVERTY

The concept of absolute poverty has three dimensions.

> In developing societies, absolute poverty is subsistence poverty, meaning that people are in poverty if they don't have regular access to basic resources such as food and clean water, because of famine, war and so on, and, consequently, they and their children are at risk of early death. The United Nations estimates that 800 million people live in a state of subsistence poverty in the developing world.

> In modern societies, absolute poverty is normally defined as having insufficient money to meet basic needs for food and shelter. For example, in 2015,

homeless people, people who are forced to use foodbanks, or pensioners who have to choose between eating or heating their homes, could be said to be experiencing absolute poverty in the UK.

› Absolute poverty is also a type of measurement of poverty. It was extensively used in the early days of poverty research in the form of the budget standards approach, when many researchers attempted to calculate how much income a person or household required to ensure they had the basics to live a healthy life. The state also uses a variation on absolute poverty in that citizens of the UK are eligible to claim benefits if their income falls below a certain level.

The definition of absolute poverty is mainly associated with two 19th-century anti-poverty campaigners, Charles Booth and Seebohm Rowntree.

Charles Booth

Booth is often described as the father of modern poverty studies. Between 1889 and 1903, he carried out a street-by-street survey of East and Inner London which documented and mapped the numerical extent of poverty, as well as grading the degree of the poverty experienced by households in these streets. Booth concluded that 31 per cent of people in the districts he examined were living in poverty.

Booth's studies showed that around a third of people in East and Inner London lived in poverty around the beginning of the 20th century.

Booth is important because he was the first researcher to apply an absolute approach to the study of poverty in the UK. This means that he set an income level below which he regarded people as living in poverty. In 1887, he described his absolute definition – "by the word 'poor' I mean to describe those who have a fairly regular though bare income, such as 18 shillings to 21 shillings per week for a moderate family, and by 'very poor' those who fall

below this standard, whether from chronic irregularity of work, sickness, or a very large number of very young children" (Glennerster *et al.*, 2004, p. 18). Glennester *et al.* note that what Booth succeeded in doing for the first time was to set a rough income level, based on a judgement about what was socially acceptable and unacceptable, that was recognised as a valid indicator of poverty by social policy makers.

Seebohm Rowntree

Rowntree was profoundly affected by Booth's work and embarked on a poverty survey of York in 1899 because he wanted to see whether the same findings could be observed outside of London. He adopted Booth's methodology of house-to-house visits, making notes about the size of the family and accommodation, the occupations of those who worked and the standard of life, cleanliness and respectability of those families. He also adopted Booth's notion of an absolute income level that would distinguish the poor from the non-poor. This was based on deciding what resources, and therefore income, were needed for a person to be able to live healthily and work efficiently. However, Rowntree used a type of absolute poverty approach known as the '**budget standards**' approach because his income level was based upon:

› the costs of a very basic diet

› the costs of purchasing a minimum amount of clothes of minimum quality

› the rent for a basic level of housing.

UNDERSTAND THE CONCEPT

The **budget standards** approach refers to a type of absolute poverty measurement that works out the minimum income required to buy the items needed to be healthy.

In other words, Rowntree worked out the minimum budget needed to be healthy. The 'poverty line' was then drawn at the income needed to meet the three costs in his definition. In addition, Rowntree's investigators were asked to make judgements from observation about whether, in their view, the family was living in 'obvious want and squalor' and the reasons for this. On the basis of these judgements, Rowntree concluded that 28 per cent of the total population of York was living in a state of poverty. However, he distinguished between two types of poverty: primary poverty and secondary poverty.

› *Primary poverty* affected 9.9 per cent of York's population. The people who experienced this type of poverty had incomes so low that even if they spent their money efficiently and wasted not a penny, they would not be able to achieve a healthy standard of living. This category of poverty distinguished Rowntree's definition of absolute poverty from that of Booth because Rowntree used scientific experts to work out the minimum nutritional intake required for a working man to be an effective worker. Rowntree then worked out the cost of the cheapest foods that would ensure consistency with the nutritional level recommended by his experts. On the basis of these criteria, he came to the conclusion that a significant number of workers in York (15 per cent) were 'underfed' and this malnutrition was a serious threat to the effective running of industrial Britain.

Below is an extract from Rowntree's 1899 diet for men. The other days of the week were equally meagre.

Sunday

Breakfast: Bread 8 oz, Margarine $\frac{1}{2}$ oz, Tea 1 pt

Dinner: Boiled bacon 3 oz, Pease pudding 12 oz

Supper: Bread 8 oz, Margarine $\frac{1}{2}$ oz, Cocoa 1 pt

Monday

Breakfast: Bread 8 oz, Porridge $1\frac{1}{2}$ pts

Dinner: Potatoes with milk 24 oz, Bread 2oz, Cheese 2oz

Supper: Bread 8oz, Vegetable broth 1pt, Cheese 2oz

Tuesday

Breakfast: Porridge $1\frac{1}{2}$ pts, Skim milk 1pt

Dinner: Vegetable broth 1pt, Bread 4oz, Cheese 2oz, Dumpling 8oz

Supper: Bread 4oz, Porridge $1\frac{1}{2}$ pts

› *Secondary poverty* was experienced by 17.9 per cent of York's population. These were families whose total earnings should have been enough to ensure health and working efficiency but a significant proportion of their earnings were spent on other things, both useful (furniture, presents for their children and so on) and wasteful (drink, tobacco and so on).

However, Rowntree did eventually acknowledge that no one could be expected to live on his primary poverty income in real life because they were expected by their community to live like a 'normal' social being. For example, their workmates might invite them to have a drink in the local pub, and children would want pocket money. Consequently, Rowntree's subsequent poverty

surveys in 1936 and 1951 incorporated the need for a social life into his minimum income level.

Advantages of an absolute definition of poverty

An absolute definition of poverty provides us with a clear measure of who is in poverty at any one time. It also provides a point of comparison that can be used in the same society at different periods in time. For example, Rowntree repeated his 1899 study in both 1936 and 1951. He adjusted his minimum income levels so that they reflected the improved standard of living experienced in these periods compared with 1899. However, by 1951, Rowntree concluded that absolute poverty had virtually disappeared from the UK because the expansion of the welfare state after the Second World War had raised most people's income levels well above his absolute poverty income line.

Some commentators suggest that the budget standards approach used by Rowntree is not really an absolute approach. Why do you think this is?

Disadvantages of an absolute definition of poverty

Critics of the absolute definition approach to poverty, such as Townsend (1979), point out the following weaknesses.

› It is a limited tool in terms of its potential global use. The most absolute definition of poverty is a measure of destitution – the failure to obtain the absolute necessities to keep life going; poverty so extreme that life itself may be threatened. But poverty in the UK is not actually destitution – someone can be poor, but still be able to struggle on. For example, a widely accepted absolute indicator of poverty in less economically-developed countries is the number of people living on less than $1.25 per day, on the grounds that people on such incomes are literally in danger of starving to death. This threshold is often termed 'absolute income poverty'. But using this measurement in the UK would be completely inappropriate because the qualitative experience of poverty is immensely different: poor people in the UK are rarely in danger of starving to death.

› The absolute approach is based on the assumption that basic needs can be identified for all people in all societies. Spicker (2012) suggests that an absolute minimum standard cannot be universally applied. He uses food as his example and points out that what is considered 'food' changes from one society to another. He notes that "in Britain, we do not eat horse-meat or snails; in France people do. Many people across the world are unable to digest cow's milk; when in the period after the Second World War, the US arranged for dried milk to be provided to help people in poor countries, it made them sick" (Haralambos and Holborn, 2013, p. 233).

Critics also point out that the nutritional demands of people living in the same society are often very different. For example, someone engaged in heavy manual work is likely to have different dietary requirements compared with a pregnant woman or an elderly person.

› The budget standards approach is arguably too dependent on the value judgements of researchers and experts. It may not reflect the real experience of poverty. Value judgements are subjective and, consequently, biased assessments about what is good or bad, or of value or not, according to one person's own standards, beliefs, upbringing, and so on.

› An absolute definition fails to take into account that what is regarded as poverty changes over time. Poverty is actually a relative concept because what is a luxury today may be a necessity tomorrow, as fashion, acceptable standards of housing and general standards of living change. This makes it very hard to decide exactly what constitutes a 'minimum' standard of clothes or an 'acceptable' diet. This observation has led to some commentators suggesting that both Booth and Rowntree actually recognised the relative quality of poverty: Booth was aware that his poverty line was the product of social judgements and expectations that might change, while Rowntree updated his definitions of what qualified as basics in 1936 and 1951, as well as budgeting for a social life to reflect how standards of living had improved since 1899.

RELATIVE POVERTY

An alternative way of looking at poverty, **relative poverty**, is to see it in terms of the normal expectations or living standards of a society at a particular time. As societies change and become more (or less) affluent, so the idea of what poverty is will change too. Central heating and colour televisions were once luxuries – yet today the majority of homes have them. More recently, mobile phones and home computers have become part of a 'normal' standard of living for a very large section of the British population. Therefore, if a person or family is unable to achieve a moderate or normal standard of living, using this definition they may be poor.

UNDERSTAND THE CONCEPT

Relative poverty means that a person lacks the material resources, such as income, to voluntarily take part in those activities that the rest of society accepts as normal routine.

Measuring relative poverty

There are two ways of operationalising (that is, measuring) the concept of relative poverty:

› the relative income measure – the official state-endorsed definition of poverty

› the consensual measure as used by sociological surveys, such as the *Breadline Britain* surveys carried out by Mack and Lansley in 1983 and 1990.

The relative income measure (HBAI)

In 1988, the government began to publish annually a report known as 'Households Below Average Income' (HBAI) which is based on evidence gathered by the Family Resources Survey (FRS) carried out on behalf of the Department of Work and Pensions. The HBAI provides various details of the low-earner experience and, over the years, politicians and social policy makers have used its data to suggest that the official poverty line should be 60 per cent of median British household income. Median means that low-income households are compared with middle-income households rather than the richest ones, because sociologists and policy makers want to compare poorer households with what can be considered a 'normal' standard of living in the UK today.

Importantly, the 60 per cent poverty line is based on disposable income – income after tax. Incomes are adjusted for household size and composition so that they can be fairly compared. For example, a single adult does not need the same income as a family of five, but similarly the larger household does not need five times the income of the single adult because they share some costs.

It was the Labour government of 1997–2010 that first proactively adopted this measure of poverty in their desire to reduce the extent of child poverty. For example, in 2009, Labour estimated that 13.5 million people in the UK (22 per cent of the population) were living in poverty, that is, in households that were below the 60 per cent low-income threshold after deducting housing costs.

FOCUS ON SKILLS: MEASURING POVERTY

Case study

Jennie lives in temporary accommodation in Redbridge, North London. She is a single mother with three sons over the age of ten, all of whom have disabilities. While she tries to make sure her sons are properly fed, she struggles: "Chicken drumsticks, which I am going to do today for the kids for their dinner, with some chips, beans and spaghetti. They mainly have fruit and veg over the weekends … they tend to eat it as soon as I get it. I can't go and get any more because I don't have the money. I have to budget".

She sometimes gets offered food by friends and neighbours, but in order to ensure that her children are properly fed, she regularly goes without herself. Jennie worked as a hairdresser when she left school, but her middle son, Mark, contracted meningitis as a baby leaving him visually impaired. Jennie, now 41, left work to care for him.

Most of the family's benefit income goes on food, fuel, school clothes and local travel, with rent paid by housing benefit. They rarely socialise and have never had a holiday. They do have a television set, a fridge and a washing machine. Jennie often runs out of money.

So are Jennie and her family in poverty? Their standard of living is well below that of most people in the UK, and they experience deprivation in a variety of ways – but are they poor? The family recognise that their situation could be worse … They have a roof – however insecure – over their head. They just get by on food – even if they run short quite regularly. They have a higher standard of living than the poor of a century, or half a century ago – they have access to health services and education. They are not starving.

Based on Lansley and Mack (2015), pp. 1–2.

Poverty charities

In September 2012, the Save the Children Fund announced that it was launching a £500,000 appeal to help poor British families with the most basic of needs – from a hot meal to blankets and beds. This was the first time in its history – nearly a hundred years – that the charity, known for its work in providing aid overseas, had intervened to provide direct help domestically. The *Daily Mail* attacked the move as 'obscene' for implying that British children were just as needy as African children. In 2009, another charity – the Trussell Trust – ran 28 foodbanks. By 2014, the number had climbed to over 400 with the charity providing help for over 800,000 people – a third of them children – in 2013–14.

Based on Lansley and Mack (2015), pp. 206–7.

Questions

1. **Identify,** looking closely at Jennie's situation, six indicators that suggest that she and her children are in poverty.

2. **Analyse** which arguments suggest Jennie and her children are not in poverty.

3. **Analyse** what basic needs most of us take for granted. Make a list of the items or services in your home that your family could not do without.

4. **Assess** whether Jennie and her family can improve their situation. Justify your answer.

5. **Identify** and **analyse**, in small-group discussion, why the Save the Children Fund and the Trusssell Trust feel the need to offer the services they do in the UK.

6. **Evaluate** whether it is possible, in your opinion, to talk about poverty in the UK when we can see such extreme deprivation in other parts of the world.

Labour also set targets to halve child poverty, defined as below 60 per cent of median income level (before housing costs) by 2011.

The fixed 60 per cent of median income suggests that this approach to poverty is an absolute one in the tradition of both Booth and Rowntree. However, the official poverty line also has a relative component in that it stays in line with median incomes. It is not a fixed sum of income that always remains the same, year in and year out. If median incomes (and consequently standards of living) rise or fall, so will the official poverty line, and consequently the number of people in and out of poverty will fluctuate. This relativity element is clearly seen when median income levels between 2002 and 2012 are examined. Data from the Department of Work and Pensions shows that median income fell from £429 in 2002 to £427 in 2012 – its lowest level for a decade, due to pay freezes and austerity cuts. This pushed a further 1 million people below the official absolute poverty line and resulted in a further 300,000 children living in households experiencing poverty.

The consensual approach to relative poverty

Townsend defined this type of poverty as lacking the resources or **necessities** to enjoy the living conditions, amenities and rituals that the majority of society take for granted, such as having carpets, a fridge, exclusive use of a toilet and bathroom, and being able to buy birthday presents for children and to celebrate Christmas.

UNDERSTAND THE CONCEPT

Necessities are the goods or resources that the majority of the general public believe everybody should be able to afford to buy; for example, a fridge is a necessity so that food can be preserved for longer. In contrast, luxury goods such as cars or jewellery are not regarded as basic necessities.

Guy Palmer of The Poverty Site (2011) argues that the relative poverty approach to defining and measuring poverty is important because "we believe that no one should live with 'resources that are so seriously below those commanded by the average individual or family that they are, in effect, excluded from ordinary living patterns, customs and activities'. In other words, we believe that, in a rich country such as the UK, there should be certain minimum standards below which no one should fall."

This consensual approach assumes that definitions of poverty are not fixed. The relative definition of poverty is very flexible because it reflects the constantly changing living standards of a particular society and the fact that cultural expectations about what things are regarded as necessities and luxuries frequently vary over time and between regions, as well as social groups differentiated by age, social class, gender and ethnicity. For example, the elderly may need access to a completely different set of resources or necessities compared with children.

Identify groups who might experience different needs and therefore a different set of basic necessities.

The poverty surveys carried out by Mack and Lansley in *Breadline Britain* (1993), and David Gordon *et al.* (2000) used a consensual approach. These surveys began by asking large samples of people what items or activities they believed were "customary, socially approved and of vital importance to social life". Mack and Lansley classed something as a 'necessity' if a consensus among the respondents was achieved, that is, if over 50 per cent of the sample said that it was essential. On the basis of this consensus (meaning that people are in broad agreement with each other on a subject), the survey identified 22 items to include in their 'deprivation index', including a damp-free home, daily fresh fruit and vegetables, a warm, waterproof coat, and so on.

The surveys asked their respondents what necessities they lacked but also whether this was a matter of choice or affordability. Mack and Lansley decided that those respondents who lacked three or more necessities were 'poor', whereas Gordon *et al.* decided to set their poverty line at the lack of two or more necessities. This meant that the *Breadline Britain* survey estimated that 11 million of the UK population lived in poverty in 1990 (up from 7.5 million in 1983), while Gordon *et al.* estimated that 24 per cent of the UK population (approximately 14 million) were poor.

Advantages of the relative definition of poverty

The relative definition links poverty to the expectations of society – it reflects the fact that most people measure their own quality of life against that of others like themselves.

It also broadens the idea of what poverty is. It is no longer a case of not being able to afford a list or a shopping basket of basic necessities.

FOCUS ON SKILLS: WHAT ARE THE REAL NECESSITIES?

Table 6.2.1 contains a list of items and activities. An adult sample was asked in 1983, 1990, 1999 and 2012 whether these should be necessities that all families or individuals should have.

Items and activities	% thinking item to be a necessity			
	1983	1990	1999	2012
Heating to keep home adequately warm	97	97	95	96
Damp-free home	94	98	94	94
Two meals a day	64	90	91	91
Replace or repair broken electrical goods	-	-	86	86
Fresh fruit and vegetables every day	-	88	87	83
Washing machine	67	73	77	82
All recommended dental work and treatment	-	-	-	82
Celebrations on special occasions	69	74	83	80
Warm waterproof coat	87	91	87	79
Telephone	43	56	72	77
Appropriate clothes for job interview	-	-	70	69
A table with chairs at which the family can eat	-	-	-	64
Two pairs of all-weather shoes	67	74	67	54
Internet connection at home	-	-	6	41
Home computer	-	5	11	40
Roast joint or equivalent at least once a week	67	64	58	36
Car	22	26	36	44
Hair done or cut regularly	-	-	-	35
Mobile phone	-	-	8	40
Television	51	58	58	51

Table 6.2.1 *Changing attitudes to 'necessities'*

Based on Lansley and Mack (2015), Fig. 2, p. 19.

Questions

1. **Identify** the items and activities in Table 6.2.1 that the majority of people agree are necessities.

2. **Analyse**, using Table 6.2.1, which of the items and activities support the view that the general public accepts that minimum living standards need to reflect contemporary and not past styles of living.

3. **Evaluate** why some sociologists might be critical of the way the items and activities are worded in this survey.

4. **Assess**, using material from this article and elsewhere, the view that consensual surveys of relative poverty are more useful in uncovering the real degree of deprivation in societies than budget standard approaches focused on the minimum income needed for a healthy lifestyle.

The consensual approach allows sociologists to track changes in what other members of society agree are the resources required so that people can voluntarily take part in activities that the majority of people take for granted.

Disadvantages of the relative definition of poverty

The relative definition of poverty does have a number of disadvantages.

> It can only be used within any one society; it does not help with cross-cultural comparisons. Consensual approaches measure poverty by asking people what is acceptable within their society – not across the world.

> It is still too researcher-based and therefore reflective of subjective middle-class judgements. Both the surveys above achieved a consensus by giving people a list of necessities produced by the researchers. It might be more productive and valid to ask panels of 'ordinary' people to produce these lists rather than sociologists or experts.

What problems might occur in defining poverty if a panel of 'ordinary' people were used to decide on a list of necessities?

> The choice of two or three necessities or more to indicate poverty seems arbitrary. It is not clear why these numbers have been chosen – why not four items?

> It was not clear why people could not afford necessities – the surveys failed to consider that they might be spending their income on non-necessities such as smoking or drinking.

> The surveys fail to state what quality the necessities need to achieve. For example, could clothing be second-hand, could a carpet be threadbare, or could food be fast-food?

> The concept of relative poverty also has the rather absurd implication that, no matter how rich people become, there will always be poverty, as long as inequality exists.

POVERTY AND SOCIAL EXCLUSION

Since 1997, the concept of relative poverty has been closely linked to that of **social exclusion**, and there is some debate over whether the term social exclusion

should replace 'poverty'. Poverty is usually seen as a lack of income to purchase the goods and services that allow people to participate fully in society. In many ways, it is a 'static' concept because it is based on an inability to purchase a socially accepted standard of living. Social exclusion, on the other hand, is a dynamic concept because it widens the horizon of analysis and looks at a range of interconnecting disadvantages from which certain groups in society suffer. These groups often have the worst housing, health, education and job prospects in society, while suffering from the highest levels of stress, crime victimisation and unemployment.

UNDERSTAND THE CONCEPT

Social exclusion refers to the range of problems experienced by the poor, beyond their everyday experiences, that undermine their future opportunities and those of their children. For example, they may have to live in inner-city areas with high crime rates and poor schools; these things, respectively, increase their chances of being a victim of crime and leaving school with few qualifications.

The idea of social exclusion comes from two sources. In the UK, it was originally developed by Townsend, who first introduced the notion of relative poverty. Townsend amended his definition of poverty to argue that poverty turned into social exclusion when it denied people full membership of society. This is the crucial distinction between the ideas of poverty and of social exclusion. For poverty campaigners, if low incomes can be eradicated, then the problem of poverty will disappear. For campaigners who wish to eradicate social exclusion (see Figure 6.2.1), extreme inequalities in health, housing, environment, crime victimisation and education also have to be tackled.

According to the government's Social Exclusion Unit: "Social exclusion is a shorthand term for what can happen when people or areas suffer from a combination of linked problems such as unemployment, poor skills, low incomes, poor housing, high crime environments, bad health and family breakdown".

Social exclusion is therefore something which manifests itself in virtually every aspect of life. This, however, makes measuring it difficult. As a result, various 'indices' or measures have been developed by the government and researchers in order to attempt to document the wide range of disadvantages that the socially excluded face in life. For example, the McInnes et al. (2014) review of poverty and social exclusion uses 50 indicators which measure levels of:

> income and poverty

> low-paid work and employment

> educational attainment

> mental and physical health

> family breakdown and poor parenting

> housing and homelessness

> discrimination

> crime

> living in a disadvantaged neighbourhood.

Those living in homeless shelters may experience social exclusion.

The Social Exclusion Unit set up by the Labour government of 1997–2010 also noted that the risk factors for social exclusion tend to cluster in certain neighbourhoods. However, not everybody at risk lives in a deprived area. Finally, social exclusion is seen as a problem that continues across generations, so that patterns of poor health, low educational attainment and high levels of victimisation continue within the same families and neighbourhoods. Social exclusion is therefore a much wider and more complex concept and issue than poverty because it explores the experience of deprivation beyond simply lacking the income to purchase necessities to include other forms of social injustice. Not all sociologists are happy with this – some argue that the focus on social exclusion is problematic because it deflects attention away from dealing with poverty. In particular, it is seen as an excuse for governments to avoid doing anything about income inequality, which some sociologists such as Wilkinson and Pickett (2010) see as the main cause of poverty in the modern UK.

CONCLUSIONS

There is no universal agreement among sociologists and social policy makers on how poverty should be defined and measured. Some sociologists today argue that the rising number of foodbanks in the UK suggests that absolute definitions and measurements should not be abandoned altogether. Other sociologists and the state continue to use variations of the budget standards approach used by Booth and Rowntree. However, surveys such as *Breadline Britain* have highlighted the strengths of a consensual relative approach to poverty, while those sociologists who argue that poverty is merely one symptom of wider inequalities in wealth, education, employment, political power, and so on, have argued in favour of a more encompassing social exclusion approach.

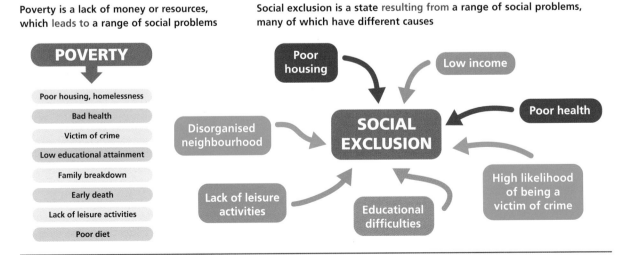

Poverty is a lack of money or resources, which leads to a range of social problems

POVERTY

Poor housing, homelessness

Bad health

Victim of crime

Low educational attainment

Family breakdown

Early death

Lack of leisure activities

Poor diet

Social exclusion is a state resulting from a range of social problems, many of which have different causes

Poor housing

Low income

Poor health

Disorganised neighbourhood

SOCIAL EXCLUSION

High likelihood of being a victim of crime

Lack of leisure activities

Educational difficulties

Figure 6.2.1 *The differences between poverty and social exclusion*

CHECK YOUR UNDERSTANDING

1. Identify three luxuries that have become necessities in the past 20 years.

2. Identify the two types of poverty revealed by Rowntree's surveys of poverty.

3. Define what is meant by 'subsistence poverty'.

4. Define what is meant by 'relative poverty'.

5. Define what is meant by 'social exclusion'.

6. Outline and explain why relative poverty was seen as a better way of measuring poverty than the budget standards approach.

7. Outline and explain why subsistence poverty does not exist in Britain.

8. Explain the methods used by Booth to distinguish the poor from the non-poor.

9. Analyse and explain the strengths of Mack and Lansley's approach to measuring poverty in the *Breadline Britain* survey.

10. Outline and evaluate the view that social exclusion is a more useful way of measuring inequality and deprivation than absolute and relative approaches to poverty.

TAKE IT FURTHER

Draw up your own list of 15 essential items that your family agree they could not do without today. Ask a representative sample of students: (a) whether they agree that your items are necessary; (b) which of your items should be affordable for all families; and (c) which items all families should not have to do without.

Find detailed information on poverty, social exclusion and further research at The Poverty Site, and at the websites of the New Policy Institute and the Joseph Rowntree Foundation.

6.3 THE EXTENT OF POVERTY

LEARNING OBJECTIVES

> Demonstrate knowledge and understanding of the extent and persistence of poverty in contemporary society (AO1).

> Demonstrate knowledge and understanding of the distribution of poverty between different social groups (AO1).

> Analyse and apply the evidence collected by surveys of poverty to work out how poverty is distributed between different social groups in the contemporary UK (AO2).

> Evaluate sociological classifications of poverty in order to make judgements and draw conclusions about the extent of poverty in the UK today (AO3).

INTRODUCING THE DEBATE

Chapter 2 documented how the numbers of people classed as living in poverty will vary depending on which definitions and measurements of poverty are used. The 'Households Below Average Income' (HBAI) approach – the number of households with incomes below 60 per cent of median income – is the method used by the government to measure an official poverty line. The 2012–13 figures indicated that 10.6 million individuals were in absolute poverty in the UK before housing costs, but this increased to 14.6 million (23.2 per cent of the population) when measured after housing costs had been deducted.

Lansley and Mack (2015) claim that nearly three out of every ten (about 18 million) people in Britain fell below their minimum living standard based on a measure of relative poverty put together by majority public opinion. This was double what their first survey in 1983 had estimated.

Whichever measurement of poverty is used, the facts support the view that poverty is very widespread in Britain and not just restricted to a few 'unfortunates'.

WHO ARE THE POOR?

The following sections present a 'snapshot' of groups who have a high risk of living in poverty, drawing examples from all of the classifications of poverty.

One-parent families

Gardiner and Evans (2011) note that children living in unemployed one-parent families are more likely to be in poverty compared with one-parent families in which the parent worked either part time or full time. There are two interrelated reasons why single mothers (who make up 90 per cent of single parents) are likely to be poor.

1. Women from poorer backgrounds have a higher risk of becoming single parents in the first place. So they are already more likely to be at risk of poverty before having children.

2. Any single parent is likely to be poorer because they have to combine childcare with employment. This means that they are more likely to be workless when their children are young, or to work part time, so their incomes on average will be lower. One-parent families are more than twice as likely to be on low incomes as couples without children, and three times as likely as single adults without children. However, HBAI official statistics suggest that paid work is not always a way of escaping poverty for single-parent families because the poverty rate for children in single-parent families in 2014 where the parent works part time was 30 per cent and 22 per cent where the parent works full time.

Poverty affects single-parent families in specific ways, according to Gingerbread, a charity dedicated to such families. Some examples are given below.

> 42 per cent of single-parent families are social tenants, that is, they are often found on council estates. However, there is some evidence that they are often allocated to 'problem' estates or neighbourhoods with social problems such as failing schools, crime (especially drug crime) and anti-social behaviour. The experience of living in such deprived areas may worsen the experience of poverty, especially for children.

What other forms of deprivation might people who live in poor neighbourhoods experience?

> Single-parent households are the most likely to be in debt and/or arrears on one or more household bills, their mortgage, or to have borrowing commitments from lending companies such as pay-day lenders or local loan sharks.

> Lansley and Mack note that many single mothers report that they have no savings and that money always runs out before the end of the week or month.

> Spencer (2005) argues that these material disadvantages lead to multiple other disadvantages. Children in one-parent families are more likely to experience health problems, to underachieve at school and to be labelled as difficult or anti-social by teachers and the police. There is also evidence that such families are **stigmatised** as dysfunctional and broken by the mass media, politicians and social policy makers, and, because of their need for welfare benefits, to be seen as an unwelcome economic burden on society.

UNDERSTAND THE CONCEPT

Stigma refers to the negative labelling or stereotyping experienced by groups who are often powerless.

However, it is important to remember that not all single parents are poor – it is just that they are more at risk of poverty.

Children

Some 27 per cent of children (3.5 million) were living in low-income families in 2013. Two-thirds (66 per cent) of children growing up in poverty live in a family where at least one person works. Charities such as the Child Poverty Action Group and End Child Poverty have identified a number of consequences of poverty that particularly blight the lives of children.

> Poor children are born too small; birth weight is on average 130 grams lower in children from poor families compared with children born into better-off families. Low birth weight is closely associated with infant death and chronic diseases in later life.

> Poor children miss out on activities that their better-off peers take for granted. For example, 61 per cent of families in the bottom income quintile would like, but cannot afford, to take their children on holiday for one week a year.

> Poverty often influences the educational development of children. Before reaching two years old, a child from a poorer family is more likely to show a lower level of attainment than a child from a better-off family. By the age of six, a less able child from a rich family is likely to have overtaken an able child born into a poor family in terms of reading, writing and mathematical ability.

> Children receiving free school meals achieve 1.7 grades lower at GCSE than their wealthier peers (DfE, 2011). Furthermore, children growing up in poverty are more likely to leave school at 16 with fewer qualifications and, consequently, are more likely to be employed in low-skilled and low-paid work or to end up long-term unemployed.

Sociologists often measure the impact of poverty on educational performance by focusing on children receiving free school meals. Why do you think this is?

The unemployed

In 2015, there were 1.91 million people out of work in the UK according to the government. About 75 per cent of these unemployed people live in poverty. Those who are unemployed for a long time face much greater problems than those who are out of work for a short period. These problems include a lower level of income; the gradual exhaustion of savings; the accumulation of debt; and a deterioration in the condition of clothing, furniture and general possessions.

After three months of unemployment, the average disposable income of a family drops by as much as 59 per cent. Lansley and Mack note that hunting for work, especially in areas of high unemployment, is an extremely "demoralising and often demeaning process. For many it means a life of low income, repetition and constant strain. Unemployment has a deadening impact on people's lives" (p. 92). It is therefore not just financial losses that occur as a result of long-term unemployment. There are psychological effects too, such as lack of confidence; loss of status; shame; loss of masculine role or purpose; feelings of uselessness; stress; and depression.

These effects further undermine people's ability to obtain work.

Since the financial crisis of 2008, youth unemployment has risen at twice the national rate. In 2014, it was nearly three times the national average. Over 50 per cent of those who left school at 16 without five GCSEs at grades A–C were unemployed in 2014. Lansley and Mack point out that many young people – 950,000 aged 16 to 24 in 2014 – are NEETS (Not in Employment, Education or Training).

Moreover, a study carried out by Barr et al. (2012) suggests that an increase in the English suicide rate, which began in 2008, may be linked to unemployment. They found that English regions with the largest rises in unemployment have had the largest increases in suicides, particularly among men, and conclude that around 40 per cent of the increase in male suicides can be attributed to rising unemployment. (See Topic 5, Chapter 3 for more on this.)

Why is suicide disproportionately high among young unemployed males?

Lansley and Mack argue that the unemployment rate in the UK gives a false picture of unemployment because of the following trends.

> There has been a rise in the level of enforced underemployment – people working shorter hours than they would like because of the growing number of part-time jobs which involve zero-hours or 'no guaranteed hours' contracts.

> There has been a rise in the number of people classifying themselves as self-employed. Lansley and Mack note that some people go down this route out of choice but there are an increasing number who are forced down this road because they have failed to find work. There is also evidence that job centres are encouraging the unemployed to become self-employed in an attempt to reduce unemployment statistics.

The low paid

Over 30 per cent of all poor people are in full- or part-time employment, but do not earn enough to live on. The Low Pay Commission estimated in 2014 that 1.4 million people were in minimum wage jobs and most of these were employed in retail, hospitality or cleaning. However, the think tank The Resolution Foundation (2014) found that one in five employees earn less than the '**living wage**'. This means that 5 million people were on such low pay in 2014.

UNDERSTAND THE CONCEPT

The **living wage** is the amount that an individual needs to earn to cover the basic costs of living. It may vary slightly across the country because living costs are, for example, higher in London. In 2015, the living wage for London was £9.15 p/h and £7.85 for the rest of the UK, compared with a minimum wage of £6.50.

Furthermore, many of the low paid are young people. Hills et al. (2013) found that the wages of young people have fallen more steeply since 2008 compared with other social groups, while Brinkley et al. (2013) found that young women were three times more likely to be employed in low-paid, low-skilled jobs in 2012 than 20 years ago. Lansley and Mack refer to young people born around 1990 as the 'jinxed' or 'jilted' generation because they are the first generation to see their incomes stagnate compared with previous generations.

Sociologists and charities have made a number of observations about the plight of the low paid.

> The low paid often have few educational qualifications and fewer skills.

> They tend to live in areas with relatively few jobs so competition keeps wages low.

> Many of the low paid are single parents because single mothers often have to take on part-time jobs due to childcare responsibilities.

> Those most at risk of low pay include female workers, the young, those in lower-skilled occupations, part-time and temporary workers and those employed in hospitality, retail and care.

According to Lansley and Mack, many of the low paid are on zero-hours contracts which "offer little or no guarantee of work or pay and have come to be widely abused. For firms they allow the circumvention of employment rights, leaving employees without entitlements to holidays, sick pay and other benefits" (p. 106). In 2014, the Office for National Statistics (ONS) estimated that one in ten employers was using this approach to employment and that 1.4 million workers were on such contracts. Lansley and Mack note that such contracts offer flexibility to some workers (especially students) but that most workers on them have little choice. Many of those experiencing poverty are on such contracts and many of them have had to take on two or three of these jobs in order to ensure a regular income.

A campaign supporting the living wage and calling for an end to exploitative zero-hours contracts

What, in your view, are the advantages and disadvantages of zero-hours contracts?

Lansley and Mack also suggest that many of the so-called self-employed earn very little.

Lansley and Mack note that 'the squeeze on pay', as symbolised by zero-hours contracts, "has been compounded by the growth of 'bad jobs' offering minimal rights and security" (p. 105). Standing (2011) refers to the low-paid workforce as the 'precariat' because the jobs they have are "marginal, precarious and irregular, offering few rights, rock-bottom wages, coercive management, intensified labour processes, unsocial hours and high rates of job turnover" (Lansley and Mack, p. 106). The **precariat** is more likely to experience a livelihood crisis than other workers because it is over represented in insecure casual and temporary jobs and over-dependent on employment agencies for work.

UNDERSTAND THE CONCEPT

The **precariat** are that part of the workforce who tend to have a succession of low-paid temporary jobs offering little security.

The 2012 Poverty and Social Exclusion (PSE) survey suggests that a fifth of those who are in work or self-employed do not think their job is secure; 34 per cent said they 'felt constantly under strain', while 31 per cent lost sleep because of worry.

A study of a large supermarket chain by Cambridge University researchers, cited in Lansley and Mack, found that the flexible working conditions experienced by the low paid damaged their mental health. They suffered enormous levels of anxiety and stress because they interpreted their job situation as highly unstable and they worried about the daily struggle to make ends meet.

Older people

About 16 per cent of pensioners (1.8 million) were in poverty in 2014 according to the ONS. However, the charity for the elderly, Age UK, claimed that 900,000 pensioners were in 'severe poverty', meaning that they were unable to afford decent food, heat their home or live an independent life.

Being old does not necessarily make people poor, but the risk increases for a number of reasons.

> People who are poor in old age are most likely to be those who have earned the least in their working lives.

> Elderly women are more likely to be in poverty than elderly men because they generally receive less from their state and private pensions, which are linked to earnings. These women probably took time out of the labour market to raise children and, consequently, did not contribute as much of their wage to this future benefit.

> Retired women in poverty often fail to claim the state benefits they are entitled to, either because they are unaware of them or because they are too embarrassed or proud to claim the money.

> Fuel poverty is a particular problem for the elderly because fuel bills in the UK are high. Age UK estimates that 2 million elderly people are so anxious about these bills that they turn their heating down when they are not warm, go to bed even if they are not tired, or use just one room in their house.

However, the numbers of elderly people in poverty has fallen over the last 30 years. Lansley and Mack argue that this is the only success story related to poverty since 1983. Free bus passes, the winter fuel allowance and better state and occupational pensions have combined to lift many pensioners out of poverty. However, the rapid ageing of the population that is currently taking place suggests that poverty among the elderly will increase again because employers are now offering less generous pension schemes to the current workforce, while people now have to work for a longer period before they receive the state pension. If this is in low-paid zero-hours contract work, their prospects will be even more compromised.

The homeless

The homeless are a group who are often neglected in studies of poverty. Lansley and Mack estimate that there were 185,000 homeless people in England in 2013. There are many different types of homelessness.

> Sleeping rough on the streets – official statistics show that on any one night in England in 2014, about 2,700 people slept rough on the streets, although London charities estimated that there were actually about 6,500 people sleeping rough in London in 2013–14.

FOCUS ON SKILLS: WHO ARE THE POOR?

Employment status	Percentage of all the poor
In full-time work	39%
In part-time work	13%
Unemployed	12%
Permanently sick/disabled	11%
Looking after family/home	10%
Retired	9%
Student	6%
All	100%

Table 6.3.1 *Adults lacking three or more 'necessities' by their employment status (UK: 2012)*

One of the most significant trends over the last 30 years has been a sea change in the groups most at risk of poverty. Despite some politicians' claims about the lack of personal responsibility, and a weak work ethic, the most striking shift has been the rise of poverty among those in work.

In the 1960s, around a third of the poor were elderly. Today, less than a tenth of those in poverty are in households where all adults are retired. Nevertheless, deprivation in older age continues for some, reflecting the inequalities experienced during their lifetimes. Today's poor pensioners are a group who were unable to build up resources during their lives and rely purely on the state pension and, when they take them, means-tested top-ups. Those most at risk of poverty are single pensioners – around twice the risk of pensioner couples. Among single pensioners, women are more vulnerable than men, because they are more likely to have been in low-paid work, to lack an occupational pension and to have paid insufficient national insurance (although the rules have improved in recent years) to get a full state pension.

Based on Lansley and Mack (2015)

Questions

1. **Identify** which social groups are most likely to be in poverty according to Table 6.3.1.

2. **Analyse** the reasons why the social groups in Table 6.3.1 are likely to be in poverty.

3. **Evaluate** the view that there has been a major change in the types of groups likely to be in poverty compared with 30 years ago.

> Many homeless single people stay in hostels – there are 38,500 beds for single homeless people in the UK.

> In 2014, nearly 61,000 homeless families were in temporary accommodation provided by local councils, such as BBs, privately rented flats and hostels.

> Many homeless families are in 'concealed housing', that is, sleeping on the floors and sofas of friends and relatives. Research by the charity Crisis suggests that about 62 per cent of the homeless are hidden in this way.

> Some homeless people live in 'squats'.

> A large number of those seeking help with homelessness are aged 25 years or under (52 per cent). The majority of them have become homeless because the relationship with their parents has broken down. A significant number have also left home because of physical or sexual abuse. Homeless young people face a range of complex problems – more than 6 in 10 are NEETS, for example. Many adults are homeless because they become unemployed and lose their homes, or because they cannot afford to buy or rent, particularly in London.

Over half of Britain's homeless are aged 25 years or under.

Sick and disabled people

According to government statistics, in 2014, there were 11 million people with limiting long-term illness, impairment or disability in the UK. About 6 per cent of children (about 770,000 under the age of 16), 16 per cent of working-age adults and 45 per cent of pensioners are disabled.

A large number of individuals who live in families with disabled members live in poverty, compared to individuals who live in families where no one is disabled. For example, in 2014, 19 per cent of individuals in families with at least one disabled member lived in poverty as defined by HBAI, compared to 15 per cent of individuals in families with no

disabled member. In addition, 21 per cent of children in families with at least one disabled member are in poverty, compared with the 16 per cent of children in families with no disabled member. Overall, it is estimated that around a third of all disabled adults aged 25 to retirement are living in low-income households. In 2011, the ONS reported that 40 per cent of disabled children and a third of disabled adults were living in poverty, although Lansley and Mack argue that over 70 per cent of people who are sick or disabled are poor, on the basis of their consensual measure of poverty.

Lansley and Mack note two trends with regard to the relationship between poverty and disability.

1. Those in poverty are likely to become long-term sick or disabled. They cite a study by Burchardt et al. (2013) which found that people in the poorest fifth of the income spread are two-and-a-half times more likely to become disabled during a year compared with those in the top fifth.

2. Ill health and disability lead to poverty. There are several reasons for the poverty of long-term sick and disabled people, and their families who are often responsible for their care.

   > Some people may be unable to work because of the nature of their disability.

   > Disabled people are less likely to be in employment than non-disabled people. For example, in 2012, only 46 per cent of working-age disabled people were in employment, compared to 76 per cent of working-age non-disabled people. Consequently, over 50 per cent of the disabled are unemployed. This may be because disabled people are around three times as likely not to have any qualifications compared to non-disabled people, and be around half as likely to have a degree-level qualification.

   > The work the disabled can do may be limited to particular kinds of low-paid employment.

   > People with disabilities often have higher outgoings, such as having to pay for a special diet or for heating to be on all day. Kaye et al. (2012) found that 87 per cent of their sample said their everyday living costs are significantly higher because of their condition.

   > Kaye et al. reported that the disabled were very badly hit by cuts in government spending in the period 2010–2012. For example, it is estimated that £500 million less was spent on the disabled by the government in 2011 compared with previous years. In addition, Kaye et al. claim that thousands of disabled people were wrongly declared fit to work by government agencies and had their benefits cut

as a result. The disabled have also seen local councils cutting up to £2 billion from their care budgets and putting up charges for essential services, such as transport and meals on wheels.

Ethnic minorities

Lansley and Mack quote PSE (2012) research that suggests there is a high risk of poverty among certain ethnic-minority groups. The PSE estimate that over half of Black or Black British households and 42 per cent of British Pakistani and British Bangladeshi households are in poverty. Barnard and Turner (2011) suggest that British Bangladeshis have the highest poverty rates of all ethnic-minority groups in the UK. Only 25 per cent have above average incomes. (In contrast, both the British Chinese and British Indian minorities are the least likely ethnic groups to be found in poverty.) The following factors probably make it harder for such groups to escape poverty.

> Ethnic minority groups have substantially higher rates of unemployment than the majority of the population. This holds true even if the person has the same educational qualifications as the majority population. For example, in 2012, unemployment rates were 7.3 per cent for White people but 15.5 per cent for Black people, 16.6 per cent for British Pakistani people and 13.5 per cent for British Bangladeshi people.

> Those of African Caribbean origin and a majority of those of Asian origin have a greater chance of earning lower wages than the majority population, and they are more likely to work in the types of employment where wages are generally low. For example, in 2012, British African, British African Caribbean and British Pakistani men earned on average up to £6,500 a year less than White men with similar qualifications.

> British Asian and British African Caribbean boys tend to underachieve at school and consequently enter the labour market with fewer qualifications.

> Some ethnic minorities may be more likely to live in areas of high unemployment.

In your view, what role does racism play in bringing about ethnic-minority poverty?

Women

Some sociologists claim that poverty has become **feminised** in recent years. This is because the majority of the poor in the UK are women – most of the groups discussed above are likely to have a majority of women

members. Single parents are overwhelmingly women who are more likely to be in part-time work, to be in low-paid work, or to be unemployed, leading to the situation where the majority of single families are poor (See the section on 'One-parent families' for more on this.). Single female pensioners are also slightly more likely to be poor (21 per cent) than single male pensioners (17 per cent). This is because they are less likely to have savings, as a result of low earnings throughout their lives (See the section on 'Older people' for more information.).

UNDERSTAND THE CONCEPT

The **feminisation** of poverty is used to describe two interrelated phenomena: the fact that women are more likely to be in poverty compared with men, and that their experience of poverty is likely to be more severe than that experienced by men.

RISK OF POVERTY AND REGION

The chances of living in poverty vary considerably across the country and within cities. In relative terms, the UK is second only to Mexico in the industrialised world for the extent of regional inequalities in living standards. People living in Wales, the North East, Inner London and Yorkshire are most likely to be poor, and those living in Outer London and the South East are least likely to be poor. These largely reflect differences in rates of pay and in levels of unemployment.

POVERTY: A RISK NOT A STATE

When we talk about poor people, it is rather misleading, because it gives the impression that there is a group of people who live in poverty all their lives. This is true for some people, but the majority of the poor are people who live on the margins of poverty, moving into poverty and out again, depending upon a range of economic factors, government decisions, family responsibilities and their earning possibilities.

However, all of the groups discussed in this chapter face the following common risks.

Inter-generational poverty

The risk of people passing down poverty to the next generation has probably increased. Blanden *et al.* (2002) investigated whether poverty persisted over generations and whether children could escape the poverty of their parents as they got older. They re-analysed two well-known longitudinal studies – the 1958 National Child Development Study and the 1970 British Cohort Study (both of which had been used for a range of purposes, including medical and educational studies).

Their research concluded that the chance of being better off than one's parents had actually reduced for those who grew up in the 1970s and 1980s, compared to the earlier cohort. More of the 1970s cohort were in poor families at the age of 16 than the older cohort. In the majority of cases, children remained in the same quarter of the income distribution as their parents. In the 1958 cohort, almost 20 per cent of males and females rose from the lowest earning quarter of families to the top. But in the 1970s cohort, the figures had fallen to 15 per cent. The increase in educational opportunities in the last 30 years has been more likely to benefit the children of the more affluent, rather than the poor.

Stigma and blame

Lansley and Mack note that there is an increasing tendency among the mass media, politicians and the general public to blame the victims of poverty for their plight. For example, Lansley and Mack observe that "successive governments – of all persuasions – have viewed those of working age in poverty less as victims than as architects of their own misfortune. Ministers have mostly blamed the problems of low pay and unemployment on individuals – on a culture of worklessness, an anti-work ethic, excessive job or wage expectations and inadequate skills and qualifications – rather than on the absence of an adequate supply of secure, decently paid jobs" (p. 114). Moreover, politicians have also implied that poverty-stricken individuals and families are both a social and criminal problem. Families that experience poverty are often described as dysfunctional families and it is strongly implied that the main causes of their poverty are poor parenting skills, promiscuity, drug addiction and general inadequacy.

There is some evidence that the general public and even the poor themselves may be influenced by the stigma of being labelled poor. Research by Shildrick and MacDonald (2013) in Middlesbrough found that people in deep poverty were reluctant to use the language of poverty to describe their situation because they associated the concept with those who were workshy, benefit scroungers and people who wasted their money on drugs and gambling. As Shildrick and MacDonald (2015) note, "poverty in other people's lives was usually viewed as a consequence of individual ineptitude or moral failure" (p. 8). The researchers concluded that the denial of poverty could be partly explained "by an emphasis on, and a pride in managing in

difficult circumstances". However, some sociologists have highlighted the media portrayal of the poor in programmes such as *Benefits Street* as the main source of the idea that poverty should be regarded as shameful.

What ideas in this section may explain why the elderly do not claim the benefits they are entitled to?

Punishing the poor

Some commentators believe that another dominant idea related to poverty is that people in poverty, especially those who are claiming benefits, deserve to be punished. The notion that these people are 'getting something for nothing' is particularly strong among government ministers and right-wing newspapers such as the *Daily Mail*.

These sentiments therefore made it easier for the Coalition government (2010–2015) to focus its austerity spending cuts on the very poorest. As Lansley and Mack observe, the Coalition government cut benefits and made the conditions for their receipt more restrictive. Sanctions were introduced so that those who were deemed to be not trying hard enough to lift themselves out of poverty could be punished.

Lansley and Mack note that these cuts have disproportionately affected the poor by making them poorer and by making it more difficult to escape the cycle of poverty. MacInnes et al.'s (2013) research confirms this – 63 per cent of families affected by spending cuts were already below the official HBAI poverty line.

Debt

Poverty is becoming increasingly difficult to escape because of debt. Lansley and Mack argue that this problem has worsened since 2000 because successive governments have allowed the loan industry to expand. There are now 240 lenders operating in the UK, often charging extremely high interest rates, which can make it difficult to keep up with repayments. Between 2009 and 2013, the size of this industry doubled. Moreover, their high street stores are disproportionately concentrated in deprived neighbourhoods. Lansley and Mack observe that growing numbers of the poor are "trapped in a debilitating cycle of debt and poverty" (p. 60). In 2014, the Financial Conduct Authority (FCA) announced tougher rules on the loan industry. The FCA capped the cost of borrowing – the interest rates – so that people should never have to pay back more than double what they had originally borrowed.

FOCUS ON RESEARCH: SHILDRICK AND MACDONALD (2015)

Shildrick and MacDonald conducted their research in Teesside's largest town, Middlesbrough, between 2008 and 2010. The region has experienced persistently high rates of unemployment, with a significant number of workers moving between low-quality, insecure jobs and periods of unemployment. Shildrick and MacDonald undertook in-depth interviews with 60 people (equally divided by gender) who had experience of these changes in the labour market. All interviewees could be categorised as working class (on the basis of their occupational histories) and all were ethnically White British, reflecting the socio-demographic profile of their neighbourhoods. Interviewees were asked to reflect on their experiences of living in poverty. This allowed some insight into how they talked about poverty – both in respect of their own experiences and that of others.

Some informants appeared to be in deep poverty: they were unable to clothe or feed themselves properly or furnish and heat their homes adequately. Day-to-day life was a juggling act which demanded strict routines (such as catching the daily reductions at the shops). Leisure lives were limited.

However, informants generally rejected the label of poverty, which they believed happened to a nameless mass of others who were generally seen as responsible for their predicament; that is, they were seen as the undeserving poor. Interviews were heavily loaded with moral assessment. Poverty in other people's lives was usually viewed as a consequence of individual ineptitude or moral failure. Others were blamed particularly for their inability – or unwillingness – to 'manage'.

Based on Shildrick and MacDonald (2015)

Questions

1. Identify the strengths and weaknesses of the research methods used in the study.

2. Analyse the impact of economic change and poverty on people who took part in the study.

3. Using information from this article and elsewhere, evaluate the view that people in poverty share a common experience.

Health problems and low life expectancy

The bare existence associated with all social groups in poverty can lead to health problems and can even lower life expectancy. Two problems which are central to this issue are poor diets and poor quality housing.

1. Food poverty – the inability to afford, or have access to, food to make up a healthy diet – is increasing according to Lansley and Mack. They note that there has been an increase in the number of poor people cutting back on food and meals because they have run out of money or because another bill has the priority. They estimate that half a million children are not adequately fed. Schools have responded to this by providing breakfast clubs. Poor diet is a major risk factor in terms of disease. For example, the Royal College of Physicians (2005) reported that it contributes to almost half of heart disease and a third of cancers. With regard specifically to poor children, poor diet contributes to low birth weight, obesity, dental problems and lack of concentration at school.

2. Poor housing is also contributing to poor health. In 2012, nearly 20 per cent of children lived in damp homes, while 2.5 million children lived in homes that were both damp and cold. Children who live in such housing are three times more likely to suffer from coughing and respiratory illnesses, and 25 per cent more likely to become seriously ill by the age of 33 compared with other children.

Poverty of resources, relationships and identity

People in poverty not only lack income but also the skills, qualifications and health to achieve a good standard of living, and the ability to make choices and to make the most of opportunities. Poverty undermines people's ability to establish strong and supportive relationships, and to successfully maintain family and community life. Instead, the poor often live in fragmented and hostile communities with all of their associated social problems. The poor are also likely to lack a strong sense of self-worth and may lack belief in their ability to escape poverty. Poverty can lead to poor self-esteem, a lack of wellbeing, poor mental health, and even drug and alcohol misuse.

CONCLUSIONS

Whichever definition or measurement of poverty sociologists adopt, there is evidence that poverty is a significant social problem in the UK that profoundly and negatively affects the daily lives of a diverse range of social groups. Moreover, this chapter points to the difficulties involved in escaping from such deprivation. The next chapter focuses on the range of sociological theories that aim to explain the persistence of poverty in the UK.

CHECK YOUR UNDERSTANDING

1. Identify three reasons why disabled people are likely to be in poverty.

2. Identify two reasons why fuel poverty is particularly a problem for the elderly.

3. Define what is meant by the 'feminisation' of poverty.

4. Define what is meant by the 'precariat'.

5. Define what is meant by the 'jinxed generation'.

6. Outline and explain the relationship between stigma and poverty.

7. Outline and explain why people are poor despite having jobs.

8. Explain why some ethnic minorities are more likely to be poor than White people.

9. Analyse and explain why inter-generational poverty occurs.

10. Outline and evaluate the view that the social distribution of poverty is diverse.

TAKE IT FURTHER

Keep up with the latest figures for poverty in the UK by visiting the websites of charities such as the Child Poverty Action Group, the Joseph Rowntree Foundation, Age UK, Scope and The Trussell Trust.

6.4 EXPLAINING THE EXISTENCE AND PERSISTENCE OF POVERTY

LEARNING OBJECTIVES

› Understand the difference between individualistic and sociological views of poverty (AO1).

› Understand the difference between dependency-based and exclusion-based sociological explanations of poverty (AO1).

› Analyse the overlap between sociological perspectives on and ideological views of the causes of poverty (AO3).

› Evaluate the strengths and weaknesses of different explanations of poverty (AO3).

INTRODUCING THE DEBATE

As we have seen in Chapter 2, people disagree about how poverty should be defined. They also disagree about how it should be explained. Two basic lines of division can be identified. The first is between those who favour individualistic explanations and those who favour sociological explanations. The second is between sociologists who think poverty can best be explained by focusing on the poor and sociologists who argue that one needs to look *beyond* the poor to how the wider social system works.

This gives rise to two basic types of sociological explanations:

› *dependency-based explanations* argue that poverty is the result of the cultural and behavioural characteristics of the poor; such explanations include the belief that there is a specific section below the working class that does not want to work, called the underclass

› *exclusion-based explanations* focus on the way in which some people are 'made to be poor' by the economic and political system.

INDIVIDUALISTIC EXPLANATIONS

Individualistic explanations are perhaps the most prevalent type of 'common-sense' explanation of poverty. Moreover, as neoliberal ideas emphasising individualism and self-reliance have become more influential in British society in recent decades, so have such explanations.

In this view, poverty is a product of the alleged deficiencies of poor people as individuals: they are, it is claimed, lazy, disorganised, unable to budget, lacking in self-control and feckless.

Criticisms of individualistic explanations

If one wished to explain, say, why one family in a street were poor while their neighbours weren't, individualistic explanations may have some value. But for sociologists they are inadequate as explanations of poverty for the following reasons:

> they tend to be *value-laden* rather than objective

> they imply that poor people are inherently different from the non-poor, ignoring the fact that people may move in and out of poverty during their lives

> they fail to recognise that people belong to groups and societies, and that their lives are shaped by social forces over which they may have little or no control

> they fail to see poverty as a *social* phenomenon.

DEPENDENCY-BASED EXPLANATIONS

These sorts of sociological explanations argue that the poor are, in some way, the cause of their own poverty. At their most extreme, they suggest that the welfare system in the UK actually makes people dependent on it by providing an attractive alternative to work. Two different approaches exist.

The culture of poverty

The idea of a culture of poverty was originally suggested by Oscar Lewis (1966) in his study of poor people in Mexico. Lewis argued that poor people in a 'class-stratified and highly individualistic society' were likely to develop a set of cultural values that trapped them in their poverty. It is important to stress these ideas of class and individualism, for Lewis is not arguing that poor people are necessarily deficient. He believes that they are caught in a society that really does put barriers in their path – but that the poor themselves help to ensure that they are trapped by developing a set of values that prevent them from breaking out of poverty. These cultural values include:

> a sense of fatalism and acceptance of their poverty

> an inability to think for the long term

> a desire for immediate enjoyment.

BUILD CONNECTIONS

The values identified as characteristic of a culture of poverty are the same as those referred to by sociologists who favour cultural explanations of working-class underachievement in education.

Educational success in this view is linked with notions of mastery (that one is in charge of one's destiny) rather than fatalism, long-term horizons rather than short-term, and deferred gratification (making sacrifices now for the sake of future gains) rather than immediate gratification. (See Topic 1, Chapter 2 for more on this.)

The underclass or 'benefits culture'

The underclass approach is a development of the cultural explanation for poverty, but it extends the analysis much further and introduces a **New Right** (or **neoliberal**) critique of the American and British welfare systems. In the culture of poverty thesis, the 'cause' of poverty lies in a cultural adaptation to a highly class-stratified society; in the underclass approach, on the other hand, poverty is a response to cultural, economic and welfare changes.

UNDERSTAND THE CONCEPT

Neoliberalism and the **New Right** are alternative ways of talking about a set of political ideas/beliefs that have, arguably, dominated political discourse in the UK, USA and beyond since the 1980s. The key idea informing neoliberalism is that individual freedom is best guaranteed by the 'free market' and that the role of the state is to promote private enterprise (through privatisation, for example) and remove barriers to the free operation of markets (by removing government regulation, for example). Beyond this, the state should do as little as possible consistent with maintaining social order and providing a minimal safety net for those genuinely unable to support themselves (because of illness or disability, for example).

The argument, developed most prominently by the American political scientist Charles Murray in 1989, is that an underclass exists in Britain and the USA consisting of people "at the margins of society, unsocialised and often violent ... and who cannot provide for themselves" (see Figure 6.4.1). These people prefer to live off the state rather than to engage in regular work. By underclass, Murray means a significant and self-reproducing group who form a distinctive element at the bottom of the class structure. Murray accepts that there are poor people who are poor through no fault of their own. Nevertheless, he believes that the bulk of poverty is caused by those who do not make the effort to earn a living, and/or waste what they do have. Murray's analysis is slightly different for the USA and the UK. His analysis of the USA focuses heavily on 'American Blacks' as the source of the underclass; in the UK, his analysis is not race based.

Murray argues that the underclass distinguishes itself through the following factors.

> *Crime* – A very high proportion of violent and property crime is carried out by a small proportion of the population.

> *Illegitimacy* – There are very high levels of children born outside marriage (and in particular to never-married women) among the underclass. These children are the outcome of casual sex, and the fathers have no interest in supporting the child or the mother.

> *Economic inactivity* – Here, Murray is referring to the high levels of long-term unemployment that characterise the same relatively small group of people. He argues that it is not that they are unemployed in any traditional sense, but that they prefer to collect state benefits and to work in the **hidden** or **shadow economy**.

In an update published in February 2000, Murray argued that the alleged British underclass continued to grow and was driven by "the breakdown in socialisation of the young, which in turn is driven by the breakdown of the family", citing the growing rate of illegitimacy as a crucial piece of supporting evidence.

UNDERSTAND THE CONCEPT

The **hidden** or **shadow economy** refers to economic activity that is both unregulated and out of sight of HMRC, where work is done for cash. A report issued by a think tank, the Institute of Economic Affairs, in 2013 estimated that Britain's shadow economy was worth about £150 billion, or 10 per cent of national income.

Murray's views – though not his use of the term 'underclass' – were reflected in David Marsland (1996), *Welfare or Welfare State*. Writing also from a New Right perspective, Marsland presented a stinging critique of the welfare state, arguing that it "undermines the psychological foundations of personal autonomy by sapping individuals of their native capacity for enterprising, self-reliant behaviour". Welfare provision was needed by a "small and changing minority of people", Marsland conceded, but it should be provided by the private sector and voluntary organisations, not by the state. (See Chapter 5 for more on this debate.)

If someone does a job for cash in the shadow economy in order not to pay VAT and income tax, they are involved in *tax evasion* and are breaking the law. Many large corporations in the UK – such as Starbucks, Google and Amazon – organise their tax affairs so that they can avoid paying corporation tax. For example, Amazon had sales of £3.35 billion in 2011 in the UK, but paid just £1.8 million in tax (BBC News, 21 May 2013). This is *tax avoidance*.

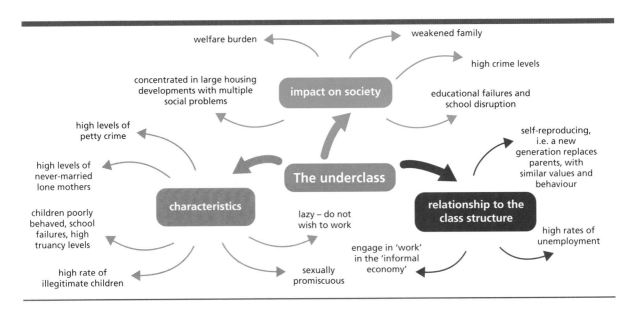

Figure 6.4.1 *Murray's view of the underclass*

Tax avoidance is legal. What do you think are the sociological implications of this distinction between tax avoidance and tax evasion?

From scroungers to skivers

The idea that there is a 'large group' of people in British society that are happy to 'play the system' and live off the state has been around since at least the 1980s. At that time, much attention was paid by the tabloid press to alleged 'scroungers'. Today, it is so-called 'skivers' or 'shirkers', who are contrasted with hard working 'strivers':

"Where's the fairness for the shift-worker, leaving home in the dark hours of the early morning, who looks up at the closed blinds of their next door neighbour sleeping off a life on benefits… We speak for all those who want to work hard and get on… They strive for a better life. We strive to help them."

George Osborne, October 2012

"Welfare is there to help people who work hard, it shouldn't be there as a sort of lifestyle choice."

David Cameron, April 2013

Source: New Economics Foundation, (2013)

That there are some people who do 'play the system' is undoubtedly true. Most people who live in deprived neighbourhoods can point to families like the fictional Gallaghers, the stars of the Channel 4 series *Shameless* that ran from 2004–2013. However, it is a big jump from this to the idea that there is a permanent underclass in UK society characterised by a distinctive subculture that keeps people more or less permanently dependent on the state. Indeed, Imogen Tyler (2013), writing about the widespread use of the underclass narrative by sections of the media to explain the 2011 riots in England, sees the term as a "powerful political myth" which is used by neoliberal governments to legitimise increasingly punitive welfare policies.

During 2014 and 2015, both Channel 4 (*Benefits Street* and *Britain's Benefit Tenants*) and Channel 5 (*Benefits Britain: Life on the Dole*) broadcast documentary series focusing on benefit recipients and streets where a high proportion of residents were dependent on benefits. Some critics described the programmes as 'poverty porn'. What do you think they meant by this? Do you agree?

Criticisms of the underclass theory

Ruth Lister (1996) has argued that the term underclass is too 'elastic' and 'imprecise' to be useful for shaping sociological research.

Empirical evidence does not support the idea that there are generations of workless, work-shy families. Research by Lindsey Macmillan (2011) based on the government's Labour Force Survey, found that in households with two or more generations of working age, there were only 0.3 per cent where neither generation had ever been in legitimate employment.

Most benefit claims are short term. The charity Elizabeth Finn Care (2012) reported that less than half of Job-Seekers' Allowance ('dole') claimants claim the benefit for more than 13 weeks and fewer than 10 per cent claim for more than a year. People in receipt of benefits in the long term (over 5 years) are generally those with long-term or severe disabilities and those who care for them informally. Moreover, over half of social security spending goes to pensioners, and the majority of children and working-age adults in poverty – as officially defined – live in working, not workless, households.

The idea that illegitimacy is confined to a group of people belonging to an underclass is implausible. The proportion of children born outside marriage/civil partnerships had reached 47.5 per cent in England and Wales by 2012.

Finally, dependency-based explanations assume that poverty can be explained without looking beyond those in poverty. The theories we will now go on to look at dispute this.

EXCLUSION-BASED EXPLANATIONS

Exclusion-based explanations come in two main groups: those deriving from consensus theories and those deriving from conflict theories. The former seek to explain poverty in functionalist terms; the latter argue that the poor are poor because they are prevented from achieving a reasonable standard of living by the actions of the more powerful or because of the way capitalism works.

The functions of poverty

According to Herbert J. Gans, poverty "survives in part because it is useful to a number of groups in society". In an article in the *American Journal of Sociology* in 1972–3, he identified a list of 15 positive functions of poverty, including:

› "Poverty helps to ensure that dirty, dangerous, menial and undignified work gets done.

> The poor subsidise the affluent by saving them money (for example, domestic servants, medical guinea pigs...).

> Poverty creates jobs in a number of professions (e.g. drug pedlars, prostitutes, pawnshops, army, police).

> Poverty helps to guarantee the status of the non-poor."

Criticisms of the function of poverty theory

Gans says little in his article about the dysfunctions of poverty and nothing about functional alternatives. A more adequate functionalist analysis would require a consideration of these points. Additionally, Gans's approach does not provide any explanation of why the extent of poverty may vary over time or from one society to another. As Peter Townsend (1979) commented, while Gans's list of functions shows that there are groups in society with a vested interest in perpetuating poverty, Gans doesn't explore "the interrelationships between groups and the sources and conditions of their power".

Conflict perspectives on poverty

Conflict theorists view societies as made up of groups with conflicting interests and unequal resources, status and power. Three broad categories can be distinguished: feminist, Marxist and Weberian. Feminists prioritise gender divisions. Marxists prioritise class divisions. Weberians argue that social divisions vary from time to time and from society to society, and involve a plurality of cross-cutting allegiances. Politically, feminism is not aligned with any single ideology, but Weberian approaches can be linked to **social democracy**, while Marxist approaches can be linked to **socialism**.

UNDERSTAND THE CONCEPT

Social democracy and **socialism** are left-wing political ideas/beliefs that are critical of capitalism. Social democrats believe that capitalism can be made to work in the public interest so long as the state takes an interventionist role in both society (for example, through welfare provision) and the economy (for example, through regulating how private companies operate). Socialists, on the other hand, think that capitalism will inevitably benefit the few at the expense of the many. Traditionally, this meant that they believed in bringing the economy into state ownership. Socialism is closely associated with Marxism, but the two are not the same: socialism is a political ideology; Marxism is a theory of society and history.

Feminist explanations of poverty

Feminist perspectives of poverty start from the recognition that it is women rather than men who are more likely to be poor. This feminisation of poverty is seen as having its roots in patriarchal social arrangements that entrench gender inequalities. See Topic 1, Chapter 4 for more on the theories of patriarchy.

An important source of such inequality is the unequal distribution of caring roles between men and women, which means that the majority of unpaid, informal caring of children, disabled people and elderly people is carried out by women. This is reflected, for example, in the fact that one-parent families are overwhelmingly female-headed – 91 per cent in 2014 (ONS).

Different strands of feminism explain these facts in different ways. Some – such as radical feminism – focus exclusively on patriarchy, others – such as socialist feminism – focus on the interaction of gender and class. However, it is postmodern feminism that has most clearly recognised that women's experiences are not all of a kind through their embrace of the notion of intersectionality (see Chapter 1).

Criticisms of feminist explanations of poverty

Feminist explanations of poverty are embedded in their general theories of gender inequality. This is both a strength and a weakness: a strength in that it avoids the mistaken belief that poverty can be explained by focusing just on the poor; a weakness in that they have nothing to say about poor men.

Marxist explanations of poverty

Marx himself, unlike Victorian philanthropists such as Charles Booth and Seebohm Rowntree, was dismissive of those at the bottom of society, characterising them as the *lumpenproletariat*. Contemporary Marxists are more sympathetic.

Marxists see poverty as an inevitable outcome of the capitalist system. According to Marxist theory, the economy is owned and run by a small ruling class, who exploit the majority of the population who work for them. Poverty cannot be explained if one focuses simply on the poor because, as Kincaid (1973) put it: "It is not simply that there are rich and poor. It is rather that some are rich *because* some are poor".

According to Ralph Miliband (1974), the poor are not separate from the working class, but simply the most disadvantaged among its members. Their position is

FOCUS ON RESEARCH: POVERTY FIRST HAND

Beresford et al. (1999) pointed out that most research undertaken on poverty had been by 'experts' and pressure groups. Typically, they collected statistics on poverty and then worked out the numbers of people in that situation. Even the definition of poverty was provided by these experts. Beresford et al. wanted to find out the views and attitudes of poor people themselves. In order to do so, they approached a wide variety of local groups across the country, mainly composed of people on low incomes, and then interviewed representatives from each. In all, 137 people were interviewed.

The results showed that living in poverty was a difficult and demoralising situation, in which people felt stigmatised by the attitudes of others. The majority of the people believed that the causes of poverty were in the way society was organised, rather than in individual failings. They vehemently rejected the notion of the underclass. They expressed a desire to find work if they could, and, for those already in employment, to find better-paid work.

Based on Beresford et al. (1999)

Questions

1. What method of primary research was used in this study?

2. How representative of the poor do you think the sample was likely to be?

3. What were the views of the sample on the causes of poverty?

4. How valid do you think this method is in terms of establishing poor people's beliefs?

5. Why might poor people's views on the causes of poverty not provide an adequate explanation of poverty?

---

a result of their lack of political power, which is itself a product of their economic deprivation. Consequently:

› their lack of economic resources means that they cannot afford to organise themselves as a pressure group

› they lack effective sanctions – such as the withdrawal of their labour, available to trade unionists – with which to threaten the powerful

› they are unable to mobilise widespread support among the working class because of policies of 'divide and conquer' pursued by the powerful

› they are politically handicapped by the stigma associated with poverty.

In addition, for Westergaard and Resler (1976), while the welfare state was a concession wrested from the ruling class by the working class after the Second World War, it is used by the rich and powerful to provide just enough in the way of services and benefits to prevent a serious challenge to their authority. In this way, the potential for the working class to become not only a **class in itself**, but

also a **class for itself** has been 'contained'. For Marxists, then, poverty will persist so long as we have capitalism.

UNDERSTAND THE CONCEPT

For Marxists, a **class in itself** is a group of people who occupy a distinctive position in relation to the economy but who lack class consciousness (that is, they don't see themselves as belonging to a class). A **class for itself** is a group who are aware of belonging to a social class and who act collectively in their class interests.

Criticisms of Marxist explanations of poverty

Critics of Marxism claim that it fails to explain why poverty is unequally distributed among different groups.

Marxist theories rightly locate poverty as a feature of the wider structure of inequality within capitalist societies, but they imply that, in the absence of socialism, poverty is unavoidable. Social democrats disagree.

For Marxists the state is inevitably biased towards promoting the interests of the rich. Critics disagree, arguing that the state is neutral and can act in the public interest.

"What thoughtful rich people call the problem of poverty, thoughtful poor people call with equal justice a problem of riches." R.H.Tawney (1913).

Why do you think that sociology textbooks – including this one – have whole chapters on poor people but not on rich people?

Social democratic theories of poverty

Where Marxists see capitalism as in need of *replacement*, social democrats see it as capable of *reform*. Similarly, where the New Right are against what they call *state interference*, social democrats are in favour of *state intervention* to tackle poverty.

Social democratic theories of poverty tend to reflect Weberian rather than Marxist perspectives, arguing that in democratic societies, power is not inevitably concentrated in the hands of the wealthy and that the state can act as a neutral mediator between competing social classes and status groups.

An example of a social democratic perspective from the last century is provided by Townsend. Townsend saw the distribution of resources through the labour market as the crucial determinant of occupational classes and consequently the distribution of income. But he also saw status as playing a role. Poverty, he argued, was concentrated in what he called 'minority groups' – elderly people, disabled people, the chronically sick, the long-term unemployed and one-parent families – who had low status and were either excluded from or discriminated against within the labour market.

An example of a social democratic perspective on poverty today is provided by Lansley and Mack (2015). In 2012, nearly 30 per cent of the population fell below the poverty threshold determined by the consensual measure used in their research (see Chapter 2), compared to 14 per cent at the time of their first study in 1983.

They attack both individualistic and New Right explanations of poverty, arguing that it is "rising inequality, especially towards the very top [of the income distribution] that lies at the heart of the spread of deprivation".

The crucial factor for Lansley and Mack is the pursuit of neoliberal economic policies by successive governments – including Labour ones – based on the idea that increasing wealth would 'trickle down' to those on lower incomes and thereby benefit everyone. As we saw in Chapter 1, this hasn't happened. Since the 2007/8 banking crisis, austerity policies have hit those at the bottom of society hardest, in proportional terms. An Institute for Fiscal Studies (IFS) report in January 2015 stated that low-income families with children had borne the brunt of the Coalition government's austerity drive.

In a statement clearly reflecting their belief that the key social agency in determining levels of poverty is government, the IFS states that "the historically and globally high levels of poverty in the UK can be traced directly to the political choices taken by successive governments over the last three decades".

Criticisms of the social democratic theory of poverty

Townsend does not adequately explain exactly how class and status interrelate to produce poverty. New Right critics would argue that the higher taxes necessary to achieve greater income equality would act as a disincentive to entrepreneurs (people who set up businesses). Marxist critics would argue that governments have limited autonomy under capitalism and that multinational corporations increasingly dictate government policies in liberal democracies.

FOCUS ON SKILLS: 'COMMENT' BY POLLY TOYNBEE

Note: *The article below is taken from a national daily newspaper,* The Guardian. *Newspapers do not provide impartial information. The article appeared in the 'Comment' section, rather than the news section, where writers are expected to express a particular point of view in a forthright way. The Guardian is generally seen as left-of-centre politically and Polly Toynbee is one of their longest-standing commentators.*

There can rarely have been a better fit for Ebenezer Scrooge than Iain Duncan Smith. He told Andrew Neil on the BBC's Sunday Politics that he wants child benefit limited to a family's first two children. It would save money and prompt "behavioural change".

Back in 1974 Keith Joseph destroyed his Tory leadership hopes with this speech: "A high and rising proportion of children are being born to mothers least fitted to bring children into the world … Some are of low intelligence, most of low educational attainment. They are unlikely to be able to give children the stable emotional background, the consistent combination of love and firmness … They are producing problem children … The balance of our human stock is threatened."

Sir Keith had four children but apparently they didn't threaten "our human stock". These days, what he said might be less controversial: it's an everyday right-wing press platitude.

Some themes deep in the heart of Toryism just never go away. Up they pop, over and over. Control the lower orders, stop them breeding, check their spending, castigate their lifestyles. Poking, sneering, moralising and despising is hardwired within Tory DNA.

The desire to extirpate the poor goes back a long way. In 1913 the eye-opening report 'Round About a Pound a Week' by Maud Pember Reeves and her group of Fabian women (republished by Persephone Books) detailed the household accounts of mothers trying to keep their families on the average £1 manual wage. The report's

irrefutable evidence showed that wages were too low to live on, puncturing the perpetual myth among the comfortable (then as now) that the working classes were "bad managers". In fact, these mothers scrimped every farthing, maximising calories in bread and dripping.

I was reminded of that book because Pember Reeves wrote angrily of middle-class assertions that no one should have children until they can afford them. She pointed out that working families would never have any if they waited for that day – but, of course, that is what Duncan Smith wants.

Pember Reeves was even more scathing about the well-off who preach what she calls contemptuously "the gospel of porridge". Ah, porridge! Right on cue, up popped Lady Jenkin, wife of Tory MP Bernard Jenkin, last week: "Poor people don't know how to cook. I had a large bowl of porridge today, which cost 4p." She was presenting the Church of England report which found that 4 million people are going hungry.

The Mail hurried to her home and she told them how to cook a three-course meal for 57p – soup, rice and lentils, and banana and custard powder. The Mail's verdict? "Simple, filling and very tasty." So here we are, back with the argument that never changes: poverty is caused by fecklessness and dependency, not by sub-survivable rates of pay.

The baroness had no wise tips for how a family on the minimum wage should procure a Christmas present for a child: home-knitted socks? Easier for people such as her to ignore the steep fall in real wages, or that only one in 40 net jobs since 2008 has been for a full-time employee, according to the TUC. Easier to overlook Monday's report from the Office for National Statistics showing the bottom 10 per cent have suffered much higher rates of inflation than the well-off, spending more on food and fuel.

Of the unthinkable £48bn cuts Osborne announced in his autumn statement, the only specific one that he, Duncan Smith and the others keep crowing about is another £12bn to be cut from benefits, confident that Tory polling finds welfare cuts still popular.

Source: Toynbee (*The Guardian*, 16 December 2014)

Questions

1. **Explain** which theory/theories of poverty are favoured by the Conservatives (Tories), according to Toynbee. (Provide evidence from the article to support your claim.)

2. **Explain** what themes from earlier times are reflected in the views of present-day Tories about the causes of poverty.

3. **Analyse**. Toynbee's article appeared in *The Guardian* newspaper and she refers to an article in the (*Daily*) *Mail*. What do these articles suggest about the political sympathies of these two newspapers?

4. **Evaluate**. How far do you agree with Toynbee's criticisms of Tory policies? (Support your answer with evidence.)

CHECK YOUR UNDERSTANDING

1. Define the 'hidden economy'.

2. Explain in your own words what is meant by individualistic explanations of poverty.

3. Identify two reasons why sociologists reject individualistic explanations of poverty.

4. What is the basic difference between dependency-based and exclusion-based explanations of poverty?

5. Identify two criticisms of dependency-based explanations of poverty.

6. Identify one strength and one weakness of feminist explanations of poverty.

7. Identify two differences between social democratic and Marxist explanations of poverty.

8. Identify two weaknesses of Marxist explanations of poverty.

9. Identify two weaknesses of social democratic explanations of poverty.

10. Some writers talk about government actions as state 'interference', some describe the *same* actions as state 'intervention'. Explain the difference. (Hint: you need to think about the different connotations – associations – of the two terms).

TAKE IT FURTHER

In order to feel confident about answering questions on this topic, it is helpful to understand something about the political background to the theoretical and empirical debates around poverty explored in this chapter and the next. The following table summarises the broad changes since 1945:

Date	Political party forming the UK government	Dominant political ideology embraced by government
1945–1979	Both Labour and Conservative governments at different times	Social democracy
1979–1997	Conservative	Neoliberal/New Right
1997–2010	('New') Labour	Third Way
2010–2015	Coalition government (between Conservatives and Liberal-Democrats)	Neoliberal/ New Right

Use the internet to find out more about the different political ideologies identified in the third column. (Make sure you think about the likely validity, impartiality, reliability and credibility of each website you use.)

6.5 WELFARE

LEARNING OBJECTIVES

> Understand the nature of welfare provision in the UK (AO1).

> Understand how the mix of welfare provision displays both continuities and changes (AO1).

> Analyse the influence of different political ideologies on the development of the welfare mix (AO3).

> Evaluate the views of neoliberals and social democrats of the Welfare State (AO3).

> Analyse the role of the voluntary sector and informal care in welfare provision (AO3).

INTRODUCING THE DEBATE

Welfare is concerned with people's wellbeing. The term refers to four related but distinct things:

> cash payments by the state to working-age people who are out of work

> cash payments by the state to anyone in need (aka social security or social protection)

> social security, plus the whole range of welfare services provided by the state, including health, housing and education

> all welfare provision, whoever provides it.

It is in the last of these senses that the term will be used here.

In any society, there are potentially four main types of providers of welfare: the state (or public sector); private (for profit) providers; not-for-profit community and voluntary organisations (also known as 'the third sector' or charities); and informal providers (family, friends and neighbours). The mix of these four providers varies across time and across societies.

In most advanced industrial societies, the state is far and away the biggest provider of welfare. In the UK, in 2014–15, total government spending was forecast to be £732 billion. Of this, £489 billion – about two-thirds – would be on state welfare (the 'Welfare State'), with 44 per cent of this going on social security and tax credits.

Given the sums involved, the state's role in welfare provision is a matter of intense political debate. This chapter will explore that debate by:

> briefly returning to the different political perspectives involved

> describing how the state came to be the biggest provider of welfare in the twentieth century, and the continuities and changes in provision since then

> examining the continuing debate provoked by New Right criticisms of the Welfare State, which have had a profound influence on the public's view of 'welfare'

> examining the role of community and voluntary organisations and informal providers.

PERSPECTIVES ON THE WELFARE STATE

To understand the changes to the welfare mix that have taken place in the UK since the Second World War, we have to understand what motivates governments' policy decisions. The starting point, arguably, is the set of political beliefs or the **political ideology** a government embraces, because this guides their view both of what is *desirable* and what is *possible*. While these beliefs/ideas do not determine a government's policies, they inevitably influence them.

UNDERSTAND THE CONCEPT

Political ideologies are sets of beliefs about how countries should be governed and what relationships should be had with other countries. They involve underlying assumptions about the nature of people and society, which are largely left unexamined by the ideology's supporters.

In representative democracies such as the UK, political ideologies alone don't determine government policy. There is a wide range of other factors that constrain any government's freedom of action, particularly public opinion, as this translates into electoral preferences. To put it simply, governments may not pursue the policies they'd ideally like to pursue because they would lose too many votes. Cabinet papers released in 2012 suggested that in 1982, Margaret Thatcher and her Chancellor, Geoffrey Howe, had asked her Central Policy Review Staff to examine the possibility of dramatically reducing the role of the state in welfare provision, particularly in relation to health and education. However, some individuals within the Cabinet who opposed the plan that was drawn up leaked details to the papers and the resulting public outcry forced her to claim that the ideas were "all a total nonsense".

The main political ideologies that have influenced the Conservative party since the Second World War have been conservatism (note the small 'c') and neoliberalism. Those that have influenced Labour have been socialism, social democracy and neoliberalism. We have already covered socialism, social democracy and neoliberalism in Chapter 4, so it just remains to briefly describe conservatism before going on to examine how welfare has developed since 1945.

Conservatism
Conservatism emphasises tradition, law and order, and duty. Human nature is seen as too imperfect to allow society to dispense with tradition and firm government. The (traditional) family, schools and churches are seen as having a crucial role to play in promoting public morality. In terms of welfare, the rich have a responsibility to help the poor (*noblesse oblige*), but conservatives prefer this to be done through charity rather than through an extensive Welfare State.

A Conservative campaign poster criticising Labour's approach to welfare

Tony Blair, as PM, claimed that New Labour was "beyond ideology... we are interested in whatever works". David Cameron, as PM, declared: "We are not driven by some theory or some ideology. We are doing this as a government because we have to." Why do you think that politicians deny that their policies are 'ideological'?

WELFARE BEFORE THE WELFARE STATE

Prior to the Second World War, the state played only a limited role in relation to social security, housing and health care. State pensions had been introduced in 1911 and there was limited state assistance for the sick and unemployed, but the poor were mainly dependent on charity and informal financial support. Council housing had been introduced in 1919, but the majority of the population, lacking the funds to buy their own home, relied on private rented accommodation. In health care, employed men had been covered by state health insurance since 1911 for primary (GP) care, and local authorities provided secondary care in the form of 'municipal hospitals' for rate-payers. But those unable to afford private health care were largely dependent on voluntary hospitals and informal care. State education, by contrast, had been introduced in 1870, but unless their parents could afford independent school fees, education for the majority of children ended at 13.

WELFARE SINCE THE SECOND WORLD WAR

During the war, the coalition government commissioned Lord Beveridge to produce a plan for the reconstruction of society after the war was over. The plan he produced – the 1942 'Beveridge Report' – provided the blueprint for a new system of welfare in which the state would be the major player.

Beveridge identified what he called the five 'evils' which he felt the government needed to wipe out (see Table 6.5.1). These were: want (poverty), ignorance, disease, squalor and idleness. The resulting policies, introduced between 1944 and 1948, brought about the NHS, an extension of schooling, the social security system, an increase in social housing and a commitment to full employment. This system became known as the 'Welfare State'.

Despite the fact that it was a Conservative politician – Winston Churchill – who led Britain to victory, a Labour government was elected at the end of the war in 1945 and, over the next six years, largely enacted Beveridge's blueprint.

Social evil	Welfare State
Want (poverty)	Poverty was to be tackled by payment of unemployment and sickness benefits, and a 'safety net' benefit that would cover everyone not covered by these other benefits known as 'national assistance'.
Ignorance	Free secondary schooling was to be extended to all (to age 15), and new schools were to be built.
Disease	A National Health Service (NHS) was to be set up, whereby everyone would have a right to free health care, both primary and secondary.
Squalor (poor housing)	A programme of house-building was to be undertaken to get rid of poor-quality housing ('slums').
Idleness (unemployment)	The government was to commit itself to ensuring that 'never again' would there be a return to the mass unemployment of the 'Great Depression' in the 1930s.

Table 6.5.1 *Beveridge's blueprint for the Welfare State*

WELFARE PROVISION SINCE 1951

1951–1979: Social democracy

While there were many switches between Labour and Conservative governments during this period, there was a dominant social democratic consensus around the idea that the state should play the major role in welfare provision. Consequently, while there were many reforms, the basic structure remained the same.

1979–1997: New right/neoliberalism

1979–1997 was a period of Conservative governments, led first by Margaret Thatcher and subsequently by John Major. The postwar social democratic consensus disappeared and New Right ideas became politically dominant. The Welfare State came to be seen by many on the right as a bad thing. Thatcher called it the 'nanny state', the implication being that it had *infantilised* people (treated adults like children), taking away their capacity for self-reliance and self-responsibility.

Thatcher and Major's governments believed that the Welfare State treated adults like children.

The term 'nanny state' carries negative connotations. Can you think of any terms used about the Welfare State that carry positive connotations? If not, why do you think this is?

While both Thatcher and Major were unsuccessful in their quest to shrink the Welfare State – the proportion of national income spent on it was actually slightly higher in 1997 than 1979 – they did introduce some significant reforms inspired by neoliberal ideas. In particular:

> council house tenants were granted the 'right to buy' their rented properties and responsibility for 'social housing' was largely transferred to third sector housing associations

> social security benefits were increasingly means-tested

> residential care was increasingly transferred from local authorities to private and voluntary providers

> an 'internal-market' was introduced into the NHS which allowed GP practices to purchase patients' health care from private providers.

1997–2010: The third way

During the period 1997–2010 there was a succession of Labour governments under Tony Blair and then Gordon Brown. Blair deliberately characterised his party as 'New Labour' because he wanted to distance the party from its previous socialist associations in the electorate's mind (although it is still officially a 'democratic socialist' party according to its constitution).

Tony Blair's New Labour aimed to distance itself from the socialist positioning of earlier Labour governments.

Blair followed an ideology he called the 'third way', which sought to position the party between neoliberalism on the right and social democracy on the left. This approach was heavily influenced by the writings of the British sociologist Anthony Giddens.

Giddens argued that enormous social and economic changes were occurring in advanced Western economies such as the UK, ushering in a new era which he called 'Late Modernity', and that new forms of social institutions, including welfare, needed to be created to respond to these changes. The changes which most heavily impacted on poverty were:

> the restructuring of the labour market with globalisation and the ending for most of a 'job for life'

> the increased rate of divorce and family breakdown, the growth of single-parent households and the growth in women's employment.

Giddens also argued that the notion of income poverty as an isolated problem for the Welfare State was misguided, and should instead be seen as just one aspect of a wide swathe of linked disadvantages better thought of as 'social exclusion' (see Chapter 2).

This new approach was spelled out in New Labour's welfare reform Green Paper in 1998: "The Welfare State now faces a choice of futures. A privatised future, with the Welfare State becoming a residual safety net for the poorest and most marginalised; the status quo, but with more generous benefits; or the Government's third way – promoting opportunity instead of dependence, with a Welfare State providing for the mass of the people, but in new ways to fit the modern world."

New Labour welfare reforms

The welfare policies introduced under New Labour reflected this desire to give people, in Blair's words, 'a hand up, not a hand out'. Among the specific policies introduced were:

> 'Welfare to work' policies, as in the 'New Deal', which required people on Jobseekers Allowance (JSA) to accept offers of work experience, voluntary experience, education or training, or face benefits sanctions

> changes designed to tackle the problem of 'working poverty' (being employed but still in poverty), such as the introduction of a statutory minimum wage and Working Families Tax Credit (subsequently divided into Child Tax Credit and Working Tax Credit) to boost low wages

> an increased role for the private sector within the NHS in England, covering both primary and secondary care

> public/private partnerships, such as the Private Finance Initiative, in which the private sector built hospitals and schools and then rented them to the NHS and local authorities respectively

> policies designed to tackle social exclusion, such as Sure Start centres, which offered support to parents of preschool children in deprived areas

> the introduction of an 'academy' programme in secondary schools in England and Wales, removing schools from local authority control.

Waiting lists for social housing increased as the reduction in stock caused by the 'right to buy' (a policy that continued under New Labour) was not matched by new builds.

Expenditure on the Welfare State was significantly higher as a proportion of national income in 2010 than it was in 1997, partly as a result of significant increases in expenditure on health care and in social security payments following the 2007–08 financial crisis.

2010–2015: The return of neoliberalism

In 2010, a coalition government of the Conservatives and Liberal-Democrats replaced New Labour, with David Cameron (Conservative) and Nick Clegg (Liberal-Democrat) as PM and Deputy PM respectively. Neoliberalism again became the dominant political ideology.

From the start, the coalition government made it clear that reform of the Welfare State would be a central focus. In their first month in office, they published a *State of the nation report: poverty, worklessness and welfare dependency*, which reiterated New Labour's focus on paid employment as the surest route out of poverty.

The report detailed a wide range of issues it wished to address, including: the fact that numbers in relative poverty (households below 60 per cent of median income) had increased since 1998/99 among single adults and couples without children; the fact that the proportion of the UK population in poverty was higher than in many other EU countries, including France, Germany and Portugal; and the fact that 4 million people in the UK had been on an out-of-work benefit for nine or more of the previous ten years.

Coalition welfare reforms

The NHS in England was reorganised, with local Clinical Commissioning Groups having the responsibility to commission (buy) health care services from any qualified provider in the state, private or voluntary sector. This resulted in a further increase in the role of private sector companies within the NHS.

In education, New Labour's academy programme was significantly expanded to include primary schools and 'free schools' – state-funded schools which could be set up by businesses, voluntary organisations or parents. By January 2014, 57 per cent of state-funded secondary schools were academies.

Numbers on waiting lists for social housing continued to rise as the austerity programme continued to cause cuts in subsidies for new social housing. Financial penalties relating to Housing Benefit were introduced in 2013 for working-age tenants of social housing for 'under-occupancy' (the so-called Bedroom Tax).

Many reforms were made to the social security system, including a benefits cap, harsher sanctions and the introduction of Work Capability Assessments for those moving from Incapacity Benefit to Employment Support Allowance. However, the major reform was the introduction of Universal Credit to replace six existing benefits for unemployed working-age people or those on a low income, and designed to simplify the benefits system and tackle the **unemployment** and **poverty traps**. Expenditure on the Welfare State as a proportion of national income was slightly lower in 2013–14 than in 2010.

UNDERSTAND THE CONCEPT

The **poverty trap** occurs when there is no financial incentive to *get a better paid job* because of the loss in benefits and the increase in taxes and other costs.

The **unemployment trap** occurs when there is no financial incentive to *get a job* because of the loss in benefits and the increase in taxes and other costs.

Note: sometimes the term 'poverty trap' is used to cover both of these circumstances.

WELFARE SINCE 1945: AN OVERVIEW

We can divide the period since 1945 into two halves. From 1945–1980, state provision of welfare became dominant, the Welfare State grew enormously and there was widespread public and political support for it. From 1980–2015, state *funding* of welfare continued, but the *provision* of welfare services was increasingly transferred from the state to the private and voluntary sectors, while social security expenditure, under the influence of neoliberal ideas, became an increasingly toxic political issue, which we will now examine.

FOCUS ON RESEARCH: WELFARE REFORMS FAIL TO MOVE TENANTS INTO WORK

Note: The following article is taken from the magazine Inside Housing *and refers to primary research carried out by social researchers at the London School of Economics. The research involved face-to-face interviews of a representative sample of working-age social housing tenants in the South-West of England. In 2013, 200 tenants were interviewed, and all those traceable and willing (123) were reinterviewed in 2014. The shortfall was made up by interviewing a further 77 tenants.*

The research produced both qualitative and quantitative data.

A Labour campaign against Conservative government

The coalition's welfare reforms have failed to help social housing tenants into work, an academic study commissioned by social landlords said today.

Research by the London School of Economics (LSE), found just one in six tenants had either found work or increased their hours in 2013/14.

The report, 'Is Welfare Reform Working?', which surveyed 200 social housing tenants in the south west of England, said the majority of the social tenants found their links with their job centre 'unhelpful'.

It found that tenants face 'persistent' barriers to work, including ill health, disability, caring responsibilities, low confidence and unaffordable transport costs.

Tenants who found work most commonly worked for family members or became self-employed and most of the new jobs were part-time and flexible hours, the report also said.

Ministers have made repeated claims that their reforms to the benefit system are helping people to find work.

A study commissioned by the Department for Work and Pensions (DWP) published in November found

19 per cent of households hit by the benefit cap in May 2013 were in work after a year compared to 11 per cent for a similar uncapped group.

However, interviews conducted by the LSE report authors suggested that benefit sanctions had shifted jobseekers' focus away from work and redirected their attention to finding alternative ways to cover basic living costs.

A total of 126 out of 200 tenants (63 per cent) said they were managing financially by reducing expenditure, in some cases on food, getting into debt to pay large bills, or borrowing from family and friends.

A DWP spokesperson said the report was "not nationally representative or suitably robust". "Our welfare reforms are restoring fairness to the benefit system and make sure that work pays," the spokesperson added.

Source: Spurr (2015)

Questions

1. What was the purpose of this research?

2. Explain how the research was able to produce both qualitative and quantitative data.

3. Suggest one advantage and one disadvantage of using face-to-face interviews.

4. A spokesperson for the government's Department of Work and Pensions rejected the report on the basis that it was "not nationally representative or suitably robust". Explain and evaluate this claim.

5. What does this study suggest about the effectiveness of the Coalition government's social security reforms?

The New Right critique of the Welfare State

The New Right have developed a series of arguments that attack the Welfare State and see it, both directly and indirectly, as one of the main causes of poverty. New Right theorists, such as Marsland (1996) (see Chapter 4) argue that in a democratic, capitalist society, wealth is created by those people who successfully run companies, and by others who innovate, have entrepreneurial ideas and start new companies. Everyone else relies upon these people for jobs, and therefore incomes. These 'entrepreneurs' (people who start new businesses) are motivated by money, and it is therefore up to government to encourage entrepreneurs and owners of successful companies to flourish. This is best done where there is a 'free market' – an economic system where there are a number of competing firms seeking to offer their services, and where the government does not interfere.

Welfare as an indirect cause of poverty

In order to ensure that entrepreneurs are well rewarded, taxation must be kept as low as possible. This is done by minimising the size of the government and keeping expenditure as low as possible. The Welfare State – including provision of state benefits for those without employment – is the largest area of government spending, employing a massive array of people to deliver benefits and services. Without the costs of employing the staff and the expenditure on welfare payments, taxes could be much lower. The Welfare State is therefore an indirect cause of poverty, because:

› it discourages the efforts of entrepreneurs to start new companies which would create new jobs

› it hinders successful, established companies by burdening them with taxes.

Welfare as a direct cause of poverty

Welfare also has a direct role in causing poverty. This is because the Welfare State actually undermines the will to work. It does this by providing free health and care services, plus financial support for those who do not want to work. So those who prefer to live on state benefits can do so, thus placing a huge burden on the rest of the population in the form of increased taxes and lost productivity. Murray (1990) coined the term 'the underclass' to describe this group (see Chapter 4).

The Welfare State as the cause of (nearly) all that's wrong with society

Perhaps the most extreme critique of the Welfare State is that provided by James Bartholomew (2013, orig. 2004) in his book *The Welfare State We're In*. He provides a long list of society's contemporary ills which, he contends, are the result of the Welfare State, among them: permanent mass unemployment; avoidable deaths in the NHS; rising illegitimacy; single parenthood; truancy; falling standards in schools; and declining standards of behaviour.

Criticisms of the New Right approach

The New Right approach has been heavily criticised on a number of grounds.

› The idea that there is a permanent underclass beneath the working class has already been evaluated (Chapter 4).

› Critics claim that poverty would increase if the Welfare State were abolished. Tax credits and the minimum wage help to protect workers from exploitative employers. If there were no Welfare State, society would be split between a wealthy minority and a mass of the poor who would have little stake in society.

› The fact that critics can point to failings in state provision of welfare does not mean that alternatives would necessarily be better. There is plenty of evidence of failings where the private sector has taken over provision.

› The fact that various social ills have appeared in society at the same time as the growth of the Welfare State does not mean that the latter has necessarily caused the former. This is to confuse **correlation** with **causation**.

› Legally, private companies' primary responsibility is to their shareholders. The resulting pressure to keep costs down may militate against the ability of private companies to provide welfare services that meet the needs of their clients.

UNDERSTAND THE CONCEPT

Two variables are correlated if when one changes the other does too. If they both move in the same direction they are *positively* **correlated**; if they move in opposite directions they are *negatively* correlated. The fact that two variables are correlated doesn't necessarily imply that one is **causing** the other. It may just be coincidence, or there may be a third variable causing both.

A SOCIAL DEMOCRATIC REJOINDER TO THE NEW RIGHT

John Hills (2015) has written a powerful rejoinder to the New Right attack on the Welfare State in his book *Good Times, Bad Times: The Welfare Myth of Them and Us*.

Hills argues that two beliefs currently dominate the public's view of the Welfare State: that most welfare expenditure goes on unemployment support, and that society can be divided into two groups (those who benefit from the Welfare State and those who pay for it.)

According to Hills, both of these beliefs are mistaken.

> State spending on all out-of-work benefits in 2014/15 was £38 billion. This represents less than a fifth of the total spent on social security (£207 billion) and less than a tenth of the total Welfare State bill (£489 billion). To put it another way, spending on out-of-work benefits and tax credits amounts to £1 out of every £12.50 of total welfare expenditure. Pensions actually account for the largest amount of the total social security and tax credits bill, amounting to £114 billion in 2014/15.

> The dominant effect of the Welfare State is to redistribute income across the life-cycle rather than from one group to another. Working-age households pay more in tax than they receive in services and benefits, but this reverses after retirement. Just about everyone contributes to the Welfare State (for example, through VAT) and just about everyone receives something back at some stage of their lives (for example, through Child Benefit or state pensions).

BUILD CONNECTIONS

The issue of objectivity is one that applies across the board in sociology. Max Weber thought that it was crucial, if sociology was to be scientific, that sociologists should seek to produce a 'value free' analysis, even if they themselves could not avoid holding values as citizens. Most contemporary sociologists are less convinced that this is possible, but nevertheless believe it is important to be impartial. Howard Becker, by contrast, argued that it was naïve to think that objectivity was achievable and that sociologists therefore had a duty to 'support the underdog' and to use their scholarship to promote their interests.

Alan Bryman has argued that objectivity is like 'perfect cleanliness': it can never be achieved, but that doesn't make it less worthwhile to pursue. What do you think?

SUMMING UP THE POLITICAL APPROACHES TO THE WELFARE STATE

Evaluating such a politically charged topic is a real challenge for sociologists and we should acknowledge that any attempt to do so is unlikely to be entirely objective. Nevertheless, a number of conclusions about the debate examined above can be suggested.

> There is little evidence to support the existence of a large, permanently excluded underclass in Britain.

> There is considerable confusion about the Welfare State because of the different ways in which the word 'welfare' is used. The Welfare State is not just a provider of cash benefits.

> The majority of social security is spent on pensions, not on out-of-work benefits.

> The number of those experiencing in-work poverty is currently higher than those in out-of-work poverty.

> There are many beneficiaries of social security besides the poor. For example, Housing Benefit subsidises private landlords and Working Tax Credit subsidises employers.

> Many people find themselves in the poverty trap and unemployment trap. An alternative solution to cutting the level of social security benefits would be to raise the minimum wage or the income tax threshold.

> Poorer people pay a bigger share of their income in tax than richer people. According to Bradshaw (2013), the poorest 10 per cent of households paid 35 per cent of their gross income in tax (including indirect taxes such as VAT), while the richest 10 per cent paid 34 per cent.

> Whether they acknowledge it or not, government policies on welfare always advantage some and disadvantage others. To pretend otherwise is disingenuous. Table 6.5.2 gives a brief summary of different attitudes to poverty and welfare.

THE ROLE OF THE THIRD SECTOR IN WELFARE PROVISION

The role played by community and **voluntary organisations** (CVOs) in providing welfare services has grown enormously in recent years. Their funding comes from donations, central government and local government. In 2010, the National Council for Voluntary Organisations reported that the sector had earned over £9 billion in income from delivering statutory contracts, a rise of 128 per cent since 2000/01.

Approach	View of Welfare State	View of poor people	Strategy to eliminate poverty	Role of government
New Right/ Neoliberal	BAD – wasteful and inefficient; undermines the will to work	Lazy or less able than successful people	To let entrepreneurs create wealth for themselves and therefore jobs for others	To create the conditions for successful commerce, e.g. low taxes, few regulations
Conservative	As above	A mixture of the feckless and the unfortunate	Charity plus minimal benefits	Provision of a safety net
Social democratic	GOOD – role is to ensure a fair society	Unfortunate people	An all-encompassing Welfare State paid for through tax	To organise, provide and fund a 'free' Welfare State
Marxist	Hides the true exploitation of the majority of the population by the rich minority	Exploited by the ruling class	REVOLUTION – Take over control of the economy and the state	Governments in capitalist societies are just there to represent the interests of the ruling class

Table 6.5.2 *Solutions to poverty: a summary of different perspectives*

UNDERSTAND THE CONCEPT

Voluntary organisations are not made up solely of volunteers; most involve a mixture of volunteers and paid staff. In 2010, voluntary organisations in the UK employed 668,000 people. They are called voluntary organisations because their existence is not required by law, so in this sense they are 'voluntary'.

There are close to 200,000 charities in the UK and the range of welfare services provided is enormous, ranging from foodbanks and refuges for victims of domestic violence, to support and advice for drug addicts, and including housing associations and academies.

THE 'BIG SOCIETY'

The Conservative Party Manifesto in 2010 talked about revolutionising the role of the third sector in welfare provision: "Our alternative to big government is the Big Society: a society with much higher levels of personal, professional, civic and corporate responsibility; a society where people come together to solve problems and improve life for themselves and their communities; a society where the leading force for progress is social responsibility, not state control."

In a paper, *Building the Big Society*, published in May 2010, the new Office for Civil Society said that the government would:

> encourage volunteering and involvement in social action

> encourage charitable giving and philanthropy

> introduce a National Citizen Service for 16-year-olds

> support the creation and expansion of mutuals, co-operatives, charities and social enterprises, and support their greater involvement in the running of public services

> use funds from dormant bank accounts to establish a Big Society Bank to provide new finance for neighbourhood groups, charities and social enterprises.

Evaluation of the Big Society

Little has been heard about the Big Society since 2013, although many of the policies associated with it are still operating.

According to the think tank Civil Exchange, in a report published in January 2015, while the programme had produced some "genuinely positive initiatives" it had failed to deliver against its original goals: "Attempts to create more social action, to empower communities and to open up public services, with some positive exceptions, have not worked. The Big Society has not reached those who need it most. We are more divided than before."

In response, the Cabinet Office claimed that the report did not fairly reflect "the significant progress made" and failed to acknowledge the success of initiatives such as the National Citizen Service, Big Society Capital, public service mutuals and the transfer of public assets to the voluntary sector.

One of the most dramatic indicators of the effects of the Coalition government's austerity drive and reform of social security has been the growth of foodbanks provided by the voluntary sector. Vouchers for food are distributed by specified agencies, such as doctors' surgeries, schools, churches, social services, Citizens' Advice Bureaux and Jobcentres, to people judged to be in crisis.

THE ROLE OF INFORMAL CARE IN WELFARE PROVISION

Before the introduction of the Welfare State, the main form of welfare provision was that provided for free by family, friends and neighbours. Far from becoming a marginal feature of welfare provision today, such informal care continues to play a vital role in society.

Economists refer to the core economy: all the unpaid time, caring, support, friendship, expertise, giving and informal teaching that underpin the formal economy.

Putting a monetary value on the core economy is impossible, precisely because it is unpaid and, by necessity, unregulated. However, there is data available on a specific part of it: informal care provided by carers – people who provide unpaid care for those who are sick, disabled or too frail to care for themselves.

According to Carers UK, in a briefing published in May 2014:

> 6.5 million people in the UK are carers

> every year over 2.1 million adults become carers and almost as many cease to be carers

> 3 in 5 people will be carers at some point in their lives

> 58 per cent of carers are female, 42 per cent are male

> almost 178,000 under-18s have caring responsibilities

> the care provided is worth an estimated £119 billion annually.

While this work is unpaid, it is supported by a social security benefit called Carer's Allowance. This can be claimed by people who act as carers for at least 35 hours per week and was worth £61.35 per week in March 2015. Research indicates that many carers feel marginalised and unsupported and, according to the New Economic Foundation (2013) "have found their time and capacity increasingly stretched by reduced local public services, changes to working and child tax credit and insecure low-paid employment".

With an ageing population and increasing rates of dementia, informal care is likely to become an increasingly significant part of welfare provision.

FOCUS ON SKILLS: ARE FOODBANKS BEING ABUSED?

Note: *Remember that newspapers are not impartial sources of information. The* Daily Mail *and* Mail on Sunday *are both generally seen as right-wing and pro-austerity. While the Toynbee article was taken from the 'Comment' pages, this article is taken from the 'News' pages. You need to think about why the* Mail on Sunday *would be keen to publish a news story that appears to cast foodbanks in a negative light.*

Volunteers for a charity that blames welfare cuts for the soaring use of its food banks have admitted that fraudsters routinely 'take advantage' of the handouts.

The Trussell Trust, the UK's biggest provider of food banks – which highlighted a 'shocking' rise in demand for emergency food packages last week – last night pledged to investigate after volunteers were filmed admitting that people could take free food without checks, and that many visitors were asylum-seekers.

One worker said that people regularly 'bounce around' locations to receive more vouchers than they are entitled to.

A Mail on Sunday investigation has also found inadequate checks on who claims the vouchers, after a reporter obtained three days' worth of food simply by telling staff at a Citizen's Advice Bureau – without any proof – that he was unemployed.

Undercover reporters posing as volunteers at food banks in London and Nottinghamshire also found:

› Staff at one centre gave food parcels to a woman who had visited nine times in just four months, despite that particular centre's own rules stipulating that individuals should claim no more than three parcels a year.

› Volunteers revealed that increased awareness of food banks is driving a rise in their use.

› Staff at a supermarket, where shoppers are encouraged to buy extra food and donate it to a local food bank, were alleged to be later turning up to claim the food themselves.

According to the Trussell Trust's statistics, more than 913,000 people received three days' emergency food from its banks in 2013–14 compared with 347,000 in 2012–13.

The charity, which runs more than 400 of Britain's 1,000 food banks, acknowledged that a third of the food was given to repeat visitors, but insisted the rise was based on genuine need for emergency food.

Individuals experiencing severe financial hardship are able to claim food vouchers but there are no clear criteria on who should be eligible. Once received, the vouchers can be exchanged for three days' worth of food at an allotted centre. The Trussell Trust has a policy that an individual can claim no more than nine handouts in a year, but undercover reporters found this limit varied in different branches.

One volunteer, who had been helping the charity for more than a year, said that he regularly saw the same people claiming more food parcels than they were entitled to. He said one woman who attended Friday's session had visited at least nine times in just four months, receiving food each time. He added: "It's got to the point where I recognised names because you see them so frequently." The volunteer also said he suspected that several people, possibly other family members, had been collecting vouchers under the woman's name.

A female volunteer showed a reporter a list of people who had claimed more than three food parcels, but she said that they would be unlikely to be refused items if they visited again. In another case, a man was given a food parcel after turning up without a voucher – only a form from the Jobcentre. He was handed the food despite a female volunteer earlier saying: "We're not supposed to give it out."

Last night the Trussell Trust said it would investigate allegations of abuse, adding: "There is no evidence to suggest that awareness of the food banks is driving an increase in visitors, rather that food bank use is meeting a real and growing need."

Source: Murphy and Marshall, No ID, no checks... and vouchers for sob stories: The truth behind those shock food bank claims *Mail on Sunday*, 19 April 2014

Questions

1. **Identify** the alleged abuses of foodbank rules uncovered by the *Mail on Sunday*.

2. **Analyse** why the *Mail on Sunday* considers it significant that 'many visitors were asylum-seekers'.

3. **Explain.** How would a) a neoliberal, and b) a social democratic perspective interpret the evidence provided in this article?

4. **Evaluate** the *Mail on Sunday's* claim that this article provides "the truth behind those shock food bank claims".

CHECK YOUR UNDERSTANDING

1. Indicate the four different ways in which the word 'welfare' is used.

2. Name the four different types of welfare provision in society.

3. Explain the difference between socialism and social democracy.

4. What were the five evils the Beveridge Report identified?

5. Identify two welfare reforms made by Conservative governments between 1979 and 1997.

6. Identify two welfare reforms made by Labour governments between 1997 and 2010.

7. Identify two welfare reforms made by the Coalition government since 2010.

8. Identify one way in which the Welfare State can be seen as an indirect, and one as a direct, cause of poverty, according to neoliberals.

9. Identify two criticisms of the neoliberal view of the Welfare State.

10. What is the Big Society?

TAKE IT FURTHER

One of the long-running debates surrounding social security is whether benefits should be 'universal' or 'selective'.

Selective benefits are benefits targeted at those most in need. Eligibility is normally established through means-testing, that is, by checking that the recipient's resources ('means') in terms of income and wealth are below a specified level. Examples of this type of benefit would be Housing Benefit and Income Support.

Universal benefits are benefits that are provided to all who are eligible, irrespective of their resources. Examples would be the State Pension and Child Benefit. Some universal benefits depend on prior National Insurance contributions (State Pension), others do not (Child Benefit).

There are arguments for and against both types:

Universalism	Selectivism
Arguments for:	Arguments for:
Ensures that all those in need receive it	Avoids giving money to those who don't need it
Avoids the stigma associated with means-testing	
Arguments against:	Arguments against:
Wastes money by providing benefits to those who don't need them	Requires an expensive bureaucracy to administer it
	Often results in significant levels of non-claiming by eligible people

Hold a class debate debating the motion: 'This house believes that Child Benefit should be means-tested'.

6.6 WORK

LEARNING OBJECTIVES

› Distinguish between work, non-work and leisure (AO1).

› Recognise the different spheres within which work takes place (AO1).

› Understand the nature of the UK as a post-industrial society (AO1).

› Examine the relationship between technology and work (AO3).

› Examine the nature and significance of worklessness (AO3).

› Understand current debates around globalisation and work (AO1).

INTRODUCING THE DEBATE

"It's true that hard work never killed anybody, but I figure, why take the chance?" (Ronald Reagan, USA President 1981–89).

Most people have an ambiguous relationship with work. On the one hand, besides being a vital source of income, it provides a structure

to their lives, social status and, if they're lucky, job satisfaction. On the other hand, it can be a source of stress, frustration and even exhaustion. However, since a significant proportion of most people's lives is taken up with working, it is clearly of importance sociologically.

WORK, NON-WORK AND LEISURE

Common sense suggests that 'work' is something that involves mental or physical effort – or both – which, on balance, we'd prefer not to have to do given the choice, but which we do because we need the money. Yet we only have to look at people who've chosen to spend their leisure time taking aerobics classes or weight training to see that effort is not limited to work, and most people whose wealth would be sufficient to allow them not to work nevertheless often choose to do so.

Similarly, work is not equivalent to paid employment. Pupils and students aren't paid to sit in class or to do assignments outside class, but nevertheless – much to the bemusement of their teachers and lecturers! – they tend to see both these activities as work rather than leisure. Domestic labour – housework, childcare, do-it-yourself (DIY), and so on – are all clearly forms of work, even if unpaid. Moreover, to complicate matters further, the same activity – singing, say – can be both a job and a leisure activity.

The way round these difficulties is to recognise that it isn't particular kinds of activities that distinguish work from leisure, but their social meanings. What counts as work and what counts as leisure is culturally and historically variable: 'work' and 'leisure' are social constructs. Campaigns as diverse as those mounted by housewives, informal carers and prostitutes ('sex workers') to get what they do recognised as 'real' work, illustrate this.

What counts as work, then, is not fixed, but it is nevertheless useful to distinguish it from leisure and non-work. Leisure activities involve some degree, at least, of choice and hoped-for pleasure. Non-work includes all of those activities which we have little or no choice about, but which we are highly unlikely to be paid for: sleeping, eating, washing, travelling, and so on.

SPHERES OF WORK

We can further distinguish between three main spheres of work-related activities: the core economy, the formal economy and the shadow economy.

The core economy

This phrase, which is a fairly recent coinage within economics (for example, New Economics Foundation (nef), 2011), refers to the many kinds of unpaid work carried out by families, friends and neighbours out of affection, duty or tradition. It includes cooking, cleaning, care work, DIY, gardening, voluntary work and many other activities which are largely taken for granted, yet are essential to the working of the wider society.

The formal economy

This is the sphere within which most of what is officially recognised as work takes place. It is the sphere of paid labour, of jobs, occupations and careers, and of income tax and national insurance. It involves employers, employees and the self-employed and it is regulated, to a greater or lesser extent, by the state.

The shadow economy

As the name suggests, this is the sphere where work that is paid but is hidden from the view of the state takes place. Such work is sometimes divided into two subcategories: the *grey economy*, which involves work that is legal but undeclared for tax purposes (for example, repair work done for cash-in-hand), and the *black economy*, which involves illegal work (for example, drug dealing and manufacturing, selling counterfeit goods or smuggling). Work carried out for the Institute for Economic Affairs estimated that the size of the UK shadow economy was £150 billion in 2012, or 10 per cent of national income.

In 2008, the UN issued a directive to member states to start including estimates of the size of the shadow economy in calculations of Gross National Income (GNI) – the total value of all incomes received by the population of a country. In order to comply with this directive, the EU required its member states to change the methods used to calculate GNI from September 2014 to include *illegal transactions to which all parties involved consented* (so it would include illegal drug purchases, say, but not theft or robbery).

Consequently, in September 2014, the Office for National Statistics (ONS) for the first time included estimates of the money spent on prostitution and illegal drugs in the UK. In 2013, it estimated that prostitution added £5.65 billion and illegal drug sales £6.62 billion to the economy, amounting to about 0.7 per cent of the total.

What problems do you think are likely to be involved in trying to estimate the monetary value of these two activities? How do you think the estimates were arrived at? (You can check out how the ONS addressed these challenges in an article by Abramsky and Drew on the ONS website published on 29 May 2014.)

EMPLOYMENT IN THE UK

Long-term trends in a global context

Over the last 50 years, the UK has undergone a process of 'de-industrialisation': there has been a substantial decline in jobs in manufacturing and a corresponding increase in jobs in the service sector.

As Table 6.6.1 shows, by 2009 the service sector as a whole provided 83.6 per cent of jobs in the UK, while manufacturing accounted for only 10 per cent.

This development was anticipated in an influential book published in 1976 by the American sociologist, Daniel Bell, entitled *The Coming of Post-Industrial Society*. Bell predicted that, in future, economic growth would depend upon the generation and application of scientific and technical knowledge. He thought that post-industrial societies would be dominated by a new 'intelligentsia' of professional and technological workers.

The increasingly important role played by information and communications technology (ICT) in contemporary society fits well with Bell's predictions, but what he didn't – perhaps wasn't able to – predict was the parallel development of globalisation and its effect on work.

	1978	1988	1998	2008	2009	Change 1978 to 2008	Change 2008 to 2009
Agriculture and fishing	1.7%	1.4%	1.3%	1.0%	1.0%	-0.7%	-
Energy and water	2.8%	1.8%	0.8%	0.7%	0.7%	-2.1%	-
Manufacturing	28.5%	20.7%	17.0%	10.5%	10.0%	-18.0%	-0.6%
Construction	5.7%	5.1%	4.4%	4.8%	4.8%	-0.8%	-
Distribution, hotels and restaurants	19.5%	21.3%	23.8%	23.6%	23.5%	4.1%	-0.1
Transport and communications	6.5%	5.9%	5.7%	5.9%	5.8%	-0.7%	-0.1%
Finance and business services	10.5%	14.8%	18.1%	21.4%	20.8%	10.9%	-0.6%
Public administration, education and health	21.1%	24.5%	24.2%	26.9%	28.1%	5.8%	1.2%
Other services[1]	3.8%	4.5%	4.7%	5.3%	5.4%	1.5%	0.1%
All industries (=100%) (millions)	24.3	23.7	24.7	27.2	26.5	2.9	-0.7

[1] *Community, social and personal services including sanitation, dry cleaning, personal care, and recreational, cultural and sporting activities*

Table 6.6.1 *Employee jobs by industrial sector (UK), 1978–2009 (%).*
Source: Social Trends (2010)

UNDERSTANDING GLOBALISATION

Globalisation is a complex process with many different strands, but one of its key features is the increasing internationalisation of the production, distribution and management of goods and services since the 1980s, facilitated by the neoliberal policies – pursued by most governments in the developed economies – of financial and labour market deregulation, trade liberalisation and privatisation.

Castells (2000) has identified three developments in particular that have been associated with this process: the integration of world financial markets, the growth of multinational corporations (MNCs) and the growth of foreign direct investment (FDI), where companies owned in one country invest in or take over companies owned in another.

Very few countries in the world (North Korea and, until 2015, possibly, Cuba are excepted) now operate outside the reach

of this system of global capitalism. Until the late 1980s there were alternatives to capitalism, notably the state socialist, centrally-planned economies of China, the USSR (Union of Soviet Socialist Republics) and Eastern Europe. However, with the disintegration of the USSR, popular revolutions in Eastern Europe in the 1990s, and growing economic liberalisation in China – dubbed by the media 'The Collapse of Communism' – capitalism has become the dominant form of economic organisation world-wide.

Globalisation: the example of KFC

KFC (originally, Kentucky Fried Chicken) is the world's second largest restaurant chain after McDonalds. It has around 19,000 outlets in 118 countries, including around 4,500 in China. It is owned by a USA company, Yum! Brands, which also owns Pizza Hut and Taco Bell. About 10 per cent of KFC outlets are owned directly by the company, the rest are operated by franchise holders. BBC1 broadcast a three-part documentary on KFC in April 2015 entitled *The Billion Dollar Chicken Shop*.

Globalisation and the labour market

These developments have led to a significant restructuring of the labour market over the last three decades. According to Lansley (2011): "there has been a rise in the number of well-paid professional and managerial jobs, a decline in the number of middle-paid and skilled jobs, and a rise in the number of routine low-paid service jobs. Alongside this 'hollowing out of the middle' has been a steady growth in the number of 'bad jobs' that offer poor conditions of work, minimal rights and little security."

We will return to these emerging features of work today at the end of the chapter, but first we need to review how sociologists' understanding of work under capitalism has developed.

ORGANISATION AND CONTROL OF THE LABOUR PROCESS UNDER CAPITALISM

Sociology emerged as a response to the enormous social changes ushered in by industrialisation in Europe in the nineteenth century. Much of the work of all three 'founding fathers' of sociology (Durkheim, Marx and Weber) explored the impact of these changes on society.

Industrialisation was associated with a number of far-reaching social and economic changes, including:

> *urbanisation* – the growth of towns and cities

> *mechanisation* – the replacement of manual labour by machinery and the growth of factories

> *specialisation* – a new 'division of labour' (how the work to be done in a society is split up) involving an ever greater narrowing of focus on specific jobs or aspects of jobs

> *rationalisation* – the replacement of traditional ways of doing things by methods based on scientific knowledge and impersonal calculations.

Durkheim and industrialisation

Durkheim was interested in the impact of industrialisation on 'social solidarity': the (assumed) need for people to feel part of a collective whole if society was to function effectively. In his book *The Division of Labour in Society* (first published in 1893), he argued that industrialisation involved the movement from a traditional to a modern society and from one form of social solidarity to another.

In traditional societies there were relatively low levels of specialisation, people lived in smaller communities and there were lower levels of social differentiation. People shared the same, religiously inspired values and identified with others. He called this 'mechanical solidarity'.

Modern society, by contrast, entailed a more specialised division of labour, larger communities and, consequently, higher levels of social differentiation. People no longer produced most of what they needed themselves, but relied on the labour of others to produce the goods and services they needed. This interdependence had the potential to produce a different form of solidarity, 'organic solidarity', based not on people's resemblance to each other, but on their different yet interdependent roles.

However, Durkheim was conscious of the fact that the greater individualism associated with industrial societies could threaten social solidarity and saw an important role for occupational associations, legal contracts and state action to counterbalance this potentially divisive force. He feared that the rapid pace of social change under industrialisation could lead to a breakdown of shared norms and values, or what he called **anomie** (literally, normlessness).

UNDERSTAND THE CONCEPT

For Durkheim, human wants and desires were potentially infinite. People needed a system of norms and values provided by society so that they could know what to expect out of life, thereby keeping these desires in check. Sometimes, however, situations arose – for example, during times of rapid social change – where society failed to provide such guidelines because social norms were unclear, conflicting or unintegrated. Durkheim referred to this as **anomie**.

BUILD CONNECTIONS

Anomie has proven to be a fruitful concept for exploring the psychologically destabilising effects of changes in status such as retirement and unemployment, where previous routines no longer provide purpose or structure to a person's life. It has also been used, most famously by Robert Merton, to suggest why deviant behaviour may occur. Merton argued that people socialised to embrace the 'American Dream' of financial success for all, but denied legitimate opportunities to be successful, would experience anomie and turn to illegitimate means of achieving success – or to other forms of deviant behaviour.

Marx and industrialisation

While Durkheim was preoccupied with the changes wrought by industrialisation, Marx was more exercised by the fact that it was a particular form of industrialisation that was occurring, namely capitalist industrialisation. For Marx, these changes involved a new stage in the history of class struggle as capitalism replaced **feudalism**.

UNDERSTAND THE CONCEPT

For Marx, history moved through a sequence of stages distinguished by different modes of production. **Feudalism** was the stage that preceded capitalism and was distinguished by class relations based on the ownership and non-ownership of land.

Where feudalism entailed the exploitation of peasants and serfs by the aristocracy, capitalism involved the exploitation of a new class of industrial workers – the 'proletariat' – by the owners of the new forces of production, machines and factories ('capital'), the 'bourgeoisie'.

They were exploited, in Marx's view, not because capitalists were 'evil' people, but because the *surplus* value produced by the workers' labour (the difference between what they were paid in wages and the value of the product their labour produced) belonged not to them, but to the owners and – once the various costs of production had been covered – generated an income for the owners in the form of profit.

It is important to recognise that the idea that capitalism is inherently exploitative is highly controversial. In orthodox economics, profit is the reward enjoyed by entrepreneurs for the risks they take in setting up a business which might or might not generate any profits. The exploitation of workers by owners may perhaps occur, but it is not – in this view – an inevitable feature of capitalism.

Marxists insist that exploitation is built into capitalism and that this is a matter of fact; critics disagree, and argue that to label a relationship 'exploitative' is not a statement of fact, but a value judgement. What do you think? Is capitalism by its very nature exploitative of workers?

Where Durkheim saw anomie as the key danger associated with industrialisation, for Marx it was *alienation*. Under capitalist relations of production, workers were inevitably alienated (estranged) from themselves, their fellow workers and even from the product of their own labour. Work, for Marx, represented the primary human activity and a vital means of personal fulfilment, but under capitalism it became merely a means to an end.

Weber and industrialisation

Weber agreed with Marx that industrialisation brought about a capitalist society, but differed significantly in his understanding of capitalism. Weber said little in his work about exploitation, disagreed about the inevitability of a proletarian revolution and, according to Lowy (2007), was much more ambivalent and contradictory than Marx in his view of capitalism.

Nevertheless, there are certainly passages in his work which indicate that, like Durkheim and Marx before him, there were features of capitalist society that concerned him, particularly those relating to rationalisation. One was the risk that the rational pursuit of profit might come to be seen not as a means to a better life for all, but as an end in itself. Another was the loss of personal freedom and autonomy he feared might occur as societies' institutions and organisations became ever more rational, impersonal and bureaucratic. Humans might find themselves trapped in an 'iron cage' of their own making.

TECHNOLOGY AND THE LABOUR PROCESS

Many of the issues explored and insights offered by Marx, Durkheim and Weber have provided inspiration for the sociological exploration of work in more recent decades.

One of these has to do with the effects of changes in technology on the level of skills required by workers. Technological change advanced rapidly after the Second World War with automation – the control of machines by machines – supplementing mechanisation and, more recently, with the growth of ICT transforming many workplaces.

Fordist production techniques

An influential take on these developments (albeit before the use of ICT in production became widespread) was provided in the 1970s by an American sociologist, Harry Braverman, writing from a Marxist perspective, in his book *Labor and Monopoly Capital: The Degradation of Work in the Twentieth Century* (1974). Braverman believed that the level of skill required in work had

439

been progressively reduced under capitalism, mainly because employers had used 'deskilling' as a method of controlling the workforce.

Employers had been strongly influenced, he claimed, by a school of management connected with an American management theorist – Frederick W. Taylor – and known as 'scientific management'. This involved breaking down the production process into numerous small steps, each of which could be performed with a minimum of training.

Such a production process was exemplified by Henry Ford's mass production of cars in the USA in the early part of the twentieth century, which succeeded in producing high volumes of affordable, reliable cars for the first time by means of the creation of assembly lines where each worker had a highly specialised and relatively simple, repetitive task to perform.

Braverman thought that this process – which had deskilled 'blue-collar' (manual) workers – was, at the time he was writing, being extended to 'white-collar' (non-manual) workers and that as much as 70 per cent of the USA workforce could be seen as having been 'proletarianised', thereby blurring the traditional status boundary between manual and non-manual work.

Production lines became very popular in the first half of the twentieth century.

Post-Fordist production techniques

Braverman's claims have been contested by sociologists who argue that, since the 1970s, production under capitalism has moved into a new 'post-Fordist' era characterised by reskilling and more flexible work roles.

Michael J. Piore (1986) argues that manufacturers have used new technology, particularly ICT, to make manufacturing more flexible. For example, computer

numerical-controlled machine tools can be reprogrammed to perform different tasks. More flexible working is therefore required of workers and such working requires a more flexible organisational structure. Firms are organised less hierarchically with more communication between departments, and workers need a wider range of skills as their work becomes more varied.

A similar view was expressed by Shoshana Zuboff (1988) who, between 1981 and 1986, studied a wide range of different kinds of firms – eight in total – that were either introducing ICT or extending its role. She argues that this technology requires workers to possess theoretical and analytical skills and that this "creates pressure for a profound reskilling" (Zuboff, 1988, p. 57).

Evaluation of technology's effect on the labour process

Stephen Wood (1989), on the basis of his study of two British steel-rolling mills, rejects the reskilling thesis. He found that new technology had helped to increase the range of products produced, but it did not significantly increase the skills needed by workers. He suggested that many of the workers doing highly skilled jobs using the new technology had been skilled workers to start with. Moreover, 'flexibility' meant little more than having to move between different semi-skilled jobs, none of which required much training.

By contrast, support for the reskilling thesis was provided by a major piece of research carried out in the UK in the 1990s using survey techniques to examine labour markets in six localities: Aberdeen, Kirkcaldy, Rochdale, Coventry, Swindon and Northampton.

According to Duncan Gallie (1994), overall, 52 per cent of employees claimed that the level of skill required in their job had increased over the last five years, compared to just 9 per cent who said that it had decreased. Moreover, he found little difference in the experience of upskilling in manufacturing (53 per cent said that they had been upskilled in the last five years) compared with services (50 per cent said they had been upskilled).

These two claims appear incompatible. However, one way round this apparent paradox lies in the possibility that new technology produces *skill polarisation*. Rather than there being either a general increase or decrease in skill levels, new technology may have led to a polarisation of skills in the workforce. Gallie himself suggested this and his view was supported by Bradley, Ericson, Stephenson and Williams (2000): "Some groups of employees, principally those working in managerial, professional and technical occupations, are witnessing an increase in their skills; many others are not."

TECHNOLOGY AND THE EXPERIENCE OF WORK

The picture that emerges of the impact of new technology on skill requirements is far from straightforward. Some see it as inevitably producing a process of deskilling, some the opposite. The picture is further complicated by the fact that some writers see technology as having a determining influence (technological determinists), while others argue that how new technology impacts on skills is dependent on how it is *applied* in the workplace (social determinists).

Similar disagreements are apparent when it comes to the effects of technology on other aspects of workers' experience, such as job satisfaction, a sense of purpose and fulfilment.

TECHNOLOGY AND ALIENATION

The foremost study of the effects of technology on workers' experience of employment in the twentieth century was that of American sociologist Robert Blauner, *Alienation and Freedom* (1964).

Blauner examined the behaviour and attitudes of manual workers in four different industries: printing, textiles, automobiles and chemicals. While not strictly a technological determinist, he nevertheless saw the type of production technology used as the major factor influencing the degree of alienation that workers experienced.

Blauner defined alienation as "a general syndrome made up of different objective conditions and subjective feeling states which emerge from certain relationships between workers and socio-technical settings of employment".

He operationalised alienation by identifying four measurable dimensions:

› the degree of control workers had over their work

› the degree of meaning and purpose they found in their work

› the degree to which workers were socially integrated into their work

› the degree to which workers were involved in their work.

Low scores represented respectively, powerlessness, meaninglessness, isolation and self-estrangement.

On the basis of questionnaire data, Blauner claimed that the lowest levels of alienation were experienced by those working in printing (this was before the introduction of ICT and automated printing processes) and the highest levels by those working in the automobile industry. The alienating effects of the machine technology characteristic of textile production were counterbalanced by workers' strong sense of community. The textile workers in his survey lived in small, close-knit communities, united by ties of kinship and religion. They felt a part of the industry because they were a part of the community.

It was the chemical industry that was the most highly automated at this time and his findings here led him to believe that automation would be associated with lower levels of alienation. Automation meant that workers had considerable control over and responsibility for production through the need for constant monitoring of the production process. Blauner argued that this restored control, meaning, integration and involvement to the workers.

Evaluation of Blauner's study

From a Marxist perspective, Blauner ignored the basic cause of alienation – the objective position of the worker within the relations of production in a capitalist economic system. From this perspective, the printer, the textile worker and the process worker are just as alienated as the assembly-line worker. All are exploited wage-labourers.

Theo Nichols and Huw Beynon (1977) challenge Blauner's claims regarding automation. In a study of seven chemical plants in Britain, they found little evidence that alienation had decreased and that the amount of skilled and rewarding work had increased. Moreover, in six of the seven plants, control-room operatives were a minority of the workforce.

One worker commented: "You move from one boring, dirty, monotonous job to another boring, dirty, monotonous job. And somehow you're supposed to come out of it all 'enriched'. But I never feel 'enriched' – I just feel knackered." (Nichols and Beynon, 1977, p. 16)

Whether workers feel alienated or not is likely to be dependent on what they expect from work. If they have low expectations of work they are unlikely to feel alienated. In a famous study of Vauxhall car workers in Luton in the 1960s, Goldthorpe and Lockwood found that workers displayed an attitude of 'privatised instrumentalism' towards their work (they viewed work simply as a way of making money to support themselves and their family). They therefore felt indifferent towards their work, rather than alienated from it.

According to Zygmunt Bauman (2007) Britain is now a **consumer society** in which identity is no longer associated with people's role as workers but with their role as consumers. If work is simply a means to provide the funds to enable us to pursue particular lifestyles, and we expect to fulfil ourselves through consumption, we would not expect people to invest much of themselves in their work and, hence, not to experience alienation.

UNDERSTAND THE CONCEPT

In a **consumer society**, buying things replaces producing things as the chief source of personal identity. In such societies, the relevance of class declines and people associate themselves with others who share the same lifestyles. Consumer societies, for Bauman, are divided between two main groups, the **seduced** – those both able and willing to embrace consumerism as the principal source of meaning in their lives – and the **repressed** – those who for various reasons are either unable or unwilling to embrace consumerism.

WORKLESSNESS

When people talk about 'worklessness' they usually have in mind the lack of *paid* employment. This is important to bear in mind as it ignores the wide range of unpaid work people undertake in the core economy.

Worklessness can take many different forms: it can be chosen or enforced (for example, voluntary redundancy and compulsory redundancy), it can involve unemployment or underemployment (that is, working fewer hours than one would like), and it can be a temporary or a permanent condition.

It might be thought that, if Bauman is right and we now live in a consumer society where identity is linked to consumption rather than employment, worklessness would be less significant today, both socially and individually. However, the ability to consume for most people is linked directly to their income from employment and, also, sociological research does not support this view.

The pattern of unemployment

Statistics on unemployment do not generally refer to all those without paid employment, but only to the proportion of those who don't have a job but are actively seeking work (defined in government statistics as those who are 'economically active').

The level of unemployment varies between groups. Broadly speaking, it is higher for men, younger working-age groups, ethnic minorities and the disabled.

The difference in unemployment rates for men and women in the UK is slight, with the rate for men this century consistently just 1 or 2 per cent higher than that for women. Other groups display a much greater gap.

For example, according to the *ONS Annual Population Survey*, the unemployment rate between October 2013 and September 2014 for all aged over 16 was 6 per cent, but for those in the 16–24 age group it was nearly three times higher. However, within the 16–24 age group there were marked variations by ethnicity, with youth unemployment at 16 per cent for White groups and twice that for Black groups.

Similarly, disability increases the likelihood of unemployment. According to the *UK 2011 Labour Force Survey*, among those of working age, 40 per cent of disabled people were working (about half the rate of non-disabled people), 25 per cent were (involuntarily) unemployed and 35 per cent were voluntarily unemployed.

There are also significant geographical variations in unemployment. The older industrial areas in the Midlands, the North of England, Scotland and Wales are significantly above the UK average, the South-East significantly below.

The effects of unemployment

Research has linked unemployment with a number of negative consequences for individuals, families and communities: reduced income; elevated rates of physical and mental health problems; loss of self-esteem; increased mortality rates; strained relationships within families; and a decline in social engagement.

Fagin and Little (1984) found through their in-depth study of 22 unemployed men and their families that unemployment impacted negatively on spouses and children as well as the men themselves. Children whose fathers had been out of work for a long time experienced more health and behavioural problems.

Communities with high rates of unemployment tend to display higher rates of crime, a decline in trust levels, an increase in drug and alcohol abuse and a deterioration in the quality of the built environment. Also, they may well experience stigmatisation at the hands of politicians.

FOCUS ON RESEARCH: GENERATIONS OF WORKLESSNESS?

Below is a brief summary of some research carried out in 2012/13 by MacDonald, Shildrick and Furlong, who set out to examine the claim by Iain Duncan Smith (Secretary of State for Work and Pensions) that in the UK there are whole communities where three generations of families have never worked. They interviewed a sample of 47 people across 20 families involving at least two generations. The researchers were unable to locate any family where three generations had been workless.

In the 1950s and 1960s, unemployment was very low – under 2 per cent.

'*Benefits Street* and the myth of workless communities' presents the findings of research which examined two commonly held perceptions about welfare in the UK: whether there are indeed families in which no one has worked for a number of generations; and whether there are whole communities where the vast majority of the population is unemployed. It draws on research conducted in Glasgow's 'Parkhill' and Middlesbrough's 'East Kelby'. Findings indicate that even in these two cases, which were chosen as they represented neighbourhoods with very high levels of worklessness, the majority of people were in work. The research notes that only 38.1 per cent of Parkhill residents were workless

(compared to a worklessness rate of 21.8 per cent in Glasgow, and 14.6 per cent in Scotland) and 30.6 per cent of East Kelby residents (compared to 20.9 per cent in Middlesbrough, and 12.4 per cent in England). The research argues that the idea of 'benefit ghettos' where unemployment is a 'lifestyle choice' is a modern day myth, used by politicians to provide the impetus for government welfare reforms and suggests that rather than assume an 'epidemic of laziness', a proper explanation of worklessness in such communities should seek to understand the rapid deindustrialisation of places and how this has resulted in the economic dispossession of the working classes among the UK's old industrial centres.

Source: MacDonald, Shildrick and Furlong (2014)

Questions

1. The researchers used what they called 'a critical case study method'. What do you think they meant by this?

2. Identify the key findings of this research.

3. Put the final sentence of the summary into your own words.

4. Evaluate the strengths and limitations of this research.

Retirement

Worklessness as a consequence of ageing may appear to be both a natural consequence of biological changes and a welcome release from the stresses and strains of employment. For many this is the case, but for others retirement is associated with both an unwelcome decline in standards of living and the experience of anomie.

The effects depend, crucially, on class and gender. For those with wealth and private pensions, retirement is not inevitably associated with a decline in income, but for others, particularly women, it is.

Also, for many people, the end of paid employment doesn't mean the end of work. Much childcare is carried out by grandparents and levels of voluntary work are significantly higher among the retired. A survey conducted

in 2013 by the Royal Voluntary Service found that two out of five people over 60 were engaged in voluntary work.

Recent changes in the relationship between age and employment illustrate the extent to which age is a social construct. For Cumming and Henry (1961), growing old was inevitably associated with increasing dependency and 'social disengagement'. Hockey and James (1993), by contrast, argue that dependency in old age has more to do with stereotypical assumptions and institutional arrangements (such as compulsory retirement).

Our ideas about old age have also been significantly modified as a result of increasing life expectancy, which increased by two years per decade in the second half of the last century (Harper, 2013). Compulsory retirement was abolished in the UK in 2011, the age at which the state pension can be claimed has been raised and employment rates for older people have been increasing. The employment rate for people aged 65 and over increased from 5 per cent in 2001 to nearly 10 per cent in 2013. The rate among those aged 65–69 was about 22 per cent, with about one-third of these in full-time employment. These trends are likely to continue.

WORK IN A GLOBALISED WORLD: CURRENT ISSUES

Current debates around work reflect the impact of globalisation on employment, the continuing effects of the 2007–08 economic crash and the associated neoliberal austerity policies of governments. They also point to the continuing relevance of earlier sociological concern about, for example, exploitation, rationalisation, flexibility and deskilling.

Rationalisation and deskilling

In *The McDonaldization of Society* (2007, first published 1993), the American sociologist George Ritzer examines how Weber's ideas about rationalisation are exemplified in the organisation of the famous fast-food chain, McDonalds. This organisation is based on the principles of efficiency, calculability, predictability and control, according to Ritzer, and globally more and more firms display these characteristics.

While this form of organisation ensures that customers can rely on a consistent and relatively cheap 'eating experience', this is bought at the cost of deskilling and dehumanisation, in Ritzer's view. Each worker is responsible for a narrowly defined range of tasks requiring little training and is required to display a positive and friendly attitude towards customers at all times.

A study by Leidner (1993) found that interactions between employees and customers were strictly scripted and that employees' compliance was closely monitored. 'Mystery shoppers' were used by McDonalds to monitor employees' self-presentation and if it was not sufficiently friendly the entire shift could lose their bonus. Hochschild (1983) has designated such work **emotional labour**.

Many large chains in the service industry use 'mystery shoppers' to monitor customer experience and workers' compliance with company policies.

UNDERSTAND THE CONCEPT

Emotional labour refers to the process by which workers are expected to manage their feelings in accordance with organisationally defined rules and guidelines. The concept was coined by Arlie Hochschild in her book *The Managed Heart:* The Commercialization of Human Feeling (1983). The sociological literature on emotional labour tends to focus on one of two themes. The first focuses on the organisation, structure and social relations of service jobs. The second focuses on individuals' efforts to express and regulate emotion and the consequences of those efforts.

Globalisation and exploitation

In *No Logo: Taking Aim at the Brand Bullies* (1999), the Canadian writer Naomi Klein argues that MNCs have become so big that they have superseded governments to become the ruling political bodies of a globalised world. Moreover, she claims that corporate rule has been associated with an assault on civic space, civil liberties and employment rights.

Klein focuses mainly on high street retail brands such as Nike, Disney, Wal-Mart, Starbucks and Levi Strauss. She argues that what these companies are selling is not so much products as lifestyles and identities, and that 'logos' (brand identities) are the mechanism by which this is done.

Klein argues that manufacturing has largely been off-shored to countries with lower labour costs and less regulated labour markets, such as Indonesia, China, Mexico, Vietnam and the Philippines. Production in these countries is concentrated in free trade zones (or export processing zones) where workers are expected to work 12-hour days, for 'military style' supervisors, at rates of pay below the minimum wage in the country where the MNCs have their headquarters.

Back home, these companies are developing two-tier workforces: a core of full-time employees enjoy high salaries, secure employment and fringe benefits, surrounded by a larger periphery of workers on part-time and temporary contracts who are often not even employed by the firms themselves but by agencies.

Flexibility and precariousness

In the 21st century, 'flexibility' increasingly refers not to the ability of firms to alter their products and production methods in response to the market, but to the *imposition* of flexible working on workers. Increasing numbers, as Klein claimed, are faced with casual employment, short-term contracts and zero-hours contracts.

FOCUS ON SKILLS: MAID IN LONDON

Below is an edited version of the first post by a blogger who calls herself 'Maid in London', available at:
http://maidinlondonnow.blogspot.co.uk/

THURSDAY, 12 FEBRUARY 2015

Hi…

I'm new here. I'm a room attendant – what may have been known in the past as a 'chambermaid' – but basically, a cleaner.

I work in the housekeeping department of a luxury Four Star hotel in London made up of 350 bedrooms for the rich, the even richer, and people who managed to get cheap internet deals.

My agency contract guarantees me a wage of £24 per week. No I didn't miss a zero there. That's four hours work at the minimum wage of £6.50 an hour.

I'm expected to clean 16 rooms in a 7.5 hour day with a 30 minute unpaid lunch break that goes in the blink of an eye. That's 20 minutes to: change a double (or Queen or Kingsize) bed, perfectly plump and press four pillows, dust two bedside tables, pictures, a desk, an office chair, a table, clean a hospitality tray and replace tea, coffee, milk, sugar and cookies, wipe and 'mop' a bathroom (with a floor duster), wash any dirty cups or glasses, replace soap, shower gel, shampoo, conditioner and body lotion, fold all towels and bath mat, wash a sink and bath/shower and toilet, polish all chrome and hoover everywhere.

Right.

The housekeeping department is all women save for a couple of supervisors and around four young male laundry porters. We're a workforce of around 45 and we're Indian, Nigerian, Sri Lankan, Italian, Romanian,

Bulgarian, Hungarian, Polish, Lithuanian, Czech and Latvian. Around 35 of us clean at least ten rooms per day, covering the entire, five floor, 350 room hotel.

The first three days are training – shadowing and working with a long-term worker.

I had my first day today, trained by a twentysomething Indian woman – Adhira* – who literally seemed to dance around the bed, the room and bathroom spraying, tucking, smoothing, straightening, hoovering and wiping.

She's been doing the job for five years on an agency contract. I learn she has a three year old daughter. I ask why she hasn't been taken on by the hotel direct. She mumbles something about how she had got pregnant so they did not take her on at the time.

I ask her if we're really expected to do 16 rooms per day. 'You cannot do it', she says bluntly. 'It is too hard. Too hard'. She is in a constant state of motion and seemingly exhausted and agitated at the same time. She drinks Red Bull for breakfast.

As I fumble along, unused to the pace, Adhira chides me, 'Faster, faster, faster.' I know that's the logic of capitalism but no one had ever said it to me, over me, like that before.

*All workers' names will be kept confidential.

Questions

1. **Explain** what is meant by an 'agency contract' and **identify** the terms of Maid in London's contract.

2. **Identify** the key features of Maid in London's work.

3. **Explain.** What does the composition of the housekeeping department suggest about the demographic characteristics of those involved in precarious employment?

4. **Explain.** Blogs represent a form of secondary qualitative data. Explain what this means.

5. **Evaluate** the uses and limitations of such data for sociological purposes. (Hint: think about issues of validity, reliability and representativeness.)

According to the ONS, about 700,000 people, or 2.3 per cent of the labour force, were employed on zero-hours contracts in the UK for their main job between October and December 2014. Zero-hours contracts were particularly associated with females and the young. Some people – for example, students – may want the flexibility that such contracts offer, but the Trades Union Congress (TUC) estimated that before the 2007 economic crash, there were 2.3 million underemployed, and by late 2013 numbers had increased to nearly 3.4 million.

According to the British sociologist Guy Standing (2011), insecurity, or what he calls **precariatisation**, is becoming the defining feature of the lives of an increasing section of society. In his book *The Precariat: The New Dangerous Class*, Standing argues that a growing number of workers in the UK and elsewhere, mainly – though not only – towards the bottom of the jobs market, find themselves "expecting a life of unstable labour and unstable living". He speculates that this group could become class conscious and, as the subtitle of his book suggests, challenge the neoliberal social order that has brought them into existence.

UNDERSTAND THE CONCEPT

Standing (2011) states that "to be **precariatised** is to be subject to pressures and experiences that lead to a precariat existence, of living in the present, without a secure identity or sense of development achieved through work and lifestyle". He uses the term in an analogous way to Marx's use of the term 'proletarianisation' to refer to the social processes within industrial society that were generating a new class of proletarians (industrial workers). The TUC has used the term 'vulnerable employment' to refer to the kind of work Standing is talking about, defined as "precarious work that places people at risk of continuing poverty and injustice resulting from an imbalance of power in the employer/worker relationship" (TUC, 2014).

CHECK YOUR UNDERSTANDING

1. Distinguish between 'work' and 'paid employment'.

2. Identify the two components of the shadow economy.

3. What is meant by a 'post-industrial society'?

4. Distinguish between 'anomie' and 'alienation'.

5. Explain what is meant by 'technological determinism'.

6. What are the key differences between Fordist and post-Fordist production techniques?

7. How does a consumer society differ from an industrial society?

8. Identify four consequences of unemployment for individuals.

9. What are the four organisational principles that McDonalds is based on, according to Ritzer?

10. Who are the 'precariat', according to Standing?

TAKE IT FURTHER

Identify a sample of people from among your classmates who have worked, or are working, in fast-food restaurants.

Interview them to find out about the nature of their contract and working conditions. Explain the concept of 'emotional labour' to them and ask whether they feel that the requirement to be unfailingly cheerful is a reasonable commercial expectation or an unreasonable imposition.

Write up your findings in the form of a research report, commenting on the strengths and weaknesses of interview research in this context.

APPLY YOUR LEARNING

AS LEVEL

1 Define the term 'relative poverty'.   [2 marks]

2 Using **one** example, briefly explain what is meant by 'corporate capture'.   [2 marks]

3 Outline **three** ways in which globalisation has impacted on the British labour market in recent decades.   [6 marks]

4 Outline and explain **two** criticisms of the claim that British society can be neatly divided
   into those who contribute to the welfare state and those who take from it.   [10 marks]

5 Read **Item A** below and answer the question that follows.

ITEM A

The welfare state

For three decades after the end of the Second World War, the welfare state was widely seen as playing a crucial role in the reduction of poverty in the UK. Since then, neoliberal ideas have gained ground and have recast the welfare state as a cause of poverty rather than a solution to it. Margaret Thatcher, for example, talked about the welfare state as the 'nanny state' which allegedly infantilised people and encouraged them to become dependent on the state.

Applying material from **Item A** and your knowledge, evaluate the claim that the welfare state
has worsened poverty in the UK rather than alleviated it.   [20 marks]

A-LEVEL

1   Outline and explain **two** ways in which paid employment in Britain has become more precarious in recent years.   [10 marks]

2   Read **Item B** below and answer the question that follows.

ITEM B

The rise of in-work poverty

One of the most significant trends in terms of poverty in the UK over the last 30 years has been a sea change in the groups most at risk of poverty. Despite some politicians' claims about the lack of personal responsibility, and a weak work ethic, the most striking shift has been the rise of poverty among those in work.

Applying material from **Item B** and your knowledge, analyse **two** reasons for the rise in in-work poverty in recent decades.   [10 marks]

3   Read **Item C** below and answer the question that follows.

ITEM C

The riots of the underclass?

Many journalists and politicians today take it for granted that an underclass exists in British society. Ironically, it is often the same journalists and politicians that argue that social classes are disappearing.

Consequently, when rioting took place across a number of English towns and cities in August 2011, the explanation for many social commentators was obvious: these were the riots of the underclass.

Applying material from **Item C** and your knowledge, evaluate the claim that there is a permanent underclass in UK society characterised by a distinctive culture.   [20 marks]

You can find **example** answers and accompanying teachers' comments for this topic at www.collins.co.uk/AQAAlevelSociology.

LOOKING AHEAD

You are reading this section of the book because you are about to begin the first year of the AQA A-level specification for Sociology. You may intend to sit only the AS examination, or alternatively you may have signed up to study the full A-level, or you may plan to see you how you progress and perhaps take both the AS and the full A-level. In all cases this section of the textbook explains what is in the specification, and what skills and knowledge you will develop through your course.

Year 1 specification content
The first year of study is divided into two units that lay out what you will learn.

> Unit 3.1 will involve the study of two compulsory topics: *Education* and *Methods in Context*. This involves the study of the educational system and how sociological research methods have been employed to study aspects of it.

> Unit 3.2 also involves a compulsory *Research Methods* section and the study of a minimum of one optional sociological topic from a choice of *Culture and Identity*, *Families and Households*, *Health*, and *Work, Welfare and Poverty*.

Year 1 assessment
You or your school or college may decide that you should sit the AS examination at the end of your first year. If this is the case, you should take a look at Table 1 which shows the structure of the AS examination.

Year 2 specification content
The second year of study is divided into two units that lay out what you will learn.

> Unit 4.2 will involve the study of a minimum of one sociological topic from a choice of *Beliefs in Society*, *Global Development*, *The Media* and *Stratification and Differentiation*.

> Unit 4.3 involves the study of a compulsory topic *Crime and Deviance* with *Theory and Methods*. This involves the study of crime and deviance, sociological research methods and sociological theories of society.

Year 2 assessment
If you are working towards the A-level qualification, you will sit three examinations in this subject, even if you have already achieved the AS qualification. You should take a look at Table 2 which shows the structure of the A-level examination.

What skills are you expected to acquire during your course of study?
The skills you will acquire and develop during this course are split into three main strands or assessment objectives. As you work through the course you will be expected to demonstrate these skills in your work and in the exams you take at the end of the course.

1: Knowledge and understanding
To meet this objective successfully, you have to show your knowledge and understanding of the chosen topic on which you are answering a question. This knowledge and understanding covers the full range of relevant sociological material, including concepts, theories, perspectives, the findings of sociological studies, relevant facts (from official sources, for example) and sociological methods.

You will also develop and be assessed on the quality of your written communication. In other words, you need to be able to express yourself clearly in writing. This is a really important skill for sociologists.

2: Application
To meet this objective successfully, you will have to apply sociological theories, concepts, evidence and research methods to the question that you have been asked. This means that while it is probably obvious that you need to know some sociological material, you need to be able to use and discuss it in ways that actually address and answer the question.

For example, you need to be able to *interpret* or work out what the question is asking and respond by selecting relevant material (theories, studies, sociological observations and so on) from what you know. Some questions will specifically ask you to use material from an attached item of information as well. You should then aim to *apply* all of this knowledge to the question in an appropriate way.

3: Analysis and evaluation
To meet this objective successfully, you will have to *analyse* and *evaluate* sociological theories, concepts, evidence and research methods in order to:

> present arguments

> make judgements

> draw conclusions.

Analysis refers to the ability to show how arguments and ideas logically fit together. Good analysis is shown by presenting an informed, detailed and accurate discussion of a particular theory, perspective, study or event, and also by the ability to present your arguments in a clear and logical manner.

Evaluation involves being able to recognise and weigh up strengths and weaknesses; advantages and disadvantages; evidence and arguments of a sociological theory, perspective, study, argument or research method to reach an appropriate conclusion.

Table 1: AS units of study and assessment

Unit	Topics covered	Forms of assessment
1 60 marks 50% of AS	› *Education* › *Methods in Context*	PAPER 1: EDUCATION with METHODS IN CONTEXT Written examination of one hour thirty minutes. All questions are compulsory. Three short questions focused on *Education* worth 2, 2 & 6 marks respectively; one question worth 10 marks and an essay question worth 20 marks partly based on a data response item. A 20 mark *Methods in Context* question focused on a data response item that describes an aspect of education and a research method.
2 60 marks 50% of AS	› *Research Methods* › *Culture and Identity* › *Families and Households* › *Health* › *Work, Welfare and Poverty*	PAPER 2: RESEARCH METHODS and TOPICS in SOCIOLOGY Written examination of one hour thirty minutes. A compulsory Section A focused on *Research Methods* containing a short question worth 4 marks and an essay title worth 16 marks. Section B will contain five questions per topic: three short questions worth 2, 2 & 6 marks respectively; one question worth 10 marks and an essay question worth 20 marks partly based on a data response item.

Table 2: A-level units of study and assessment

Unit	Topics covered	Forms of assessment
1 80 marks 33.3% of A-level	› *Education* › *Methods in Context* › *Theory and Methods*	PAPER 1: EDUCATION with THEORY and METHODS Written examination of two hours. All questions are compulsory. Two short questions focused on *Education* worth 4 & 6 marks respectively; one question worth 10 marks based on a data response item and an essay question worth 30 marks partly based on a data response item. A 20 mark *Methods in Context* question focused on a data response item that describes an aspect of education and a research method. A 10 mark question focused on an aspect of *Theory and Methods*.
2 80 marks 33.3% of A-level	SECTION A › *Culture and Identity* › *Families and Households* › *Health* › *Work, Welfare and Poverty* SECTION B › *Beliefs in Society* › *Global development* › *The Media* › *Stratification and Differentiation*	PAPER 2: TOPICS in SOCIOLOGY Written examination of two hours. All questions need to be answered from *one* topic from Section A and *one* topic from Section B. Both sections will contain three questions per topic: one question worth 10 marks; one question worth 10 marks partly based on a data response item and one question worth 20 marks partly based on a data response item.
3 80 marks 33.3% of A-level	› *Crime and Deviance* › *Theory and Methods*	PAPER 2: TOPICS in SOCIOLOGY: CRIME and DEVIANCE with THEORY and METHODS Written examination of two hours. All questions are compulsory. Two short questions focused on *Crime and Deviance* worth 4 & 6 marks respectively; one question worth 10 marks partly based on a data response item and an essay question worth 30 marks partly based on a data response item. Two questions focused on *Theory and Methods*: one is worth 10 marks and the other that is partly based on a data response item, is worth 20 marks.

Understanding questions and instructions

It is really important that you become familiar with the meaning of the 'command words' that you will use during your course. Command words tell you how to go about a task or how to approach an answer to a question. The following command words are used throughout this book:

> *Analyse* – separate sociological information into components or sections and identify their characteristics.

> *Define* – Specify the meaning of a concept.

> *Identify* – Name whatever you have been asked for, such as a concept or theory. It is often a good idea to include an example to illustrate your understanding.

> *Explain* – Set out the reasons or distinguishing features of a theory, sociological study, and so on and say why they are important.

> *Outline* – Set out the main features or characteristics of something.

> *Outline and explain* – Set out the main features of something such as a sociological theory and explain the reasons why these features are important.

> *Using one example, briefly explain* – Give a brief account of something.

> *Examine* – Look at the advantages and disadvantages of a theory, or look at evidence for and against a sociological view contained in an essay title.

> *Evaluate* – Judge the strengths and weaknesses of something from the evidence available and/or by looking at all sides and come to an informed conclusion.

> *Assess* – Look at all sides, or all theories that relate to the sociological debate in question and come to an informed conclusion.

> *Applying material from Item A* – Draw on material from the data or information in the item that accompanies the question. Remember: there may be more than one useful point in the item. Also, bear in mind that this is an *instruction*, not a suggestion, so make sure you use the information that you have been given to its full potential.

The command word descriptions above may not match the definitions in the AQA specification. A full list of AQA command words and definitions can be found on the AQA website.

Communication tips

> Read the whole question or instruction very carefully before you begin your answer. Reading the question thoroughly will help you to recognise which aspects of the topic are covered. Identify any command words and decide what type of answer is required.

> Read the item(s) provided. They are there to help you and contain essential information. Think of them like a map that gives you clues to the direction in which to take your answer. To make the most of the items, read them through several times, picking out or underlining key points and letting your mind digest them. Then, try to link them up with your own knowledge.

> When you have read the question and items, make a brief plan for any longer questions before you begin writing. As you write your other answers, you may well remember things that you wish to slot into these answers. Stick to your plan and refer back to it when writing.

> Plan your time carefully. Make sure you have time to answer all of the questions to the best of your ability.

> If you are giving multiple reasons or suggesting several examples to make your point, you may wish to use bullet points. This will help you set out and deliver your argument clearly.

> Start each point on a separate line or begin a new paragraph. By doing so, the structure of your writing will be much easier to follow.

> When writing longer, more involved arguments, you should refer to appropriate theories, perspectives, studies and evidence to support and inform your point. Where possible, bring in examples of recent or current events, policies and so on, to illustrate the points you are making.

> Finally, make sure that you answer the question that is being asked, rather than the one that you wished had been set! It is very easy to want to write down everything you know about a topic, particularly if you have studied hard, but this does not show that you have understood the topic as well as a carefully-constructed response.

REFERENCES

Abbott, D. (1998) *Culture and Identity*, London: Hodder & Stoughton

Abraham, J. (1995) *Divide and School: Gender & class dynamics in comprehensive education*, London: Routledge Falmer

Abraham, J. (2009) 'Partial progress: governing the pharmaceutical industry and the NHS, 1948–2008'. *Journal of Health Politics, Policy and Law*, 34 (6): 931–77

AcademicTUC (2014) *The Decent Jobs Deficit*, London: TUC

Acheson, Sir Donald (1998) *Independent Inquiry into Inequalities in Health: Report*, London: The Stationery Office

Adams, P. (2014) *Policy and Education*, Abingdon, Oxon: Routledge

Adorno, T.W., Frenkel-Brunswik, E., Levinson, D. and Sanford, N. (1950) *The Authoritarian Personality*, New York: Norton

Aiden, H. and McCarthy, A. (2014) *Current attitudes towards disabled people*, London: Scope UK

Alcock, P. *Understanding Poverty*, London: Palgrave Macmillan

Alford, R.R. (1975) *Health Care Politics: Ideological and interest group barriers to reform*, Chicago: The University of Chicago Press

Ali, N., Burchett, H., (2004) 'Experiences of Maternity Services: Muslim Women's Perspectives', *The Maternity Alliance*, London

Ali, S. (2002) 'Interethnic families', *Sociology Review*, 12(1)

Althusser, L. (1971) 'Ideology and ideological state apparatuses', in *Lenin and Philosophy and Other Essays*, London: New Left Books

Anderson, M. (1971) 'Family, Household and the Industrial Revolution', in M. Anderson (ed.) *The Sociology of the Family*, Harmondsworth: Penguin

Anderson, P. and Kitchin, R.M. (2000) 'Disability, space and sexuality: Access to family planning services', *Social Science and Medicine*, 51

Annandale, E. (1998) *The Sociology of Health and Illness*, Cambridge: Polity Press

Ansley, F. (1972) quoted in Bernard, J. (1976) *The Future of Marriage* Harmondsworth: Penguin

Antle, B.J. (2004) 'Factors Associated with Self-Worth in Young People with Physical Disabilities', *Health Social Work*, 29(3): 167–175

Arber, S. and Ginn, J. (1993) 'Class, caring and the life course' in S. Arber and M.E. Vandrow (eds.) *Ageing, Independence and the Life Course*, London: Jessica Kingsley

Archer, L. (2003) *Race, Masculinity and Schooling: Muslim Boys and Education*, Maidenhead: Open University Press

Archer, L. and Francis, B. (2007) *Understanding Minority Ethnic Achievement: Race, Gender, Class and 'Success'*, Abingdon: Routledge

Aries, P. (1962) *Centuries of Childhood*, London: Random House

Arnot, M., Gray., J., Hames, M. and Rudduck, J. (1998) *A Review of Recent Research on Gender and Educational Performance*, OFSTED research series, London: The Stationery Office

Askham, J. (1984) *Identity and Stability in Marriage*, Cambridge: Cambridge University Press

Atkinson, J.M. (1978) *Discovering Suicide: Studies in the Social Organization of Sudden Death*, London: Macmillan

Aune, K. and Redfern, C. (2013) *Reclaiming the F Word: The New Feminist Movement*, London: Zed Books Ltd.

Babb, P., Butcher, H., Church, J. and Zealey, L., (2006) *Social Trends*, 6, National Statistics

Baker, S. and MacPherson, J. (2000) 'Counting the Cost: Mental health in the media', Mind: London

Ball, S.J. (1981) *Beachside Comprehensive*, Cambridge: Cambridge University Press

Ball, S.J. (2008) *The Education Debate*, Bristol: Policy Press

Ball, S.J. (2012) *Global Education Inc.: New Policy Networks and the Neo-liberal Imaginary*, London, Routledge

Ball, S.J. (2013) *The Education Debate*, Bristol, Policy Press (2nd edn.)

Ball, S.J., Bowe, R. and Gerwitz, S. (1994) 'Market forces and parental choice' in S. Tomlinson (ed.) *Education Reform and its Consequences*, London: IPPR/Rivers Oram Press

Barber, B. (1963) 'Some problems in the sociology of professions', *Daedalus*, 92(4)

Barker, D.J. and Clarke P.M. (1997) 'Foetal undernutrition and disease in later life.' *Reviews of Reproduction*

Barlow A. & Duncan S. (2000) Supporting families? New Labour's communitarianism and the 'rationality mistake': Part I, Journal of Social Welfare and Family Law, Volume 22(1) pp.23–42

Barnard, H. and Turner, C. (2011) 'Poverty and Ethnicity: A review of evidence', *Policy and Research*, York: The Joseph Rowntree Foundation

Barnett, S. and Curry, A. (1994) *The Battle for the BBC: a British Broadcasting Conspiracy?*, London: Aurum

Barr, B. et al. (2012) 'Suicides associated with the 2008–10 economic recession in England: Time trend' in *Suicide Research: Selected Readings, Vol. 8*, ed. by D.M. Skerret, E. Barker and D. De Leo

Barrett, M. and McIntosh, M. (1982) *The Anti-social Family*, London: Verso

Barry, A.M. and Yuill, C. (2012) *Understanding the Sociology of Health: An Introduction*, London: Sage Publications

Bartholomew, J. (2013) *The Welfare State We're In*, London: Biteback Publishing

Bartlett, W. and Le Grand, J. (1993) *Quasi-markets and Social Policy*, London: Palgrave Macmillan

Bartley, M., Blane, D. (2008) 'Inequality and social class' in Scambler, G. (ed.) *Sociology as applied to medicine*, Amsterdam: Elsevier Limited

Basit, T.N. (2013) 'Educational capital as a catalyst for upward social mobility amongst British Asians: a three-generational analysis' *British Educational Research Journal*, 39(4)

Bauman, Z. (1988) *Freedom*, Milton Keynes: Open University Press

Bauman, Z. (1996) 'From pilgrim to tourist: a short history of identity' in Hall, S.& du Gay, P. *Questions of Cultural Identity*, London: Sage Publications

Bauman, Z. (1997) *Postmodernity and its Discontents*, Cambridge: Polity Press

Bauman, Z. (1998) *Globalization: The Human Consequences*, Cambridge: Polity Press

Bauman, Z. (2004) *Identity*, Cambridge: Polity Press

Bauman, Z. (2007) *Consuming Life*, Cambridge: Polity Press

Bauman, Z. (2011) *Collateral Damage: Social Inequalities in a Global Age*, Cambridge: Polity Press

Baumeister, R. (1986) *Identity: Cultural Change and the Struggle for Self*, Oxford: Oxford University Press

Beaujouan, E. and Bhrolchain, M. N. (2011) 'Cohabitation and marriage in Britain since the 1970s', *Population Trends*, 145

Beck, U. (1992) *Risk Society: Towards a New Modernity*, London: Sage Publications

Beck, U. and Beck-Gernsheim, E. (1995) *The Normal Chaos of Love*, Cambridge: Polity Press

Becker, H. (1970) *Sociological work: Method and substance*. Chicago: Aldine Publishing

Becker, H. (1971) 'Social class variations in the teacher-pupil relationship', in B. Cosin (ed.) *School and Society*, London: Routledge & Kegan Paul

Bell, D. (1973) *The Coming of Post-Industrial Society*, New York: Basic Books

Beharrell, P. (1974) *Bad News*, Abingdon: Routledge

Ben-Galim D. and Thompson S. (2013) 'Who's breadwinning? Working mothers and the new face of family support', London: IPPR

Ben-Galim, D. and Silim, A. (2013) 'The Sandwich Generation: Older Women Balancing Work and Care', London: IPPR

Bennet, T. and Holloway, K. (2005) *Understanding Drugs Alcohol and Crime*, Milton Keynes: Open University Press

Bennett, A. (2004) 'Rap and Hip Hop: community and identity', in S. Whiteley, A. Bennett and S. Hawkins (eds.) *Music, Space and Place*, Aldershot: Ashgate

Bennett, R. 'Too much TV can cause emotional turmoil for children', *The Times*, 18th March 2014, http://www.thetimes.co.uk/tto/health/child-health/article4036495.ece

Bennett, R. 'Many immigrants "are better qualified than white Britons"' *The Times*, 11th March 2014, http://ww.thetimes.co.uk/tto/education/article4029336.ece

Bennett, T. et al. (2009) *Culture, Class, Distinction*, Routledge: London

Benston, M. (1972) 'The political economy of women's liberation', in N. Glazer-Malbin and H.Y. Waehrer (eds) *Women in a Man-Made World*, Chicago: Rand McNally

Beresford, P., Green, D., Lister, R. and Woodward, K. (1999) *Poverty First Hand: Poor People Speak for Themselves*, London: Child Poverty Action Group

Bernard, J. (1982, originally 1972) *The Future of Marriage*, Yale: Yale University Press

Bernstein, B. (1971) *Class, Codes and Control* (Vol. 1) London: Routledge & Kegan Paul

Berthoud, R. (2000) 'Family formation in multi-cultural Britain: three patterns of diversity', *Working Paper of the Institute for Social and Economic Research*, Colchester: University of Essex

Berthoud, R. (2003) Lecture at ATSS Conference 2004, based on research conducted in 2003

Best, L. (1993) '"Dragons, dinner ladies and ferrets": Sex roles in children's books', *Sociology Review*, 2(3) Oxford: Philip Allan

Best, S. (2005) *Understanding Social Divisions*, London: Sage Publications

Bhatti, G. (1999) *Asian Children at Home and at School: An Ethnographic Study*, London, Routledge

Bicknell, B. (2014) 'Parental Roles in the Education of Mathematically Gifted and Talented Children', *Gifted Child Today*, 37(2), pp. 82–93

Bielewska, A. (2012, originally 2011) 'National identities of Poles in Manchester: Modern and postmodern geographies', *Ethnicities*, 12(1), pp. 86–105

Billington, R., Hockey, J. and Strawbridge, S. (1998) *Exploring Self and Society*, Basingstoke: Macmillan

Blackman, S. (1997) 'An ethnographic study of youth underclass' in R. McDonald (ed.) *Youth, the Underclass and Social Exclusion*, London: Routledge

Blackman, T. & Wistow, J., 'Health Inequalities in the UK', *Sociology Review*, April 2009, 18(4)

Blanden, J., Goodman, A., Gregg, P. and Machin, S. (2002) 'Changes in intergenerational mobility in Britain', *CEE DP 26*, London: Centre for the Economics of Education

Blanden, J., Gregg, P. and Machin, S. (2005) *Intergenerational Mobility in Europe and North America*, London: The Sutton Trust

Blauner, R. (1964) *Alienation and Freedom*, Chicago: Chicago University Press

Blaxter, M. (1990) *Health and Lifestyles,* London: Routledge

Bleach, K. (1998) *Raising Boys' Achievement in Schools,* Stoke: Trentham Books

Blumer, H. (1969) *Symbolic Interactionism: Perspective and Method,* Englewood Cliffs, NJ: Prentice-Hall

Boffey, D. (2014) Institutional racism and history teaching, *The Observer,* 22nd March 2014

Book Marketing Limited (2000) 'Reading the Situation: Book Reading, Buying and Borrowing Habits in Britain', *Library and Information Commission Research Report 34,* London: Book Marketing Limited

Bourdieu, P. (1977a) 'Cultural Reproduction and Social Reproduction' in Karabel, J. and Halsey, A.H. (eds.), *Power and Ideology in Education,* Oxford: Oxford University Press

Bourdieu, P. (1977b) *Outline of a Theory of Practice,* Cambridge: Cambridge University Press

Bourdieu, P. (1984) *Distinction: A Social Critique of the Judgement of Taste,* London: Routledge

Bourdieu, P. and Passeron, J.C. (1990) *Reproduction in Education, Society and Culture* (2nd edn.), London: Sage Publications

Bourgois (2003) *In Search of Respect: Selling Crack in El Barrio,* Cambridge: Cambridge University Press

Bowlby, J. (1951) 'Maternal Care and Mental Health', *Bulletin of the World Health Organisation,* 3, pp. 355–534

Bowles, S. and Gintis, H. (1976) *Schooling in Capitalist America: Educational Reform and the Contradictions of Economic Life,* New York: Basic Books

Bradley, H. (1996) *Fractured Identities: Changing Patterns of Inequality,* Cambridge: Polity Press

Bradley, H. (2013) *Gender,* Cambridge: Polity Press

Bradley, H., Erickson, M., Stephenson, C. and Williams, S. (2000) *Myths at Work,* Cambridge: Polity Press

Bradley, J.M. (1997) 'Political, religious and cultural identities: The Undercurrents of Scottish Football'. *Politics,* 17(1), pp. 25–32

Bradshaw, J. (2012) 'Child wellbeing in the 2000s' in *Ending child poverty by 2020: Progress made and lessons learned',* ed. by Linsday Judge, London: Child Poverty Action Group

Bradshaw, J. (2013) cited in Crossley, S. (2014) 'The 'un-politics' of child poverty', *Poverty* (149), London: CPAG

Bradshaw, J. et al (2013) *The Good Childhood Report 2013,* The Children's Society and University of York

Brah, A. (1993) 'Race and culture in the gendering of labour markets: South Asian young women and the labour market', *New Community,* 19(3)

Brannen, J. (2003) 'The age of beanpole families', *Sociology Review*

Brannen, J. and Heptinstall, E. (2003) 'Family Life – what the children think', *Young Minds Magazine,* 54

Braverman, H. (1974) *Labor and Monopoly Capitalism: The Degradation of Work in the Twentieth Century,* New York: Monthly Review Press

Brinkley et al. (2013) *The Gender Jobs Split,* London: The Work Foundation

Brinkworth, L., 'Scared their boys will go to Syria, scared to go to the police', *The Times,* 20th January 2015

British Social Attitudes Survey (2013) 'Trends in British Social Attitudes', 30

Britland, M. 'Shorter holidays will stop private tuition widening the achievement gap', *The Guardian,* 2nd August 2013, available at http://www.theguardian.com/teacher-network/teacher-blog/2013/aug/02/shorter-holidays-private-tuition-achievement-gap

Brooks-Gunn, J. and Kirsch, B. (1984) 'Life events and the boundaries of midlife for women', in G. Baruch and J. Brookes-Gunn (eds.) *Women in Midlife,* New York: Plenum Press

Brookman, F. (2000) 'Dying for Control: Men, Murder and Sub-Lethal Violence', *British Criminology Conference: Selected Proceedings,* 3 (http://www.lboro.ac.uk/departments/ss/bsc/bccsp/vol03/brookman.html)

Brooks, D. (2001) 'The Organization Kid', *The Atlantic,* April 2001 issue, available at http://www.theatlantic.com/magazine/archive/2001/04/the-organization-kid/302164/

Brown, D. (1994) 'An ordinary sexual life? A review of the normalization principle as it applies to the sexual options of people with learning disabilities', *Disability and Society,* 9(2)

Brown, G.W., Harris, T.O. and Hepworth, C. (1995) 'Loss, humiliation and entrapment among women developing depression', *Psychological Medicine,* 25, pp. 7–21

Brown, S. (1997) 'High and low quality performance in manufacturing firms', *TQM Journal,* 9(4), pp. 292–9

Brückner, H., and K. U. Mayer (2005) 'De-standardization of the life course: what it might mean? And if it means anything, whether it actually took place?', *Advances in Life Course Research,* 9

Bryant, I., Johnston, R. and Usher, R. (1997) *Adult Education and the Postmodern Challenge: Learning Beyond the Limits,* London: Routledge

Bryson, V. (1999) *Feminist Debates,* London: Macmillan

Buchan, I. E., (2011) 'Trends in mortality from 1965 to 2008 across the English north-south divide: comparative observational study', *British Medical Journal,* 342

Buchanan, R. 'Vocational qualifications to be dropped', *The Times,* 7th March 2013, available at www.thetimes.co.uk/tto/education/article370668.ece

Buck D., Dixon A. (2013) 'Improving the allocation of health resources in England: How to decide who gets what', London: The King's Fund.

Bull, A. (2014) 'Reproducing class? Classical music education and inequality', November 04, 2014

Burchardt, T., Evans, M., Holder, H. (2013) 'Public policy and inequalities of choice and autonomy', CASEpaper 174, London: Centre for Analysis of Social Exclusion, London School of Economics

Burns, J. and Bracey, P. (2001) 'Boys' underachievement: Issues, challenges and possible ways forward', *Westminster Studies in Education,* 24, pp. 155–66

Busfield, J. (1988) 'Mental illness as a social product or social construct: a contradiction in feminists' arguments?', *Sociology of Health and Illness,* 10, pp. 521–42

Busfield, J. (2002) 'The Archaeology of Psychiatric Disorder: Gender and Disorders of Thought, Emotion and Behaviour

Buswell, C. (1987) *Training for Low Pay,* Basingstoke: Macmillan

Butler, E. (2010) 'The family is the best agent of welfare', *The Spectator online,* 24th August 2010, available at http://blogs.spectator.co.uk/coffeehouse/2010/08/the-family-is-the-best-agent-of-welfare/

Butler, J. (1999) *Gender Trouble,* London: Routledge

Cadario, B (2011) *The Tablet,* 20(2), pp. 12–13

Calhoun, C. (2003) *Feminism, the Family and the Politics of the Closet: Lesbian and Gay Displacement,* Oxford: Oxford University Press

Cangiano, A. (2014) 'Migration Policies and Migrant Employment: Conceptual Analysis and Comparative Evidence for Europe', *Comparative Migration Studies,* Uitgave: Amsterdam University Press

Cant, S. and Sharma, U. (2002) 'The state and complementary medicine: a changing relationship?', in S. Nettleton and U. Gustafsson (eds.) *The Sociology of Health and Illness, A Reader,* Cambridge: Polity Press

Carrington, B. et al (2007) 'A Perfect Match? Pupils' and teachers' views of the impact of matching educators and learners by gender', *Research Papers in Education,* 23(1).

Castells, M. (2000) *The Rise of the Network Society,* Oxford: Blackwell

Centre for Social Justice (2013) *Fractured Families: Why stability matters,* London: The Centre for Social Justice

Chahal, K. and Julienne, L. (1999) 'We Can't all be White!': Racist Victimisation in the UK. York: YPS for the Joseph Rowntree Foundation

Chambers, D. (2012) *A Sociology of Family Life,* Cambridge: Polity Press

Chapman, T. (2004) *Gender and Domestic Life: Changing Practices in Families and Households,* Basingstoke: Palgrave Macmillan

Charlesworth, S. (2000) *A Phenomenology of Working Class Experience,* Cambridge: Cambridge University Press

Cheal, D. (2002) *Sociology of Family Life,* Basingstoke: Palgrave Macmillan

Chesler, P. (1972) *Women and Madness,* New York: Doubleday

Chew-Graham C., Bashir C., Chantler K., Burman E, et al. (2002) 'South Asian women, psychological distress and self-harm: lessons for primary care trusts, *Health and Social Care in the Community,* 10(5),339–47

Chitty, C. (2014) *Education Policy in Britain,* Basingstoke: Palgrave Macmillan

Chubb, J.E and Moe, T.M. (1988) 'Politics, Markets and the Organization of Schools' *American Political Science Review,* 82(4)

Civil Exchange (2015) *Whose Society? The Final Big Society Audit,* London: Civil Exchange

Clarke, A. and Clarke, A. (2003) *Human Resilience a Fifty Year Quest,* London: Jessica Kingsley

Clarke, J. & Critcher, C. (1985) *The Devil Makes Work: Leisure in Capitalist Britain,* London: Macmillan

Coard, B. (1971) *How the West Indian Child is Made Educationally Subnormal in the British School System: The Scandal of the Black Child in Schools in Britain,* London: New Beacon, for the Caribbean Education and Community Workers' Association

Coffey, A. and Delamont, S. (2000) *Feminism and the Classroom Teacher: Research, Praxis and Pedagogy,* London: Routledge Falmer.

Cohen, M. (1998) 'A Habit of Healthy Idleness', in J. Elwood, D. Epstein, V. Hey & J. Maw (eds.) *Failing boys? Issues in gender and achievement.* Buckingham: Open University Press.

Cohen, P. (1984) 'Against the new vocationalism', in I. Bates, J. Clarke. R. Moore and P. Willis *Schooling for the Dole? The New Vocationalism,* Basingstoke: Macmillan

Cohen, S. (1980) *Folk Devils and Moral Panics* (2nd edn) Oxford: Martin Robinson

Coleman-Fountain, E. (2015) 'What's the difference? Lesbian and gay youth "after equality"' *Discover Society,* 1st March 2015 available at http://discoversociety.org/2015/03/01/whats-the-difference-lesbian-and-gay-youth-after-equality/

Collee, Dr J. (1992) *The Observer* 15th March 1992

Colley, A. (1998) 'Gender and Subject Choice in Secondary Education', in J. Radford (ed.) *Gender and Choice in Education and Occupation,* London: Routledge.

Collier, R. (2002) 'Masculinities', *Sociology,* 36(3), pp.737–42

Connell, R. W. (2009) *Gender: Short Introductions,* Cambridge: Polity Press

Connolly, P. (1998) *Racism, Gender Identities and Young Children: Social Relations in A Multi-Ethinc, Inner-City Primary School,* London: Routledge

Conrad, P. (2004) 'On the medicalization of deviance and social control.' In Ingleby, D. (ed) *Critical Psychiatry: the Politics of Mental Health.* (2nd edn.). London: Free Association

Cooper, Z. (2010) 'The NHS White Paper: evolution or revolution?', *CentrePiece:* 14–17

Corlett, A. and Whittaker, M. (2014) 'Low Pay Britain 2014', London: The Resolution Foundation

Corsaro, W.A. (2011) *The Sociology of Childhood,* London: Sage Publications

Cote, J. (2000) *Arrested Adulthood: The Changing Nature of Maturity and Identity,* New York: New York University Press

453

Cotton, D., Winter, J. and Bailey, I. (2013) 'Researching the hidden curriculum: intentional and unintentional messages' *Journal of Geography in Higher Education* 37(2)

Coughlan, S. (2013) 'Teacher's attack' "rebranded sexism" ' *BBC News*, 2nd April 2013

Craig, L. (2007) 'Is there really a 'second shift', and if so, who does it? A time-diary investigation', *Feminist Review*, 86, pp. 149–170

Crinson, I. (2008) *Health Policy: a Critical Perspective*, New York: Sage Publications

Cronin, A. (1997) 'Sociology and Sexuality', *Sociology Review*, 16(4)

Crook, S., Pakulski, J. and Walters, M. (1992) *Postmodernization: Changes in Advanced Societies*, London: Sage Publications

Culley, L. & Dyson, S. (1993) 'Race, inequality and health', *Sociology* Review, 3(1), pp. 24–27

Cumberbatch, G. and Negrine, R. (1992) *Images of Disability on Television*, London: Routledge

Cumming, E. and Henry, W. (1961) *Growing Old*, New York: Basic Books

Cunningham, H. (2006) *The Invention of Childhood*, London: BBC Books

Curtice, J. and Heath, A. (2000) 'Is the English Lion about to roar? National identity after the devolution', in R. Jowell *et al.* (eds.) *British Social Attitudes, 17th Report: Focusing on Diversity*, London: Sage Publications

Davey Smith, G. (2003) ed. *Health inequalities: Lifecourse Approaches*, Bristol: The Policy Press.

Davies, C.A., Charles, N. and Harris, C. (2006) 'Welsh identity and language in Swansea (1960–2002)', *Contemporary Wales*, 18, pp. 28–53

Davies, T. (2006) 'Curse or cure: the medicalisation of social life' *Sociology Review*, 15(3)

Davis, K. and Moore, W.E (1945) 'Some Principles of Stratification', *American Sociological Review*, 10(2)

De'Ath, E. and Slater, D. (1992) *Parenting Threads, Caring for Children when Couples Part*, London: Stepfamily Publications

Delphy, C. and Leonard, D. (1992) *Familiar Exploitation: A New Analysis of Marriage in Contemporary Western Societies*, Oxford: Polity Press

Dench, G., Gavron, K. & Young, M. (2006) *The New East End: Kinship, Race and Conflict*, London: Profile Books

Department for Education (2007) *Departmental Report 2007*

Department for Education (2010) *Youth Cohort Study & Longitudinal Study of Young People in England: The Activities and Experiences of 19 year olds: England 2010*

Department for Education (2012) *Cash Boost for Disadvantaged School Children*

Department for Education (2013) *Early Years Foundation Stage Profile Attainment by Pupil Characteristics, England 2013*

Diez-Roux, A. V., Link, B. G., & Northridge, M. E. (2000) 'A multilevel analysis of income inequality and cardiovascular disease risk factors', *Social Science & Medicine*, 50, pp. 673–687

Dillner, L. 'Should I use health apps?', *The Guardian* online, 20th January 2013

DisabilityRightsUK (2013) *Risk of major disability poverty rise* available at http://www.disabilityrightsuk.org/news/2013/june/risk-major-disability-poverty-rise

Dittmar, H. (2007) 'Consumer Culture, Identity and Well-being' *European Monographs in Social Psychology Series*, New York: Psychology Press

Dixon, A., Le Grand, J., Henderson, J., Murray, R. and Poteliakhoff, E. (2007) 'Is the British National Health Service equitable? The evidence on socioeconomic differences in utilization', *Journal of Health Services Research & Policy*, 12(2), pp. 104–9

Dobson, B., Beardsworth, A., Keil, T. and Walker, R., (1994) 'Diet, Choice and Poverty: Social, Cultural and Nutritional Aspects of Food Consumption among Low Income Families.' London: Family Policy Studies Centre

Donald Hirsch (2007) Hirsch, D. (2007) *Experiences of Poverty and Educational Disadvantage*, York: Joseph Rowntree Foundation

Donin, A.S. et al (2010) 'Nutritional composition of the diets of South Asian, black African-Caribbean and white European children in the United Kingdom: the Child Heart and Health Study in England (CHASE).' *British Journal of Nutrition* 104, pp. 276–285

Donnelly, M. (2014) 'The Road to Oxbridge: Schools and Elite University Choices', *British Journal of Educational Studies*, 62(1)

Donzelot, J. (1979) *The policing of families*, New York: Pantheon Books

Dorais, M. (2004) *Dead Boys Can't Dance: Sexual Orientation, Masculinity and Suicide* Montreal: McGill Queens University Press

Dorling, D., Mitchell, R., Shaw, M., Orford, S., and Davey Smith, G. (2000) 'The ghost of Christmas past: health effects of poverty in London in 1896 and 1991' *British Medical Journal*, 7276(23–30), pp. 1547–1551

Douglas, J.W.B. (1964) *The Home and the School: A Study of Ability and. Attainment in the Primary Schools*, London: MacGibbon and Kee

Dowler, E. (2008) 'Policy initiatives to address low-income households' nutritional needs in the UK', *Proceedings of the Nutrition Society*, 67(3), pp. 289–300

Doyal, L. and Pennell, I. (1979) *The Political Economy of Health*, London: Pluto

Drotner, K. and Livingstone, S. (2008) *The International Handbook of Children, Media and Culture*, London: Sage Publications

Dumit, J. (2012) *Drugs for Life: How Pharmaceutical Companies Define our Health (Experimental failures)* Durham: Duke University Press

Duncan, S. and Barlow, A. (2000) 'Family law, moral rationalities and New Labour's communitarianism', *Journal of Social Welfare and Family Law*, Part I 22(1), pp. 23–42, Part II 22(2), pp. 129–143

Duncan, S., Carter, J., Phillips, M., Roseneil, S., & Stoilova, M. (2013) 'Why do people live apart together?' *Families, Relationships and Societies*, 2(3), pp. 323–338

Duncombe, J. and Marsden, D. (1995) 'Women's "triple shift": paid employment, domestic labour and "emotion work"', *Sociology Review*, 4(4)

Dunne, M. et al. (2011) 'The teaching and learning of pupils on low-attainment sets', *The Curriculum Journal*, 22(4), pp. 485–513

Durkheim, E. (1893, reprinted 1933) *The Division of Labour in Society*, Glencoe: Free Press

Durkheim, E. (1897, reprinted 1952) *Suicide: a Study in Sociology*, London: Routledge

Durkheim, E. (1912) *The Elementary Forms of Religious Life*, London: Allen & Unwin

Durkin, K. (1995) *Developmental Social Psychology, from Infancy to Old Age*, Oxford: Blackwell

Economic and Social Research Council (ESRC) (2012) *Poverty and Social Exclusion (PSE) survey*

Education Journal (2013) 'Pupil Premium Latest' *The Education Journal*, 170

Edwards, R., Alldred, P. and David, M. (2000) 'Children's understandings of parental involvement in education', in *Children 5–16 Research Briefing Number 11*, ESRC

Ehrenreich, B. and English, D. (1979) *For Her Own Good: 150 Years of Experts' Advice to Women*, London: Pluto

El-Gingihy, Y. 'Health Act means the death of the NHS as we know it', *The Guardian* online, 30th March 2013

Elias, N. (1978) *The Civilising Process*, Oxford: Blackwell

Elizabeth Finn Care Annual Review 2012/2013, Elizabeth Finn Care

Ellis, A. and Fry, R. (2010) *Regional health inequalities in England*, Office for Nation Statistics

Elston, M. A. 2009, 'Remaking a trustworthy medical profession in twenty-first-century Britain?'. J. Gabe and M. Calnan (eds.). *The New Sociology of the Health Service*. London: Routledge

Emslie, S., Knox, K. and Pickstone, M. (2002) *Improving Patient Safety: Insights from American, Australian and British Healthcare*, Herts: ECRI

Epsom, J.D. (1978) 'The Mobile health clinic: a report on the first year's work' in D. Tuckett and J. M. Kaufert, *Basic Readings in Medical Sociology*, London: Tavistock

Epstein, D. (1998) 'Real boys don't work: "underachievement", masculinity and the harassment of "sissies"', in D. Epstein, J. Ellwood, V. Hey and J. Maw (eds.) *Failing Boys? Issues in Gender and Achievement*, Buckingham: Open University Press

Equality and Human Rights Commission (EHRC) (2010) *How Fair is Britain?*

The Equality Trust (2015) *The scale of economic inequality in the UK*

Erens B, Primatesta P and Prior G (2001) The Health Survey for England. The Health of Minority Ethnic Groups 1999. London: TSO

Evans, G. (2007) *Educational Failure and Working Class White Children in Britain*, London: Palgrave Macmillan

Evans, J. and Chandler, J. (2006) 'To buy or not to buy: family dynamics and children's consumption', *Sociological Research Online*, 11(2)

Faculty of Public Health of the Royal College of Physicians of the United Kingdom, 'Food Poverty and Health', May 2005

Fagin, L. and Little, M. (1984) *The Forsaken Families*, Harmondsworth: Penguin

Feinstein, L. (2003) 'Inequality in the early cognitive development of British children in the 1970 cohort', *Economica*, 70(277), pp. 73–98

Finch, N. (2003) 'Family Policy in the UK' for the project 'Welfare Policy and Employment in the Context of Family Change', Social Policy Research Unit, University of York

Fine, C. (2011) *Delusions of Gender: The Real Science Behind Sex Differences*, London: Icon Books

Fine, G. (2006) 'Friends, impression management and preadolescent behaviour' in Handel. G. *Childhood Socialization* New Brunswick: Aldine Transaction

Finkelstein, V. (1975) *To Deny or Not to Deny Disability - What is disability?* www.independentliving.org/docs1/finkelstein.html

Finkelstein, V. (1980) *Attitudes and Disabled People: Issues for Discussion*, New York: World Rehabilitation Fund

Finn, D. (1987) *Training without Jobs*, Basingstoke: Macmillan

Firestone, S. (1971) *The Dialect of Sex*, London: Women's Press

Fletcher, R. (1988) *The Shaking of the Foundations: Family and Society*, London: Routledge

Flouri, E. & Buchanan, A. (2002) 'What predicts good relationships with parents in adolescence and partners in adult life: Findings from the 1986 British birth cohort', *Journal of Family Psychology*, 16, 186–198

Fone et al. (2013) 'Socioeconomic patterning of excess alcohol consumption and binge drinking: a cross-sectional study of multilevel associations with neighbourhood deprivation', *British Medical Journal Open*, 3(4)

Ford, R. 'Babies born on right side of north-south divide live years longer', *The Times*, 20th November 2014

Ford, R. and Millar, J. (1998) (eds.) *Private Lives and Public Responses*, London: Policy Studies Institute

Foucault, M. (1965) *Madness and Civilization*, New York: Random House

Foucault, M. (1973) *The Order of Things: An Archaeology of the Human Sciences*, New York: Vintage/Random House

Foucault, M. (1976) *The Birth of the Clinic*, London: Tavistock

Fox Harding, L. (1996) *Family, State and Social Policy*, Basingstoke: Macmillan

Fox, N.J. and Ward, K.J. (2008) 'What governs governance, and how does it evolve? Towards a dynamic sociology of governance', *British Journal of Sociology*, 59(3), pp. 519–538

Francis, B. (2000) *Boys, Girls and Achievement. Addressing the Classroom Issues*, London: Routledge Falmer

Francis, B. and Hutchings, M. (2013) 'Almost a third of professional parents have moved home for a good school', London: The Sutton Trust

Francis, B. and Hutchings, M. (2013) 'Parent Power?', London: The Sutton Trust

Francis, B. and Skelton, C. (2005) *Reassessing Gender and Achievement*, London: Routledge/Farmer

Francis, B., Hutchings, M. and De Vries, R. (2014) 'The impact of academy chains on low income students', London: The Sutton Trust

Francis, B., Hutchings, M. and De Vries, R. (2014) 'Chain Effects', London: The Sutton Trust

Francis, R. (2013) *Report of the Mid Staffordshire NHS Foundation Trust Public Inquiry*, London: The Stationery Office

Francis, R. (2015) *The Freedom to Speak Up review, Final Report*, London: The Stationery office

Friedson, E. (1965) 'Disability as social deviance', in M.B. Sussman (ed.) *Sociology of Disability and Rehabilitation*, Washington, DC: American Sociological Association

Frosh, S. and Phoenix, A. (2001) 'Positioned by 'Hegemonic' Masculinities: A Study of London Boys' Narratives of Identity', *Australian Psychologist*, 36

Frosh, S., Phoenix, A. and Pattman, R. (2002) *Young Masculinities: Understanding Boys in Contemporary Society* London: Palgrave

Frost, L. (2001) *Young Women and the Body: A Feminist Sociology*, London: Palgrave

Fuller, C. (2009) *Sociology, Gender and Educational Aspirations: Girls and their Ambitions*, London, Continuum International Publishing Group.

Fuller, M. (1984) 'Black girls in a London comprehensive', in R. Deem (ed.) *Schooling for Women's Work*, London: Routledge

Gaine, C. and George, R. (1999) *Gender, "race", and Class in Schooling: A New Introduction*, London: Psychology Press

Gallie, D. (1994) 'Patterns of Skill Change: Upskilling, Deskilling or Polarisation?' in Penn, R., Rose, M. and Rubery, J. (eds.) *Skill and Occupational Change*, Oxford: Oxford University Press

Gans, H. J. (1972–3) 'The Positive Functions of Poverty', *American Journal of Sociology*, 78(2), pp. 1972–3

Gardiner, K. and Evans, M. (2011) 'Exploring poverty gaps among children in the UK', Working Paper No. 103, London: Department for Work and Pensions

Ghuman, P. A. S. 1993 *Asian Adolescents in the West*, Leicester: BPS Books

Giddens, A. (1991) *Modernity and Self-Identity: Self in Society in the Late-Modern Age*, Cambridge: Polity Press

Giddens, A. (1992) *The Transformation of Intimacy: Sexuality, Love and Eroticism in Modern Societies*, Chicago: Stanford University Press

Giddens, A. (1997) *Sociology* (3rd edn) Cambridge: Polity Press

Gillborn, D. (1990) *'Race', Ethnicity and Education: Teaching and Learning in Multi-ethnic Schools* , London: The Stationery Office

Gillborn, D. (2002) *Education and Institutional Racism*, London: Institute of Education

Gillborn, D. (2008) *Racism and Education: Coincidence or Conspiracy?*, London: Routledge

Gillborn, D. and Mirza, H.S. (2000) *Educational Inequality: Mapping Race and Class*, London: OFSTED

Gillborn, D. and Youdell, D. (1999) *Rationing Education: Policy, Practice, Reform and Equity*, Milton Keynes: Open University Press

Gillborn, David (2002) 'Racism in Education' *ACE Bulletin*, 110, p. 9.

Gillespie, R. 'Childfree and Feminine: Understanding the Gender Identity of Voluntarily Childless Women', *Gender and Society*, February 2003, 17(1), pp. 122–136

Giroux, H. (1984) *Ideology, Culture and the Process of Schooling*, London: Falmer Press Ltd

Glaser, B. and Strauss, A. (1967) *The Discovery of Grounded Theory*, Chicago: Aldine

Glennerster, H., Hills, J., Piachaud, D. and Webb, J., 'One hundred years of poverty and policy', York: Joseph Rowntree Foundation, 14th December 2004

Goffman, A. (2014) *On the Run: Fugitive Life in an American Country*, Chicago: Unversity of Chicago Press

Goffman, E. (1963) *Stigma: Notes on the Management of Spoiled Identity*, New York: Prentice Hall

Goffman, E., (1983) 'The Interaction Order', *American Sociological Review*, 48

Goldacre, B. (2012) *Bad Pharma: How drug companies mislead doctors and harm patients*, London: Fourth Estate

Goldthorpe, J. H., D. Lockwood, F. Bechhofer and J. Platt (1968) *The Affluent Worker: Industrial Attitudes and Behaviour*, Cambridge: Cambridge University Press

Goodman, A., and Gregg, P. (2010) *Poorer Children's Educational Attainment: How important Are Attitudes and Behaviour?*, York: Joseph Rowntree Foundation.

Gordon, D., Adelman, L., Ashworth, K., Bradshaw, J., Levitas, R., Middleton, S., Pantazis, C., Patsios, D., Payne, S., Townsend, P. and Williams, J. 'Poverty and Social Exclusion in Britain', York: The Joseph Rowntree Foundation, 11th September 2000

Gordon, D. et al., (1999) *Inequalities in health: Where are we now and what can be done*, Bristol: The Policy Press

Goulbourne, H. and Chamberlain, M. 1999 'Living arrangements, family structure and social change of Caribbeans in Britain', ESRC Population and Household Change for Research, Swindon: Economic Social Research Council

Gouldner, A. (1970) *The Coming Crisis of Western Sociology*, New York: Basic Books

Gove, W.R. (1982) 'The current status of the labeling theory of mental illness', in W.R. Gove (ed.) *Deviance and Mental Illness*, Beverly Hills, CA: Sage Publications

Graham, H. (2002) 'Inequality in Men and Women's Health', in S. Nettleton and U. Gustafsson (eds) *The Sociology of Health and Illness, A Reader*, Cambridge: Polity

Graham, H., Kelly, M. P. (2004) *Health inequalities: concepts, frameworks and policy*, London: Health Development Agency

Gramsci, A. (1971) *Selections from the Prison Notebooks*, London: Lawrence and Wishart

Gray, J. M. (1999). 'Postmodern medicine', *The Lancet*, 354(9189), pp.1550–1553

Green, H., McGinnity, A., Meltzer, H., Ford, T. and Goodman, R. (2005) 'Mental health of young people in Great Britain, 2004', London: Office for National Statistics

Green, L. (2015) 'Age and the Life Course: Continuity, Change and the Modern Mirage of Infinite Choice' in Holborn, M. (ed.) *Contemporary Sociology*, Cambridge: Polity Press

Greer, G. (2000) *The Whole Woman*, New York: Anchor Books

Grice, E. 'Cry of an enfant suavage', *The Telegraph*, 17th July 2006

Griffin, C. (1985) *Typical Girls: Young Women from School to the Job Market*, London: Routledge & Kegan Paul

Guibernau, M. and Goldblatt, D. (2000) 'Identity and nation', in K.Woodward (ed.) *Questioning Identity: Gender, Class, Nation*, London: Routledge/Open University Press

Guilliford, J., Shannon, D., Taskila, T., Wilkins, D., Tod, M. and Bevan, S. 'Sick of Being Unemployed: The health issues of out of work men and how support services are failing to address them', June 2014, The Work Foundation

H. Connor, C. Tyers, T. Modood and J. Hillage (2004) *Why the Difference? A Closer Look at Higher Education Minority Ethnic Students and Graduates*, Department for Education

Hakim, C. (1995) 'Five feminist myths about women's employment', *British Journal of Sociology*, 46, pp. 429–55. Reprinted pages 11–37 in *Women and Management* (eds) C Gatrell, C L Cooper and E E Kossek, Cheltenham: Edward Elgar

Hakim, C. (1996) *Key Issues in Women's Work*, London: Athlone

Hakim, C. (2010) 'Erotic Capital', *European Sociological Review*, 26(5), p. 19

Hall, S. (1992) 'Our Mongrel Selves' *New Statesman*, 19th June 1992

Hallam, S., Ireson, J. and Davies,. J. (2004) 'Primary pupils' experiences of different types of grouping in school', *British Journal of Educational Research*, 30, pp. 515–33

Halsey, A. H. (1961) *Education, economy, and society: a reader in the sociology of education*, New York: Free Press of Glencoe

Halsey, A. H., Heath, A. & Ridge, J. (1980) *Origins and Destinations*, Oxford: Oxford University Press

Hammersley, M. and Gomm, R. (2004) 'Recent radical criticism of the interview in qualitative research', *Developments in Sociology: Annual review*, 20, pp. 91–102.

Handel, G. (2006) *Childhood Socialization*, New Brunswick: Aldine Transaction

Hannan, J. (2000) *Improving Boys' Performance*, Dunstable: Folens

Haralambos, M. and Holborn, M. (2008) *Sociology: Themes and Perspectives*, London: Collins Educational (7th edn.)

Haralambos, M. and Holborn, M. (2013) *Sociology: Themes and Perspectives*, London: Collins Educational (8th edn.)

Hardey, M. (1998) *The Social Context of Health*, Buckingham: Open University Press

Hardey, M. (1998) *The Social Context of Health*, Buckingham: Open University Press

Hargreaves, D. (1967) *Social Relations in a Secondary School*, London: Routledge & Kegan Paul

Hargreaves, D.H. (1967) *Social Relations in a Secondary School*, London: Routledge & Kegan Paul

Hargreaves, David H., Hester, Stephen K., and Mellor, Frank J. (1975) *Deviance in Classrooms*, London: Routledge

Harper, S. (2013) *Future Identities: Changing Identities in the UK the next ten years*, London: Government Office for Science

Hart, N. (1976) *When Marriage Ends*, London: Tavistock

Harvey, D. and Slatin, G. (1976) 'The relationship between a child's SES and teacher expectations: A test of the middle class bias hypothesis', *Social Forces*, 54(1), pp. 140–159

Haskey, J., 'One parent families – and the dependent children living in them – in Great Britain', London: Office for National Statistics

Haug M., Lavin B., (1983) *Consumerism in medicine: Challenging physician authority*, Beverly Hills, CA: Sage Publications

Healey, J. and Yarrow, S. (1997) *Family Matters: Parents Living with Children in Old Age*, Bristol: Policy Press

Heath, S. (2004) 'Shared households, quasi-communes and neo-tribes.' *Current Sociology*, 52(2), pp. 161–179

Hennink, M. et al. (1999) 'Young Asian women and relationships: traditional or transitional', *Ethnic and Racial Studies*, 22(5)

Herzlich, C. (1973) *Health and Illness: a social psychological analysis*, London: Academic Press

Hetherington, K. and Harvard, C. (2014) 'Consumer Society? Identity and Lifestyle' in J. Allen and G. Blakeley (ed.), *Understanding Social Lives 1*, Milton Keynes: The Open University, p.125

455

Heywood, C. (2001) *A history of childhood: Children and childhood in the west from medieval to modern times*, Bristol: Policy Press

Hicks, J. and Allen, G. (1999) *A Century of Change: Trends in UK statistics since 1990*, London: House of Commons Research Paper

Higgs, P. (2008) 'The limits and boundaries to medical knowledge' in *Sociology as Applied to Medicine*, G. Scambler (ed.) (6th edn.) London: Saunders

Hill, M., Ross, N., Cunningham-Burley, S., & Sweeting, H. (2005) 'Grandparents and teen grandchildren: exploring relationships', ESRC

Hills, J. (2010) 'An anatomy of economic inequality in the UK: Report of the National Equality Panel.' London, Government Equalities Office

Hills, J. (2015) *Good Times, Bad Times: The Welfare Myth of Them and Us*, Bristol: Polity Press

Hinksman, M. (2015) 'The Difference between a Consultant and a Doctor in a Hospital', www.gapmedics.co.uk, 2nd April 2015

Hoban, M., James, V., Pattrick, K., Beresford, P. and Fleming, J. 'Shaping our age: Voices on well-being - A report on research with older people', Cardiff: Royal Voluntary Service

Hochschild, A. (1983) *The Managed Heart: The Commercialisation of Human Feeling*. Berkeley: University of California Press

Hockey, J. and James, A. (1993) *Growing Up and Growing Old*, London: Sage Publications

Hollingworth, S. & Williams, K. (2009) 'Constructions of the working class "other" among urban white middle class youth: "chavs", subculture and the valuing of education', *Journal of Youth Studies*, 12(5), pp. 467–483

Holman, J. *Educating Yorkshire*, Review in *The Yorkshire Times*, 6th September 2013

Holmes, J. and Kiernan, K. (2010) 'Fragile Families in the UK: evidence from the Millennium Cohort Study', SCHMI University of Manchester, University of York

Hough, J.M. and Roberts, J.V (2004) *Juvenile Delinquency in England*, Oxford: Polity Press

Hunt, S. (2001) 'Dying to be thin', *Sociology Review*, 10(4)

Hunt, S. and Lightly, N. (1999) 'A Healthy alternative? A Sociology of Fringe Medicine, *Sociology Review*, 8(3)

Hurst, G. 'Anxious UK pupils lag behind in maths', *The Times*, 4th December 2013

Hurst, G. 'Boys expected to narrow the gap at GCSE as English grades fall' *The Times*, 21st August 2013

Illich, I. (2002) 'Medical Nemesis', *Journal of Epidemiology and Community Health*, 57(12)

Illsley, R. (1986) 'Occupational class, selection and the production of inequalities in health', *Quarterly Journal of Social Affairs*, 2(2), pp.151–64

The Independent Commission of Fees (2014) 'Analysis of trends in higher education applications, admissions, and enrolments'

Ireson, J. and Hallam, S. et al. (2009) 'Ability grouping in the primary school: a survey', *Educational Studies*, 29(1), pp. 69–83

Ireson, J., Hallam, S. and Hurley, C. (2002) *Ability grouping in the Secondary School: Effects on GCSE attainment in English, mathematics and science*, Paper presented at the British Educational Research Association Annual Conference, Exeter University, Exeter, 10–14 September 2002.

Jackson, C. (2006) *Lads and Ladettes in School: Gender and the fear of failure*, Milton Keynes: Open University Press

James, O.W. (1998) *Britain on the couch: Why we're unhappier compared with 1950, despite being richer*, London: Arrow

Jamieson, L. et al (2002) 'Cohabitation and commitment: partnership plans of young men and women', *The Sociological Review*, 50(3)

Jasper, L. 'School system failing black children', *The Guardian*, 16th March 2002

Jefferis, B., Power, C. and Hertzman, C. (2002) 'Birth weight, childhood socioeconomic environment, and cognitive development in the 1958 British birth cohort study', *British Medical Journal*, 325, p.305

Jenkins, R. (1996) *Social Identity (Key Ideas)* London: Routledge

Jenks, C. (1993) *Culture*, London: Routledge

Jerrim, J. (2013) 'Family Background and access to 'high status' universities', London: The Sutton Trust

Jivraj, S. and Khan, O. (2013) *Ethnicity and deprivation in England: How likely are ethnic minorities to live in deprived neighbourhoods?* Centre on Dynamics of Ethnicity briefing paper.

Johal, S. (1998) 'Brimful of Brasia', *Sociology Review*, 8(1)

Johnson, J. and Bytheway, B. (1993) 'Ageism: concept and definition', in J.Johnson and R.Slater (eds.) *Ageing and Later Life*, London: Sage Publications

Jones G. and Wallace, C. (1992) *Youth, Family and Citizenship*, Milton Keynes: Open University Press

Jones, L. and Green, J. (2006) 'Shifting discourses of professionalism: a case study of general practitioners in the United Kingdom' ,*Sociology of Health and Illness*, 28(7), pp. 927–50

Jordan, B. (1992) *Trapped in Poverty: Labour Market Decisions in Low Income Households*, London: Routledge

Judge, L. (2012) 'Introduction' in 'Ending Child Poverty by 2020: Progress made and lessons learned', Child Poverty Action Group

Jylhä, M. (2009). 'What is self-rated health and why does it predict mortality? Toward a unified conceptual model.' *Social Science & Medicine*, 69, pp. 307–316.

Kai J., Beavan J., Faull, Dodson L., Gill P., Beighton A. (2007) 'Professional Uncertainty and Disempowerment Responding to Ethnic Diversity in Health Care: A Qualitative Study', *PLoS Medicine*, 4(11)

Kallianes, V. and Rubenfeld, P. (1997) 'Disabled women and reproductive rights', *Disability and Society*, 12(2)

Karlsen, S. & Nazroo, J. Y. (2004), 'Fear of racism and health', *Journal of Epidemiology and Community Health*, 58, pp. 1017–1018

Karlsen, S., and Nazroo, J. (2014) 'Ethnic and religious variations in the reporting of racist victimization in Britain: 2000 and 2008/2009', *Patterns of Prejudice*, 48(4), pp. 370–97

Katz, M.M., Cole, J.O. and Lowery, H.A. (1969) 'Studies of the diagnostic process: the influence of symptom perception, past experience, and ethnic background on diagnostic process.' *American Journal of Psychology*, 125, pp. 109–19

Kaye, A., Jordan, H., Baker, M. (2012) 'The Tipping Point: The human and economic costs of cutting disabled people's support', London: The Hardest Hit Coalition

Keddie, N. (1971) 'The Organization of Classroom Knowledge' in *English in Education*, 5(2), pp. 63–68

Kelly, A. (2009) 'Globalisation and education: a review of conflicting perspectives and their effect on policy and educational practice in the UK Globalisation', *Societies and Education*, 7(1)

Kersley, H. and Shaheen, F. (2014) Addressing Economic Inequality at Root. London, New Economics Foundation

Khan, M. (2014) *The Men with Many Wives: the British Muslims who practise polygamy*, Channel 4 television

Kincaid, J. (1973) *Poverty and Equality in Britain*, Harmondsworth: Penguin

Kindlon, Daniel J. and Thompson, M. (1999) *Raising Cain: Protecting the Emotional Life of Boys*, New York: Ballantine Books

Kirby, R. (2000) *Underachievement in Boys*, www.practicalparent.org.uk

Kirkby J. 'I'm in the Technical Middle Class … get me out of here', *The Times* online, 4th April 2013

Klein, N. (1999) *No Logo*, New York: Picador

Krause, I.B. (1989) 'Sinking heart: a Punjabi communication of distress', *Social Science and Medicine*, 29, pp. 563–75

Kyaga et al., (2012) 'Mental illness, suicide, and creativity', *Journal of Psychiatric Research*

Kynaston, D. 'What should we do with private schools' *The Guardian Review*, 5th December 2014

Kynaston, D. (2014) *Modernity Britain: Book Two: A Shake of the Dice, 1959–92 (Modernity Britain Book 2)*, London: Bloomsbury Publishing

Langley, S. and Mack, J. (1983, 1990, 1993 and 2015) *Breadline Britain: The Rise of Mass Poverty*, London: Oneworld Publications

Lansley, S. and Reed, H. (2013) *How to Boost the Wage Share*, London: TUC

Lareau, A. (2011) *Unequal Childhoods: Class, Race, and Family Life, With an Update a Decade Later*, Berkley: University of California Press

Larkin, M. (2011) *Social Aspects of Health, Illness and Healthcare*, Maidenhead: McGraw-Hill Education.

Laslett, P. (1972) 'Mean household size in England since the sixteenth century', in P. Laslett (ed.) *Household and Family in Past Time*, Cambridge: Cambridge University Press

Lees, S. (1986) *Losing Out: Sexuality and Adolescent Girls*, London: Hutchinson

Leidner, R. (1993) *Fast Food, Fast Talk: Service Work and the Routinisation of Everyday Life*, Berkeley: University of California Press

Leonti, M., and Casu, L. (2013) 'Traditional medicines and globalization: current and future perspectives in ethnopharmacology', *Front. Pharmacol*, 4(92)

Leung, G. and Stanner, S. (2012) 'Is diet to blame for poor health of minority ethnic groups in the UK?', London: British Nutrition Foundation.

Levine, R. (1956) 'Body language of the Nacirema', *American Anthropologist*, 58

Levitas, R. (2012) 'Policy Response Series No. 3: There may be "trouble" ahead: what we know about those 120,000 "troubled" families', Poverty and Social Exclusion in the UK,

Lewis, J. (2007) *Families and Labour's Family Policies*, posted on www.lse.ac.uk/collections/pressAndInformationOffice/newsAndEvents/archives/2007/BlairsLegacyJune07.htm

Lewis, O. (1966) *La Vida*, New York: Random House

Lewis, P., Newburn, T., Taylor, M., Mcgillivray, C., Greenhill, A., Frayman, H. and Proctor, R. (2011) 'Reading the riots: investigating England's summer of disorder', London: The London School of Economics and Political Science and *The Guardian*

Lievesley, N. (2013) 'The ageing of the ethnic minority populations of England and Wales: findings from the 2011 census: a briefing paper', London: Centre for Policy on Ageing

Ling et al (2012) 'The "other" in patterns of drinking: A qualitative study of attitudes towards alcohol use among professional, managerial and clerical workers', *BMC Public Health*, 12(892)

Link, B. and Phelan, J. (1995) 'Social conditions as fundamental cause of disease', *Journal of Health and Social Behaviour*, pp.80–94

Lister, R. (ed.) (1996) in *Charles Murray and the Underclass: The Developing Debate*, London: IEA Health and Welfare Unit

Littlewood, R. and Lipsedge, M. (1997) *Aliens and Alienists: Ethnic Minorities and Psychiatry*, 3rd edn. London: Routledge

Litwak, E. (1965) 'Extended kin relations in an industrial democratic society', in E. Shanas & G.F. Streib (eds.) *Social structure and the family*, Englewood Clifs, NJ: Prentice-Hall

Livingstone, S. (2009) *Children and the Internet: Great Expectations, Challenging Realities*, Cambridge: Polity Press

Lockwood, D. (1966) *The Blackcoated Worker*, Sydney: Allen & Unwin

Longmore, F. (1987) 'Screening stereotypes: images of disabled people in TV and motion pictures', in A. Gartner and T. Foe (eds.) *Images of the Disabled, Disabling Images*, New York: Praeger

Lowy, M. (2007) *Marx and Weber: Critics of Capitalism*, New Politics, (11)2

Luck, M., Bamford, M. and Williamson, P. (2000) *Men's Health: Perspectives, Diversity and Paradox*, Oxford: Blackwell Science

Lupton, D. (1994) *Medicine as Culture: Illness, Disease and the Body in Western Societies*, London: Sage Publications

Lury, C. (2011) *Consumer Culture*, Cambridge: Polity Press

Lyng, S. (1990) 'Edgework: a social psychological analysis of voluntary risk-taking', *American Journal of Sociology*, 95(4), pp. 851–6

Lyotard. J. (1979) *The Postmodern Condition: A Report on Knowledge*, Paris: Les Éditions de Minuit

Mac an Ghaill, M. (1994) *The Making of Men: Masculinities, Sexualities and Schooling*, Milton Keynes: Open University Press

Mac an Ghaill, M. (1996) *Understanding Masculinities: Social Relations and Cultural Arenas*, Buckingham: Open University Press

Mac an Ghaill, M. (1998) *Young Gifted and Black: The Schooling of Black Youth*. Buckingham: Open University Press.

Macaskill, M. (2014) 'Teenage boys strain to meet body ideals', *The Sunday Times*, 16th November 2014

MacDonald, R., Shildrick, T. and Furlong, A. (2014) 'Benefits Street' and the myth of workless communities', *Sociological Research Online*, 19(3), pp. 1–6

Machin, S. and McNally, S. (2006) *Gender and Student Achievement in English Schools*, London: LSE

Machin, S. and McNally, S. (2006) *Education and Child Poverty: A Literature Review*, York: Joseph Rowntree Foundation

McInnes, T., Aldridge, H., Bushe, S., Tinson, A. and Barry Born, T., (2013) 'Monitoring poverty and social exclusion 2014', York: The Joseph Rowntree Foundation

MacKenzie, R., Stuart, M., Forde, C., Greenwood, L., Gardiner, J. & Perrett, R. (2006) '"All that is solid?" Class identity and the maintenance of a collective orientation among redundant steelworkers', *Sociology*, 40(5)

Macmillan, L. (2011) 'Measuring the intergenerational correlation of worklessness', *CMPO Working Paper No. 11/278*, Bristol: University of Bristol

Marcuse, H. (1964) *One-Dimensional Man*, Boston: Beacon

Marmot, M. and Shipley, M. (1996) 'Do Socio-economic Differences in Mortality Persist after Retirement? 25 Year Follow-up of Civil Servants from the First Whitehall Study', *British Medical Journal*, 313, pp. 1177–80

Marsh, I. and Keating, M. (2006) *Sociology: Making Sense of Society* (3rd edn) Harlow: Pearson

Marshall, G. (1998) *Oxford Dictionary of Sociology*, Oxford: Oxford University Press

Marsland, D. (1996) *Welfare or Welfare State?*, Basingstoke: Macmillan

Martin, W. 'Banning the 'blended' family: why step-families will never be the same as first families, *The Telegraph*, 23 January 2013, available at http://www.telegraph.co.uk/women/mother-tongue/9820359/Banning-the-blended-family-why-step-families-will-never-be-the-same-as-first-families.html

Marx, K. & Engels, F. (1848) *Manifesto of the Communist Party*, Moscow: Foreign Languages Publishing House

Marx, K. and Engels, F. (1974) *The German Ideology* (2nd edn) London: Lawrence & Wishart

McAllister, F. with Clarke, L. (1998) *Choosing Childlessness*, York: Family Policy Studies Centre and Joseph Rowntree Foundation

McCrone, P., Dhanasiri, S., Patel, A., Knapp, M. and Lawton-Smith, S. (2008) 'Paying the Price: The cost of mental health care in England 2006', London: King's Fund

McDonald, A. Saunders, L. and Benefield, P. (1999) 'Boys' achievement, progress, motivation and participation: Issues raised by the recent literature', *Journal of the National Foundation for Educational Research*

McDonald, Dwight (1957) *The Responsibility of Peoples, and other essays in political criticism*, London: Victor Gollancz

McHale, S., A.C. Crouter, and S.D. Whiteman. 2003, 'The family contexts of gender development in childhood and adolescence', *Social Development*, 12, pp. 125–148

McHardy, F. *Surviving Poverty – The Impact of Parenthood*, Poverty Alliance

McKenzie, R. et al (2006) 'Redundancy as a critical life event: moving on from the Welsh steel industry through career change', *Work Employment & Society*, 23(4) pp. 727–745

McKeown, T. (1979) *The Role of Medicine: Dream, Mirage or Nemesis*, Oxford: Blackwell

McKinlay, J.B., and Arches, J. (1985) 'Towards the proletarianization of physicians', *International Journal of Health Services: Planning, Administration, Evaluation*, 15(2), pp.161–95

McMahon, B. 'ADHD: Diagnosis of a generation driven to distraction', *The Times*, 8th January 2014

McNamara, R.P. (1994) *The Times Square Hustler: Male Prostitution in New York City*, Westport: Praeger

McNight, A., Glennerster, H. and Lupton, R. (2005) '"Education, education, education": An assessment of Labour's success in tackling education inequalities', in J. Hills and K. Stewart (eds.) *A More Equal Society: New Labour, Poverty Inequality and Exclusion*, Bristol: Policy Press

McRobbie, A. (2000) *Feminism and Youth Culture*, London: Palgrave Macmillan

Mead, G.H. (1934) *Mind, Self, and Society*, Chicago: University of Chicago Press

Mercer, S., Watt, G. (2007) 'The inverse care law: Clinical Primary Care encounters in deprived and affluent areas of Scotland', *The Annals of Family Medicine*, 5(6), pp. 503–510

Meyer, H. 'House prices near top 30 state schools are '12% higher'', *The Guardian*, 27th October 2013

Miliband, R. (1974) 'Politics and Poverty' in Wedderburn, D. (ed.) *Poverty, Inequality and Class Structure*, Cambridge: Cambridge University Press

Millett, K. (1970) *Sexual Politics*, Champaign: University of Illinois Press

Milner, C., Van Norman, K. and Milner, J. (2012) *The Media's Portrayal of Ageing in Global Population Ageing: Peril or Promise?* Agenda Council on Ageing Society and World Economic Forum

Mirza, H. (1992) *Young, Female and Black*, London: Routledge

Mitsos, E. and Browne, K. (1998) 'Gender differences in education: the underachievement of boys', *Sociology Review*, 8(1)

Modood, T. (1997) *Ethnic Minorities in Britain: Diversity and Disadvantage*, London: Policy Studies Institute

Modood, T. (2004) 'Capitals, ethnic identity and educational qualifications' *Cultural Trends*, 13(2)

Modood, T. (2005) *Multicultural Politics Racism, Ethnicity and Muslims in Britain*, Minneapolis: University of Minnesota Press

The Money Charity (2014) *The Money Statistics September 2014*, http://themoneycharity.org.uk/money-statistics/september-2014/

Mooney, A., Oliver, C. and Smith, M. (2009) 'Impact of Family Breakdown on Children's Well-Being: Evidence Review', London: Thomas Coram Research Unit, Institute of Education, University of London for the Department for Children, Schools and Families

Moore, S. (2004) 'Hanging around: the politics of the busstop', *Youth and Policy*, 82, pp. 47–59

Morgan, D.H.J. (1996) *Family Connections: An Introduction to Family Studies*, Cambridge: Polity Press

Morgan, P. (2000) *Marriage-Lite: The Rise of Cohabitation and its Consequences*, London: Civitas

Morgan, P. (2002) 'Children as trophies? Examining the evidence on same-sex parenting', The Christian Institute

Morgan, P (2007) *The War between the State and the Family: How Government Divides and Impoverishes*, London: The Institute of Economic Affairs

Morris, D. (1968) *The Naked Ape*, London: Corgi

Morrow, V. (1998) *Understanding Families: Children's Perspectives*, York: National Children's Bureau in association with the Joseph Rowntree Foundation

Mort, F. (1996) *Cultures of Consumption: Masculinities and Social Space in Late Twentieth-Century Britain*, London: Routledge

Mortimore, J. and Blackstone, T. (1994) *Disadvantage and Education*, London: Paul Chapman

Mount, F. (2004) *Mind the Gap: The New Class Divide in Britain*, London: Short Books

Murdock, G.P. (1949) *Social Structure*, New York: Macmillan

Murphy, M. quoted in '"Marriage still the best way to play happy, healthy families", says study', Polly Curtis, *The Guardian*, 5th October 2007

Murray, C. 'Underclass: A Diasater in the Making', *The Sunday Times Magazine*, 26th November 1989

Murray, C. (1990) *The Emerging British Underclass*, London: IEA

Murray, C. (1994) *Underclass: The Crisis Deepens*, London: IEA

Murray, C. (1996) *Charles Murray and the Underclass: The Developing Debate*, London: Civitas

Myers, J. (1975) 'Life events, social integration and psychiatric symptomatology', *Journal of Health and Social Behaviour*, 16, pp. 121–7

Myhill, D. (2002) 'Bad boys and good girls? Patterns of interaction and response in whole class teaching', *British Educational Research Journal*, 28, pp. 350

Navarro, V. (1977) *Medicine under Capitalism*, London: Martin Robertson

Nazroo, J Y. (2008) "Ethnic Inequalities in Health." In *Encyclopedia of Life Sciences*, Wiley & Sons Ltd: Chichester,

Nazroo, J.Y. (2001) *Ethnicity, class and health*, London: Policy Studies Institute

Nelson, M. K. (2010) *Parenting Out of Control: Anxious Parents in Uncertain Times*, New York: NYU Press

Nettleton, S. (1995) *The Sociology of Health and Illness*, Cambridge: Polity Press

New Economics Foundation (2011) *The Great Transition: social justice and the core economy*, London: New Economics Foundation

New Economics Foundation (2013) *Surviving Austerity*, London: New Economics Foundation

New Economics Foundation (2014) *NEW Review of the Year 2013–2014*, London: New Economics Foundation

Nichols, T. and Beynon, H. (1977) *Living with Capitalism*, London: Routledge and Kegan Paul

O'Brien, M., Jones, D., Sloan, D. and Rustin, M. (2000) 'Children's independent spatial mobility in the urban public realm', *Childhood: A Global Journal of Child Research*, 7(3), pp. 257–277

O'Brien, R., Hunt, K., Hart, G. (2005) '"It's caveman stuff, but that is to a certain extent how guys still look to operate"': men's accounts of masculinity and help seeking', *Social Science and Medicine*, 61, pp. 503–516

O'Byrne, D. (2015) 'Globalisation' in M. Holborn (2015) *Contemporary Sociology*, Cambridge: Polity Press

O'Connor, J. (1973) *The Fiscal Crisis of the State*, Basingstoke: Macmillan

O'Donnell, M. (1991) *Race and Ethnicity*, Harlow: Longman

O'Donnell, M. and Sharpe, S. (2000) *Uncertain Masculinities: Youth, Ethnicity and Class in Contemporary Britain*, London: Routledge

457

Oakley, A. (1981) *Subject Women*, New York: Pantheon Books

Oakley, A. (1982) *Subject Women*, London: Fontana

Oakley, A. (1985) *The sociology of housework*, New York: Basil Blackwell

Oakley, A. (1986) 'Feminism, motherhood and medicine – Who cares?', in J. Mitchell and A. Oakley (eds) *What is Feminism?*, Oxford: Blackwell

Office for National Statistics (2005) *Annual Abstract of Statistics*, Basingstoke: Palgrave Macmillan

Office for National Statistics (2012) 'Statistical Bulletin: Families and Households, 2012', *Families and Households, 2012 Release,* London: Office for National Statistics

Office for National Statistics (2012) 'Short Report: Cohabitation in the UK, 2012', *Families and Households, 2012 Release*, London: Office for National Statistics,

Office for National Statistics (2012) *Marriages in England and Wales (Provisional) 2010*, London: Office for National Statistics

Office for National Statistics (2013) *National Population Projections, 2012–based Statistical Bulletin*, London: Office for National Statistics

Office For National Statistics (2014) *Analysis of Employee Contracts that do not Guarantee a Minimum Number of Hours*, London: Office for National Statistics

Office for National Statistics (2014) *National Life Tables, United Kingdom, 2010–2012*, London: Office for National Statistics

Office for National Statistics, (2013) *What does the 2011 census tell us about older people?*, London: Office for National Statistics

Office for National Statistics, (2014) *Divorces in England and Wales, 2012'*, London: Office for National Statistics

Office for National Statistics, (2014) 'Living Alone in England and Wales', Part of the *2011 Census Analysis, Do the Demographic and Socio-Economic Characteristics of those Living Alone in England and Wales Differ from the General Population?*, London: Office for National Statistics

Office for National Statistics, (2014) *UK Wages Over the Past Four Decades*, London: Office for National Statistics

Office for National Statistics, *Household Satellite Accounts - Valuing Household Clothing and Laundry Services in the UK*, London: The Office for National Statistics

Oliver, M. (1990) *The Politics of Disablement*, Basingstoke: Macmillan

Oliver, M. (1996) *Understanding Disability*, London: Macmillan

Oliver, M. (2009) *Understanding Disability, from Theory to Practice Second Edition*, Basingstoke: Palgrave Macmillan

Olney, M.F. and Kim, A. (2001) 'Beyond adjustment: integration of cognitive disability into identity', *Disability and Society*, 16

Ormston, R. and Curtice, J. (eds.) (2015) *British Social Attitudes: the 32nd Report*, London: NatCen Social Research

Osler, A. (2006) *Response to the Equalities Review Interim Report of the Cabinet Office* sponsored by the Joseph Rowntree Foundation, Centre for Citizenship and Human Rights Education, University of Leeds

P. Woods (1983) *Sociology and the School: An Interactionist Viewpoint*, London: RKP

Pahl, R. and Spencer, L. (2001) *Rethinking Friendship: Personal Communities and Social Cohesion*, ESRC Report

Palmer, G. (2015) 'The Poverty Site', www.poverty.org.uk

Palmer G., Carr J. and Kenway P. (2005) 'Monitoring poverty and social exclusion 2005', York: Joseph Rowntree Foundation

Palmer, G., MacInnes, T. and Kenway, P. (2007) 'Monitoring poverty and social exclusion 2007', York: Joseph Rowntree Foundation

Palmer, S. (2007) *Toxic Childhood. How the modern world is damaging our children and what we can do about it*, London: Orion

Park, K., (2005) 'Choosing childlessness: Weber's typology of action and motives of the voluntarily childless', *Sociological Inquiry*, 75(3), pp. 372–402

Parker, S. (1976) 'Work and leisure' in Butterworth, E. and Weir, D. *The Sociology of Leisure*, London: Allen and Unwin

Parry, N. and Parry, J. (1976) *The Rise of Medical Professions*, London: Croom

Parsons, T. (1951) *The Social System*, Free Press: New York

Parsons, T. (1965) 'The normal American family', in S.M. Farber (ed.) *Man and Civilization: the Family's Search for Survival*, New York: McGraw Hill

Parsons, T. (1975) 'The sick role and the role of the physician reconsidered', *Millbank Memorial Fund Quarterly: Health and Society*, 53, pp. 257–78

Paton, C. (2014) 'At What Cost? Paying the Price for the Market in the English NHS', London: CHPI

Pell., J., Pell, A., Norrie, J., Ford, I., Cobbe, S. (2000) Effect of socioeconomic deprivation on waiting time for cardiac surgery: retrospective cohort study, *BMJ*, 320, pp. 15–18

Perry, E. and Francis, B. (2010) 'The Social Class Gap for Educational achievement: a review of the literature', London: The RSA

Phillips, M. (1997) *All Must Have Prizes*, London: Little Brown

Philo, G, Miller, D & Happer, C (2015) 'The Sociology of the Mass Media: circuits of communication and structures of power' in Holborn, M. (ed.) *Contemporary Sociology*, Cambridge: Polity Press

Philo, G. and Berry M. (2004) *Bad news from Israel*, London: Pluto Press

Philo, G. and Glasgow University Media Group (1982) *Really Bad News*, Michigan: Writers and Readers

Philo, G. and Secker, J. (1999) 'Media and mental health' in B. Franklin (ed.) *Social Policy, The Media and Misrepresentation*, London: Routledge

Phoenix, A. and Frosh, S. (2001) Positioned by 'Hegemonic' Masculinities: A Study of London Boys' Narratives of Identity Australian Psychologist, 36, pp. 27–35

Pilcher, J. (1996) *Age and Generation in Modern Britain*, Oxford: Oxford University Press

Pilgrim, D. and Rogers, A. (1999) *A Sociology of Mental Health and Illness* (2nd edn) Buckingham: Open University Press

Pilkington, A. (2002) 'Cultural representations and changing ethnic identities in a global age' in Holborn, M. (ed.) *Developments in Sociology Volume 17*, Ormskirk: Causeway Press

Pilkington, A. (2011) 'David Cameron and multiculturalism: reproducing the new orthodoxy', *Social Science Teacher*, 40(3) pp. 22–25, 2043–8931

Pill, R. & Scott, N. (1982) Concepts of illness causation and responsibility: Some preliminary data from a sample of working class mothers, *Social Science and Medicine*, 16(1), pp. 43–45

Piore, M. J. (1986) 'Perspectives on Labour Market Flexibility', *Industrial Relations*, 25(2), pp. 146–66

Pirie, M. 'How exams are fixed in favour of girls', *The Spectator*, 20th January 2001

Platt, L. (2009) 'Ethnicity and family: relationships within and between ethnic groups: an analysis using the Labour Force Survey EHRC unumbered research reports', Manchester: Equality and Human Rights Commission

Platt, L. (2011) 'Inequality within ethnic groups', *JRF programme paper: Poverty and ethnicity, 2607*, York: Joseph Rowntree Foundation

Platt, L. (2011) *Understanding Inequalities: Stratification and Difference*, Cambridge: Polity Press

Platt, S. (2012) 'Trends in national suicide rates for Scotland and England & Wales, 1960–2008, *The British Journal of Psychiatry, 200.3)* pp. 245–251

Plummer, K. (1982) *Documents of Life*, London: George Allen & Unwin

Plummer, K. (1995) *Telling Sexual Stories: Power, Change, and Social Worlds*, Abingdon: Psychology Press

Pollock, L. (1983) *Forgotten Children: Parent-Child Relations from 1500 to 1900*, Cambridge: Cambridge University Press

Postman, N. (1982) *The Disappearance of Childhood*, New York: Delacorte Press

The Poverty Site, Educational Attainment at 16, available at http://poverty.org.uk/26/index.shtml?6 accessed 01/10/2014

Pudney, S. (2002) *The Road to Ruin? Sequences of initiation into drug use and offending by young people in Britain*, London: The Home Office

Pugh, A. (2002) *From 'Compensation' to 'Childhood Wonder': Why Parents Buy*, Working Paper No 39. University of California Berkeley: Centre for Working Families

Punch, K. (2009) *Introduction to Research Methods in Education*, London: Sage Publications

Punch, S. (2002) 'Youth transitions and interdependent adult-child relations in rural Bolivia', *Journal of Rural Studies*, 18, pp. 123–133

Putnam, R. (2000) *Bowling Alone*, New York: Simon and Schuster

Radford, L. et al. (2011) *Child abuse and neglect in the UK today*, London: NSPCC

Ranson, S. (2005) 'The participation of volunteer citizens in school governance', *Education Review*, 57

Rapoport, R. N., (1976) 'Dual-Career Families Re-examined: New Integrations of Work and Family', London: Martin Robertson

Ratcliffe, R. 'Eton headmaster: England's exam system unimaginative and outdated', *The Guardian*, 5th August 2014

Ratcliffe, R. 'Pupil premium funds diverted, illegally large classes and fantasy curriculum', *The Guardian Online*, 13th June 2014

Reay, D., David, M. et al. (2005) *Degrees of Choice: Social class, race and gender in higher education*, New York: Oxford University Press

Reay, D., Davies, J., David, M. and Balls, S.J. (2001) 'Choices of Degree or Degrees of Choice? Class, "Race" and the Higher Education Choice Process', *Sociology*, 35(4) pp. 855–874

Reay, D., David, M.E. and Ball, S. (2005) *Degrees of Choice: social class, race and gender in higher education*, Stoke-on-Trent: Trentham Books

Rector, R. 'How Welfare Undermines Marriage and What to Do About It', the Heritage Foundation, November 17th 2014

Reed, H. (2012) 'In the eye of the storm: Britain's forgotten children and families: A research report for Action for Children, the Children's Society and NSPCC', June 2012

Reynolds, D. (1984) *Constructive Living*, Hawaii: Kolowalu Books, University of Hawaii Press

Richards, C. (2012) 'Playing under surveillance: gender, performance and the conduct of the self in a primary school playground'. *British Journal of the Sociology of Education*, 33, pp. 373–90

Ridge D, Emslie C, White A. (2011) 'Understanding how men experience, express and cope with mental distress: where next?' *Sociology of Health and Illness*, 33, pp. 145–59

Rikowski, G. *Methods for Researching the Social Production of Labour Power in Capitalism*, School of Education Research Seminar, University College Northampton, 7th March 2002

Rikowski, G. *Distillation: Education in Karl Marx's Social Universe*, Lunchtime Seminar, School of Education, University of East London, Barking Campus, 14th February 2005

Ritchie, J. and Lewis, J. (eds.) (2003) *Qualitative Research Practice: A Guide for Social Science Students and Researchers*, London: Sage Publications

Ritzer, G. (2007, orig. 1993) *The McDonaldisation of Society*, Newbury Park: Pine Forge Press

Rivell, P. 'The hidden curriculum', *The Guardian*, 30th April 2004

Roberts, K. (1986) 'Leisure' in M. (ed.) *Developments in Sociology Volume 2*, Ormskirk: Causeway Press

Roberts, K. (2011) *Class in Contemporary Britain 2nd Edition*, Basingstoke: Palgrave Macmillan

Roberts, K., Cavill, N., Hancock, C. and Rutter, H. 'Social and economic inequalities in diet and physical activity', London: Public Health England, November 2013

Robertson, R. (1992) *Globalization: Social Theory and Global Culture*, London: Sage Publications

Rogers, A., May, C. & Oliver, D. (2001) Experiencing depression, experiencing the depressed: the separate worlds of patients and doctors. *Journal of Mental Health*, 10, pp. 317–333

Rogers, S. 'Government Spending by Department 2011–12: get the data', *The Guardian*, 4th December 2012

Rojek, C. (1995) *Decentring Leisure*, London: Sage Publications

Rosenhan, D.L. (1973/1982) 'On being sane in insane places', *Science*, 179, pp.250–8; also in M. Bulmer (ed.) (1982) *Social Research Ethics*, London: Holmes and Meier

Rosenthal, R. and Jacobson, L. (1968) *Pygmalion in the Classroom: Teacher Expectation and Pupils' Intellectual Development*, Carmarthen: Crown House Publishing

Ross, N., Hill, M., Sweeting, H. and Cunningham-Burley, S. (2006) *Grandparents and Teen Grandchildren: Exploring Intergenerational Relationships*, Edinburgh: Centre for Research on Families and Relationships

Rothermel, P. (1999) 'A nationwide study of home education: Early indications and wider implications', *Education Now*, 24

Rowe, D & Lynch, R (2012), 'Work and play in the city: some reflections on the night-time leisure economy of Sydney', *Annals of Leisure Research*, 15(2), pp. 132–47

Rutter, M. (1979) 'Protective factors in children's responses to stress and disadvantage' in M.W. Kent & J. E. Rolf (eds.) *Primary prevention of psychopathology (Vol. 3) Social competence in children*, Hanover, NH: University Press of New England.

Salway, S. Carter, L. Powell, K., Turner, D., Mir, G. and Ellison, G.T.H. (2014) 'Race inequalities and health inequalities: towards more integrated policy and practice', London: Race Equality Foundation

Sanders, T. (2004) 'The risk of prostitution: punters, police and protesters', *Urban Studies*, 41(8), pp. 1703–17

Sanders, T. (2005) *Sex work: A risky business*, Devon: Willan Publishing

Sardar, Z. 'First Person', *The Guardian online*, 13th September 2008, available at http://www.theguardian.com/lifeandstyle/2008/sep/13/family1

Savage, J. (2007) *Teenage: The Creation of Youth Culture*, London: Chatto & Windus

Savage, M. (1995) 'Class analysis and social research', in Butler, T. and Savage, M. (eds.) *Social Change and the Middle Classes*, London: UCL Press

Savage, M. (2005) 'Working class identities in the 1960s: revisiting the affluent worker study', *Sociology*, 39(5), pp. 929–946

Savage, M., Devine, F., Cunningham, N. Taylor, M., Li, Y., Hjellbrekke, J., Le Roux, B, Friedman, S., and Miles, A.. (2013) 'A New Model of Social Class? Findings from the BBC's Great British Class Survey Experiment', *Sociology*, 37(2), p. 230

Scambler, G. (2008) *Sociology as Applied to Medicine*, Saunders Ltd., Philadelphia: Saunders Ltd.

Scambler, G. and Higgs, P. (2001) '"The dog that didn't bark": taking class seriously in the

health inequalities debate', *Social Science and Medicine*, 33, pp. 275–96

Schudson, M. (1994) 'Culture and integration of national societies', in D. Crane (ed.) *The Sociology of Culture*, Oxford: Blackwell

Scott, J. (1991) *Who Rules Britain?*, Cambridge: Polity Press

Scott, R.A. (1969) *The Making of Blind Men*, New Brunswick: Transaction Publishers

Scraton, S. & Bramham, P. (2001) 'Changing work and leisure relations' in Haralambos, M. (ed.) *Developments in Sociology Volume 17*, Ormskirk: Causeway Press

Scraton, S. & Watson, B. (2015) 'Leisure and Consumption: A critical analysis of "free time" in M. Holborn (2015) *Contemporary Sociology*, Cambridge: Polity Press

Seddon, N. (2007) 'Quite like heaven: options for the NHS in a consumer age', Civitas

Self, A. and Zealey, L. (eds) (2007) *Social Trends 37*, Basingstoke: Office for National Statistics/ Palgrave Macmillan

Sewell, T. (1997) *Black Masculinities and Schooling: How Black Boys Survive Modern Schooling*, Stoke-on-Trent: Trentham Books

Shaheen, F. (2014) The embarrassing truth of trickle-down'. London: New Economics Foundation

Shakespeare, T. (2013) *Disability Rights and Wrongs Revisited*, London: Routledge

Sharpe, S. (1976, 1994 2nd edn) *Just Like a Girl*, Harmondsworth: Penguin

Shaw, A. (2000) *Kinship and Continuity: Pakistani Families in Britain*, London: Routledge

Shaw, M., Dorling, D., and Davey Smith, G. (2006) 'Poverty, social exclusion and minorities' in Marmot M. and R. Wilkinson (eds.) *Social determinants of health (Second edition)*, Oxford: Oxford University Press

Shildrick, T. and MacDonald, R. (2015) 'Talking About Poverty', *Sociology Review*, 24(3)

Shildrick, T., MacDonald, R. (2013) 'Poverty talk: how people experiencing poverty deny their poverty and why they blame "the poor"', *The Sociological Review*, 61(2)

Shilling, C. (2003) *The Body and Social Theory* (2nd edn), London: Sage Publications

Singer, P. W. (2006) *Children at War*, Berkeley: University of California Press

Singh Ghumann, P.A. (1999) *Asian Adolescents in the West*, Leicester: BPS Books

Skeggs, B. (2015) 'The Idea of Class: A measure of value' in Holborn, M. (ed.) *Contemporary Sociology*, Cambridge: Polity Press

Skelton, C., Francis, B. and Valkanova, Y. (2007) 'Breaking down the stereotypes: gender and achievement in schools', Manchester: Equal Opportunities Commission

Smart, C. (2007) *Personal Life*, Cambridge: Polity Press

Smith, J. (2003) *The Shipman Inquiry: Second Report*

Smith, T. and Noble, M. (1995) *Poverty and Schooling in the 1990s*, London: Child Poverty Action Group

Smithers, A. 'A-level results show shifting balance between sexes', *The Guardian*, 15th August 2014

Smyth, C. 'Thousands of patients killed by drug equipments and errors', *The Times*, 24th December 2014

Smyth, C., 'Chummy young doctors are bad for your health', *The Times online*, November 24th 2014

Social Exclusion Unit (2004) *Mental Health and Social Inclusion*, London: Office of the Deputy Prime Minister

Somerville, J. (2000) *Feminism and the Family: Politics and Society in the UK and USA*, Basingstoke: Palgrave Macmillan

Sontag, S. (1978) 'The double standard of ageing', in V. Carver and P. Liddiard (eds.) *An Ageing Population*, London: Hodder & Stoughton

Soothill, K. and Walby, S. (1991) *Sex Crime in the News*, London: Routledge

Sorhagen, N.S. (2013) 'Early Teacher Expectations Disproportionately Affect Poor Children's High

School Performance' *American Psychological Association*, 105(2)

Spencer, N. (2005) 'Does material disadvantage explain the increased risk of adverse health, educational, and behavioural outcomes among children in lone parent households in Britain? A cross sectional study', *Journal of Epidemiology H and Community Health*, 59(2), pp. 152–157

Spender, D. (1983) *Invisible Women: The Schooling Scandal*, London: Writers and Readers

Spicker, P. (2012) *Social Policy: Themes and Approaches*, Bristol: The Policy Press

Sproston, K. and Mindell, J. (2006) *Health Survey for England 2004: the health of ethnic minorities*, Leeds: The Information Centre

Spurr, H. (2015) 'Welfare reform "failing to move tenants into work"', *Inside housing* http://www.insidehousing.co.uk/welfare-reform-failing-to-move-tenants-into-work/7008974.article

Standing, G. (2011) *The Precariat: The New Dangerous Class*, London, Bloomsbury

Stanko, E. (2000) 'The day to count: a snapshot of the impact of domestic violence in the UK', *Criminal Justice*, 1(2)

Stanworth, M., (1990) *Gender and schooling: Study of sexual division in the classroom*, London: Routledge

Starkweather, K. E. and Hames, R. (2012) 'A survey of non-classical polyandry', *Human Nature*, 23(2), pp. 149–172

Statham, J. (1986) *Daughters and Sons: Experiences of Non-Sexist Childraising*, Oxford: Blackwell

Statham, J. (2011) 'Grandparents providing childcare', Childhood Wellbeing Research Centre, Briefing Paper, Working Paper No. 10

Steel, E. and Kidd, W. (2001) *The Family*, Basingstoke: Palgrave

Stein, S. (2002) *Sociology on the Web*, London: Routledge

Stevenson, F., Barry, C., Britten, N., Barber, N., Bradley, C. (2000) 'Doctor-patient communication about drugs: the evidence for shared decision making', *Social Science & Medicine*, 50, pp. 829–840

Stewart, K. (2013) 'Labour's record on the under fives: policy, spending and outcomes 1997–2010', Social Policy in a cold climate working paper, SPCCWP04, Centre for Analysis of Social Exclusion (CASE) London

Stirling A, Wilson P, McConnachie A (2001). 'Deprivation, psychological distress, and consultation length in general practice', *British Journal of General Practice*, 467, pp. 456–60

Stone, M. (1981) *The Education of the Black Child in Britain*, Glasgow: Fontana

Strand, S. (2007) *Minority Ethnic Pupils in the Longitudinal Study of Young People in England LYSPE)* Centre for Educational Development Appraisal and Research, University of Warwick/ Department for Children, Schools and Families

Strand, S. (2012) 'The White British–Black Caribbean achievement gap: tests, tiers and teacher expectations', *British Educational Research Journal*, 38(1), pp. 75–101

Strinati, D. (1995) *An Introduction to Theories of Popular Culture*, London: Routledge

Sugarman, B. (1970) The Cloistered Elite, *Sociology*, 4(3), p. 434

Sukhnanda, L., Lee B. and Kelleher, S. (2000) 'An Investigation into Gender Differences and Achievement: phase 2: School and classroom strategies', Slough: NFER

Sullivan, A. (2001) 'Cultural Capital and Educational Attainment', *Sociology*, 35(4), pp. 893–912

Sullivan, A., Ketende, S. and Joshi, H. (2013) 'Social Class and Inequalities in Early Cognitive Scores' *Sociology*, 29, Online Preview

Summerfield, C. and Babb, P. (eds.) (2004) *Social Trends 34, 2004 edition*, London: National Statistics

The Sunday Times, 'The Sunday Times Rich List', *The Sunday Times*, 11th May 2014

Susman, W. (1973) *Culture as History*, Washington DC: Smithsonian Books

Sutton et al (2007) A child's-eye of social difference, York: Joseph Rowntree Foundation

The Sutton Trust (2010) Responding to the new landscape for university access

The Swann Report (1985) Education for All, London: The Stationery Office

Szasz, T. (1973) The Second Sin, New York: Anchor Press/Doubleday

Szcezepura, A. (2005) 'Access to health care for ethnic minority populations', Postgraduate Medical Journal, 81(953), pp. 141–47

Tawney, R. (1913), 'Poverty as an industrial problem', inaugural lecture, reproduced in Memoranda on the Problems of Poverty, London: William Morris Press.

Taylor, L. (1984) In the Underworld, London: Royal National Institute for the Blind

Taylor, P. (1997) Investigating Culture and Identity, London: Collins Educational

Tebbel (2000) The Body Snatchers: How the Media Shapes Women, NSW: Finch Publishing

Thakar, M., & Epstein, R. 'How love emerges in arranged marriages: A cross-cultural follow-up study' presented at the 73rd annual meeting of the National Council on Family Relations, Orlando, Florida, November 2011

Thiel, D. (2007) 'Class in construction: London building workers, dirty work and physical cultures' British Journal of Sociology, 58(2)

Thornes, B. and Collard, J. (1979) Who divorces?, London: Routledge & Kegan Paul

Thornton, S. (1995) Club Cultures: Music, media and subcultural capital, Cambridge: Polity Press

Tikly, L., Haynes, J., Caballero, C., Hill, J. and Gillborn, D. (2006) Evaluation of Aiming Higher Report, University of London Research Report RR801, London: DFES/HMSO

Tizard, B. and Phoenix, A. (1993) Black, White or Mixed Race: Race and Racism in the Lives of Young People of Mixed Parentage, London: Routledge

Tomlinson, S. (2005) Education in a Post-welfare Society (2nd edn), Maidenhead: Open University Press

Townsend, P. (1979) Poverty in the UK, Harmondsworth: Penguin

Toynbee, P. 'The Tories' plan for poor people: stop them breeding', The Guardian, 16th December 2014

Trowler, P. (1996) Investigating Health, Welfare & Poverty, London: Collins Educational

Tudor Hart, J. (1971) 'The Inverse Care Law', The Lancet, 297, pp. 405–412

Tunnell, K. (1998) 'Reflections on Crime, Criminals, and Control in Newsmagazine Television Programs', in F. Y. Bailey and D. C. Hale (eds.) Popular Culture, Crime and Justice. Belmont, CA: West/Wadsworth

Turnbull, C. M. (1987) The Mountain People, New York: Touchstone

Turner, B.S. (1992) Regulating Bodies: Essays in Medical Sociology, London: Routledge

Tyler, I. (2013) 'The Riots of the Underclass? Stigmatisation, Mediation and the Government of Poverty and Disadvantage in Neoliberal Britain', Sociological Research Online, 18(4)

Universities UK (2005) Survey of higher education students' attitudes to debt and term-time working and their impact on attainment, A report to Universities UK and HEFCE by the Centre for Higher Education Research and Information (CHERI) and London South Bank University

Urban, M. 'Which is the true face of England?', The Guardian, 5th May 1999

Valentine, G. (1999) 'Oh please Mum. Oh please Dad'. Negotiating children's spatial boundaries', In L. McKie et al. (eds.) Gender, Power and the Household, Basingstoke: Macmillan

Van Rompaey, V., Roe, K. 'The Home as a Multimedia Environment: Families' Conception of Space and the Introduction of Information and Communication Technologies in the Home', Communications, 36(4), pp. 351–369

Veblen, T. (1899) The Theory of the Leisure Class, New York: Macmillan

Venkatesh, S. (2009) Gang Leader for a Day, London: Penguin Press

Victor, C. (2010) 'The Demography of Ageing', in Dannefer, D. & Phillipson, C. (eds) The Sage Handbook of Social Gerontology, London: Sage Publications

Victor, C. (2014) 'Ethnicity and ageing: what is life like for older people in Britain?', Sociology Review, 24(1)

Victor, C; Scambler, S; Bond, J & Bowling, A (2005) 'The prevalence of, and risk factors for, loneliness in later life: a survey of older people in Great Britain' in Ageing & Society, 25, pp. 357–375

Vincent, C., Ball, S. '"Making Up" the Middle Class Child: Families, Activities and Class Dispositions', Sociology, 41, pp. 1061–1077

Virdee, S. (1997) 'Racial harassment', in T. Modood, R. Berthoud, J. Lakey, J. Nazroo, P. Smith, S. Virdee and S. Beishon (eds) Ethnic Minorities in Britain: Diversity and Disadvantage, London: PSI

Wall, R. (1998) 'Intergenerational relationships past and present' in A. Walker (ed.) The New Generational Contract: Intergenerational Relationships, Old Age and Welfare, London: UCL Press

Wallander, E. in Paul, P. (2001) 'Childless by choice', American Demographics, 23, pp. 45–50

Walter, N. (2010) Living Dolls: The Return of Sexism, London: Virago Press

Wanless Report (2007) Getting it, Getting it Right, London: Department for Education and Skills (HMSO)

Washbrook, E. and Waldfogel (2010) J. 'Low Income and Early Cognitive Development in the UK', London: The Sutton Trust

Waters, M. (1995) The Death of Class, London: Sage Publications

Watson, N. (1998) 'Enabling identity: disability, self and citizenship', in Shakespeare, T. (ed.) The Disability Reader: Social Science Perspectives, London: Cassell

Watt, N. 'Pupil premium struggling to close GCSE attainment gap', The Guardian, 28th January 2014

Weaver, N.F., Hayes, L., Unwin, N.C. and Murtagh, M.J. (2008) '"Obesity" and "clinical obesity": men's understandings of obesity and its relation to the risk of diabetes: a qualitative study', BMC Public Health, 8, p. 311

Webber, R. and Butler, T. (2007) 'Classifying pupils by where they live: how well does this predict variations in their GCSE results?', Urban Studies, 44(7), pp. 12–29

Weber, M. (1958) Theory of Social and Economic Organisation, New York: Free Press

Weeks, J., Heaphy, B. and Donovan, C. (2001) Same Sex Intimacies: Families of Choice and other Life Experiments, London: Routledge

Weiner, G. (1995) 'Feminisms and education', in Feminism and Education, Buckingham: OUP

Wells, K. (2009) Childhood in a Global Perspective, Bristol: Polity Press

Wertz, R.W. and Wertz, D.C. (1981) 'Notes on the decline of midwives and the rise of medical obstetricians', in P. Conrad and R. Kerns (eds) The Sociology of Health and Illness: Critical Perspectives, New York: St Martin's Press

Westergaard, J. and Resler, H. (1976) Class in a Capitalist Society, Hardmonsworth: Penguin

Wheater, R., Ager, R., Burge, B. and Sizmur, J. (2013–revised 2014) 'Achievement of 15–Year Olds in England: PISA 2012 National Report (OECD Programme for International Student Assessment)', Paris: OECD

Whelehan, I. (2000) Overloaded: Popular Culture and the Future of Feminism, London: Women's Press

Whitty, G. (2002) Making Sense of Education Policy, London: Paul Chapman

Whitty, G., Power, S. and Sims, S. (2014) 'Lasting benefits: The long term legacy of the assisted places scheme for assisted place holders', London: The Sutton Trust

Whyte, B. and Ajetunmobi, T. (2012) 'Still "the Sick man of Europe?" Scottish Mortality in a European Context 1950 – 2010: An analysis of comparative mortality trends', Glasgow: Glasgow Centre for Population Health

Wilkins D., Payne S., Granville G., Branney P. (2008) 'The Gender and Access to Health Services Study', London: Men's Health Forum and University of Bristol for the Department of Health

Wilkinson, H. (1994) No Turning Back: Generations and the Genderquake, London: Demos

Wilkinson, R. and K. Pickett (2010) 'Reply to the Critics', Equality Trust, available at http://gemensamvalfard.se/wp-content/uploads/2012/10/Responses-to-all-critics-Wilkinson.pdf

Wilkinson, R. and Pickett, K. (2010) The Spirit Level: Why Equality is better for Everyone, London, Penguin

Wilkinson, Richard (1996). Unhealthy societies: the afflictions of inequality, London, New York: Routledge

Willis, P. (1977) Learning to Labor: How Working Class Kids Get Working Class Jobs, Cambridge: Cambridge University Press

Willis, P. (2005) Learning to Labor: How Working Class Kids Get Working Class Jobs, Cambridge: Cambridge University Press

Wilson, A. (1980) 'The infancy of the history of childhood: An appraisal of Philippe Ariès', History and Theory, 19, pp. 132–153

Witz, A. (1992) Professions and Patriarchy, London: Routledge

Wolf, A. (2002) Does Education Matter?: Myths About Education and Economic Growth, London: Penguin

Wood, L. (2012) 'Media Representations of Disabled People: A Critical Analysis', Disability Planet, available at http://www.disabilityplanet.co.uk/critical-analysis.html

Wood, S. (1989) 'The Transformation of Work?' in Wood, S. (ed.) The Transformation of Work?, London: Unwin Hyman

Woods, P. (1983) Sociology and the School: An Interactionist Viewpoint, London: Routledge & Kegan Paul

Woodward, C. (2000) 'Questions of Identity' in Woodward, K. (ed.) Questioning Identity: Gender, Class and Nation, Milton Keynes: Open University Press

Woodward, K. (2000) Questioning Identity: Gender, Class, Nation, London: Routledge

Woolcock, N. 'Free schools are failing to serve neediest' The Times, 7th August 2014

Wragg, T. (1997) Oh Boy!, Times Educational Supplemente

Wragg, T. (1997) The Cubric Curriculum, London: Routledge

Wright, C. (1992) 'Early education: multi-racial primary classrooms', in D. Gills., B. Mayor and M. Blair (eds.) Racism and Education: Structures and Strategies, London: Sage Publications

Young, M. and Willmott, P. (1957) Family and Kinship in East London, Harmondsworth: Penguin

Young, M. and Willmott, P. (1973) The Symmetrical Family, Harmondsworth: Penguin

Young, R. (2012) 'Can Neds (or Chavs) Be Non Delinquent, Educated or Even Middle Class? Contrasting Empirical Findings with Cultural Stereotypes', Sociology, 46(6), pp. 1140–1160

Youth Cohort Study & Longitudinal Study of Young People in England, 2011

Zaretsky, E. (1976) Capitalism, the Family and Personal Life, London: Pluto Press

Znaniecki, F. (1919) The Polish Peasant in Europe and America, Boston: The Gorham Press

Zuboff, S. (1988) In the Age of Smart Machines, New York: Basic Books

INDEX

Page numbers in **bold** refer to definitions/explanations of key terms.

William Collins' dream of knowledge for all began with the publication of his first book in 1819.

A self-educated mill worker, he not only enriched millions of lives, but also founded a flourishing publishing house. Today, staying true to this spirit, Collins books are packed with inspiration, innovation and practical expertise. They place you at the centre of a world of possibility and give you exactly what you need to explore it.

Collins. Freedom to teach

HarperCollins*Publishers*

The News Building, 1 London Bridge Street, London, SE1 9GF

Browse the complete Collins catalogue at www.collins.co.uk

© HarperCollins*Publishers* 2015

10 9 8 7 6 5 4 3 2 1

ISBN 978-0-00-759747-5

Collins® is a registered trademark of HarperCollins Publishers Limited

A catalogue record for this book is available from the British Library

Contributing author: Tim Davies

Commissioned by Alexandra Riley and Tom Guy

Project managed by Elektra Media

Development edited by Kim Vernon

Copyedited by Sarah Patey

Proofread by Faye Cheeseman

Illustrations by Elektra Media and Oxford Designers & Illustrators

Typeset by Jouve India Private Limited

Design and cover design by We Are Laura

Indexed by Indexing Specialists (UK) Ltd

Production by Rachel Weaver

Printed and bound by Grafica Veneta S.p.A

HarperCollins does not warrant that www.collins.co.uk or any other website mentioned in this title will be provided uninterrupted, that any website will be error free, that defects will be corrected, or that the website or the server that makes it available are free of viruses or bugs. For full terms and conditions please refer to the site terms provided on the website.

The publishers gratefully acknowledge the permissions granted to reproduce copyright material in this book. Every effort has been made to contact the holders of copyright material, but if any have been inadvertently overlooked, the publisher will be pleased to make the necessary arrangements at the first opportunity.

The Department for Education do not accept responsibility for any inferences or conclusions derived from the NPD Data by third parties. The EHRC content in this publication has been adapted from and all other intellectual property rights in that material are owned by, or licensed to, the Commission for Equality and Human Rights, known as the Equality and Human Rights Commission. HESA cannot accept responsibility for any conclusions or inferences derived from the data by third parties.

Approval Message from AQA

This textbook has been approved by AQA for use with our qualification. This means that we have checked that it broadly covers the specification and we are satisfied with the overall quality. Full details for our approval process can be found on our website.

We approve textbooks because we know how important it is for teachers and students to have the right resources to support their teaching and learning. However, the publisher is ultimately responsible for the editorial control and quality of this book.

Please note that when teaching the AS and A-level Sociology course, you must refer to AQA's specification as your definitive source of information. While this book has been written to match the specification, it cannot provide complete coverage of every aspect of the course.

A wide range of other useful resources can be found on the relevant subject pages of our website: www.aqa.org.uk

Photo credits: p2 Blend Images/Superstock, p3 Mike Booth/Alamy, p13r East Lancashire Newspapers, p17r TravelStockCollection - Homer Sykes/Alamy, p37 Ingram Publishing/Alamy, p42 Manchester Daily Express/Getty Images, p52 Janine Wiedel Photolibrary/Alamy, p60 Stonewall, p65 Photofusion, p66 Janine Wiedel Photolibrary/Alamy, p67 Oli Scarff /Getty Images, p69l Haywood Magee/Picture Post/Getty Images, p69r Fox Photos/Getty Images, p74 Rupert Hartley/Bloomberg via Getty Images, p75 Laurence Griffiths/Getty Images, p78 Paul Rogers - WPA Pool/Getty Images, p80 LEON NEAL/AFP/Getty Images, p81 Matt Cardy/Getty Images, p89b Channel 4/REX, p94 Nicolas McComber/Getty Images, p95 Photofusion Picture Library/Alamy, p114 Nigel Cattlin/Alamy, p115 Ian Canham/ Alamy, p118 Hero Images/Getty Images, p120 Oli Scarff/Getty Images News, p124 John Swart/AP/Press Association Images, p126 Dave J Hogan/Getty Images, p148 Guy Corbishley/Alamy, p156 ANDREJ ISAKOVIC/AFP/Getty Images, p159bl © AF archive/ Alamy, p170 Yuri Arcurs/Getty Images, p199 Peter Macdiarmid/ Getty Images, p201 CARL COURT/AFP/Getty Images, p208 INDRANIL MUKHERJEE/AFP/Getty Images, p217 © Everynight Images/Alamy, p218 © Barry Lewis/Alamy, p225 Cultura RM/ Russ Rohde/Getty Images, p230 © Homer Sykes/Alamy, p232 Kurt Hutton/Picture Post/Getty Images, p235 Fred W. McDarrah/ Getty Images, p242 Kate Geraghty/Fairfax Media/Getty Images, p244 Stephen J. Boitano, LightRocket/Getty Images, p288 Jeremy Young/News Syndication, p293 DeAgostini/Getty Images, p296 © Jeff Gilbert/Alamy, p299 MOHAMED DAHIR/AFP/GettyImages, p312tr Courtesy Miss You Can Do It, p312br Hill Street Studios/ Getty Images, p323 Yellow Dog Productions/Getty Images, p336 Javier Larrea/Getty Images, p341 JW Ltd/Getty Images, p346 Guy Corbishley/Getty Images, p347 Edward G Malindine/Getty Images, p358 Tim Whitby/Getty Images, p360l BSIP/UIG/Getty Images, p360r Jean Pierre FOUCHET/RAPHO/Gamma-Rapho/ Getty Images, p372 Thomas Barwick/Getty Images, p397 © David White/Alamy, p401 © Janine Wiedel Photolibrary/Alamy, p406 © Matthew Chattle/Alamy, p411 © Peter Jordan_NE/Alamy, p418 © Adam Bronkhorst/Alamy, p420 PAUL ELLIS/AFP/Getty Images, p423 Chris Ware/Keystone/Getty Images, p427 Photoshot/Getty Images, p432 Matt Cardy/Getty Images, p442 Malcolm Dunbar/ Picture Post/Getty Images